Historical Perspectives on Business Enterprise Series

BFGoodrich

TRADITION AND
TRANSFORMATION
1870–1995

MANSEL G. BLACKFORD

K. AUSTIN KERR

OHIO STATE UNIVERSITY PRESS

COLUMBUS

Copyright © 1996 by the Ohio State University Press.
All rights reserved.

Library of Congress Cataloging-in-Publication Data

Blackford, Mansel G., 1944–
    BFGoodrich : tradition and transformation, 1870–1995 / Mansel G.
Blackford and K. Austin Kerr.
        p.   cm. — (Historical perspectives on business enterprise
series)
    Includes bibliographical references and index.
    ISBN 0-8142-0696-4 (alk. paper). — ISBN 0-8142-0697-2 (pbk. :
alk. paper)
    1. B.F. Goodrich Company—History.   2. Rubber industry and trade—
United States—History.   3. Tire industry—United States—History.
I. Kerr, K. Austin (Kathel Austin)   II. Title.   III. Series.
HD 9161.U54B143   1996
338.7'6782'0973—dc20   96-13482
                                                                              CIP

Type set in Goudy Oldstyle by The Composing Room of Michigan, Inc.
Printed by Braun-Brumfield, Inc.

The paper used in this publication meets the minimum requirements of
American National Standard for Information Sciences—Permanence of
Paper for Printed Library Materials.
ANSI z39.48–1992. ∞

9   8   7   6   5   4   3   2   1

For the men and women of BFGoodrich

CONTENTS

PREFACE

This book is an authorized history. In 1990 John Ong, the Chairman and Chief Executive Officer of BFGoodrich, asked us to explore the possibility of writing a scholarly history of the company, in time for its 125th anniversary in 1995. Ong explained that he wanted a scholarly book, one subject to peer review by other scholars, and published by his alma mater's University Press. This volume is our answer to his request.

We are deeply indebted to John Ong. A historian and an avid reader of the fruits of historical scholarship, Ong repeatedly insisted that the judgments in this book were to be ours, and not his or the company's. Ong generously gave his time for extensive interviews about his impressions of Goodrich's past and, especially, his career as an executive with the firm. At our request, he read drafts of our manuscript and told us where he thought we had gotten the facts wrong. He also challenged our interpretation and characterization of those facts at a number of points, but was always clear that the decision about what to say in the book was ours, and ours alone. We could not have written this book without his help as a source, as a reader, as a critic, and, finally, as a friend.

There were many other generous Goodrich people who helped us. The list of persons we interviewed is a long one, and we have appended it. In every case interviewees were generous with their time, their energy, and their insights. This book would not have been possible without their help, and we are in debt to many good, able men whose memories of their careers enriched our own knowledge.

Goodrich supports an archive of many of its important records in the University of Akron library. The archivist, John Miller, advised us, and he and his staff provided cheerful assistance whenever we needed it. The company has maintained minute books of meetings of the board of directors, and of high-level executive bodies, and other legal records to which we had full access. In fact, the company allowed us access to any records we thought important for the project. In what may be unprecedented access for any business historian, Ong even loaned us files from his office.

The company also provided generous financial support for this project. Funds donated to Ohio State University allowed us to take time off from teaching to do research and writing. Those same funds allowed us to employ student assistants. At different points in the project, we enjoyed wonderful help from Eric Neff, Stephen Trenta, Albert Churella, Jonathan Bean, Jonathan Silva, Douglas Smith, Terence Kehoe, and David Stefacek. Without their assistance this book would have taken much longer to complete, and their expertise in several subject areas greatly enhanced our insights into the company's history.

Daniel Nelson and David Sicilia read drafts of the manuscript and gave us the benefit of their informed and critical eyes, for which we are grateful.

We are especially grateful to Joan Taffi, Gary L. Habegger, Rob Jewell, and Maryann Morgart of Goodrich, and Thomas Waltermire, who is now with Geon. Tab Lewis and other professional archivists at the National Archives in Washington, D.C., went out of their way to help us. The *Akron Beacon Journal* generously granted access to its clipping files. To all of these people, and others, we say thank you.

Furthermore, we note that the project has greatly enriched our scholarly lives as business historians, and it was a tremendous opportunity for the students who worked with us. Although both of us had taught business history for a number of years, and had written both specialized and general works in the field (sometimes in collaboration), neither of us had enjoyed the chance to explore the history of a big firm whose history was large in both economic scale and historical scope. Completing the project has given us many examples to use in our classes. It has also enlarged our understanding of how industries grow and change, of how companies respond to economic and social challenges and market opportunities, and of how the legal and political environment shapes the history of even a big business. Our own understanding of history in general will be forever changed because of this particular history. For the opportunity to have this personal and professional growth we thank the men and women of BFGoodrich.

Finally, we have endeavored to provide a factual and scholarly history of a large, old, and complex institution. In doing so, Austin Kerr assumed principal responsibility for the introduction and chapters 5, 6, 7, 8, and 11, and Mansel Blackford for chapters 1, 2, 3, 4, 9, and 10. We accept joint responsibility for whatever failings this book may have, and give credit for whatever successes it may enjoy to our assistants, referees, and, most of all, to the men and women, past and present, of BFGoodrich.

As we begin, let us observe that BFGoodrich experienced several name changes over its long history. In the 1870s the company was a partnership known by several names. With its incorporation in 1880, the firm was known as the B.F. Goodrich Company. Most recently, beginning in 1974, the company has used BFGoodrich as its logo.

Introduction:
Exploring the History of
the BFGoodrich Company

The BFGoodrich Company's 125th anniversary on 31 December 1995 marked a significant milestone in its evolution. The company stood as an important manufacturing concern employing over 13,000 men and women and enjoying about $2.2 billion in annual sales. The stockholders of the company, through their board of directors and executive officers, controlled about $2.5 billion in total assets. BFGoodrich was truly a "big business," an economic institution that commanded an important position in two industries, specialty chemicals and aerospace. Its facilities were at sites from coast to coast, and it sold goods and services to other companies on four continents.

The company celebrating its anniversary was a sophisticated human organization. Goodrich workers used complex machinery and advanced technology to accomplish their tasks. They communicated with one another and with other business counterparts at the speed of electricity. Managers employed sophisticated accounting and financial techniques to monitor their businesses. They related to one another in a matrix of organizational structure, with managers held accountable for special areas by a small staff working in discrete, comfortable offices in a quiet suburban area. Executives in corporate headquarters decided policies for the entire company, coordinated the work of the firm's specialized divisions, and presented the affairs of BFGoodrich to stockholders, capital markets that electronically transferred huge sums of money across the globe, and the public at large.

The BFGoodrich Company of 1995 was a far cry from the fledgling partnership, Goodrich, Tew & Co., formed in Akron, Ohio, on 31 December 1870. The founding entrepreneur, Dr. Benjamin Franklin Goodrich, a physician turned businessman, could not have foreseen how the firm would evolve over the next 125 years. Dr. Goodrich had come to Akron seeking his fortune after failing to establish a successful medical practice. He stumbled into the rubber business, and struggled in it, as did other ambitious manufacturers in many other industries. His was a small business, founded in an area of the nation that was in the early stages of the industrial revolution. Goodrich, Tew & Co. employed a mere handful of people, operated largely with local capital, stood close to the central business district of a small town, and sold its first products in a limited region. Responsible for the firm's daily management, Benjamin Franklin Goodrich personally worked with raw rubber and handled finished goods.

There was still another Goodrich that contrasted sharply with the fledgling firm of 1870 and with the sophisticated modern enterprise of 1995. This B.F. Goodrich Company was a giant rubber fabricator, an industrial behemoth, one of four firms that dominated the American tire industry from the 1920s, after the growth of the automobile age, to the 1970s. Goodrich as a rubber giant employed more than fifty thousand men and women. Its headquarters were in a large, multistoried brick factory building that grew almost hodgepodge from the original small plant established in 1871. There, and in factories located in every one of the nation's regions, thousands of workers built tires, made rubber belts and hoses, fabricated other rubber goods demanded by an advanced industrial economy, and even made shoes for thousands of customers. In offices housed in the Akron factory, managers, working within a hierarchical bureaucratic system of decision making and authority, swept the grime of carbon black from their desks, perspired in the heat of summer, and guided a company whose full complexity was beyond the knowledge of any one individual.

The striking differences between the Goodrich of 1870, of the middle years, and of 1995 are so remarkable as to leave few similarities. Perhaps the only common aspect was that all three institutions were manufacturing businesses whose leaders invested capital in land, buildings, raw materials, and machinery; who recruited, motivated, disciplined, organized, and rewarded workers; and who arranged the distribution of finished goods in order to earn a profit. Aside from the elemental fact that the institutions were manufacturing businesses, the differences between them were startling. The most obvious difference was that by 1995 BFGoodrich was no longer a rubber company.

This difference is one of the central themes in the exploration of the company's history: the gradual movement of Goodrich into chemicals and aerospace and, in the 1980s, the deliberate shucking of the traditional rubber manufacturing activities. From its earliest days Goodrich was something of a "chemical" company, albeit a far cry from the firm participating in the modern chemical industry that arose in the middle of the twentieth century. Reflecting the transformation were the careers, at different times, of the founder's two sons. Benjamin Goodrich, and for a time his son Charles Cross Goodrich, worked in a laboratory on the problems of compounding and fabricating crude rubber into useful commodities. Benjamin's other son, David Goodrich, served the company until his death in 1950, supporting policies of investment in the development and manufacture of petroleum-based plastics and synthetic rubber, and overseeing the company's participation in the expansion of the aircraft industry during World War II.

Goodrich has always been a diversified manufacturing company. The company's first products were a diverse set of rubber goods, ranging from hoses to belts. Later, in the early twentieth century when the growth of the tire industry accelerated, Goodrich chose to remain a diversified rubber manufacturer and eschew aggressive investments in that one product line. In the 1930s, as an outgrowth of its diverse rubber manufacturing businesses, Goodrich executives decided to lead their company into the chemical business. Still later, starting from a historical base as a rubber fabricator, Goodrich consciously chose to become a manufacturer of goods for the aerospace industry. True to its tradition of diversity, Goodrich at the time of its 125th anniversary was a diversified company. It was also a transformed company, no longer in its traditional rubber fabrication businesses.

We shall explore the significant strategic courses taken by BFGoodrich over the decades that transformed the company. During the early automobile age, the company chose to be a diversified rubber manufacturer, one that spread its resources across a broad line of products and did not aggressively invest in the tire industry before World War I. In the 1930s, Goodrich executives decided to enter the chemical industry. Somewhat later, they chose to enter the aerospace business, a decision that evolved slowly in the period after World War II. These strategic decisions were sometimes consciously and carefully planned and executed; at other times they were reached almost haphazardly and inadvertently, and later solidified with careful planning and execution. In the 1930s the officers decided to invest in the chemical industry when a revolution in petrochemical production possibilities was barely on the horizon. Goodrich had performed a small role in the American aircraft industry from its earliest days, and its role increased during the mobilization of World War II and the creation of a huge American aircraft industry. However, the company reached a strategic decision to focus attention on the aerospace industry slowly, and only in the 1980s decided that aerospace would become one of its chief lines of business. At about the same time executives plotted the company's strategic departure from all rubber manufacturing, including tires.

With the company's remarkable growth in size and scope, transformations in corporate strategy are a theme central to the history of the firm. From its founding, BFGoodrich had objectives that went beyond the simple truism of earning a return on investment. Rubber manufacturing and the demand for rubber products varied markedly over the years, and with changing opportunities came difficult questions about company goals. What markets should the company pursue, and with what vigor and resources? How much return on investment should Goodrich seek? How much of the earnings should be reinvested or expended as personal rewards for the officers and owners? Decisions about corporate strategy lie at the heart of the history of BFGoodrich, and those decisions framed the history of the company. The executives who set the course of BFGoodrich encountered opportunities for investing in new product lines and even new industries themselves. The modern company became a chemical company because of the traditional requirements of rubber chemistry, and it became an aerospace company because of the rubber materials used by aircraft. Goodrich executives also faced traditional boundaries built over the years. Their opportunities in some rubber fabricating activities, especially tire making, diminished when investment decisions reached in the early days of the automobile age caused the company to lose a leadership position that could never be regained.

The transformation of Goodrich, Tew & Co. from a fledgling venture into a modern "big business" frames our historical exploration. Goodrich became a "big business" during the first decade of the twentieth century, a time of rapid institutional growth among American manufacturing companies in several industries. Big businesses were firms that developed a hierarchical organization of departments specializing in the firm's functions of purchasing, manufacturing, distribution, and sales. In Goodrich, and similar large American firms, top officers paid attention to the company's strategic decisions while lower-level executives tended operations. A third, or "middle," level of managers coordinated work among the departments. As opportunities enlarged for the investment of capital and the employment of workers, business executives struggled with complex problems of human organization, of how to structure the work of the business to meet their objectives.

The struggle of executives to devise a structure appropriate for their objectives as BFGoodrich became a big business provides another theme in its history. The problems of corporate structure appeared slowly at first, and their solutions were not always readily apparent. Opportunities for rubber manufacturing broadened rapidly in the expanding industrial economy of the late nineteenth century, and then exploded in the first three decades of the twentieth century as the automobile became the preferred mode of transportation. Any rubber company taking advantage of those opportunities had to grow in both the scale and scope of its manufacturing and distribution operations. Growth brought on the problems of corporate structure, of how to organize the people in the firm according to the company's functions and goals. That strategy was far from static, especially when the company entered the infant petrochemical and aerospace industries and as those markets expanded. Corporate structure—the story of how the people who operated the company were organized to work together—is a subject that pervades the entire history of BFGoodrich.

The history of any institution is one of continuity and change. For a company as old and as complex as BFGoodrich, not all themes recur throughout the story of its evolution. The original company, for instance, was one in which the firm and the Goodrich family were closely intertwined. The firm was also intimately connected to the leading citizens of Akron, who supplied some of its capital and much of its leadership. When it changed from a partnership to a corporation in 1880, Goodrich was still a closely held company with comparatively few stockholders, most of whom resided in northeastern Ohio. Even after Goodrich grew by merging with its Akron neighbor, Diamond Rubber, in 1912 and was incorporated in New York with headquarters in the nation's biggest city, it remained closely tied to its familial roots and Akron origins.

The personality of any leader makes some imprint on the organization he or she is leading, and a collection of these personalities over the years forms the corporate culture. The personal values and practices of the Goodrich family, the early executives, and their immediate successors profoundly affected the fortunes of the historic BFGoodrich Company. All business firms exist to earn profits, but the decisions of what to do with profits differ among firms according to the perspectives of the men and women most immediately responsible for them. There developed a long tradition in BFGoodrich of taking funds from the company, which was not always to the long-term benefit of the owners of the firm. While the company's competitors took funds and reinvested them, for decades Goodrich's approach was one of reducing risks, and of taking money from the company to enjoy the privileges associated with the American upper-class lifestyle. Those decades during which the profit-taking, risk-reduction orientation prevailed were also marked by the most explosive growth in the nation's economy, closely linked to the growth of the automobile industry. Between 1908, when Henry Ford introduced the Model T—the first mass-produced automobile—and the early 1930s (years that saw American industry emerge as the strongest in the world), Goodrich slipped from being the nation's largest rubber manufacturer to only the fourth largest.

Nevertheless, Goodrich remained a very large firm indeed. It was one of four large firms dominating the rubber industry during the automobile age. Between 1920 and 1970 the "big four" rubber manufacturers—Goodyear, Firestone, U.S. Rubber (later Uniroyal), and Goodrich—integrated production and distribution to varying degrees in an effort to moderate business risks through economic efficiency. Goodrich pioneered in the development of petrochemical-based synthetic rubber, an industry created by the federal government during World War II, and after 1954 invested in the production of natural rubber in the African nation of Liberia. Goodrich went into the retail trade, building a distribution system for its rubber products, especially tires, aimed at individual consumers through a system of independent dealers and company-owned stores. The strategy of backward vertical integration into raw materials and forward into retail distribution enabled each of the "big four" rubber companies to develop more durable and better products at lower prices. After 1970 the rubber, and especially the tire, industry changed fundamentally with the successful rise of firms headquartered outside the United States. After 1970 American companies ceased to dominate rubber manufacturing even in the American market, and Goodrich left the field altogether.

The strategy of vertical integration proved effective in an economic sense and also ensured that each rubber firm would grow large. This growth, in turn, involved Goodrich and its major competitors in a series of political and policy disputes with government officials in Congress, the executive branch, and the regulatory agencies. In an age of powerful giant enterprises, Americans have used public power in an attempt to ensure fair play and democratic traditions and have imposed social responsibility on large companies. The fact that these "big four" companies could potentially act as an oligopoly, or behave like a monopoly, to control markets and prices subjected them to ongoing attacks from smaller firms and ambitious politicians. Thus, not only did the business environment change dramatically from the days of the company's founder, so did the political environment. Although antitrust issues involving its size receded as Goodrich changed in the latter part of the twentieth century, the company still faced government regulators concerned about such matters as occupational health and a livable environment.

Along with regulation, growth brought other consequences. Growth spurred conflict in human relationships, as industrial processes estranged workers on the shop floor from the executives in charge of the company. As Goodrich added thousands of employees to its payroll, it faced major problems. Not the least was the challenge of recruiting able workers and of securing a steady supply of labor. With workers recruited by the tens of thousands, Goodrich executives, like their counterparts in other growing manufacturing firms, learned that personal relationships between employer and employee no longer sufficed to train, motivate, discipline, and organize workers on the shop floor. For decades the history of labor relations was one of strain and conflict, exacerbated as production workers formed independent unions to engage in collective bargaining with their employers. The target of union activity, Goodrich suffered from periodic strikes throughout its history as a rubber manufacturer, entering a period of relative harmony only in 1979 when the firm's position in rubber manufacturing ebbed in the face of international competition.

The "big four" companies also competed vigorously, and sometimes viciously, with one another over prices and technological advances. Vertical integration—backward into raw material sources and forward with distribution facilities, including, for many years, even retail stores—helped guard against the wounds that competition threatened. However, although important for all of the large rubber manufacturers during the twentieth century, vertical integration could not fully protect Goodrich. As Firestone and, especially, Goodyear grew so much larger than Goodrich, they were able to prevent their smaller competitor from taking full advantage of its own resources, especially the technological advances in tire design and construction that after 1950 did so much to make driving safer and less expensive. After the World War I, the fact that Goodrich was third, and sometimes fourth, in its industry meant that it could not withstand the full force of competition in tire manufacturing. Eventually, in the 1980s, it was forced to withdraw from that industry.

Our history of BFGoodrich, thus, explores many interrelated themes, as the company grew from a small firm to a national and international corporation and as the nature of its products changed over time. Our history focuses on the basic question faced by nearly all successful American businesses: How have such companies transformed themselves over time? Other questions follow from this basic question. How have companies altered their product lines and their approaches to marketing? How have they reacted to the changing political and social environments in which they have operated? As their very natures have changed, how have they altered their management structures and styles? How have they changed their relationships with labor? How have they reached out to foreign markets? Although the theme of transformation dominates our history of BFGoodrich, the theme of continuity is also present. Certain values and approaches to doing business pervaded long stretches of the firm's history, especially in its earlier years, and those values shaped what Goodrich as a company became. During the 1920s and the 1930s, a corporate culture opposed to most risk taking meant that Goodrich would fall behind several of its major competitors in rubber manufacturing, and especially in tire manufacturing.

The corporate culture of BFGoodrich was, like almost every aspect of the firm, not a static phenomenon. Changes in the corporate culture were an important part of the company's transformations. The company's culture reflected not only the values and attitudes of the company's leaders but also the ideological and intellectual currents in American business of production, marketing, and finance. As Goodrich was a manufacturing firm, its executives always had to be concerned about production, distribution (marketing), and the company's finances. What changed over time, however, were both unspoken assumptions and articulated strategies about these business functions. In general, executives responsible for American manufacturing companies were concerned about the overwhelming problems and opportunities associated with production during the first decades of growth. By the 1920s some companies, led by General Motors, developed top executives who were oriented more toward distributing, or marketing, goods than toward production. Later, in the 1960s and beyond, a finance mentality swept through the ranks of American corporate executives, which meant that large companies like Goodrich came to be seen as portfolios of businesses, since the means used to control them were financial instruments.

The corporate culture of Goodrich reflected these trends. With the growth of the American industrial economy, and the explosion of the automobile industry after 1908 and its voracious demand for rubber goods, executives had to focus attention on the problems of organizing production processes. The route for advancement for an ambitious executive lay in solving production problems. When the rubber goods, and especially the tire, industry matured in the middle of the 1920s and suffered from overexpansion of productive capacity, Goodrich executives had to focus on marketing. Still, the production orientation persisted, and it was not until after 1957 that marketing became a consciously stated focus of the company's leaders, and solving problems of distribution became a route of advancement for ambitious managers. In 1971, after the company had staggered from vicious competition in the tire industry, leadership changes brought a finance mentality to the executive suite.

We offer, then, a history of a leading big business in the United States—a history of a firm that prospered during many years and that survived in others, the story of a company that has gone through dramatic transformations over the past 125 years. Those transformations were indicative of changes taking place in American business, especially as executives in various industries faced growing competition from foreign-based multinational firms. The BFGoodrich of 1995, so different from the firm of 1870, was a product of the rapid growth of the midwestern and American economies in the company's first century. It was also a product of the dramatic changes in the industrial scene after 1970 when markets for capital and manufactured goods became truly global. The opportunities for manufacturing in the United States had changed irrevocably, and Goodrich executives faced enormous difficulties in reshaping their firm.

I

Goodrich and the Akron Elite: Entrepreneurial Opportunities in Rubber, 1870–1907

On a November day in 1870, Dr. Benjamin Franklin Goodrich alighted from a train in Akron determined to found a rubber manufacturing company in that midwestern town. He went to the offices of George Crouse, the president of Akron's Board of Trade, where the two men talked. Crouse called a meeting of Akron's business leaders at the Empire Hotel the next evening. At that gathering Goodrich outlined his plans to build a rubber factory in Akron: a two-story brick factory building with a single-story adjoining structure for a boiler room would house a substantial plant. Goodrich predicted a rosy future for his firm: gross profits of $90,000 on sales of $225,000 within just two years, large sums in those days.[1] Akron's business elite responded enthusiastically. Twenty-three businessmen pledged financing for Goodrich's proposed venture. Their funds, augmented by his own money and capital from family and friends in the East, allowed Goodrich to form the partnership of Goodrich, Tew & Co. on the last day of 1870. Goodrich, Tew & Co., the predecessor of today's BFGoodrich Company, began manufacturing rubber products on 19 February 1871 and was the first rubber manufacturer west of the Appalachians.

Success did not come easily for B.F. Goodrich (as Goodrich, Tew & Co. was reorganized in 1874). Beyond the many difficulties associated with founding new enterprises, the company's officers, like their competitors, faced basic challenges in the nascent rubber industry: developing a reliable supply of raw rubber at a reasonable price, finding new processes (sometimes through the application of science) to make a broadening array of new products, and opening markets for those products. B.F. Goodrich almost failed in the mid-1870s, but by the time of his death in 1888, Dr. Goodrich had established the company as a healthy concern of regional importance. Under its second president, George T. Perkins (1888–1907), B.F. Goodrich became a prosperous national corporation. From a partnership capitalized at $40,500 with sales of $49,000 in 1871,

B.F. Goodrich became a corporation worth $12.5 million with sales of $13 million in 1907.[2]

BENJAMIN FRANKLIN GOODRICH AND THE FOUNDING OF A RUBBER COMPANY

Benjamin Goodrich was the initial guiding force in the company that came to bear his name. That such would be the case was not at first apparent. Only after experimenting with careers in medicine and real estate did Goodrich stumble into the rubber business, and only after failing in efforts to develop rubber companies at two sites in New York did he move to Ohio.[3] Chance, not planning, dictated many of the early developments at B.F. Goodrich. As events would show, the move to Akron brought Goodrich luck, landing him at the right place at the right time for the type of business he wanted to develop.

Dr. Goodrich: Entrepreneur

Born 4 November 1841 on a farm near the small town of Ripley in upstate New York, Benjamin Goodrich was the son of Anson Goodrich and Susan Dinsmore Goodrich. Named after Benjamin Franklin—his mother greatly admired Franklin and often read to her son from Franklin's autobiography and *Poor Richard's Almanac*—Goodrich as a boy performed chores on his family's farm and attended the local school. He enjoyed making maple syrup in the spring, swimming and fishing in the summer, and ice-skating in the winter. He even devised a wind-powered sled.[4] Goodrich's father died in 1847, and his mother two years later, when he was eight. He then went to live with his mother's brother, John Dinsmore, not far from Ripley. In the Dinsmore household Goodrich found a supportive family. Writing a cousin, he observed, "You know I love Uncle John Dinsmore as a father and I think he cares nearly as much for me as for his own boys."[5] Educated first by a teacher tutoring Dinsmore's children at home, Goodrich went at the age of fifteen to attend a boy's boarding school at Austinburg, Ohio (his first contact with the state), and a year later attended the Academy in Fredonia, New York, another private school.[6]

Medicine attracted Goodrich. He first studied the subject in 1858 with his cousin, Dr. John Spencer in Westfield, New York, and later that year returned to Ripley to work with Dr. George Bennett. Such personal preparation for the medical profession was common in the nineteenth century. Goodrich went further by enrolling in the highly regarded Cleveland Medical College in 1859 (later known as the Medical School of the Case Western Reserve University), from which he graduated in the following year. In July 1860 he opened a medical practice in Mayville, New York, with his office and rooms in a hotel. Goodrich's initial foray in medicine proved discouraging. According to one biographer, a year after Goodrich entered the field "his practice amounted to nothing and he was without both money and necessary clothing."[7]

At the nadir in his life, the Civil War intervened to improve Goodrich's

Dr. Benjamin F. Goodrich is pictured here as a young
man. (BFG Co.)

fortunes. With the gift of a twenty-dollar gold piece from his sister, Goodrich
traveled to Albany, where he was accepted as a hospital steward in the Ninth
New York Cavalry, serving in the same company as his cousin Dr. John Spencer, with whom he had earlier studied. Soon promoted to assistant surgeon,
Goodrich was transferred to a battalion of engineers. Goodrich continued his
medical studies at the University of Pennsylvania while on leave in late 1862
and early 1863. After returning to duty he served with the Army of the Po-
tomac as a commissioned assistant surgeon, taking charge of a small hospital
for a short time.[8]

Like so many Americans in both the North and the South, Goodrich found
his life disrupted by the Civil War. David Goodrich recalled that his father was
possessed by "a sort of restlessness" after the conflict.[9] If Goodrich resembled
many of his countrymen in this respect, he differed from them in others: even
after the death of his parents he benefited from an upbringing in what he later
described as "comfortable circumstances" and from a superior education.[10] At
a time when few Americans went beyond grammar school, he attended college. The personal and family connections so important in providing advantages in his early life would continue to aid Goodrich in the postwar years. But
while differing from most Americans in his background, he was similar to

America's leading business executives of the late nineteenth and early twentieth centuries. Like him, most came from upper- or middle-class families and were well educated. Few were the sons of immigrants, and none came from minority groups. Then, as now, "rags to riches" careers were rare in American business.[11]

After the war, Goodrich continued to struggle for a foothold in medicine. He moved to Jamestown, New York, a commercial center not far from Ripley. Then he forged on to newly developing boomtowns in the oil fields of Pennsylvania, where E. L. Drake had sunk America's first commercial oil well in 1859. Tideout, Rouseville, and Pit Hole attracted Goodrich's attention, and by the fall of 1865 he was practicing in Pit Hole. Conditions there were primitive but expensive. Writing a relative, he observed that "there are no women here . . . the food is so bad . . . and the life is so hard that you would not last here a month." Goodrich found it difficult to make ends meet because of the high cost of living. He and a partner paid the astronomical sum of $1,000 for one year's rent for two office rooms. Although they hoped to erect their own office building, Goodrich lamented, "I have not the money to do it."[12] The young man's aspirations as a doctor finally died, and he entered the employ of Brown Brothers Oil Company, a firm he had become acquainted with in Pit Hole, as a member of its shipping department in New York City.[13]

Goodrich's career change and move to New York City set the stage for his entrance into the rubber industry. He boarded in the home of a Mrs. Sanderson and there became friends with a young attorney, John P. Morris. The two men dabbled in real estate enterprises together, several of which appear to have been quite profitable.[14] At least one such venture was not, however. Ironically, it was this one that first involved Goodrich in the rubber industry. Goodrich had come to know Ezra Frost and others owning the Hudson River Rubber Company, whose production works were at Hastings-on-the-Hudson but whose head office was in New York City. Possessing $11,000 worth of machinery and capitalized at $42,000, the company produced rubber fire hoses, belting and steam packing (seals and gaskets) for factory machinery, and railroad car springs.[15] Intrigued by what he saw in the company, Goodrich persuaded Morris to join him in offering to trade $10,000 worth of real estate in New York City for an equal value of stock in the company. Hudson River Rubber Company officers, facing intense competition and desperate for capital, eagerly accepted Goodrich's offer in July 1869.[16] Presumably, they sold the lots acquired from Goodrich and Morris to raise cash for their company.

According to Morris, Goodrich was "anxious to make this trade"—perhaps too eager. The Hudson River Rubber Company, burdened by rundown machinery and suffering from severe competition, was found by the new shareholders to be "in bad shape financially." To protect their investments, Goodrich and Morris became more deeply involved in the rubber business by buying out all of the other stockholders through a further exchange of New York City real estate for shares in the rubber company. Goodrich then became president and manager of the company, while Morris served as its secretary and treasurer.

Morris played an inactive role, remaining in New York City in the real estate business. As Morris later recalled, "Dr. Goodrich immediately took charge of the works at Hastings," even though he possessed no previous knowledge of how to manufacture rubber products. Problems continued to hurt the company: worn-out machinery, high rents, and ever-present competition. Seeking to salvage the operation and perceiving opportunities elsewhere, Goodrich closed the Hastings plant, leased a small rubber factory in Melrose, New York, and moved all of the Hastings equipment there. This relocation accomplished little. "The Melrose factory did not succeed any better than the Hastings factory," Morris later recalled, "and the Doctor said we would either have to have some more money or close up and sell the business out."[17]

Goodrich entered the rubber business just a few decades after its beginning in the United States. By the 1820s and 1830s merchants in eastern seaboard cities were offering rubber shoes, bottles, and syringes for sale in America. Made from latex obtained by tapping wild rubber trees growing in the Amazon River basin, these items were waterproof. Constructed in the Amazon's interior, the goods were shipped downriver to the port city of Para on the Atlantic, where they were transshipped to Europe and the United States. By 1827 nearly 70,000 pounds of rubber shoes were leaving Para each year. Because the liquid latex from the trees could not be transported very far, American rubber makers soon sought chemical and mechanical ways to break down the shoes and other rubber items coming from the Amazon as the first step in making new products from them. The first American factory to try to do so was established by Edwin Chaffee in Boston in 1833, and others soon followed. Still, there were problems: goods made from reconstituted crude rubber softened in the heat of summer and became brittle in the cold of winter.[18]

Scientific, and especially chemical, advances were essential to the development of the rubber industry. In the late 1830s and early 1840s a number of rubber manufacturers, of whom Charles Goodyear became the best known, discovered how to vulcanize crude rubber. Vulcanization toughened the rubber, ending problems with softness and brittleness. The rubber men added sulfur to cut-up rubber as it was being prepared in mixing mills and then baked the new finished rubber goods in ovens. With this discovery, the manufacturing of rubber products took off. By 1870 the United States had fifty-six manufacturers of rubber and elastic goods capitalized at $7.5 million and employing 6,025 people.[19]

The Move to Akron

Far from discouraged, Goodrich sought rubber manufacturing opportunities farther west. It is likely that Morris inspired Goodrich to look beyond New York. As Morris later explained, "I thought that if one was started out West where there were then no factories and he could get enough money so he would not be cramped for two or three years, that he would succeed in business." In part, the competition of well-established eastern companies drove

Goodrich and Morris to look westward. Perhaps Goodrich's earlier experiences in Ohio also led him to venture across the Appalachians. Goodrich was a young man on the make, only twenty-eight years old, and not easily dispirited by what he saw as temporary setbacks. He harbored no doubts about his new industrial profession, never giving serious consideration to going back to medicine or real estate.[20]

Goodrich was optimistic enough about his future to marry Mary M. Marvin of Jamestown, New York, the daughter of one of the state's leading jurists, in November 1869. The two had met in Jamestown during Goodrich's search for a place to practice medicine right after the Civil War. Before long the couple had children: Charles Cross, born in August 1870; Isabella, in February 1874; and David, who arrived in June 1876 (twins born in 1872 died in infancy). Less resilient than his partner, Morris resumed his real estate work in New York City, hoping to recoup his investment in the rubber company at a future date.[21]

Goodrich spent much of 1870 seeking a new location for rubber manufacturing, eventually choosing Akron. Perhaps, as legend at the BFGoodrich Company suggests, he was traveling by train to Cleveland when by chance an Akron businessman entered into conversation with him and convinced him to visit his town. More likely, Goodrich learned about Akron through a broadside that was widely distributed in the East by the town's Board of Trade. Touting Akron as being "at the beginning of greatness," the one-page flyer praised the town as possessing all of the prerequisites of a manufacturing center: abundant coal resources, transportation facilities, and a government responsive to the needs of industry (only two other comparable Ohio towns, the flyer pointed out, had lower tax rates than Akron).[22]

Akron had much to offer a budding industrialist like Goodrich. As the Board of Trade boasted, the city had canal and railroad connections to coal and other raw materials, and to regional and national markets for finished goods. Sitting astride the intersection of the Ohio & Erie and the Pennsylvania & Ohio Canals, Akron had grown as the "City on the Summit," perched on the crest of Ohio's watershed and linked to the rest of the state by mule-drawn canal boats. By the late 1860s and early 1870s, however, the canals were falling into disuse and were replaced by railroads. The coming of the Cleveland and Pittsburgh Railroad in 1852 provided connections to regional markets, and the Atlantic & Great Western Railway offered direct links to New York eleven years later. Although canals declined in significance for transportation purposes, they remained important as sources of clean, mineral-free water drawn from reservoirs such as Portage Lake and Long Lake. Copious supplies of pure water were needed in the making of rubber, especially in the first stage of work, when dirt and other impurities were washed out of the natural rubber gum.[23]

Probably most important to Goodrich, Akron was emerging as an industrial town and thereby had the people, businessmen and laborers, needed to support manufacturing advances. During the 1860s Ferdinand Schumacher put up the first of the great cereal mills on South Summit Street, naming his enterprise the Empire Barley Mill. The clay industry, established before the Civil War, was expanding, making Akron one of America's centers for sewer pipe production. Several entrepreneurs opened a branch of the Aultman works of Canton under the name of Aultman, Miller & Company to produce the Buckeye mower and reaper. John F. Seiberling, another manufacturer of reapers and mowers, moved his company to Akron from Massillon. Many of the businessmen involved in these industries would soon support Goodrich in his nascent rubber manufacturing venture. With industrial development came population growth. From an overgrown village of 3,500 in 1860, Akron became a goodsized town of 10,000 a decade later. Akron thus had a growing industrial workforce ready for employment in Goodrich's projected rubber factory.[24]

Akron possessed another key asset as well, an industrial business elite eager to attract Goodrich's plant and willing to provide Goodrich with financial backing. When Goodrich visited Akron in November 1870, he sought out George Crouse on his first day in town because, as president of the Board of Trade, Crouse had signed the board's promotional flyer. In approaching Crouse, Goodrich made a fortunate choice, for Crouse was well connected to the rest of Akron's business leaders and would soon become instrumental in the founding and early development of Goodrich's enterprise. Born in 1832 in Summit County, Crouse, like Goodrich, had been raised on a farm. Like Goodrich and many other late-nineteenth-century Americans, however, Crouse left the farm for town life, working as a teacher, deputy treasurer, auditor, and treasurer for Summit County in the late 1850s. During the Civil War he served briefly in the 164th Ohio Volunteer Infantry. He later turned most of his attention to business affairs. In 1863 he became the local agent for the Atlantic & Great Western Railroad in Akron. A few months later he became the financial manager for the Akron branch of Aultman, Miller and was made its secretary and treasurer in 1865. Crouse's interests extended beyond manufacturing reapers. In 1863 he was elected president of the Board of Trade, and seven years later helped organize the Bank of Akron.[25]

Crouse set up the meeting at which Goodrich successfully presented his ideas to Akron's business elite. After making his presentation, Goodrich called on those at the gathering for support. Their response was favorable, but the businessmen wanted to know more about Goodrich and his previous experiences. They selected George T. Perkins, who had just replaced Crouse as president of the Board of Trade, to travel to Melrose to look over Goodrich's operations.

Perkins was a logical selection for the task. Like Crouse, he would play a key role in the first several decades of Goodrich's rubber company's evolution, including a stint as the firm's second president. As a grandson of the founder of Akron and a son of one of Summit County's largest landowners and leading businessmen, Perkins understood Akron's development firsthand.[26] Born in 1836, he was only five years older than Goodrich. In 1859, after graduating from local schools and briefly attending Marietta College, Perkins went to work in an uncle's coal company. Enlisting as a private in the Civil War, he served capably and at times heroically. At an action in Perrysville, Kentucky, he had his horse shot out from under him, and at the Battle of Chickamauga he was wounded while leading a crucial charge. Upon his return to Akron, Perkins solidified his family's economic status by marrying the daughter of Levi Rawson, a former mayor of Akron and a businessman in the shipping trade. From 1867 to 1870 Perkins was the secretary of Taplin, Rice & Company, and in 1870 he became the president of the Bank of Akron (the same bank Crouse had founded).[27]

After inspecting Goodrich's plant at Melrose, Perkins urged his fellow businessmen to invest in Goodrich's proposed venture. As the head of one of his town's financial institutions, Perkins proved persuasive. Altogether twenty-three business leaders pledged $15,000 to Goodrich (of which $13,600 was actually paid in). Those providing funds included Crouse and Miller of Aultman, Miller; John Seiberling, the reaper manufacturer (whose sons would form Goodyear Tire and Rubber in 1898); Nelson Stone, the treasurer of the Weary-Snyder-Wilcox Manufacturing Company, a lumber manufacturing firm; Erhard Steinbacher, a prominent druggist; Alexander H. Commins of Allen & Commins, millers; Schumacher, the owner of Schumacher Mills; William T. Allen, the treasurer of the Webster, Camp & Lane Machine Company; Henry Clark of Clark & Barber, grain dealers; David King, the secretary of the Akron Sewer Pipe Company; and George Bates and John Pendleton, the president and the vice president of the Second National Bank, respectively. Perkins loaned $500 of his own funds.[28]

It is high testimony to the spirit of the midcentury boosterism sweeping through American towns and cities, especially in the Midwest, that businessmen in industry, trade, and finance all supported Goodrich's plans. Like Goodrich, Akron's business leaders were extremely optimistic about the future of their town and of the rubber industry. They had to be: after all, they were backing a man who, while successful in real estate, had struggled as a physician and had twice experienced difficulties in the rubber business. Goodrich's own commitment and enthusiasm—his willingness to uproot himself and his family, to invest all of his own capital in the venture, and his pledges of additional financial support from friends and family in New York—helped his case immensely. Still, backing Goodrich was a gamble.[29]

The Formation of Goodrich, Tew & Co.

Assured of the needed financing, Goodrich dismantled the Melrose plant and moved to Akron to begin anew. On 31 December 1870, Goodrich and four others set up the partnership Goodrich, Tew & Co. under Ohio law to manufacture various kinds of rubber goods. Goodrich contributed $22,500 to the partnership in the form of equipment from Melrose. Joining him as active partners were Harvey W. Tew, a brother-in-law from Jamestown who invested $7,500, and Henry Sanderson, the son of Goodrich's former landlady in New

York City, who contributed $2,500. Robert Newland, an uncle of Goodrich's wife's who lived in Jamestown, came in as an inactive partner, investing $5,000, as did David Marvin, a brother of Goodrich's wife's practicing law in Jamestown, who invested $3,000. It was to this group that the Akron businessmen loaned the $13,600. The partnership agreement was to be renewed annually, and under its terms the partners were to share in the profits or losses of their company proportional to their investments. The active partners were to devote themselves solely to the business of their new company, for which Goodrich and Tew would each receive annual salaries of $1,500 and Sanderson $858.[30]

Goodrich derived much of the support for the founding of Goodrich, Tew & Co. from family and friends. At its inception Goodrich, Tew & Co. resembled most new American companies, then and now: personal trust was essential in securing the starting capital. Goodrich, his wife's family, and his friend Sanderson accounted for three-quarters of the financing. A persuasive businessman, Goodrich reached beyond his immediate acquaintances to tap additional sources of capital in Akron. The key lay in his relations with Crouse and Perkins, two businessmen whose lives would become increasingly intertwined with the development of Goodrich's company. Connections with influential businessmen were important to Goodrich's success. Through their intercession he won the backing of the Akron group. However, even with their support, Goodrich, Tew & Co. began operations short of capital, a weakness soon exposed by unexpected events during the 1870s.

SURVIVAL AND EXPANSION, 1871–1888

Benjamin Goodrich formed his company at an auspicious time. The late nineteenth to the early twentieth century was a period of tremendous expansion for American business, as the United States became a predominately industrial and urban nation. From a country based on farms and small towns before the Civil War, America became a nation of factories and large cities by the time of World War I. In the 1880s, for the first time, more people worked in nonfarm than in agricultural jobs; by 1920 more people came to live in towns and cities than in villages and on farms. Between 1870 and 1920 America's gross national product (GNP) increased eightfold, and GNP per capita tripled. Manufacturing output rose nearly tenfold. B.F. Goodrich's two leading products for much of this period, fire hoses and rubber belting for machinery, benefited immensely from this growth.

Yet, the late nineteenth century was also a risky time for American business, a period full of dramatic ups and downs in the business cycle. A major depression shut down many industries in the mid-1870s, and a recession hurt many businesses a decade later. A very severe depression hit in the mid-1890s. There were winners and losers in the playing out of America's business cycle. With Goodrich's persistent entrepreneurship, the company survived the 1870s and expanded during the 1880s to become a regional industrial corporation of some repute. Under Perkins's leadership, the firm continued to grow in the 1890s and early 1900s.

Making and Selling Rubber Goods

Goodrich, Tew & Co. began operations on four lots on the north side of what was then called Factory Street, later renamed Rubber Street, in South Akron. Located near the upper basin of the Ohio & Erie Canal, the site provided the company the space and water needed to begin work. In February 1871 Goodrich, Tew & Co. finished construction of a factory building and moved in machinery. Described by an Akron newspaper as "machinery . . . of the heaviest description," this equipment was driven by a 150-horsepower steam engine.[31] Goodrich purchased raw rubber from brokers in New York City, which was then shipped to Akron by railroad and hauled from Akron's railroad station to the factory in mule-drawn wagons.

Manufacturing at the Goodrich plant progressed through several stages. The initial factory work took place on the first floor, where the crude rubber was soaked in warm water and then run through rough roller washers until all of the dirt had been removed. Next, the clean raw rubber was hung to dry for two weeks to six months over a large heater. Once dry, the rubber was ready to be made into usable items. The first step was to mix the raw rubber with sulfur and other chemicals and pass it through heavy rollers, from which it came out in thin layers. Depending on what the final products were to be, the remaining steps varied. If rubber belting or hoses were desired, the strips of rubber were fed, along with cotton duck, into calenders made up of three massive rollers kept continuously hot. These rollers pressed the rubber and cotton duck together, according to a contemporary account, "filling every fibre of the cloth with the rubber." For products not using cotton duck this step was skipped. Next, the rubber or rubber-impregnated duck was taken upstairs, where it was made into finished products. Last, the products were taken downstairs for heat curing in vulcanizers.[32]

Two specialty goods dominated Goodrich, Tew & Co.'s product line: fire hoses and industrial belting. The Midwest was rapidly urbanizing and industrializing in the early 1870s. Consequently, the region's burgeoning cities required fire hoses, and its factories needed miles of belting to connect steam engines to pieces of machinery. The Hudson River Rubber Company and the Melrose plant had made hoses; and, from the first, Goodrich, Tew & Co. manufactured them as well. However, Goodrich Tew & Co.'s thorough impregnation of the cotton duck with rubber through intensive calendering produced what the firm's publications correctly called "the first really serviceable conductor of fluids" made out of rubber. Labeled the "White Anchor" brand, the hoses became well known for their high quality.[33] Goodrich also made rubber belting from its earliest days, another product inherited from the Hastings and Melrose factories.

Although fire hoses and industrial belting were their leading products, the

The original workforce in Akron pose in front of their factory. (BFG Col. UAA)

firm's executives followed a policy of diversified production and sales. Initiating a strategy that would long distinguish his company from later entrants into the rubber business—such as Goodyear Tire and Rubber and Firestone Tire and Rubber, which in their early years made only tires—Benjamin Goodrich spurned excessive specialization. Goodrich, Tew & Co. made whatever rubber goods its owner-managers thought they could sell profitably. In addition to hoses and belting, the company made wagon springs, steam packing, wringer rolls for washing machines, valves, billiard cushions, tubing, gas bags, and fruit-jar rings. Footwear was one of the few rubber items the company did not make. Large eastern firms specializing in boots and shoes sold footwear at prices that it could not then match. Most of Goodrich's sales occurred through word-of-mouth to prospective customers in Akron and nearby towns such as Canton and Cleveland.[34]

The early 1870s were prosperous years for Goodrich, Tew & Co. Sales in 1871 came to nearly $50,000, an amount smaller than that predicted by Goodrich but a respectable sum. Within its first few months the company increased the size of its workforce from twenty to forty and maintained that number over the next few years.[35] About half of the original workers migrated from Goodrich's Melrose plant and trained new employees in Akron. Observers thought the new company had an auspicious future. A credit reporter for R.G. Dun noted in January 1872 that the company "appear[s] to be doing well."[36]

But a nationwide depression in the mid-1870s temporarily shattered hopes for expansion. America's GNP came to about $9.1 billion in 1869–73 and rose only slightly to $11.2 billion in 1872–76.[37] The slump slowed the development of America's rubber industry. In 1870 America had 56 rubber manufacturers capitalized at $7.5 million and employing 6,025 workers. By 1880, despite considerable recovery in the late 1870s (America's GNP came to $16.1 billion in 1877–81), little growth had occurred. More rubber companies had come into existence—there were 90 altogether, increasing competition in the industry—but their total capitalization had fallen to only $6 million, and their employment of 6,265 was about the same as ten years before.[38]

For Goodrich, Tew & Co., which was still trying to establish itself in the rubber trade, the results of the depression were little short of disastrous. By mid-1874 the company teetered on the brink of failure. A credit reporter explained the situation succinctly: "These parties are and have been cramped for ready means. Slow pay. Their net profits last year 10 [thousand]. Nearly all spent in repairs. . . . Prospts [prospects] not flattering."[39] These problems brought immediate changes to the company. Thoroughly discouraged, Tew and Sanderson dropped out of the partnership, which was reorganized in the fall of 1874 as B.F. Goodrich & Co. Goodrich was now the only active partner, with Newland and Marvin continuing as inactive ones.[40] This shake-up did little to improve the rubber company's finances. In November 1874 the partners were said to have "all the debts they can carry."[41] Their problems were not unusual. All of Akron's industrial establishments were hit hard by the depression. "In 1873 the panic which disrupted business throughout the whole nation had its effect on Akron," noted one chronicler. "Manufacturers and merchants— everyone—faced hard times; growth was temporarily at a standstill."[42]

Finally, in the spring of 1875, relief came when George Perkins agreed to endorse the notes of the partnership to a total of $35,000, a move that helped the company reestablish its credit and prosperity.[43] By the end of the year the company had earned a profit estimated by one outsider at $20,000 and was considered safe and responsible.[44] In large part, the company's return to profitability resulted from economic recovery in the United States during the late 1870s. As their tax bases were restored, municipalities bought fire hoses once again. The superiority of its fire hose gave B.F. Goodrich & Co. what one observer called "almost a monopoly" in that market.[45] The quality of its products thus gave Goodrich some limited control over its market niches. The company also became more aggressive in pushing its products. Goodrich brought Henry F. Wheeler into the company as a fire hose salesman, and he was quite successful. By 1877 cities across the United States—from Jackson, Mississippi, to Indianapolis, Indiana, and from Topeka, Kansas, to Oil City, Pennsylvania—had purchased Goodrich hoses. The market for industrial belting also picked up, and Goodrich was able to sell to such emerging national companies as the Standard Oil Company of Ohio and the E. Anheuser Company– Brewing Association of St. Louis, as well as to hundreds of smaller industrial ventures in the Midwest.[46] B.F. Goodrich & Co.'s sales rose to $234,000 in

1879, and the firm posted profits of $24,000.[47] The company finally was achieving the sales Benjamin Goodrich had projected a decade before.

Prosperity brought managerial changes to B.F. Goodrich & Co. In 1876 Wheeler became a minor partner with a claim to 5 percent of the company's profits, as did Benjamin T. Morgan, who had been acting as the office manager for some time. Morgan and Wheeler bought out most of the partnership shares of Newland and Marvin. However, this attempt to bring in new managerial talent to assist Goodrich in running the growing company did not work out well.[48] While deeply involved in starting up his company, Goodrich did not supervise his new junior partners closely enough. Wheeler and Morgan were, according to a contemporary credit reporter, "a little careless and did not fill their positions with satisfaction to the Concern." In fact, "some crookedness" was suspected in their dealings with the company, and by the close of the 1870s Goodrich was looking for a way to get rid of them.[49]

In spite of its successful weathering of the depression, B.F. Goodrich & Co. remained cash-poor, a situation that led to additional managerial changes. Once again Goodrich looked for someone to guarantee his company's notes. Perkins could not help because of financial reverses suffered by one of his enterprises. This time Crouse rescued the firm. In the fall of 1878 he agreed to endorse the partnership's paper in return for receiving 45 percent of its profits, up to a total of $45,000. Recognizing that B.F. Goodrich & Co. did not "have sufficient capital to carry on its business," Crouse looked to the incorporation of the company as soon as he had received his specified profits from the partnership. Crouse and Goodrich anticipated that they would each receive 45 percent of the stock in the corporation; Wheeler and Morgan, they agreed, would get 5 percent apiece.[50]

The Incorporation of the B.F. Goodrich Company

In early 1880 Goodrich and Crouse thought that the time had arrived to incorporate their firm, and on May 10 they transformed the partnership into an Ohio-chartered corporation, the B.F. Goodrich Company. Capitalized at $100,000 (1,000 shares of stock valued at $100 apiece), the company had seven stockholders. Goodrich received 333 shares. Crouse and Perkins held 202 shares each (Perkins received his shares as a gift from his friend Crouse). Richard P. Marvin Jr. (a brother of Goodrich's wife's), Morgan, and Wheeler obtained one share apiece. In addition, Alanson Work Jr., whom Goodrich had brought into the company as its plant manager in 1879, received 100 shares. The remaining 160 shares were not distributed at that time.[51]

Certainly one reason for incorporation was the chronic need for capital. As the company expanded, it required money. The corporate form of organization, with its promise of limited liability to investors, offered a potential means to secure the desired additional capital. Indeed, the capitalization of the new company was raised to $200,000 just two years after its founding. Goodrich explained, "the exigencies of business [have] compelled us to increase our capacity to such an extent that we find our present capital entirely inadequate to our wants."[52] Incorporation, however, initially brought in little new investment. Loathe to yield control of their company to outsiders, the owners were unwilling to dilute ownership in the corporation. The firm was, as one observer noted, very much "a close corporation" in its early years.[53] When the capitalization of the company was increased, the original stockholders were allowed to buy additional shares, paying for them over time with the dividends they generated. Moreover, whenever old shares came on the market, the original stockholders purchased them, again usually paying for them over time.

Perhaps more important in explaining the timing of the formation of the corporation was the desire of Goodrich and Crouse to rid themselves of Morgan and Wheeler. Despite the 1878 agreement, which pledged 5 percent of the new corporation's shares (fifty of the one thousand shares) to each of them, Wheeler and Morgan were allowed only one share apiece in the 1880 incorporation. After threatening a lawsuit against Goodrich and Crouse for their failure to honor the terms of the 1878 agreement, Wheeler and Morgan dropped all charges in return for a substantial cash payment. In early 1881 they sold their shares in B.F. Goodrich back to the firm.[54]

The management of B.F. Goodrich was standard. Stockholders elected a board of five directors each year, who, in turn, chose the officers of the corporation: the president, a vice president, a secretary, and a treasurer. On a daily basis, power rested with the president, who was assigned the "general supervision and charge of all the affairs and business of the Company," and the vice president, who doubled as the general plant superintendent.[55] At B.F. Goodrich the owners managed their corporation. Goodrich was the company's president, receiving an annual salary that reached $7,500 by the time of his death in 1888. Work served as vice president and superintendent, receiving an annual salary of $3,000, until he died unexpectedly in 1881. Crouse then became the company's vice president, serving without pay. Perkins was the firm's secretary and treasurer, receiving $1,000 annually until 1884, when Henry C. Corson, who had joined the company as its sales manager three years earlier, became the secretary at $2,000 per year, after which time Perkins was the company's treasurer. Throughout these years the board of directors—initially composed of Goodrich, Crouse, Perkins, Work, and Marvin—changed little.[56]

Alanson Work Jr. was by far the most important addition to B.F. Goodrich's management. Born in Quincy, Illinois, in 1842, Work was one year younger than Goodrich. He soon moved with his family to Connecticut, where he was educated in Hartford's public schools and at Trinity College. After clerking in New York City, Work relocated in 1869 to Cincinnati, where he served for four years as an engineer building railroads across Ohio. Returning east, he served first as an engineer for a company putting up railroad bridges, and then as the superintendent of the Allen Fire Department Supply Company at Providence, Rhode Island. The Allen Company, which made fire engines for fire departments across the nation, was where Work probably first learned of Goodrich's venture.[57]

Work joined Goodrich's company in Akron on 1 January 1879, as the plant superintendent, a position he held (along with that of vice president from 1880) until his death from illness in the fall of 1881. A bundle of energy, Work got along well with Goodrich. The two men lived near each other, and the first telephone line strung in Akron was a private line connecting their homes.[58] Given a free hand by Goodrich, Work expanded the Akron rubber company. Described by the company's bookkeeper as a man of "indomitable will and fertile brain," Work was a production man.[59] He moved quickly to increase the size of the company's factory and to make it more efficient. In 1881 the corporation put up its first office building, added a three-story brick factory building to handle "a large and growing increase" in business, and made major improvements to its power plant.[60] The improvements begun by Work continued after his death. In 1884 hydraulic presses replaced hand-powered ones in vulcanizing, for an estimated annual savings of 5 percent, and a year later Murphy Smokeless Furnaces were installed in the boiler room to "effect a saving in fuel."[61]

Upon Work's death, Goodrich resumed direct supervision of the rubber factory's daily operations, assisted by Frank H. Mason. Born in 1852 in Littlefield, New Hampshire, Mason had lived in Vermont, Pennsylvania, and California as a young man. In 1879 he came to Akron to take a job with Seiberling's mower and reaper company. On the way to that plant, however, he saw a help-wanted sign in the window of the Goodrich office and applied for work. Starting as a laborer in the mill room, he became a foreman within six months, the plant superintendent in 1882, and the general manager of the works in 1893, a position he held until his retirement in 1907. Like Work, Mason got along well with Goodrich. Goodrich's son David later recalled that his father even tutored Mason in "an old house near the factory . . . many a night." Mason was, however, not able to take as much of the management burden off of Goodrich's back as had been hoped, for he was often ill.[62]

Prosperity in the 1880s

Work, Mason, and Goodrich led their corporation into a period of substantial growth and prosperity. By 1881, at the close of its first full year of operations, B.F. Goodrich possessed assets of $233,000, made sales of $319,000, and posted profits of $69,000. A month before Benjamin Goodrich's death in August 1888, the company had assets of $564,000 and in that year earned profits of $107,000 on sales of $696,000.[63] Goodrich hardly exaggerated when in 1882 he called the company's operations "exceedingly prosperous," or when two years later he observed that his company was in a "most satisfactory condition."[64] Throughout the 1880s outside observers noted that B.F. Goodrich "was doing well + making money" and that it was "prompt in meeting all obligations."[65]

By 1883 the Goodrich factory and its workforce had grown in size. Notice the Goodrich fire hose in the lower right-hand corner. (BFG Co.)

B.F. Goodrich's growth occurred as part of the general industrial development in Akron. In 1881 the Valley Railroad (later part of the Baltimore & Ohio Railroad) provided additional transportation facilities for the city, and by the close of the decade, five lines linked the city to the outside world. New factories followed. Seiberling put up a six-story cereal mill, later converted into an oatmeal factory. The Diamond Match Company was formed in 1881 as a combine of twenty-eight formerly independent companies, with Ohio C. Barber as its president from 1888. (Barber would soon help found the Diamond Rubber Company, which quickly became a major competitor of B.F. Goodrich and which B.F. Goodrich acquired in 1912.) During the 1880s Akron's population rose from 16,500 to 27,600.[66] As one booster publication noted in 1886, the city's recent growth had been "marvelous," and the "future of the city is bright with the bow of promise."[67]

As it grew, Goodrich continued to make a diversified range of rubber products, still dominated by specialized products for niche markets. Fire hoses and industrial belting headed the list. In 1883 Goodrich was granted a patent on a type of industrial belting that achieved greater flexibility without any loss in its strength through a new method of vulcanization.[68] As before, however, company executives were reluctant to tie their firm's future too closely to any one or two products. Consequently, Goodrich made a wide range of rubber goods, expanding its scope of production by moving into manufacturing hard rubber items: combs, rods, tubing, and sheeting.[69]

To sell its products, Goodrich moved beyond word-of-mouth recommendations. At the time of its incorporation, the company engaged Henry C. Corson, a New York City newspaper reporter, to take charge of sales. Corson moved to Akron, where he composed letters soliciting the business of fire departments and industrial firms across America. Clerks—there were eight by the mid-

1880s—then copied his letters in their own handwritings, had them lithographed (typewriters came into common use at Goodrich only in the 1890s), filled in the names and addresses of the prospective customers, and sent them out.[70] These letters stressed the "quality and serviceability" of the Goodrich products. Unlike some rubber companies, Goodrich refused to offer discounts, preferring instead to emphasize what one epistle called its "high standard of quality."[71] Presumably, although no records have survived to show it, Goodrich also sold its goods across the United States through independent wholesalers. Such was the common practice at the time for nascent manufacturers that could not afford the costs of setting up their own national sales networks. Hard rubber products, however, as specialized items quite different from Goodrich's other goods, were handled separately. All hard rubber sales were made through a commission house in New York City.[72]

For the most part, Goodrich's strategy—a diversified product line and a strong emphasis on quality—resulted in healthy profits and an expanding enterprise. Nonetheless, problems plagued the young company, problems that persisted for rubber manufacturers for decades. Before the introduction of synthetic rubber in the mid-twentieth century, volatility in the supplies and prices of raw materials presented a basic business problem. The crude rubber used by Goodrich and other manufacturers came from wild trees in the Amazon River basin. Only in the early twentieth century did raw rubber, made from latex gathered from plantation trees in Southeast Asia, replace this source. Goodrich bought its crude rubber from New York City importers—more than thirty brokers in 1878 but only eleven in 1885—in lots ranging from 1,000 pounds to as many as 40,000 pounds at a time. In the 1880s Goodrich was just one of many rubber manufacturers in the United States. By 1890 there were 139 makers of rubber and woven elastic goods in America, capitalized at $13.7 million, employing 9,800 people, and turning out $18.7 million worth of goods.[73] In this competitive situation, Goodrich could exercise no control over the price of its most important raw material. That price varied tremendously from year to year, and even within a single year. In 1878 the company paid anywhere from 45½¢ to 55½¢ per pound for crude rubber, and at one point in 1882 the price touched $1.17.[74]

To lessen competition and moderate the swings in raw rubber prices, the corporation's owner-managers considered cooperating with their counterparts in other rubber companies. Like many American businessmen of the late nineteenth century, Goodrich's officers looked to combinations as one way to stabilize their business and make it more profitable. Through pools and trade associations, America's business leaders often sought to limit competition and bolster prices. As recessions bit into profits in the mid-1870s and mid-1880s, railroad executives formed America's first pools to apportion traffic and bolster sagging rates. Similarly, in many of the nation's major industries, such as the steel industry, business leaders shared market information and tried to set prices. Only in the late 1880s and early 1890s, with the establishment of the Interstate Commerce Commission to regulate railroads (1887) and the passage of the Sherman Antitrust Act (1890), did the federal government intervene to prevent such actions.

From its earliest days, competition hurt B.F.Goodrich, and in times of crisis the company's management considered cooperation as a way out of their troubles, as they would well into the twentieth century. In 1882 Benjamin Goodrich wrote the heads of various rubber companies proposing the formation of a single "central company," which would absorb sixty-two makers of rubber goods, including B.F. Goodrich.[75] Early in the following year he attended a meeting of rubber makers in New York City "to consider the propriety of consolidating the entire Rubber Manufacturing interest of the United States into one company." His company's directors gave Goodrich "full authority to bind the Company by signing any agreement which he might think for its best interest."[76] Although they still hoped for "ultimate success" in arranging a merger as late as April, no such combination emerged.[77] The idea of combination resurfaced in 1886. Seven important rubber manufacturers in Trenton, New Jersey, formed a pool for mechanical rubber goods, including industrial belting. The company's officers seriously considered joining the pool, and executives from two of the member companies were elected as directors of the corporation to facilitate the action. In the end, however, Goodrich's officers withdrew from committing their company to the pool.[78] Most likely, they thought they could do better on their own, for their company never suffered as much as many of their competitors during hard times. B.F. Goodrich earned profits even during 1885 and 1886. Then, too, the swings in the price of crude rubber temporarily lessened in the mid-1880s.

The Death of Benjamin F. Goodrich

Goodrich lived to see his company benefit from several years of accelerating growth before his death in 1888, and as the major stockholder in the company he enjoyed the fruits of that expansion. Some remembered Benjamin Goodrich as "a gentleman of quiet dignity," but there was more to him.[79] He also was known as one of the best poker players in Akron, probably enjoying games with Ohio Barber, another devotee of stud and draw. As his prosperity increased, Goodrich enjoyed driving fast horses hitched to his buggy and, his health permitting, trips to Europe, where he bet on horse races. He was successful in at least some of his wagers, for his son David later recalled that after visiting a Parisian track in 1885 his father returned to his hotel with his "clothing completely padded out with huge French bank notes" after he "picked winners in five out of six races."[80]

Goodrich's health had been seriously deteriorating since the mid-1880s. Never robust, he suffered from tuberculosis. Goodrich traveled to Europe for his health several times in the 1880s, but in the end exhaustion and illness overtook him. In January 1888 he sailed to Europe one last time, and five months later went west to a Colorado sanitarium, where he died.[81] Goodrich was buried in his wife's family plot in Jamestown, a resting place befitting a man who had depended so much on his in-laws during his early years in the rubber business. Among his pallbearers were George Perkins and his old partner in real estate, John Morris. For Goodrich's grave, the employees of his Akron firm contributed a white anchor made of flowers shaped to resemble the "White Anchor" trademark of Goodrich's fire hose.[82]

Goodrich had in a scant eighteen years built up one of Akron's leading businesses, a firm known throughout the Midwest for the scope and quality of its products. He could be justifiably proud of his accomplishments, and to his dying moments the company was his life. On 11 July 1888, just three weeks before he died, Goodrich called several of the officers of his company to his bedside in Colorado, with the certainty that his health was rapidly failing. At this final conference he gave his executives advice on how to continue operations after his death. He emphasized the need to maintain the high quality of products. "The only anxiety I have," Goodrich observed, "is whether the discipline is kept up, whether the repairs are kept up to the mark and whether the standard of quality is right up to the mark." When the firm's general plant superintendent asked if standards might not be too high, Goodrich replied that, to the contrary, "that is just where you are mistaken. By God, the standard can not be too high."[83]

B.F. GOODRICH AND TIRE MAKING, 1888–1907

Management succession proceeded smoothly, and, driven by an expanding product line, B.F. Goodrich increased its assets, sales, and profits fourfold during the 1890s, despite a very severe depression. Goodrich continued to manufacture many specialized products, but new commodity products made for a growing mass consumer market—bicycle tires, automobile tires, and footwear—ensured its prosperity. It went where promising markets and, increasingly, industrial research, especially in rubber chemicals, led it. Rapid growth continued during the opening years of the twentieth century, as sales doubled and assets and profits tripled between 1900 and 1907.

A New Management Team

Experienced men guided B.F. Goodrich's expansion, as the company continued to be led by a closely held group of owner-managers. George Perkins served as president until he stepped down in 1907, and Crouse acted as a vice president and director for many of these years. Corson rose to become the secretary, treasurer, and vice president of the company, while remaining a director. These leaders successfully attracted talented new people to Goodrich. Walter Folger replaced Corson to become the treasurer in 1894 and the assistant secretary five years later. Family ties and personal friendships remained of considerable importance to the firm's management. Richard Marvin Jr. became the secretary in 1889 and a director in 1890; and Goodrich's son Charles set up the company's first laboratory a few years later.

Nowhere were family ties more apparent, however, than in the rise of Bertram G. Work, the son of Alanson Work and his wife, Henrietta. Born in 1868, Bertram was just finishing his freshman year at Yale University when his father died. Rather than return to Yale, he joined B.F. Goodrich as a clerk. After about eighteen months of routine bookkeeping, he came close to quitting and even bought a red neckerchief and sombrero to wear on a trip out west. Benjamin Goodrich intervened and convinced Work to stay with the company. Like his father, Work was tireless, arriving at the factory well before its opening and often staying until midnight. He became general superintendent of the plant in 1893 and a vice president in 1902. David Goodrich later remembered Work as "one of the most diffident and bashful men I have ever known," a person who "hid behind an exterior gruff and forbidding." Work, he recalled, "barked at people on the telephone and he barked at people who came into his office." When under too much pressure on the job, he "would grab his hat, get on the train and go to Chicago or Cleveland or St. Louis. There he would get just about as boiled as a man could get. He'd stay at it until he had completely relaxed, then he'd go back to Akron and to the factory and go to work again." Hard-driving, Work also had charisma, despite his bashfulness. According to Goodrich, on one occasion Work talked the mill room employees out of going on strike. He "got up on a box and made a half hour speech. When it was finished, every worker took off his coat and went back to work." More than any other single individual, Work was the spark plug behind B.F. Goodrich's growth in the 1890s and early 1900s. As Goodrich recalled, "B.G. just about ran the plant." When Perkins retired, Work became the company's president.[84]

Research at Goodrich

Scientific research, as in the development of vulcanization, has always been important to the rubber industry. Chemical research, in particular, played a significant role in the industry's evolution. Goodrich established one of the first research laboratories in the rubber industry, indeed one of the first laboratories in the United States, to develop new products. (Boston Woven Hose and Rubber set up the first laboratory in the rubber industry in 1880. Goodrich's was the second.) By 1907 the cost of operating Goodrich's laboratory had risen to $16,000 annually, a significant increase over the $4,600 spent seven years before. Although it was significant, the laboratory was not yet as important a part of B.F. Goodrich's operations as it would later become.[85]

Goodrich was one of a few American industrial firms that pioneered in the use of research laboratories in the late nineteenth and early twentieth centuries. New products developed in their laboratories were used to maintain or increase their market shares in their industries. General Electric set up a laboratory in 1900 to advance the technology that would maintain its domination of the American electrical-lighting market, and American Bell set up a research laboratory in 1911 to increase its lead in telephone communications.[86]

At Goodrich, most of the early laboratory work was aimed at giving the company an advantage over its competitors in a broad range of rubber products.

Charles Goodrich founded the company's laboratory in 1895 and remained its head for the next twelve years. He graduated from Harvard in 1893, trained in chemistry and physics, and did a year of postgraduate work in science at the Massachusetts Institute of Technology and the Lawrence Scientific School at Harvard. Charles's first laboratory was a small room on the second floor of a three-story building on the north side of Factory Street, where he worked alone for three years. In 1898 he set up a larger laboratory on the second story of a new brick building that faced the canal. One room was a chemical laboratory well equipped with two long white tile-top tables for experiments, cupboards to store chemicals, suction pumps, and a still to supply distilled water. A second room was devoted to mixing, curing, and testing rubber compounds. Goodrich hired Ludwig Peterson, a chemist with Boston Woven Hose, in 1898. Several years later he hired two assistants, Arthur Warner and John Thomas, who held chemistry degrees from Buchtel College (later the University of Akron).[87]

Under Charles Goodrich's supervision the chemists tested and prepared new rubber compounds for their firm's growing array of products. They also tested pigments, oils, and fabrics and inspected the quality of raw materials coming into the company.[88] They performed limited basic research on ways to speed up the vulcanization process and to reclaim old scrap rubber for use as a material in manufacturing new rubber products, but enjoyed only limited success. Most of the problems they faced, Warner later recalled, were "mainly practical studies in rubber compounding."[89]

Secrecy long remained a byword in research at Goodrich and other rubber companies. David recalled that the factory, continuing a practice begun by Benjamin Goodrich, "actually had a series of secret recipes for rubber compounds kept in cypher or code."[90] As one early-day scientist recalled, "formulas or recipes for rubber compounds were guarded with unusual precautions . . . only top laboratory and factory executives knew what they were. Every ingredient had a number which was used in mixing and processing." This concern for secrecy went so far that William Geer, who replaced Charles Goodrich as the head of research in 1907, was allowed to attain the post only after marrying Bertram Work's sister, thus insuring his loyalty to the firm.[91]

Additional Diversification: Footwear

The officers at Goodrich followed a strategy of diversified production as the most fruitful way to achieve growth. As opportunities for new products—many of them specialty items for niche markets—opened up, they took advantage of them. The firm added rubber matting and tiles in 1897, and rubber thread a year later.[92] By 1898 Goodrich was also turning out what the rubber industry's leading trade journal described as "a high grade" golf ball; and further improvements soon made this ball the industry leader in the United

States.[93] Nevertheless, Goodrich also made commodity products for America's emerging mass consumer market.

Footwear was a new commodity product for Goodrich, produced as the firm grew in strength. Too weak at first to go head-to-head with United States Rubber and the other leading American rubber footwear makers, Goodrich entered the fray in the early 1900s. Goodrich's executives first gave "serious consideration" to making rubber footwear in 1898, and in 1905 the directors approved the establishment of a department "for the manufacture of boots and shoes." Later in the year they set up the Akron Rubber Shoe Company as a wholly owned subsidiary.[94] The company began making lightweight footwear under the "straight-line" label for sale in 1906. A year later, when boots and shoes accounted for 4 percent of Goodrich's total sales, the subsidiary was worth $470,000.[95]

Goodrich Manufactures Bicycle Tires

The expansion of its traditional product lines alone would not have brought prosperity to Goodrich in the 1890s, for the depression, the worst to that time in American history, shattered American business in the middle of the decade. Between 1893 and 1897 some eight hundred banks failed, industrial production fell by about 25 percent, and 20 percent of the workforce was unemployed.[96] Many companies producing well-established rubber goods saw their earnings drop. Goodrich thrived despite the depression. Sales increased yearly, and earnings only fell off slightly in 1896 and 1897.[97] Much of the reason for Goodrich's success lay in the company's rapid movement into the production and sale of bicycle tires—like footwear, a commodity product for a mass market. Following a minor bicycle craze in the 1880s, the United States experienced a major one in the 1890s. Despite the depression, Americans found money to buy bicycles. As "safety" bicycles replaced older "ordinary" bicycles with high front wheels, the output of bicycles in the United States soared from 12,000 in 1881 to 1.2 million in 1896. The bicycle craze created a demand for rubber tires.

The bicycle tire evolved rapidly. The ordinary bicycle of the 1870s used hard rubber strips cemented into metal channels around wheel rims. Improvements came with the development of the pneumatic (inflatable) tire, whose commercial use is usually credited to John Boyd Dunlop, a Scot, in 1888. The development of the clincher rim in 1890 made it easier to attach tires to and remove them from wheel rims. Two additional improvements in 1893 were of particular significance for Goodrich. P. W. Tillighast was granted a patent on single-tube tires (tires without inner tubes), and John F. Palmer acquired both the British and American patents needed to make cord tires. In cord tires internal friction and heat were reduced by using fabric layers nearly parallel to each other, rather than crossing each other at right angles, thus increasing greatly the life of the tires.[98]

Goodrich was among the companies that pioneered the manufacture of bicycle tires. Goodrich was making solid rubber bicycle tires by 1888 then switched to pneumatic tires in the early 1890s. It became one of the first American companies to make pneumatic tires as a licensee under the Palmer and Tillighast patents. As the *Akron Beacon Journal* correctly observed in late 1893, "With the introduction of the pneumatic tire into America a little over three years ago, the Goodrich people were among the first to grasp the idea and to realize that it was the tire of the future."[99] Goodrich produced single- and double-tube tires (double-tube tires had inner tubes) for some of America's leading bicycle makers.[100] In 1898, Goodrich executives, following their company's tradition, decided to make only high-grade bicycle tires. In February of that year, they announced that "although the trade generally seem inclined toward a lower-priced tire than was offered last year, which necessarily means a cheaper tire, the Goodrich company have [sic] decided that it would not be to their own or their customers' benefit to offer a lower-priced tire."[101] Later in 1898 Goodrich purchased sole rights to manufacture bicycle tires under the Palmer patents in the United States.[102]

By the mid-1890s the bicycle tire market had become very competitive, and Goodrich's officers worked with the executives of other companies to try to limit that competition. Here they went further than they had in their cooperative efforts to try to control raw rubber prices and competition a decade earlier. In 1896 Goodrich became one of seventeen companies to found the Rubber Tire Association. Perkins served as the organization's second vice president, and Corson was a member of its executive committee. The association, which lasted for two years, sought to decrease competition by devising and holding its members to a standard customer guarantee on tires and by improving the quality of bicycle tires. However, companies making about a third of the bicycle tires in America remained outside of the association and undercut its efforts. By 1898 it was no longer important.[103] Growth in the sales of bicycle tires necessitated improvements to Goodrich's factory and its workflow during the late 1880s and early 1890s. Physical improvements included the installation of electric lighting and a telephone system and additional mixing mills to wash the raw rubber, warming mills and calenders in which to work the rubber, and vulcanizers to cure the finished products.[104] In 1892 the company increased the size of its tire making room and three years later made extensive additions to two other buildings to provide still more space for bicycle tire making.[105] In 1899 the firm erected a new tire making facility at a cost of $240,000.[106] By the close of 1898, 2,200 Goodrich employees worked in factory buildings covering nearly ten acres.[107]

Just as the rubber industry pulled out of the depression of the 1890s, America's bicycle industry entered a long-term slump, causing the collapse of bicycle tire demand. The value of bicycle tires sold in the nation fell from $26 million in 1898 to only $3.7 million in 1904.[108] Bicycle tires accounted for 25 percent of Goodrich's total sales and generated 20 percent of its profits in

1902, but by 1907 they composed a scant 3 percent of its sales and 6 percent of its profits. The collapse of the market for bicycle tires taught Goodrich's management lessons they would carry for decades. The market slump reaffirmed their desire to keep their company diversified so that it would never rely too much on one product for its sales and profits. This determination to remain diversified would, in the second decade of the twentieth century, lead Goodrich's executives to hesitate in going full tilt into the booming automobile tire market.

A Pioneer in Making Automobile Tires

That Goodrich eventually would fall behind other companies in making automobile tires was far from apparent in the late 1890s. As the first American firm to make pneumatic automobile tires (Michelin had already made such tires in France), Goodrich pioneered in making automobile tires in America. Its work on bicycle tires led Goodrich into manufacturing automobile tires. The facilities constructed to make bicycle tires could be used in the production of automobile tires, for in its infancy automobile tire making did not need much specialized machinery. In 1896 Alexander Winton, a former bicycle maker who headed the newly founded Winton Automobile Company of Cleveland, visited the Goodrich production works to ask Bertram Work to make tires for his cars. Although Goodrich had never made such tires, Work agreed to do so; but he insisted that Winton bear the development expenses. For $400, which included the cost of making new tire molds, Winton took delivery of a set of 36" by 4" tires (double-tube clinchers) by the end of the year.[109]

Goodrich benefited greatly from the early-twentieth-century expansion of the automobile industry. Car registrations in the United States rose from 14,800 in 1901 to 140,300 six years later, and in the same period the annual sale of tires increased from 97,000 to 593,000.[110] By 1904 the value of automobile tires sold in America was nearly double that of the value of bicycle tire sales. Goodrich rode the crest of this change. Its output surged from 45,000 automobile tires in 1904 to nearly 140,000 three years later, when the product accounted for over one-third of the company's sales and profits.[111]

Goodrich faced several major competitors in the automobile tire business, but its fiercest rival was the United States Rubber Company. Formed in 1892 as a consolidation of footwear manufacturers, U.S. Rubber entered tire production when it acquired the Rubber Goods Manufacturing Company in 1905. The Rubber Goods Manufacturing Company, in turn, had resulted from the 1898 merger of most companies making mechanical rubber products, such as belting. As with the rubber goods merger talks of the 1880s, the officers of Goodrich initially considered joining the Rubber Goods Manufacturing Company, only to stay out at the last minute.[112] U.S. Rubber produced bicycle tires but, like Goodrich, switched to automobile tires in the opening years of the

THE WINTON MOTOR-GARRIAGE CO.

Winton automobiles were the first to use Goodrich tires. (BFG Co.)

twentieth century. While the company sold its tires as original equipment directly to automakers, a system of branch stores sold replacement tires directly to automobile owners. Like Goodrich, U.S. Rubber was a diversified rubber producer, for whom automobile tires became increasingly important.[113]

None of the other tire makers was as large or as diversified as U.S. Rubber. Frank and Charles Seiberling—the sons of John Seiberling, one of the Akron industrialists who had loaned money to Benjamin Goodrich in 1871—formed the Goodyear Rubber Company in 1898 as an Akron corporation. They named it in honor of Charles Goodyear, who had developed vulcanization. (Charles Goodyear thus had no ownership or management tie to the company that bore his name.) Impressed by Goodrich's sales and profits, the Seiberlings quickly took Goodyear into the production of bicycle tires. Like Goodrich, Goodyear was hurt by the slump in bicycle sales in the early twentieth century and turned its attention to automobile tires. By 1908 the company was making nine hundred tires a month, mainly for Ford, Reo, and Buick.[114] Harvey Firestone, who had extensive experience as a salesman for several makers of rubber carriage tires in Chicago and Akron, formed his own company in Akron in

1900. His firm began business by first attaching rubber tires made by other companies (including Goodrich) to carriage wheels and then selling them. Firestone Tire moved into making rubber tires in 1903, using supplies of prepared rubber and fabric purchased from Goodrich. The company's initial growth was modest, but in 1906 Firestone landed a major order from Ford Motors, setting the stage for rapid development.[115] Former Goodrich employees founded Diamond Rubber, a final rival firm, in 1894, putting up a small factory on land acquired from the Diamond Match Company right across the street from the Goodrich plant. With an infusion of capital from Ohio C. Barber, Diamond Rubber quickly developed into one of Akron's leading rubber companies. By 1909, the company possessed a workforce of 1,685 and had become a major competitor of Goodrich in the field of automobile tires.

B.F. Goodrich's pioneering efforts in bicycle and automobile tires in the 1890s gave it advantages over many of its competitors that did not enter the automobile tire business until the early 1900s. In addition to its edge in production technologies (derived from manufacturing bicycle tires), Goodrich also enjoyed ties to major companies that allowed it to place its tires on their cars as original equipment. High-end companies such as Winton, Pierce Arrow, Franklin, Stanley, and Packard bought mainly from Goodrich. Like U.S. Rubber, Goodrich also established a national system of branch houses to market replacement tires to consumers. These advantages allowed Goodrich to control 21 percent of America's automobile tire market in 1908. U.S. Rubber was the nation's other large producer of tires, making 25 percent of America's total as late as 1912. In 1909 the combined output of Goodyear and Firestone came to only two-thirds of Goodrich's output of automobile tires.[116]

Even as it competed with other rubber companies in manufacturing tires, B.F. Goodrich cooperated with them. In the late 1890s and early 1900s the company joined with others, including Goodyear, in an effort to limit competition by purchasing from the Single Tube Automobile and Tire Company the right to manufacture automobile tires under the Tillighast patents. Companies not so licensed were excluded from making certain types of tires.[117] Similarly, in 1903 Goodrich joined the Rubber Goods Manufacturing Company and several others in setting up the Clincher Tire Association. This body tried to limit competition by acquiring patents that gave its members the sole right to make clincher automobile tires. It also set production quotas and prices. Goodyear was given a very small allocation, and Firestone was excluded altogether.

The plan backfired. Goodrich was no more successful in limiting competition in automobile tires than it had been in bicycle tires. Companies left out of the association were motivated to develop ways to attach tires to wheel rims not covered by the clincher patents. Led by Goodyear and Firestone, they developed a "straight-side" tire that was much easier for motorists to change than the clincher tire. It was through its development of the straight-side tire that Firestone was able to secure its first orders from Ford and emerge as a strong competitor in the automobile tire industry. Membership in the Clincher Tire

Association thus hurt Goodrich by stifling innovation and spurring several small, new rubber companies to develop into major competitors.[118]

Expansion of the Sales Network

The expansion of Goodrich's operations and the alterations of its product mix brought changes to its sales system. The sales staff in the Akron office was reorganized as an advertising department in 1890 and had grown to thirty-two people by 1910. As before, the salesmen mailed solicitations to potential customers, especially those who might be interested in hose and belting.[119] They sent out increasingly elaborate brochures, folders, circulars, and pictures proclaiming the merits of their company's goods. The company also used more and more national advertising in rubber industry trade journals such as the *India Rubber World* to push its products. Such efforts were not enough, however, to sell footwear and tires as commodity products to consumers. Goodrich took special pains to show off these new wares at national trade shows. The company was well represented at the meetings of the League of American Wheelmen and the National Cycle Association, for example.[120]

Like U.S. Rubber, B.F. Goodrich set up a system of branch houses to sell its automobile tires (the branch houses sold some other Goodrich products, but tires were by far most important). Car manufacturers, recognizing the importance of tire service to successful car operations, required tire makers seeking their original equipment business to provide field service and sales through branch houses. Equally important, the establishment of branch houses fit in with the desires of the tire makers. Setting up branch houses was a typical strategy used by many late-nineteenth-century manufacturers to achieve greater control over the sale of their products. Instead of selling through sometimes unreliable independent wholesalers, they established their own distribution systems.[121]

For Goodrich the use of branch houses began in New England. For a number of years, the Columbia Rubber Works Company of New York City had been selling Goodrich's products to consumers in the region. In an effort to control those sales, Goodrich purchased Columbia Rubber in 1898 and turned it into its first company-owned branch house.[122] By 1907 Goodrich also had branch houses in Boston, Buffalo, Denver, Detroit, Philadelphia, Cleveland, and St. Louis.[123] Branch houses accounted for 52 percent of the total value of Goodrich's automobile tire sales in 1907. However, in areas with less immediate sales potential, usually sparsely populated regions, Goodrich remained dependent on others to sell its goods. In 1900, to tap the growing West Coast market, Goodrich designated the Gorham Rubber Company of San Francisco as its selling agent.[124] To supervise this expanding network of sales outlets, the office of manager of sales was created in 1901.[125]

Goodrich also devised a new marketing channel for boots and shoes. The firm's subsidiary, Akron Rubber Shoe, sold its footwear through an independent company, the Mishawaka Rubber Shoe Company of Indiana. Founded in

1897, Mishawaka Rubber employed more than 1,300 workers by 1901 and had the capacity to produce more than 3,600 pairs daily, giving the firm sales of $3 million a year.[126] Only in the 1910s did Goodrich begin selling footwear directly through its own outlets.

Foreign markets first attracted attention from Goodrich in the 1890s. In 1892 the company sold 1,500 pneumatic bicycle tires in Great Britain.[127] In 1896 Work made extensive trips to Europe to explore marketing possibilities there. Two years later, with the Hartford Rubber Company and the Boston Hose and Rubber Company, Goodrich established the Single Tube Tire Company to sell tires in Great Britain.[128] In 1899 Work returned to Europe on a month-long visit to look into both sales and production opportunities. After going to France, Germany, Austria, and Britain—where Goodrich was selling tires through independent agents—he recommended setting up a foreign department in the Akron office. He urged Goodrich's executives to consider moving more deeply into the European market "through already established concerns," finding prospects in France particularly enticing. Although little came immediately from Work's trip, his journey laid the groundwork for Goodrich's overseas expansion at a later date.[129]

Akron: America's Rubber Center

With its entrance into the manufacture and sale of new products, especially tires, by 1907 Goodrich was a vastly different company from that at the time of Benjamin Goodrich's death. In 1907 bicycle and automobile tires made up 41 percent of the firm's sales and earned 40 percent of its profits. By contrast, hoses and belting declined in importance. Tubing and hoses composed only 17 percent of the company's sales and earned but 14 percent of its profits that year. Belting accounted for even less, just 5 percent of sales and 4 percent of profits. By that time B.F. Goodrich employed about 2,500 workers making rubber products in the following major production departments: automobile tires, druggists' supplies, footwear, hose and tubes, molded goods, and bicycle tires. Some 104 employees composed the office force in 1905.[130]

Goodrich's diversified growth made Akron America's rubber center. In 1891 the rubber industry, with only B.F. Goodrich there then, was the city's fourth-largest industrial employer, after the mower and reaper industry, the clay products industry, and the match industry.[131] The depression of the mid-1890s severely injured many of Akron's established industries (at one point industrial unemployment in the city reached 51 percent), thus increasing the relative importance of the rubber industry. Schumacher's Jumbo Mill, the largest cereal mill in America, burned in 1886, and in the 1890s his business became part of the American Cereal Company (later Quaker Oats), headquartered in Chicago. John Seiberling's reaper and mower company failed, and Aultman, Miller was acquired by International Harvester.[132] Rubber companies took up the slack, beginning, by the early 1900s, to make Akron the rubber capital of Ohio and the United States. By 1905 Goodrich had been

B.F. Goodrich was well known as a diversified rubber manufacturer in the
early twentieth century. (BFG Col. UAA)

joined by twenty-six other rubber companies in Ohio, making the manufacture of rubber products the fourteenth-most-important industry in the state.
Thirteen of the rubber companies were located in Akron and accounted for
about one-third of the city's industrial capital and workforce.[133] The development of the rubber industry brought continuing population growth to Akron.
About 43,000 persons lived in the city by 1900; there were 69,000 Akronites a
decade later.

Numerous factors accounted for Akron's rise as a rubber city. The availability of clean water, good transportation facilities, cheap fuel from Ohio's coal
mines, and a relatively inexpensive labor supply (Akron rubber companies
paid their workers 20 percent less than the national average for rubber workers
in 1899) enticed would-be rubber manufacturers to Akron. The biggest attraction, however, was B.F. Goodrich's success. Entrepreneurs, well aware of the

Sales and Profits by Major Departments, 1902 and 1907

	1902 Department Sales	% of Total BFG Sales	1902 Department Profits	% of Total BFG Profits	1907 Department Sales	% of Total BFG Sales	1907 Department Profits	% of Total BFG Profits
Bicycle tires, etc.*	$1,468,251	25	$216,374	20	$719,989	6	$78,709	3
Tubing & hose	1,197,836	20	204,498	19	1,862,030	14	273,210	12
Molded goods	834,041	14	202,392	19	1,082,224	8	233,513	10
Druggist sundries	624,000	11	14,865	1	878,107	7	115,399	5
Solid tires	415,295	7	22,571	2	513,962	4	12,962	1
Golf balls	399,040	7	125,328	11	221,531	2	30,039	1
Rubber belting	286,134	5	21,997	2	603,408	5	82,920	4
Handmade goods	266,316	5	47,054	4	309,674	2	59,182	3
Cotton hose	166,097	3	22,329	2	353,873	3	49,942	2
Matting, tiling, packing	59,860	1	3,995	0	486,262	4	77,620	3
Rubber thread**	19,694	0	2,380	0	111,315	1	4,706	0
Auto tires	0	0	0	0	4,461,428	35	869,220	37
Rubber boots & shoes	0	0	0	0	549,152	4	404	0
Major division total	$5,736,564	98	$883,783	80	$12,152,995	95	$1,887,826	81
Total company sales	$5,888,209		$1,093,855		$12,930,046		$2,323,889	

Source: P. W. Leavitt, "History of and Statistics Appertaining to the B.F. Goodrich Co.," BFG Col., box NA-1, file 14.

Note: Columns of percentages do not total 100% because a few minor product lines are not included.

*1902 figure includes automobile tires.

**Intercompany sales excluded.

company's growth and profitability, located in Akron hoping to duplicate the firm's enviable record.

MANAGING GROWTH

In running their company, the executives at B.F. Goodrich successfully balanced a quest for growth with a desire to enjoy a life in Akron's high society. The strategy first annunciated by Benjamin Goodrich of producing a diverse range of high-quality goods proved to be a viable formula for success. Goodrich's closely knit group of officers presided over a growing and very prosperous company. The tremendous profitability of Goodrich from the 1880s into the early twentieth century allowed its officers both to substantially increase their company's productive facilities and to pay out large dividends. As first and second generation owner-managers, Goodrich's executives worked hard, putting in long hours. Risk-taking entrepreneurs, they had a direct personal stake in the success of their company and their community and identified very closely with them. They regarded B.F. Goodrich as "their" company.

Personal Management

Those owning shares in B.F. Goodrich benefited enormously from their stake in the company. As investors they received generous cash and stock dividends. Even during the depression of the 1890s, the average annual dividend paid on common stock came to nearly 20 percent. Moreover, as the capitalization of the company was increased in steps from $100,000 in 1880 to $10 million in 1906, stockholders were allowed to buy the newly issued shares—paying for them over time with the earnings from those shares, as was then customary in American business.[134] By the late 1890s and early 1900s, the company was no longer quite the closed corporation it had been in the early 1880s. Stock ownership had become more dispersed as a result of inheritance and sales. Nonetheless, the Goodrich, Perkins, Mason, Corson, Work, and Crouse families owned over 90 percent of the company's stock as late as 1899.[135] Officers benefited from high salaries. In 1907 the president received $25,000, the first vice president $20,000, the second vice president $12,500, the treasurer $8,500, and the secretary $8,000.[136] A survey conducted by Harvard University economists showed that the chief executive officers of American companies capitalized at $1.5 million or more received average salaries of about $10,000 during the years 1904 through 1914.[137]

The management style at Goodrich was characterized by informality in its early years. Especially in the 1870s and 1880s the company's operations were small and simple enough to be run without many managerial hierarchies or detailed rules. Business was conducted on a personal, face-to-face basis. When Benjamin Goodrich needed to buy additional boilers in 1881 between the board of directors' quarterly meetings, he had "an informal talk" with several of the directors, after which he purchased the equipment.[138] Even in the late

TABLE 1.2

Ratios of Financial and Operating Performances, 1881–1907

	Return on Assets* (%)	Return on Average Stockholder Equity** (%)
1881	30	43
1882	29	38
1883	25	30
1884	26	31
1885	20	26
1886	17	21
1887	10	14
1888	19	28
1889	29	36
1890	20	25
1891	19	25
1892	21	29
1893	24	32
1894	24	29
1895	29	33
1896	18	21
1897	14	17
1898	21	29
1899	20	27
1900	16	21
1901	19	24
1902	27	31
1903	14	16
1904	23	26
1905	26	29
1906	20	22
1907	19	21

Sources: "Directors Meetings," 1881–1907; P. W. Leavitt, "History of and Statistics Appertaining to the B.F. Goodrich Co.," BFG Col., box NA-1, file 14.
*Return on Investment on Total Assets: Income + Interest Expense (Net Income Tax)/Total Average Assets (Interest Expense and Income Tax figures not available).
**Return on Stockholder Equity: Net Income/Average Stockholder Equity.

1880s the factory grounds were used as a play area by neighborhood children. Fishing for bluegills was good in the upper canal basin, and workmen in the nearby Goodrich factory took time to cut rubber pieces for the boys' slingshots. Old discarded sugar barrels held "great attractions for the boys."[139]

Labor relations, like the management of the company, were informal, with paternalistic, personal relations as the norm. Benjamin Goodrich gave turkeys or dollar bills to all employees each Thanksgiving and Christmas.[140] In 1878 company workers took out a notice in the *Akron Beacon Journal* to "return their sincere thanks to Messrs. B.F. Goodrich & Co., who so amply supplied their families and tables with excellent turkeys, given to them as a token of esteem and goodwill."[141] In the 1880s the company maintained a baseball diamond for neighborhood boys and a grocery store for its employees.[142] Annual company picnics, featuring athletic contests during the day and dances in the evening, were well attended by management and labor alike. Beginning in 1892 the company supported a brass band that offered a regular program of summer concerts to all Akronites each year. The company also opened a "light airy lunch room" for factory employees in early 1899.[143] Despite these practices, some problems arose. Walkouts occasionally took place.[144] Thefts of tools and even of crude rubber were a nuisance.[145]

Bureaucratic Management

As B.F. Goodrich grew in size and complexity, informal management practices gave way to more bureaucratic ones. New management positions were created: general manager of the works in 1894, second vice president a year later, and assistant secretary and assistant treasurer in 1901. In 1901 a four-member board of control, composed of the president and three directors, was established "to assist the President in the management of the business" between meetings of the board of directors, and the size of the board of directors was increased from five to seven members.[146] Two women, Mrs. Benjamin Goodrich and Mrs. Alanson Work, served on the board of directors for short periods, though neither played much of a role in policy making.

At the operating level, B.F. Goodrich adopted a departmental structure in 1898, formalizing a direction in which the company had been moving for over a decade. By the early 1880s, Benjamin Goodrich had come to rely heavily on foremen placed in charge of what were already being called departments: the mill room, the press room, hose and belting, wringer rolls, tubes, the machine shop, and shipping.[147] This structure was elaborated in the early 1890s, and near the end of the decade a departmental organization was fully implemented. As the company's chief accountant explained, "in the fall of 1898 it was decided to divide the business into different departments in order to definitely know the cost and profits on the many and various classes of goods manufactured."[148] Twenty-five departments existed by 1907. The departments were based on individual product lines or on specific functions performed for the entire company. Some, such as the washing, milling, and calendering departments, prepared materials for other departments to use. Others, such as the bicycle tire, automobile tire, and boots and shoes departments, manufactured the finished goods. Still others, such as the shipping, advertising, and research departments, provided support services. "A very thorough [internal] cost [accounting] system" was set up to keep track of company operations.[149]

Labor relations also grew in complexity as Goodrich expanded. Much of the paternalism lasted into the twentieth century. As late as 1902, for example, it was common for management to shut down the company's plants for thirty minutes so that the workers could go outside to view passing circus parades.[150] Goodrich officials mixed their paternalism with a steadfast opposition to unionism, as did officers in other Akron rubber companies. Akron's rubber company managers first encountered unionism with the formation of the Amalgamated Rubber Workers' Union of North America in 1902. The Akron local claimed that its membership list was stolen and that employers used it as the basis of blacklisting and firing union members. Union officers accused Goodrich of engaging in discriminatory firing.[151] B.F. Goodrich and the other rubber companies took the lead in forming the Akron Employer's Association, which aimed at preventing the formation of unions.

SUCCESS

By the early twentieth century, B.F. Goodrich had emerged as one of the most successful rubber companies in the United States. Second in size only to U.S. Rubber, Goodrich was one of the most profitable firms in the American rubber industry. Goodrich was part of a rapidly growing industry. By 1904, 265 U.S. rubber companies capitalized at nearly $100 million employed 44,000 workers to produce nearly $150 million worth of rubber goods.[152] With assets of $12.5 million in 1907, B.F. Goodrich was not quite yet a big business by national standards, but it was rapidly becoming one.

No single factor accounted for B.F. Goodrich's success. How Goodrich was run partly explained its success. Benjamin Goodrich and the other executives were persistent entrepreneurs. They were willing to take risks and never despaired, even during the hard times of the mid-1870s when their company came close to failing. Benjamin Goodrich's greatest contribution to his firm was his optimism. Despite the problems he encountered in the rubber industry in New York in the 1860s and in Ohio during the 1870s, he continued to work hard to make his company a success. Goodrich, the Works, and others in management also proved innovative and flexible in their approaches to business. They aimed at making high-quality goods through advanced production processes, whether those products were fire hoses, belting, or tires. While committed to producing a wide variety of rubber goods, they were flexible in the mix of goods they made—specialty and commodity products alike—in any particular time period. They were willing—indeed, eager—to take the lead in manufacturing new products as soon as markets existed for them. Having a re-

TABLE 1.3

Comparison of Major Rubber Companies' Financial Performance, 1907

	Net Sales	Net Income	Net Income as a Percentage of Net Sales
U.S. Rubber	$39,716,000	$4,590,000	12
B.F. Goodrich	12,930,046	2,323,889	18
Goodyear	2,190,000	NA	NA
Firestone	1,681,000	214,287	13

Sources: Allen, *House of Goodyear*, unpaged appendix; Babcock, *United States Rubber*, 421; "Directors Meeting," 1912; Lief, *Firestone Story*, 416.
Note: NA = not available.

search laboratory aided in this respect and would become still more important in later years.

Nonetheless, companies headed by owner-managers that were just as hardworking and innovative as those at B.F. Goodrich have failed; there was more to the company's success than how it was managed. The social and economic environments within which B.F. Goodrich operated aided the development of the firm. Benjamin Goodrich's acceptance by the Akron business elite was especially important. Like Goodrich himself, Perkins, Crouse, and many other Akronites were young men on the make, adventurous entrepreneurs seeking out opportunities in commerce, finance, and, increasingly, in industry. They supported Goodrich's enterprise as a way of improving their own fortunes, as well as those of Akron. They readily accepted Benjamin Goodrich as one of their own. In fact, Goodrich served on Akron's city council in 1880 and 1881, acting as the body's president in the latter year. Such positions of respect brought advantages to the business. For instance, when B.F. Goodrich needed more land for factory expansion, company officers were able to get the city of Akron to vacate a nearby street, which they then purchased.[153]

National economic developments also proved favorable to the growing company. Despite the economic downturns that punctuated the middle of each of the closing decades of the nineteenth century, the late nineteenth and early twentieth centuries were a time of tremendous economic growth in the United States. B.F. Goodrich was in the right place at the right time with the right products to participate in this growth. Its fire hoses and industrial belting served well the burgeoning cities and factories of the Midwest in the 1870s and 1880s, and its footwear and tires appealed to consumers with money to spend in the 1890s and early 1900s. By seizing on key emerging markets, Goodrich executives succeeded in expanding their firm.

2

The Growth of the Tire Industry: Diversification in Rubber Products, 1908–1918

Rubber manufacturing experienced a fundamental transformation in the early twentieth century. With the advent of the automobile age, automobile tires became the most important product for rubber makers. Henry Ford began making his famous Model T in 1908 and over the next decade applied moving assembly-line production techniques. As the mass production of automobiles became the norm in America, the production of passenger cars rose from 356,000 in 1912 to 1.5 million just four years later.[1] The value of tires and tubes made in the United States nearly tripled in the four years following 1912; by 1914 they accounted for nearly one-half the value of the rubber products made in America.[2] B.F. Goodrich participated only partially in this change. Stung by the collapse of their bicycle tire business, Goodrich executives hesitated to commit fully to automobile tires. That reluctance opened the door for other rubber manufacturers to lead in tire production.

As the president of B.F. Goodrich for two decades (beginning in 1907), Bertram G. Work left a strong imprint on the corporation. Writing to members of the executive committee in 1915, Work reaffirmed the company's commitment to a broad range of rubber goods and warned against becoming too dependent on automobile tires. He observed that "some years ago it became evident that our tire business was becoming too large a factor of our total and that we might at any time find ourselves at the mercy of the automobile industry." B.F. Goodrich was fortunate, Work thought, "in having a diversified business."[3] At a time when several of its competitors—most notably Goodyear and Firestone—focused their energies on making automobile tires, Goodrich consciously chose to remain a diversified rubber goods manufacturer.

THE
GOODRICH

VOL.1   June-July   Nº 10

1912

The automobile, pictured in this Goodrich publication, revolutionized the rubber industry. (BFG Co.)

THE NEW COMPANY: PERSONAL VALUES AND RISK TAKING

When he assumed the presidency of B.F. Goodrich, Work changed the nature of the firm's organization and operations. The alterations he made profoundly shaped the company for decades to come. Work and the other Goodrich executives held a new conception of their firm. They were adverse to taking many risks and became profit takers lured by high society life, often in locales removed from Akron. Work began at Goodrich in 1881. Hard driving and sometimes explosive in his early days with the firm, Work sought relaxation and became more conservative in his business views in the 1910s and beyond. In a letter to company stockholders in 1904, Work expressed his stand-pat attitude. "Without question," he observed, "we now have the largest and best equipped rubber factory in the world, and we can well afford to stop our improvements for a while and cash up what we have put into it."[4] Content with the large profits the company was earning and the high dividends it was paying, officers saw little need to alter operations. While Benjamin Goodrich's entrepreneurial leadership had spurred his company to success a generation earlier, Work's desire to take company profits limited its development in the opening decades of the twentieth century.

New York and Life in High Society

In 1909 Work moved Goodrich's headquarters to New York City. In late 1908 Goodrich purchased a sizable lot on West Fifty-seventh Street and Broadway and by the end of the following year had erected a palatial twelve-story building.[5] A large portion of the building was devoted to the storage, sale, and servicing of automobile tires, but the structure also served as a corporate headquarters. The exterior was done in white and green marble with bronze decorations; marble, oak, and mahogany trim graced the interior. The new building symbolized Goodrich's rise to national prominence and stood as "a conspicuous achievement by the leading rubber company in the city."[6]

In part, economic motives prompted the move. As Goodrich grew it needed more capital, and New York was the nation's chief financial market. In 1910 the company doubled its capitalization to $20 million by issuing 200,000 shares of preferred stock.[7] Existing stockholders, who were given priority rights to purchase the stock, oversubscribed the issue. This was one of the last stock increases handled directly by B.F. Goodrich. Thereafter, the company worked through established underwriters, the most important of whom were located in New York. Then, too, New York City was the home of the United States' raw rubber market. Work fancied himself to be a particularly astute buyer of raw rubber and wanted to be near the market.

Social considerations also spurred the relocation. Work was a social climber. Akron offered opportunities too limited for his aspirations; only New York City would suffice. As one observer of Akron's rubber scene reported, Work "cleared out of the city [Akron] as swiftly as possible, came back as seldom as possible thereafter."[8] In December 1912 Work moved into a mansion on New York's prestigious Fifth Avenue, and he soon acquired a thirty-acre estate at Oyster Bay on Long Island, then one of the nation's most fashionable retreats. Work became known as "a prominent figure in club circles." He often traveled to Europe for months at a time with his wife and family. On one such trip in August 1914, he was nearly caught in the battle zone when World War I broke out. Perhaps befitting his lifestyle, Work died in 1927 while vacationing in St. Moritz, Switzerland.[9]

Work's quest for the high society life affected the company. Goodrich executives emulated Work, when they could. David Goodrich, a powerful member of the board of directors, lived near New York City and paid only part-time attention to business affairs. Because so many officers were spending their time there, the corporation found it necessary to rent a lavish apartment in Manhattan.[10] It became difficult even to hold the required meetings of the board of directors in Akron because Work and other board members were not present. A 1913 meeting had to be delayed when the train bringing Work and Goodrich from New York was involved in an accident.[11] On another occasion members of the executive committee went to New York City "to relieve Mr. Work of the necessity of coming to Akron."[12]

A New York Corporation

After erecting the New York building, Work reincorporated B.F. Goodrich as a New York business and again increased the company's capitalization. In March 1912 the board of directors entered into an agreement with a banking syndicate consisting of the Lehman Brothers, Kleinwort Sons & Company, and Goldman, Sachs. (From this underwriting originated a long-standing reliance of B.F. Goodrich on Goldman, Sachs for its financing.) The agreement specified that all the assets of B.F. Goodrich (Ohio) would be transferred to a newly created B.F. Goodrich (New York), which would possess $45 million in capital stock, composed of $15 million in preferred stock and $30 million in common stock.[13]

Several reasons lay behind the reorganization. The change appealed to Goodrich's officers, who thought that managing a New York firm would bestow on them a higher status than running an Akron company. The company's officers and stockholders also reaped a windfall from the recapitalization. For each common share they had owned in the Ohio Goodrich, they received 2.7 shares of common stock in the New York Goodrich and $78 in cash. Preferred shareholders received 1.2 shares in new preferred stock or $120 in cash for each share of old stock, whichever they chose. Other financial advantages also accrued. By the spring of 1912, executives were negotiating a merger with Diamond Rubber. The New York reincorporation agreement stipulated that if Goodrich merged with another company, Goodrich would redeem its preferred stock, issued with a par value of $100 per share, at $125 per share. Beyond the shares they automatically received from the reincorporation, existing Goodrich shareholders were granted first priority in purchasing additional preferred shares at par. Should a merger take place, they could then have Goodrich redeem these preferred shares, as well as their other preferred shares, at $125 each. As an Akron newspaper aptly put it, B.F. Goodrich had "a large melon cut among the stockholders."[14]

Goodrich's owners could well afford such moves, for the first four years of Work's presidency were ones of growth and profits—sales more than doubled and returns on assets averaged about 22 percent annually. The market for automobile tires boomed, and Goodrich operated its "huge plant night and day."[15] In 1909 the company purchased a large tract of land adjoining its existing Akron holdings, and over the next two years spent nearly $1 million erecting new factory buildings.[16] By May 1912 the corporation employed over six thousand workers.[17] Goodrich continued to use its branch houses, which numbered twenty-four by 1911, to sell its goods, and in addition set up a chain of twenty-seven tire depots as distribution points serving retailers across the nation.[18]

While benefiting from the exploding demand for tires, Goodrich remained a diversified rubber manufacturer. In 1908 Work warned stockholders against becoming too dependent on automobile tire sales and urged caution in preparing for the future. "It is believed by the management," he wrote, "that in years to come we will look back upon the present era as a few years when the advent of automobiles made our business abnormally profitable." Work concluded that "the only wise and safe policy to pursue during these years is to conserve our resources."[19] This meant remaining a full-line maker of rubber products: tires, hoses, belting, mechanical rubber goods, footwear, and golf balls.

THE ACQUISITION OF DIAMOND RUBBER

Former Goodrich employees incorporated Diamond Rubber as an Ohio company in early 1894. Goodrich purchased Diamond Rubber in 1912, a move that would influence Goodrich's development for decades. The acquisition reinforced management's decision to keep the company diversified and not risk too much on automobile tires. The purchase led to the creation, during World War II, of a separate chemical division—Diamond Rubber's chemists were world leaders in rubber chemistry—from which many of Goodrich's chemical efforts derived.

The Rise of the Diamond Rubber Company

Diamond Rubber was founded by the Sherbondy brothers (George, Walter, and William), who were workers in Goodrich's bicycle tire department. In 1893 Walter Sherbondy was granted a patent for a new way of making bicycle tires, and the brothers wanted to strike out on their own. They did so on land acquired from the Diamond Match Company across the street from Goodrich.[20] Diamond Rubber began operations during the summer of 1894, turning out bicycle tires. From this base the company branched out into the production of hoses, belting, mechanical goods, and druggists' supplies. As Diamond Rubber expanded, it required additional capital, and changes in the company's capital base brought far-reaching alterations to its ownership and management. Much of the new funding initially came from Ohio C. Barber of Diamond Match. By 1898 he had become a major stockholder in Diamond Rubber, and the Sherbondys had left the company. That same year, however,

Barber sold half of his stock to Bostonians. The two principal investors were the brothers Frank and Walter Hardy. Walter became the plant manager, and the Hardys brought in two other Boston men, William Miller and Arthur H. Marks, as the chief sales manager and head chemist.[21]

Marks's work was of utmost importance. He graduated in chemistry from Harvard University in 1896, just three years after Charles Goodrich. His most important discovery at Diamond Rubber was a new way to reclaim scrap rubber, a process also sought by B.F. Goodrich's scientists. Crude rubber prices were rising in the late 1890s; and, even more disturbing to rubber manufacturers, the price of raw rubber was volatile, with large, unpredictable swings from year to year. Using reclaimed rubber could reduce rubber manufacturers' dependence on crude rubber, thereby making their businesses more predictable and profitable.[22]

The basic problem that Marks solved was how to separate the rubber in scrap goods from other materials with which it had been combined, such as cotton fiber and chemical additives. Some companies had achieved partial success in the 1880s and 1890s by dissolving scrap rubber in acids. In 1899 Marks developed a far superior alkali process, in which the old rubber was heated in a dilute caustic soda solution. As one scientist noted, "this treatment simultaneously destroyed the fabric, plasticized the rubber, and dissolved the uncombined sulfur and some of the lead compounds." This process gave Diamond Rubber a distinct cost advantage over its competitors in making tires and other goods.[23]

Marks recruited others to develop Diamond Rubber's technological prowess. Of note, George Oenslager was hired in 1905 to study methods to improve vulcanization. Trained as a chemist at Harvard—where he had gotten to know Marks, with whom he graduated—Oenslager worked on accelerating the vulcanization process developed sixty years before. Two advantages would accrue to whoever developed a workable process. First, more rubber could be made in any given period, thereby permitting a more efficient utilization of plant facilities. Second, better vulcanization could increase the strength of rubber, thereby allowing less-expensive grades of raw rubber to be substituted for the expensive, stronger Para fine crude rubber. In 1906 Oenslager devised a new way to use organic materials, especially anilines, to speed up and improve vulcanization (previously, only less-efficient inorganic accelerators had been used). Although anilines were toxic when used by themselves, Oenslager later developed a nontoxic derivative, thiocarbanilide powder. Like Marks's development of a new way to reclaim rubber, this discovery gave Diamond Rubber a major cost advantage over other rubber companies.[24]

These scientific developments took place in strict secrecy. Marks and Oenslager even delayed securing patents on their processes, lest they alert competitors of their progress. Most of the work was conducted in Mill 3 (later called Plant 3), Diamond Rubber's research building, located for safety reasons some distance from Diamond's production facilities. Materials were brought in and taken out in disguised boxes and cans. Diamond Rubber's officers kept purchasing Para fine crude rubber in normal amounts so that those at Goodrich would not realize that they had made breakthroughs in the utilization of raw materials. The unneeded Para fine was then smuggled out of the Diamond plant and resold on the open market, some even reaching Goodrich.[25]

In the still-small rubber world in Akron, Goodrich officers, while not fully understanding what was going on at the Diamond plant, soon realized that something new was afoot and took steps to work more closely with their counterparts there. In 1904 Goodrich and Diamond executives formed a new corporation called the Alkali Rubber Company to manufacture reclaimed rubber through Marks's alkali process. The Alkali Rubber Company was to build a reclaiming plant in Akron, and Diamond Rubber and B.F. Goodrich would each own half of the new firm. Goodrich paid for its share in cash—$250,000 right away, another $250,000 as needed. Diamond's payment was more complex. In exchange for assigning Marks's patent to the new company, Diamond was credited with having contributed $83,333 to the new firm; and Diamond was credited for the buildings and equipment it had been using in reclaiming rubber, as these now passed into the possession of Alkali Rubber. In the end, Diamond Rubber put up very little cash. Diamond Rubber was also granted a royalty of ½¢ for every pound of reclaimed rubber produced.[26] Both Diamond Rubber and B.F. Goodrich obtained what they desired from this agreement: Goodrich received access to an important technical process that it had not been able to develop, while Diamond obtained a growing source of income from royalties, funds it desperately needed for growth.

Diamond Rubber continued to expand in the early 1900s. When sales of bicycle tires slumped, the company broadened its product line to include hard rubber goods, steam packing, and insulated wire. Like Goodrich, Diamond Rubber also entered the production of automobile tires. By 1901 Diamond Rubber was reported as experiencing "phenomenal growth" and a year later put up a new factory devoted entirely to tire making. Diamond increased its workforce from 293 employees in 1900 to 1,685 in 1909.[27] By 1911 Diamond Rubber's tangible assets of $17.5 million rivaled Goodrich's $18.8 million.[28]

As it developed, Diamond Rubber both competed and cooperated with B.F. Goodrich. In 1910 Diamond Rubber defeated Goodrich in winning exclusive American rights to use a cord tire machine developed by Chris Gray at his tire factory in Silvertown, England. After merging with Diamond Rubber, Goodrich took over those rights and began making its famous "Silvertown" automobile tires. Goodrich would use this brand name for its highest quality tires into the 1970s.[29] Cooperation, rather than competition, became the norm. In 1910 Diamond and Goodrich executives joined forces to arrange the merger of the Alkali Rubber Company and the Philadelphia Rubber Works Company, assuming the name of the latter firm. The Philadelphia Rubber Works controlled the acid process for reclaiming rubber, and the goal of the merger was to combine in one company the alkali and acid reclaiming methods.[30] This move gave Goodrich and Diamond each a quarter-interest in Philadelphia Rubber.

Factors Affecting the Acquisition of Diamond Rubber

Drawn together by their growing cooperation, Diamond Rubber and B.F. Goodrich merged in 1912. At the same time that Goodrich officers were reorganizing the company as a New York corporation, they were looking into acquiring Diamond Rubber. Goodrich was officially reincorporated on 2 May 1912. Just six days later, its board of directors approved a merger agreement arranged by the same banking syndicate that had handled the reorganization.[31] On 3 June Goodrich's stockholders unanimously approved the agreement, along with a doubling of Goodrich's capital necessary to effect it. B.F. Goodrich purchased Diamond Rubber for $45 million in Goodrich stock ($15 million preferred, $30 million common).[32] Goodrich was now capitalized at $90 million, making it the nation's second-largest rubber company after U.S. Rubber.

Several factors led Goodrich to acquire Diamond Rubber. Goodrich had developed increasingly close ties with Diamond Rubber, and Work was a good friend of Marks's. According to the *India Rubber World*, "it was largely his [Work's] influence that eventually brought both Mr. Marks and the Diamond into the Goodrich fold."[33] There was, however, more to the merger. Through the acquisition, Goodrich obtained the greatly desired research capabilities of Diamond Rubber. It provided Goodrich with direct access to Diamond Rubber's reclaiming and vulcanization methods, as well as to its Silvertown cord tire patents. It also brought the research scientists Oenslager and Marks to Goodrich.[34] In addition, a desire for personal gain may have motivated Goodrich's executives and owners. Goodrich shareholders could now sell their holdings of preferred stock at $125 per share—the market value of Goodrich preferred was $106 per share at the time of the acquisition—back to their company, for the merger agreement committed Goodrich to redeeming a large number of preferred shares each year.[35] The acquisition, too, served less tangible interests for those associated with Goodrich. Like Goodrich's reorganization as a New York company, the merger illustrated management's determination to win national recognition for themselves and their corporation. With assets of $94 million in 1913, B.F. Goodrich was clearly a big business by American and international standards (generally speaking, any business with at least $20 million in assets was considered a big business then). With assets of $146 million in 1917, Goodrich had become the twenty-second-largest company in the United States.

Diamond executives were also willing to sell their company, for they had much to gain financially from the sale. Their shareholders received 2.7 shares of new common stock in B.F. Goodrich for each share they held of Diamond Rubber's common stock. Diamond Rubber's preferred stockholders secured a one-to-one exchange, plus a 50 percent cash dividend. The president of Diamond Rubber, Frank Hardy, benefited from a special provision that entitled him to purchase 25,000 shares of preferred stock in Goodrich at par.[36] Then, too, for the first time Diamond Rubber was encountering difficulty in making tires, its leading product. A chemical compounding ingredient that had promised great improvements in automobile tire life instead caused the rapid deterioration of tires. Complaints from buyers were beginning to flood Diamond's offices. According to rumors at that time, this sales disaster prompted Diamond's officers to sell out quickly to Goodrich.

Contemporary accounts suggest that Diamond's executives went so far as to employ deception. "To get it [the merger] done quickly, before news of the failing product could become public, two Diamond executives," a Goodrich manager later reported, "learning that a Goodrich officer was going on a trip to New York, managed to book a section in a New York sleeper next to him. . . . They carried on a conversation with each other, ostensibly private, but deliberately loud enough so that the Goodrich man could hear it, revealing their intention to offer Diamond to the United States Rubber Company. . . . The ruse was successful. Goodrich quickly bought Diamond."[37]

Goodrich emerged from the merger weaker than its capitalization indicated. Just before the merger, the combined tangible assets of B.F. Goodrich and Diamond Rubber amounted to $38.5 million. The merger created a Goodrich capitalized at $90 million. The discrepancy between tangible assets and capitalization supports Goodyear Tire president Frank Seiberling's contention that the reorganization involved a great deal of stock "water."[38] Until 1920 Goodrich carried $58 million in assets on its books as goodwill. Responding to this overcapitalization and to a decline in the company's earnings, the price of Goodrich stock dropped on the New York exchange. By February 1913 a share of common stock was selling for $54, and a year later for only $23.[39]

Over the next three or four years, Goodrich's management consolidated Diamond Rubber with their company. Three months after the merger, the executive committee voted to discontinue the designations "Goodrich Division" and "Diamond Division," and in early 1913 the electric sign that shone over Diamond Rubber's factory buildings was altered to read "The B.F. Goodrich Company, Everything in Rubber."[40] In a letter to company stockholders in 1914, Work reported that "the definite purpose of combining and assimilating the facilities [of the two companies] has been continued until now the combined organizations are operating practically as a unit."[41] The last parts to be consolidated were the laboratories, which were combined in 1919.

In the process of consolidation, Goodrich initially retained Diamond Rubber's executives, but they soon left. Frank Hardy became the new chairman of the board of directors, and Marks became the company's general manager and first vice president.[42] However, Marks and Hardy left the active management of the company in 1917.[43] Just weeks after the merger, William Miller, Diamond Rubber's former secretary and sales manager, left to start the Norwalk

Tire & Rubber Company in Connecticut. Three years later, Cliff Mathewson, Diamond Rubber's former Pacific Coast manager, and John Lanier, who had been the sales manager for Diamond Rubber in the Southwest, joined Miller in this new venture.[44] Over the next few years still others left Goodrich to swell the management ranks of the Pennsylvania Rubber Company, the Boston Belting Company, and the McGraw Tire & Rubber Company.[45] By 1917 there could be little doubt that the men of B.F. Goodrich, not Diamond Rubber, controlled the new consolidation.

The merger was a watershed in Goodrich's evolution. Before 1912 the company had expanded through internally generated growth: earnings were plowed back to improve and expand the company's Akron factories. From 1912 much of Goodrich's growth came largely through acquisitions. As the officers increasingly put a desire for personal gain ahead of needed improvements in their plants, they found acquisitions as a new route to achieve growth for their company. For decades to come, acquisitions at home and abroad would be an important part of Goodrich's management strategy.

RESPONDING TO THE AUTOMOBILE BOOM

The mass production of automobiles fundamentally altered the rubber manufacturing industry in America. The automobile boom, and with it the rapidly growing importance of automobile tires for rubber manufacturers, presented a range of new challenges that Goodrich executives had not fully experienced earlier: increased difficulties in acquiring crude rubber, labor problems, marketing problems, and the complexities of foreign operations.

Akron Manufacturing Operations

Goodrich expanded its tire manufacturing operations shortly after acquiring Diamond Rubber. By 1915 Goodrich was running its plants at full capacity, with Work calling that year "the most successful since the formation of the present Company."[46] The corporation's tire production rose to an average of 12,000 per day in June 1915, a 50 percent increase over its average daily tire output in the previous year.[47] By the spring of 1916 Goodrich was making 17,000 tires daily.[48] By this time most of the tires were cord tires. Goodrich and the major tire makers introduced cord tires in the early 1900s and made increasing numbers of them after 1910. Cord fabric was composed of longitudinal threads held in place by tiny cross threads. In a cord tire, the first ply was laid out so that its cords ran at a forty-five-degree angle to the core of the tires. The second ply was laid so that its cords lay at a ninety-degree angle to those of the first ply, thus reinforcing it, and so forth for each ply. Cord tires generated less internal friction and heat than earlier tires and were less prone to blowouts. Cord tires also lasted for about 8,000 miles as opposed to 3,500 miles for earlier tires.

Despite the growing importance of tires, Goodrich remained diversified.

Hurt by the turn-of-the-century collapse in the market for bicycle tires, Goodrich officers were determined not to become too dependent on automobile tires. In early 1915 Work pressed his company to expand in footwear. Within a year Goodrich had built a new boot and shoe plant that was expected to bring "a big increase in gross sales."[49] The company also continued to produce hose (including a new gasoline hose), belting, golf balls, and other long-established products.[50]

While less willing than their counterparts at Firestone and Goodyear to expand their automobile tire operations, Goodrich executives entered the new area of airplane industry products. Little risk was involved in doing so. The market for rubber airplane products was small, and those products could be made mainly by hand, calling for few investments in new machinery or buildings. In 1909, just six years after the Wright brothers' first powered flight at Kitty Hawk, Goodrich produced tires for Curtis airplanes. Within a few years, the company was making "Lumina" cloth, a fabric made of cotton covered by high-grade rubber solutions, to cover the wings and bodies of airplanes. In early 1917 Goodrich recognized the growing importance of this work by establishing a small aeronautics department. From these modest beginnings would emerge Goodrich's aerospace division decades later.[51]

Goodrich's expansion in operations led to significant plant additions. In 1912 the Akron factory was housed in six multistory buildings with a floor space of seventy acres. At the "heart of the whole plant" lay the mill room, which prepared rubber for all of the production departments. The pneumatic tire department was the largest in the world. A department in a separate building manufactured solid tires for trucks and was "rapidly growing." Smaller buildings serving specialized functions clustered around these large factory buildings.[52] Additions brought factory floor space to one hundred acres by the end of 1913.[53] Two years later, officers authorized the expenditure of $800,000 for two new five-story factory buildings designed mainly to make tires.[54] These were large structures: one measured 360 feet long, 100 feet wide, and 100 feet high.

In the plants, rubber manufacturing became increasingly mechanized and capital-intensive. This was especially true in making automobile tires, as the manual methods suitable for bicycle tires no longer sufficed. For Goodrich, as for its competitors, more heavy equipment was needed than ever before.[55] Two innovations were of crucial importance. The development of core-building machines allowed the partial mechanization of manufacturing tire casings, permitting workers to begin making tires more by machinery than by hand. John R. Gammeter, the engineer in charge of mechanical innovations at Goodrich, devised one of the first such machines, and by 1909 his company was using thirty of them. At about the same time, Goodyear's chief engineer, W. C. State, developed a rival core-building machine that was widely adopted in the industry. The machines increased a worker's output of tire casings from around seven per day to over twenty.[56] As important was the introduction of the Banbury mixer, pioneered by Goodyear in 1916. This piece of equipment mixed chemicals and rubber in an enclosed container for the first time. The prepared rubber could then be used in making tires and other products. The Banbury mixer permitted the more precise formulation of rubber compounds, greatly sped up the preparation of rubber, and saved on labor expenses. Goodrich, too, was soon using the mixers.

The use of core-building machines and Banbury mixers heralded a new future for rubber makers, especially tire makers. Tire making, like the production of automobiles, was fast becoming an industry based on mass production. Only those companies that invested heavily in the new mass-production technologies could hope to reap the benefits of reduced unit costs of production. Only those firms willing to spend liberally to constantly update their production facilities could remain competitive for very long. As we shall see, Goodrich proved unwilling to go as far as Goodyear and Firestone in these respects and so lost ground to them in tire production. Goodrich did improve its Akron plant. The benefits of locating tire production in one place rather than in scattered plants—again, lower unit tire costs resulting from grouping expensive machinery in one factory close to centers of automobile production—dictated this approach. But, Goodrich failed to invest as heavily in tires as some of its major competitors.

The Problem of Crude Rubber

The failure to invest fully enough in tires was not, however, Goodrich's most pressing problem. As Goodrich expanded its production of tires and other rubber products, the acquisition of raw materials, especially crude rubber, assumed a new urgency. The predictability of the supplies of essential raw materials worried executives. They wanted to secure stable supplies of their basic raw materials to ensure that they would be able to keep their capital-intensive manufacturing plant running at as near to full capacity as possible. Any interruption in production would, they feared, cut into production and profits. In their assumptions Goodrich's officers resembled their counterparts in large industrial enterprises across the United States. As industrial ventures became increasingly capital-intensive, it became important for their managers to achieve a smooth flow of raw materials to finished goods through their plants.

Wide swings continued in the price of crude rubber. Prices generally rose between 1907 and 1910, with most of the raw rubber used by American manufacturers coming from wild rubber trees in the Amazon River basin. As the demand for rubber soared, this supply proved inadequate. Over the next five to six years rubber from plantations in the Far East, especially in Malaya, largely replaced Amazon rubber, and crude rubber prices dropped. By 1916 the plantations supplied three-quarters of the crude rubber grown in the world, of which Akron companies purchased over one-half.[57]

Some of America's rubber manufacturers responded to the price fluctuations by developing their own plantations, a form of backward vertical integration. In 1910 U.S. Rubber bought 80,000 acres of plantation land in Sumatra, making it the first American company to own an overseas rubber plantation. Goodyear followed with the purchase of a 20,000-acre plantation in Sumatra in 1916. Firestone explored the possibility of buying plantations in the Far East, especially in the Philippines, but made no purchases until the 1920s— and then in Liberia.[58]

Goodrich executives were deeply concerned about the volatility of crude rubber prices. As early as 1910 Work decried "the work of speculators in London" in raising crude rubber prices.[59] Three years later, he sent a company officer on an extended trip to investigate the possibilities for growing and buying crude rubber in the Far East. After looking at Ceylon, the Malay Peninsula, Sumatra, and Java, the executive recommended against buying rubber plantations because "the risks are too great to justify a manufacturer in going into the production of a raw material." He did, however, suggest that Goodrich move its major buying operations from New York City to Singapore. There the company could make arrangements to take the output of high-quality rubber in assured supplies from the best plantations. Such a buying office would also be close to Singapore's growing auction market for crude rubber.[60]

The onset of World War I in Europe heightened concerns about the supply of crude rubber. Just three months after the war began, Great Britain declared an embargo on the shipment of raw rubber from its Far Eastern plantations to any place other than London. The goal was twofold: to ensure British rubber makers of the raw material they needed, and to deny its use to Germany and its allies.[61] Working with representatives of the U.S. State Department, American rubber manufacturers, led by Work and Marks, set up a committee that persuaded the British to lift their embargo. In part, the Americans succeeded because British growers were eager to restore raw rubber shipments to the United States, and in part because the British government did not want to unduly antagonize the U.S. government, which actively pressed the cause of the American companies. In January 1915 the British lifted their embargo, following the issuance of guarantees by the American firms that they would not ship raw rubber to Great Britain's enemies.[62]

The embargo goaded Goodrich executives to consider actions on their own, as well as to cooperate with other American rubber manufacturers. In 1915 they sent a company representative on a six-month trip to India, Africa, and the Far East to look into crude rubber opportunities.[63] Three years later, another Goodrich officer visited Far Eastern plantations, and later that year the company established a buying office in Singapore.[64] Goodrich did not, however, purchase any plantations. As one company executive later recalled, "considerable sums of money were spent in investigations which came to naught." The reason, he believed, was that "Mr. Work considered himself such a clever buyer of crude rubber in the New York market that there could be no need for us to grow our own."[65] More was probably involved. The purchase and development of rubber plantations were expensive and required long-term commitments. Goodrich's officers were loathe to make the necessary investments of money and time.

Labor Relations

As Goodrich grew in size with the production of automobile tires, labor relations at the company became more complex. In this realm of activity, Goodrich followed patterns set by its competitors. Officers combined a commitment to employee benefit programs (then known as "welfare" work) and improvements in production efficiency with opposition to independent labor unions. Goodrich's executives were ambivalent about paternalistic overtones in the more ambitious welfare programs, but after a major strike in 1913 they embraced welfare programs, especially in the realm of health care.

A major strike crippled Akron's rubber manufacturers during the winter of 1913. Located in downtown Akron, the Goodrich plant was an attractive target for the strike leaders, and most of the violence and disruptions that took place during the strike occurred near Goodrich's factory gates. Workers had numerous grievances against Goodrich and the other rubber manufacturers: unhealthy working conditions, work speedups, the lack of a fixed wage scale, and the importation of cheap labor into Akron. Most Goodrich workers, like those on strike at the other companies, hoped simply to redress specific grievances. Women workers in Goodrich's shoemaking operations, for example, complained of low wages and work-induced illnesses. For some, however, more was involved. A minority of workers viewed the strike as a means to radically alter the economic system under which they labored. Many strikers, while not going that far, were alienated from the management of the rubber companies, which they pictured as "soulless corporations." The officers of Goodyear and Firestone, living in Akron and deeply tied to their community, were largely able to deflect such criticism. But Goodrich's officers, then more divorced from Akron, had a difficult time defusing such attacks on their company.[66]

The strike surprised Goodrich's officers, most of whom thought they had a contented, loyal workforce. Refusing to accept reality, E. C. Shaw, Goodrich's plant manager, blamed the strike on "outside agitators."[67] Goodrich and the other rubber manufacturers successfully resisted the strikers' poorly formulated demands. Rent by disagreements over strike goals and strategies, the workers failed to win their objectives. Nonetheless, the strike greatly influenced labor relations in Akron's rubber industry for the next two decades. It was partly in response to the strike that rubber manufacturers, including Goodrich, vastly expanded welfare programs for their workers during and after World War I.

A Sales System for Automobile Tires

Selling automobile tires, especially replacement tires, presented new challenges to Goodrich's officers. (Goodrich and the other major tire producers continued to rely on personal connections to sell their original equipment tires to automobile companies.) In earlier times, Goodrich had offered some mass-produced rubber products, such as bicycle tires, directly to consumers.

But many of its products, such as rubber belting and fire hoses, were not sold to the general public, and still other goods were made only for specialty markets. Selling commodity consumer goods required a considerable adjustment in thinking and sales methods. Over time, executives came to realize that more was involved than selling the tangible properties of their products. Especially in the case of replacement tires they found themselves selling a way of life. "Modernity," as represented by the automobile and the mobility it provided Americans, became part of their sales pitch.

To sell replacement tires, tire manufacturers expanded their systems of branch houses. They increasingly substituted branch houses for jobbers and distributors, because independent middlemen were unable to push tire sales adequately. The middlemen would not build up dealer networks, did not carry complete tire stocks, and were unwilling to extend credit to dealers.[68] Goodrich's branch houses increased in number from fifty-nine in 1913 to seventy-two three years later.[69] Beginning in 1910, Goodrich also set up a chain of tire depots to supplement the work of the branch houses. The depots were smaller than the branch houses—a typical depot carried $20,000 worth of merchandise—and were subordinate to them.[70]

The branches and depots took tire deliveries from the factory, broke them down into small batches, and sold them either to customers or to independent retail dealers. In the larger cities the branches became what Goodrich's officers called "factories in miniature, fully equipped with repair shops for repairing automobile tires."[71] The Boston branch was typical. A basement contained repair facilities and storage areas for solid tires. The first floor was used as the office, sales room, and shipping department. The second and third stories were storage areas for pneumatic tires.[72] To standardize sales practices and create enthusiasm among the salesmen at its branches and depots, Goodrich began holding regional and national sales conferences. At one such gathering in early 1916, some five hundred salesmen converged for a two-day sales conference in Akron, replete with parades, speeches, and dinners.[73]

While making many of the sales on their own, the branches and depots also worked with independent tire dealers. In 1916 the corporation's executive committee authorized the treasurer to extend credit up to $500 "to at least one dealer in every town in the United States, irrespective of the actual credit risk."[74] The company did not want to lose those dealers it secured, and so often guaranteed them against any losses they might incur in their inventories, should tire makers lower prices. Goodrich, Goodyear, Firestone, and U.S. Rubber each had about thirty thousand tire dealers by the time of World War I. At first, many of the dealers were bicycle retailers and repair shops with whom the tire makers had well-established relationships, but they soon came to include automobile dealers, gasoline distributors, hardware stores, farm implement sellers, and others.[75]

Direct advertising became more important as Goodrich's officers tried to reach out to consumers. Goodrich continued to send out a wide variety of promotional literature and advertised broadly in national rubber trade journals

To encourage driving, B.F. Goodrich marked highway routes across the United States. (BFG Co.)

such as the *India Rubber World* and the *India Rubber News*. It also placed advertisements in popular magazines. In another new departure, Goodrich prepared route books distributed free to the public showing the best ways to travel by car over 45,000 miles of roads, and marked some of the roads, including transcontinental ones such as the old Santa Fe Trail, with Goodrich signs. Executives were depicting a new way of living for Americans: a lifestyle based on frequent travel. No longer tied to the railroad, Americans could and *should*, the Goodrich advertisements suggested, travel often and far. It was the modern thing to do.[76]

Beginning a trend that would last into the 1980s, Goodrich became stronger in the replacement tire than in the original equipment tire market. This situation resulted both from the strength of its branch house network and from the emphasis its competitors, especially Firestone and Goodyear, placed on sales to mass producers of automobiles. Goodrich probably had the best-established branch house system in the tire industry. While this insured Goodrich's dominance in the replacement tire field, it did not help much in the original equipment area. Here Firestone and Goodyear rose to prominence. Goodrich too long emphasized tires for luxury automobiles, continuing to sell to Winton, Packard, Reo, Pierce Arrow, Franklin, Stoddard Dayton, and other makers of expensive cars.[77] In contrast, beginning in 1906, Harvey Firestone established long-lasting personal ties with Henry Ford, who made less-expensive, mass-produced automobiles. For decades, Firestone received the bulk of Ford's tire orders. Similarly, Goodyear established connections with General Motors, as did U.S. Rubber not long after.[78]

Overseas Sales and Manufacturing

As part of its emergence as a large, complex industrial giant, Goodrich stepped up its foreign sales at the start of the twentieth century. Growth in sales abroad led American rubber manufacturers to set up production ventures overseas as they sought to get closer to their foreign markets. In doing so, the rubber manufacturers were in step with American industrialists in other fields. American multinational corporations greatly increased their presence in Latin America, Europe, and Asia during the first two decades of the twentieth century.[79] U.S. Rubber bought Canadian Consolidated Rubber in 1907, and Goodyear purchased a tire making plant in Ontario in 1910.[80] Goodrich did still more. There were several reasons for Goodrich executives' being eager to make overseas investments at a time when they were reluctant to finance needed plant investments in Akron. They hoped that by making tires abroad they could circumvent tariff barriers and eliminate shipping costs from Akron. Then, too, overseas investments were inexpensive, at least at first. Finally, they hoped to make large and quick profits from such investments to offset declining profits at home.

Goodrich began its overseas expansion by bolstering foreign sales. In 1913 Goodrich operated its own sales branches in London, Paris, Toronto, Montreal, Marseilles, Frankfurt, Brussels, San Juan, and Tokyo; and, in addition, the firm sold through independent sales agencies in Austria, Switzerland, Holland, Italy, and France. By the time America entered World War I, the company had twenty-one branches and seventy-six agencies outside of the United States.[81]

Goodrich's officers worked hard to develop overseas sales, particularly for their company's tires. They made sure their firm was well represented in foreign trade shows and mounted extensive advertising campaigns. They adapted to the demands of local cultures. As the head of foreign marketing for Goodrich noted, the success of an overseas sales representative depended "largely on the quality of his product and proper methods of economical distribution, as well as the adaptation of his merchandise to the service needs of the countries into which it goes."[82] Since no records segregating Goodrich's foreign sales from its domestic sales have survived for the 1910s or the 1920s, it is impossible to judge the importance of overseas sales. For American rubber manufacturers as a whole, foreign sales came to about 3.5 percent of total sales by the 1920s.[83] Since Goodrich had a more fully developed foreign sales network than most of its competitors, it is likely that considerably more of its sales were made abroad.[84]

Goodrich began manufacturing abroad with a factory in France, where it first established a branch house in 1908.[85] Two years later, Goodrich spent $300,000 to buy and equip a factory to produce tires in Colombes, just outside of Paris. The Colombes factory was intended to provide tires for Italy, Germany, England, and France. Set up as a wholly owned subsidiary of B.F. Goodrich, the French company operating the factory was named the Société

Française B.F. Goodrich. Management came from Goodrich's Akron tire works, while financing came from a line of credit from the French branch of the House of Morgan and was guaranteed by Goodrich.[86] The Colombes factory manufactured both solid and pneumatic tires. In early 1913 Work reported that its French manufacturing represented "the greatest development" in Goodrich's foreign operations, and later that year an outside reporter observed that the plant was "having marvelous success."[87] By the summer of 1914, Goodrich's investment in the factory came to $634,000.[88]

Nonetheless, problems surfaced. The Colombes factory was designed to produce two hundred tires per day but for several years managed to turn out only half that many, owing to production difficulties. The Société Française manufactured tires of inferior quality. As the American manager of the French plant explained, "we ran into trouble; in fact, much trouble. A good many tires came back and we lost our good reputation." Part of the problem may have been that Akron executives expected the Colombes factory to be an instant success and were not willing to allow much of a break-in period. A second difficulty lay in fierce competition from Michelin, the French tire maker, which cut prices to meet Goodrich head-on. Only after Work and E. C. Shaw, Goodrich's general production manager, spent months in France helping the Colombes plant get running were its operations ironed out.[89]

World War I partially disrupted the work of the French factory. In early 1915 the French government began operating the plant to make military tires. Nonetheless, the factory earned a profit for Goodrich that year.[90] Two years later, the Colombes factory began making heels for shoes and boots to enter what was hoped would become a major civilian market after the war.[91]

Beginning a trend that would become pronounced in later decades, Goodrich showed interest in licensing its technical knowledge to foreign rubber manufacturers. In March 1917 Goodrich entered into an agreement with a Russian rubber maker, Bogatyr, in Moscow. Bogatyr made footwear and wanted to diversify into tires. Joseph Talalay, the chief engineer for Bogatyr, approached Goodrich through contacts he had with executives in its French subsidiary. (His son, Anselm Talalay, would become important at Goodrich after World War II.) Goodrich was to supply Bogatyr with plant specifications, equipment, and technical advice needed to "build a first class cover, tube and truck tyre equal in quality to the Goodrich tyre." In return, Goodrich was to receive 5 percent of all net sales of the tires. The machinery was shipped to Bogatyr via Vladivostock. However, the Russian Revolution intervened, the equipment was lost, and the tire plant was never built. In 1919 Joseph Talalay signed over Bogatyr to Lenin's new Soviet government and left Russia for Germany.[92]

Goodrich's Relationships with Its Competitors

As Goodrich's operations grew in size, scope, and complexity, so did the firm's relationships with its competitors, particularly those companies engaged

in tire making. Making and selling automobile tires became increasingly competitive. In fact, intense competition in tire making would grow still more pronounced in the 1920s and 1930s, and after World War II the revival of such
competition would lead Goodrich to emphasize chemical over tire production. In the 1910s officers sought to limit that competition to protect their
company's profits. Rather than pour retained earnings into new plants and
equipment, which might have allowed them to compete more effectively with
Firestone and Goodyear, they sought through various agreements to stop price
cuts by their competitors—a tactic that was only partially successful.

Goodrich and Goodyear executives sometimes worked together informally.
They shared price lists, offered similar tire warranties, sought to standardize
tire and rim sizes, and divided markets. On one occasion in 1914, Goodyear's
Boston branch house went after all of the automobile tire business of the White
Company in its region. R. E. Raymond, Goodrich's vice president, complained
to Frank Seiberling, the president of Goodyear, that this action violated an
understanding between their two companies, and he threatened that
Goodrich would retaliate by seeking more Boston business. "If it is to be a race
to absorb this business I sought to divide fairly," Raymond wrote, "we might as
well sprint ourselves. Shall we?" Seiberling replied that it had all been a mis-
understanding between Goodyear's head office and its branch house. He instructed the branch house to accept no more than a third of White's business
and replied to Raymond that he hoped that "this will straighten out the situation."[93]

In addition to hammering out individual agreements with their competitors, Goodrich officers worked with them as officers and members of trade associations and professional groups, including the Mechanical Rubber Goods
Manufacturers' Association (which in 1915 became a division of the Rubber
Club of America), the Rubber Club of America, the Associated Manufacturers
of Electrical Supplies, the Society of Automobile Engineers, and the American
Society for Testing Materials.[94] These organizations spread market information and sought to standardize products. For example, the Society of Automobile Engineers tried with some success to standardize tire and rim sizes.[95]
Through their cooperative work, Goodrich officers were able partially to protect their firm's present profits. The years just before World War I were ones of
prosperity and growth for B.F. Goodrich. Assets, sales, and earnings all rose significantly, with 1915 and 1916 being particularly prosperous. Returns on assets
and equity, if not as high as in earlier years, remained respectable. Nonetheless, Goodrich's growth rate, while keeping pace with the diversified U.S. Rubber, fell far behind that of the tire makers Firestone and Goodyear, a gap that
would widen more in later years.[96]

Most ominous for the future, Goodrich officers did not keep up with their
counterparts at Goodyear and Firestone in building new factories equipped
with modern machinery. It was not that Goodrich stopped making improvements—significant additions were made to the tire making and footwear facilities—but it did not make as many or as effective additions as did its

TABLE 2.1

Ratios of Financial and Operating
Performances, 1908–1918

	Return on Assets* (%)	Return on Average Stockholder Equity** (%)
1908	23	25
1909	24	29
1910	20	26
1911	NA	NA
1912	NA	NA
1913	8	4
1914	15	16
1915	29	33
1916	18	23
1917	12	14
1918	12	14

Sources: "Directors Meetings," 1908–18.
Note: NA = not available.
*Return on Investment on Total Assets: Income + Interest Expense (Net Income Tax)/Total Average Assets (Interest Expense and Income Tax figures not available).
**Return on Stockholder Equity: Net Income/Average Stockholder Equity.

competitors. Firestone built new factories from the ground up in 1909–10 and in 1917 to make tires for Ford's Model T. Similarly, Goodyear opened a brand-new tire plant in 1916. In fact, the Goodyear additions of 1915–17 nearly equaled the size of the entire Goodrich plant.[97]

At Goodrich improvements came in the form of additions to its existing plant. By 1916 the factory group was a hodgepodge of fifty-eight buildings, which did not benefit fully from the economies of scale available in the more logically laid out tire plants operated by Firestone and Goodyear. A typical factory problem caused by Goodrich's haphazard operations arose in late 1916. The washing line, where the raw rubber was cleaned before manufacture, broke down due to faulty foundations upon which it had been built. Though about eight years old in 1916, the washing line was supposed to have been only temporary; it had been intended to be replaced quickly with a properly constructed permanent line. This was not done, and the failure of the line slowed factory operations for months.[98]

Why did Goodrich's officers not invest more of their company's earnings in tire making? Why did they not erect a modern tire plant? In part, they wanted their firm to remain diversified. In part, too, funds were needed to service obligations resulting from the acquisition of Diamond Rubber. From 1914 to

TABLE 2.2
B.F. Goodrich Expenditures, 1914–1918

	Increase in Tangible Capital Assets*	Increase in Investments in Other Companies	Preferred Stock Redemption	Dividends Paid	Interest Expenses
1914	$(287,000)	$645,000	$900,000	$2,069,000	$123,000
1915	890,000	931,000	1,100,000	1,960,000	47,000
1916	2,944,000	1,042,000	700,000	4,311,000	1,046,000
1917	2,101,000	33,000	900,000	4,248,000	1,333,000
1918	(1,265,000)	797,000	900,000	4,185,000	1,993,000

Sources: "Directors Meetings," 1914–18; "Annual Reports," 1914–18.
Note: Numbers in parentheses are negative numbers.
*Real estate, buildings, plant, machinery, and equipment minus reserve for depreciation.

1916, Goodrich paid out $8.3 million in dividends on its preferred stock, spent $2.7 million redeeming preferred stock, and paid out $1.2 million in interest charges. In contrast, the company invested only $3.5 million in net additions to real estate, buildings, and machinery.[99] Officers had become profit takers, who failed to prepare their company for the future. Eager to enjoy a comfortable life, they rewarded themselves liberally with dividends and stock redemptions. Altogether, they allocated about 40 percent of Goodrich's net earnings to dividend and stock redemption payments. By comparison, Firestone paid out only 6 percent of its net earnings as dividends.[100]

Goodrich's share of the American tire market shrank, as the shares of Goodyear and Firestone rose. Goodyear's share increased from 12 percent in 1910 to 21 percent in 1916, the year it overtook Goodrich as the nation's leading tire maker. Firestone's share rose from 8 percent to 20 percent during the same years. With the development of specialized tire makers such as Firestone and Goodyear, the positions of the more diversified companies that engaged in tire making eroded. U.S. Rubber made about 25 percent of America's tires in 1910, but a scant 11 percent by 1917. Goodrich's market share rose from 18 percent in 1909 to perhaps 25 percent with its merger with Diamond Rubber in 1912, but fell thereafter. This division between Firestone and Goodyear as expanding tire makers and U.S. Rubber and Goodrich as more diversified rubber goods manufacturers would widen over the next six decades.[101]

Rubber Chemical Research

Goodrich executives continued to support research during Work's tenure as president, although they were far from alone in setting up research facilities. By World War I, about a hundred manufacturers—mainly companies in chemicals, oil refining, communications, photography, and rubber manufacturing—operated research laboratories. Apart from the nation's chemical companies,

America's rubber manufacturers probably sponsored the most far-reaching research programs. In 1913 U.S. Rubber's executives established a general research laboratory in New York City, where it remained for fifteen years. Goodyear executives also set up an experimental department to produce an alternative to the cotton cord fabric, whose patents Goodrich controlled, and this department developed into a research laboratory. Firestone officers hired their first research chemist in 1908, and by World War I the Firestone laboratory employed forty people.[102]

While it fell behind Firestone and Goodyear in tire making, Goodrich surpassed them in rubber chemical research. As in earlier years, chemical research was important in the making of rubber products, especially in the production of automobile tires. Several reasons explain Goodrich's success in rubber chemicals. The company inherited a particularly talented group of chemists when it acquired Diamond Rubber. Moreover, it required only a modest investment in laboratories for the company to succeed in rubber chemistry. Like their investments in airplane products and overseas manufacturing, this limited investment appealed to Goodrich executives. Finally, the laboratories were physically separate from the rest of the company, giving the chemists some freedom in their work.

William C. Geer, hired as Goodrich's chief chemist in 1907, was instrumental in the company's research efforts. Educated at Cornell, where he earned his doctorate in 1905, Geer was employed by the U.S. Forest Service when contacted by Work. Geer became the manager of Goodrich's development department in 1912 (replacing Charles Goodrich, who became a company director), the director of development of goods and processes four years later, and the vice president in charge of research in 1918. More than any other individual, Geer organized Goodrich's research drive in rubber chemicals.[103]

Under Geer's guidance, laboratories expanded considerably. By 1909 they employed thirty-seven researchers and their assistants. Two years later, Goodrich constructed an experimental plant consisting of three steel buildings on its property on Exchange Street, with the turret of one of these buildings serving as the laboratory. Earlier, executives had set up a subsidiary laboratory for hazardous experiments on a five-acre plot at the corner of East Exchange and Carroll Streets, considered a safe distance from the Goodrich factories. Here, solvent naptha, an unstable and flammable liquid, was used to extract gutta-percha and balata, used in making golf ball covers. When this laboratory burned to the ground in 1909, it was not rebuilt. Instead, the land became an athletic field for Goodrich employees. With the acquisition of Diamond Rubber in 1912, many research activities moved to that firm's Mill 3, which, being outside of Akron at that time, was deemed a safer location for potentially hazardous experiments. Some work continued at the Goodrich laboratory as well.[104]

Over the next few years, Geer combined the Diamond Rubber and Goodrich laboratories and systematized research efforts, and in doing so he separated basic from applied research. Geer set up three laboratories by 1915, each with distinct functions. There was, as Geer stipulated, an "operating laboratory," established to "cooperate with the operating departments and purchasing department." This was the company's "general laboratory," designed to "deal with any special problems" Goodrich faced or anticipated. Second, there was a "research laboratory," set up to conduct basic research, a laboratory not to be "incumbered [sic] with production problems." It was to "follow up its work into commercial operations only so far as necessary to insure proper safeguarding and uniformity of new processes or new materials." Once established, those processes and materials were turned over to the operating laboratory, leaving the research laboratory "free for the study of new problems." Finally, a compounding laboratory prepared rubber compounds for the company.[105]

Most of the research revolved around well-established needs in the rubber business, but tires increasingly attracted the attention of Goodrich's researchers. In the vulcanization of rubber, Goodrich experimented with new types of accelerators to speed curing, with cold vulcanization techniques, and with continuous curing methods. While applicable to the making of all rubber products, advances in these fields were especially important in helping speed up automobile tire making, as it became a mass-production undertaking.[106] Ways also were found to make tires last longer and resist damage by abrasion. A major breakthrough came when Oenslager developed carbon black as an abrasion-resistor in automobile tire treads. Oenslager began experiments along this line while at Diamond Rubber in 1910 and perfected the use of carbon black after Diamond's acquisition by Goodrich. As a result of using carbon black, tires lasted considerably longer than before. A side effect was that automobile tires became black for the first time. Previously, they had been milky white.[107]

The beginning of World War I in Europe heightened Goodrich's research efforts. In 1915, with their German supplies cut off, Goodrich scientists set up one of the first aniline-manufacturing plants in the United States to produce the much-needed accelerator. A year later they started making their own thiocarbanilide, a nontoxic derivative of aniline first discovered a decade earlier, which they called "Lagos powder." Because it was not poisonous, thiocarbanilide soon replaced aniline as an accelerator. Experiments with new ways to reclaim rubber continued. Goodrich's scientists also began to investigate methods to get rubber to adhere to metal surfaces, experiments that would later pay off handsomely.[108]

B.F. GOODRICH AT WAR

Unlike World War II, which would revolutionize Goodrich's operations, World War I brought few changes to the company's work. Instead, it reinforced existing trends in its operations and in its relations with competitors. The complexity of Goodrich's operations continued to grow, but the firm failed to capitalize on wartime opportunities and, as a result, continued to fall behind Firestone and Goodyear.

Making and Selling Rubber Goods during Wartime

With America's entry into World War I in 1917, Goodrich began large-scale production of war materials. In its most notable departure from past operations, Goodrich, along with Goodyear and several other companies, made nonrigid dirigibles for the navy. Goodrich had been producing rubberized fabric and tires for airplanes, but its move into the production of entire airships was a step not easily taken. Only after receiving assurances from the federal government that they would not be responsible for the inflation and test flying of the dirigibles did Goodrich executives consider making them. Even then, they hesitated, worried that the prices would not cover their production costs. Finally, the argument of Howard Raymond, a vice president, that the company "ought to take our allotment and not be underrated in the minds of the Navy Department as to our ability to cope with the unusual or the big operation" carried the day, and Goodrich's officers agreed to make airships.[109]

Nonetheless, Goodrich remained a hesitant participant in dirigible and balloon manufacturing.[110] Built to government specifications, the dirigibles were 160 feet long and 50 feet high. Originally intended for patrols along America's Atlantic coast, they were employed along the North Sea in antisubmarine duty as well. Goodrich eventually produced eight of the craft.[111] The company also manufactured 362 smaller "kite-type" observation balloons, which the army manned with artillery spotters on the front lines in Europe.[112] In late 1918, still worried about the profitability of manufacturing dirigibles and balloons, company officers agreed to their production "only as a war measure" and determined "that the program should not be continued further than required by the needs of the Government."[113] Goodyear, which pursued the dirigible and balloon contracts more aggressively, produced sixty airships and more than one thousand balloons during the war and remained a major producer of dirigibles after the conflict.[114]

Goodrich showed less reluctance to enter the production of other war materials and manufactured a broad range of war items. Army and navy officers requested that the company make gas masks; working from British gas mask designs, Goodrich was soon turning out 4,000 per day.[115] During 1917 and 1918 the company also made hard-rubber battery casings for tanks and submarines, millions of pieces of surgical tubing, hundreds of thousands of feet of hose, some 50,000 raincoats, over 800,000 pairs of rubber footwear, and thousands of tires for airplanes, cars, trucks, and bicycles.[116]

As a mechanized war, World War I increased the demand for tires by the military; at the same time domestic consumer demand for tires continued to rise.[117] The number of tires produced by American firms soared from 8.2 million in 1916 to 24.5 million in 1918. Most were replacement tires, whose production nearly doubled from 10.8 million in 1916 to 20.5 million two years later.[118] Goodrich participated in the boom, but not to as great an extent as Firestone and Goodyear. For the first time in its history, Goodrich experienced major problems with the quality of its tires. As we have seen, the company's

Like Goodyear, Goodrich made blimps during World War I. (BFG Co.)

early development was marked by its emphasis on high-quality manufacturing. This eroded following the acquisition of Diamond Rubber. In 1917 Goodrich encountered great difficulties in making cord tires that would last as long and handle road hazards as well as those made by Goodyear and Firestone. Its immediate response was to offer its customers costly rebates on faulty tires. Then, over the next several years, Goodrich tried to improve the quality of its tires by changing production processes and by instituting intensive road testing before offering them for sale.[119]

During the war Goodrich relied on earlier sales practices. Branch houses became increasingly important for tire makers; by 1920 they accounted for 80 percent of their replacement tire sales.[120] Goodrich continued to support company-owned branch houses and depots that made replacement tire sales to car owners and supplied independent dealers who also made such sales. The company's branch houses rose in number from 72 in 1916 to 108 two years later.[121] Concerned about the cost of making sales, company officials tightened controls over the branch houses. Unlike Firestone, which allowed its outlets to operate as independent units, Goodrich standardized the billing for depots in each region. All invoices were handled for the depots by the regional branch houses—a move designed, according to W. O. Rutherford (who became Goodrich's vice president in charge of sales in 1917), to be "in harmony with the general plan of economizing in our operations."[122] National advertising, regional and national sales conferences, and participation in trade shows spurred sales of mechanical goods, druggists' sundries, footwear, and hose, as well as truck and automobile tires.[123]

18,000 Man Power

Goodrich's factory force is pictured here around the time of World War I. (BFG Col. UAA)

As sales nearly doubled between 1916 and 1919, the officers sought better ways to coordinate production and sales. In early 1918 they declared that "as a general policy our volume of sales should guide and govern the volume of production in all lines."[124] As part of their efforts to mesh production and sales, they sought to standardize pricing policies. In 1917 and 1918 the executive committee empowered the president and vice president to set prices for all of the pneumatic tires, boots, and shoes sold in the United States. The executive committee also established a new selling price committee—composed of the second vice president in charge of production, the second vice president in charge of sales, and the comptroller—to set prices for all other goods sold in the nation.[125]

As Goodrich's overseas sales rose, despite wartime disruptions, company officers modified sales efforts. In 1917 they set up a foreign department, "separate and distinct from domestic sales," to oversee all of the company's overseas sales. Through this department, Akron officers set the prices and terms for sales made through foreign branches and agencies.[126] Several of Goodrich's competitors took similar steps. U.S. Rubber had established a foreign sales department in 1914, and Goodyear did so in 1921.[127]

The Expansion of Welfare Capitalism at B.F. Goodrich

For Akron's rubber manufacturers, expansion during World War I caused twin labor problems, labor shortages and high turnover rates, as workers moved from job to job and company to company. In 1916 Goodrich estimated that the annual turnover rate for the company as a whole was 180 percent and more than 300 percent for some departments. Recruiting and retaining workers had become a major, unwanted expense.[128] By far the most vexing problem facing Goodrich as it sought to retain workers was housing, for Akron suffered from an acute housing shortage during World War I.

Goodrich considered two possible solutions to the housing crisis. One was to provide company housing in the manner of Goodyear and Firestone. In late 1916 Goodrich executives seriously considered a proposal to build houses for employees. Company housing would, its proponents argued, provide workers with a "home steak [stake]" and thus reduce the turnover rate. At the same time, the personal contact that would occur between workers and managers in administering a housing program would, they thought, foster mutual understanding that could prove valuable in times of industrial unrest—the disruptions caused by the 1913 strike remained very much on their minds.[129] The second possibility was to move some of the operations out of Akron. Work suggested that footwear be relocated, possibly to Brooklyn. "My idea," he wrote other company officers, "is that it would be fundamentally more economical to move a certain part of our work into a community where the scale of wages is lower. If we bring labor from outside it immediately commands the scale of wages prevalent in Akron." Work concluded that "if we move some of our production into a large labor market we can easily afford to offer attractive inducements to get all we want of both men and girls and still pay much less than we would in Akron."[130]

In the end, Goodrich rejected the two options. Officers concluded that it would cost too much to provide adequate housing. Moreover, they doubted that their workers would appreciate new housing. Goodrich's plant manager believed that it was "unreasonable to expect that these people [recent immigrants] could come over here and accept our standards and way of living. . . . I should rather expect that if you provided these people with the type of houses I understand are being planned for them . . . you would probably find their coal supply in the bath tub, and a lot of things of that nature."[131] Similarly, the executives decided not to move any operations from Akron because this, they concluded, would in fact save very little money. Lower wages would not offset the costs involved in making the move.[132]

Instead, Goodrich officers relied on welfare capitalism to solve their labor problems. They were hardly alone. In the first three decades of the twentieth century, many American business leaders, including Goodrich executives, rejected the idea of bargaining with labor leaders. Instead, some businessmen promoted the concept of welfare capitalism, which meant that businesses, not independent trade unions, should look after the best interests of workers. Welfare capitalism came to include a broad range of activities: housing, educational, recreational, and religious facilities for employees; profit sharing plans; and retirement pensions.[133]

To lessen the turnover rate and keep workers loyal to their company, Goodrich managers built on earlier programs. Firestone and Goodyear led the way in these activities, but by the end of World War I Goodrich was close behind. Goodrich centralized hiring and personnel services in a single department of

125 employees, including 23 nurses and 9 doctors by 1917. This department offered insurance and medical care to most employees and gave them free legal advice. Goodrich's foremen solicited suggestions from their workers on how production processes might be improved and rewarded those with the best ideas. The company also sponsored a broad range of athletic activities and teams, ranging from track and field to bowling. By 1917, 2,107 men and 506 women had joined the Goodrich Athletic and Field Association. A company newspaper, the *Circle*, published monthly from June 1916, sought to give Goodrich employees a sense of belonging to one big, contented family.[134]

As was true in many large industrial companies across the United States, an "Americanization" campaign was an important part of welfare capitalism at Goodrich. In part a wartime phenomenon aimed at insuring the loyalty of recent immigrants to the United States, Americanization campaigns were widespread in the Midwest and the nation. They often had a dark side, forcing immigrants to give up their native languages and cultures. Goodrich was the largest employer of immigrants in Akron: by 1917 some 7,250 of the company's workers, nearly half of the total, were noncitizens. Goodrich enrolled 1,500 of its employees in English classes, worked with Akron's city government to speed up the process by which its workers might become citizens, and cooperated with an Americanization campaign mounted by an Akron newspaper.[135]

In addition to engaging in welfare capitalism, Goodrich executives attacked labor problems through a program of wage-and-hours adjustments and personnel reform. They corrected discrepancies between wages in an effort to insure that workers received equal pay for similar jobs, instituted a forty-eight-hour workweek, and had the members of Goodrich's industrial relations department interview all workers who gave notice of leaving. This effort had a strong psychological impact on foremen, who became "more careful than ever before to assure themselves that they have personally used every possible means to retain the employee and to relieve any causes of dissatisfaction before the employee finally makes request for his pay in full."[136]

B.F. Goodrich, Its Competitors, and the Federal Government

America's rubber companies standardized their products to provide for the nation's wartime needs. Goodrich cooperated with Goodyear and other companies to limit competition and standardize products before World War I. Now, for the first time, the work of the federal government became critical to Goodrich and the other rubber companies. The significance of federal government actions would deepen more in later years.

During the war, federal government officials worked with rubber company officers to standardize their products as a matter of convenience on the fighting fronts and to conserve scarce supplies of rubber. In July 1918 rubber company officers serving on an industry committee of the War Industries Board, the federal agency in charge of mobilizing industry for the war, agreed to discontinue making many sizes and types of truck tires. Four of the five classes of truck tires were discontinued. Only one class—made, however, in fourteen different sizes—was produced thereafter.[137] Goodrich officers took a leading part in this standardization drive. Shortly after the July meeting, Goodrich's executive committee instructed company officers to "push this matter" of tire standardization "in all ways possible."[138] Although truck tires attracted the most attention, officers labored for the standardization of other rubber products as well. They worked, with varying degrees of success, with government officials to persuade executives in other firms to standardize the production of airplane tires, insulated wire, waterproof clothing, druggists' supplies, and some types of mechanical rubber goods.[139]

To achieve unity among themselves, the rubber manufacturers worked through their trade associations, of which the Rubber Association of America was the most important. Evolving from predecessor bodies dating back to 1900, this organization had 231 member firms by 1917 and a year later boasted a fully developed divisional structure, in which each division represented a separate rubber product line (such as the pneumatic tires division, the solid tires division, the mechanical goods division, the medical goods division, and the aircraft division).[140] Through this trade association, the companies worked independently and with the federal government to standardize procedures and products. In 1917, for example, the association's officers drafted a standard contract for their members to follow in buying crude rubber from their British suppliers. Although composed of representatives from all lines of rubber manufacturing, the Rubber Association came to be dominated by the large tire makers. Harvey Firestone served as the body's president in 1916–18, and Bertram Work was president 1918–19.[141]

Despite their efforts to work with federal government officials and with their counterparts in competing rubber companies, Goodrich officers failed to reap many profits from World War I. Except for the dirigibles, which Goodrich produced for a set amount arrived at through competitive bidding against other companies, Goodrich manufactured rubber goods for the federal government for a 10 percent profit.[142] While the company's net earnings rose considerably in absolute terms, its returns on both assets and stockholders' equity fell from those of previous years. As before, the company officers paid out most of their firm's earnings as dividends rather than reinvesting them in new plant facilities. A few plant improvements were made. In 1917 the company installed new mixing mills and connected its Akron factory buildings with underground tunnels to speed the flow of work. However, Goodrich's tangible capital assets increased by only $836,000 during the war. Despite the new tunnels, Goodrich's production complex remained a jumble of poorly coordinated buildings, a problem that would plague the company into the 1980s.[143] As before, the newer rubber manufacturers that focused more on tire production, Goodyear and Firestone, did better than the older, more diversified firms, Goodrich and U.S. Rubber, in terms of growth in sales, profits, and assets.[144]

TABLE 2.3
America's Leading Rubber Companies, 1913–1919
(in millions of dollars)

	Goodrich	U.S. Rubber	Goodyear	Firestone
		Assets		
1913	95	185	19	NA
1916	116	222	49	35
1919	139	320	120	73
		Sales		
1913	40	92	33	16
1916	71	127	64	44
1919	141	226	169	91
		Profits		
1913	2.6	7.5	2.0	1.6
1916	9.6	10.4	7.0	6.0
1919	17.3	17.7	23.3	9.3

Sources: Annual reports of the companies; Calvin W. Neiman, "A Study of Rubber Industry Profits with Emphasis on Correlation to Sales and Capital Investment" (M.B.A. thesis, Kent State University, 1965).

MANAGING EXPANSION

The growth strategies followed by most twentieth-century American businesses have greatly influenced their organizational structures, and such was certainly the case at Goodrich. As the company became larger and more complex in its operations at home and abroad, its administrative organization became, of necessity, increasingly bureaucratic. Company officers developed more highly organized and standardized ways to handle their firm's work. As important as a new bureaucratic organization was the development of a new corporate culture, a way of thinking and acting. These second- and third-generation managers, less closely tied to their company and Akron than their predecessors, shared a new set of values that deeply influenced how they perceived their company's future and what their roles in that firm should be.

A Changing Corporate Structure

The expansion that occurred during World War I was a special impetus to reorganization at Goodrich. In 1916 the press of work led Goodrich officers to establish an operating committee to relieve the executive committee of much of its responsibility for directing the daily operations of the firm. The executive committee could focus more on strategic matters.[145] More far-reaching was the adoption of a functionally departmentalized management structure in 1916. To deal with the growing size of their company's operations, officers established six major departments—sales, production, costs, development, plant administration, and chemical laboratories—each headed by a director (not to be confused with members of the board of directors). In 1918 members of the executive committee decided that there should be an even "more definite line of cleavage between the various divisions of the company" and modified the departments to become simply sales, production, plant administration, and development. Those in charge of the departments were designated as second vice presidents in the company (and from 1919 on simply as vice presidents). The vice presidents reported to the executive committee that oversaw and coordinated the work of the departments. The company's executives also adopted Goodrich's first formal organizational chart, designed to clearly delimit the responsibilities of the departments and to smooth communications between them.[146]

Information flow and financial matters grew in importance. In 1918 the office of comptroller was created and Harry Hough, who had been a partner in Goodrich's outside auditing firm, was elected to the position. Hough established a new budgeting system for Goodrich, by which each part of the company was judged by the results of its operations. "He put each division on a budget so that it either makes money and continues to thrive, or shows up in red and attracts to itself the remedy."[147] (Hough would become Goodrich's president after Work's death in 1927.)

In making these organizational changes, Goodrich was in line with other rubber manufacturing firms and companies in other industries. Most large manufacturing firms established centralized management systems based on departmental organizations. Only later, in the 1920s and 1930s, would American businesses begin developing decentralized management structures. U.S. Rubber, then the largest and most diversified rubber manufacturer, established an executive committee in 1906 and set up footwear, development, tires, and mechanical goods departments nine years later. Goodyear had vice presidents in charge of sales, production, and finances by 1915 and a controllers office six years later. Work was departmentalized at Firestone during the war, with department heads meeting with an executive committee each week to discuss common problems and issues.

Corporate Management and Corporate Culture

The top management of Goodrich remained largely inbred. The company depended on recruiting men at an early age, with executives typically climbing their way up the corporate ladder. Harold Joy, who was Goodrich's general superintendent for a number of years shortly after Work became president, was described as "having worked his way up," thus "understand[ing] every detail of the business."[148] E. C. Shaw came to Goodrich as an engineer in 1894, became the assistant plant superintendent in 1901, the general manager in 1907, and vice president in charge of factory operations in 1917, before retiring a year later.[149] Similarly, Charles Raymond joined Goodrich in 1890, became the secretary in 1907, and one of the second vice presidents in 1916.[150] His brother, Howard Raymond, began as a clerk at Goodrich in 1896, became the assistant general superintendent in 1912, and was made the second vice president in charge of production in 1916.[151] A. B. Jones joined Diamond Rubber in 1908, became the assistant to the manager of production works after Goodrich acquired Diamond, and the manager of the works a few years later.[152] All of these officers also served as members of Goodrich's board of directors, which continued to be composed mainly of inside directors.

Work's presidency did, nonetheless, bring changes to Goodrich's management and ownership. Outsiders, especially businessmen trained in finance, grew in significance. Harry Hough, who had been an outside auditor, took over as comptroller in 1918. Hough also served as a company director. The use of brokerage houses to arrange its acquisition of Diamond Rubber resulted in the placement of investment bankers on its board of directors in 1912, Henry Goldman of Goldman, Sachs and Philip Lehman of Lehman Brothers.[153] As Goodrich expanded, the firm became less of a family enterprise. With the acquisition of Diamond Rubber, ownership became more dispersed. From just a handful in 1907, the number of stockholders grew to several hundred by 1918, with no single family or group of families dominating the company to the same extent as had been true earlier.[154]

As the sense of family identity dissipated in the twentieth century, a new corporate culture grew at the company. Much of the older personal commitment to the development of the company and Akron eroded as the firm's officers increasingly placed personal satisfaction above the needs of their firm and their community. The officers of Firestone and Goodyear, while certainly enjoying a life based on conspicuous consumption, did so as members of the Akron community and for the most part continued to identify with Akron as their hometown.

In contrast, Work left Akron to enjoy life in New York's high society, and other Goodrich officers sought to emulate him. Although they were not necessarily atypical of American businessmen of the time, their upper-class lifestyle sometimes detracted from their ability to manage the company with full effectiveness—in sharp contrast to their rivals at Goodyear and Firestone. David Goodrich did not go regularly to his office in New York. Rutherford was known as a person who "traveled extensively," a frequent visitor to Bermuda, where he stayed for up to a month at a time, and to Europe. He toured England, France, Germany, and Scotland, where he and his son John were described as "good golfers." Rutherford won repute as a club man, belonging to the Portage Country Club in Akron and the Detroit Athletic Club. Howard Raymond became renowned as a yachtsman in New York City's social circles, serving as commodore of the Shelter Island Yacht Club. He was also a member of the New York Yacht Club and the Columbia Yacht Club.[155]

A. H. Marks's way of life epitomized the aspirations of many Goodrich executives. After the acquisition of Diamond Rubber by B.F. Goodrich, Marks promptly purchased a country estate known as "Elmcourt" outside of New York City, where he passed most of his time. Known for its artificial brook and bathing pool, the estate boasted a prize herd of dairy cows. Marks also owned a summer home in Marblehead, Massachusetts, and he traveled in style. A member of the Eastern Yacht Club, Marks owned a 98-foot, twin-screw gasoline yacht. When this boat proved inadequate, he bought the 157-foot-long yacht *Aramis* in 1916. Built entirely of steel, this ship had several dining rooms, a music hall, and a reception room.[156]

A NEW COMPANY WITH NEW VALUES

By 1918 B.F. Goodrich was much larger and more complex than it had been just a decade before. Profitable growth remained central to its development as assets, sales, and earnings increased. Nonetheless, Goodrich fell behind Goodyear and Firestone as tire makers. The continued adherence to diversification, combined with the alteration in the personal goals of management, led Goodrich into a period of relative decline. Goodrich missed a golden opportunity in automobile tires, then the most rapidly expanding segment of rubber manufacturing. Capital investments needed to insure Goodrich's success in the future were not made. More strongly committed than Goodrich to tires, Goodyear and Firestone outstripped Goodrich in the business. America's leading tire maker in 1913, Goodrich fell to second place just three years later, to third place during the 1920s, and to fourth place in the early 1930s—a relative decline from which the firm would never fully recover.

3

Expansion in Rubber Making, Relative Decline in Tire Making, 1919–1929

Basic changes in the business environment faced by Goodrich executives before World War I accelerated after the close of the conflict. Their responses to change during the 1920s hurt the company in the long term. Most important was their failure to take advantage of the growing importance of tire making. After World War I the American automobile industry continued to expand rapidly. Improvements in automobile technology made cars ever more appealing, and the nation embarked on a major public works program of highway construction and road paving. Automobile use soared. The opportunities for rubber manufacturing grew dramatically, and by 1925 tires accounted for nearly three-quarters of the nation's production of rubber goods. Goodrich, however, chose to avoid aggressive investments in both new tire technologies and modern tire manufacturing facilities and lost its position in what was potentially the most lucrative rubber manufacturing market.[1]

Structural transformations also occurred in the rubber manufacturing industry, a change that Goodrich did not lead. Rubber manufacturing became increasingly concentrated in the hands of fewer firms as the use of expensive machinery raised capital requirements, making it difficult for small companies to compete. America's tire industry became an oligopoly, an industry whose markets were effectively controlled by just a handful of firms, a shape it would long retain. By 1929 the "big four" companies of Goodyear, Goodrich, Firestone, and U.S. Rubber produced three-quarters of the tires sold in the United States.[2] Tire making also became an industry characterized by excess capacity. As demand for tires soared, rubber manufacturers, especially Goodyear and Firestone, tried to seize opportunity by building new plants. However, they misjudged and built plants far in excess of demand. Consequently, the expansion of the tire industry did not bring high profits to most rubber manufacturers, including Goodrich. Only those that could afford the new equipment, keep unit costs low, and establish national marketing networks prospered. In none of these respects was Goodrich a pacesetter, and the company grew less rapidly than Goodyear and Firestone.[3]

In their main operations, making automobile tires and other rubber products for the American market, Goodrich executives faced the challenge of working in an increasingly concentrated and competitive industry. Led by Bertram Work, their responses to this situation proved, in the long run, inadequate. Diversification was a deliberate strategy, part of a desire to lessen the impact of competition in the domestic tire industry. Rather than fully revamp their Akron tire operations—a very expensive proposition, given the growing obsolescence of that factory complex—Goodrich officers opted for a growth strategy through acquisitions and foreign investment that they hoped would pay quicker dividends at less cost. While expanding its output of rubber goods in absolute terms, Goodrich fell farther behind Goodyear and Firestone, who were aggressive in their investments. Several acquisitions within the United States broadened the range of Goodrich's product offerings, and the opening of manufacturing ventures in Japan, Canada, and Great Britain were designed to bring greater financial stability to the firm. This strategy failed, however, to compensate fully for growing difficulties in tire production in Akron. Decisions to eschew aggressive investments would haunt the company for a long time to come, leading to a very dramatic transformation decades later: Goodrich's departure from the tire industry altogether. Only in fields beyond rubber manufacturing did Goodrich surpass its rivals. Building on the firm's research tradition, a Goodrich chemist named Waldo Semon discovered how to plasticize polyvinyl chloride (PVC) in 1926, thus helping lay the foundation for the world's modern plastic industry and heralding a new future for Goodrich.

GOODRICH IN THE POSTWAR RECESSION

A brief but sharp recession hurt American businesses after World War I. Automobile sales dropped from 2.2 million in 1920 to just 1.6 million a year later, and sales of automobile tires fell from 29 million to 28 million.[4] The recession temporarily curbed the growth of America's rubber manufacturing companies, who not only saw their largest single market, automobile tires, contract, but were also caught holding overvalued stocks of raw materials, especially crude rubber and raw cotton. As the prices of these commodities dropped, rubber manufacturers wrote down the values of their inventories. Company after company reported reduced earnings, and their assets and sales fell. Firestone escaped bankruptcy only when Harvey Firestone hurriedly returned from a European vacation and pledged his personal fortune to save the firm. Frank Seiberling was ousted from Goodyear, and the company was reorganized with new management.[5]

Goodrich was hurt severely by plummeting tire sales. Throughout 1919 Goodrich turned out about 30,000 tires per day, but by the fall of 1920 the company was making only 4,000 tires daily.[6] Continuing problems with the quality of its tires exacerbated recession-related difficulties. Goodrich faced "serious complaints regarding the failure of Solid Tires" in 1919 and a year later suffered from the production of a "large number of blemished tires."[7] Declining sales also afflicted Goodrich's footwear operations. In late 1920 Goodrich was turning out about 17,000 pairs of boots and shoes each day, but by the close of 1921 this output had halved.[8]

The Response to the Recession

Goodrich officers mounted an ineffective response to their company's problems. They shelved a major plant modernization program begun in the fall of 1919 even as they continued to pay themselves hefty dividends on their common and preferred stocks. That year they tore down a number of buildings dating back to the 1880s and 1890s, intending to replace them with new facilities costing $10 million. The recession, however, delayed the construction, and much of it was never undertaken.[9] Officers also tried to cut overhead expenses, especially factory costs, which on occasion included shutting factories down.[10] Like their counterparts, Goodrich officers reduced their inventories of raw materials and revalued the raw rubber and cotton that they kept, taking multimillion-dollar losses in doing so.[11]

The company reorganized its distribution system while placing renewed emphasis on sales. Work, who rarely left New York City, traveled to Detroit to try personally to secure original equipment tire business for his company.[12] Goodrich officers appointed the first advertising director in 1919, and boosted the advertising budget from $1.75 million to $2.25 million between 1919 and 1920.[13] Even so, Goodrich trailed far behind the other large rubber makers in magazine advertising. In 1920 Goodyear spent $2 million on magazine advertisements, nearly as much as Goodrich's entire advertising budget.[14] In some respects, Goodrich was forced by financial exigencies to contract sales operations. At the conclusion of World War I, Goodrich had 108 branch houses or depots in 21 sales districts across the United States; by early 1921 these had been reduced to 33 branch houses and 31 depots in 12 sales districts.[15]

The Impact of the Recession

These steps only partially met the challenge of the postwar recession, as Goodrich's cherished strategy of diversification failed to protect the company from hard times. Goodrich reported a record loss of nearly $9 million in 1921, a year in which all of its major competitors—Goodyear, Firestone, and U.S. Rubber—earned profits.[16] Goodrich also suffered more than the others from the deflation of its assets and the decline of its sales. The results of the postwar recession confirmed Goodrich's ten-year decline relative to other major American tire producers. During 1912–21 Goodrich's profits-to-assets ratio was only 5.8 percent, but Goodyear's reached nearly 12 percent and Firestone's stood at 9.6 percent. Only U.S. Rubber had a lower ratio of 5.6 percent.[17]

TABLE 3.1

America's Leading Rubber Companies, 1919–1928
(in millions of dollars)

	Goodrich	U.S. Rubber	Goodyear	Firestone
		Sales		
1919	141	226	169	91
1922	94	169	123	25
1925	136	206	206	126
1928	149	193	251	126
		Profits		
1919	17.3	17.7	23.3	9.3
1922	3.0	7.0	4.4	7.3
1925	12.7	17.3	13.5	12.8
1928	3.5	(10.8)	13.3	7.1
		Assets		
1919	139	320	120	73
1922	92	316	169	61
1925	109	353	193	72
1928	117	343	211	111

Sources: Annual reports of the companies; Calvin W. Neiman, "A Study of Rubber Industry Profits with Emphasis on Correlation to Sales and Capital Investment" (M.B.A. thesis, Kent State University, 1965).

Goodrich emerged from the recession in poor shape to meet competition. The firm needed capital to support its operations, and in 1919 the company's stockholders authorized a $25 million increase in preferred stock ($15 million worth was actually sold). With the funds raised from this sale, company officers retired a $15 million loan of two years before. Realizing that Goodrich was still short of capital, they issued an additional $30 million in five-year notes in 1920, an action that further raised the interest charges Goodrich had to meet each year.[18] Despite the company's record losses in 1921, the firm paid large dividends. As a consequence, few funds were available for plant improvements. In 1921 Goodrich paid out $10.2 million for dividends, preferred stock redemption, and interest charges, but spent only $731,000 to modernize its factories.

This failure to invest for the future hurt Goodrich. Goodyear and Firestone, despite facing serious financial problems of their own, continued to outstrip Goodrich. In 1919 Goodyear made 49 percent of the nation's original equipment tires, up from 32 percent three years before.[19] In 1920 Goodyear's factories had the capacity to make 25,000 tires per day, Goodrich's and U.S. Rubber's plants could turn out 20,000, and Firestone's could make 18,000.[20] Fragmentary information suggests, however, that the two large tire specialists

THE B. F. GOODRICH COMPANY, AKRON. OHIO

In the early 1920s B.F. Goodrich had the world's largest single factory making rubber goods, but the company was no longer the world's or America's largest tire maker. (BFG Co.)

made more tires. In June 1921 Firestone manufactured 20,000 tires daily, Goodyear produced 19,000, and Goodrich made only 15,000.[21]

PARTIAL RECOVERY IN THE MID-1920S

Prosperity—although leavened by growing competition in automobile tires—returned to large rubber manufacturers during the mid-1920s. Buoyed by the prosperity, Goodrich executives sought to modernize their production facilities and went farther in trying to reach the public through mass advertising. They introduced a new method of assessing factory workers' performance, the Bedaux system, which remained in place well after World War II. They also tried to gain greater control over the raw materials needed in making rubber products.

Making and Selling Tires

The rubber industry began to recover from the postwar recession in 1922, and Goodrich participated in the upswing. In 1923 the editor of the *India Rubber Review* reported that "the pulse of the rubber industry is steadier and stronger today than it has been for months" and that "its temperature is back to normal."[22] In the same year Work wrote Goodrich's stockholders that "the earnings for the past year may be regarded as satisfactory."[23] Stung by their recession experiences, Goodrich's officers sought to revamp their company's operations. Work returned from New York City to live in Akron in 1924, after a twelve-year absence, "so as to be more constantly in direct contact with Goodrich affairs."[24] He and his staff reduced inventories of raw materials, refi-

TABLE 3.2

Ratios of Financial and Operating Performance, 1919–1927

	Return on Assets (%)	Return on Average Stockholder Equity (%)
1919	12	13
1920	4	3
1921	−4	−16
1922	6	6
1923	7	6
1924	14	18
1925	9	11
1926	7	8
1927	14	20

Sources: "Annual Reports," 1919–27.
Note: On accounting at B.F. Goodrich: In 1920 intangible capital assets ceased to be listed separately on the asset side of the balance sheet. Instead, they were listed as reductions to the Common Stock account on the liability side of the balance sheet. This had the effect of reducing owners equity, total liabilities, and total assets.

nanced their company's debt, and tried to achieve "economies throughout the organization"—steps that permitted them to lower the costs of their products while earning higher profits.[25]

For the first time in years, Goodrich officers poured substantial sums into plant improvements. In 1925 the *India Rubber Review* reported that "during the past year the Goodrich Company has materially reduced its overhead expenses and operating cost through the installation of new and more modern machinery," concluding that "the Company now produces practically the same number of tires with half as many employees as a few years ago."[26] In May 1926 Moody's Investment Services, while rating Goodyear and Firestone as better-managed companies than Goodrich, noted that Goodrich had made considerable progress in recent years and that "the company is one that during the next period of prosperity in business should be able again to show an expanding earning power."[27] Between 1922 and 1927 Goodrich officers invested about $4.4 million in net capital improvements, a marked increase over the previous five years. As a result of these investments, Goodrich compared more favorably with its major competitors than it had for some time.[28] Even so, Work continued the tradition of taking large sums out of Goodrich. Between 1922 and 1927 Goodrich executives allocated about $7.2 million to redeem preferred stock, paid out roughly $21 million in dividends, and paid over $15 million in interest charges.

TABLE 3.3

B.F. Goodrich Expenditures, 1919–1927

	Increase in Tangible Capital Assets*	Increase in Investments in Other Companies	Preferred Stock Redemption	Dividends Paid	Interest Expenses
1919	$2,424,000	$4,179,000	$900,000	$4,647,000	$1,200,000
1920	13,342,000**	(3,232,000)**	1,188,000	6,293,000	3,727,000
1921	731,000	(1,706,000)	1,188,000	3,528,000	4,746,000
1922	(689,000)	378,000	—	2,606,000	2,094,000
1923	(432,000)	(460,000)	1,204,000	2,543,000	2,895,000
1924	(726,000)	1,149,000	1,188,000	2,361,000	2,460,000
1925	705,000	1,585,000	2,367,000	3,516,000	1,928,000
1926	3,347,000	494,000	1,188,000	4,966,000	2,976,000
1927	1,768,000	(1,951,000)	1,188,000	4,885,000	2,927,000

Sources: "Directors Meetings," 1919–27; "Annual Reports," 1919–27.
Note: Numbers in parentheses are negative numbers.
*Real estate, buildings, plant, machinery, and equipment minus reserve for depreciation.
**Beginning in 1920, the account of the French company and some other foreign holdings were consolidated with those of the Akron company.

Meanwhile, Goodrich officers remained committed to diversification as a way of escaping growing competition in tires. In the late 1920s Goodrich made 34,000 different rubber products in six major lines: tires, footwear, druggists' sundries, hard rubber goods, aeronautical supplies, and mechanical rubber goods.[29] As Work explained, diversification was necessary because of "the great importance of developing new articles and products not subject to the keen competition that the tire business is experiencing at the present time."[30] To spur the development of new products, he formed a new products division.[31] Among the goods Goodrich developed were hard rubber bodies for radios and the largest airplane tire then made, one over five feet in diameter.[32] The company's most important nonautomotive product was footwear. Goodrich began making tennis shoes and introduced zipper boots to the American public. By 1928 its factories had the capacity to turn out 34,000 pairs of footwear daily.[33]

Automobile tires and tubes remained most important, nonetheless, accounting for about 55 percent of sales. In 1923 Goodrich purchased the Brunswick Tire Corporation of Muskegon, Michigan, which had a well-established brand name. Goodrich moved Brunswick's tire making operations to Akron and continued to sell its tires under the Brunswick label.[34] Tire sales increased in the face of stiff competition. In the fall of 1922, Goodrich executives decried "the keenness of the competition" in the tire business, a lament they voiced throughout the next two decades.[35] They responded by bringing out new grades of tires. Before World War I, only two main types of tires were made in the United States: well-recognized "standard brands" and "gyps" of dubious quality. Major tire makers, including Goodrich, produced only standard brands. In the postwar recession, however, the majors, including Goodrich, began turning out second-line tires; and in the mid-1920s third-line tires appeared.[36]

In the face of intense competition, the problems of distribution, or marketing, began to receive more and more attention. Brand identification became critical for success. Thus, Goodrich employed mass advertising designed to reach consumers directly, maintaining an annual advertising budget of about $2 million throughout the 1920s. The funds mostly paid for advertisements in major newspapers and national magazines. Goodrich was also among the large manufacturers of consumer products who used the new technology of radio to promote its image and its Silvertown brand. The company owned a chain of radio stations in New York City, Buffalo, Boston, Providence, Philadelphia, and Pittsburgh, where listeners could hear the company's Silvertown Cord Orchestra and a comedy team known as the "Goodrich Zippers."[37]

The Continuing Quest for Raw Materials

During the boom years of the 1920s, the scarcity of raw materials at stable prices, especially crude rubber, continued to trouble Goodrich. The demand for crude rubber had fallen during the postwar recession. In response to declining raw rubber prices, the British government appointed a committee chaired by Sir James Stevenson—the managing director of John Walker and Sons, a major British trading house—to investigate conditions in its colonial rubber planting industry.[38] The Stevenson Committee called on the British government to restrict crude rubber exports from British colonies in Southeast Asia, by then the source of 85 percent of the world's supply of crude rubber, in hopes of increasing prices. Through the "Stevenson Plan" the British government limited raw rubber exports to just 60 percent of 1920 production, with the goal of raising the price of raw rubber to 30¢ per pound.[39]

American rubber manufacturers were divided in their responses to the Stevenson Plan. Harvey Firestone demanded its repeal and called for greater American investment in rubber plantations. However, the other rubber manufacturers accepted British arguments that restriction would stabilize prices and encourage additional rubber planting.[40] Work declared that the "Stevenson Plan [had] been generally misunderstood. It did not provide for a restriction of production . . . but merely prevented the dumping of crude rubber on the market in quantities that would cause the price to slump to the point where it would kill off the producers."[41] Work believed that British planters deserved a 15 percent rate of return in order to encourage them to increase production, which would require a crude rubber price of approximately 30¢ per pound.[42]

The crisis in crude rubber supplies and prices climaxed in 1925 and 1926 as the British increased their restrictions. American manufacturers tried to stabilize

The problem of obtaining an adequate supply of crude rubber worried Goodrich officers in the 1920s. (BFG Col. UAA)

prices by pooling resources. General Motors and five rubber companies—U.S. Rubber, Goodyear, Goodrich, Firestone, and Fisk—established a purchasing pool, and three New York banks provided a credit of $40 million.[43] American companies also expanded their rubber plantations. U.S. Rubber had the largest investment in rubber planting, increasing its production to 54,000 acres by 1927. Goodyear began planting rubber in the Philippines, Henry Ford established his own rubber plantation in Brazil, and Firestone secured a million-acre lease of rubber land in Liberia.[44] Only Goodrich held back. As before, Work hesitated to commit his company to long-term, expensive projects. In 1923 Goodrich even closed its Singapore buying operation. "In the future," members of the company's executive committee decreed, "orders will be handled either out of London or Akron."[45]

Goodrich responded to rising crude rubber prices by bolstering its rubber reclaiming capabilities, a form of backward integration that was less costly and faster than developing plantations. As we have seen, Goodrich joined with Diamond Rubber in financing the Philadelphia Rubber Company's acquisition of the Alkali Rubber Company in 1910. In 1916 Goodrich sold quarter-interests in Philadelphia Rubber to Goodyear and Firestone as a way of bringing together "the skilled information which all may have or may hereafter acquire."[46] A year later, Philadelphia Rubber abandoned its inferior acid process and closed its Philadelphia plant; it became an Akron company using the superior alkali process developed by Diamond Rubber. Over the next decade, Philadelphia Rubber expanded its operations in Akron and added a reclaiming plant in Oaks, Pennsylvania, named the Perkiomen Rubber Works Company after a stream running through its property.[47] In 1926 Goodrich purchased total control of Philadelphia Rubber, thus increasing its access to reclaimed rubber.[48]

Crude rubber prices finally declined in 1927–28. The work of the rubber pool may have been partly responsible for this welcome turn of events. More important, however, was the development of new supply sources. In addition to expanding their own plantations, American rubber manufacturers turned to other sources, especially Dutch plantations in the Far East. The share of the crude rubber market controlled by British planters dropped to only 53 percent by 1927. In the face of growing competition, the British repealed the Stevenson Plan in late 1928. The American purchasing pool promptly lost $19 million as crude rubber prices plummeted, lessening the value of its rubber inventory, and the rubber manufacturers disbanded the pool. Goodrich and other rubber manufacturers also lost money on their own raw rubber inventories. U.S. Rubber nearly failed after losing $21 million, surviving through a bailout and reorganization by the DuPonts.[49]

Goodrich and leading U.S. rubber manufacturers also had to contend with problems in obtaining sufficient supplies of raw materials other than crude rubber. They encountered difficulty in securing enough pure water from Akron sources—a serious impediment, since their companies used a great deal of water in washing raw rubber to remove dirt and impurities. Goodrich joined with other rubber manufacturers in lobbying the state government to finance improvements to Summit Lake and the nearby Tuscarawas Lake, another reservoir, efforts which proved partially successful. In 1926 Goodrich managers also received permission from the state to increase the amount of water their company withdrew from the Ohio and Erie Canal each year.[50]

Cotton textiles supplies presented a still greater challenge. By 1920 Goodrich alone was using two million pounds per month.[51] Many tire makers integrated backward to control their sources of cotton textiles. In 1917 U.S. Rubber acquired a controlling interest in the Winnsboro Mills of South Carolina, becoming the first tire maker to own its sources of cotton cord.[52] Similarly, Firestone purchased the Sanford Mills in Fall River, Massachusetts, in 1924.[53] Goodyear went the farthest, owning a large cotton plantation in Arizona and three fabric making mills in Georgia by the late 1920s.[54] In 1929 Goodrich paid $2 million for a cotton fabric plant in Thomaston, Georgia, called the "Martha Mills." The purchase would, Goodrich's president predicted, "enable the Company to effect substantial savings in fabric costs." By the end of the year, the plant was supplying 60 percent of Goodrich's cotton fabric needs.[55]

Like their competitors, then, Goodrich executives sought to ensure that their company had the necessary raw materials at reasonable prices. But they did not go as far or as quickly as their competitors. They hesitated to fully push backward vertical integration, a hallmark of many successful American manu-facturing companies in the early twentieth century. While willing to invest modest sums in rubber reclaiming works and more substantial funds in cotton textile factories, Goodrich officers lagged far behind their major competitors in investing in rubber and cotton plantations. Satisfied with current profits, they failed to prepare their firm for the future as well as they might have.

Introducing the Bedaux System in Labor Relations

With production increases, Goodrich faced the renewed challenge of labor relations. With the return of prosperity came a resurgence of labor militancy. In 1922–23 nine strikes hit Akron's tire making plants. The most important strike occurred at Goodrich, when the company cut wages in December 1922. At the peak of the strike, seven hundred Goodrich workers left their jobs, only to return in January 1923 to work at lower wages.[56] Responding to the strikes, Goodrich mounted a two-pronged attack on labor activism in the mid-1920s.

Welfare capitalism remained important. The company continued to spon-sor a broad spectrum of athletic activities. Bowling, baseball, boxing, horse-shoes, tennis, roller polo (hockey on roller skates), and even cricket won company support.[57] Goodrich's comprehensive health program became a mod-el for other firms, with the health department having nine divisions: statistics, dispensaries and hospitals, medical research, physical examinations, nursing, tuberculosis, life insurance, disability compensation, and service annuities. The company also initiated a profit sharing plan.[58]

Scientific management was another approach to controlling labor matters. Increasing competition in tire making led Goodrich and others to refine their shop-floor management methods to squeeze more productivity out of workers. At Goodrich the movement toward scientific management began before World War I but expanded greatly in the 1920s. As early as 1916 Goodrich had instituted such practices in its machine shop.[59] Three years later, it spent $10,000 to train foremen in "methods of handling labor problems, team work and present-day management of the factory." In 1926 it allocated $70,000 for a preliminary production study to be done by the Bedaux Company, an American consulting firm. At the completion of this study, Goodrich officers brought Charles Bedaux and five industrial engineers to Akron to institute the "Bedaux System" and between 1926 and 1930 spent $240,000 to implement the system in their plants.[60]

The Bedaux system became the basis for the payment of most Goodrich workers well past World War II. It was a piecework system with a guaranteed minimum wage. Production experts made time-motion studies of each job to determine the amount of time workers should take to complete one hundred units (or Bs) of their work. Workers could earn more money by turning out one hundred units more quickly than at the company's par rate. Jobs were subdi-vided in an attempt to make workers more efficient. As one Goodrich manag-er recalled, "in studying an operation we'd break it down. For example, walk to the desk, break it, pick up a pencil, break it, return, break it, put it down on the table, break it. We broke it down pretty fine." By 1936 about 85 percent of the employees labored under some variant of the Bedaux system; the rest were paid by the hour.[61]

Goodrich and Its Competitors

The steps Goodrich's officers took to improve operations, although narrowing the gap, did not allow Goodrich to catch up with Goodyear and Firestone.[62] The efforts to increase productivity came too late and amounted to too little. Firestone and Goodyear continued to increase their market shares in tires. Goodyear's share of the tires made in America rose from 16 percent in 1921 to 22 percent in 1926, and Firestone's share increased from 8 to 14 percent during the same period. U.S. Rubber produced 9 percent of the nation's tires in 1921, but only 7.4 percent in 1926. Goodrich's market share stood at 10 percent in 1926 (no reliable figures are available for 1921).[63]

Symptomatic of Goodrich's problems was its failure to keep pace in introducing the most revolutionary tire of the 1920s, the low-pressure balloon tire. Smaller but wider than cord tires, balloon tires provided a more comfortable ride and allowed motorists to travel at higher speeds. Made up of fewer plies, they generated less internal friction, thus lessening the danger of blowouts. They were more pliable and better able to handle road hazards. Balloon tires also lasted longer. Tire makers guaranteed cord tires for 8,000 miles in 1919; by 1931 balloon tires lasted 15,000 miles. The balloon tires caught on rapidly. "No matter whatever else may be said about it," observed the *India Rubber Review* in early 1924, "the new type of balloon tire is sweeping the American continent with such an amazing and wholly unexpected wave of popular favor that it seems destined to become perhaps the ultimate pneumatic tire."[64] Ford adopted balloon tires as original equipment that year.

Firestone developed the first balloon tire in 1922, and within two years was making 25,000 per week.[65] Goodyear also moved quickly into making balloon tires. Goodrich hesitated. Making balloon tires required some new types of equipment, especially molds used to cure the tires, which were expensive. In the summer of 1923 Goodrich publicly attacked balloon tires as experimental and untried. The following year the company was making only 7,500 per week, one-third of the number Firestone was turning out.[66] By 1929 balloon tires accounted for about three-quarters of the tires sold in the United States, and Goodrich's reluctance to enter this field had probably cost the company significant market share.[67]

MANAGEMENT SUCCESSION AND CORPORATE DEVELOPMENT IN THE LATE 1920S

Management succession dominated the thoughts of Goodrich executives as the 1920s closed. Bertram Work died unexpectedly in August 1927. Strategies

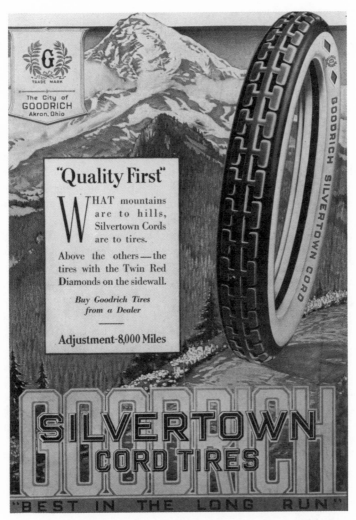

B.F. Goodrich was one of the first companies to make cord tires. (BFG Co.)

put forward by Work had steered Goodrich's development for about three decades. His willingness to enter the automobile tire market served the company well in the late 1890s and very early 1900s, but his unwillingness to invest as heavily in making automobile tires as competitors had later hurt Goodrich. His increasingly stand-pat, conservative outlook contributed to B.F. Goodrich's decline relative to the much more energetic tire makers Goodyear and Firestone. With Work's death, Goodrich directors had a chance to reassess the future of their company through their choice of a new president. It was an opportunity they missed. Satisfied with Goodrich's current earnings and dividends, they chose an executive who would perpetuate Work's strategies into the late 1930s.

New Presidents: Harry Hough and James Tew

Goodrich's directors promoted Harry Hough to president in an action described by a leading business journal as "a natural thing."[68] Hough was originally recruited by Work. As a senior partner in Lovejoy, Mather, Hough & Stagg, the firm that handled Goodrich's accounting, Hough came to know Work in New York City. In 1918 Work persuaded Hough to leave his position to become Goodrich's comptroller. Hough was only forty-five years old when promoted to Goodrich's presidency. Described as "quiet and likable," Hough enjoyed golf, automobiling, and listening to the radio. An "easy-going man," he disliked controversies. Far from resolving management succession matters at Goodrich, however, Hough's election set off "a great struggle for power."[69] Contemporary observers noted that with Hough's election, management at Goodrich became "a hotbed of internal politics."[70]

James D. Tew challenged Hough for the presidency. Unlike Hough, Tew was a production man with a long career at Goodrich. Born in Jamestown, New York, in 1882, he was a nephew of Benjamin Goodrich and the son of Harvey Tew, one of the original partners in the rubber business with Goodrich. After graduating from Harvard with a bachelor of science degree, Tew spent eight months as a mining engineer in Mexico. He joined Goodrich in 1906 as a factory worker, only to leave two years later for Diamond Rubber, where he worked with A. H. Marks on special tire problems. After Goodrich acquired Diamond Rubber, Tew took charge of the cord tire division. He became the general superintendent of all tire making in 1918, the assistant works manager in 1925, the works manager in 1926, and a vice president in 1927.[71]

Hough lasted as president for a scant seven months. Complaining that "for several years the responsibilities of my work have been exceedingly heavy and have exacted an increasing toll on my strength and nervous energy," he resigned in March 1928.[72] At the same meeting at which they accepted Hough's resignation "on account of the condition of his health," members of Goodrich's board of directors voted Tew president, a post he retained until 1937. Hough left Akron for the more congenial atmosphere of his former accounting firm in New York.

In running B.F. Goodrich, Tew was joined by David M. Goodrich, Benjamin Goodrich's youngest son. Born in 1877, David Goodrich was raised in Akron, where he attended local schools. Upon his father's death, he moved to New York City with his mother. After graduating from Harvard University in 1898, David joined Theodore Roosevelt's Rough Riders during the Spanish-American War. His service won him the rank of lieutenant and a commendation from Roosevelt. During World War I he served on the general staff of the American Expeditionary Force with the rank of colonel. He was elected to Goodrich's board of directors in 1913 and became the chairman at the same meeting that Tew became president.[73] Observers of the rubber industry initially described Goodrich's position as chairman as "chiefly ornamental," and perhaps it was.[74] It is unclear what role, if any, Goodrich played in Hough's resignation and Tew's election as president. During the 1930s, however, Goodrich would emerge as one of the strongest directors, and, by the close of the decade, he would spur far-reaching management changes at B.F. Goodrich.

Corporate Growth and Competition in the Late 1920s

The late 1920s were years of growth for America's major rubber manufacturers. In September 1927 a reporter for the *Akron Beacon Journal* observed that "it is like old times to read the balance sheets of the Akron rubber companies."[75] With the exception of U.S. Rubber, which inherited financial problems stemming from poor managerial decision-making earlier in the decade, the leading companies benefited from soaring sales and profits. No one observing the rubber or tire industries in the late 1920s foresaw the Great Depression. All were planning for an expansionary future. At the close of 1928, Moody's newsletter stated that "the long range outlook for the rubber industry is better than it has been at any previous time in the last decade. . . . the industry may still be rightfully considered a young industry and has by no means exhausted its possibilities."[76]

Anticipating a prosperous future, big rubber companies reinvested their earnings in new equipment and factory buildings. Altogether, such investments rose a remarkable 50 percent in just three years (1927–29). These investments, and the overcapacity they created, would contribute to virulent competition in America's tire industry during the 1930s.[77] Firestone spent $4 million in 1929 to construct a seven-story addition to one of its Akron factory buildings. The firm devised a new way to make balloon tires called the "flat-band" method. Cord fabric was applied to the tire building drums in endless bands rather than, as had been done earlier, in batches. These bands were then joined automatically to the beads, treads, and sidewalls in a process that saved factory space and production time. The process gave Firestone and Goodyear, which also soon invested in it, cost advantages over their competitors.[78] Goodrich constructed a three-story building to house more Banbury mixers and a nine-story warehouse for tires. However, the firm did not invest in machinery needed to institute the flat-band process.

Goodrich enjoyed prosperity during the late 1920s but, nonetheless, continued to trail Goodyear and Firestone in its performance. Goodrich's profits, when measured as a percentage of either sales or assets, were consistently lower than those of Goodyear and Firestone. In late 1928 Moody's noted that Firestone's record of earnings was "impressive," that the company's stock "represents a strong equity issue," and that "the company is capable of reporting large per share earnings." Goodyear garnered similar praise. "The management has been progressive," observed Moody's, "and the business of the company has shown very consistent growth." In contrast, Moody's noted that Goodrich had suffered a loss on its operations for the first six months of the year and judged that its stock should be considered only from "the long range investment standpoint." Only U.S. Rubber, of the "big four," was deemed to be in worse shape.[79]

Goodrich's fortunes varied by product line. A mild winter in 1928–29 led to "severe losses in volume" in footwear sales, which then constituted about 8 percent of Goodrich's total sales. Over the next year, however, they rebounded. Footwear sales may have been helped by endorsements from the famous Native American football and track star Jim Thorpe for the "Chief Long Lance" athletic shoe. In advertisements appearing in such popular magazines as Boy's Life and the American Boy, Thorpe attributed the "secret of a strong and athletic body" to his rubber-soled Goodrich sport shoes. Sales of mechanical goods and druggists' sundries "held up very well" in 1928 and 1929.[80]

Tire sales, which continued to make up about one-half of Goodrich's sales, became increasingly competitive. Sales of new automobiles slumped in 1926 and 1927, cutting into original equipment tire sales. The fact that tires lasted longer also bit into Goodrich's replacement tire sales, as did a revolutionary sales agreement that Goodyear reached with Sears, Roebuck in 1926. Goodyear gained all of Sears's business by agreeing to sell tires to the national marketer for their cost of production plus a 6 percent profit. Sears then resold the tires under its "Justice" and "Master Justice" labels. This was the first major agreement of a tire maker's selling its tires through another party as "unbranded" goods. Goodyear renewed its contract with Sears in 1928.[81]

The Silver Fleet and the Silvertown Stores

Goodrich mounted a spirited marketing attack against the growing competition in tire sales. It sponsored trips by a caravan of cars, all equipped with Goodrich tires, across the United States. In 1929 a "Silver Fleet" (also called the "Silvertown Fleet") of fourteen silver-sheened automobiles mounted on Goodrich Silvertown tires cruised over 30,000 miles of American roads to advertise the firm and its products to consumers across the nation. A similar caravan toured the United States in 1930. According to Philip Kelly, Goodrich's advertising director, up to this point the company's sales work had been "honest, but dull." The Silver Fleet, he thought, represented "the first dramatic demonstration by any tire company."[82] Executives for J. Walter Thompson, the company's marketing consultant, concurred. "I don't know of any account or campaign with which I have ever been associated," remarked one Thompson executive in the fall of 1929, "where there has been anything like the publicity break that we are getting on the Silver Fleet."[83] Like the company's efforts to reach the consumers directly in the 1910s, this advertising campaign presented Goodrich's tires as icons of modernity, something to which all Americans should aspire.

In a still more far-reaching marketing move, Goodrich officers lessened their dependence on branch houses, continuing a trend begun in the recession following World War I. The branch houses' selling expenses rose in the 1920s, as they offered more rebates and discounts to convince dealers to push their

The Silver Fleet is pictured here crossing the Sierra Nevadas into California. (BFG Col. UAA)

tires. In 1924 Goodrich's vice president in charge of sales estimated that his company could save $5 million annually by closing many of its branches.[84] Moreover, the houses came to be seen as unresponsive to market and demographic changes. The houses had made sense when Goodrich was pioneering markets for automobile tires, because they had allowed the firm to provide better service and more products for customers than did most independent middlemen. A relatively small number of branch houses sufficed in the limited initial market for tires. But as a larger, more mature, and more competitive market for replacement tires developed, it became important for Goodrich to reach consumers directly at the local level.

Goodrich, and other leading tire companies, turned to smaller company-owned retail outlets to replace the branch houses. Called "Silvertown Stores," Goodrich's outlets sold replacement tires directly to customers—not to independent retailers. By the end of 1929 Goodrich had invested $4.4 million in 109 stores across the nation. As competition intensified and more and more independent dealers failed, Goodrich expanded its company-owned retail network. These stores would remain important outlets for Goodrich products into the 1980s.[85] By 1929 Firestone had invested $8.8 million in 337 stores, and Goodyear had 98 company-owned retail outlets. Goodyear continued to sell many of its replacement tires through Sears. The switch to selling through mass retailers, such as Sears, and through their own retail stores marked a major shift in marketing replacement tires, one that would continue for decades. The share of replacement tires handled by independent dealers dropped from 91 percent of the total tire sales in 1926 to just 76 percent in 1929.

Goodrich's marketing efforts bore mixed results. Replacement tire sales remained more important to the company than original equipment tire sales, and its share of the nation's replacement tire sales rose slightly in the late 1920s. However, Goodrich lost ground in the original equipment market, and this hurt. Firestone maintained its close ties to Ford, and Goodyear remained linked to General Motors. Goodrich's declining position in original equipment tire sales caused its overall share of tire sales in the United States to slip from 10 percent in 1927 to just 7 percent in 1929.[86]

Goodrich and the Rubber Institute

Intensifying competition in tire sales led Goodrich to cooperate with other firms to form the Rubber Institute during the summer of 1928. The preamble to the institute's constitution stated that, too often, rubber manufacturers had "practically been forced to engage in ignorant and often ruthless competition, which has resulted in unsound and uneconomical merchandising trade practices." Those founding the institute embraced "open pricing." They agreed not to give any rebates to tire retailers, and they outlawed "unfair discrimination" and "secret price concessions." The institute's founders also promised to draft a "code of trade practices," which would "definitely describe certain practices as unfair."[87]

The Rubber Institute sustained the cooperation among tire makers that had begun much earlier. Tire makers had worked together to standardize tire sizes and limit competition even before World War I. The war heightened the cooperative impulse and brought the federal government into the picture. Government officials were intimately involved in the work of the Rubber Institute. Throughout the summer of 1928 institute officers conferred with representatives of the U.S. Attorney General's office and the Federal Trade Commission. Only after receiving the assent of these officials did the institute's officers proceed with their open-pricing plans.[88]

Like many American businessmen of the 1920s, the tire makers sought to solve their economic problems through cooperative action involving the federal government. In what became known as "associationalism," business leaders often worked voluntarily with government officials, led by then–Secretary of Commerce Herbert Hoover, to rationalize their industries and businesses. They hoped to make their firms more efficient, standardize their products, and limit competition. Hoover, in particular, called for "cooperative competition" and had the Department of Commerce participate in programs designed to stabilize the nation's economy while maintaining individual business autonomy. Far from being adversaries, businessmen and government officials often worked together in the 1920s to try to stabilize business practices and dampen competition.

Goodrich executives had high hopes for the Rubber Institute. Tew, who participated in its founding, proclaimed that "I am sure the Institute will prove to be a very stabilizing influence in the rubber industry."[89] In the late fall of 1928, Tew chaired a committee of tire makers to devise a new open-price list for original equipment tires. Under his direction, representatives of ten tire makers met in Cleveland. The conference accomplished little, however. After "due discussion of the economic difficulties of the operation of the present plan," those at the meeting "unanimously agreed to suspend its operation effective immediately." They could not decide on any alternative plan, and price-cutting quickly recurred.[90]

Faced with the collapse of its primary objective, the Rubber Institute merged with the Rubber Association of America, the industry's leading trade association, in the spring of 1929.[91] The forces of competition proved too powerful for containment by voluntary cooperation, even with the approval of the federal government. America's tire industry simply was overbuilt. Tire prices dropped 5 percent in November 1927, starting a long-term trend: major price cuts would average two per year over the next decade.[92] The interaction between competition and cooperation would, nonetheless, continue throughout the 1930s, with federal government officials playing important roles. The work of the institute expanded the role of the federal government in Goodrich's affairs and set the stage for further government involvement in the future.

New Rubber Manufacturing Plants

In the late 1920s Goodrich built or acquired three new rubber manufacturing plants, including two outside of Akron. In part this move resulted from its policy of diversification. Goodrich purchased two well-established companies, the Hood Rubber Company of Watertown, Massachusetts, one of America's leading footwear makers, and the Miller Rubber Company of Akron, which had a strong position in druggists' sundries. The acquisitions were made to lessen Goodrich's dependence on the tire market. At the same time, however, Goodrich opened a brand-new factory in Los Angeles whose major product was tires. With these moves, and with a growing involvement in foreign operations, Goodrich began a dispersal of its production facilities out of Akron, a process that would accelerate in later decades. In the 1920s Firestone, Goodyear, and U.S. Rubber also established new factories outside of Akron, mainly in low-cost labor areas in the South and Far West.

Goodrich's Los Angeles Plant

On 2 May 1928, Goodrich opened a new rubber manufacturing plant in Los Angeles, the first tire making factory built by the company outside of Akron, with great fanfare. At a ceremony attended by the mayor of Los Angeles and the lieutenant governor of California, and broadcast live by thirty radio stations nationwide, Tew spoke of the importance of the new facility. Over the next five days, fifty thousand Angelenos toured the spacious single-story factory.[93] Measuring 400 by 1,800 feet, employing 1,500 workers, and costing $4 million, the factory was the largest plant to open in Los Angeles in eighteen years. By early 1929 the facility was operating at its full capacity of 5,000 tire casings and 7,500 tubes per day.[94]

Numerous factors drew Goodrich to Los Angeles. City officials, dubbed by one historian as "urban political entrepreneurs," were eager to attract industry. They pushed their city's vast supplies of clean water, brought in by aqueduct from the Owens River, and cheap electric power to prospective manufacturers. Los Angeles was also situated near cotton grown in California's Imperial Valley and was within easy reach of crude rubber shipped from Malaya. Furthermore, the city was located in the largest and fastest-growing market for tires on the Pacific Coast, and was well connected by water and rail to the rest of the Far West.[95] By the late 1920s Goodrich's rivals were beginning to exploit this market with their own plants. Goodyear operated a tire making plant in Los Angeles beginning in 1920 (the company also opened a plant in Gadsden, Alabama, in 1929), and Firestone opened one there seven years later. In 1930 U.S. Rubber followed by buying Samson Tire and Rubber.[96]

While many considerations lured Goodrich to Los Angeles, the most important was the low cost of labor. Los Angeles was well known as an antiunion, open-shop city, and the perception that labor would be cheap and manageable appealed to Goodrich. During the plant's opening ceremony Tew declared with pride that "the American Plan open shop system is to be in effect." Speaking at a luncheon for Los Angeles businessmen a day later, he informed the audience that "freedom from industrial disputes" dictated his company's decision to build in Los Angeles.[97]

The Los Angeles plant was, according to many accounts, a "model of efficiency," a real contrast to Goodrich's antiquated Akron works. Such an efficient plant, officers reasoned, would be able to do well in the increasingly competitive times. According to one contemporary description, "The layout permits a continuous straight-line flow of progress from the raw materials warehouse at one end, through the various stages of compounding, milling, calenders, and vulcanizing, inspection and wrapping to the finished goods

The Los Angeles plant, pictured here, was a model of efficiency in the late 1920s. (BFG Col. UAA)

warehouse shipping department at the other end."[98] While intended mainly to be a tire making plant, the factory also turned out mechanical rubber goods. Tew estimated that lower labor, power, and water expenses would enable the Los Angeles plant to "operate at a cost of from 15 to 20 percent less than at Akron."[99]

Goodrich considered building additional factories elsewhere. In late 1929 the company made plans to open a new tire plant in Atlanta, at a projected cost of $4 million, and had purchased a plot of land; the Great Depression ended the venture.[100] With the coming of hard times, it turned instead to the less expensive and faster route of expansion via acquisition.

The Purchase of Hood Rubber

One year after opening the Los Angeles factory, Goodrich purchased the Hood Rubber Company of Watertown, Massachusetts. Two members of the Hood family, A. N. Hood and Frederick Hood, together with other investors, had incorporated Hood Rubber in 1896. Their father, George Hood, was a pioneer in rubber manufacturing and the founder of the Boston Rubber Company, one of the firms that merged to found U.S. Rubber in 1892.[101] Looking to the future, Hood Rubber soon established a rubber chemical research laboratory that became well regarded over the first two decades of the twentieth century.[102]

Growth was rapid for Hood Rubber. By 1899 the company's Watertown factory produced nearly 20,000 pairs of rubber footwear daily.[103] Fourteen years later, Hood Rubber had net tangible assets of $6 million, on which it earned net profits of $2 million. The firm expanded during World War I, with its sales increasing from $9 million in 1915 to $32 million just five years later.[104] In 1917 Hood Rubber began tire production, and in the following year its tire division boasted sales of nearly $5 million, one-fifth of the company's total sales. Nonetheless, Hood Rubber remained famous for its footwear. By 1920 its footwear factory, the largest such plant in the world, was turning out 65,000 pairs of boots and shoes each day. Hood Rubber's production accounted for one-fifth of the rubber footwear sold in America.[105]

However, Hood Rubber faced increasing difficulties during the 1920s, leading to its purchase by Goodrich. Building on their earlier move into tires, Hood Rubber's executives sought further diversification, and by 1928 their company was producing a variety of footwear, tires, inner tubes, and battery containers. But despite this strategy the company lost $1.5 million on sales of $30 million in 1928. Like most other major rubber companies, Hood Rubber suffered from inventory losses brought on by the repeal of the Stevenson Plan. Moreover, the same mild, dry weather that cut into Goodrich's footwear sales also hurt Hood Rubber's.[106] Hood Rubber's declining fortunes, combined with the retirement of its president, Frederick Hood, made possible its acquisition. In April 1929 Hood offered to sell his company to Goodrich. Goodrich was eager to buy, and four months after Hood approached them, Goodrich executives acquired Hood Rubber in exchange for 100,000 shares of their firm's common stock.[107]

Underlying the purchase, Tew told his company's stockholders, was Goodrich's "long established policy of diversification."[108] Through its acquisition of Hood Rubber, Goodrich hoped to increase its share of the footwear market and lessen its reliance on automobile tire sales. By 1928 Goodrich had become the nation's third- or fourth-largest producer of rubber footwear, and the purchase of Hood Rubber made it America's second-largest maker of rubber boots and shoes, after only U.S. Rubber.[109] With the acquisition, Goodrich's market share rose from 7 percent to about 18 percent of the total.[110] Goodrich also expected to reduce labor costs by moving footwear production to Watertown, where wage rates were lower than in Akron. It wanted, as well, to earn profits by revamping Hood Rubber's tire operations. Hood Rubber had sold $8 million worth of tires in 1928 but had earned no profits on the sales. Goodrich thought that by relocating Hood Rubber's tire production in Akron it could reduce expenses substantially. Altogether, Goodrich expected to earn about a 15 percent annual return from its purchase of Hood Rubber.[111]

The Acquisition of Miller Rubber

Goodrich's second acquisition was the Miller Rubber Company. Jacob Pfeiffer and his brother William, both retail druggists, had joined with Harvey and Leo Miller to found the Miller Rubber Manufacturing Company in 1898.[112] Miller Rubber soon produced a wide range of druggists' supplies, mechanical rubber goods, surgeons' equipment, and toys. The company began to make automobile tires in 1912. During World War I, Miller Rubber's business rapidly expanded as the company produced tires, surgical goods, and gas masks. Sales soared from $2 million in 1914 to $31 million just six years later.[113] By 1924 the company produced over three hundred items.[114] Nonetheless, like Hood Rubber, Miller Rubber experienced severe difficulties during the recession of the early 1920s. Sales declined by nearly half, and the company lost money. Sales recovered mildly during the mid-1920s, but Miller Rubber continued to suffer, as crude rubber prices fell and the company endured heavy write-offs on its inventory. Losses in 1928 totalled $2 million, a daunting sum for a company having sales of just $25 million.[115]

In early 1930 Goodrich took advantage of Miller's sorry financial state to snap up the company at a bargain price. Goodrich exchanged $4.8 million worth of its common stock and assumed all of the liabilities of Miller Rubber, approximately $10 million, for full ownership of the firm. Goodrich's total offer amounted to $14.8 million, then, for a company whose net tangible assets were $18.3 million.[116] A committee representing Miller Rubber's stockholders noted that a "continuation of its present operations would only result in further losses," and the stockholders quickly approved the sale. Like the acquisition of Hood Rubber, the purchase of Miller Rubber was, as Tew explained, a way of "following our policy of diversification."[117] With the purchase, Goodrich took over Miller Rubber's thirty factory buildings in Akron.

The purchases of Hood and Miller indicated continuity in Goodrich's development: they reaffirmed Goodrich's commitment to diversification. Diversification fit well into the corporate strategy that had developed over the past generation, for it was easier and less expensive to grow via acquisitions than by plowing back retained earnings into manufacturing plant and equipment. Only in its Los Angeles venture did Goodrich stray from this strategy, and only after Goodyear had shown the desirability of Pacific Coast operations.

OVERSEAS EXPANSION

Goodrich proved more successful in its foreign than in its domestic operations during the 1920s, as the company's continuing success in foreign sales lured it into overseas manufacturing. As in the case of its French operations before World War I, Goodrich hoped to reap large, quick profits from foreign ventures at relatively little cost to the company. By the end of the 1920s, Goodrich had expanded its overseas enterprises considerably from what they had been a decade before. By 1928 Goodrich sold through 40 foreign branches and 120 foreign agencies.[118] The firm was also established as a manufacturer in Japan, Great Britain, Canada, and France.

In its overseas activities Goodrich was hardly alone. As the United States emerged as the world's chief creditor nation after World War I, American multinationals successfully challenged European, especially British, interests around the globe. Using mass-production, marketing, and organizational capabilities first honed in America's huge domestic market, firms turned their attention abroad. American investments in Canada exceeded those of Great Britain for the first time in 1922, and by 1929 the investments of United States companies in Latin America also surpassed those of Great Britain. The direct investments of American firms in Europe nearly doubled in the 1920s. In short, as the American economy prospered, American companies pushed abroad. This was certainly true in the rubber industry. Goodyear increased its foreign presence through the ownership of three Canadian factories by the close of the 1920s. British tariff barriers posed a particular challenge to American tire makers, and they responded by setting up manufacturing operations in England. Goodyear established a British tire making factory in 1927, as did Firestone a year later. Goodyear also opened a factory in Australia in the late 1920s.[119]

Manufacturing in France

With the end of World War I, Goodrich expanded its French operations. In 1919 it initiated improvements to the Colombes plant to raise output of tires and tubes, and over the next few years production increased greatly despite the postwar recession. Even larger production increases occurred with the return of prosperity in 1922. By January of that year, the factory was making 600 fabric tires, 250 cord tires, 160 solid tires, and 450 tubes per month.[120] When Ford's Bordeaux factory called upon Goodrich for tires in 1923, it was the Colombes plant, not the Akron factory, that supplied them. By the mid-1920s Colombes's tires were selling in England, Spain, Switzerland, Belgium, Italy, and France.

As the French operation matured, it was granted increasing autonomy from Akron. In 1923 the Société Française was allowed to set up its own operating committee and to stop sending routine reports to Akron.[121] As Work explained, "the management and responsibility of the business should be placed squarely with the French management."[122] Later in the same year, the subsidiary was permitted to establish a development department to prepare compounds needed in the construction of solid tires. The French laboratory could "proceed independently of any activity along the same line at Akron."[123]

The Asian Market: Manufacturing in Japan

Japan became home to Goodrich's second overseas manufacturing venture. Goodrich had sold rubber products there before World War I, and by 1914 company officers were contemplating establishing a manufacturing operation.[124] In late 1917 Goodrich entered a joint venture with Yokohama Electric Wire, a member of the Furukawa zaibatsu, to establish a new company, Yokohama Rubber, to manufacture and sell a wide range of rubber products.[125] Goodrich was looking beyond Japan to China and Manchuria, where Yokohama Rubber was to establish sales outlets. Yokohama Electric Wire's officers were seeking ways to diversify their product lines and markets. Rubber items seemed promising, for at the time only a handful of small Japanese companies and a branch of the British company Dunlop Rubber were making rubber products in Japan.[126]

The Asian market, which had beckoned to American businessmen since at least the mid-nineteenth century, still proved magnetic.[127] Goodrich executives were far from alone in going into Japan. Many American manufacturers entered Japan during the first three decades of the twentieth century, often through joint ventures. The Japanese generally proved willing hosts, eager in those years to acquire western technology and business expertise. Only in the 1930s and later did they close the door to foreign investment.[128]

Officers from Goodrich and Yokohama Electric Wire initially shared in policy making for Yokohama Rubber; however, a Japanese manager from Yokohama Electric Wire soon took charge of the enterprise's daily operations. Profits were divided evenly between the two companies.[129] Over the next several years, Yokohama Rubber built a modern rubber factory with equipment supplied by Goodrich on land owned by Yokohama Electric Wire in Yokohama, just south of Tokyo. Goodrich sent technicians to Japan to explain the production processes to their counterparts in Yokohama. Most important was the work of George Oenslager, who remained an active researcher for Goodrich after the acquisition of Diamond Rubber. Oenslager spent most of 1920–22 overseeing Yokohama Rubber's work. Experts from Akron in calendering, belt manufacturing, tire making, rubber processing, and hose making also helped Yokohama Rubber get started. In addition, Japanese representatives visited Goodrich's Akron plant to learn American production methods. For their part, the Japanese set up sales offices for Yokohama Rubber in Tokyo, Osaka, and Ogura. Moreover, Furukawa became the dealer for Yokohama Rubber in China and Manchuria.[130]

Yokohama Rubber began manufacturing in 1920: belting; rickshaw; bicycle, automobile, and truck tires; hoses; gaskets; tubes; thread; and footwear. The output was substantial by Japanese standards, with the plant designed to make 132 automobile tires and 50 truck tires per month.[131] (In 1920 there were only 6,000 private automobiles in Japan. By 1929 the number had risen to 52,000.) As in the case of the French factory, start-up problems hindered the work of Yokohama Rubber. Wartime shortages of raw materials delayed the completion of the factory. Meanwhile, Yokohama Rubber sold goods made in Akron. When the plant began operations, there were quality control problems. In the early 1920s Yokohama Rubber's dealers complained that the company's bicycle tires could not compete with those made by Dunlop. Disputes between Americans and Japanese over what type of tire to manufacture delayed the making of cord automobile tires until 1921. When production began, "unexpected difficulties" arose because their construction "required many new technologies." Then, too, the postwar recession hindered efforts to create a market for Yokohama Rubber products.[132]

In the early years of the joint venture, a major concern was just how much

An outlet for Goodrich tires in Japan is shown here. (BFG Col. UAA)

knowledge Goodrich executives should share with those in charge of Yokohama Rubber. As was typical in joint ventures with Japanese firms, the Japanese partner sought complete access to western technologies. Taiji Komuro,
sent by Yokohama Rubber to study Goodrich's practices in Akron, pressed
Goodrich executives to show him all of their operations and to allow Yokohama Rubber to enter all phases of rubber manufacturing. Goodrich leaders
partially rebuffed him. Howard Raymond, Goodrich's vice president in charge
of production, explained to the head of his firm's research laboratories, "while
we want to handle Mr. Komuro in such a way that his energy will not be curbed
or his feelings hurt, he cannot run loose or have anything contrary to OUR best
judgment." Yokohama Rubber, he thought, should "start along very simple
lines."[133] Accordingly, Raymond informed Komuro, "Yokohama Rubber must
crawl before it can walk." Yokohama Rubber was specifically forbidden access
to Goodrich's rubber compounding formulas, except those absolutely needed
for production purposes. Referring to the formulas, Raymond told Komuro,
"These you *cannot* have . . . it is clearly understood that Compounds are only
to be supplied *when* the new Company *is ready to manufacture* . . . we shall send
a man over to start the manufacture with you."[134]

   Yokohama Rubber nearly went out of business in the 1920s. The Kanto
earthquake of 1 September 1923 leveled the company's factory. "The buildings
toppled over like a file of dominoes," remembered one executive.[135] The anticipated cost of rebuilding, combined with an unexpected slowness in the development of the Asian markets, nearly convinced Goodrich executives to

abandon manufacturing in Japan. Profits had been lower than expected, and even before the earthquake some Goodrich officers complained that the Japanese market required too much "strengthening and improving" before it would be profitable.[136] Nor had the China market developed as well as had been hoped. For Goodrich executives, as for most American businessmen, it proved elusive. Dissatisfied with progress there, Goodrich took direct control of the China market away from Yokohama Rubber in 1922. In return for a 3 percent commission on all sales made in China, Yokohama Rubber ceded all rights to the market to B.F. Goodrich.[137] The postwar recession also weakened the Furukawa zaibatsu, making its leaders reluctant to invest in rebuilding. In early 1924 Goodrich executives declared that they "would not make any further manufacturing investments in Japan" and began seeking sales outlets beyond Yokohama Rubber for Goodrich products in Japan.[138] In 1928, only after lengthy, painful discussions, did Goodrich and Furukawa officers decide to rebuild Yokohama Rubber's factory.

The Beginning of Production in Great Britain

Goodrich explored making rubber products in European nations other than France in the 1920s. In 1923 they considered setting up a tire making factory in Spain but decided not to because "it did not seem advisable to make any commitments along this line."[139] A similar investigation into Australian possibilities led to similar results.[140] Other possibilities bore fruit. After several years of negotiations, Goodrich invested in the Continental Caoutchouc & Gutta Percha and the Continental Rubber companies of Germany. The German companies served as outlets for Goodrich products, as well as producing their own rubber goods.[141]

In Europe, beyond the continuing expansion of its factory in Colombes, Goodrich went furthest in its manufacturing in Great Britain. As in other areas in which it entered manufacturing, Goodrich began by selling products made in Akron. By World War I, the company had well-established depots in London, Manchester, Bristol, Leeds, and Glasgow.[142] By 1916 Goodrich's sales in England reached $2.5 million, mostly from pneumatic tires.[143] During the war, officers considered building a tire making factory in Great Britain, for, as the head of Goodrich's sales department warned in early 1917, "it appears that after the war is concluded there is every probability that England will place a tariff on the import of manufactured rubber goods."[144] However, they took no immediate steps to begin manufacturing in Great Britain because the war effort soon left their firm overextended even in Akron.

Goodrich renewed its quest for a British factory after the war. In 1919 it looked into factory sites, only to reject those "not sufficiently attractive."[145] But, five years later it set up the British Goodrich Rubber Company, Ltd., to manufacture and sell rubber products in Great Britain. Goodrich acquired a factory in Leyland employing three thousand workers by purchasing the Ajax Rubber Company, which had been owned by the Wood-Milne Tyres &

Manufacturing Company. Sir Walrond Sinclair was the deputy chairman of Wood-Milne, and with Goodrich's purchase of Ajax he became a director of British Goodrich—thus beginning a long, at times stormy, relationship.[146]

B.F. Goodrich gave the new firm Goodrich's already existing sales organization in Britain and provided it with the technical expertise needed to begin manufacturing. British Goodrich experienced start-up problems, and Sinclair took over as its managing director (a position analogous to that of president in an American company) in 1925 and became chairman in 1927. Over the next few years, Sinclair reorganized the company's factory operations to put them on a profitable basis and revamped its network of dealers. By 1927 British Goodrich's Leyland plant was turning out 750–1,000 tires per day, as well as large quantities of belting and hose.[147]

Manufacturing in Canada

Canada was the final nation in which Goodrich began manufacturing during the 1920s. Company officers seriously considered building a factory at St. Catharines, Ontario, in 1913. They went so far as to buy thirty-two acres there, only to abandon the project, according to members of the executive committee, "because of the opportunity offered the Company here [in the United States] for putting forth all its energy, which would give quicker and more profitable returns." By this time, Goodrich had branch houses in Toronto, Montreal, and Ottawa and dealers in every province.[148] Immediately after World War I, Goodrich's executives looked into manufacturing possibilities to the north as a way to reach a significant and growing market.[149]

Goodrich bought a major interest in the Ames Holden Tire & Rubber Company of Montreal in early 1923. The firm's research expertise may have been what appealed most to Goodrich's executives. William Wiegand, its president, was well versed in chemistry and had placed great emphasis on the development of new rubber compounds in the early 1920s.[150] Ames Holden was licensed to make and sell tires to Goodrich's specifications in Canada, with Goodrich providing any technical expertise and equipment needed.[151] After overcoming initial quality control problems in the production of cord tires, Ames Holden's factory at Kitchener, Ontario, proved a success. In 1925 Goodrich secured nearly all of the company's stock and changed its name to the Canadian Goodrich Company, Ltd., and a bit later to the B.F. Goodrich Company of Canada, Ltd. Goodrich soon expanded and modernized the Kitchener plant, aimed at producing 1,500 tires per day along with a substantial output of footwear and mechanical goods. Rapid growth in the factory's business required further additions in 1928.[152]

The Formation of International B.F. Goodrich

Goodrich had set up a foreign department during World War I, as had other large American rubber manufacturers. But as the scope and complexity of its overseas operations continued to grow, Goodrich went further, well beyond what its competitors were doing. In 1921 Goodrich established the International B.F. Goodrich Company, a wholly owned subsidiary, which took over the management of all foreign sales and manufacturing operations except those in Canada. Initially capitalized at $10 million, International B.F. Goodrich imposed centralized controls over Goodrich's overseas sales outlets and manufacturing subsidiaries. Within a year of its formation, International B.F. Goodrich had established a management structure composed of both regional divisions (e.g., Latin American sales) and functional divisions (e.g., the plant operation and extension division, the foreign service department, and the technical division).[153]

Foreign Expansion Late in the Decade

During the late 1920s foreign sales and manufacturing prospered. Tew observed in mid-1929 that "commendable progress has been made by the International Corporation in volume of business and earnings," and six months later he reported that for 1929 as a whole "the operations of our foreign plants generally, as well as the Export Division, showed marked improvements."[154]

Its European sales and manufacturing remained the most important of Goodrich's foreign operations. The French subsidiary (together with a Spanish sales outlet) reported sales of $5.5 million during the first nine months of 1929. These were profitable sales. The French subsidiary earned a net profit of $236,000 on sales of $2.7 million during the first six months of 1929.[155] British Goodrich earned a net profit of £73,000 in 1929, up from only £6,000 in the previous year.[156] Goodrich did withdraw from one European operation. In early 1929 the company sold its share in the German rubber companies. Goodrich officers had been using these connections to help market their products in Europe but saw no need to continue the ties after their French subsidiary began maturing.[157]

Still other operations caught Goodrich's attention. In 1929 it spent $500,000 to expand its Canadian plant and transferred a "substantial part" of the export business previously handled by the Akron factories to that facility.[158] After long deliberations, Goodrich managers decided to work with Yokohama Rubber in rebuilding their Japanese plant, and by the summer of 1929 the plant was once again turning out mechanical rubber goods and was gearing up to make three hundred tires per day as well.[159] At this point, Goodrich increased its stake in the venture to 70 percent, with Furukawa having the remaining 30 percent.[160] Following a new bearing, Goodrich executives gave serious consideration to the Latin American market. In 1929 the head of International B.F. Goodrich traveled widely south of the U.S. border and returned to Akron very favorably impressed with prospects there. Later that year, Goodrich purchased a sixty-acre site for a tire factory just outside of Buenos Aires, Argentina. While Tew announced that "we do not expect to build at once," he said that Goodrich was "prepared to erect a branch factory there in the near future." At about the same time, Goodrich granted a license to Compania Manufacturera de Atefactos da Hule Euzkadi to manufacture tires in Mexico. Organized in 1925, the firm had one of the largest rubber factories in Latin America.[161]

It may well be that Goodrich's officers hoped that expansion overseas would offset the problems of competition at home during the 1920s. They certainly wanted to make profits quickly in their overseas manufacturing ventures. These hopes were only partly realized. Setting up foreign manufacturing enterprises, whether on their own or as joint ventures, proved more difficult than had been anticipated. In many cases quality control problems initially hindered progress. In some instances, as in Japan, unexpected difficulties nearly led Goodrich to abandon overseas manufacturing when immediate profits were not forthcoming. Nonetheless, by the late 1920s Goodrich's overseas operations were profitable—more so, perhaps, than those in the United States.

RESEARCH AND SALES IN RUBBER CHEMICALS

In rubber chemicals Goodrich also proved more successful than its competitors during the 1920s. Goodrich scientists conducted important research on rubber chemicals, and that research increasingly had commercial applications. Research became more closely integrated with manufacturing and sales than before; in this integration may be seen the origins of new marketing concepts that Goodrich would more fully develop after World War II. Even so, as Goodrich's experiences with polyvinyl chloride (PVC) illustrated, commercialization did not always follow hard on the heels of discovery.

The Commercialization of Rubber Chemical Research

Writing in 1922, William Geer, who headed Goodrich's research efforts in the 1910s, observed that "the rule-of-thumb methods are gone."[162] Research was fast becoming standardized and commercialized. In that year Goodrich advertised that its chemical manufacturing division, operating out of Mill 3, sold a "complete line of organic accelerators" to speed vulcanization. Goodrich made these available to other rubber companies, and within a year sales reached $750,000. Goodrich remained the nation's largest producer of accelerators throughout the 1920s.[163] How to minimize the deterioration of rubber surfaces also engaged Goodrich chemists. Cracks sometimes developed in tire sidewalls, allowing water to enter and rot the cotton cord, resulting in blowouts. Goodrich discovered how to make an antioxidant, Agerite resin, that prevented such problems. First produced in 1923, by 1927 Agerite was produced in commercial quantities by Mill 3, in powdered form, as phenyl betanapthylamine (PBNA). That year Goodrich sold $500,000 worth of Agerite at 33 percent net profit. Valuable though it was in the 1920s and 1930s, PBNA became more important in later years in the production of synthetic rubber tires, for synthetic rubber could not be processed without the use of an antioxidant.[164]

Another new research area for Goodrich was making rubber through the anode process. Developed first in Europe, the method consisted of immersing a metal item in liquid rubber latex and passing an electric current through it so that the latex would coagulate on the surface. Irregularly shaped items could thus be coated with rubber, making them resistant to corrosion. The anode method was far superior to dipping the item in latex a number of times to build up layers of rubber, because all too often bubbles formed between rubber layers serially constructed, weakening the rubber coating. The anode method proved especially useful in making surgical supplies, gloves, and inflatable toys. It also provided a way to coat small metal surfaces. Goodrich commercialized the anode process in 1926. Together with the Anode Rubber Company, Ltd. (a subsidiary of Dunlop Tire), and Eastman Kodak, Goodrich set up the American Anode Company, of which Goodrich bought full control in 1938.[165]

With its work both in well-established areas such as accelerators and in new fields like the anode process, Goodrich retained its lead in rubber chemical research, and especially in its commercialization. One scientist later recalled that in the 1920s, Mill 3 became "an integrated plant . . . which would make and sell any chemical, if it could be done profitably."[166] Research, production, and sales became increasingly interlinked; and, adopting a new strategy, Goodrich began selling chemical building blocks, such as the organic accelerators, to other companies.

Sales were made through the chemical division, not through the sales outlets used for tires and rubber products. Chemicals were too different technologically from rubber goods to be handled in accustomed ways. The independence of chemicals from the rest of Goodrich's operations, already apparent in the 1920s, would increase in later decades. Indeed, chemists sometimes found themselves acting as salesmen. J. R. (Bob) Silver Jr. is one such example. After graduating from Pennsylvania State University with a degree in chemical engineering in 1914, he served in the army's chemical warfare service during World War I. There he became well versed in the mass production of chemicals, and Goodrich hired him in 1918 to expand production at Mill 3. His charge was to move Mill 3 into "large capacity type manufacturing." Silver ran Mill 3 for several years, but then went into the sale of chemical products made by Goodrich.[167] Goodrich's chemical sales were profitable. By the close of the 1920s Goodrich laboratories sold their products at a 20–45 percent net profit, far more than was being earned in the sale of tires and other rubber goods.

Waldo Semon and PVC

By far the most important discovery made by a Goodrich scientist in the 1920s was that of a way to plasticize PVC, one of the bases for the world's modern plastic industry. Goodrich's involvement with PVC began with the company's quest for synthetic rubber and for a method to make rubber adhere to metal. (If rubber could be adhered to metal, metal pipes, tubes, and tanks could be lined with rubber, making them resistant to any acids or chemicals they might hold or carry.)

Harlan Trumbull was key in both efforts. A professor of chemistry at the University of Washington, Trumbull was recruited to head Goodrich's chemical research efforts in 1919. Looking for methods to bond rubber to metal, Trumbull tried to develop a synthetic rubber, for he thought that synthetic rubber would adhere to metal better than natural rubber. Goodrich scientists had been researching synthetic rubber even before World War I, when natural rubber prices were high. When natural rubber prices collapsed in the postwar recession, they cut back their investigations. Then, as crude rubber prices mounted again in the mid-1920s, the chemists renewed their efforts. Trumbull observed that "no matter what our commercial policy is going to be concerning synthetic rubber, it is time we started work along this line. The advantage will be one of far-reaching scope."[168] At about the same time, Trumbull began looking for another way to make rubber adhere to metal—the anode process was practical only for small surfaces that could be completely immersed in latex.[169]

Goodrich's conservative management team had some difficulty understanding the potential value of these investigations and only with some reluctance supported them. Work once remarked, "You can never compete with Nature."[170] Nonetheless, even Work came to see market possibilities for pipes and tanks lined with rubber and in 1924 called for an acceleration of such research. These investigations led to the creation of the "Vulcalock" process, and by 1927 Goodrich was selling $114,000 of rubber tank linings annually.[171] However, Howard E. Fritz, who had a background in chemicals and who was a salesman for Goodrich's rubber-lined tanks, hoped that a still better process could be discovered.[172]

For this purpose Trumbull hired Waldo Semon, soon destined to become the most illustrious chemist in the rubber industry. Semon had studied chemistry with Trumbull at the University of Washington and was teaching there when Trumbull contacted him. Arriving in Akron during the summer of 1926, his task was to try to find a material with a nonrubber base that would adhere to metal. Semon first experimented with reclaimed rubber and German methyl rubber, a synthetic rubber. As summer turned into fall and then winter, these substances proved unpromising, and Semon went on to work with synthetic organic polymers, one of which was the polymer of vinyl chloride. Semon found this polymer insoluble at room temperature and so proceeded to heat it. He hoped that in doing so he would derive a synthetic adhesive, but he failed in that quest. More important, Semon noticed that when his solution cooled, it formed a flexible, jellylike substance. By "accident," as he later recalled, Semon had discovered how to plasticize PVC—giving a large boost to the development of the modern plastic industry.[173]

Still, just how Semon's discovery might be commercialized was unclear for some time. The plasticized PVC had valuable qualities: it was elastic like rubber but much more resistant to corrosion. Intrigued by what he had found, Semon tried making things with it, such as a golf ball and shoe heels, and he coated handles of pliers and screwdrivers and lengths of wire with PVC. Semon found it more difficult than he had expected to line a tank with PVC, but in this, too, he eventually succeeded. (The Vulcalock project temporarily became a sideline for Semon; but by 1934, when the project ended, he had uncovered over a hundred ways to make rubber adhere to metal—giving Goodrich a jump in this line of work.) Goodrich executives began to commercialize Semon's discovery in the 1930s, but only in the 1940s and 1950s did PVC resins and compounds develop into one of Goodrich's leading product lines—a position maintained into 1993. In the late 1920s it was much clearer to researchers than to those in management that something momentous had been discovered.[174]

Goodrich enjoyed the most advanced chemical research effort of America's rubber companies. Both in rubber chemicals and in new areas such as PVC, Goodrich scientists were ahead of their counterparts. However, this edge did not always give Goodrich a competitive commercial advantage. As David Goodrich observed, "One of the strange things about Goodrich is that, throughout its history, the Company has shown an astonishing inability to consolidate satisfactorily."[175] By this he meant that the company often failed to capitalize fully on its scientific discoveries. So it was, all too often, with research. While beginning to commercialize more established developments in accelerators and antioxidants, management failed to commercialize rapidly the breakthrough discovery of how to plasticize PVC.

GOODRICH ON THE EVE OF DEPRESSION

Tew and the other executives at B.F. Goodrich could look upon their accomplishments in the late 1920s with a modicum of satisfaction. Financially, their company was in better shape than it had been for some time. Although troubled by the overcapacity and growing competition in tires, Goodrich earned profits (whether measured as a percentage of sales or assets) closer to those of Firestone and Goodyear than in earlier years and higher than those of U.S. Rubber. Goodrich was a more diversified and complex company than ever before, with growing operations abroad and several manufacturing plants outside of Akron in the United States for the first time.

Even so, Goodrich continued to fall behind Goodyear and Firestone in what had become the major market for rubber goods in America and the world, automobile tires. Executives remained reluctant to invest the firm's earnings in new machinery, production methods, and factories in Akron. Their hesitancy to move into the making of balloon tires was unfortunate. While recognizing the need to change some ways of doing things—he took Goodrich in new directions in sales—Tew did not radically alter corporate strategy. Rather than thoroughly modernize the Akron tire factory so it could compete effectively, Goodrich chose instead to diversify into nontire fields. As a consequence, despite some modernization efforts in the 1920s, Goodrich entered the Great Depression with its main plant in worse shape than those of its major competitors.[176]

The decisions to emphasize diversification at the expense of losing its position in tire manufacturing proved to be shortsighted. To be sure, in the short run diversification helped Goodrich escape some of the worst effects of competition in the tire industry. However, the loss of market share in tires was a consequence from which Goodrich would long suffer and never recover. Nor did diversification protect Goodrich from the hard times of the 1930s. When the Great Depression struck, as in the recession of the early 1920s, Goodrich suffered more than Goodyear and Firestone.

4

Coping with the Great Depression, 1930–1939

As the Great Depression blanketed American industry, Goodrich and its officers were beleaguered. Sales fell by more than half in the early 1930s, and the firm reported crippling losses. Unprecedented in its severity, the depression hurt nearly all of American business and greatly limited available choices for business leaders. Between 1929 and 1932 the nation's gross national product declined from $104 billion to just $76 billion, and industrial production fell by half, throwing at least a quarter of all laborers out of work. As Americans stopped buying new cars, tire sales collapsed. Sales of original equipment tires fell from 21 million to just 6 million, and replacement tire sales dropped from 47 million to 33 million. The sales of all other rubber products dropped from $323 million in 1929 to $171 million three years later.[1] Consequently, the depression accelerated the shakeout in rubber manufacturing which was already under way. Of the twenty-two rubber footwear makers in the United States in 1929, thirteen were left in 1933, and the number of tire makers dropped from ninety-one to only forty.[2] An observer of the Akron scene concluded, in 1936, that this was a period "of collapsing demand, vanishing companies, and the readjustment of a billion-dollar industry on a fairly permanent basis of half size."[3]

The depression presented Goodrich executives the dual challenge of dealing with a precipitous decline in demand for their firm's products and of handling the competition of better-positioned and better-equipped companies. In their responses to the problems, officers reaffirmed themes growing out of the company's earlier history. Behind many of their actions was a continued commitment to diversification, but the depression was so pervasive that this strategy failed to protect the company. Moreover, management problems, first apparent in the 1920s, persisted throughout the 1930s. Improvements and investments needed for long-term growth continued to be slighted. Instead,

Goodrich executives worked with officials in the federal government to try to end competition and price wars, thus heightening the importance of governmental actions for their company's development. In particular, they participated in efforts to stabilize prices through the National Recovery Administration, a federal government agency set up as part of President Franklin D. Roosevelt's New Deal in 1933. They also reduced the relative importance of operations in Akron by opening factories elsewhere in the United States, a move that would continue during and after World War II.

These measures proved unsuccessful in protecting the company from the hardships of the depression. To make matters worse, both employees and stockholders challenged management's authority. Goodrich workers joined unions in unprecedented numbers and questioned management's authority to set wages, determine working conditions, and govern the factory and office workplace. In short, acrimonious labor relations appeared that would trouble the company for over four decades. Stockholders, appalled by the company's performance, mounted a serious challenge to management's authority from another direction.

Not all was bleak in the 1930s, however. Bad as the tire market was during the depths of the depression, there was some recovery by the middle of the decade in both the original equipment and replacement tire markets. Goodrich was not as well positioned as its larger competitors, Goodyear and Firestone, to profit from the recovery, but nevertheless some years saw at least modest profits. Moreover, the company continued to lead the industry in technological changes, developing aircraft deicers and other products. As we shall see in chapter 5, they launched what proved to be a significant venture in what was then a fledgling petrochemical industry.

In the final analysis, the 1930s were poor years for Goodrich management and employees. The market crisis of the Great Depression, the rebellion of hourly employees, and the challenges of a stockholder revolt exhausted top management and produced a crisis of leadership—a crisis not resolved until the end of the decade.

THE INITIAL RESPONSE TO THE GREAT DEPRESSION

Like the recession after World War I, the Great Depression of the 1930s raised perennial challenges for Goodrich executives. How should they reshape their product lines and sales? Should they continue their strategy of diversification? How should they deal with competitors? And what should they do about their foreign operations? When officers addressed these issues, they changed their company's operations a bit; but in the end they failed to solve the problems they faced, and the Great Depression nearly overwhelmed them.

Goodrich in the Early 1930s

That a major depression would hurt the firm was not apparent in the late 1920s. During the fall of 1929, Goodrich operations were, Tew noted, "far from satisfactory," but he thought these problems were only temporary.[4] Like most of America's business leaders, Tew was convinced that his company and the industry were fundamentally sound. Goodrich had no plans to slow its expansion program; rather, it continued to prepare for prosperous times, which Tew believed were right around the corner. In the summer of 1930 Goodrich successfully floated $30 million in convertible debentures, the proceeds of which were used to liquidate debts incurred in purchasing Hood Rubber and Miller Rubber.[5]

Only in 1930 and 1931 did officers begin to realize that they faced unprecedented problems. In 1930 sales fell for the first time in years, and Goodrich posted a loss of $8.4 million. At the same time, Goodrich suffered from a 50 percent fall in the price of crude rubber and a 40 percent drop in cotton prices. Although the price decreases would later help Goodrich by lowering its raw material costs, the initial impact was harmful. Inventory write-downs for rubber and cotton totalled nearly $2 million.[6] In 1931 sales slumped in field after field: original equipment tires experienced a 56 percent decline, footwear a 40 percent drop, and mechanical rubber goods a 29 percent fall. A $3.8 million loss in footwear, a $1.7 million deficit on foreign operations, and a $300,000 loss in original equipment tire sales contributed to Goodrich's staggering $8.8 million loss in 1931. The prices of raw materials continued to slide, forcing Goodrich to write down the value of its raw materials inventories by an additional $4.9 million.[7]

Events in 1932 reinforced the recognition that something was fundamentally wrong. In January Tew told his company's directors that he did "not look for an up-turn in business during the present year."[8] Goodrich's bath in red ink persisted. Nearly all of the company's operations showed deficits in 1932, but three areas accounted for most of Goodrich's $6.9 million in losses. Footwear sales lost $3.6 million, and foreign operations lost nearly $1 million. In addition, continuing raw materials inventory write-offs cost Goodrich $1.1 million.[9]

During the economic downturn of the early 1930s, as was the case during the competitive times of the late 1920s, Goodrich's experiences varied by market and product line. Footwear, foreign operations, and automobile tires caused the most headaches for Goodrich. Unable to solve fully problems in these three areas, Goodrich retrenched its operations.

Disaster in Footwear

The Great Depression temporarily killed the company's aspirations of developing a profitable position in footwear. After purchasing Hood Rubber, Goodrich transferred its boot and shoe operations to Watertown, Massachusetts. The goal was to save on labor costs, for, as Tew observed, in Watertown "the labor market is more favorable than in Akron."[10] A mild winter in 1931 combined with the deepening of the depression upset such plans. By early 1932 Goodrich's footwear division was operating only four days per week, at just 40 percent of its capacity. Hurt by the same problems, U.S. Rubber,

Goodrich's major competitor, slashed prices, setting off a price war that destroyed profits. Goodrich was the loser in this competition, as its share of the American market for rubber footwear slid from 30 percent to just 26 percent during 1931. By the end of the year, Tew was calling footwear "an almost insurmountable problem."[11]

Losses in footwear worsened during 1932. Another mild winter bit into sales, as did a twelvefold increase in imports of rubber footwear from Japan and Czechoslovakia.[12] Representatives of Goodrich, U.S. Rubber, and other companies lobbied Congress to raise import duties, which was done in 1933. Goodrich executives also acted on their own. As the footwear division's hemorrhaging dragged his company down, Tew decided in late 1932 to remove the division's miserable showing from Goodrich's balance sheet, and through an accounting sleight of hand the division's performance was separated from Goodrich's. Only in 1935, when conditions in boots and shoes improved, were the results of the footwear division once again included in Goodrich's consolidated financial statements.[13]

Problems Overseas

Overseas operations, which had been so promising during the 1920s, collapsed during the depression. As the depression became global, the economic downturn hurt Goodrich's foreign manufacturing and sales. At the same time, currency exchange rates shifted against the American dollar, especially from 1931, adding to Goodrich's losses.

Results varied considerably by country in 1930. Tew reported that Goodrich's French and British plants were "doing a good job and making a good return on sales and invested capital" in the early fall of that year. For its fiscal year ending in September 1930, British Goodrich reported net profits of £88,000. As late as January 1931, a Goodrich director visiting France found his company's plant there "busy and prosperous." By way of contrast, Yokohama Rubber was incurring losses due to "a very serious business recession" in Japan; and Goodrich's Canadian plant experienced difficulties as a result of "poor business conditions" in that country. Nonetheless, as in domestic operations, the magnitude of the depression was not yet fully perceived by Goodrich officers. In January 1931 Tew announced that he expected foreign operations to earn $500,000 on sales of $26 million during the coming year.[14]

The deepening of the depression shattered any such hopes. In the summer of 1931 Tew admitted that "the foreign companies, outside of France and England, are not operating profitably." This sorry state of affairs was due, he thought, to "poor business conditions abroad and partly to our own organization."[15] Tew could do little about the spread of the depression, but he did try to improve Goodrich's overseas organization. He moved International B.F. Goodrich's offices from New York City to Akron and sought to provide closer supervision of the subsidiary's operations.[16] Still, the situation worsened. "Foreign business is of course very unsatisfactory," Tew reported in late 1931.[17]

Anticipating no improvements in overseas sales, Tew withdrew Goodrich products from Italy, Germany, Austria, Hungary, and Argentina in the winter of 1932. Later in the year he announced that Goodrich was "continuing to restrict operations in Foreign fields" and said that he hoped the company would be able to withdraw from Brazil, Denmark, Norway, Sweden, India, and Chile.[18]

Competition in Tire Making

Tires presented a third major challenge.[19] A price war between Goodyear and U.S. Rubber led to a 10 percent reduction in original equipment tire prices in 1930, causing Tew to complain that "the condition of the original equipment field is worse than it has ever been."[20] Moody's reported in 1930 that "little ground for optimism" could be found in the tire industry, for "stocks of goods on hand are large [and] productive capacity is excessive."[21] The situation soon deteriorated more, as the new capacity added by tire companies in the late 1920s came back to haunt them in the early 1930s. "Special deals and discounts" meant that Goodrich's earnings from original equipment sales were "badly impaired."[22] In the replacement tire market, where Goodrich had historically been stronger, profits were eliminated by almost continuous price cuts, made worse by special rebates to independent dealers. Longer-lasting tires combined with increased competition devastated Goodrich.[23] A report by Standard and Poor's observed that "few industries have had to face the destructive, cut-throat price warfare prevalent in the retail distribution of replacement tires and tubes."[24]

Goodrich sought to limit competition through cooperation with rival firms. Officers joined representatives of other tire makers in sponsoring a "war room" in Akron. Consisting of "a battery of telephones, all directly connected to the rubber companies' district offices," the room was moved from company to company month by month. Using a secret code, representatives of each major tire maker were in constant contact with their firms' retail outlets. In this room company officers shared price information and used their phones to try to quash local price wars that threatened to broaden into widespread price-cutting, actions most likely in violation of America's antitrust laws.[25] Goodrich officers were also active in the Rubber Manufacturers' Association. Tew was elected president of the organization in 1931, and under his leadership the association tried, over the next two years, to end "unethical advertising" and "unsound merchandising."[26] The association's efforts were of little avail, however. By early 1933 Tew could only hope that the "conditions resulting from these price wars are so serious" that the tire makers would jointly devise some sort of "constructive policy" to deal with them.[27]

In the meantime, Goodrich sought to boost its sales in the replacement tire market. Though a production man, Tew recognized the importance of better tire distribution. Between 1928 and 1932 Goodrich employed J. Walter Thompson, a pioneer in marketing research in America, as its advertising agency. In report after report the firm recommended ways to improve Goodrich's sales. A seminal report completed in June 1930 found that Goodrich's tire advertising efforts were ineffective, when compared with those of the company's competitors, and recommended that Goodrich adopt a new sales strategy aiming at "profit rather than more sales volume as the ultimate objective."[28] Another report showed that Goodrich lagged far behind Goodyear and Firestone in consumer brand recognition for replacement tires.[29]

Responding to these reports and to the findings of his own investigations, Tew sought to increase the effectiveness of the dealers through which Goodrich sold many of its replacement tires.[30] He initiated an "aggressive Dealer and Advertising program," consisting of dealer conferences held across the nation. Altogether, dealers marketing three-quarters of the dealer-sold Goodrich tires attended the conferences. The meetings revived flagging spirits among the dealers, and by early 1932 Goodrich had three thousand more dealers than a year earlier.[31] Goodrich also funneled a larger share of its tire advertising budget into activities supporting the dealers. By 1932, 61 percent of Goodrich's tire advertising expenditures went for "dealer material, signs, [and] sales promotions." Goodrich spent the rest on direct consumer advertising in newspapers, magazines, and on the radio.[32]

Goodrich also relied on the company-owned Silvertown stores to tap the replacement tire market. In early 1931 Tew announced that in the future Goodrich's policy would be "to continue opening Silvertown stores, with diversified service, in large markets."[33] The worsening of the depression, however, limited the resources available to carry out this policy; after the company-owned stores lost $700,000 during the first six months of 1931, Tew halted store expansion. The number of Silvertown stores dropped from 180 in the summer of 1931 to 156 a year later.[34] Losses still mounted. By 1933 the Silvertown stores, organized as a wholly owned subsidiary, owed $6.5 million to B.F. Goodrich.[35] At the same time, Goodrich tried to sell replacement tires through new distribution channels. In 1930 it reached an agreement with the Atlas Supply Company, a subsidiary of the Standard Oil companies, to handle Goodrich tires as one of its special brands. (Atlas also took tires from U.S. Rubber.)[36]

Goodrich's sales efforts were only partially successful. The company's share of America's shrinking tire market rose from 12 percent in 1931 to 13 percent a year later. Even so, Goodrich dropped from third to fourth place among the nation's tire sellers in 1931, the position it held for the rest of the 1930s.[37] Part of the problem lay in the attitudes of top managers. Despite the changes begun by Tew, most Goodrich executives were not, at heart, marketers. As Philip Kelly, the head of Goodrich's advertising program, later explained, "for years, on the executive committee, the Board of Directors, or the Executive Staff, there was not one single executive who had ever had actual experience at retail selling." In fact, he thought, "to be a successful retailer was considered the end of the road by the stuffed shirts who controlled the business."[38] Then, too, Goodrich's competitors were advancing in marketing. For all of the major tire

Goodrich's Silvertown stores were hit hard by the Great Depression, and they dropped in number. (BFG Col. UAA)

makers, company-owned stores became more important than branch houses in making sales, and Goodyear and Firestone owned more of them than Goodrich. When compared to Goodyear and Firestone, Goodrich lacked adequate retail outlets to move its replacement tires at a profit.[39]

Retrenchment

Like their competitors, Goodrich officers responded to the Great Depression with retrenchment. Despite calls from President Herbert Hoover for increased capital spending projects to help Americans deal with the depression, most companies cut back on spending and employment in the early 1930s. In the fall of 1930, Tew reduced the number of salaried employees by about 10 percent in Akron and more at Watertown.[40] Further cutbacks soon followed. A program begun in January 1931 aimed at saving $1.3 million over three months by reducing operating expenses.[41] The wages of all salaried employees were cut by 10 percent in February 1931, an additional 10 percent in late 1932, and another 10 percent in January 1933.[42] Other rubber companies took similar actions. U.S. Rubber closed its least efficient factories and sold its equipment. U.S. Rubber, Firestone, and Goodyear also reduced salaries and shortened the hours of work.[43]

Tew judged his retrenchment work to be successful, but it failed to solve the problems facing Goodrich. In a report to company directors in early 1932, Tew observed with pride that over the past fourteen months Goodrich had reduced its salaried employees by 16 percent and actual salaries by 29 percent, for an-

TABLE 4.1
Rubber Companies' Performance, 1929–1939

	Goodrich	U.S. Rubber	Goodyear	Firestone
	Profit as a Percentage of Sales			
1929	4.5	(1.7)	7.3	5.3
1930	(5.4)	(11.5)	4.9	6.1
1931	(7.6)	(8.3)	0.8	5.3
1932	(8.8)	(13.2)	(0.8)	6.1
1933	2.9	(0.7)	5.5	3.2
1934	2.4	(0.5)	3.3	4.2
1935	2.9	1.7	3.3	4.6
1936	5.2	6.3	5.8	6.7
1937	(0.6)	4.6	3.6	3.7
1938	1.9	4.0	3.6	3.7
1939	4.9	5.4	4.9	4.2
	Profit as a Percentage of Assets			
1929	4.5	(1.1)	7.7	4.8
1930	(5.3)	(8.5)	4.4	1.0
1931	(6.3)	(5.1)	0.6	4.3
1932	(5.8)	(6.2)	(0.4)	3.9
1933	2.0	(0.4)	3.0	1.8
1934	2.1	0.3	2.3	3.1
1935	2.7	1.4	2.8	4.0
1936	5.2	5.9	5.5	6.2
1937	(0.6)	4.8	3.7	5.6
1938	1.7	3.6	3.2	3.1
1939	4.7	5.8	5.1	3.8

Sources: Annual reports of the companies; Calvin W. Neiman, "A Study of Rubber Industry Profits with Emphasis on Correlation to Sales and Capital Investment" (M.B.A. thesis, Kent State University, 1965).
Note: Numbers in parentheses are negative numbers.

nual savings of $5.1 million.[44] Nonetheless, Goodrich suffered more than Goodyear or Firestone from the onset of the Great Depression. Goodrich's sales, assets, and profits fell faster than those of the two tire makers. Its profits, whether considered as a percentage of its assets or its sales, were considerably lower than Firestone's and Goodyear's. Among major American rubber manufacturers, only U.S. Rubber performed worse than Goodrich during the early 1930s. Moody's concluded in 1931 that Goodyear and Firestone "have shown considerably more stable and generally more satisfactory results" than Goodrich or U.S. Rubber.[45]

In short, Goodrich's strategy of diversification failed to protect the firm from the economic collapse of the early 1930s, just as it had proven inadequate during the 1920s recession. From the days of Benjamin Goodrich, executives had prided themselves on having a diversified company turning out a wide range of goods for a variety of markets. In the 1910s and 1920s Bertram Work had consciously kept Goodrich diversified, being careful not to make it too dependent on the automobile tire market. In part, it was this desire to further Goodrich's diversification that led Tew to purchase Hood Rubber, with its footwear operations at Watertown. Unfortunately, the depression was too widespread for Goodrich to avoid hard times. Like Goodyear and Firestone, Goodrich was hurt by slumping tire sales and falling tire prices. In addition, Goodrich incurred major losses (as did U.S. Rubber) from footwear sales. Here diversification undoubtedly hurt Goodrich. Goodrich purchased Hood Rubber at an unfortunate time, for the depression combined with mild winters and foreign imports to devastate the sales of rubber boots and shoes.

RECOVERY FROM THE GREAT DEPRESSION

The United States recovered from the Great Depression slowly. The nadir was reached in 1933. By 1937 the nation's gross national product had risen to its 1929 level. After a slump in 1938, economic growth was robust, with full recovery taking place during World War II. Trends in the rubber industry mirrored those in the nation's economy. As Americans began buying new cars again, original equipment tire sales more than tripled in the four years following 1932. Replacement tire sales lagged behind, as technological advances meant that tires lasted longer. The number of factories making tires increased from forty-four to forty-six between 1933 and 1936. Even so, the amount of capital invested in tire plants in 1937 remained substantially less than it had been eight years before. Recovery occurred faster in nontire rubber goods, and by 1937 the capital invested in factories was 22 percent higher than in 1929. Employment in rubber manufacturing rose well above the 1930 level by 1940.[46]

Goodrich participated in America's economic recovery. Between 1933 and 1937 the company's sales nearly doubled to $150 million. In 1933 the firm earned its first profits in three years, and by 1936 profits stood at a healthy $7.3 million. During 1937 Goodrich undertook a $600,000 plant modernization program in Akron, the largest of its type since 1929.[47] Defense spending boosted Goodrich's expansion. Hood Rubber began developing a new type of rubber casing for submarine batteries in 1938, and the casings came into general use during World War II. Goodrich developed an endless band track used by tanks and other military vehicles. Derived from a track designed for agricultural tractors in 1931, over one hundred pairs had been produced by 1937. Field tests in the late 1930s led to refinements that paid off with use of the tracks by the amphibious "Weasel" vehicle during the war.[48]

Three domestic issues concerned Goodrich the most: ending continuing competition in automobile tire sales, securing stable supplies of raw materials, and dealing with a unionization drive by its workers. In facing these issues, officers worked on their own and with their competitors. At times, as in their effort to limit competition, they turned to the federal government for help; at other times, as in the unionization campaign, they found themselves at odds with federal officials. Foreign operations offered little respite from domestic problems and formed yet another challenge for Goodrich.

Competition and Marketing in Tire Sales

Continuing competition in tire sales presented a major challenge to Goodrich's officers in the mid- and late 1930s. In early 1933 Firestone and the mail-order houses slashed their tire prices, and Goodrich responded by cutting its prices later in the year.[49] What Tew described as "disturbed conditions" in tire prices brought about by additional "discounts by the large mail-order houses" persisted into the winter of 1934.[50] At this time Sears and Montgomery, Ward began offering 25 percent trade-in allowances on all purchases of new tires, a move most tire manufacturers met quickly. But not Goodrich. Calling this practice "detrimental," Goodrich advised its store managers and dealers not to grant such allowances.[51]

Goodrich reacted to the competition by expanding the coverage of the Silvertown stores. The Silvertown stores took on new functions, as did the stores of Goodrich's competitors. The tire makers' stores increasingly served as distributors to independent outlets or subdealers, that is, they sold at wholesale as well as at retail. In fact, by 1934 about one-third of all of Goodrich's store sales were made at wholesale. Still, retailing remained the core of store activities, and in 1934 Silvertown stores began allowing installment buying of tires. Two years later there were 431 Silvertown stores, nearly equal in number to Firestone's 561 retail outlets, the most of any tire company. But the Silvertown stores were not very profitable. In late 1936 Goodrich had to pump $4.5 million into the facilities, and the stores continued to incur losses in 1937 and 1938.[52]

As in the early 1930s, Goodrich's sales efforts proved only partially successful. Sales rebounded as economic recovery took place, but not as quickly or as fully as those of its major competitors. Even U.S. Rubber, led by new management, experienced more rapid sales growth. Goodrich's profits as a percentage of its sales also generally lagged behind those of the other large rubber manufacturers during the mid- and late 1930s.

Goodrich and the Federal Government

Faced with the continuing problem of competition, Goodrich turned to the federal government for help. Its major vehicle was the National Industrial Recovery Act, a piece of New Deal legislation passed by Congress in June 1933. The goal of the act was to foster planning and cooperation among firms, and with federal officials—planning that would boost business profits by decreasing competition and raising prices. The law established a new federal government agency, the National Recovery Administration (NRA). NRA officials met with industry representatives, usually trade association officers, to draft codes of fair business competition for each industry. The codes stipulated practices that would cut back production and, as their proponents hoped, raise prices and business profits. Initially, most business leaders supported the work of the NRA as a patriotic way to fight the Great Depression and as a method of increasing their earnings.[53]

Rubber manufacturing was one of the major industries affected by the work of the NRA. As early as the summer of 1932, Tew noted approvingly, an "Advisory Committee" composed of the "larger units" in rubber manufacturing was formed to search for "constructive and beneficial solutions" to competition.[54] Shortly after its formation, the NRA asked the large rubber manufacturers to report on the needs of their industry; in June 1933 a three-man committee of the Rubber Manufacturers' Association (RMA), which included a Goodrich officer, issued a report finding competition to be "the outstanding evil of the industry which should be corrected." The RMA committee urged the NRA to standardize product lines, set prices, and establish production quotas for firms making rubber tires, footwear, mechanical goods, druggists' sundries, and miscellaneous goods.[55] NRA officials, in turn, requested that the RMA establish committees to draft codes for the various sectors of rubber manufacturing. The RMA responded by setting up an eight-man committee—composed of the presidents of Goodrich, Goodyear, Firestone, General Tire, and four smaller companies—to draw up a code of fair competition for tire making.[56] The committee submitted a proposed code in late July, and a month later Moody's predicted that "successful adoption of the code will materially alleviate the severe competitive conditions that have prevailed for some years."[57]

However, disagreements among the companies surfaced at private committee meetings and public hearings during the fall of 1933. The manufacturers were divided over whether to allocate production through quotas or simply to set prices. Once the decision was reached to rely on pricing, disagreements arose on how best to set prices to cover the costs of production. Here the major difficulty was a lack of agreement on how to value inventories of crude rubber, for large and small producers wanted different approaches. Only on Christmas Day was the head of the NRA able to force agreement on a greatly revised code, and then only because amendments to the original code had rendered it virtually meaningless. As approved, the code called on all tire manufacturers to maintain their current prices for ninety days and to agree on some unspecified form of price stabilization within sixty days.[58]

Efforts to draft a code of competition for the retail tire trade formed a second prong in the attempt to stabilize tire prices.[59] The National Tire Dealers' Association led the campaign for price setting at the retail level. Tire manufacturers who relied the most on independent dealers to sell their tires backed the work of the association. Goodrich executives wrote NRA officials that

"adoption of the Retail Code [w]as absolutely essential."[60] J. Penfield Seiberling, the sales manager for Seiberling Rubber, rallied support among small- and
medium-sized companies. Condemning price cuts then being made by Sears as
comprising the "most demoralizing sales policy" the tire industry "has ever
faced," he concluded that "in the last analysis it is going to be necessary for the
Government to intervene."[61] Some twenty tire makers responded to Seiberling's call by petitioning the NRA to speed up the preparation of a retail code
to prevent "destructive price-cutting."[62]

Nonetheless, many divisions between the various types of retailers—large
dealers versus small ones, chain stores and mail-order houses versus independent dealers—hindered the preparation of a code. The president of Sears argued
that his company was helping consumers by cutting tire prices. Writing the
head of the NRA, he explained, "we have prospered because we have adapted
mass distribution to mass production and have kept prices to the consumer
down. . . . Which is more important, the welfare of 50,000 or 60,000 tire dealers or 23,000,000 car owners?"[63] When little agreement could be reached
among the retailers, the NRA issued an administrative order establishing minimum prices in May 1934. The order remained in effect until October but did
not stop price-cutting, for, as Tew observed just a few weeks after the issuance
of the decree, "the N.R.A. was inactive in enforcing code complaints."[64]

The tire making and tire retailing codes had only a limited impact on the
tire industry. There was initial optimism. In January 1934 Moody's noted that
"the possibilities of a substantial improvement in the earnings of tire and rubber companies during 1934 are considered reasonably good."[65] Such optimism
faded in the face of renewed competition. By July 1934 Moody's observed with
dismay that "severe competition . . . has not permitted an increase in tire
prices."[66] Tew remained optimistic longer, observing that "widespread efforts
[were] being made to hold the price structure" when the administrative code's
retail order lapsed in October 1934, but by April 1935 he was again complaining about "the chaotic condition of the tire price structure all over the
country." When the U.S. Supreme Court declared the National Industrial
Recovery Act unconstitutional in May 1935, Goodrich did not miss the NRA,
whose short existence was thereby ended. Moody's concluded that the "recent
dissolution of the NRA is not expected to have any important influence upon
the tire industry . . . tire prices were not aided by the NRA."[67]

The demise of the NRA did not end government involvement in the work
of the tire makers. After a two-year investigation, the Federal Trade Commission (FTC) issued a "cease and desist" order in April 1936 specifying that
Goodyear cancel its contract to supply Sears with replacement tires. The
commission ruled that the cost-plus contract discriminated against small tire
makers. Sears's actions, the commission argued, "substantially lessened competition and tended to the creation of a monopoly."[68] The passage of the
Robinson-Patman Act by Congress in the summer of 1936 more directly affected Goodrich's sales operations. This act forbade tying contracts between
manufacturers and distributors that might limit competition in retailing.

Goodrich interpreted the law to mean that it could no longer make replacement tires for the Atlas Supply Company and canceled its contract with Atlas.
Not all tire makers did so. U.S. Rubber continued supplying tires for Atlas until challenged by the FTC in 1939.[69]

Unionization and the Move out of Akron

Federal government involvement in the operations of the rubber companies extended well beyond the work of the National Industrial Recovery Act.
Government support of unionization fundamentally altered the nature of industrial relations in rubber manufacturing during the 1930s. Large unions
came to dominate many of America's mass production industries during the
depression. The rubber industry, especially tire making, was no exception. The
United Rubber Workers (URW), a Congress of Industrial Organizations (CIO)
affiliate, brought mass unionism to the industry. As unionization raised labor
costs in Akron, manufacturers, including Goodrich, accelerated the dispersal
of their factories out of the city. Searching for cheaper supplies of labor, the
companies accelerated their migration to low-wage areas.

Large rubber manufacturers differed in their labor policies. The historian
Daniel Nelson has shown that they responded to unions in one of three ways.[70]
Management either bitterly opposed unions, adopted a realistic if grudging re-
sponse to them, or saw a silver lining in the storm cloud of their formation.
Nelson described Goodyear as following the first path, Firestone the second,
and U.S. Rubber the third. Goodrich's labor policy resembled Firestone's.
Goodrich management consistently tried to prevent unionization, but avoid-
ed the charged rhetoric and confrontational style of Goodyear managers. Like
Firestone executives, they dealt with the union once it became clear that they
had no choice, but hoped to use the threat of production relocation to bend
the union to their will. When this gambit failed, Goodrich, like Goodyear and
Firestone, continued the move out of Akron.

Work Sharing, Reduced Wages, and Welfare Capitalism

When the Great Depression deepened in the early 1930s, one response of
the rubber manufacturers was to reduce the hours worked by their employees
in a "share the work policy."[71] Goodyear led the way, reducing the workday in
its Akron plant to six hours in 1930. Firestone and General Tire followed in
late 1932, and Goodrich in early 1933. In February 1933 Goodrich's T. G. Graham, the vice president in charge of production, estimated that spreading
work had enabled some four thousand employees to retain their jobs.[72] Management's motivation was not purely altruistic. Executives liked the new six-
hour day because they thought that workers were more efficient during the first
six hours of work than they were later in their shifts.[73]

Like other major rubber manufacturers, Goodrich assisted its employees
through welfare programs. During the winter months, Goodrich financed em-

ployee coal purchases.[74] Goodrich's cooperative gardening program was another approach to employee welfare. In 1932 the company sponsored the
Akron Community Gardens, a two-hundred-acre plot where employees and
former employees could grow food for themselves and their families. Nearly
1,000 families received foodstuffs from the 1932 growing season, and 750 did
so in the following year.[75] Goodrich also contributed to welfare relief in
Akron through the participation of its employees in the city's community
chest campaign. Employees pledged 1 percent of each paycheck for the year,
and the company added an unspecified amount to the total.

Goodrich's Company Union

While Akron's rubber manufacturers battled over the new tire industry
codes of fair competition drafted by the NRA, the city's rubber workers began
joining the American Federation of Labor (AFL) in record numbers. By the
fall of 1933 the AFL had added 23,000 rubber workers to its rolls. With 7,500
members, the Goodrich local was the largest unit, while the Goodyear and
Firestone locals followed with 6,500 and 5,000 members, respectively. Goodrich union members elected Sherman Dalrymple as their president, and he
later became head of the United Rubber Workers.[76] As Nelson correctly ob-
serves, the unions liked much about the large rubber manufacturers. They paid
relatively high wages for short work days. Still, the unions had real grievances.
Foremen sometimes treated workers unfairly, promoting and laying them off
with little respect for seniority. Most important, union members wanted to
bargain collectively with management as a group. Behind specific grievances
lay the unease engendered by the Great Depression. Nelson notes that the
hard times they saw around them led workers into unionization activities.[77]

The large rubber manufacturers fought the formation of AFL unions through
the sponsorship of company unions. Goodrich, Firestone, and General Tire introduced employee representation plans in the fall of 1933, while Goodyear
expanded a plan already in existence. Goodrich's Graham was willing to meet
with Dalrymple and other Goodrich union officers, and even helped them set
up grievance committees; privately he believed the company could defeat
unionization efforts. Graham's introduction of the Goodrich Cooperative
Plan as a company union in October 1933 was part of his larger strategy to un-
dermine the AFL. The plan offered a simple format. Elected departmental representatives would work with management to try to resolve problems. Any
unresolved issues could be appealed to Goodrich's president and board of directors. This plan gave workers little power. As a laborer on Goodrich's factory floor recalled, "if you had a grievance, it would go to the general foreman or
the superintendent and there it ended."[78] In Goodrich's company union, as in
most, the real power lay with management.

Still, the Cooperative Plan won gains for Goodrich's workers. Late in 1933
Goodrich granted annual paid vacations to employees with more than five
years of continuous service.[79] In the fall of 1934 executives agreed to use se-

niority as the basis for their firm's employment policies. The program mandated that "in all dealings between The B.F. Goodrich Company and its employees with respect to transfer, layoff, rehiring, and shift assignment 'seniority' shall govern." The seniority program recognized the changed character of Goodrich's workforce. Managers were dealing with a veteran group of workers. By early 1935, 3,230 Akron factory workers had been with Goodrich between five and ten years; 2,169, between ten and fifteen; 1,315, between fifteen and twenty; and 518, between twenty and twenty-five.[80] With some recovery under way, Goodrich raised wages. While the degree of collusion is unclear, Akron's major rubber firms moved in concert in granting a number of wage increases between 1933 and 1936.[81]

Goodrich disbanded the Cooperative Plan after the U.S. Supreme Court upheld the Wagner Act in 1937. The Wagner Act was a piece of New Deal labor legislation passed by Congress in 1935. It gave workers the right to form unions of their own choice to bargain collectively with management, and severely limited the activities of company unions. An important question is how much support the plan enjoyed among Goodrich employees. Nelson states that in spite of the Cooperative Plan's well-publicized accomplishments, "most employees remained skeptical about the legitimacy of the plan and the independence of the representatives."[82] Nonetheless, as late as April 1935, just under 85 percent of Goodrich's workers took part in elections under the Cooperative Plan. At least some Goodrich employees viewed the plan seriously.[83]

Labor Militancy and Union Avoidance

In 1934 William Green, president of the AFL, and Coleman Claherty, president of the United Rubber Workers' Council, responded to the growing impatience of the rubber workers and to the RMA's rejection of a proposed industrywide labor agreement by seeking employee elections under the auspices of the newly created National Labor Relations Board (NLRB), a federal government agency. They hoped that NLRB-sponsored elections would generate publicity favorable to unionization and provide it with the stamp of government approval. The AFL sought elections at Goodrich and Firestone in the fall of 1934, but executives at the two firms announced that elections were unnecessary, due to the formation of company unions.[84]

Intense legal and political maneuvering led to a temporary compromise. The three largest Akron locals made contract demands on management, only to have corporate officials refuse to bargain with them. Instead, the executives used the early months of 1935 to prepare for a strike.[85] In response, the locals called a strike vote, but at each company the strike resolution failed to poll the 75 percent required by the AFL, and union officials kept the results of the elections a secret.[86] In April 1935, to head off a rubber industry walkout, Secretary of Labor Frances Perkins met with executives from Goodyear, Firestone, and Goodrich (including Tew and Graham of Goodrich) and with union leaders.

Perkins conferred with each group separately; at no time during the three days of meetings did the union and business leaders speak directly to each other. The pact that emerged was a compromise. The unions agreed not to strike; both sides agreed to postpone unionization elections; and the manufacturers agreed to negotiate individual grievances with their workers and terminate financial support for company unions until the courts determined their legality. Many of Akron's union members thought they had been sold out by the AFL's national leadership, but each local approved the pact.[87] Goodrich executives, on the other hand, believed "the matter had been exceptionally well handled, and that the result was entirely satisfactory."[88]

Objecting to the Perkins agreement, some rubber workers formed the URW in September 1935 (the URW affiliated with the CIO in 1936), and Local 5 of the URW sought to represent workers in Goodrich plants. The establishment of the URW as an aggressive union led to a resurgence in rubber worker militancy that came to a head in a sit-down movement. The Goodrich plant experienced its first major sit-down strike in February 1936. Workers in the tire department sat down at their job stations and refused to leave their buildings, forcing Graham to close the plant for the weekend. Graham had initially acceded to the tire workers' demand that Goodrich pay them for time lost when the tire department was changing machines, but the strikers then demanded that they be paid as well for the time lost during their sit-down. Graham refused. As with many of the future sit-downs, the strikers acted without the approval of Local 5 officers, who opposed the strikers' second demand and eventually succeeded in persuading the strikers to leave the plant.[89]

Sit-down strikes, while not yet common, were not unknown in American industry during the mid-1930s. Some automobile plants, for example, were hit with them even before Goodrich workers sat down on the job; and auto workers attracted the most attention. In late 1936 auto workers at General Motors's Flint, Michigan, Fisher Body plant initiated what became a successful sit-down strike. Winning national attention, this strike dramatized the new tactic employed by workers, as they contested with management for control of the workplace.

Goodrich's sit-down strike, and a larger one against Goodyear, imbued union members with a new sense of confidence that manifested itself in more aggressive bargaining and acts of militancy. The URW leadership found it increasingly difficult to control the activities of rank-and-file members who were ready to engage in unauthorized sit-downs at the slightest provocation. Company managers, on the other hand, tried to avoid major confrontations during this period. In May 1936, when workers in Goodrich's mechanical goods department sat down to protest the layoff of several veteran employees and Local 5 president Callahan subsequently threatened a larger strike, Graham rehired the men.[90] Unlike his counterparts at some of Akron's other rubber plants, Graham favored a low-key approach in his dealings with union members.

Nonetheless, the sit-down movement spread, and there were at least fifty-two Akron sit-downs between March and December 1936. The sit-downs achieved their goals. After signing a contract with Firestone in April 1937—the first formal contract between a major tire manufacturer and a union—the URW entered into negotiations with Goodrich and Goodyear. Both firms agreed to abide by the results of employee elections held under the auspices of the NLRB, and in August workers at each company overwhelmingly voted for the URW locals as their bargaining agents. Goodrich workers rejected the company union in this vote. Local 5 drew 75 percent of the vote at Goodrich, and from this point on represented Goodrich's Akron workers in their labor negotiations with management.[91]

URW members experienced less success at Goodrich's Watertown plant. Management blunted the union's organizing drive through the formation of a company union. Even after the U.S. Supreme Court ruled that company unions could not be forced on workers as substitutes for independent unions, Goodrich officers were able to transform their company union into a so-called independent union. Only in 1939, under orders from the NLRB, did Goodrich disband the union. During the following year an AFL (not CIO) local won a decisive victory in a representation election and was certified by the NLRB as the sole collective bargaining agent for Goodrich's Watertown employees.

Plant Dispersal out of Akron

In the long run, the most important way in which Akron rubber executives responded to unionization was to keep moving production to new, usually nonunion, plants outside of Akron.[92] As late as 1935 almost 53 percent of the rubber industry's total wage earners and about 60 percent of the industry's output were in Akron and nearby towns.[93] Despite paying higher wages, Akron rubber plants enjoyed the lowest unit costs in the industry until 1933. Until then, Akron rubber workers were more productive than their counterparts elsewhere. With unionization, however, wages rose faster than labor productivity, which dropped in Akron between 1936 and 1938. Executives at the major tire manufacturers attributed the decline in productivity to frequent sitdowns, the deliberate restriction of output, and other manifestations of labor militancy—factors which, in fact, appear to have contributed to productivity losses.[94]

The concern of Goodrich's management with labor costs became pronounced in the mid- and late 1930s, as concessions to the URW forced up Akron wages. The declining productivity of their Akron workers also worried Goodrich officers. With unionization, the Bedaux system proved less effective than before in controlling labor costs. Workers, guided by union leaders, made sure that they approached, but did not surpass, Bedaux norms. If workers averaged 90 percent or more of the norm, Goodrich officers reevaluated the standard for the job upward, a situation workers wanted to avoid. As one labor specialist for Goodrich later recalled, the Bedaux system "started to go downhill in Akron particularly" during the 1930s.[95]

Goodrich opened new operations outside of Akron and in 1936 established a factory at Oaks, Pennsylvania, near Philadelphia, capable of producing 5,000 tires a day. Goodrich already had a sizable plant there through its ownership of the buildings formerly used by the Philadelphia Rubber Works. Goodrich had the six structures revamped, then moved in modern tire making machinery. The establishment of the factory cost $1 million, but it was estimated that the new plant would result in annual savings of $140,000. Executives reasoned that "a substantial volume of business will be lost to the company if it does not establish greater tire production facilities outside of Ohio."[96] In the same year Goodrich spent about $500,000 to buy and reequip a factory that had been operated by the Acme Motor Car Company in Cadillac, Michigan. This plant was soon making mechanical rubber goods for the automobile industry. Cost considerations prompted officers to invest. In 1938 they approved improvements totalling $33,000, but expected to bring annual savings of $40,000.[97] The final new plant opened by Goodrich before World War II was in Clarksville, Tennessee. At a cost of $1.4 million, it built a new factory there in 1939 to manufacture rubber heels and soles for the footwear division. The lures were "cheap power rates and lower wage costs."[98]

Even though they were smaller, these plants were more efficient than the Akron factory. They used more modern machinery and were laid out in a manner allowing the smooth flow of work through them. Speaking about the Oaks plant, one Goodrich labor expert noted, "we could put all the modern equipment to start with, which we couldn't do in Akron." Oaks was, as a result, a "very efficient operation." All of the plants used the Bedaux system, but the standards were set higher than was possible in Akron: "We used some standard [Bedaux] values, but at all the plants we had improvements . . . and we'd include those improvements."[99]

The Unions and Plant Dispersal

Even with the opening of the new plants, Goodrich retained a larger percentage of its production in Akron than did Goodyear or Firestone. By 1938 Goodyear and Firestone were manufacturing only one-third of their tires in Akron, while Goodrich still made two-thirds of its tires in the city.[100] Goodrich also kept most of its mechanical goods production in Akron. In early 1938 Graham presented Goodrich workers with a stark choice: either make concessions on wages and hours or have Goodrich move most of its production out of Akron.

Graham argued that the only way to make Goodrich more competitive was to reduce the selling price of its rubber goods, and it was in the area of labor costs, he claimed, that savings would have to be found. Graham sought approval for a flexible workweek of between thirty and forty hours that would allow Goodrich to handle temporary production peaks without hiring new workers. Graham warned that visits to numerous competitors' plants revealed that Goodrich's rivals were "taking advantage of the latest developments in machinery, processes, and layouts in order to reduce their costs." If Goodrich were to stay competitive, modernization of its Akron facilities was essential.

Graham concluded that Goodrich officers had prepared plans to update many of the company's Akron operations, but that they would not proceed with the improvements unless assured of labor concessions.[101] In a meeting with representatives from Local 5, Graham laid out a roster of demands. Goodrich executives needed assurances that new and existing equipment and facilities would be operated efficiently and that all employees would cooperate with management in finding ways to cut production costs. Moreover, wages had to be lowered by about 15 percent. If these provisions were not accepted, Graham threatened, Goodrich would slash its production of tires and mechanical rubber goods in Akron by half.[102]

Throughout 1938 and 1939 Goodrich and Local 5 officials negotiated on these issues before reaching an agreement. Union leaders questioned the importance of higher wages in raising Goodrich's costs of production and countered with their own plan, one that called for smaller wage concessions and a pledge by Goodrich officers to keep production in Akron for at least two years. In May 1938 Goodrich workers voted to accept a contract, the first formal union contract agreed on between labor and management at Goodrich. The contract failed to incorporate any of Graham's demands, leaving pay scales and working hours untouched.[103] Goodrich continued to move production out of Akron; and, under continuing pressure, Local 5 accepted a new contract in early 1939. This contract, while declaring that Goodrich would treat the six-hour day and thirty-six-hour week as "normal," made provisions for "flexible working schedules," as desired by company officers.[104]

By this time, Goodrich was no longer the Akron company it had once been. Goodrich was committed to continuing the dispersal of operations out of the city. The changing relationship between Goodrich and Akron was highlighted in March 1939 when city officials asked the company to contribute $30,000 to the building of a municipal stadium designed to seat 35,000. In return for help in funding the stadium, city officers pledged to dedicate it as a memorial to Dr. Benjamin Goodrich. However, company officers declined "with regret" to contribute to the project.[105]

Obtaining Raw Materials: Rubber and Cotton

Raw materials presented a third major domestic challenge for Goodrich. Falling crude rubber prices had created problems for Goodrich in the early 1930s, as inventory values shrank dramatically; but by the mid-1930s, with the firm's inventories fully devalued, it was able to benefit from continuing low prices. Crude rubber prices stayed under 10¢ per pound in 1933 and remained lower than 15¢ per pound during most of the following year. Goodrich bought heavily, and by the fall of 1934 the company had a ten-month supply of crude rubber on hand, several months more than the normal supply. With recovery, the problem once again became how to secure stable supplies of raw materials at reasonable prices.

When Tew became Goodrich's president, he reopened the company's Singapore buying operations, and Goodrich soon had a two-man office on the city's waterfront. Every evening agents in Goodrich's Akron purchasing office cabled their Singapore buying office about the amounts and grades of rubber they needed. The buyers, in turn, purchased from dealers who acted as middlemen for the plantation owners. If rubber supplies were inadequate in Singapore, buyers bought it on the New York or London markets. But by the 1930s Singapore had clearly emerged as the major crude rubber market for American manufacturers. Working through a committee of the Rubber Manufacturers' Association, the manufacturers standardized the grades of rubber they purchased. Buying rubber remained very competitive, however. Nearly sixty years later, Elmer Stevens, who purchased crude rubber for Goodrich in the 1930s, remembered his excitement when he was able to buy a large shipment for only 2 9/16¢ per pound.[106]

Faced with ruin from the collapse in raw rubber prices, rubber growers in the Far East formed the International Rubber Regulation Committee (IRRC) in 1934. This association was much more inclusive than the Stevenson Plan of the previous decade, for even American companies owning plantations belonged. The IRRC sought to raise crude rubber prices by cutting back on rubber exports. Export quotas combined with a growing demand, resulting from the recovery in rubber manufacturing, to lift crude rubber prices to nearly 25¢ per pound by 1937.[107] Realizing that crude rubber growers needed to earn profits to stay in business, Goodrich supported the work of the IRRC, just as it had backed the work of the Stevenson Plan. As Stevens recalled, Goodrich executives believed that "nothing is ever good that's going to drive your suppliers out of business."[108]

Goodrich officers did, however, explore alternatives to buying from the members of the IRRC. In 1930 they looked into the possibility of planting rubber trees on Haiti and Santa Domingo, and in 1934 they investigated buying rubber plantations in Malaya.[109] The possibility of making rubber from a guayule, a bush that grew in Mexico and the American Southwest, briefly caught their attention in the mid-1930s. Officers considered building a plant to extract rubber from guayule in Mexico, but abandoned the idea "due to the present political situation."[110] Instead, as in the 1920s, they focused on expanding Goodrich's rubber reclaiming capabilities. Most of the money spent on plant expansion and modernization in Akron in 1937 went to improve reclaiming operations.[111]

Cotton was the second raw material used in great quantities by Goodrich. During the mid-1930s the company benefited from low cotton prices, and by late 1934 Goodrich had stockpiled a ten-month supply.[112] Seeking a stable source of cotton fabric with which to make tires, Goodrich expanded the company's cotton textile factory, Martha Mills, in Georgia. Hoping to save money by buying from its own factory, Goodrich invested $1 million in Martha Mills during 1933 and 1934, until the plant could supply all of the firm's needs.[113] Further expansion, costing another $1 million and expected to save $200,000 annually, came in 1936.[114]

Goodrich thus continued to vertically integrate operations. Its actions resembled those of other major rubber manufacturing concerns, but were not enough to enable the company to catch up with its rivals. During the hard times of the 1930s Goodrich lacked the resources needed to undertake such a major, long-term investment as the development of rubber plantations. Consequently, Goodrich fell further behind its rivals in this field. Goodyear experimented with rubber plantations in Panama and Costa Rica as a way of circumventing the restrictions of the IRRC. After briefly shutting down rubber-growing operations in Liberia because of low crude rubber prices in 1934, Firestone expanded them in the mid- and late 1930s. Like Goodrich, Firestone increased its cotton-textile operations through the purchase of a large mill in Gastonia, North Carolina, in 1935. U.S. Rubber added a number of textile mills, setting up a separate textile division in 1941.[115]

Problems in Goodrich's Overseas Ventures

Overseas manufacturing and sales difficulties exacerbated domestic problems. By the close of 1936, International B.F. Goodrich, the subsidiary that ran most of Goodrich's foreign operations, had accumulated a deficit of $3.8 million and was forced to reduce its capital stock from $10 million to $5 million.[116] Most likely, foreign operations improved in the late 1930s as many countries partially recovered from the depression.

In Europe, Goodrich's French operations were most important. After difficult times in 1933 and 1934, the situation improved in late 1935 when the French subsidiary won a contract to supply Renault with one-quarter of its original equipment tires. Thereafter, the French plant operated profitably, and Goodrich poured in substantial funds for its modernization and expansion.[117] By the end of 1937 the French subsidiary was the third-largest tire maker in France, turning out 2,000 tires per day. It trailed only Michelin, which made 7,000 tires daily, and Dunlop, which produced about 3,500.[118] Goodrich expanded its operations elsewhere in Europe by providing technical assistance. In 1932 it considered entering into an agreement with the Kudrnac-Everit Rubber Company to make tires in Czechoslovakia. Two years later, several Goodrich executives visited the Soviet Union to look into the possibility of offering technical assistance to the Soviet Union Rubber Company. In the summer of 1939, Goodrich provided assistance for the Romanian government to build that nation's first tire making facility.[119]

In contrast, Goodrich greatly decreased its British presence. In early 1934 the British Tyre and Rubber Company (BTR), headed by Walrond Sinclair (the former chief of British Goodrich), acquired a number of British rubber manufacturers, including British Goodrich, through stock exchanges.[120] As the owner of British Goodrich, B.F. Goodrich thereby became a major shareholder in BTR. Over the next six years, however, Goodrich divested itself of most of these shares, selling them back to BTR at Sinclair's urging. The divestiture, and with it Goodrich's near exit from manufacturing in Great Britain, appears to have been voluntary. Goodrich saw the stock sales as a desirable way to raise cash for faltering operations at home.[121] B.F. Goodrich executives left a profitable company. BTR earned profits of £127,000 in 1934 and paid an 8 percent dividend, and its profits climbed in later years.[122]

Latin America, Oceania, and Africa attracted increased attention but did not emerge in the 1930s as major centers of activity for Goodrich. In 1935 Goodrich supplied technical know-how and a small amount of capital to aid a Mexican rubber company's move into tire making, receiving in return 35 percent of its stock.[123] In another venture a year later, Goodrich engineers constructed a tire making factory in Montevideo for Uruguay, as they did for Argentina in 1939.[124] Goodrich gave technical assistance to a tire making company in New Zealand in 1934–37.[125] World War II cut short explorations to establish Goodrich factories in Chile, Peru, Cuba, Brazil, New Zealand, and Australia.[126]

Goodrich maintained a stake in Japan up to the outbreak of World War II through its joint venture in Yokohama Rubber. That presence was a reduced one, however. In September 1935 Goodrich owned 59 percent of the shares in Yokohama Rubber, with Furukawa holding the other 41 percent. Over the next four years, Goodrich sold most of its shares to Furukawa, until by 1939 Goodrich held only 9 percent of Yokohama Rubber's stock. Those sales appear to have been involuntary: in the late 1930s the Japanese government passed laws limiting foreign investments in many industries.[127] At the same time the Japanese government also reduced the amount of money that foreign companies could take out of Japan, but allowed silk to be exported instead. This situation affected Goodrich, as the company brought silks back to Akron. Goodrich's new chemical operations began coating the silk with plasticized PVC. All the colors of the rainbow came out of two coating machines, and other manufacturers eagerly awaited the coated silks for use in making everything from draperies to evening gowns.[128]

For Goodrich the mid- and late 1930s was a time of retrenchment in foreign operations. Only in France did the firm expand its foreign manufacturing base (no records have survived for Goodrich's Canadian operations, so it is impossible to tell what occurred there). Substantial contraction occurred in Japan and Britain. For the first time, Goodrich fell behind Goodyear and Firestone in foreign operations. Hit harder in the United States by the depression than these two firms, Goodrich could not keep up with them abroad. Firestone opened a Spanish factory in 1933, a South African one two years later, and plants in Brazil and India as the 1930s came to a close. Firestone also expanded its operations in Britain and Argentina.[129] Goodyear similarly expanded its manufacturing overseas, especially in South America, Canada, and Asia.[130]

A LEADER IN AIRPLANE PRODUCTS

In making airplane products Goodrich clearly surpassed its competitors throughout the 1930s. Here Goodrich's strong research tradition served the company well. After World War I, Goodrich abandoned the realm of lighter-than-air dirigibles to Goodyear, focusing instead on airplanes. In 1922 Goodrich joined other companies in forming the Aeronautical Chamber of Commerce, a New York–based trade association promoting civilian air travel. In the late 1920s, after a flurry of interest among optimistic investors in civil aeronautics was dashed by disappointing sales of aircraft, advances in aircraft technology came mainly from risk takers in small, personally owned firms. Goodrich was one of the very few large American companies to remain involved in the fledgling aircraft industry.[131] By doing so, Goodrich got in on the ground floor of an expanding industry. The number of airplanes produced in the United States rose from 290 in 1920 to 4,216 in 1928. As Moody's observed in July 1928, there had recently been "tremendous gains in air mail, express and passenger transportation."[132]

The number of airplanes produced in America rose to more than 6,000 in 1929, but tumbled with the onset of the Great Depression to just 1,000 in 1933. During the 1930s, despite the hard times, American airplane manufacturers moved ahead of their European competitors in the design of large planes. American airplane makers greatly increased the weight (payload) carried by their planes. The DC-2 entered service in 1934, and within just three years American carriers using American airplanes had started transatlantic and transpacific service, well ahead of their European rivals. Further advances made during World War II would enhance the advantages American manufacturers had secured by the mid-1930s.[133] American airplane production recovered to nearly 3,000 aircraft in 1936, and by 1937 Moody's could accurately report that airplane manufacturing was in its "second phase of expansion."[134]

Tires and Brakes

Airplane tires emerged as a leading aircraft product made by Goodrich. In 1927 Charles Lindbergh landed his *Spirit of St. Louis* near Paris on Goodrich tires, becoming the first aviator to cross the Atlantic alone. Three years later Goodrich made the largest airplane tire in the world, and Goodrich's Silvertown tires quickly became standard equipment on many of America's airplanes. In 1937 Goodrich came out with a tire capable of carrying fifteen tons. Adopted as standard equipment by Douglas Aircraft, this model was soon in use on the planes flown by major American airlines. By 1938 Goodrich produced 142 different airplane tires.[135]

Goodrich's work on tires led the firm into making brake parts for airplanes. The company entered this market in 1937 with what it called an "expander tube" brake system. A series of brake shoes pressed outward against a circular brake drum when a rubber expansion tube in the center of the mechanism was inflated with a hydraulic fluid. According to Goodrich officials, the advantage of this system was that all of the braking surfaces received equal pressure from the expander tube, insuring quicker, smoother stops than were available from competing systems. They also emphasized that the brake was reliable under a

Charles Lindbergh's Spirit of St. Louis *used Goodrich tires. (BFG Co.)*

wide range of conditions and that it automatically adjusted itself for wear.[136] Goodrich linked up with Hayes Industries, an automobile parts manufacturer in Jackson, Michigan, to produce the brake.[137] Goodrich made the rubber expander tube, but lacked the machinery needed to build the other brake parts. By 1938 Goodrich-Hayes brakes ranging from five to twenty-five inches in size were standard equipment on many airplanes, including the Douglas DC-4. A year later the army air force adopted them for the Boeing B-17 "Flying Fortress." In addition to brakes, Hayes Industries made airplane wheels, a field Goodrich would later enter.

Pioneering in the Production of Deicers

Three days before Christmas in 1930, Wesley Smith, the superintendent of the eastern division of the National Air Transport Company, later part of United Airlines, went aloft in one of his company's airplanes to test a new device made by Goodrich. "We took off at 12:53 and in ten minutes had attained an altitude of about 4000 feet," reported a Goodrich technician on board. "At this point we were flying at 80 m.p.h. thru dense clouds and ice was forming rapidly on all projecting edges." These atrocious flying conditions were perfect for the test. Smith engaged Goodrich's invention, the world's first deicer for airplanes, and within seconds "all accumulated ice from the wings and struts" was removed.[138]

Consisting of a rubber "boot" or bladder attached to the leading edges of wings and other parts of airplanes on which ice accumulated, the deicer was inflated to break the ice away. The deicer spurred the development of commercial aviation by allowing airplanes to fly in higher altitudes and in colder weather. As a grateful pilot for Southwest Pacific Airlines wrote his father, who worked in Goodrich's aviation department, "There would have been sixteen guys floating down on parachutes if it hadn't been for your De-Icers. It is swell to see ice form on the wings and then—flooie—see the boots break it off."[139] Important though tires and brakes were, the deicer was by far Goodrich's greatest contribution to aviation during these years, for as airplanes had begun flying higher and in the winter, icing had become a very serious problem.

William Geer, the former head of Goodrich's research laboratories, worked on developing a deicer as a retirement project at his personal laboratory in Ithaca, New York, for several years in the late 1920s. His interest was stimulated by reports of ice hazards encountered by Lindbergh during his transatlantic crossing. Working with officials of the National Air Transport Company, Geer first experimented with paint that he hoped would be slippery enough to shed ice, to no avail. Supported by the Daniel Guggenheim Fund, Geer next built a small refrigerated wind tunnel at Cornell University, near his home. Here he carried out tests on mechanical means to break off ice using "a rubber overshoe containing an inflatable tube." Using deicer boots required sophisticated techniques. If the boot was inflated too soon, it might push the ice outward just as it froze, creating an air tunnel at the limit of the boot's expansion. Conversely, if the boot was inflated too late, the ice build-up would be more than the boot could handle.[140]

To go further, Geer needed the cooperation of a rubber goods manufacturer. Goodrich officials he approached gave him "immediate and cordial cooperation." In the fall of 1930 Geer used a refrigerated wind tunnel built at a Goodrich laboratory to demonstrate the potential of the deicer.[141] Upon watching the test, Wesley Smith of the National Air Transport Company summed up the importance of Goodrich's deicer. "That device," he observed, "means we can fly safely through air levels that are laden with ice and snow. That means fewer lives will be sacrificed in the air lanes." Smith and others conducted successful flight tests in the winter of 1930–31, and the deicer won ready acceptance by makers of civilian and military airplanes.[142] By 1935 Lockheed, Northrup, Boeing, and Douglas were using Goodrich deicers. Four years later, an even broader range of airplanes employed Goodrich deicers, small Taylorcrafts to large DC-2s, and the still bigger and more famous DC-3s and DC-4s.[143]

Their invention of the deicer led Goodrich scientists into the development

This National Air Transport plane, used to carry mail, had Goodrich deicers on its wings and tail. (BFG Co.)

of related devices. To attach the rubber deicers to metal wings, they devised "rivnuts," internally threaded tubular rivets made from corrosion-resistant aluminum, which could be employed when only one surface was accessible. To keep ice from forming on propeller blades, they found a way to spray a liquid deicing solution on the blades while airplanes were in flight. In 1935 Goodrich won a federal government contract to supply the Bureau of Air Commerce with the tool, called a "slinger ring." Transcontinental and Western Air immediately ordered slinger rings for sixty airplanes.[144]

Goodrich made more than tires, brakes, and deicers for the aviation industry. In the 1930s the company produced fuel hoses, shock absorbers, and engine mounts. Altogether, Goodrich was making fifty items for airplanes by the late 1930s. In 1935 company scientists even made a pressurized rubber suit, a forerunner of suits it would build for the Mercury astronauts decades later, in which Wiley Post set the world's altitude record.

Selling Airplane Products

Goodrich was quick to publicize the successes of its airplane products. Similar to the way the Silver Fleet advertised automobile tires, Goodrich used airplanes to attract attention to its aviation products. In the summer of 1928 it

Goodrich made Wiley Post's high-altitude suit. (BFG Co.)

purchased a Fairchild airplane, capable of carrying four passengers. Emblazoned with the words "Goodrich Silvertowns" in silver letters on its bright blue fuselage, the airplane ferried Goodrich executives to business meetings in Canada and the United States.[145] In 1929 Goodrich tires graced forty of the fifty airplanes in the "Ford Reliability Tour," in which aviators visited thirty-two airports across America. Goodrich also owned a racing airplane, the "Miss Silvertown." By 1930 this airplane held six of the nation's eleven air speed records and in that year made a nonstop crossing of the United States from Cleveland to Los Angeles in a record thirteen and one-half hours.[146]

Goodrich sold its airplane products through personal connections, especially those forged by James S. Pedler. A veteran flier from World War I, Pedler maintained close ties with other former wartime fliers through an informal group called the "Quiet Birdmen," which later developed into a professional association and still existed in the early 1990s. Jimmy Doolittle and Eddie Rickenbacker were among the group's members. As the body's members became important executives in commercial airlines, Pedler was able to sell Goodrich products to their companies through his personal connections with them.[147] Pedler's importance to Goodrich differed from the sales situation at other rubber companies. None had the personal links to the emerging airlines that Goodrich enjoyed. Instead, about half of America's pilots purchased airplane tires only from wholesalers and another quarter only from retailers. Just one-fifth bought directly from tire manufacturers. Most of that fifth bought from Goodrich.[148]

Still, the airplane market remained small before World War II. Even with economic recovery, American companies produced only about 5,000 airplanes in 1939.[149] Not until after World War II did airplane and aerospace products emerge as a commercially significant segment of Goodrich's business. The very insignificance of airplane products to Goodrich's overall sales picture helps explain its success in the years before World War II. At a time when it was stumbling in many areas, Goodrich succeeded in airplane products. In part this was due to the research of one person, Geer, for whom the development of the most important product, the deicer, was a personal hobby. In addition, the sales work of Pedler was crucial; airplane products was one field in which Goodrich beat the sales efforts of its competitors. Perhaps most important, Goodrich's top management, uninterested in such an insignificant part of their company, allowed aviation products to develop more or less on its own, with little interference from above—a situation soon to be replicated, on a larger scale, in the development of a chemical division.

MANAGEMENT CHANGES

As their company became more complex in terms of its products and markets, Goodrich executives experimented with management styles during the 1930s. They moved briefly to a decentralized management system in the early 1930s, only to abandon it later in the decade. As problems multiplied during the Great Depression, they hired outside consultants and set up special internal committees to examine their company's difficulties.

Experiments with a New Company Structure

During the 1930s Goodrich experimented with a new corporate structure. Goodrich had adopted a fully departmentalized structure during World War I: vice presidents ran sales, production, plant administration, and development departments. Few changes occurred in the 1920s. During the early 1930s, however, the firm briefly adopted a decentralized management system similar to those pioneered by General Motors and DuPont in the previous decade. As Goodrich came to manufacture a broader range of goods for wider markets, its management probably realized that the simple centralized departmental system could not adequately handle the complexity of the firm's operations.

Movement toward decentralization began in 1929. In part, this was due to the growing stress placed on distribution. General managers in charge of both production and sales were set up for Goodrich's major product lines to bring about "a closer relationship . . . on production and sales problems, thereby ensuring prompt decisions on major problems and improved service to the trade."[150] By 1930 Goodrich had separate product divisions for tires, footwear, and mechanical rubber goods. A year later, another division had been set up for druggists' sundries. However, as the Great Depression deepened, this multidivisional structure was abandoned. As Goodrich retrenched, it returned to its more traditional centralized management based on functional departments.[151] Even so, some lasting changes occurred. In 1930 and 1931 Tew revived the operating committee, which had existed during and shortly after World War I, to relieve the executive committee of some of the pressure of routine decision making. He also specified that, for the first time, the executive committee be composed mainly of outside directors rather than company officers to bring more objectivity to decision making.[152]

Questioning Management

The many problems Goodrich faced in the 1930s, and how they were handled, led to an unprecedented questioning of management. In 1935 directors proposed refinancing Goodrich's debt to take advantage of lower interest rates, and controversy from this proposal brought tensions between stockholders and management into the open. The directors urged the company's stockholders to approve issuing up to $45 million in first mortgage bonds. Some $28 million would be immediately issued to pay off debts and provide Goodrich with new operating capital.[153] This proposal engendered bitter opposition from several quarters among stockholders. Cyrus Eaton opposed the plan, because his Cleveland-based Otis & Company, which had helped handle a 1930 bond offering, was to be cut out of handling any of the transactions. John Weed, a large preferred stockholder living in California, objected, as did many other owners of preferred stock, to having new obligations on corporate income placed ahead of theirs. William Hunt, a Cleveland stockholder, offered the most vehement opposition. Pointing out that Goodrich's management and directors had done a much worse job in running their company than had their counterparts in other major rubber manufacturing firms for well over a decade, he called for their removal from office.[154]

In a dramatic move, Eaton's Otis & Company obtained a court order forcing Goodrich to reveal the names and addresses of its stockholders, and mounted a proxy fight against management's proposal—a most unusual step in American business. Otis & Company nearly succeeded in challenging Goodrich's management, but in the end common stockholders voted 75.3 percent in favor of refunding and preferred stockholders voted 76.1 percent in favor (a three-quarters favorable vote of both classes of stockholders was required for approval).[155]

The election did not end stockholder opposition to management. Hunt, in a series of statements reported in the *Akron Beacon Journal*, continued to criticize management for running Goodrich poorly. "While two of Goodrich's leading competitors [Goodyear and Firestone] in the last five calendar years were showing profits of approximately $20,000,000 and $17,000,000, Goodrich showed operating losses of $25,000,000."[156] Arguing that Goodrich executives had engaged in improprieties during the proxy fight, Hunt and other disgruntled stockholders tied up the refunding plan in New York courts. Eventually, a referee for the Supreme Court of New York ruled in favor of Goodrich.[157]

Meanwhile, officers put forward a new refunding plan at the company's annual meeting in the spring of 1936. Like the 1935 scheme, this plan called for stockholder approval for the issuance of up to $45 million in first mortgage debt. But, Goodrich executives also sought to satisfy the demands of preferred stockholders. The company had paid no dividends on preferred stock since 1931 and was by 1936 more than $10 million behind on such payments. Goodrich officers urged that stockholders ratify a plan by which the firm's preferred stockholders would exchange their stock for new preferred stock in Goodrich. For each share of their old preferred stock, they would receive 1.4 shares of new preferred plus, as a bonus, half a share of common stock, then selling at $23 a share. In making the exchange, the preferred stockholders would relinquish any claim on the arrears in dividends on the old preferred stock. Stockholders overwhelming approved this plan.[158]

Hunt continued his fight against management, nonetheless. At the 1937 stockholders meeting he denounced Goodrich executives for putting their best interests ahead of the stockholders. He claimed that the company had fallen under the baleful influence of Sidney Weinberg. The head of Goldman, Sachs, Weinberg had become a Goodrich director in 1930. Goldman, Sachs exercised, Hunt claimed, "a stranglehold" over Goodrich. "Broker's squeeze and the profits of insiders," Hunt asserted, had over the years amounted to "many millions of dollars."[159] Hunt also issued a thirteen-page report castigating how executives were running the firm, pointing out again that Goodrich had fallen far behind Goodyear and Firestone in profitability.[160] Few stockholders were listening. The 1936 plan had taken care of the claims of the preferred stockholders. Moreover, with recovery from the depression both common and preferred stockholders once again were receiving dividends.

Still, stockholder challenges, although defeated, combined with the dismal showing of their firm in the early 1930s, led Goodrich directors to question management's handling of company affairs. The executive committee had Rudolph S. Rauch, an outside company director, look into the effectiveness of Goodrich's sales system. Writing David Goodrich in June 1936, Rauch observed that B.F. Goodrich was performing poorly and urged him to have the board of directors hire an outside engineering firm to investigate all aspects of the company's operations.[161] Goodrich acted on Rauch's suggestion. In the summer of 1936 the directors employed McKinsey, Wellington & Company (the forerunner of today's management consulting firm McKinsey & Company) "to make a preliminary survey of the conduct of the company's retail operations."[162] The report, issued in the spring of 1937, recommended changes in how Goodrich sold its replacement tires. Rather than adopt the McKinsey plan, Goodrich executives called for McKinsey to study the matter further.[163]

A New President: Samuel B. Robertson

In the midst of this questioning, a new president assumed office. James Tew, long wishing to retire at the age of fifty-five, stepped down in May 1937. As Tew explained, "an executive of a big corporation burns up about two years of his life every twelve months." Above all, Tew wanted "more leisure and what goes with it."[164] Thus, Tew's retirement does not appear to have been directly related to the financial problems plaguing his company, although he must have been stung by the criticisms of stockholders like Hunt.[165] Tew hand-picked his successor, Samuel B. Robertson. Following Tew's recommendation, the board appointed Robertson as executive vice president in early 1937.[166] When Tew declined to be renominated for the presidency a few months later, the board nominated Robertson and the stockholders duly elected him.

Like Tew, Robertson was a production man unlikely to alter established ways of conducting business at Goodrich. Born in 1878 in Milton, Massachusetts, he was educated at MIT. Robertson had been with the Pennsylvania Railroad for twenty years before joining Goodrich as the assistant to the Akron works manager in 1919. In 1920 he became the director of engineering in Akron; eight years later he oversaw the construction of Goodrich's Los Angeles plant and for the next three years managed that plant. Robertson returned to Akron in 1931 as a vice president and the general manager of the tire division.[167]

GOODRICH BEFORE WORLD WAR II

"Punctuated by roaring exhausts and rubber screaming on asphalt . . . was the thrill demonstration put on by Jimmie Lynch and his automobile troupe on a paved and banked arena, which introduced into the transportation area of the fair an attraction more in tempo with the crowd magnets of the Fair's midway section." With these words, a press release described the opening night of Goodrich's exhibit at the 1939–40 World's Fair in New York City. Watched by Samuel Robertson, David Goodrich, and several of Goodrich's vice presidents, the demonstration designed to show the durability of Goodrich tires was dramatic. "Jimmie Lynch and Jimmie, Jr., father and son 'auto tamers,' careened around the banked track, righting cars after hurtling off ramps at different levels, and climaxed the act by gunning a car into an 85-foot leap over a parked truck."[168]

The theme of the World's Fair was "Building the World of Tomorrow." The central structures were the Trylon (a triangular pylon) and the Perisphere, supposed to be a modern-day Eiffel Tower. Modernity was a major motif at the New York fair. The General Motors "Futurama" exhibit tried to show guests the world of 1960 from moving chairs, while General Electric put on a show complete with lights, arcs of electricity, and thunderous noise. Streamlining was important in exhibits of everything from automobiles and trains to architecture and toasters. Altogether forty-four million people attended the fair. Covering 120,000 square feet, Goodrich's exhibit was one of the largest. Located next to the Ford and General Motors exhibits, it had two parts. At an outdoor proving ground, up to five thousand fairgoers could watch demonstrations of Goodrich tires. Jimmie Lynch staged his automobile antics six times a day. Fairgoers could even ride around the track in cars equipped with Goodrich tires, going through water hazards and over mechanically controlled bumps. An adjacent exhibition hall showcased Goodrich products.[169]

Goodrich's exhibit hall highlighted the recent scientific advances made by the company and, like the fair, took modernity as its cue. "Spectacular aspects of the company's research activities," said the company's press release, were shown in the building. At the center of the structure was a ninety-foot-high tower housing a "tire guillotine" similar to one used in Goodrich's Akron laboratory. The blade fell on tires from varying heights to demonstrate the resistance of the tires to injury. The exhibit claimed data from the test was used "in improving tire construction to afford greater resistance to stone bruises and the wear and tear of modern, high-speed motoring." Another exhibit illustrated bonding metal to rubber: photographs showed a 10" by 4" strip of rubber lifting a car and "dangling it in the air." Other exhibits showed rubber gloves made by the anode process, rubber springs made of rubber bonded to metal, and rubber parts for "a new streamlined subway car."[170]

Goodrich also showed off its growing line of plastic products. As we have seen, Goodrich discovered how to plasticize polyvinyl chloride (PVC) in 1926, and during the 1930s, Goodrich began, hesitantly, to commercialize this discovery. At the fair the company had on display PVC-covered fabrics claimed to be "waterproof, sunproof, stain proof, and acid proof."[171] On the exhibit's opening night, Goodrich had many products made from PVC for sale: tablecloths, shower curtains, umbrellas, aprons, raincoats, golf jackets, bowl covers, tobacco pouches, and artificial flowers. Throughout the fair, Goodrich gave away souvenir ties and bracelets made of PVC.[172]

Its exhibits at the World's Fair summed up well what Goodrich had become in the sixty-nine years since its founding: a corporation firmly grounded in a variety of products developed by modern science. Goodrich nurtured a strong research tradition. It was one of the first rubber companies to maintain a research laboratory, from which came a stream of inventions and innovations. This placed Goodrich far ahead of Firestone and Goodyear in commercializing the production of rubber chemicals. Goodrich also was the first American rubber company to develop a long line of products, from pneumatic tires to airplane deicers. As it emerged from the Great Depression, Goodrich remained what it had been since its inception in the 1870s, a diversified company. In the late 1930s about 60 percent of the firm's sales came from tires, 15 percent from footwear, and another 15 percent from other rubber products ranging from belting to druggists' sundries.[173] The variety of Goodrich's products on display at the fair set it apart from Goodyear and Firestone.

A continuing commitment to research and diversification was, however, only part of the ledger. While quick to invent, Goodrich encountered difficulty, especially after World War I, in staying abreast of its major competitors, particularly those in tire making, in sales and profitability. Much of the entrepreneurial energy that had motivated management during the firm's early years dissipated. Many of the company's top executives lacked either the desire or the imagination needed to keep Goodrich moving ahead. New developments continued, but usually only if they did not cost too much and only if they seemed to promise quick returns. Goodrich entered overseas manufacturing in a major way in the 1920s and began building competencies in chemicals, PVC, and airplane products during the 1920s and 1930s. However, in its main business of making rubber products, especially tires, Goodrich lagged behind its competitors in making the capital investments needed to modernize its plant. By the late 1930s, as its executives and stockholders were coming to realize, Goodrich faced an uncertain future.

5

The Crises of World War II: Planting the Seeds of Transformation

On Monday morning, 8 December 1941, Elmer Stevens awoke as usual, prepared to face another steamy day in the B.F. Goodrich office overlooking the waterfront of the British colony of Singapore. There Stevens, with the help of an assistant and a small clerical staff, would bargain and arrange rubber purchases from nearby plantations. Although the clouds of war had been gathering for months across the Pacific Ocean, Stevens and his wife felt safe. While Scottish regiments prepared to defend against land attack, the British navy had sent two of its prize warships, the *Prince of Wales* and the *Repulse,* to protect the colony's shores and shipping lanes. Monday appeared to be a routine but busy day because the volume of rubber purchase orders was large. Back in the United States, the Rubber Reserve Corporation, a special agency of the U.S. government, was stockpiling rubber to insure against a possible disruption of supplies for factories.

Monday, 8 December 1941, proved anything but a routine day in Singapore or, for that matter, much of the world. As Stevens drove to his office, he discovered that Japanese aircraft had bombed the city at 4:00 A.M., apparently missing their targeted government buildings but destroying part of the business district. Simultaneously, across the international dateline Japanese airplanes were destroying much of the American fleet docked at Pearl Harbor. When he arrived at the office, Stevens learned that the Japanese army had landed on the Malay peninsula and was marching toward Singapore. Stevens quickly arranged for a bomb shelter to be dug into the hill behind the company house where he lived. On 10 December Japanese aircraft sank the *Prince of Wales* and the *Repulse;* several weeks later the Japanese bombers renewed their attacks on the city, often at night, sometimes during the day. Stevens decided to book passage for his wife to return to the United States, and to inquire of his superiors in Akron if he should return home. Mrs. Stevens was able to leave by ship on 20 December and had a safe voyage to the United States.[1]

When permission to depart Singapore arrived by cable, Stevens arranged passage for himself on an American freighter loading rubber and tin that was nearly ready to cast off. Executives charged with managing the Dunlop plantation up-country in Malaya had fled the advancing Japanese army, now just a few days' march from Singapore itself, and happily purchased the furniture that Goodrich provided its expatriate executive. On 17 January 1942, Stevens no sooner had boarded his ship, crowded with sixteen other passengers eager to escape the immediate danger of the war, when the air raid sirens warned of another attack. Ordered to crouch behind a bulkhead, Stevens and the others on board remained safe as the bombers attacked warehouses instead of ships. When the planes returned to base, the vessel departed for the Indian Ocean. More than forty days later, having rounded the Cape of Good Hope and escaped German submarine attack in the Atlantic and Caribbean, Stevens landed in New Orleans on the last American ship to carry bales of Asian natural rubber to American shores before peace returned over three years later.

World War II had come to B.F. Goodrich and its people with a vengeance. Stevens's personal crisis was but one of thousands of stories of Goodrich people and the war. Before the war ended in August of 1945, twelve thousand Goodrich employees had or were serving in the American armed forces. Nor were the misfortunes simply personal. For Goodrich, and all Americans, the crises of World War II were institutional, national, and international.

World War II became a turning point in the history of Goodrich, for the company as an organization changed in ways that proved fundamental. During the war the B.F. Goodrich Chemical Company was organized, and the modern aerospace business began to take shape. At Goodrich, payrolls climbed, older factories hummed, and new ones were built.

For Goodrich the war involved more than simply taking advantage of new business opportunities, however. The reshaping of the company into a chemical firm came about because of national crisis. As a rubber company, Goodrich was dependent on overseas supplies for its raw material. To fight the war, U.S. armed forces required myriad rubber products, from truck tires to airplane de-icers to simple belts and hoses. The rubber supply was cut off by the Japanese, while the rubber demand was voracious and seemingly ever mounting. The shortfall in rubber supply was an acute national crisis. Goodrich's response, the development of synthetic rubber and the promotion of polyvinyl chloride as a substitute material, was permanently etched on B.F. Goodrich.

By 1941, the war had already deeply affected Goodrich. The outbreak of the European war in September 1939 had caused the company to forgo its usual profits from that continent, and Akron lost Colombes Goodrich during the successful German invasion of France in the spring of 1940. In addition newspapers soon reported that the British Royal Air Force was damaging the French tire factory, now serving the German cause, in bombardments of its own.

The war changed domestic operations as well. When the war ended in 1945, the company was dramatically different. While still a diversified rubber manufacturer, the outlines of what was to become the new Goodrich of the late twentieth century, a chemical and aerospace firm, were clearer than in 1939. Another important event was the rise of John L. Collyer, a new leader.

Collyer and other industrialists faced wartime business conditions that were dramatically different from those of peacetime. The only parallel was with the mobilization effort of World War I, which was both short-lived and small in comparison. Goodrich and the other rubber companies not only had to provide essential goods for wartime industries and the armed forces, but they had to do so in an industry whose basic raw material, rubber, was no longer available following the Japanese naval victories.

The war meant that the federal government intervened in the affairs of Goodrich and other firms as never before. Eventually, government officials took charge of the nation's rubber supply and required collaboration among rubber manufacturers through trade groups, especially the Rubber Manufacturers' Association, in effect suspending the antitrust laws. The government eventually controlled the company's prices, labor relations, and, through special taxes, profits.

This important government intervention evolved slowly at first. In 1939 the American government began to move away from a policy of isolationism and, with hesitant steps, toward military mobilization and intervention abroad. Spending for war brought the country out of the depression and quickly confronted rubber manufacturers with an unprecedented involvement in government affairs. In 1940 federal policy makers realized that rubber was a critical raw material, and they organized the Rubber Reserve Corporation to stockpile supplies. The possibility of constructing a synthetic rubber industry was also on the national agenda, and the military services promoted plastics, including polyvinyl chloride.

After the attack on Pearl Harbor, the government intervened with an unprecedented speed and thoroughness. The construction of a synthetic rubber industry began in earnest. Through the spring and summer of 1942, the nation was swept with controversy concerning rubber policies, and President Franklin D. Roosevelt, following the recommendations of a special committee headed by Bernard Baruch, appointed William Jeffers as a "rubber czar" to coordinate and expedite the construction of a successful synthetic rubber industry. Even though engineers at B.F. Goodrich and other manufacturers successfully built and operated synthetic rubber factories during the war, problems continued to plague rubber manufacturers almost until the end of the war. The synthetic rubber manufactured during the war was not suitable for all purposes, especially tires, and the stockpile of natural rubber was rapidly consumed. Meanwhile, orders for rubber products were simply overwhelming, all the more so in 1944 and 1945 when fleets of trucks were required to supply advancing armies.

Important as the war's events were in framing the company's affairs, howev-

er, traditions, business opportunities, and the executives' own values continued to shape and reshape the institution. Goodrich tried to adhere to its traditions in rubber manufacturing. When huge military markets for aircraft and
munitions opened, Goodrich held back from becoming an airframe manufacturer, stayed out of the wheel, rim, and brake businesses for the time being, and
agreed to help supply ordnance only under duress. True to tradition, Goodrich
executives were more cautious than their counterparts at Firestone and
Goodyear in taking advantage of opportunities to use public investments in
manufacturing facilities to expand the company lest markets shrink precipi-
tously in peacetime. Nevertheless, John Collyer, the new president recruited
in 1939, made B.F. Goodrich a leader in public relations and influenced the
nation's rubber policy. Collyer eventually seized wartime opportunities in the
burgeoning field of petrochemicals.

RECRUITING JOHN COLLYER

The predicaments and opportunities of the war years were still in the future
when David Goodrich and other members of the board of directors contem-
plated the condition of their firm in 1938. The deep recession of 1937–38 had
been hard on his company, compounding accumulated problems, as we have
seen. David Goodrich reluctantly concluded that a change in leadership was
required. The company had lost money again in 1937, it had lost position in
important markets, and labor relations remained strained. Perhaps worst of all,
morale in the executive ranks was low. At the end of June 1938, the executive
committee decided to act. David Goodrich appointed a special committee of
Arthur Marks, R. S. Rauch, and A. B. Jones to investigate the firm's ills and report to the board of directors. The committee concluded that management
was having difficulty keeping track of the firm's diverse operations and had
failed to take full advantage of opportunities to reach profitable markets for
chemical products, including polyvinyl chloride (whose trade name was Koroseal). The financial control of the company also concerned the board, which
removed the company comptroller from Robertson's control. The board also
created an independent vice president for finance. Finally, the board decided
in December 1938 to dismiss Samuel B. Robertson as president and to look for
new leadership.[2]

Once Goodrich and the board decided to dismiss Robertson, two problems
loomed: finding a new leader, and ensuring that the action did not damage
the company's relations with its customers, especially the automobile manufacturers. David Goodrich knew he needed to act quickly. He and other board
members did not believe that any current Goodrich executive had the vision
or ability to lead the company, and they sought to recruit a talented new
executive. From his wide contacts in American and British business circles,
the chairman learned that John L. Collyer might be available. Collyer, after
his graduation from Cornell University in 1917 in mechanical engineering,
worked briefly in the shipbuilding industry. He then enjoyed a successful

career with Dunlop, first in the United States and after 1929 in England,
where he was joint managing director. Through Walrond Sinclair, head of
British Tyre and Rubber, Goodrich learned that the expatriate wished his children to live in the United States and was interested in returning home. After
discussing the matter in New York, the chairman telegraphed Sinclair, who
was returning to England from the United States aboard the Queen Mary, and
requested that he inquire of "John most confidentially."[3]

Sinclair discovered that Collyer was indeed interested in the Akron job, so
David Goodrich went to England aboard the Queen Mary in the summer of
1939 to discuss the leadership of the firm with him. Goodrich and Sinclair met
with Collyer at the Savoy Hotel in London on 11 July, and Collyer and
Goodrich quickly consented on terms. Goodrich agreed to confine his activities as chairman to board matters and relations with shareholders, the public,
and "the financial structure of the Company." Collyer was to be responsible for
the operations of Goodrich "subject only to major policy, which would be decided by the board of directors."[4]

Collyer was a fitting person for the tasks that soon faced his company. Collyer's background was in production, and the overriding problems that the war
would produce were production problems. Furthermore, unlike the typical industrial executive of his day, Collyer sought public notice for himself and his
company. Collyer brought a strong desire for self-promotion in public relations
to his job, a vision that, like his background in production, would serve his
company well in the wartime policy disputes surrounding the rubber supply.

Collyer required a few months before leaving Dunlop. In the meantime,
Goodrich mended fences with important Detroit customers, who expected to
have direct contacts with the presidents of tire companies. The chairman took
active charge of the company until the new president arrived from England,
and Robertson stayed on briefly as a salesman in the Detroit market. David
Goodrich believed that Robertson, whatever his failings, had succeeded in
establishing good relationships for the important original equipment tire
market. After he arrived in Akron, Collyer would have to establish his own
relationships with the auto magnates.[5]

THE ARRIVAL OF JOHN COLLYER

When Collyer arrived in Akron to take command of Goodrich, after a brief
period of observation he worked to install policies intended to overcome the
shortcomings that David Goodrich and others had explained to him. With the
chairman's clear support, Collyer moved to place Goodrich on a sound financial basis and improve manufacturing operations. Improving operations during wartime mobilization proved to serve not only the company well but the
country as well. The end of the depression and the wartime boom, of course,
did much to improve the company's performance. Changes in management
also played an important role in guiding Goodrich through the crises associated with the war.

Setting an Example

John Collyer immediately set an example in leadership, loyalty, and behavior. A sense of purposeful expectation spread quickly through the company's offices. Collyer set standards for punctual performance on the job and held formal social occasions to praise accomplishments and build an esprit de corps. Collyer was not personally friendly with his executives. Those who worked under Collyer quickly learned that he demanded polite behavior; blunt talk about the company's affairs was unwelcome. No longer were they free to leave the plant for long luncheons; Collyer expected to see them in the executive dining room.[6]

The new president soon made administrative changes to bring about greater managerial professionalism and accountability. Before he arrived in Akron to take the reins, friends in the rubber industry filled John Collyer's ear with reports about the poor leadership in the firm's headquarters, rife with politics among the executives. In Akron, Collyer learned that the top officers had functioned through an operations committee where votes were cast. He realized that this procedure was conducive to logrolling among executives seeking support for pet projects and lent itself to departmental fiefdoms functioning at the expense of the well-being of the company as a whole. Soon he made it clear that once issues had been discussed in regular meetings among the heads of divisions, he, as president, would make the decisions. Collyer then had the executive responsible for a major recommendation make a presentation to the board of directors.[7]

Collyer discovered firsthand the serious problems of which Goodrich, Sinclair, and his friends in the rubber industry had warned. Collyer quickly learned the details of the company's weak financial position and set out to correct the situation. His goal was to get the firm out of debt by reducing costs and improving earnings in order to follow a strategy of expansion through retained earnings. Collyer believed it important especially for an international company to have cash reserves in the face of unpredictable tax and exchange rates. Executive rewards would be commensurate with performance.[8]

The changes involved more than procedures for the Akron executives. Working with David Goodrich, Collyer began to reshape the board of directors. Although the company already had an unusually high proportion of outside directors, due to its need to have the support of large banks, the two leaders favored removing management directors and replacing them with additional outside directors. Collyer sought diversity on the board in terms of experience in finance, sales, and manufacturing. He wanted people with talent and expertise who would not simply ratify management decisions but with whom he could freely discuss the company's problems and prospects.[9]

Changes in Management

Collyer believed that changing the company involved more than revamping decision-making processes. He recognized a need to recruit new executive talent from outside. Two management changes seemed most pressing. First, Collyer wanted to recruit an executive experienced in managing chain stores who could halt the stores' drain on resources and turn them into profitable ventures. Second, Collyer wanted an executive with broad experience to help strengthen the firm's financial position.

Collyer solved the problem in one stroke by departing from the company's long-standing tradition of advancing local executives from production areas. He turned for help to the nation's most successful retailer, General Leonard Wood of Sears, Roebuck, with whom Collyer had become acquainted in England. In the spring of 1940, Collyer read in the newspaper that top officers of Montgomery Ward had resigned. Collyer called Wood, who once worked for Ward's, for a recommendation. Wood suggested George Vaught, who became vice president and treasurer 1 July 1940. Vaught brought a wealth of experience in the problems of distribution, and he was known in the executive suite as first among the vice presidents.[10]

John Collyer's new ideas for Goodrich did not involve basic structural changes during the World War II years, although there was one important exception. Full-scale restructuring into quasi-independent divisions remained for the postwar years. The company retained a centralized organization, and executives responsible for different aspects of operations reported to the head office. However, a major change was the formation of the chemical division in 1942, and early in 1945 the organization of the B.F. Goodrich Chemical Company, headquartered in Cleveland. This was done to take fuller advantage of opportunities, in production, marketing, and scientific areas, in what was amounting to a different line of business.

Emphasis on Manufacturing and Research

Collyer made important improvements in manufacturing efficiency during his first three years at Goodrich. Expenditures for expanded and improved manufacturing facilities nearly doubled in 1940, 1941, and the first half of 1942 when compared to depression-era levels. In that thirty-month period Goodrich spent $15 million to manufacture traditional rubber products at lower costs and, especially, to expand the capacity to manufacture polyvinyl chloride. The company calculated the savings on prior production levels from lowered costs at $2,256,000.[11] In the early months of the war, the company reported an improving sales and expense ratio. Sales in 1942 rose at about 75 percent above their level in 1939, yet there was a "net cost reduction of $4,613,356" on an annual basis. The figures revealed that profits were rising significantly before substantial war orders arrived in Akron, thanks to improved management.[12]

Collyer differed from his predecessors, and his immediate successor, with respect to research. He took a personal interest in the research efforts of the company's technical personnel. Collyer visited laboratories, asked informed questions, and tried to understand the answers. During the war years research remained a focus of the company. The president's knowledge of the work of the

firm's scientists and engineers afforded him important opportunities in promoting the company to the larger public. These came often, for Collyer was an
active public speaker and, when the occasion arose, was a witness before congressional committees.[13]

Public Relations

John Collyer was more involved with public relations than any other top
executive in the history of B.F. Goodrich. When he arrived in Akron, the president quickly became familiar with the firm's advertising and public relations
resources, and within months put them to use to promote his own stature as an
industrial statesman, direct the image of his company, and effect changes in
American public policy. Throughout the war, and after, Collyer had the firm
prepare a series of so-called "easel talks"—short presentations that he made to
congressional committees, trade audiences, and the like—the main points of
which he illustrated with placards placed on an easel in front of the room. The
company printed and widely distributed these messages. Young executives
learned quickly that Collyer expected good news about the company to be attributed to him.[14]

Collyer's attention to public relations and policy served the nation and the
company well during the early years of war preparation. Unlike some of his
counterparts and some military officers, Collyer thought the nation's rubber
supply was in danger. More than any other rubber executive, the Goodrich
president used his position effectively to force public attention on the need to
develop a petrochemical industry capable of producing synthetic rubber. Nor
did his activities as a publicist stop after Collyer and other leaders had persuaded the Roosevelt administration and Congress that the nation faced a raw
materials crisis. Collyer used the public recognition he had earned to remain
in the spotlight for the remainder of his career.

During the war Collyer encouraged other executives to make public ap-
pearances, and he had the public relations staff in Akron keep the company in
the public's eyes as a willing leader in patriotic causes. For instance, Goodrich
prepared and distributed films to educate Americans about the vital part that
rubber played in the war effort. In 1942, Collyer forwarded a Goodrich advertisement and booklet to federal officials to demonstrate how the company was
cooperating with the national effort to conserve natural rubber and to boost
synthetic rubber research and production. The company also offered a free
booklet, similar to an easel talk, entitled "Will America have to jack up its
29,000,000 automobiles?" The booklet touted conservation, and in it Collyer
explained that as early as 1940 Goodrich had urged the government to build
synthetic rubber factories.[15]

COLLYER AND THE RUBBER SUPPLY PROBLEM

Collyer's favorable public relations gave him a central presence in addressing
the nation's rubber supply problem and earned him the respect of public offi-

cials. Working with a few other key figures, including David Goodrich and Harry Truman, Collyer tried to stir American public policy from its lethargy on this issue. Collyer stressed the importance of developing a synthetic rubber industry. He drew on the company's long research tradition and its experience in polymer research (as well as his own public relations skills) to promote effectively the need for public discussion and action on what portended to become a major national crisis. Collyer was frustrated, however, by the cautious Jesse Jones, secretary of commerce during the fateful months before Pearl Harbor.

The Context

As an experienced rubber executive, Collyer realized that both his company and his country were dependent on overseas supplies of basic raw materials. By the end of the 1930s, American rubber companies imported about 95 percent of their rubber from plantations in southeast Asia, where rubber trees were free of the blight that had plagued latex harvests in the Western Hemisphere. American officials in both government and industry believed that the British navy, supported by American warships, would protect the world commerce in rubber.[16]

Collyer and David Goodrich were less sanguine. Even if the United States successfully maintained its isolationist posture, war would disrupt channels of trade and create a substantial new demand for rubber products. Both a stockpile of natural rubber and a synthetic rubber industry seemed in the national interest. When David Goodrich recruited Collyer, he liked the fact that Collyer recognized the possibilities of building a synthetic capability. As a European rubber executive, Collyer knew of German successes in developing synthetic rubber, and Dunlop scientists kept him abreast of the promises it held for rubber companies. The problem was cost: there was no foreseeable prospect of the cost of synthetic rubber becoming competitive with that of natural rubber.[17]

Eventually, the government became significantly involved in the rubber supply problem. When the Japanese conquered Asian rubber plantations and controlled sea lanes, obtaining new supplies of rubber was essential to victory. The answer involved several approaches. The government launched a scrap rubber drive for remanufacturing. Civilian uses were controlled through rationing. Most significant, however, was the government construction of a huge synthetic rubber industry during the war, a construction that occurred with the close cooperation of the rubber companies, including Goodrich. By the summer of 1942 government officials and rubber company engineers agreed on a recipe for synthetic rubber, so-called GR-S, and a standard plant design for its manufacture. By 1943 synthetic rubber was becoming a significant source of raw material for Goodrich and other manufacturers, and by 1944, in one of the most significant scientific and industrial achievements ever, American synthetic rubber factories were producing materials that, literally, made victory possible.

The Goodrich Synthetic Rubber Program

When Collyer took charge, Goodrich's established program of research in synthetic rubber provided him with an excellent base of support for improving the firm's manufacturing position. The company did not have its own rubber plantations, and if Collyer could persuade the government to invest in promising petrochemical processes to meet defense requirements, the company would be in a better position, in the long run, to compete against firms with captive supplies of natural rubber. Goodrich scientists, like others in the industry, had worked with synthetic processes in their laboratories for at least a generation. Arthur Marks, arguing that the price of natural rubber was cyclical, persuaded David Goodrich and other members of the board of directors in 1934 to establish a laboratory focused on the problems. The result might well be a "chemical plantation." Waldo Semon, the chemist who had discovered the way to plasticize polyvinyl chloride, was assigned the task of exploring avenues for freeing the company from its dependence on rubber supplies controlled by other firms. To maintain secrecy, Semon's project was given the code name "Guaylex," suggesting that the company was really exploring the southwestern desert shrub guayule, which produced a usable latex.[18]

Semon organized the laboratory in 1936 with four experienced scientists as his associates. Their company already had some valuable experience in the field. Butadiene, a chemical that could be manufactured from either alcohol or petroleum, was a key ingredient in synthetic rubber explorations. Having a rubber based on oil was an exciting prospect at a time when the United States had surpluses of crude oil, and alcohol manufactured from grain might become a much more valuable product for American farmers, who were suffering from the Great Depression. In Watertown, Hood Rubber scientists manufactured butadiene using a process developed in Germany during World War I, but the rubber that resulted proved unsatisfactory both in footwear and in tires. In Akron, the company had a similar legacy.[19]

His review of the scientific literature informed Semon that German scientists, especially those employed by I. G. Farben, were the leaders in research on butadiene manufacturing and its application. Their company was actually making tires from a synthetic rubber, Buna-S, a copolymer made from butadiene and styrene. In 1937 Semon went to Germany to learn more about their work and to try to arrange a contract to allow Goodrich to manufacture Buna-S using Farben patents. Semon was not allowed to witness Farben's manufacturing process, and he failed to win a contract. Nevertheless, because of Semon's reputation as the father of polyvinyl chloride, German scientists welcomed him warmly. What the German scientists did not realize was Semon's knowledge of their language. Although Semon did not see what he wanted to see, he learned much by simply listening to conversations. "I came back," Semon later recalled, "more enthused than ever and convinced that if Germany would not give us their method for making synthetic rubber that we could develop a method of our own."[20]

Despite the depression, Goodrich continued to invest in Semon's efforts. The chemist learned that the oil companies were interested in butadiene production but unwilling to make substantial investments. Nor were the military procurement agencies able to invest. With the support of senior management, Semon expanded his staff to eight chemists, and they ambitiously began to explore the scientific problems. By December 1941, the firm had conducted 14,492 experiments, 111 of which showed promise. The problem was to avoid the Farben patents while making a rubber that was a compound using butadiene and a comonomer.[21]

David Goodrich also remained enthusiastic about the project, and he even predicted that synthetics would play an important part in rubber manufacturing. He supported the construction of a pilot plant adjacent to Plant 3, where the firm had produced rubber chemicals since World War I. The pilot plant began operating on 5 October 1937. It included facilities that allowed engineers to work out the manufacturing processes required for both butadiene rubber and polyvinyl chloride. The plant produced its first large batch of rubber by Christmas 1938. Within a month, the factory had a capacity of one hundred pounds a day.[22]

The outbreak of war in Europe in September 1939 offered the company its first commercial opportunity in synthetic rubber. Natural rubber, no matter how vulcanized or compounded, tended to swell and disintegrate in the presence of oil. In 1938 Goodrich had begun to purchase an I. G. Farben product called Perbunan (a Buna-N synthetic made from butadiene and an expensive chemical known as acrylonitrile), which had oil-resistant properties superior to those of any other known product, to manufacture gasoline hose. The war cut off the supply, and the company faced the prospect of losing a profitable business to rivals. Semon's laboratory had developed a substitute, Nipol, which was also competitive with DuPont's neoprene. Semon and research director J. W. Schade observed that a plant capable of making three tons of Nipol a day would cost $248,000. Although this particular project never materialized, it provided a basis for expanding the production of synthetic rubber soon after Collyer's arrival.[23]

The most promising results of Semon's experiments were from "copolymerizing about 70 percent of butadiene and 30 percent of methyl methachrylate." The resulting rubber could be vulcanized and was resistant to abrasion. Although expensive to produce, it was potentially useful in the huge tire market. Thus, when Collyer arrived in Akron he found a company with a well-established base in synthetic rubber research and production that might serve the nation well in a future crisis. Early in 1940 Collyer decided to go "all out" for the tire rubber from Semon's laboratory, and the company by March had expanded production of its man-made rubbers to 250 pounds a day.[24]

Promoting a Synthetic Rubber Industry

Commercial obstacles were ever present. With the substantial capital investments required for a new industry, there was simply little prospect of artifi-

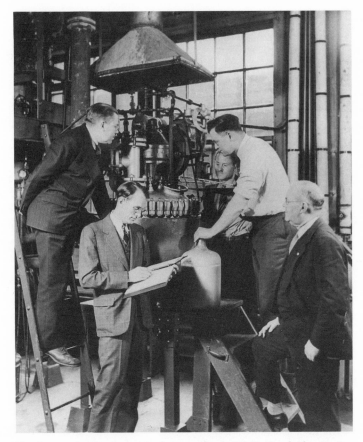

Dr. Semon, in shirtsleeves, is shown with other B.F. Goodrich scientists during the development of synthetic rubber in 1940. (BFG Co.)

cial rubber becoming competitive in price with natural rubber grown on colonial plantations. Collyer, David Goodrich, and other leaders in the rubber manufacturing industry—and soon some key executives in the petroleum industry—realized that it was essential to challenge public indifference and promote government investments to build an industry for national defense. In this regard, John Collyer and his staff proved masterful in commanding attention.

One of the problems that Collyer encountered was a rivalry with Standard Oil of New Jersey. Esso, as that company was commonly known, was the nation's largest oil refiner. Its management, seeking significant ventures in petrochemicals, had developed a prewar alliance with I. G. Farben, then the world's leading chemical manufacturer. After the war began in Europe, the oil giant purchased the American rights to Farben's patents on the manufacture of synthetic rubber, and its executives hoped for a time to control the new industry as it emerged with commercial products. The Farben patents included rights to manufacture Buna-S, a promising synthetic for the enormous tire market.

*Waldo Semon demonstrates one step in creating synthetic rubber at a 5 June 1940 press con-
ference. Looking on (from left to right) are T. G. Graham, David M. Goodrich, John L. Collyer, and James W. Schade. (BFG Co.)*

The competing desires of Standard Oil and B.F. Goodrich (and the other
large rubber manufacturers) to control the production of Buna rubbers, as all
butadiene rubbers were then known, meant that the companies were unable to
agree on the necessary investments. Just as Collyer was arriving in Akron at
the end of 1939, Dr. M. B. Hopkins of Standard Oil met with Goodrich executives to explore the possibility of joint ventures in Buna rubbers, with Standard controlling all of the patents. Confident that some of their own processes
avoided those patents, and wanting to enjoy the fruits of their own research,
Goodrich executives found Standard's terms unacceptable. In 1940, Standard
Oil served formal notice of patent infringement on Goodrich and other manufacturers who had refused its licensing terms.[25]

After an initial round of quick German military victories in Europe, the
war had quieted, until the spring of 1940. Then suddenly Germany defeated
France and threatened to invade Great Britain. As the war clouds loomed
darker and British power diminished dramatically, Collyer staged an announcement intended to shock the nation into action on its rubber policy to the benefit of Goodrich. On 5 June 1940, as France was falling to German armored
columns, the company gathered five hundred industrialists, scientists, military
experts, and journalists in the Empire Room of New York's Waldorf-Astoria
Hotel. There the Goodrich president and the firm's top scientist, Waldo
Semon, announced the introduction of Ameripol, a synthetic polymer
manufactured in America. Also called "Liberty Rubber," the new material

was a butadiene rubber that could be used in tires, which Collyer claimed could alone reduce by half the nation's dependence on imported natural rubber.[26]

At the press conference, Collyer parted blue plush curtains to reveal a map of the world. Tiny lights showed the path that natural rubber took to reach the United States, with a miniature freighter travelling from Singapore through the Suez Canal before eventually reaching America. To vivify the peril the nation faced, the freighter exploded in mid-Atlantic. Then Semon explained the new American polymer, Ameripol, made from butadiene. Butadiene came from petroleum. Cracking petroleum produced a "black, sticky material [that] is broken down to a mixture of simple molecules. From this mixture can be separated a gas which under pressure liquefies to give butadiene. This is mixed with other ingredients prepared from natural gas and air and then made into a milky emulsion using soap produced from American agricultural sources. Upon heating and agitation, these ingredients react to form an emulsion of synthetic rubber, which is similar to the latex obtained from rubber-producing trees."[27]

One function of the announcement was, again, to promote the image of B.F. Goodrich as a scientific leader in rubber manufacturing. Presenting tires made with "Liberty Rubber," Collyer appealed to other companies to purchase them to put the compound to a variety of severe tests. He also suggested that patriotic Americans buy the tires, even though they suffered from a 30 percent price premium, in order to demonstrate the nation's ability to free itself from a dependency on foreign goods. The company was able to make eighty Ameripol tires a day and would expand its capacity to four hundred per day should the market warrant the volume, said Collyer. The announcement became part of a savvy advertising campaign to promote the company as "First in Rubber." Eventually, the Ameripol test tires during the war allowed Goodrich copywriters to claim that the company's wartime synthetic passenger car tires had withstood 80 million miles of actual road testing.[28]

A second important function of the press conference was somewhat less self-serving. Collyer announced that "today, July 5, we are forwarding to the Chairman of the Advisory Commission to the Council on National Defense, an outline of a proposal to get the job underway." Collyer genuinely wanted his government to change policy quickly and finance the construction of a synthetic rubber manufacturing capability of 36,000 tons annually. This capability would serve the country as a standby resource should war actually come to America's shores. In Collyer's vision, placing the program on a "competitive basis" among the rubber companies would promote the technical learning required for the expansion of the industry and the application of its products. As for Goodrich, the company would sell its product from a government-financed plant on a cost basis to allow fabricators to learn how to use it. Collyer told the president of the Rubber Manufacturers' Association that Ameripol might cost three times as much as natural rubber, but volume production would bring down the price substantially.[29]

Within days of the dramatic announcement, Collyer, Semon, David Goodrich, and the vice president for manufacturing, T. G. Graham, were in Washington to promote government financing of a synthetic rubber industry. Granted an audience by Senator Harry S. Truman of Missouri, the Goodrich executives spoke to the Senate's Committee on Military Affairs about the dangers to the nation's rubber supply and the commercial difficulties of private investments in synthetic rubber. Standard Oil and DuPont executives warned the senators that investments might easily go for naught should the war clouds recede, but Collyer pressed his case. Collyer and Graham met with the National Defense Council's synthetic rubber committee, which was sympathetic and recommended funding facilities capable of making 100,000 tons annually. Collyer wanted the new industry built on a "competitive basis" to encourage each manufacturer to improve both the chemical engineering and the end product.[30]

Meanwhile, the government had begun to act, although not in a manner favorable to synthetic rubber advocates. In July 1940, persuaded by the international rubber cartel that synthetic plants were undesirable in the long run, Secretary of Commerce Jones arranged for the Reconstruction Finance Corporation to set up the Rubber Reserve Corporation to begin building a stockpile of natural rubber. Henceforth, Elmer Stevens and other buyers purchased rubber at a government-controlled price and with the approval of Rubber Reserve, with the manufacturers actually holding the inventories.

The synthetic question still lingered, however. Representatives of the "big four" rubber companies—sometimes joined by DuPont and Standard Oil—began holding joint meetings in which Collyer explained his pessimism about the length of time the economy could function in the event of the loss of crude rubber supplies. Goodrich's competitors were more optimistic about solving the technical problems quickly and building a synthetic industry. Standard Oil urged that, to control the quality, rubber manufacturers operate synthetic rubber plants, with oil firms supplying the raw materials. All of the industrialists agreed that the government must finance new facilities capable of making 100,000 tons annually. (Goodrich offered at one point to operate a plant on a cost basis.) The recommendation finally went to President Roosevelt in September 1941, but Jones, advised by his rubber expert, E. G. Holt, persuaded the president to delay lest the government waste its funds and rely instead on the stockpiling of natural rubber. As a consolation, Jones's Reconstruction Finance Corporation agreed to fund four 10,000-ton synthetic rubber plants. Goodrich, in the meantime, was pushing ahead with its own program of manufacturing synthetic rubbers.[31]

Beginning Synthetic Rubber Manufacturing

There were large problems in venturing into manufacturing synthetic rubber in commercial quantities and at a price competitive with natural rubber.

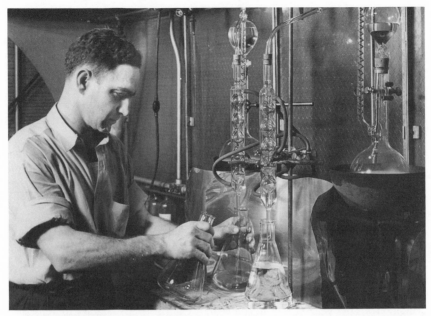

A Goodrich chemist, Dr. G. L. Browning, is seen here purifying one of the ingredients in a synthetic rubber experiment. (BFG Col. UAA)

For example, butadiene was in short supply. Fortunately, Frank Phillips, the Bartlesville, Oklahoma, oil magnate, was interested in petrochemical manufacturing. Phillips Petroleum could supply small quantities of the vital ingredient butadiene, and it was interested in expanding capacity. Goodrich and Phillips formed a joint venture, the Hydrocarbon Chemical and Rubber Corporation, announced in 1940. With butadiene arriving in carload quantities from Phillips refineries, the new venture used acrylonitrile to produce Hycar, an oil-resistant synthetic rubber of high cost and high value, in a small factory adjacent to the pilot plant. Semon was appointed vice president and director of research for the new venture.[32]

Eventually, in the summer of 1941, Collyer's campaign to persuade government officials to finance a synthetic rubber facility succeeded. The Defense Plant Corporation, the agency set up to finance new factories for essential military products, provided $2,750,000 for a plant initially capable of making 10,000 tons of rubber annually. Hycar, as the Phillips joint venture was renamed in 1942, also began constructing a synthetic rubber plant in Louisville, Kentucky, to manufacture tire rubber. At the same time, Hycar was expanding its capacity in Akron to 7,000 tons annually. These efforts meant that after the bombing of Pearl Harbor Goodrich was the first rubber company to come on line with a synthetic factory. In the first two years of the war, B.F. Goodrich manufactured more synthetic rubber than any other American firm.[33]

After Pearl Harbor

As smoke from the Pearl Harbor bombing was clearing, the government reversed its policy and launched a full-scale synthetic rubber industry. The principal vehicle was the Rubber Reserve Corporation of the RFC, which provided the capital and the coordination for building an entirely new petrochemical industry to supply butadiene and styrene. The wartime product was labeled GR-S, for Government Rubber-Styrene. Goodrich was, of course, heavily involved in this program.

The issue of whether to spend public funds for a product that might not have peacetime commercial potential now vanished. With supplies of natural rubber virtually eliminated, the government rallied industry executives to emergency action. The first task was to arrange the sharing of technical expertise and patents. In the autumn of 1941, Standard Oil had sued both Goodyear and Goodrich for infringement on its Buna-N patents. (Semon privately expressed his confidence that Goodrich would win the suit.) By mid-December, Rubber Reserve officials had cleared the way for the patent suit to be dropped in favor of wartime cooperation. In January 1942, the federal government authorized the construction of synthetic rubber plants capable of producing 400,000 tons per year. (Later in the year, the authorized capacity increased to 705,000 tons.) In early February the "General Butadiene Agreement," a formal collaboration among competing firms sanctioned by the war's emergency, included Standard and other oil companies and Hycar and Goodrich, paving the way for the production and distribution of that vital chemical.[34]

In the development of a government-owned synthetic rubber industry, Goodrich scientists and engineers played a leading role. The government policy was for the companies involved to cooperate fully, share their knowledge, and decide upon a standard formula and factory design. Semon headed the committee to choose the recipe. The group decided on butadiene-styrene rubber instead of the superior formula Semon had developed for Ameripol because styrene was more plentiful than methyl methachrylate. Similarly, although Goodrich had developed a "cold rubber" process in its own plant, which produced a superior compound more quickly, GR-S was made at warmer temperatures because of the shortage of refrigeration equipment. Representatives of the rubber manufacturers formed a group located in Pittsburgh to work closely with Blaw Knox, the construction firm selected to build the actual plants, and scientists from the Mellon Institute. William I. Burt, who had managed the Ameripol plant, chaired the committee to design and construct the government factories. Walter Piggott of Goodrich headed the engineering effort, while William Scull took charge of purchasing. Always, the atmosphere was one of crisis. The Pittsburgh group developed a standard factory design to produce units of 30,000 tons per year.[35]

Although the building of a synthetic rubber industry during the war was a major achievement of emergency cooperation among Goodrich and other firms, crises initially plagued the program. Shortages of butadiene nagged the

In October 1940 Goodrich was using its synthetic rubber research in advertisements. (BFG Co.)

program into 1944. The chemical engineering of butadiene from petroleum was difficult, especially in achieving the necessary purity. High octane aviation fuel, in such extraordinary demand in the war, also required the chemical. While oil refiners struggled to meet the demand for butadiene, the government in 1942 turned to a proven technology of producing butadiene from alcohol, although the process was more costly.

Administrative decisions were easier. The government decided that each of the "big four" firms would operate plants of equal capacity, and Goodrich and its competitors rushed the construction of standard design plants at sites near sources of butadiene. Eventually, Goodrich operated plants in the following locations: Borger, in the panhandle of Texas, near a butadiene supply from Phillips Petroleum; Port Neches, on the Texas gulf coast and near a supply from Gulf Oil; and Louisville, Kentucky, where Union Carbide was manufacturing butadiene from alcohol. By the end of the war, Goodrich operated factories capable of an annual production of 165,000 tons of rubber, while its other large rivals were capable of making 150,000 tons. Smaller firms also operated smaller plants, providing the nation with a synthetic rubber capacity of 705,000 tons at the end of the war.[36]

THE CONVERSION TO A WARTIME COMPANY

From the start, Goodrich management made a basic decision about the firm's wartime strategy: to focus on what the company knew best—rubber and its related products—and to avoid launching into fields distant from rubber. Goodyear, in contrast, decided to become an aircraft manufacturer as the defense program boosted that industry. In 1942 Collyer and the other executives believed that results justified their policy. Company employees were playing a leading role in the design and construction of the new synthetic rubber industry. The wartime policy had allowed the company to develop new products from rubber and plastic and to accelerate production in the existing manufacturing plant. Within this policy, of course, serious adjustment problems occurred, both in adapting the factories to war products and in negotiating with the firm's powerful new customers, the military procurement agencies. The one significant deviation from rubber-related products was Goodrich's operation of the Lone Star Defense Corporation, a bomb- and shell-loading plant, for the ordnance bureau of the army.[37]

Following this strategy, Goodrich made substantial contributions to the mobilization effort. The company manufactured a long list of products for the military services, the aircraft industry, and for its traditional markets in the industrial, medical, automotive, and shoe industries. In the early part of the mobilization effort, however, the company lagged behind two of its larger competitors. A study conducted by the War Production Board indicated that from June 1940 through November 1942 Goodrich had received government war contracts valued at $85.1 million ($130.5 million when $45.4 million for the Lone Star Defense Corporation was included). In contrast, Goodyear totalled $474.4 million and U.S. Rubber $549 million. Firestone was last among the "big four" rubber companies, with $126.3 million in contracts.[38]

The war brought about increased demands for rubber goods, and both the company and the government had to make substantial capital investments. Early in the war Goodrich chose to finance production from its own resources. For instance, the company spent about $1 million to modernize its reclaimed rubber plant alone, continuing a previously established policy, which served Goodrich and the nation well; the improved ability to recycle rubber was vital to victory. Self-financing, however, was impossible in the face of the military's voracious demands. In the summer of 1941, the army allotted $1.5 million to the company for equipment to build tubes and casings. The federal government financed the new synthetic rubber factories (although Goodrich proudly pointed out that at the end of 1942 its private facility was producing more general-purpose synthetic rubber than all other American plants combined) and the Lone Star Defense Corporation facilities. The government also rented some special-purpose machinery to Goodrich.[39] Eventually, in 1943 and 1944, the government financed new factories at Miami, Oklahoma, and Tuscaloosa, Alabama, that, along with similar ventures for competitors, provided facilities needed for meeting military tire requirements.

The war effort severely taxed both the workers and the company's equipment. The all-out effort to produce goods for the military meant that Goodrich accumulated considerable amounts of deferred maintenance within a short period of time. The company operated its facilities six to seven days per week, twenty-four hours a day. Although workers' earnings boomed as a result, wartime pressures proved stressful on individuals, families, and communities. Inside the factories there was little opportunity for proper maintenance of equipment. The company found that even when equipment was shut down for repair or renewal, skilled workers were often away in uniform or already overburdened with tasks.[40] One of Goodrich's proudest achievements was in reclaiming scrap rubber. Soon after the declaration of war, the government launched a drive to collect scrap rubber, and the company responded to reclaim the extra tonnage. In the summer of 1942, Goodrich announced that it had met the challenge.[41]

Problems of Doing Business with the Government

Industrial mobilization for the war involved much more than meeting the raw materials crisis. Civilian business necessarily dropped dramatically for Goodrich, and what remained was conducted under strict government controls of allocation, rationing, and pricing. Even the firm's profit margins were effectively under government scrutiny during the war. In the first two months of 1942, the tire business, which accounted for roughly 75 percent of the dollar value in the rubber industry, dropped 80 percent from its peacetime level. Thus, from a business viewpoint, mobilizing for war presented substantial challenges.[42]

The combination of wartime conditions and having the government as nearly the sole customer presented unusual hazards, against which Goodrich wished to retain earnings. Dealing with the government's procurement agencies brought a new way of doing business. Early in the war, Goodrich learned that when a military service canceled a product, the supplier could suffer. Goodrich had contracted to supply tires for an army vehicle that proved unsatisfactory under combat conditions. When the army canceled the contract, Goodrich found itself uncompensated for the funds it had spent to convert passenger-car tire-building machinery to build a new size of tire for the army vehicle. "Today," a company report complained, "this conversion cost represents dead loss."[43] Executives knew, moreover, that a sudden end to the war could magnify such problems, with lost revenue and new expenses arising from conversion to civilian operations. Government officials were not easily persuaded to allow Goodrich to retain earnings to carry it through the reconversion period.[44]

Goodrich and the other rubber manufacturers faced special problems because of the inventory requirements of their business. This fact was brought home in 1942 when the government (which controlled wages and prices during the war) announced sudden price changes for reclaimed rubber. Lobbying through the Rubber Manufacturers' Association led to a reversal of the decision. The standard government contract for war production also included a clause allowing cancellation at any time "for the convenience of the government." The manufacturers feared that the standard contract did not guarantee payment for those inventory and processing costs should mobilization agencies decide to cancel a contract. James J. Newman, vice president of Goodrich, chaired a special committee of the RMA, which petitioned the government for clarification and special consideration in its contracts.[45]

Goodrich's connections to officials in Washington proved useful in these matters. Like other industrial firms, Goodrich sent experienced executives to government service. Board member Sidney Weinberg was closely connected to the Democratic Party and the Roosevelt administration, and he served the government in important advisory capacities. Arthur B. Newhall, who before the war had served as executive vice president, joined the War Production Board (the agency responsible for the overall supervision of industrial mobilization) as rubber coordinator, with wide-ranging responsibilities for production and conservation. Most noticeably, Collyer served the government in prominent capacities. When the mobilization agencies faced a nagging crisis in the supply of large truck tires in 1945, Collyer served for three months as special director of rubber programs on the War Production Board. This position afforded Collyer accurate information about his entire industry, knowledge he could put to good use for Goodrich when competitive peacetime conditions returned.[46]

Research Traditions and Patent Pools

The war brought about a fundamental change in Goodrich's ability to use scientific research to gain an edge over its competitors. Goodrich and its competitors had to suspend their traditional secrecy and instead share knowledge about synthetic rubber and rubber manufacturing. Collyer was reluctant to share patent information, for he believed that Goodrich scientists were the leaders in their industry, and he disliked the prospect of conceding their edge over the firm's larger competitors. However, once government leaders agreed to face the nation's rubber supply crisis, Collyer and other industrialists agreed to cooperate. Again, as in so many other areas of business activity, the war meant that the company interacted with the government in novel ways, eventually sharing over two hundred patents.[47] Collyer's concern was well founded: in the 1950s Goodrich was unable to enforce patents on its 1954 discovery of synthetic natural rubber because of the role the government had played in research during the war.

Although the government redirected and even funded some of its efforts, the company remained true to its research tradition. In May 1943, with federal funds and facilities provided by the school, the company set up a laboratory for twelve company chemists at Kent State University to probe synthetic rubber. Research continued in Akron as well, both in rubber and new synthetics. Still, the company abandoned some of its prewar projects, such as research in so-called cold rubber, when it realized that there would be no postwar advantage to the results, given the sharing of scientific information.[48]

Guarding the Political Front

The war mobilization and doing business with the government changed but did not suspend the firm's political problems. In 1942 small-business opponents and the other integrated tire manufacturers tried to use the rubber shortage to their advantage, and Goodrich executives had to respond with a concerted lobbying effort in Washington. Working with the self-appointed defender of independent tire dealers, George Burger, three members of the Senate's Small Business Committee—Allen J. Ellender of Louisiana, Arthur Capper of Kansas, and Thomas Stewart of Tennessee—formed a special subcommittee on tires. Ellender introduced a bill that, among other measures, would require regular inspections of all civilian tires by independent tire dealers for the duration of the war. The stated goal was to provide for conservation and retreading of civilian tires, but the effect would be to weaken the distribution system of Goodrich and the other large manufacturers who had invested in an integrated system of stores.[49]

Goodrich assigned vice president James J. Newman the task of coordinating the firm's attack on the Ellender bill. Although Burger hoped that Roosevelt would support the cause in the name of boosting small business, the president was wary. When Roosevelt appointed Bernard Baruch to recommend a direction to expedite synthetic rubber production, Baruch opposed the small business advocates. So too did the United Rubber Workers, whose leaders observed that the large tire manufacturers had technical expertise useful in helping civilians conserve their tires. By the end of 1942, Newman could report that Burger and his friends were defeated.[50]

PERSONNEL ISSUES DURING THE WAR

Personnel problems also loomed over Goodrich as it faced the issue of meeting the nation's mobilization requirements. The need to retain the organization's capabilities both on the shop floor and the executive's desk was a challenging task as the military services threatened to strip all businesses of capable employees. Compounding the problem was the fact that during the depression

Goodrich, like so many other firms, had not been able to recruit large numbers of young engineers and executives. Following a brief period of threatened sharp cutbacks in the workforce due to the raw material shortages, Goodrich faced substantial shortages in human resources. Despite enormous pressures from the government and the public at large to maintain full production, wage and work-rule issues continued to plague the company, especially at its Akron base.

In one sense the war years were very good years for the firm's employees, as they were for most Americans. The boom in manufacturing meant that work-weeks were full, with considerable overtime pay. The war brought expanded employment opportunities for women and African Americans, traditionally victims of employment discrimination. Paychecks were regular and, with the government successfully dampening inflationary pressures, fat. Company executives were also poised to profit personally from the growth in war orders; only U.S. Rubber compensated its officials more than Goodrich.[51]

Retaining and Recruiting Employees

Although the restrictions on raw material supply during the autumn of 1941 and the first months after Pearl Harbor caused company and government officials alike to worry about furloughing employees, the boom in war production soon created acute labor shortages. The shortages progressively worsened as the war persisted and military services reached further into the nation's population for servicemen. B.F. Goodrich saw its payrolls climb dramatically from about 31,500 employees at the end of 1940 to about 50,000 in the spring of 1945, including 10,000 in government-owned plants and 20,000 in the Akron plants. Akron became a boomtown once again.[52]

Because rubber and plastic manufacturing were so vital to the war effort, Goodrich and its rivals were able to retain some personnel that other industries would have lost to the draft. Younger chemical engineers whose expertise was vital were released from military obligations. In fact, because the depression had retarded the recruitment of young technical personnel, managerial opportunities for young scientists arose. Soon after his appointment as federal rubber director, William Jeffers noted that skilled rubber workers and executives should remain in their key civilian jobs. He arranged deferments with the War Manpower Commission.[53]

Nevertheless, the company found that it lost key employees to the military services and had to recruit and train new workers, resorting even to sending recruiters into the South. The rubber companies generally found that many of the recruited employees had never done factory work. The company reported that the proportion of its women employees had grown from 18–20 percent to 28–30 percent by the middle of 1943, with an anticipated rise to 40 percent in 1944. Opportunities for women were still limited, however, because of assumptions about the physical strength required in tire building. In mid-1943

Goodrich workers are seen here leaving the Akron factory during World War II. (BFG Col. UAA)

the company employed only 165 women in jobs previously performed by men, usually building smaller tires, at male wage rates.[54]

Recruiting new workers also brought about increased racial tensions. African Americans constituted an underutilized source of skills to which industrial employers turned to meet their labor requirements. The black population of Akron doubled between 1940 and 1950, from twelve thousand to twenty-four thousand, as rubber manufacturers recruited new workers. As civil rights organizations pressed for equality, tensions in the Akron area were sharpest at Goodrich. "Near riots" occurred on the shop floor, where blacks were employed for the first time in 1942.[55]

In spite of the efforts to recruit, train, and retain new workers to meet the huge volume of business, by the spring of 1944 the labor shortage in the Akron area was acute. Seiberling Rubber found that both the "man and woman-power shortage in this area has reached critical proportions and that we are scraping hard the bottom of the barrel." Shortages were affecting manufacturers' ability to meet production schedules.[56] Combined with the near exhaustion of the natural rubber supply and the truck tire crisis of 1944 and 1945, the labor shortages hampered the ability of Goodrich and other rubber firms to meet the war emergency even as Germany was starting to fall. The military services cooperated by discharging tire builders over the age of thirty so they could return to factory jobs. But labor scarcity problems could not be fully resolved until war orders started dropping in 1945.

Motivating Workers in Wartime

Goodrich instituted special programs to motivate and reward its workforce during the war. In large part, these programs were a response to pressure from the government, which hoped that patriotism would prove a powerful enough incentive to override the traditional prewar antagonisms between labor and management that had disrupted production at Goodrich. Even President Roosevelt tried occasionally to win the Goodrich workers' support for the war effort. As early as October 1941, when sixteen thousand Goodrich workers in Akron held a one-day strike to protest a beating at the Oaks tire plant, Roosevelt wrote to union leaders stressing that production in the defense program could be limited by "only one factor—the amount necessary to overwhelm the Nazi hordes."[57] The programs, combined with a continuing barrage of patriotic pressures, were partly successful. The programs failed when union members saw their collective bargaining rights weaken.

The principal program instituted was in the shape of a Labor-Management Committee for the War Production Drive in March 1942. Formed in response to a call from Donald Nelson, head of Washington's War Production Board, the committee was the first such effort in the rubber industry. The committee had six management and six labor members, with alternating chairmen. It divided its work into subcommittees that paralleled the plantwide organization. The committee decided that its first priority was communication, and it launched *War Production News* to convey to employees their continuing vital roles in the mobilization effort.[58]

The joint labor-management program enjoyed some success. Subcommittees worked on problems of waste and material savings, transportation, safety, production, and publicity. With a dramatic photograph of a French worker mourning his loss of freedom, the first issue of the *War Production News* "enlisted" employees "as soldiers of production" and carried messages from prominent officials imploring full cooperation. Soldiers, sailors, and airmen who had left the company provided short quotations exhorting continuous production. Workers were assured that the committee was neutral regarding disputes that had divided labor and management over the years. Cooperation, supported by individuals' suggestions for improvements, was to be the order of the day. Very soon the committee proudly announced that suggestions had risen dramatically, and later articles explained how individuals had made a substantial difference in meeting and even exceeding production goals.[59]

The cooperation between labor and management during the war was always filled with tension, however. Within weeks of its launch, George R. Bass, president of Local 5 of the United Rubber Workers, announced that the union was withdrawing from the joint committee. The immediate issue involved draft deferments, which the workers felt were being issued arbitrarily; the union wanted a joint committee to decide on them, which management, wary of giving up prerogatives, refused. The union had tried for six weeks to resolve the matter, without success. To Bass the failure indicated that cooperation meant little beyond exhortations to work hard during the war.[60] The company continued the cooperation program independently, meeting with union representatives on a problem-by-problem basis. Although this approach suspended the immediate dispute, the episode was indicative of tensions throughout the course of the war, tensions that were of ongoing concern to public officials, who thought that the problems stemmed from faults of both management and union.[61]

The principal means available to both Goodrich and the government of engendering worker cooperation were exhortation and reward. The company exhorted workers especially to refrain from absenteeism—"A Saboteur Slowing BFG War Production"—and to report to work on time and avoid loafing. A parade of dignitaries and celebrities, from Hollywood stars to war heroes and high mobilization officials, came through the company's plants to maintain pressure on workers. When the army and navy awarded Goodrich its "E" banner for excellence in war production, the company made an "E" emblem available for each employee.[62]

Goodrich and the Union Movement during the War

The legacy of acrimonious disputes between Goodrich and its workers did not augur well for its ability to maintain full production. The differences did not disappear during the war, and they flared occasionally into full-scale strikes that seriously threatened the war effort. However, hostilities did recede somewhat, in part because of the pressures of patriotism, but largely because of federal officials' enormous pressure on both sides—and particularly on the company—to give ground.

The government in effect forced Goodrich (and other manufacturers) to concede to labor on the fundamental issue of union recognition. The immediate issue was the closed shop—a requirement that all workers in a firm join the union—long a goal of unions, who believed that all people benefiting from collective bargaining should support the organizations bringing about improved contracts. Goodrich, like virtually every industrial firm, did not want the United Rubber Workers, or any union, so strengthened. In order to ensure full production, the government formed a War Labor Board to arbitrate disputes between labor and management. The Labor Board forced executives in Akron to accept the union shop. The euphemism during the war was "maintenance of membership," a procedure through which all workers in a plant with a collective bargaining contract were required to join a union after a certain period of time. Despite this national policy, and the government's ruling on 28 September 1942 that the firm follow it, Goodrich consistently opposed the "maintenance of membership" requirement whenever it faced collective bargaining.[63]

Although the company's resistance to union growth failed, government intervention did not always work against management interests. Union leaders, including United Rubber Workers's president, Sherman Dalrymple, pledged that their organizations would refrain from strikes for the duration of the war. This promise gave executives at Goodrich and other firms powerful allies in trying to meet production schedules. Dalrymple, in fact, worked closely with the War Labor Board and engaged in a prolonged, though largely unsuccessful, attempt to suppress labor militancy in Akron. His cooperation with the government won an important victory for Goodrich and other rubber manufacturers during the early months of the war. Workers wanted premium pay for weekend work, which the War Production Board ordered eliminated in March 1942; the War Labor Board and Dalrymple offered the workers no support.[64]

This proved a minor victory for the company, however, compared to that won by its Akron workers in 1942 regarding overtime pay. In the annual contract renewal negotiations, with the factories running full twenty-four-hour days, Goodrich wanted to change the standard from three six-hour shifts per day to three eight-hour shifts. Management had argued since 1940 that the change was necessary to prevent waste and avoid production delays. The union resisted, and on 19 May, the day their collective bargaining contract expired, union leaders forced the issue by sending workers home after they had performed six hours of service. Management claimed that the action brought a 25 percent reduction in war production. The disruption lasted only two days while negotiations continued. Finally, both sides agreed to send the dispute to the War Labor Board for resolution, and the government ruled in favor of the union. Thereafter, the Akron factories operated on a six-hour shift, with overtime pay for additional hours of service.[65]

In spite of the no-strike pledge, labor-management disputes led to production disruptions during the war. The most serious occurred over wage issues in 1943 in all of Akron's rubber factories and resulted in a directive from President Roosevelt to both the companies and the union to resume full-scale war production. The conflict arose first with Goodrich, where wage issues had been simmering since the 1942 contract negotiations. The United Rubber Workers's local unions in Akron had pressed unsuccessfully for wage increases, finally agreeing to allow government panels to resolve the differences with management. As was its usual practice, the War Labor Board created a special local panel of six members, two from the union, two from management, and two representing "the public." With the management representatives dissenting, the panel recommended that all Goodrich production and maintenance workers receive a pay increase of 8¢ per hour retroactive to 17 June 1942, the date the union and the company signed their contract. In Akron, union officials expected the wage increase to set the pattern for the seventy thousand workers across the rubber industry. They were soon to be disappointed, however. Goodrich executives, joined by their counterparts in the other Akron-based rubber firms, appealed to the War Labor Board in Washington.

The dispute soon led to a showdown that revealed fissures in the ranks of union leaders and brought about White House intervention. On 21 May the War Labor Board ordered wages increased by only 3¢, apparently in an attempt to equalize Akron and "war-born" wage rates. Union president Dalrymple tried to restrain Local 5 president George Bass, but to no avail. Bass and other militant Akron union leaders believed that their union must retain its independence and power to strike even in the war. Accordingly, on 22 May they defied Dalrymple and led a strike of more than fifty thousand workers from the four largest Akron rubber companies. Dalrymple, even with the support of the War Labor Board, could not persuade the strikers to return to work, and production resumed only after Roosevelt threatened to have the army seize the Akron factories. Goodrich Local 5 agreed to end the strike on 29 May.[66]

Although the threatened intervention ended the strike, conflict over shop-floor control still swirled through the Goodrich factories in Akron. Overtime assignments were a persistent issue that eventually required further federal intervention. Since 1938 the union contract had required the company to submit for union approval the names of those whom management wished to have work overtime. Originally, this procedure was to ensure against favoritism. Management, however, soon came to believe—and eventually the War Labor Board agreed—that Local 5 was using the procedure politically to force employees to join the union and pay union dues, to force the company to concede to union demands on unrelated issues, and to force Goodrich to pay unjustified overtime expenses. The company believed that in 1943 alone the union's stance had cost it $3 million in double-time-wage penalties just to meet production schedules for the war. Vice president Graham observed that the issue involved "the fundamental right" of management to schedule production "to maintain War Production . . . consistent with National Policy, without interference from the union." In June 1944 the regional War Labor Board in Cleveland disagreed with Graham's position, but the company won an appeal to Washington in 1945.[67]

Management knew that despite pressure from federal officials on workers to maintain production, and despite some minor victories in War Labor Board rulings, the company was in danger of losing power to the United Rubber Workers permanently. It fought on two fronts. Executives succeeded in keeping the United Rubber Workers out of the new chemical factories, except in Borger, in favor of other, less militant unions. They also began to cooperate more fully with other firms to prevent the union from playing one company against another. In 1944 and 1945 the firm's top executives and labor relations specialists developed a formal structure in the Rubber Manufacturers' Association for exchanging information between companies about employee contracts and compensation.[68]

Goodrich executives witnessed two more significant and troublesome developments before the war was over. In the summer of 1944, the URW began successfully to organize the company's office workers and appealed especially for protection of seniority rights. The Goodrich office workers' union was the first of its kind in the industry, and with its establishment executives encountered union power in even their most routine activities.[69] Then in April 1945, before the war was over and while the nation was still experiencing a tire supply crisis, production workers in Akron struck again, idling the Goodrich factories for three days. The most significant issue involved discipline, especially management's authority to reprimand and dismiss workers. The company insisted that it was abiding by the terms of its collective bargaining contract; the War Labor Board agreed and ordered the strike ended.[70]

Overall, the war strengthened the rubber workers' union in its collective-bargaining power with Goodrich. In this respect, Goodrich's experience with labor relations during the war was typical of large American manufacturing firms. Labor was in short supply owing to the booming economy and the expansion of the armed services, and the government demanded full, uninterrupted production. Both circumstances strengthened the hand of the union, and URW power grew accordingly. The URW leadership was not, however, always able to control the rank and file. After the war, these circumstances would lead to acrimonious labor relations and strikes.

THE IMPACT OF THE WAR ON PRODUCTS

The war had a serious impact on the company's product lines, even before the United States officially declared war. Government controls over rubber in 1941 required a reduction in the manufacture of passenger car tires, although military orders for rubber goods and polyvinyl chloride were substantial. In more traditional rubber products, Goodrich was able to take advantage of new, if temporary, opportunities and to make the required adjustments to preserve its civilian business for the postwar years. Tire production continued, but with different markets and raw materials. The demand for belts, hoses, and other industrial products boomed as American manufacturing volume rose over 250 percent from 1939 to 1944. The expansion of the aircraft industry planted Goodrich firmly in a profitable and enduring line of work. The military services bought a range of items from gas masks to life preservers that Goodrich was in a position to supply.

Lone Star Defense Corporation

In 1941 government officials asked B.F. Goodrich to assume responsibility for constructing and operating a $30 million bomb- and shell-loading plant to be constructed near Texarkana, Texas. Collyer initially resisted—it would place burdens on the company's management and technical teams, and the company's more traditional product lines were flourishing—but he finally acceded to the government's request. "We were pressured into doing it," Collyer recalled. Failure to comply with the request threatened the company with "sharp governmental criticism."[71]

The Lone Star Defense Corporation was organized as a subsidiary under a cost-plus-a-fixed-fee contract. A small group of managers, led by Arthur Kelly, went to the site to help plan construction. While there, the army trained them in newly developed methods of statistical quality control, which would later become important in manufacturing operations in the United States and abroad. After the United States entered the war, a somewhat larger cadre of several dozen skilled workers embarked from Akron by train. When they first arrived in Texas in the spring of 1942, the plant had few buildings and no paved roads. The Akron workers were first trained in the hazardous work of loading bombs and ammunition and then sent to learn their new trade at operating government arsenals. Arms production began on 27 July 1942. At the peak of production, Lone Star employed about nine thousand workers, mostly women. Soon after the war ended, Goodrich turned the plant over to the government. Lone Star continued to serve the nation's military forces under different management.[72]

War Products Division

When the war began seriously to affect the company's markets for tires and other civilian rubber goods in 1941, Collyer instructed his executives to plan for reduced operations to substantially control the company's costs. At this stage of the nation's mobilization, it was unclear to what extent the critical shortages looming in the rubber supply would mean for the firm's ability to operate at full capacity. E. F. "Tommy" Tomlinson, a young executive just returned from sales duty in Chicago, suggested that B.F. Goodrich form a war products division to obtain military orders for special products. George Vaught, who cautioned his colleagues not to be hasty in cutting back their staff, supported the idea, and Collyer told Tomlinson to choose six executives, start the new operation, and seek sales. Already a substantial business before the attack on Pearl Harbor, this area became a centerpiece of the Goodrich war effort.[73]

Collyer had assigned Peter Brunner to government sales, excluding aircraft products, and Tomlinson reported to him. The war products division focused on rubber tracks for military vehicles. The company first developed the endless rubber track (called the band track during the war) for use on slow-moving agricultural vehicles in 1931 and won contracts with army ordnance to experiment with their use. The device allowed machinery to move at speeds of fifty miles per hour without damaging pavements, making it superior to the older metal tracks. In late 1940 the army began massive purchases. Because they used less rubber than conventional large tires, while giving superior performance on rugged terrain, the band tracks became a principal contribution of Goodrich during the war. The company also made the bogey wheels on which the band tracks for trucks and tanks were mounted.[74]

There were other important items developed for special sale to the armed services. Goodrich was especially proud of its work on inflatable rubber products, for which it was praised by the army. The company's engineers developed

Goodrich workers pose proudly around their fuel cells. (BFG Co.)

a way of producing a pneumatic float with vulcanized construction, replacing the older methods that used cement. The resulting pontoons formed temporary bridges for combat forces. Innovative lightweight life vests carried by air force crews and life-saving suits used by the navy were also devised.[75]

The Expansion of the Aircraft Industry

With only five thousand airplanes manufactured in the United States in 1939, enormous wartime expansion created the modern American aircraft industry. Although Goodrich supplied key products to this new market in addition to tires and deicers, the company's response to the aircraft industry's growth was less aggressive than its competitors', and less aggressive than its own reaction to the burgeoning PVC demand. Although Firestone and Goodyear formed subsidiary companies in 1939 and 1940 to seize opportunities in the aircraft industry, Goodrich did not organize a separate aerospace division until 1956. The organization of aircraft supplies remained within the traditional operating structure of the company, and the management style in aircraft markets continued to be the personal one practiced by James S. Pedler before the war.[76]

Before the war, Goodrich hoped to realize significant sales to the aircraft industry. But as long as that industry remained small, Goodrich's sales had more

Goodrich deicers were important equipment on air force planes during World War II. (BFG Col. UAA)

impact in image than on the corporate balance sheet. The company had sustained its research interest in aviation rubber markets and in 1939, in line with its advertising strategy of associating its products with the leading edge in scientific developments, reported that it enjoyed the largest sales of aircraft tires in the nation. From this base the company expanded its supply of aircraft products, some of which were for special military applications and others that would prove of continuing value in civilian applications. Self-sealing fuel tanks—called fuel cells during the war—were an especially important device that Goodrich technicians helped to pioneer. Goodrich, along with Goodyear, made some significant advances in fuel cell design and acceded to a government request to share its patents.[77]

The Wartime Tire Business

The tire business remained central to Goodrich's wartime efforts. The modern army required tires, and in huge numbers. Moreover, the army's demand for tires grew significantly as the war progressed, especially after the successful landing on the Normandy coast in the summer of 1944. As allied forces penetrated Europe, long lines of trucks carried supplies. Equipping those trucks, and all the other military vehicles, while maintaining production for essential civilian purposes, posed a very large challenge to Goodrich and other tire manufacturers.

In 1943 Goodrich reminded civilians of its war efforts. (BFG Co.)

At the same time, in the United States passenger car transportation remained an essential part of the national transportation system during the war. Government planners and tire industry officials alike recognized that civilians still needed their automobiles, especially those driving to work in plants supporting the mobilization. But somehow rubber usage had to be curtailed sharply, for the natural rubber stockpile was inadequate for the wartime demand, and no one knew how long it would take for synthetic rubber production to meet national requirements. Rubber conservation was thus in order, and rubber manufacturers cooperated in a full-scale advertising campaign to reinforce the government's conservation orders. (In its ads, Goodrich reminded Americans of the company's prewar experience with synthetic rubber tires.) After much dispute, in 1942 the federal government finally instituted tire and gasoline rationing as twin weapons to enforce driver conservation of scarce rubber resources.[78]

Synthetic rubber proved difficult to adapt to tire manufacturing. The GR-S that the synthetic industry began producing in substantial volumes in 1943 was satisfactory for tire treads, but its uses in sidewalls were limited. Large truck tires still required substantial amounts of natural rubber throughout the war. Goodrich had discovered that its Ameripol proved more satisfactory in truck tires than GR-S and offered to share its knowledge with government officials. But supplies of methyl methacrylate were insufficient to justify converting synthetic rubber plants. From a manufacturing standpoint, two problems faced tire producers: adapting machinery to synthetic rubber and building tires from both types of rubber, which required more time. Goodrich found that the use of GR-S in tire building was no more than 85 percent efficient when compared with prewar manufacturing.[79]

By the middle of 1944, mobilization officials were aware that a crisis loomed. Rubber consumption was exceeding prewar levels as manufacturers tried to supply both the booming economy and the military's needs. Although Goodrich had a better record than other firms in meeting production requirements for truck tires, overall tire production was only at about 60 percent of demand, and there was no prospect for immediate improvement. As the army advanced deeper into Europe, officers warned that operations might halt for lack of tires and tire repair facilities. Although the government increased the labor supply in tire factories and worked to improve working conditions and solve wage disputes, at the end of 1944 the nation still faced a shortfall of 1.1 million truck and bus tires. It was at this point that Collyer was called to serve as special director of rubber programs for the War Production Board. In the spring of 1945, Collyer's team of executives from the rubber industry put together a program for ensuring the coordination of production facilities, raw materials, manpower requirements, and the needs of tire consumers. However, it was only the conclusion of the European war that ended the crisis.[80]

Footwear

Goodrich, which through its subsidiary Hood Rubber was one of the nation's thirteen manufacturers of rubber footwear, faced critical shortages in that line of business as well. Working through the RMA, the government restricted the styles of footwear manufactured, and companies agreed to refrain from promoting sales. The government relied on existing inventories to fill the gap between production volumes and essential civilian needs. By 1945, however, inventories were exhausted, and the manufacturers warned of a population of war workers suffering from wet feet. The end of the war that summer allowed the industry to begin focusing attention again on its traditional markets.[81]

The war years set the stage for what Goodrich would eventually become,

Goodrich Silvertown tires are pictured being installed on a B-29 bomber in 1945. (BFG Col. UAA)

decades after the war was over. In the short term the company did not change its product lines very much; it remained true to its traditional strategy of being a diversified rubber manufacturer. But the fact that it produced aircraft products during the war offered postwar opportunities to stay and invest in those businesses. In the short run, Goodrich became a more important chemical company as a result of the war.

DOMESTIC EXPANSION

During the war, Collyer and Goodrich resisted the temptation to greatly expand manufacturing capacity to fill war orders, deciding instead to improve the firm's existing facilities. Nevertheless, the wartime manufacturing boom combined with the emergency in truck tires led to a substantial expansion of Goodrich's manufacturing capacity in its traditional rubber businesses. The rubber industry as a whole invested private funds, and the government public funds, to enlarge capacity. Collyer and the other officers worried that the policy would "create a substantial post-war problem" of "excess production capacity." As the market for aircraft products grew, the plants at Hood Rubber and the tire plant at Los Angeles began manufacturing deicers and fuel cells. Although the growth in employment outside of Akron was less dramatic, by the end of the war the Los Angeles plant was employing about 1,800 and the Oaks, Pennsylvania, factory about 1,000 workers.[82]

Most noticeable in the expansion was the construction of two entirely new factories, which Collyer observed were "required to follow Government direction." This expansion followed the policy of dispersing rubber manufacturing away from Akron. Fearful that investments of its own capital might be wasted should the postwar rubber market return to 1930s levels, the company followed a policy of restraint in its own investments. With government encouragement, the company in 1943 began to construct a new $6 million tire manufacturing plant at Miami, Oklahoma, close to synthetic rubber plants and capable of producing large "off-the-road" tires and tubes, which were in such high demand. Then, in 1944, as the truck tire crisis mounted and Goodrich reported that it had no room for enlarging production volumes, the government funded a new facility at Tuscaloosa, Alabama. Construction was under way by early 1945, but when the war in Europe ended that spring, the government notified Goodrich that the project would cease. Management decided that having the new plant in the South would allow the company to "expand along constructive lines to balance our production" to satisfy a peacetime market. Newman telegraphed the War Production Board in July to request continuation of the Tuscaloosa plant, and soon thereafter the company was able to take over full responsibility for the new facility.[83]

INTERNATIONAL EXPANSION

The war had a substantial impact on Goodrich as a multinational firm. As the American flag followed American armed forces around the globe, American companies soon followed the expansion of American power. Goodrich was no exception, spurred by its chairman's continuing interest in international operations. When the United States declared war, the company shut its International B.F. Goodrich Company, transferred its assets to the parent firm, and assigned its responsibilities to an international office in Akron.[84]

That decision did not preclude taking advantage of international opportunities that arose as a result of the war. Especially important was Latin America, where Roosevelt's "Good Neighbor" policy was encouraging American investments for economic development. The company had been expanding its operations in the region before the war, working through joint ventures with local investors. In 1940 it announced construction of a tire plant in Chile, and it planned another plant in Cuba. During the war, to help meet the supply crisis, the government encouraged Goodrich and other American rubber manufacturers to invest in return for local cooperation in harvesting wild rubber. Moreover, the company had a long-standing relationship with a group of Spanish Basque families, the Euzkadi group, interested in rubber manufacturing investments in Latin America—a relationship that allowed company officers to make personal and institutional investments in new joint ventures. Thus, by the end of the war, Goodrich enjoyed a good position in rubber manufacturing in the region, with tire plants in Cuba, Colombia, Peru, and Mexico.[85]

European operations also resumed with allied military victories. With the successful invasion of France in 1944, the company discovered that Colombes-Goodrich, reportedly bombed and written off as a loss, was operational. Late that summer military authorities reported that the plant was capable of recapping about 250 tires a day and could easily start production of 400 truck tires per day, helping to relieve the crisis. The key personnel were present; all that was lacking was an adequate supply of rubber. By the summer of 1945, the plant was employing almost 2,500 people and making 500 tires and tubes daily as well as "a substantial quantity of industrial rubber goods."[86]

During the war, operations in Canada lagged somewhat because of the shortage of rubber. The Canadian government responded actively to the rubber supply crisis only after the Japanese attack on Pearl Harbor brought the United States into World War II. Then, cooperating with American officials, the Canadians built a synthetic rubber factory at Sarnia and organized Canadian Synthetic Rubber. By the end of the war, Canadian operations were at full capacity.[87]

THE BIRTH OF B.F. GOODRICH CHEMICAL

In retrospect, the birth of the B.F. Goodrich Chemical Company during World War II was the event that transformed the company. No executive forecast the changes that would spring from this endeavor. In fact, the modern-day chemical company was slow in evolving as a quasi-independent enterprise. Products that senior management expected to develop from its PVC patents never materialized as important sources of profit. On the other hand, sizable PVC markets not anticipated did materialize in peacetime. The military services' voracious demand for PVC, along with other synthetic products, did more than anything to push the development of B.F. Goodrich as a major chemical enterprise. The chemical company operated the company's synthetic rubber plants and took charge of a substantial wartime expansion of PVC capacity.

Before Collyer arrived, Goodrich had been hesitant to invest in the chemical business. At one time senior management considered eliminating rubber chemicals entirely from the firm's portfolio of products. By the 1930s only U.S. Rubber had made a clear decision to manufacture chemicals, through its Naugatuck Chemical Company; Goodyear also had considered leaving the field to other firms. In the end the deciding factor was profits; the chemical business earned higher returns than rubber manufacturing. Goodrich management eventually caught on to the promises of Semon's discoveries and began to explore ways of manufacturing PVC and of developing useful products from it.

Learning about PVC occurred slowly. Partial credit for demonstrating the practical nature of the material went to Waldo Semon. Facing resistance from senior executives to work further on the new plastic, Semon one day confronted vice president "Vic" Montenyhol. The scientist took a curtain impregnated with the material, draped it over the executive's in-basket, and poured a pitcher of water into the reservoir. Montenyhol was amazed that his paper suffered no damage and immediately suggested trying impregnated cloth on a forthcoming camping trip. Montenyhol took charge of the plastic's development. In August 1931 J. W. Schade, the director of research at Goodrich, suggested the trade name Koroseal for the firm's PVC. The company registered the name as a trademark, and Semon obtained the basic patent on behalf of the company on 10 October 1933.[88]

In the meantime, other firms were slowly entering the plastics field with vinyls. In 1927 Carbide and Carbon Chemicals Corporation (Union Carbide) began to produce polyvinyl resins and in 1928 distributed samples under the trade name Vinylite. In 1930 Dow introduced vinylidene chloride as Saran (which subsequently became a generic term). Also, Monsanto was indirectly involved in the field through its half ownership of Shawinigan Resins Corporation, a Canadian venture of Shawinigan Chemicals. Vinyl resins saw their first commercial application from Carbide and Carbon Chemicals in sound recordings, and in the 1930s uses slowly expanded. Shawinigan began selling vinyl resins as magnet wire enamel; after 1936 the preferred material for safety glass was polyvinyl butyral. By 1939 it was the most widely used such material and was made by Shawinigan, and by DuPont and Union Carbide under Shawinigan licenses.[89]

None of these materials had the plastic qualities of Goodrich's PVC. However, Goodrich still did not know how to manufacture PVC in commercial quantities or how to apply it to industrial and consumer uses. In 1934 the company assigned Koroseal development and sales to Howard Fritz, and he began with a one-man sales department.[90] A 1914 graduate in engineering from Ohio State University, he lettered in football and was captain of both the basketball and baseball teams. Fritz turned down a career as a professional athlete to earn a doctorate in chemical engineering instead. It was Fritz who first assigned Semon the task of learning how to bond rubber to metal, which led the chemist to discover how to turn the rigid PVC into a plastic material.[91] The most significant early products were small molded gaskets for shock absorbers. The company announced PVC commercially in Business Week on 12 January 1935, and interest from customers accelerated from there.

Before the company could itself make polyvinyl chloride, it purchased the material from Union Carbide and plasticized it in small batches at Plant 3.[92] Goodrich made small amounts of PVC from ethylene dichloride, but scientists believed the method held little commercial promise. Semon learned during a trip to Germany that acetylene and hydrogen chloride seemed the most promising raw materials for large-scale production.[93] The product had enough commercial potential that senior management allocated significant capital resources to it after 1935. In 1937 the company sold $750,000 worth of Koroseal, with a 30 percent profit, and projected an annual business of $2 million at the same profit; with costs cut in half, the market was projected to expand to $8 million with a 25 percent profit.[94] The company handed Archie Japs, a young chemical engineer, the task of exploring possible production techniques in the laboratory. After the usual trial and error, Japs learned that it was possible to manufacture vinyl chloride from acetylene and hydrogen chloride using a catalytic process. In 1938 the company built a small pilot facility at Plant 3 in south Akron, where Japs's team of engineers moved their project, working alongside other engineers under Harry Warner (who eventually rose to become the company's president), researching ways of manufacturing synthetic rubber.[95]

By 1939 the group had successfully demonstrated commercial techniques for manufacturing PVC. Before Collyer arrived as president, B.F. Goodrich's board of directors authorized the construction of a plant at Niagara Falls, New York. The new plant would permit the company to produce 50,000–150,000 tons of PVC per month or more, as the market justified. Niagara Falls proved a favorable location because of the proximity of Hooker Electrochemical, which could supply Goodrich with anhydrous hydrochloric acid at a good price.[96] When Japs turned down the chance to manage the new factory in favor of continuing work in research and development, the company posted another young engineer, Harry Warner. Markets for the new plastic were growing so rapidly that the company decided less than a year after Collyer's arrival to expand the Niagara Falls facility; the expansion cost an additional $125,000, with the anticipated annual profits of $152,000 quickly amortizing the expense. With a further investment of $300,000 in 1941, a plant was built in Akron capable of making coated fabrics and film for packaging.[97]

At this point the company was uncertain about the range of commercial uses for PVC. A young electrical engineer working for Anaconda Wire and Cable in New England, George Fowles, had already demonstrated the usefulness of PVC in insulation for electrical wire. Although Goodrich's efforts to win a patent for PVC insulation failed, applications in the chemical, steel, automobile, and electrical industries (supplied through fabricators) seemed quite promising.[98]

Goodrich executives also wanted to manufacture Koroseal items. But the final uses for PVC were unclear, and it was toward PVC applications that Japs turned his attention in the Akron laboratories. No one was even sure how to classify PVC; some copywriters called it a "synthetic elastic," while others used the term "plastic." By 1939 the invention already had a range of applications, from tank linings to textiles, and the firm was touting it as an especially desirable packaging material because it could be sealed with heat. Goodrich featured vinyl as a material of the future at its 1939 World's Fair exhibit. According to David Goodrich and John Collyer, "new markets are also being developed for its use in the home furnishings and apparel fields." By 1941 the company was promoting Koroseal clothing to its own employees.[99]

The Polyvinyl Chloride Boom

Soon Goodrich executives did not have to worry about finding PVC markets. The government promoted the development of the PVC industry during the war, and the navy, which had begun experimenting with PVC in shipboard cables in 1935, was especially interested. Goodrich became a significant producer of PVC during the war in part because navy procurement officers eventually pushed Goodrich to expand production well beyond the goals set by planning for civilian markets. By midsummer 1940, Goodrich was making three tons of polyvinyl chloride per day and shipping large quantities to General Electric for use in electrical insulation. Navy officers realized that the product was essential in the expansion of the fleet, where ship construction was slowed by a shortage of insulating materials.[100]

In 1941 the navy decided to expand production of PVC. At the time, Goodrich was manufacturing about three million pounds annually, and its only rival was Union Carbide, with a capacity of five million pounds. Although Goodrich felt that Union Carbide had violated Semon's PVC patent, Collyer preferred to compete with Union Carbide than contest the violation, and the executive committee had already authorized expenditures to build a new 750,000-pound PVC plant before the navy committed the firm to an even larger capacity. The navy needed fifteen million pounds per year, and it preferred the Goodrich compound because of its superior properties. The navy offered to fund the factory fully, to have it built as quickly as possible, and to guarantee purchases for five years. This demand in the growing defense emergency pushed Goodrich into quadrupling its capacity by building a plant near Louisville, Kentucky.[101]

The company proceeded with the Louisville venture without risk, financing the project itself with "tax amortization." The plant was to provide material for heat- and flame-resistant cable for use aboard ships. But construction did not proceed as quickly as hoped. Collyer reluctantly told the navy that the "very complex and hazardous" project would suffer delays. In the "best interests of National Defense, we must not lose it by explosion or fire through hasty construction or faulty control equipment." Although production did not begin until March 1942, during the war the Louisville plant produced about half of the synthetic resin used by the navy in shipboard cable.[102]

Strategy and Structure in Chemicals

In the meantime, the demand for PVC remained voracious, and Collyer and other executives realized that the company had entered a new and different line of business. Their response—forming the separate chemical company during the war—was innovative for the rubber industry. They understood that a previous generation of rubber executives had missed an important opportunity when Bakelite was developed in 1908 and did not want to leave the development of newer plastics to other firms. "Rubber is a plastic," Collyer observed, and "we no longer have any fixed ideas that any one commodity is the best for use in our many products." Collyer also wanted Goodrich, not Hycar, to assume the enormous new responsibilities in synthetic rubber manufacturing. The company formed a separate chemical division in 1942 to take charge of these areas, coordinate the personnel required for chemical manufacturing, and service customers' needs. In doing so, Collyer was developing a multidivisional structure pioneered two decades earlier by DuPont and General Motors, a structure proven appropriate for pursuing strategies in different lines of business.[103]

Collyer chose W. S. "Bill" Richardson to take charge of the chemical division. Rivals grumbled that Richardson had no substantial experience in the tire business, the firm's usual route for executive advancement. But at a time when winning acceptance of Goodrich PVC among customers seemed the most pressing problem, Richardson brought experience in industrial sales. Richardson enjoyed a reputation as an accessible, open man who valued scientific research highly as the basis for expanding into new markets and who fought "like a tiger" for the independence of the new chemical division. Although their personalities were opposite, Richardson and Collyer felt compatible working together, and Collyer trusted Richardson and delegated responsibility to him.[104]

The new chemical division was slow to emerge as a fully independent unit until it was physically moved to Cleveland in 1944, however. The division was logically divided into the two areas of synthetic rubber production and plastics. Organizing synthetic rubber production provided fewer problems than plastics. Plant design was coordinated by the government, so the chief problem was assigning the needed engineers. As the synthetic rubber factories came into production, first at Louisville toward the end of 1942, engineers were assigned and gained experience that they took to the newer plants as they were opened at Port Neches and Borger, Texas. When the rubber manufacturing arms of the company obtained GR-S, there were established organizations for handling it, with the new chemical operation personnel playing a minor role.

PVC was another matter. The company already had a Koroseal operation, and dividing chemicals from the parent firm was more difficult. One difference between PVC and rubber was that Union Carbide was the only company offering serious competition in PVC, and opportunities for profitable expansion seemed boundless. Because of the relative newness of the material, its uses remained to be explored, and there was little established tradition in fabricating final products. Before the company announced its chemical division, it was building another organization to follow leads into promising new markets. Most important were wire and cable insulation, products so important in the war effort. The new nature of the business meant that Goodrich needed not just a staff to manufacture PVC but one to market it as well.

In organizing the new chemical division for marketing PVC, a basic strategy evolved in the company: produce chemical products for fabrication by other Goodrich divisions or other firms. Initially, Goodrich built the PVC factory to supply a plastic materials section for its industrial products area, and the idea of focusing separately on industrial sales and consumer goods developed slowly during the war. Industrial products executives were interested in manufacturing products from PVC that traditionally had been made of rubber, such as shock absorber seals. For goods that were new, especially coated fabrics, Goodrich contracted with a New York–based firm called Comprehensive Fabrics to distribute Koroseal items. Thus, a plastics materials division headed by John R. Hoover at first included sales of finished products, under L. H. Chenoweth, and technical service and raw plastic distribution under S. L. Brous. By 1944 industrial sales, under Hoover, were separated under the chemical division, and consumer sales, now headed by Tomlinson, were left under industrial products.[105]

Hoover's responsibilities had already included building the necessary marketing organization for industrial sales. The company faced a basic problem in winning the acceptance of its PVC—its product was hard to fabricate into finished goods. Union Carbide already dominated the field, with a vinyl copolymer containing vinyl acetate to make it more workable, and fabricators preferred it to the Goodrich compound. Goodrich was selling PVC to General Electric for wire and cable insulation, but Union Carbide controlled the market otherwise. To overcome this disadvantage, Hoover hired George Fowles, the electrical engineer who had first demonstrated the application of vinyl polymer as electrical insulation in 1935. Fowles began work in early 1942, first learning more about PVC and what the navy, and soon the air corps, needed for their wire and cable. The chemical company and the navy realized that Goodrich's PVC enjoyed advantages over Union Carbide's product. Union Carbide's compound with vinyl acetate resulted in a plastic easier to fabricate into electrical insulation, but one whose waterproof qualities were inferior to Goodrich's.[106]

As Fowles learned about PVC and the Goodrich product's advantages, he realized that he would need to teach wire and cable manufacturers how to use it successfully. The extrusion of rubber for insulation took place at cold temperatures, whereas Goodrich's PVC had to be extruded while it was hot. Thus, the new chemical division had to employ a small, technically trained sales force to work closely with the companies that purchased its product. In the meantime, as an electrical engineer knowledgeable about the new plastic, Fowles worked with armed forces procurement officers to write the specifications for the new types of wire and cable.[107]

Even with Fowles's marketing efforts, fabricators resisted using Goodrich PVC during the war. Robert Kenney, a young chemist hired by the War Production Board to direct the allocation of vinyl resins, found that he "had to beat them over the head to use Goodrich materials." Much of the Goodrich resin thus went overseas to British manufacturers. Nevertheless, when the government sought to expand PVC capacity in 1944 by one million pounds a month, it turned to Goodrich over several other firms seeking the bid. This expansion placed Goodrich's capacity just slightly behind Union Carbide's.[108]

In the hurry to satisfy the needs of the war machine, Richardson and the other executives never lost sight of postwar possibilities and the desire to have PVC become a mainstay of the larger company. The firm shipped its plastic to England, where PVC was also in high demand. In October 1942, for instance, 40.3 percent of Goodrich PVC went abroad, 49 percent to the navy, and 2.5 percent to the army, with the remainder going to civilian uses.[109] Even in these conditions, the company kept its eventual industrial civilian markets in sight. Lawyers advised Richardson that his division should have a trade name other than Koroseal, which suggested finished products. Told one weekend in 1943 to decide on another name, Hoover and Fowles recommended Geon, Geo for earth and eon for long life.[110]

Independence from corporate headquarters seemed especially desirable if the chemical division was to foster the entrepreneurial spirit needed to tap new markets. Richardson and the other chemical executives considered the corporate offices to be an encumbering bureaucracy. They especially wanted to be free of the company's traditional industrial products approaches and be able to expand the new business as an industrial producer of plastic. It was with this in mind that, on 4 July 1944, plastics executives loaded their cars with files and moved into new quarters in Cleveland. Thomas Nantz, who eventually headed the chemical company, later recalled the move as one "to maintain our integrity" and to avoid "a co-mingling in anything," so that they could reach customers well beyond the parent company. Finally, in the spring of 1945, Collyer announced the formation of the B.F. Goodrich Chemical Company as a separate entity, "to coordinate its expanding interests in this field," tied to the Akron headquarters only in a financial sense. Later that year it acquired the trade name and goodwill of Hycar, which was then dissolved.[111]

Planning for the Postwar World of PVC

The move to Cleveland symbolized the entrepreneurial independence of the scientists, engineers, and salesmen working with PVC and their desire to follow opportunities in what seemed almost limitless markets. The PVC business held certain advantages over the postwar rubber business. As executives expressed, "there will be no plant conversion problem; no fight to rebuild a distribution system lost in the war; no question of product re-design and modernization." Consumer uses of the plastic had already been explored and were expanding, and industrial sales during the war seemed only the start of an enlarging market.[112]

Back in Akron, executives were planning to take advantage of the firm's leadership in PVC, a position gained before the war with Goodrich's introduction of Koroseal. The arrangement with Comprehensive Fabrics to reach directly into consumer markets gave the firm an edge "in establishing contacts." That advantage was reinforced during the war with the expansion of resin manufacturing facilities. Making items of Koroseal was similar to the traditional rubber fabricating business. E. F. Tomlinson, now charged with the Koroseal business, reported on inquiries at retail stores and forecast a large demand for coated fabrics and paper and plastic film, among a wide range of products. Profit opportunities seemed most promising. Executives planned an investment of $16 million into what eventually became a Koroseal manufacturing plant in Marietta, Ohio, that would result in an annual operating profit of $2.87 million before taxes.[113]

International expansion was also an important part of planning for the postwar world of petrochemicals. In 1944 the company was able to hire Robert Kenney away from the War Production Board to work on international sales. Having allocated PVC to overseas users for the War Production Board, Kenney knew of important market opportunities.[114] Aware that there was a small market for Geon in Mexico, Kenney quickly set up a distribution system there. Then he used his government connections to obtain permission to travel to England, where he and Frank Schoenfeld worked out an arrangement with the Distillers Company to form British Geon, a joint venture to manufacture PVC for the postwar European market.

PLANNING FOR POSTWAR MARKETS

While the new chemical company planned for plastics and petrochemicals as an important source of growth for the firm, during the war Goodrich also began to make projections about how a diversified rubber firm should function in peacetime. The first step involved the formation of a department for business research. J. Ward Keener, an Ohio Wesleyan University economics professor whom the company had hired as a consultant in 1937, left academic life to work as the company's sales research analyst from 1939 to 1942, when he began to build the new department. Keener eventually succeeded Collyer as president and chairman. Planning began to affect all departments in the company during 1943, as Collyer required managers to consider ways to expand markets in the postwar environment. Keener's appointment meant that the company was, as an institution, trying to focus more on marketing, an orientation that would gain even more influence when Keener became president in 1957.[115]

Planning for postwar markets involved enormous risk, for expert economists were sharply divided about the future prosperity of the nation. An influential group, closely connected to the federal government, feared that the stagnant conditions that had befallen the American economy in the 1930s would return once the enormous market for war goods disappeared. When Goodrich planners looked at marketing surveys of consumers, the results were divided. Some reports indicated that personal savings accumulated during the war would result in substantial purchases of consumer durable goods and housing; other reports showed that consumers' fear about their future financial well-being would lead again to stagnation. Goodrich executives knew that the demand for some rubber and plastic products would be strong after the war, but they also knew that rubber manufacturing facilities had been expanded across the nation to meet war demands. Overcapacity once again threatened to keep Goodrich prices and profits down once the immediate pent-up civilian demand was satisfied. The one certain bright spot was synthetic rubber: with America now a rubber producer, its manufacturers were less likely to operate at the mercy of a foreign cartel.[116]

Amidst this uncertainty, the company proceeded to push ahead on several fronts. Managers sought prudence, and in 1945 they announced a $35 million bond issue to retire more expensive debt and pay for new facilities. They expressed confidence that current earnings would easily handle the obligations. In a dramatic turnaround from the troubles of the 1930s depression years, and thanks in part to its war earnings, Goodrich was again considered a "blue-chip" firm. This standing was strengthened by Goodrich's reputation earned from its work with synthetic rubber and the panache of modernity suggested by PVC.[117]

Its research tradition also would play a role in Goodrich's postwar planning. Research efforts had continued during the war, albeit skewed to some extent by military requirements, providing Goodrich with a solid basis.[118] The pilot plant facilities in south Akron had served the firm—and the nation—well, but were now worn-out and outdated, so the company developed plans for new facilities. Having been granted War Production Board priorities, on 28 July 1945 the B.F. Goodrich Chemical Company announced construction of a $600,000 "semiproduction" facility at Avon Lake, Ohio. The company planned to install versatile equipment to refine production processes prior to full-scale manufacturing at other sites.[119]

Construction of a new corporate research facility to rival those recently opened at Goodyear and Firestone also began during the war. Executive officers, working with Howard Fritz (now head of research) and his research department managers, Waldo Semon and other scientists, had surveyed prospective sites and decided on land in Brecksville, a suburb between Cleveland and Akron. While Collyer was in Washington serving as special director of rubber programs, the company employed former congressman Dow W. Harter to try to use his influence with officials. Harter, pleading successfully that Goodrich research was important to the military services, obtained the necessary priorities to schedule design and construction. Ground was finally broken on 3 January 1946, soon after the war was over. [120]

The new research facility was to operate directly under corporate headquarters. Serving the entire company, it allowed Goodrich to take advantage of advances made during the war. The development of a successful tubeless tire was one important example of how the war stimulated a technical advance that would have important marketing implications in the postwar world. For generations, tire companies had sought to develop a successful tubeless tire, which potentially would provide a safer tire with longer life at lower cost. Research had lagged because of discouraging results, but early in the war the army pushed for a tubeless tire with self-sealing capabilities. Goodrich technicians succeeded in making such a tire for heavy vehicles with an "Air-Seal Beadlock." When Collyer walked through the tire division one day, Frank Herzheg told him of the project, and the president instructed his subordinates to keep him informed of developments. An added appeal to this invention was the fact that the new technology conserved rubber.[121]

THE END OF WORLD WAR II

By the end of the war, people at B.F. Goodrich had accomplished a great deal. Twelve thousand employees had served in the armed forces. In the meantime, payrolls had grown from 31,500 in 1940 to 50,000 in 1945, with about 10,000 people working in government-owned facilities. Subsidiary Hood Rubber added another 5,500 employees. Sales had risen, and the company had earned substantial profits. Nor was the conversion to peacetime manufacturing likely to pose significant hardships. Geon and other chemical products would go to the same industrial customers who had bought them in such large volumes during the war. Goodrich, like other American manufacturers, had insisted that the government finance any expansion that was not sure to be needed in peacetime, so there were few extraordinary capital costs that mobilizing for the war had required. Goodrich's textile facilities were making the cotton and rayon yarns its plants needed, and the development of synthetic rubber capacity had added to the company's vertical integration. Even the retail distribution system stayed fairly intact during the war, with 465 company stores serving dispersed markets.[122]

Financially, Goodrich had advanced its position in the rubber and plastics manufacturing industry. During the war government controls ensured that none of the large firms would earn extraordinary profits. Although Goodyear's and Firestone's sales had grown much more than the sales of Goodrich during the war (1939–45), owing to their participation in aircraft and other businesses outside of rubber manufacturing, Goodrich's profits as a percentage of sales were higher, at 3.3 percent. Goodrich's assets in 1945 had grown 57 percent over the assets of 1939, a growth rate higher than any other "big four" company, and only Firestone had outstripped Goodrich in the important measure of growth in return on assets. (Goodrich's rivals had operated government-owned factories—built to make military products such as airplanes—to a much greater extent, and their gross sales figures had grown much more than those of Goodrich.) The mobilization for the war had left Goodrich in a better competitive position than that of 1939.[123]

As a company with a superior reputation for national service, an experienced executive corps, and a brilliant tradition in scientific and technical development, Goodrich stood to profit in the postwar world. Collyer had given the company a sense of direction as well as a favorable image, features sorely lacking during the prewar years. The predictions of economists that the nation would return to stagnation and high rates of unemployment proved unfounded; after the war the domestic economy experienced a truly amazing growth. And there were no serious rivals abroad, as the United States stood as the only healthy economy in a world that had been so badly devastated by a war fought with industrial might.

6

Strategies for a Peacetime Economy: The Traditional Company, 1945–1959

The business environment that John Collyer, David Goodrich, and other top executives faced at the end of World War II was unique to the American experience. The country had survived the Great Depression, which had left the economy deeply wounded and the fortunes of B.F. Goodrich seriously eroded. Mobilization for the war had rescued the economy from the depression, and government purchases had allowed Goodrich to strengthen its position as a manufacturer. However, no one knew what would happen with the war's conclusion. Would the nation slip back into stagnation, with all that implied for a manufacturing firm dependent on prosperous consumers? Or had the invigorated economy unstuck the elevator of prosperity from its basement moorings? Had the upswing in the business cycle opened new horizons for enterprising manufacturing companies, including Goodrich?

It was only in hindsight that Collyer and other American leaders knew the answers to these questions. In fact, during the war John Collyer predicted that, after a brief postwar surge in the replacement tire market, sales for his company would be only "somewhat" higher than in 1940.[1] But soon he saw that Americans had entered a new automobile age—one in which increasing numbers of families would own more than one vehicle, driving on express highways through metropolitan areas and from coast to coast. In 1945 the United States still had systems of public transportation, and American businesses still relied on common carriers, especially the railroads, for much of their freight requirements. That flexible modes of conveyance like the private automobile and the motor truck would come to characterize American transportation was not something any investor could be certain of at the close of World War II.

For John Collyer the future must have seemed especially murky in 1945, filled with both hazards and opportunities. Only one prospect in the near future was certain: the market for replacement tires was temporarily enormous, and it would take American tire manufacturers operating at the 1939 production rate twenty-one months to fill the demand. Beyond that temporary period lay an uncertain future. As a tire producer, B.F. Goodrich stood to gain less from that market, or from any expansion of motor vehicle use, than did its main rivals, for it was more diversified into rubber and chemical products than the other "big four" companies. The mechanical rubber goods manufactured and distributed by Goodrich's industrial products division were relatively more important, yet their profitability was heavily dependent on the business cycle. Moreover, the company faced the highest manufacturing costs of any firm in the "big four" simply because a greater proportion of its manufacturing capacity was in Akron, where operating costs were the highest of any location in the rubber industry and where union turmoil disrupted production. An added hazard lay in public policy, as large tire manufacturers faced continuing antitrust threats from the Federal Trade Commission and the Department of Justice.

The principal opportunity Collyer saw was in chemicals. The growing uses for polyvinyl chloride and Goodrich's ability to manufacture high-quality resins at low cost were proven outcomes of wartime mobilization. Collyer had charted an independent course for the chemical company as a division under William Richardson, a structural decision that signaled a strategic move. The investments in chemical manufacturing, particularly the new polyvinyl chloride business, would allow Goodrich to reap benefits from a more general revolution in petrochemical manufacturing that was a direct outgrowth of national emergency, scientific research, engineering expertise, and government policy.

The prospects for rubber manufacturing were less enticing. The company's goal of developing a "chemical plantation" of synthetic rubber factories had been significant in meeting the allies' wartime emergency. But at the end of the war, the federal government controlled the synthetic rubber industry and B.F. Goodrich was little closer to backward integration into raw materials supplies than earlier. The existence of the synthetic rubber industry would offer a more stable price structure for raw materials, but even then public policy would influence the fortunes of Goodrich in ways not typical in the experience of rubber industry business leaders. For Collyer the raw materials supply issue meant personal involvement in postwar public service and an ongoing public relations campaign. As a result, Collyer was the best-known American rubber executive until his retirement.

Nor, with the return to peace, were labor relations likely to remain quiescent. Mobilization and international emergency had brought intervention by the federal government to ensure continuous production of vital war materials. With the emergency over, some American industrial unions, especially the United Automobile Workers and the United Rubber Workers, were proposing a political agenda of social democracy by which, among other considerations, managers like Collyer would have to share power with their workers over the direction of their corporations. Almost as soon as the Japanese surrendered,

Collyer faced employees militant in their desire to reshape socioeconomic relations at Goodrich. No one could be certain of the outcome of renewed labor-management struggles, especially because Democratic Party officeholders had close ties to the union movement.

Although the end of the war brought almost staggering uncertainties for Collyer, peacetime also meant continued opportunity to revitalize Goodrich as a rubber manufacturer. The company quickly moved to purchase the government-built tire plant at Miami, Oklahoma, operated by Goodrich. Similarly, although the factory at Tuscaloosa, Alabama, was not yet completed, buying and finishing the facility would give Goodrich a modern tire factory without the high operating costs of Akron. The Miami plant, built to make very large tires, improved the firm's ability to tap the large farm-equipment tire market (which was still not fully rubberized). In addition, the Tuscaloosa plant allowed the company's tire business at least to stay abreast of Goodyear and Firestone; both had moved more aggressively away from Akron's high costs and union turmoil than had Goodrich.

Collyer and other Goodrich executives decided not to stray from their company's tradition but to remain a diversified manufacturer with a strong base in scientific research and technical innovation. The company took advantage of experience gained during the war and the prospects for an enlarged peacetime aviation industry to cultivate the seeds of what would eventually grow into the modern BFGoodrich Aerospace. The company continued to support research by constructing the corporate research center at Brecksville, Ohio, where, Collyer hoped, new discoveries would give the company competitive advantages. In rubber goods the basic strategy was to be a technological leader in applying new materials to improve products. A few years later, with the economy prosperous and the company buoyed by profits from PVC, the executives considered diversifying into electronics and atomic energy but ultimately rejected these options.

CORPORATE BUSINESS STRATEGY

Under Collyer's leadership the general strategy of B.F. Goodrich was cautious, conservative, and traditional. Although the executives felt they had a clearer sense of direction, and that Goodrich's reputation had improved in financial circles, practices established long before Collyer's arrival continued to hold sway. With the end of the war, the company sought to complete the four-point long-range plan adopted in 1940, taking advantage of the investments fostered by the federal government. Executives wanted the firm to remain diversified in order to guard against cyclical instability in particular product lines, ensuring a steady rate of sales and income. The company also continued to retire long-term debt and to pay its stockholders a greater share of earnings than either Goodyear or Firestone. The firm invested substantial sums of capital but, with perhaps the exception of the chemical company and corporate research efforts, was not aggressive in doing so.

In following a general strategy of diversification, Goodrich during the 1940s and 1950s was to an extent similar to other large American manufacturing firms. Diversification was the investment trend as American capitalists enjoyed substantial profits and sought new, lucrative outlets for them. Goodyear, for instance, expanded into aircraft manufacturing and atomic energy, explored prefabricated housing markets, and pursued attractive opportunities in polymer science. In its particular approach to diversification, however, Goodrich was different; its executives eschewed aspirations "to become producers of aircraft, refrigerators, prefabricated homes, and any one of industrial activities that might be open to our company." The Goodrich strategy was instead "to engage only in those undertakings in which we have outstanding and unique qualifications."[2] This meant expanding in lines of business closely associated with rubber and polymer sciences to take advantage of new synthetic materials. This strategy was most apparent in the now independent chemical company and also in the traditional rubber fabricating areas.[3]

Although Goodrich was already diversified while other large American industrial firms were exploring new businesses, this did not protect the company from competition. Goodrich faced new rivalries not only in the important tire business, which consistently produced a majority of the company's sales, but in industrial products and footwear as well. Because so many of its product lines were in highly competitive fields, Goodrich had to make substantial investments simply to stay even. When combined with the desire to pay out a substantial portion of earnings as dividends and to reduce long-term debt, this situation meant that Goodrich was not especially aggressive in improving its position in any of its traditional product lines.

Nowhere was this policy more apparent than in the company's largest line of business, tires. By 1949 it was clear that the trends in both automobile production and in motor vehicle usage were upward both at home and abroad, and that all three tire markets—original equipment, replacement, and export—were expanding. As George Vaught explained to security analysts, tire markets were relatively easy to predict, and all indications were that the number of automobiles on the road was growing, and that Americans were increasing their use of automobiles. Aware of the industry's previous overexpansion in tires, Goodrich executives chose not to risk more investments than were necessary to maintain their share of the market. Aggressive investments, in their view, might contribute to industry overcapacity and encourage price wars that would damage Goodrich profits.[4]

Important prewar and wartime themes in the company's history remained. As Goodrich pursued its business strategy in the decade and a half after the end of the war, Collyer maintained himself as a visible American "captain of industry," promoting his company as a blue-chip industrial stock. The company earned handsome profits during some of these years, especially in its polyvinyl chloride business. Collyer's public posture served the company well when public policy issues threatened to harm its viability as an integrated manufacturer. Collyer received favorable notice in the press. Government au-

These giant rollers at the Miami, Oklahoma, tire plant kneaded and mixed raw rubber. (BFG Col. UAA)

thorities, concerned about rubber supply and tax policies, listened to his testimony.

Collyer was much more than a public figure during these years, however. He played an important role in the broader attempts of the rubber fabricators—and, more generally, American manufacturers—to reduce the influence of trade unions. Goodrich, under Collyer's direction, continued to focus its investments outside of Akron where too much equipment was "obsolete and inefficient," labor costs were higher, and union relations were worse than elsewhere. The board believed that investments away from Akron would produce dramatic annual savings, allowing the company rapidly to recoup its investment costs in modernization.[5]

Collyer commanded B.F. Goodrich in ways that his predecessors and successors did not. The "Sir John" nickname that employees used behind his back was appropriate, for Collyer listened to the views of other executives but never operated in a democratic manner either in the daily functions of the firm or with the board of directors. The operations council (and later a separate authorization council that approved capital expenditures) met weekly to evaluate policies; Collyer made the decisions.

Collyer's relationship with the board of directors was not much different. Collyer, presumably in consultation with David Goodrich before his retirement in 1950, decided to have a board unusual for a large American industrial firm of the time—one composed mostly of "outside" directors with no operational responsibilities. The membership of the board fluctuated from thirteen to fifteen members. Only the most senior operating executives sat on it with Collyer. Sidney Weinberg continued to play an important role on the board, taking more than a casual interest in the company outside of board meetings. The combined connections of Weinberg and David Goodrich allowed the company to attract a luminous group of executives to serve it, or to attract younger men thought to be ascending in the larger American corporate world. For instance, David Rockefeller, grandson of the founder of Standard Oil and himself an aspiring young banking executive, was delighted when he received an invitation to join the board, because of the company's blue-chip reputation and because of the influential men with whom he would associate.[6]

Even with a distinguished board of directors, Collyer remained firmly in control. Although the agenda of board meetings always included time for a general discussion of company business, there was no freewheeling criticism or searching evaluation of its course. Collyer planned each meeting carefully, and once the time allotted for each agenda item passed, he ended the matter. Deane Malott, the president of Cornell University who served on the board from 1951 to 1968, recalled the meetings as "boring."[7]

HIGH FINANCE: DEBT RETIREMENT AND STOCK SPLITS

The strategy of Collyer and the other Goodrich executives was largely successful throughout the 1950s. Most important, Goodrich's taxable income as a percentage of gross assets either led or was a close second among the large rubber manufacturers between 1945 and 1955. Its best year was in 1951, when its taxable income as a percentage of gross assets hit 23.8 percent. (By comparison, Goodyear had 14.5 percent; Firestone, 23.9 percent; and U.S. Rubber, 14.1 percent.) By another measure, the company's total tangible assets grew from $214 million in 1946 to $614 million in 1960, a rate of increase higher than that of U.S. Rubber and just slightly below Firestone; only the much larger Goodyear grew faster. In 1950 the company enjoyed its strongest earnings in a decade, $34.7 million, and dividends to stockholders were rising. Collyer liked to say that the firm's goal was profits—"we are not volume worshipers," was the expression the press quoted—and Goodrich's profits, due largely to spectacular earnings in polyvinyl chloride, were better than any of its larger competitors for the years 1946–54.[8] In a decision that fit a pattern among American businesses during the period, the company retired all of its preferred stock in 1952. By converting the preferred stock to bonds, Goodrich improved the value of its common stock, for the interest paid on the bonds was deductible under the tax laws as a business expense. "BFG already is looked upon in financial circles as being in exceptionally good financial condition," the *Akron Beacon Journal* reported. Retiring the preferred stock would "bolster this position."[9]

The same profits that allowed B.F. Goodrich to retire its long-term debts also allowed the company to split its stock twice, a three-for-one split on 10 January 1951 and a two-for-one split on 5 January 1955. The official reason given for the action was to lower share prices, allowing more people to own shares and thereby increase interest in Goodrich and its products. While the stock splits may have had that result, they also allowed the company's executives to profit personally from their firm's well-being. With the adoption of an employee stock option plan in 1949, they began to own a larger personal stake in the company's stock and enjoyed dividends commensurately. The profits to shareholders from the splits were substantial. Before the company announced its 1951 split, the share price of common stock on the New York Stock Exchange was 124¼. After the three-way split, each share at the end of December was trading at 61 ¾, for a total increase of $61 for each share owned at the start of the year. Similar share prices resulted after the 1955 split, with shares rising from 67½ to 86¾ at the end of the year, for a total increase of $106 for each share owned at the start of the year.[10]

By other measures, however, the company's long-term prospects were less favorable. Collyer's policy was to finance expansion from retained earnings, even in the face of stockholder criticism that dividends should be higher. Nevertheless, the company paid relatively handsome dividends. Of the "big four" firms only U.S. Rubber paid out a higher percentage of earnings as dividends during those years. Firestone invested in its gross plant more aggressively than any other large rubber manufacturer, and Goodyear's investments in its gross plants, although not as aggressive as those of Firestone as a percentage, were very substantial given its great size. After Collyer retired, the generation of executives who succeeded him were heard to criticize Collyer's reluctance to keep pace with competitors in the important area of manufacturing capacity and efficiency, especially in the cash-rich tire business.[11]

A NEW STRUCTURE FOR GOODRICH

In pursuing its strategy of diversification, Collyer sought help through a new structure. He turned to William S. Richardson, the successful chief of the chemical company, and brought him to the corporate office as president in 1954. Richardson, a believer in delegating authority, was key in redesigning the firm's management organization. Although during the 1930s Goodrich had briefly flirted with the decentralized divisional structure pioneered so successfully by DuPont and General Motors in the 1920s, the action by Collyer and Richardson, taken initially in 1953, changed the company permanently. The chemical company had become quasi-independent during the war. Now other parts of Goodrich were to achieve similar status. Goodrich followed the norm for large postwar American manufacturing firms by dividing its business into product lines and markets, and assigning executives to each separate "company" to operate with considerable autonomy, responsible for production and distribution, supported by staff officers in the central corporate offices. In this scheme, corporate headquarters set the firm's strategy, assigned responsibility for operations to the division officers, and evaluated their performance. Collyer remained as chairman and chief executive officer responsible for overall strategy, and Richardson moved to the corporate office as president, responsible for daily operations.[12]

The reorganization into decentralized divisions actually occurred in steps. As we have seen, the chemical company was a semiautonomous unit before the entire corporation was decentralized. By 1952 the Hood Rubber Company, B.F. Goodrich International, and B.F. Goodrich Canada were also operating as semiautonomous units that combined line and staff functions in their own organizations, each reporting to executive vice president Richardson. The larger portion of the firm, however, remained a centralized line and staff organization, in which some executives directed day-to-day operations supported by "staff" executives. Tires and industrial products operated under the direct supervision of Collyer, supported by the staff executives in the corporate office.[13] Senior vice president J. Ward Keener supervised employee relations, the legal department, the controller and treasurer, advertising, public relations, business research, and purchasing, all staff functions in support of the company.

The decentralized company had a very different organization. At first there were seven divisions, led by the tire and equipment division, each of which had a president, line officers responsible for daily operations, and a supporting staff organization. (Sometimes the firm referred to these entities as "division," and sometimes as "company.") The tire and equipment division was responsible for the firm's largest single sales area, including all tire production and distribution, including the hundreds of retail stores. The chemical company focused on plastic, rubber, and rubber chemicals and sought exclusively to sell its products to other manufacturers. The industrial products division had a variety of products, ranging from conveyor belts to semifinished Koroseal for raincoats, luggage, and the like. The footwear and flooring division was the old Hood Rubber Company facility at Watertown, Massachusetts, where the company concentrated its footwear production and added lines of vinyl and rubber tile in hopes of profitably supplying the booming construction industry. In 1954, the company acquired what became the sponge products division, an established producer of latex foam then nearing the peak of its market in upholstery and other consumer products. B.F. Goodrich Canada functioned as a miniature version of its parent in that nation, while the International B.F. Goodrich Company sought to sell all of the firm's products abroad (except those of the chemical company, which had its own international operation) as well as manage manufacturing investments in other nations. In 1956 the company added a separate aviation products division.[14] The corporate headquarters developed staff offices, which remained small under Collyer, to help the managers of the operating divisions achieve manufacturing and marketing goals. The most innovative of those offices was the statistical quality control group under Leonard Freeman. During the war the army had promoted the use of statistical techniques to provide precise, uniform, and impartial information by which to judge manufacturing techniques and the quality of products. Freeman had, when posted to the wartime ordnance plant, learned the army's methods, and in the postwar years his assignment was to introduce them to the entire company. His group of mechanical, chemical, and industrial engineers in Akron was available to help all parts of the company improve processes and products.[15]

Whatever form the company's organization took, Goodrich remained a manufacturing company under Collyer's leadership. Collyer did not attempt to take the company into service or transportation fields. Under his leadership Goodrich was conservative, true to its roots in manufacturing. As we have seen, James Tew tried to emphasize the importance of distribution for the success of the company. Other successful American firms were fostering a so-called "marketing conception" in which executives were to think of their company as one that manufactured products for sale. Under Collyer's leadership, ideas of having management leaders with a marketing orientation never matured. Goodrich retained its reputation as a firm in which advancement for executives was most likely to occur through manufacturing.

In practice the marketing conception required structural changes in the firm, and it meant promoting executives with a merchandising background in addition to those with a background in production. The development of decentralized divisions was intended, in part, to foster a marketing orientation. Personnel decisions did not always conform to a full-blown marketing strategy, however. Arthur Kelly, one of the firm's rising executives, is a good example. With experience in establishing a number of important production facilities, including the Lone Star ordnance plant, Kelly had joined the company in 1925 as a chemist. Kelly, however, had no sales or merchandising experience. A brilliant man with a keen analytical mind, Kelly was a penurious bachelor who delighted in playing bridge competitively (and was pleased to have responsibilities for Martha Mills, in whose southern climate he could play golf during the winter); he was production- not market-oriented. Collyer named Kelly as the first president of the tire and equipment division, the division generating the largest volume of sales. In contrast, Clyde O. DeLong, the first president of the industrial products division, had a merchandising background. Both Kelly and DeLong assembled a staff of experienced sales executives to assist them. Goodrich did not consciously develop a full-blown "marketing conception," however, until J. Ward Keener replaced Collyer as president.[16]

In creating and refining a multidivisional structure for Goodrich, Collyer and his colleagues had to face an inevitable tension between the central, or corporate, office and the division managers—a tension that was present in every company that decentralized authority. Under Collyer's leadership, the divisions received somewhat greater autonomy than would be the case under his successor, J. Ward Keener, and the staff functions of the corporate headquarters were not fully developed. There was one important exception: research. Collyer favored and funded a strong research effort at the corporate level focusing on basic scientific problems and searching for new products and even new businesses for Goodrich to enter.

CORPORATE RESEARCH: BRECKSVILLE

The development of a modern corporate research center became a centerpiece of both the company's new divisionalized structure and its business strategy for the postwar years. The company's research scientists and engineers had complained for years of their inadequate facilities. Scattered across several buildings that were part of the factory complex in Akron, the laboratories were unsuited for work that required delicate measuring instruments or dust-free conditions, the very sort of work that was occurring in the rapidly developing fields of organic chemistry and polymer science. Led by Howard Fritz, Goodrich research scientists began seriously agitating for new facilities in 1942. Manufacturing executives, led by Tim Graham, disputed the wisdom of expenditures for a new facility. Eventually, Fritz persuaded Collyer, who, cognizant of the firm's contributions to synthetic rubber and plastics, planned to trumpet those achievements as a focal point of the company's larger business strategy after the war. Moreover, both Goodyear and Firestone opened modern research laboratories in 1944 and 1945, respectively, and if Goodrich failed to do likewise, its image as a company "first in rubber" might well suffer.[17]

Thus, the decision to develop a central, corporate research facility came before the decision to restructure the company into divisions. During the war, Howard Fritz had consulted with the firm's 240 research scientists and engineers and developed a set of criteria for the new facility. They finally decided on a site in Brecksville, Ohio, midway between the corporate offices in Akron and the chemical company headquarters in Cleveland. The 260 acres seemed ideal, remote enough to avoid the vibrations that upset delicate instruments and spacious enough to allow expansion. For Fritz the suburban site was far enough from the company's factories to forestall production managers' asking for help with minor problems, yet close enough to allow regular consultation among managers and engineers companywide. In 1945 the company's officers used their Washington connections to obtain the necessary priority permits to begin construction, and the board of directors announced a bond issue to pay for the project (and other matters). Finally, on 3 January 1946 the company broke ground for its new research center.[18]

Both Goodrich scientists and executives were proud of their accomplishment and advertised it as the most modern research facility in the rubber industry. The facility exemplified senior management's strategy of achieving leadership in science and technology, if not in manufacturing or marketing. Collyer explained that the investment in the Brecksville research center was made in order to take advantage of growth opportunities in the rubber industry. Future growth would not be dependent only on crude rubber and cotton consumption but also on "consumption of American rubbers, Plastic materials and rayon." Goodrich scientists would thus be opening "even wider fields for the rubber industry and for B.F. Goodrich."[19] Initially, the research center had five buildings. There were air-conditioned laboratories and meeting rooms, a sizable technical library, and, eventually, virtually all of the equipment necessary for testing and developing company products (the facility had expanded to thirteen buildings by 1990). As the company evolved in these years, each division retained technical service personnel who worked on specific manufacturing problems while the scientists at the corporate level worked on longer-range product developments. Regular weekly meetings between divisional executives and research executives ensured coordination. Moreover, the firm's scientists and engineers thought of Fritz as an excellent manager.[20]

LABOR RELATIONS

As a manufacturer employing tens of thousands of workers—44,696 at the end of 1955—Goodrich was plagued by confrontational labor relations during Collyer's term. The labor problems were partly a result of tradition, a legacy of the Great Depression years. The way Goodrich measured and rewarded the performance of factory workers, the Bedaux system, was also conducive to conflict between employees and their supervisors. And labor problems occurred in part because of the animosity of senior executives toward the United Rubber Workers in particular and unions in general—to which some, particularly local, union leaders responded in kind. The result was a continuing round of acrimonious battles that almost annually threatened production. Major strikes occurred in 1949, 1952, 1956, and 1959.

John Collyer stayed aloof from contact with the United Rubber Workers, and it was clear to all employees concerned that he was unsympathetic to the very idea of collective bargaining. In that respect Collyer was typical of American industrialists for the period (Firestone and Goodyear also had poor labor relations); however, under his leadership acceptance of union contracts was probably more grudging than was typical. Some of the managers responsible for conducting the labor negotiations were skilled in building personal relationships with union leaders. However, Collyer chose executives to supervise labor relations who were personally hostile to the principle of collective bargaining. Ward Keener, who became vice president in charge of labor relations in 1947 and who was being groomed for even larger responsibilities, was so antagonistic toward the union that he viewed factory workers purely as union members, a class apart; in his view only the management were loyal Goodrich employees.[21]

Beyond personal antagonism, however, two special circumstances augmented discord. The Bedaux system created constant friction over the standards of measurement and therefore of reward. As factory managers pressed to improve production efficiencies they also pressed to renegotiate workers' performance standards. Especially troublesome were the plant at Miami and the large complex in Akron. When the Miami plant was first opened, management had developed Bedaux standards that were theoretical, not based on actual observations, and which proved expensive. When management tried to change the standards, however, the workers resisted. In the old Akron factory complex, it was the physical layout that produced the most woes. Moving materials through a factory, from raw materials storeroom to finished product, was an expensive matter in rubber fabrication, and engineers constantly sought ways to lower the costs. The Akron plant, with its multiple stories and different departments devoted to different rubber products, was ill-suited for improvement, however. When engineers tried to modernize it, they quickly encountered resistance from the union, whose leaders, suspicious of management's motives, tried to protect members' prerogatives.[22]

Trends in the postwar national economy also produced labor-management antagonism. During the war the government had successfully controlled inflationary pressures, but those measures collapsed in peacetime, and the American cost of living soon began to soar. As workers sought commensurate wage increases, management wanted to ensure steady production to satisfy civilian demand for rubber products, especially tires. The size of those increases, and whether or not price increases levied by B.F. Goodrich and other firms were justified, was a constant source of friction between labor and management.

Conflict with the United Rubber Workers, 1945–1959

Particularly troubling to B.F. Goodrich executives immediately after the war was the threat of losing control over foremen. Collyer and his colleagues viewed foremen as members of management, but foremen were dissatisfied with their relationship to senior management and voted to join the Foremen's Association of America, a union, and to seek their own contract. The company won a twenty-two day strike in September 1945. Five months later, in an election supervised by the National Labor Relations Board (which ruled that foremen were employees entitled to union representation), the majority of the foremen voted to have the FAA as their sole bargaining agent. The issue was not resolved until 1947 when Congress passed the Taft-Hartley Act, which declared foremen part of management and ineligible for union representation. In the meantime, the company responded to the complaints of the foremen by organizing its own Foremen's Club and ensuring that top officers met regularly with its members.[23]

Although the problem of foremen organizing a union was not unique to Goodrich, Goodrich was exceptional in having its office workers organized by the United Rubber Workers. In 1946 B.F. Goodrich clerical workers in Akron, looking for standard pay rates and pension benefits, voted to join Local 5 of the United Rubber Workers. This action very much upset John Collyer, who immediately sought ways to eliminate union representation. The company fought the representation with legal action, but the National Labor Relations Board was unsympathetic, and Goodrich was forced to go to federal court to fight its ruling. Finally, during the Korean War and at the height of anticommunist hysteria, the time seemed ripe to rid the offices of union representation. In 1952 Collyer told his lieutenants that he wanted the office workers' union broken—Goodrich thought it could win a court battle because some union officers had refused to sign the anticommunist affidavits required by the Taft-Hartley Act. The company informed the union that it refused to bargain with the clerical workers. The result was a strike and a shutdown of the Akron factory as members of Local 5 refused to cross picket lines.[24]

When picketing clerical workers blocked access to the firm's offices, Goodrich attorney Ray Jeter found a sympathetic local judge who issued an injunction. Union members still refused to allow access, and Jeter had a photographer record their actions, including the participation of George Bass, president of Local 5. The judge, angered by the union's behavior, ordered Bass jailed and his organization fined. Finally, both sides agreed to an election supervised by the National Labor Relations Board, and on 1 May 1952 the majority of the clerical workers voted against representation by Local 5.[25]

Aside from the conflict over office workers, Goodrich's conflict with the United Rubber Workers seems not to have been unusual. The URW took cues from the United Automobile Workers (UAW) headquartered in Detroit, and in 1946, when the UAW failed to win the right to participate in shaping the business strategy of General Motors, the issues between the URW and the rubber companies tended to revolve around "bread and butter" matters. The workers wanted improved wages in addition to cost of living increases, and generally won those improvements. Benefits also followed those won by the UAW from the automobile industry. Workers' pensions improved, and after 1956 the rubber workers joined their counterparts in the automobile industry in winning supplemental unemployment benefits (an especially important measure protecting men and women victimized by downturns in the business cycle from loss of their income). The rubber companies agreed in times of layoff to supplement government-provided unemployment benefits with private benefits up to 65 percent of the worker's income.[26]

Much conflict revolved around those matters, however. In 1946 the union won an industrywide contract, but B.F. Goodrich fought to have only company-wide bargaining, which became the practice after 1948. Nevertheless, the effect was the same. The URW policy committee decided on its goals for the next contract and selected a target company upon which it focused pressure to win its objectives. Typically, the union issued a strike deadline, with both sides resisting one another's positions until the last minute. When it won a contract from one of the "big four" firms, the union usually obtained a very similar contract from the competitors.

During this period Goodrich was not usually the union's target company. Since Goodrich had an excellent earnings record, the union preferred to target other firms. At least once, however, the union surprised the company, apparently because of union politics. George Bass, the head of the Goodrich local in Akron, had ambitions for the presidency of the international union and sought to take the lead by winning improved pension benefits for his members, thereby increasing his popularity among members of other local unions. In August 1949, without much warning, Local 5 struck the Akron plants for three weeks over Goodrich's refusal to add money to pension funds.

Goodrich, in effect, was a victim of union factionalism and Bass's ambitions, but finally had to agree to a pension package that cost it 10¢ per hour per employee.[27]

Relations between B.F. Goodrich and the URW worsened beginning in 1957 as the company, now suffering from a weakening financial position, began to resist accepting the same terms accepted by its competitors. Early that year Goodyear had granted concessions to the union with which Goodrich disagreed. After a fifteen-day walkout the two sides came to terms somewhat less generous than those of Goodyear. The situation worsened in 1959. Again, Goodyear agreed to terms with the union, which again Goodrich (and now Firestone and U.S. Rubber also) refused to accept. Publicists for B.F. Goodrich complained that accepting the union's demands would cost the equivalent of a dollar an hour per employee and would effectively end the firm's ability to compete in the rubber business. The strike against Goodrich lasted eight weeks until the company finally acceded to the contract terms first negotiated by Goodyear.[28]

The results of the union negotiations were good for Goodrich employees. The rubber workers were participating in the prosperity that generally characterized the American industrial economy of the 1940s and 1950s. In 1959 Goodrich workers earned an average wage of $2.70 per hour, with an additional 75¢ in benefits. They were significantly protected from the uncertainties of the business cycle and enjoyed retirement pensions to supplement federal social security payments in their old age. The wage and benefit costs to B.F. Goodrich were on a par with the company's large competitors. But later, as the company stiffened its resistance to the union, especially after Ward Keener assumed the presidency and as the profits began to wane, labor relationships would become very troubled.

RUBBER SUPPLY

All of the company's newly formed divisions would benefit from backward integration into raw materials supply, especially in rubber. Finding a way to accomplish this important goal, however, was a source of nagging frustration to the company. Having invested in the prospect of a "chemical plantation" before the war, government control of the synthetic rubber industry prevented Goodrich from immediately realizing the full potential of its efforts. Problems with synthetic rubber tires reported by consumers in 1946 did not help matters either, although Goodrich and other tire companies were soon able to make reliable passenger car tires with synthetic rubber that used rayon instead of cotton cords.[29]

Goodrich and the Government Rubber Policy

Goodrich's strategy regarding the development of a "chemical plantation" required that Collyer and the company remain engaged in the political process, advising on the nation's rubber supply policies. Collyer and other rubber executives vacillated in their recommendations. At first, confident in the ability to win consumer acceptance of synthetic rubber tires, they called for the government to abandon controls over natural rubber supplies. When consumer acceptance did not immediately transpire, Collyer led in developing industry arguments regarding natural rubber. Collyer asserted that the government needed to maintain a stockpile of natural rubber to guard against interruptions in its supply and the rapid swings in its price that had so wounded Goodrich during the early years of the Great Depression and before. Moreover, the government needed to release control over synthetic rubber operations, including both research and productive capacity, to private industry in order for Goodrich to take profitable advantage of its expertise in rubber chemistry. To these ends Collyer and the company devoted much energy to persuade public opinion and political leaders through continued use of "easel talks," testimony before congressional committees, pressure on executive branch committees, and Collyer's own public service on the Department of State's International Rubber Study Committee.[30]

Several factors impeded the ability of the rubber companies, including Goodrich, to achieve their objectives quickly. Public officials faced considerable pressure to use the synthetic rubber industry as a lever to advantage small business firms. Those pressures would have forced wrenching changes in the rubber manufacturing industry by preventing the large firms, including Goodrich, from taking full advantage of vertical integration. Officials also faced another rivalry. Petroleum companies wished to expand their capabilities in the promising postwar petrochemical business, while rubber fabricators wished to control their raw material supplies by assuming ownership of government synthetic rubber plants. Then, if those political problems were not difficult enough, international considerations intruded. The postwar years saw political instability in southeast Asia, where most of the rubber plantations were located. By 1948 the cold war was beginning, requiring government officials to rethink national defense considerations; and the outbreak of the Korean War in the summer of 1950 complicated matters still further.[31]

Goodrich and the other rubber companies achieved their basic objective with the Rubber Act of 1948. Congress affirmed a national policy of supporting "a free, competitive, synthetic rubber industry," while stipulating that the government maintain a minimal reserve capacity to be used in the event of another wartime emergency. Still, there was delay, as officials in the Truman administration responded to pressures to use the disposal of the government plants to force greater competition upon the rubber manufacturing industry. The outbreak of the Korean War brought a temporary supply crisis that caused further pause, and the final decision was not made until after the 1953 truce, with the government offering the synthetic rubber facilities for sale in 1955.[32]

Meanwhile, Collyer observed more rapid progress in the important area of patent policy. Goodrich and other private firms wanted to pursue promising lines of research in synthetic rubber without having to share patents with competitors, as wartime arrangements had required. As soon as the war ended,

Collyer and other industry executives began mounting pressure to abandon the emergency patent-sharing arrangement that had helped foster the rapid development of synthetic rubber capabilities. Goodrich scientists claimed that they had supplied "the lion's share" of patents to the pool during the war, noting that they had contributed two hundred patents. Officials in the executive branch, cautious because they believed that Standard Oil's control of patents before the war had retarded scientific advances, stalled. Finally, Congress gave Collyer and the other rubber executives what they wanted, though, and the patent-pooling arrangements were lifted between 1946 and 1952.[33]

Integrating Backward: The Liberian Plantation

In 1954, in light of the firm's experience with rubber supplies and prices, Collyer decided to launch a major investment in the company's first rubber plantation, located in Liberia, where Firestone was reaping substantial profits from its own plantation. This decision was a reversal of earlier policy. As late as 1948 Goodrich executives had expressed disdain for plantation investments because of synthetic rubber developments, but by 1950 Collyer realized that competitors were enjoying very high profits from investments in natural rubber production. Natural rubber, used in the sidewalls of tires and a variety of other products, still comprised about 40 percent of the nation's rubber supply. Company planners forecast a growth in the total tonnage of tree rubber required far in excess of what existing plantations around the world could supply. Moreover, the plantations in Malaya, Indochina, and Indonesia were in a part of the world experiencing considerable political instability—further threatening the future supply of the vital commodity—whereas the United States had strong ties to the Liberian government.[34]

Nevertheless, the decision to invest in Liberia was controversial among Goodrich officers. The company was a leader in rubber research, and its chemists believed that in the foreseeable future they would be able to synthesize a polymer that mimicked the qualities of natural rubber for its largest tire and industrial markets. Collyer, although appreciative of their arguments, was ultimately less sanguine. Crude rubber use was actually rising in the 1950s, and its price remained volatile. He knew from advising the federal government on rubber supply policy that foreign producers continually threatened to form a cartel and charge high prices. Goodrich had experimented with rubber trees in the Dominican Republic during the first years of World War II, and there was reason to believe that new tree varieties would dramatically increase productivity. Still, Collyer did not wish to force such an important decision on the board of directors; he introduced the proposal at one meeting and postponed the ultimate decision. In 1953 the board finally agreed to an investment of $3,548,000 to plant 10,000 acres, forming a wholly owned subsidiary, B.F. Goodrich Liberia.[35]

The company's first rubber plantation, about forty-five miles from the Liberian capital of Monrovia, began to take shape by the spring of 1955, with production scheduled to begin in 1963 as the first rubber trees matured. The company had a concession of 600,000 acres (of which only a small portion were ever planted). The small quantity initially produced would go into the manufacture of surgical gloves, with the balance being sold on the open market. The plantation was to produce high-grade rubber selling at premium prices on world markets, as well as to supply factories at home. "We expect," Richardson explained, "to have the lowest pound cost and the highest yield per acre of any plantation in the world." Eventually the plantation would have more than four thousand employees, administered by a cadre stationed in Liberia from Akron and guided by experienced managers hired away from competitors' Asian plantations. The company developed a settlement complete with a hospital, housing, and schools for expatriate children.[36]

Integrating Backward: Goodrich-Gulf and Synthetic Rubber

With the government decision to sell the synthetic rubber facilities it had financed during World War II, Goodrich could finally establish the "chemical plantation" its executives had envisioned almost two decades earlier. In 1952, while the Korean War was delaying the disposal of the plants, Goodrich formed a new partnership with the Gulf Oil Company, based in Pittsburgh. Gulf—one of the giant petroleum refiners and distributors that arose with the discovery of the Texas oil fields in the early twentieth century—and Goodrich already had a business relationship with tire distribution through Gulf service stations. Now that relationship extended into the important new petrochemical industry, with each of the industrial giants owning an equal share of the new joint venture and cooperating in research efforts. William I. Burt, who was serving Goodrich Chemical as vice president for manufacturing, became the first president of Goodrich-Gulf.[37]

For Goodrich the alliance with Gulf had an important advantage: it could be a supplier of rubber for the first time in the company's history, and do so by sharing the capital costs. When the government sold the plants at the end of 1955, Goodrich-Gulf acquired a production capacity far in excess of the rubber fabricator's own needs. Goodrich-Gulf purchased the plant at Port Neches, Texas, with a capacity of 90,000 long tons. In contrast, its larger competitors had less capacity proportionate to their rubber use: Goodyear purchased plants with 114,800 tons; Firestone with 129,600; and U.S. Rubber just 22,200 tons.[38] There was also a disadvantage, however. Synthetic rubber manufacturing proved to be as competitive as rubber manufacturing, and by 1959 the capacity of the synthetic rubber industry exceeded even optimistic projections of demand.[39]

STRATEGIES FOR THE TIRE BUSINESS

The tire business for the postwar period was a difficult one for all of the rubber manufacturers. The overexpansion of the industry before World War II pro-

This tire builder at the Miami, Oklahoma, plant is shown applying rubber and cord fabric around a collapsible drum. (BFG Col. UAA)

vided a cautionary note. When the war ended, Goodrich executives met with other manufacturers under the auspices of the Rubber Manufacturers' Association and asked that the government either scrap the additional plant capacity it had built during the war or allow some scheme of "arbitrary control of production in the public interest." This initiative failed, and throughout the period of Collyer's leadership, except for the brief postwar bulge in demand for replacement tires, the industry generally remained overexpanded, especially as Firestone aggressively sought to overtake Goodyear as the nation's number one producer.[40]

Nevertheless, there were substantial opportunities in the tire business for Goodrich. Although the tremendous growth in motor vehicle use that occurred could not have been predicted with certainty, the trend toward larger and larger markets for all segments—original equipment, replacement, and export—was certainly clear by 1950.[41] The company gained two new, modern manufacturing plants in Miami, Oklahoma, and Tuscaloosa, Alabama, from the government's expansion program of the war. Executives had learned advanced logistical procedures from the mobilization experience, and Goodrich along with the other large manufacturers learned to apply scientific manage-

At the Miami, Oklahoma, plant in 1947, one worker places a "green" tire in a curing mold, while another removes a cured tire. (BFG Col. UAA)

ment to tire distribution in the replacement market, thereby lowering their business costs. The development of synthetic rubber stabilized the price of raw materials, and the firm's first significant investments in a rubber plantation promised to offer profits never before realized by the company.

The company chose not to use its resources to enlarge its share of any part of the tire market, however. Chemicals remained a favored line of business when executives made hard choices. In general, the company's decision in tire manufacturing was to maintain a strong fourth position in the industry, where the company had stood for over a decade. The executives had a notion of what was Goodrich's "rightful" percentage of the market and were willing to fight (and even temporarily lose money) to obtain that share. Even so, cautious investment decisions meant that they were willing to lose modest amounts of market share. As the Korean War dragged into its second year and the nation continued its re-armament program, Goodrich executives conducted a study that projected the tire market for the next five years. They concluded that the company needed to expand its production facilities, particularly in truck tires. The "most economical means" of expansion was to enlarge capacity at existing plants—Miami, Los Angeles, Oaks, and Tuscaloosa—"though such in-plant expansions as were practical would still leave us short of capacity to some degree." The company decided, in effect, to cede some market share in tires to avoid large expenditures in new manufacturing capacity.[42]

Nevertheless, the investments in tire manufacturing capacity to meet the anticipated market expansion were substantial. Following the 1952 tire market projections, the directors agreed to expand the Oaks and Tuscaloosa plants to a daily capacity of 15,765 and 15,784 tires, respectively. The capital allocation of $12,843,500 was anticipated to produce annual sales of $20,938,500, with an after-tax income of $1,741,392.[43]

The company, in line with its competitors, did not report its results by division or product line. Collyer, however, could take some satisfaction in improved results in tires, even if those results lagged behind the overall performance of American manufacturing in the postwar years. Operating income as a percentage of sales was never spectacular, given the price competition, but did rise from 3.4 percent in 1940 to 4.2 percent in 1955. Income as a percentage of capital employed improved from the miserable results of the prewar years. In 1940 operating income as a percentage of capital employed stood at just 3.9 percent, but from 1951 through 1955 hovered just over 6 percent. In 1955 the tire and equipment division earned 37.4 percent of Goodrich's operating income.[44]

Tubeless Tires: Innovation and Business Failure

With little hope of expanding its share of the cash-rich tire market without enormous investments over an extended period of time, Collyer hoped that a major breakthrough in tire technology would improve the company's business. The development of the tubeless tire, led by Frank Herzegh, was an important innovation that Collyer sought to introduce to help improve the firm's position in the tire market. In fact, the 1952 investments were made in large part to expand tubeless tire manufacturing capacity. Because this innovation produced tires of superior safety and service, Goodrich expected its patents to bring in royalty payments from its larger competitors. In the end, however, the tire division was unable to take full advantage of the technology. Although Collyer was willing to risk a sizable investment in the innovation, the company was simply too small a tire manufacturer by the postwar years to capitalize fully on the tubeless tire.

Problems associated with inner tubes had plagued tire engineers for decades. The interaction of the tire carcass and the inflated inner tube generated friction and therefore heat, the main enemy of tire life and safety. Inner tubes were prone to failure and when hot could suddenly weaken and "blow out," with the tire collapsing suddenly and causing drivers to lose control. Since the advent of high-speed driving, to overcome these problems engineers at Goodrich and elsewhere had experimented with ways of eliminating inner tubes. Advances in material science showed promise, especially the development of the synthetic butyl rubber, which was more impervious to air than any other flexible product. In 1943 the Goodrich engineer Frank Herzegh began trying new ways of building a tire that army vehicles could run "flat" for short

Goodrich produced inner tubes at its Los Angeles plant. (BFG Col. UAA)

distances. He experimented with ways of applying a liner of butyl rubber to a tire carcass and eventually developed an airtight bead to prevent the loss of pressure around the wheel rim.[45]

Herzegh's efforts proved successful. At the end of 1946 the company applied for a patent (granted in 1952) for a tubeless tire with an impervious lining combined with sealing ribs on the beads; and in 1947 Goodrich introduced its new tubeless tire to the market. This event was significant, for it demonstrated executives' new willingness to collaborate to integrate marketing with manufacturing and development—and to take risks with substantial investments.

Because Goodrich's manufacturing capacity was limited, the company decided to introduce the innovation in one market at a time, and only in its most expensive and profitable line of replacement tires. (Tubeless tires had to be cured with water in the tire mold, unlike conventional tires, which could be removed while hot.) It was not yet known how to attach the butyl rubber reliably to the carcass without any threads from the tire fabric accidentally penetrating the liner and causing eventual leaks. Initially, the engineers solved this problem by including a puncture sealant in the tire. Meanwhile, development engineers learned that they needed to compound a butyl rubber that remained fully flexible in cold weather. Finally, the company developed a new skid-resistant tread design. The resulting "Life Saver Tube Less," although selling at a premium, was cheaper than competing brands that attempted to provide similar qualities.

The single-market approach assured both an adequate supply of tires and thorough field-testing before the company expanded investment. Goodrich chose the Cincinnati, Ohio, market first and introduced the tire to taxis and other fleet customers while preparing advertisements for wider public distribution. Collyer personally introduced the tubeless tire to General Motors executives at a luncheon meeting in Detroit on 8 April 1948; he was accompanied by Herzegh, who showed a film demonstrating the important development. Collyer knew that General Motors would not adopt the tire as long as there was only one supplier, but he looked forward to the day when new cars were equipped with tubeless tires and B.F. Goodrich could earn royalties on its patents from competitors.[46]

Meanwhile, Goodrich publicists were successfully bringing attention to the tubeless tire. They hoped to expand sales in the lucrative replacement tire market and, eventually, to persuade automobile manufacturers to place the tires on original equipment. *Life*, then one of the most widely circulated magazines in the nation, ran a feature article on Frank Herzegh early in 1949, little more than a year after the initial market introduction in Cincinnati and before the company was able to supply the tires in large volumes. Then the International Edition of *Reader's Digest* picked up the story in the spring of 1949. With so much publicity, Goodrich executives felt compelled to issue statements explaining the firm's inability to supply the product. Nevertheless, the product was so promising that beginning in 1949 the firm devoted almost all of its advertising budget to Goodrich's "Life Saver Tube Less Tire."[47]

Herzegh's success prompted no small consternation among the firm's larger competitors. Goodyear, the leader in both the original equipment and replacement tire markets, downplayed the importance of Herzegh's work. The company advised its dealers to tell customers that the Goodrich product was inadequately tested and unproven, and that they were well advised to purchase a proven product from Goodyear. "If and when the Tubeless principle is proven practical and economical Goodyear will have one," was Goodyear's defense.[48]

Although Goodyear executives tried publicly to downplay the Goodrich breakthrough, they, Firestone, and U.S. Rubber quickly sought to develop tubeless tires of their own—and to do so without resorting to the Goodrich patents. By 1953 all of the large tire manufacturers were distributing tubeless tires in every replacement tire market; what remained was persuading Detroit automobile manufacturers to place the tires on new cars. With every supplier able to manufacture tubeless tires in large volume, the 1955 models of passenger cars rode on tubeless tires.[49]

Goodrich, however, was unable to realize the full advantage of the innovation. Acceptance in the replacement tire market was slow until Detroit adopt-

In 1949 Frank Herzegh tested the puncture-sealing quality of Goodrich's tubeless tire for the press. (BFG Co.)

ed tubeless tires as original equipment. Moreover, as the smallest of the tire manufacturers, Goodrich was unable to introduce tubeless tires into the original equipment market without its larger rivals being equipped to do so also. Collyer hoped that the firm could profit from royalties from its patent. But when the rival manufacturers announced their tubeless tires, they were careful to state that they had avoided the Goodrich patents. Goodrich responded by filing suit in federal court against both Firestone and U.S. Rubber; the latter case went to trial, where Goodrich lost in district court and again in the appeals court. U.S. Rubber attorneys argued that tubeless tire development had a long history in all of the major tire firms, and that their client's innovation went beyond the Goodrich patents. The judges agreed that the Goodrich patents were not so tightly drawn as to require royalty payments, and Goodrich soon dropped the Firestone suit.[50] Goodrich's innovation was real, but its patents were poorly drawn.

In the final analysis, the entire episode proved a business disappointment. As the smallest of the "big four" tire manufacturers, Goodrich was unable to use Herzegh's breakthrough to gain a larger share of the tire market. With its huge sales volume, Goodyear had an advertising voice too powerful to overcome. Although there were some short-term gains in profits from the replacement market, the long-range goal of earning patent royalties proved a chimera. What Herzegh accomplished was important, finally, in terms of safety. Tubeless tires proved economical while saving uncounted lives.

Tire Manufacture and Distribution

Although Collyer directed substantial sums toward improving the tire business, Goodrich's strategy remained conservative. The company was saddled with an inefficient, multistoried factory in Akron, where Goodrich suffered from high labor costs and hostile union negotiations. Goodyear and Firestone, while maintaining substantial tire production facilities in Akron until the early 1980s, had moved a greater proportion of their tire production to more efficient locations, and Goodrich suffered in comparison. The trend toward rayon cords that began before the war accelerated, and the fabric operation at Martha Mills had to be converted accordingly. Then, after 1945, nylon began to replace rayon as a tire cord material. Although automation in tire making lagged behind automation in other manufacturing industries, engineers were learning how to make tire plants less dependent on manpower. Automated tire curing presses, for instance, appeared at the end of Collyer's tenure.[51]

The growth of Goodrich's tire business, when not compared with the other firms, was substantial. The capital employed by the tire and equipment division, rose from $131 million in 1945 to $277 million in 1947. The company made almost 51 million passenger car tires in 1940, which went up to over 97 million tires in 1955. Although Goodrich lost market share to its larger competitors slightly, with smaller manufacturers declining, the company's share of the total tire tonnage actually rose in the postwar period, going from 11.4 percent in 1946 to 14 percent in 1955.[52]

However, Goodrich still lagged behind other companies in its manufacturing capabilities. Although Collyer, with his background in manufacturing, was sympathetic to capital investments for the tire division and to considering particular improvements, all of the other executives were reluctant to put funds into the outmoded Akron factory. In general, Goodrich made substantial improvements in its tire manufacturing technologies in the 1940s and 1950s, but its principal competitors widened the gap in efficiency. Partly the problem was bad luck, and partly it was arrogance. Goodrich had supreme confidence in its engineers' ability to develop manufacturing tools. It relied on its own developers while competitors bought machinery from outside suppliers that was sometimes superior. The bad luck came with investments in the "iron horse" tire building machines located at Oaks and Tuscaloosa. These were large devices suitable for making a few sizes of tires efficiently. When automobile manufacturers began to expand the range of tire sizes in the 1950s, Goodrich plant managers were stuck with inflexible machinery.[53]

There were both important advances made and disappointments. After the war Collyer insisted on modernizing tire fabrication. Goodrich had the "best step by step passenger tire building machine in the industry" at the Oaks and

Tuscaloosa plants, as well as "very good" truck tire building machines at Miami.[54] Manufacturing executives were enthusiastic about the possibilities of applying electronic controls to automate tire manufacturing. Although it announced a major innovation in applying rubber to nylon thread for use in truck tires in 1955, Goodrich did not take a lead in any other area. Even statistical quality control was incompletely introduced. Freeman's quality control group received little cooperation from the plant manager at Tuscaloosa, the company's largest new tire plant. Freeman was forced to pull aside boxcars filled with tires after they had left the plant in order to run the statistical tests on the product, shipping tires back to the factory that did not meet the standards.[55] It was not surprising that Goodrich earned a reputation during this period of having significant shortfalls in its tire manufacturing ability.

Goodrich also suffered distribution problems. Although the company invested substantial sums to modernize distribution facilities—like the other large tire manufacturers building fewer but larger warehouses from which it sent tires to dealers—Goodrich's smaller size hindered its ability to sell tires in the profitable replacement market. Nor were its stores as profitable as those of Goodyear and Firestone. E. F. Tomlinson, who spent his career with Goodrich in sales and who led the tire division for a time, complained that senior management never viewed the stores as profit centers; rather, the executives simply saw them as outlets for tires. The result was that Goodrich investments in stores did not pay the same returns earned by Goodyear and Firestone stores.[56] In 1955, Goodrich spent 12.9 percent of its gross sales on advertising and administrative costs, whereas the larger Goodyear and Firestone spent 13 percent and 12.6 percent, respectively. Goodrich was too small to participate fully in the new (and expensive) television advertising medium, although the company did try to stake out a reputation there. Its advertising campaign was "First in Rubber," a play on the company's introduction of the first synthetic rubber tire in 1940 and its deserved reputation as the industry leader in new tire design technologies.[57]

THE POLITICS OF ANTITRUST

Government threats to apply the antitrust laws against the "big four" tire companies posed substantial hazards to B.F. Goodrich. The independent tire dealers, led by an aggressive ex-tire dealer named George Burger, were the principal thorn in the side of the tire manufacturers. Small tire dealers complained that their wholesale cost for tires too often was higher than the retail prices charged by large competitors. There were two main areas of concern: the executive branch and the Federal Trade Commission, both with powers to act. The domination of tire markets by the four firms had long aroused suspicions about anticompetitive behavior, and in the administration of Harry S. Truman, attorney general Tom C. Clark responded by launching antitrust suits in several industries, including tires in 1947. In general, wartime mobilization had augmented the domination of the American industrial economy by large manufacturing firms like Goodrich, and Clark was responding to fears that large firms were gouging consumers and preventing small businesses from prospering.

The 1947 suit accused Goodrich and nine other companies of fixing their prices for tires and inner tubes, as well as collusion on other matters such as warranty terms. The industry's response was one of outrage. E. J. Thomas, Goodyear president, said the suit "seems utterly preposterous." While the cost of living had risen since 1939, tire prices had actually declined.[58] Government lawyers, Goodrich publicists told employees, seemed to be responding to political pressures to hold down inflation. "Those associated with the tire business in the United States hardly need any reassurance as to the fierce competition traditional in this industry." The executives vowed to fight the charge against their company's integrity even though the fight would distract from the firm's main purpose. This proved to be a "stale" case, however, for the violations alleged had occurred a decade earlier, and Goodrich and other companies had already changed their distribution strategies in response to those complaints.[59]

After a year of legal maneuvering, B.F. Goodrich and the other firms named in the suit, still refusing to admit any guilt, settled for fines totaling $50,000.[60] More serious were the actions of the Federal Trade Commission, which sought to enforce the confusing provisions of the Robinson-Patman Act of 1936. In response to retailers who were being squeezed out of business by more efficient distributors—so-called "chain stores"—Congress had included a poorly defined "quantity limit rule." After the war, Walter G. Ploeser, a Republican representative from Missouri and chairman of the Small Business Committee, continued to pressure the FTC to eliminate "the monopoly problems in the industry."[61] Although the issue was controversial among the commission's staff members, the FTC in a landmark decision eventually found Goodrich and the other large tire manufacturers guilty of violating the "quantity limit rule" by having given large-scale distributors overly large discounts on volume tire purchases. The FTC sought to protect small retailers by sharply curtailing the discounts Goodrich and the other firms could provide.[62]

Knowing that the established distribution system reflected economic realities, rubber industry executives did not allow the matter to rest. They hired White & Case, a prestigious New York law firm that often represented Goodrich, to appeal the FTC ruling in the federal courts. The companies hired independent experts who demonstrated that the costs of supplying large volumes of tires to distributors were substantially below the costs of supplying tires to small retailers. Finally, in 1955 the matter was resolved in favor of the tire manufacturers. Never again did the Federal Trade Commission invoke a quantity limit rule on American industry.[63]

STRATEGIES FOR INDUSTRIAL PRODUCTS

Although the tire business brought the largest share of the company's operating income in the decade after the war, with chemical earnings coming in a close second, industrial products remained important in the company's ac-

In 1951 Goodrich promoted a new use for its vinyl garden hose. (BFG Col. UAA)

counts. (In 1955, the operating income from the tire division was $16,850,000; from the chemical company, $14,614,000; and from the industrial products division, $4,525,000.) Industrial products, when it became a separate division in 1953, included the variety of rubber goods that the company had been producing for decades. Goodrich also entered the vinyl fabricating business more seriously than before the war under its trade name Koroseal.

There were several attractive features about this area of the company's business. Perhaps most important to a management concerned with diversification was that the product lines sold on a somewhat different business cycle, lending a measure of stability to the firm's consolidated results.[64] Moreover, some of the division's products enjoyed profitable replacement markets, especially those with industrial applications such as conveyor or transmission belts, and these goods provided the core of the division's business.[65] Goodrich also had opportunities as a technological leader in the rubber industry, for new synthetic materials provided exciting opportunities to make an impact on the market. Finally, Goodrich and other manufacturers of "flat belts" collaborated on prices between 1949 and 1957, raising prices by 67 percent (the largest price increases came during the Korean War, when demand for industrial belts was high).[66]

The business of industrial products, however, also had drawbacks. The manufacture of industrial rubber goods was much less concentrated than was tire making, which meant that the competitive situation was potentially volatile. In some lines, especially molded goods, smaller competitors could beat Goodrich in the market; the only advantage Goodrich had, with its high overhead and labor costs, was its ability to advance and control the compounding of rubber.[67] In 1959, the company was forced to close its plant in Cadillac, Michigan, where small suppliers were selling goods to the automobile industry at prices below Goodrich's costs; the plant had lost money for three years before the managers decided to close it, costing 396 employees their jobs.[68]

Distribution also posed problems. The most profitable aftermarket sales were in the hands of over one hundred independent, regional distributors, and each of the large rubber companies aggressively competed to secure able local representatives. To keep those sales outlets, Goodrich executives believed they had to be able to supply a full line of industrial rubber goods. "The need to satisfy *all* of the distributor's requirements in order to keep out competition made it difficult for a manufacturer to discontinue products that were losing money," Edgar Perry recalled from his experience in the field. Making competition more severe, Firestone, the most aggressive of the large rubber manufacturers in the postwar period, was determined to increase its industrial rubber sales. Firestone business planners sought a volume in 1949 five times the total volume of 1939, the last depression year. And Goodyear had an established lead in virtually every area of the industrial products business, with a sizable sales force and a strong commitment to manufacturing excellence.[69]

When the war ended in 1945, most of the rubber goods in Goodrich's product line were little different than they had been in the latter part of the nineteenth century, save for advances in natural rubber compounding. Soon after the war that situation began to change dramatically, as advances in polymer science transformed the field. The variety of new synthetic rubbers and fibers offered engineers an opportunity to redesign the division's most important products. Flat belts and v-belts, in particular, were improved; they were made lighter, more flexible, long-lasting, and resistant to temperature extremes and harsh chemicals. B.F. Goodrich was the industry leader in this regard. It was the first firm, for instance, to make a transmission belt with an all-rayon fabric. (Ironically, technological advances in material science occurred largely within a division whose engineers benefited little from the fact that some of the new materials were coming from their own firm's research expenditures.) When flame-resistant belts were sought because of the high risks of mine fires, engineers were able to develop various conveyor belts made of Koroseal.[70] The company proudly announced the introduction of the first "moving sidewalk" of conveyor belts in the coliseum in Houston, Texas.[71]

Although Goodrich exhibited some innovation in these products, the industrial products division was, in general, a very traditional part of the business. Conveyor belts were the most profitable industrial product, and executives ensured that their development and manufacture received capital, even if that meant shortchanging another product line. The belt plant that opened in 1950 "housed equipment and machines unlike anything else in the industry."[72] The industrial products business was organized along functional and not product lines. Executives tended to guard their interests against the men in charge of the larger tire division; as one former head of the division recalled, they were "a tight little group."[73]

Collyer was concerned that the company maintain its share of the business, especially as a leader in conveyor belts. The substantial opportunities in the field did not go unnoticed, although, as was the case in tires, Goodrich was not especially aggressive in trying to enlarge its market share. Rubber products other than tires consumed less than 30 percent of the rubber used by American manufacturers in 1946, but thereafter climbed, in 1955 reaching just under 40 percent. The number of motor vehicles on the road grew during the decade after the war, but as engineers devised new uses for rubber compounds between 1945 and 1955 the growth of rubber markets outside of tires was also larger.[74] The board of directors authorized capital expenditures accordingly, deciding to raze old facilities and build a new building in Akron for $4,475,000.[75]

Plastic Products

Next to expanding the chemical company's business, the manufacture of plastic products seemed the most promising investment for B.F. Goodrich. Senior executives were genuinely excited about the prospects that finished and semifinished polyvinyl chloride products presented to the company. Collyer believed that the plastic industry was a growth industry more promising than traditional rubber products. James J. Newman observed in 1946 that vinyl markets had increased tenfold since 1940, and the company expected even more spectacular growth in peacetime. The war had interrupted the move initiated in 1940 to boost investments in plastic manufacturing, but as soon as the war ended the company began to head in that direction. In the meantime, even during the war the industrial products sales force had emphasized the prospects of Koroseal. Collyer formed a plastic products division in 1946, shortly after executives began looking for a suitable site so that they could more seriously enter the fabrication field. While the chemical company stayed with industrial sales, its parent firm would purchase vinyl resins and manufacture them into semifinished or finished goods.[76]

In the immediate aftermath of the war, Goodrich executives expressed no little excitement about their decision to enter plastic fabrication. They anticipated a 12 percent return on the investment in the field. This seemed an excellent opportunity for a strategy of vertical integration. The continuation of the prewar contract with Comprehensive Fabrics meant that Goodrich could use outlets in the consumer products markets not yet available to competitors. The executives first searched for a government surplus factory to house the operation, but when they failed to find a suitable plant at a favorable price Goodrich decided to build a new plastic factory at Marietta, Ohio. The new facility, when completed in 1947, was designed for expansion. New products, such as vinyl hose, announced in 1946, were being developed. Meanwhile, Collyer expressed his belief that research scientists in Brecksville would develop new uses for vinyl, while the chemical company supplied the fabricating plant in Marietta through internal sales.[77]

Nor did the company rest on its initial postwar investment. From capital of $6,548,000 employed in the plastic products division in 1947, the company added funds to come to a total of $9,919,000 in 1955. (Investments in Koroseal floor material went to the footwear and flooring division in Watertown, Massachusetts.) In 1954 it commenced manufacturing rigid PVC pipe and sheet materials. A new factory in Salem, Indiana, opened to make vinyl extrusions.[78]

The dream of having a new venture comparable to the success of the chemical company proved unfounded, however. Although plastic sales generally outpaced rubber sales, and Goodrich's net sales showed growth, competition was keen. Both Firestone and Goodyear had entered the plastics field with their own products, as did oil producers and other chemical companies; smaller firms, too, rushed to enter what they projected as a lucrative field. Nor were Goodrich chemical executives enamored with the idea of forward integration into plastics products lest their non-Goodrich customers be alienated. After earning impressive profits in 1947 and 1948, Goodrich's plastic products division became a disappointment, with operating income falling as low as 0.4 percent of capital employed in 1954. Moreover, the anticipated advantage of using Comprehensive Fabrics to gain a market position did not materialize. Senior executives began to question the arrangement with Comprehensive Fabrics seriously in 1952, and they terminated the distribution contract in 1954 in hopes of resuscitating the business.[79]

Shoe Products

In addition to the company's own brand of shoes, produced in Watertown, Massachusetts, B.F. Goodrich continued to manufacture shoe products for sale to the shoe manufacturing and repair industry. With the factory located in Clarksville, Tennessee, the results were similar to those of the other rubber products. In 1955 the 468 employees in Clarksville made heels, soles, and other products that sold for $7,296,000—about a 20 percent share of the market. But the investment of $5,783,000 of capital produced disappointing results. The after-tax operating income that year was a 2.9 percent return on the capital invested.[80] This was not an area of the company's operations that gained a substantial amount of attention from senior executives. Nor were its profits sufficient to aid the company's image among investors. However, Goodrich was willing to continue the business, for shoe products kept it in competition with Goodyear, which also had a product line for shoe manufacturers, and allowed Goodrich to continue to claim that it offered a full line of rubber products.

Results in Industrial Products

The industrial products businesses were not, overall, especially profitable. In 1955 the division had 13.5 percent of the firm's capital and 12.6 percent of its sales. Goodrich earned 10 percent of its operating income that year from industrial products. The after-tax operating income as a percentage of capital employed fluctuated from a high of 11 percent in 1947 to a low of 3.6 percent in 1954; in 1955 the figure stood at 6.9 percent.

AEROSPACE DEVELOPMENTS

Aerospace evolved more clearly as a focus of Goodrich's corporate strategy in the postwar years. This focus fit with the strategy of diversification and with the desire to capitalize on the firm's traditional research abilities and its image as a technological leader among major rubber (and now chemical) manufacturers. Although aviation had received an enormous boost during the war and was a growing postwar industry, Goodrich's aeronautical business grew slowly at first. It was housed as the aeronautical products manufacturing division within the functional corporate organization and was not even separated when the company decentralized in 1953 but was instead placed in the tire division. When aerospace became an independent division in 1956, it remained a small part of the larger firm.[81]

Immediately after the war the company decided to diversify into manufacturing aircraft wheels and brakes. As far back as 1937, Goodrich announced what proved to be an important innovation in aircraft brakes. The expander-tube brake system was a series of brake shoes that pressed smoothly and evenly against a brake drum when an expansion tube, made of neoprene, in the center of the mechanism was swollen under hydraulic pressure. This technology went on every four-engine bomber produced during World War II. Goodrich, however, did not manufacture the system, instead sending the rubber parts to

Jackson, Michigan, where Hayes Industries machined the brakes and aircraft wheels.

In 1946 Goodrich decided to enter this business itself. Hayes's price quotations for original equipment installations were high, damaging Goodrich's ability to sell its tires and expander tubes for civilian aircraft. To protect its significant share of the aircraft tire market, Goodrich decided to offer airframe manufacturers an entire assembly; especially attractive was the fact that the tires, brakes, and wheels were consumable and provided potentially lucrative replacement sales. (Aircraft wheels must be made of lightweight materials and are subject to cracks from the stress of landings.) Goodrich executives were confident that they could lower manufacturing costs and offer competitive prices for wheel and brake assemblies. At the end of the war, Goodrich was able to purchase the business from Hayes Industries for $225,000. Then, in 1946 the company leased a government-owned factory in Troy, Ohio, built during the war to manufacture army gliders, relocating the business there.[82]

The investment in Troy provided a small but steady business for the company. Goodyear and Bendix were the principal competitors. Goodrich stayed with the expander tube technology for some time, even after Goodyear had introduced disk brakes, because disk brakes posed substantial problems of overheating. Goodrich placed its brakes on some of the air force B-52 bombers. Generally, however, the expander-tube drum brake systems were unsatisfactory for the large aircraft then being designed, and Goodrich risked losing the business to its competitors. In 1953 the company began a spirited effort to develop its own disk brake system. Heat buildup was still a great problem; but Goodrich engineers solved this with an innovative liquid-cooled brake system, which reduced temperatures from as high as 2,000°F to 500°F.[83]

The tubeless tire was another important safety innovation for the airplane industry. As aircraft grew larger, the heat buildup in tires proved just as critical as it did in brakes: overheated tires could explode and ruin the airplane's landing gear, causing disaster. Once Goodrich technicians learned how to manufacture a tubeless tire, however, they could also place fusible plugs in aircraft wheels. These plugs would melt upon overheating and release the air pressure before an explosion could occur.[84]

Goodrich also remained in the deicer business during the 1940s and 1950s, even as the technology was changing. The principal problem with the early deicers was their size, which changed the air foil of wings. Engineers refined the inflatable deicer by working with new rubber materials and adhesives to utilize higher air pressures, and with smaller tubes that provided a better air foil. These high-pressure deicers went on the Lockheed Constellation and other successful postwar civilian aircraft until, on newer designs begun in 1956, airframe manufacturers learned how to transfer engine heat into the wings to prevent ice formations from developing. Inflatable deicers, however, remained the least expensive solution and continued to be used on smaller aircraft in the general aviation market. Goodrich engineers also pioneered placing rubber-coated heating elements that pilots could activate to remove ice formations in propellers, engine cowls, and tail sections.[85]

Goodrich's aerospace business did not have a separate identity until 1956, when Collyer formed the aviation products division. The reorganization reflected a desire to give more focused attention to the company's profitable businesses in the field and to have the structure in place to enter new businesses. Until this time responsibility for aeronautical products was held by other areas in the company, which management handled in Goodrich's traditional ways. Such was the case with sales. James Pedler still ran sales and still relied on his personal friendships in the industry. Because rival Goodyear focused on Douglas, then the largest builder of civilian transport aircraft, Goodrich concentrated its efforts on winning contracts from Boeing. Pedler's friendships in the field allowed Goodrich to supply some brakes for Douglas's DC-3 and DC-4 models, although the company lost the business for the DC-6, DC-7, and DC-8 aircraft. But by 1958 the company was selling disk brakes to Boeing for the 707, a commercially successful jetliner.[86]

About half of the company's aerospace sales in these years were to the military services, and the separate division was formed in part to facilitate defense sales. Collyer, who disliked having to work with government procurement regulations, was persuaded to try to tap the market by the continuing high levels of defense expenditures. Rocketry seemed especially promising. Some forecasters believed that rocket propulsion would supplant, if not replace, existing aircraft in the foreseeable future, and the guided missile market was clearly emerging. Whatever the case, the Defense Department was investing in rocketry, and Goodrich held no position in the field. Yet the company's expertise in polymer chemistry offered possibilities for profitably entering the solid rocket propulsion business, so the board decided to buy the 160-acre site of the West Coast Loading Corporation at Fontana, California, and begin testing rocket fuels. Soon the company contracted to supply fuel for a new air-to-air missile, the "Sidewinder." This was the only profitable sale, however; in 1962, with the operation losing money, Goodrich retreated from the business (although the chemical company continued to sell the materials for manufacturing propellants to other firms).[87]

THE FOOTWEAR AND FLOORING DIVISION

By the war's end B.F. Goodrich had concentrated its manufacturing of footwear and flooring materials in the old Hood Rubber plants at Watertown, Massachusetts. In 1953 Hood Rubber became the footwear and flooring division of B.F. Goodrich. The Hood brand name, however, was still used along with the Goodrich brand and the "P.F." line of canvas sport and athletic shoes. Like so many other areas of the company's business, footwear and flooring offered opportunities to introduce new materials, and the company invested in its plant to try to take advantage of them.

Footwear manufacturing continued, as in the 1930s, to be subject to foreign competition. Manufacturing of waterproof rubber boots and canvas athletic shoes was a complex process requiring detailed coordination. Labor costs were significant despite efforts to introduce machinery at every possible step. Foreign competitors enjoyed two advantages: lower costs in raw materials (federal price supports for cotton raised domestic prices) and in wages. Goodrich tried to hold down its manufacturing costs by introducing teamwork and machinery wherever possible and by using women, then generally paid less than men, in the tasks of inspecting and boxing the finished products.[88]

There was still reason to believe that the business would remain profitable. Political pressures for tariff protection for the American shoe industry remained substantial. Also, Koroseal and other synthetic polymers offered prospects for new products. Designers expected that the addition of pigments would introduce colorful products to the marketplace. In the early 1950s the sales of canvas and casual shoes were running ahead of projections, and of manufacturing capacity, necessitating the use of second and even third shifts in Watertown. Goodrich enjoyed a slightly better than 20 percent share of both the waterproof and canvas footwear business in the United States in 1954 and 1955, not an insubstantial source of revenue.[89]

Floor tile was a more promising business. As soon as the war ended, Goodrich technicians began exploring ways of making vinyl tile. Koroseal enjoyed better color retention and durability than the rubber tile then in use. By 1953 the company was satisfied that it had a good product, and, as demand for vinyl tile grew, executives decided to build a new plant at Watertown to make Koroseal vinyl tile. In 1953 and 1954 the company invested more than $1.2 million to manufacture Koroseal flooring. At the end of 1955 the division's sales seemed clearly on the rise, and the return on capital employed was over 5 percent. In 1957 president Bill Richardson observed that the division's sales were likely to increase because of population growth and the boom in construction and home remodeling.[90]

BRANCHING INTO SPONGE RUBBER

In being a diversified rubber manufacturer, Goodrich was missing a significant product line, sponge rubber. The company had made some efforts to produce sponge rubber but could not compete successfully against firms that used an innovative manufacturing technology known as the Talalay process—especially the Sponge Rubber Products Company of Shelton, Connecticut, which employed the patent owners, Anselm and Leon Talalay. The Talalay brothers learned how to make sponge rubber from synthetic rubber latex, and the use of sponge rubber grew enormously after the war in products such as automobile upholstery and mattresses. In 1955 latex foam products consumed 15.4 percent of the nontire rubber in the country, second only to mechanical goods.[91]

Although there was some disagreement among senior executives, Collyer and the board of directors determined to acquire the Sponge Rubber Products

Company. They arranged through Goldman, Sachs to purchase the company's assets and business in 1954 for 180,000 shares of stock. Henceforth, the operation continued as the sponge rubber products division of B.F. Goodrich, with the existing management intact. The move gave Goodrich about a 30 percent share of the sponge rubber business in the United States.[92]

The merger proved unfortunate for Goodrich. Sponge rubber was a product whose expansion was peaking just about the time Goodrich made its acquisition. In 1955 the company spent $3.5 million to expand capacity. Worse, executives from Akron were appalled at the condition of the plant in Shelton, Connecticut, and were determined to improve it. Additional capital expenditures (a total of $4,731,000 in 1955) to bring the factory up to corporate standards added overhead costs that reduced profits. Soon the sponge division was a problem child for Goodrich. In retrospect, Collyer may have agreed to a purchase price that was too high; in any event, some executives recalled that the company, which had operated successfully as a medium-sized business employing abut 2,600 people, began to fail in the face of management controls imposed from Akron.[93]

INTERNATIONAL EXPANSION

The growth of American interests and power that the war brought provided opportunities for B.F. Goodrich and other American industrial firms to enlarge their overseas business. David Goodrich took a personal interest in his company's expansion as a multinational firm and encouraged Collyer to develop business relationships to that end. Forecasters saw foreign markets for rubber products growing even faster than domestic American markets, especially as Latin American and Asian nations industrialized and motor vehicle use rose across the globe.[94]

By the 1930s Goodrich had become a minor player on the international scene compared to its larger American rivals, and it would remain so after the war. After 1945, the senior executives saw the most profitable opportunities occurring through joint ventures in which the company could use its technical knowledge to leverage its capital investments. While the chemical company embarked on its own multinational program, the rubber company, which had expanded into Latin America during the war, looked forward to reestablishing its position in Asia and on the European continent after the war. After World War II B.F. Goodrich Canada was the only significant wholly owned international subsidiary.

The basic approach was set in 1945 through the Colombes-Goodrich experience. The French factory had suffered serious war damage from British air force bombers (Goodrich men had helped the crews locate the factory). The board of directors wanted to reestablish the firm's presence in France but recognized the advantages of associating with French investors, both in response to political considerations of French nationalism and to help leverage capital. New investments were required to repair the wartime damage and to expand the factory to meet the forecasted growing rubber market in France. The result was an association with the "Giros group" and the formation of Pneumatiques et Caoutchouc Manufacturé Kleber-Colombes. B.F. Goodrich owned one-fourth of the firm's shares; both firms agreed to share technical knowledge and patents. However, the Goodrich board insisted that the B.F. Goodrich name be dropped from products, and that advertising simply observe that Kleber-Colombes was "associated with B.F. Goodrich."[95]

The only change from the Kleber-Colombes agreement in the multinational policy that evolved concerned the use of the Goodrich brand name, which other joint ventures did use. Thus in 1946, even before the U.S. government launched its European recovery program known as the Marshall Plan, the company established a joint venture in the Netherlands for tires and rubber products using the brand name Goodrich-Vredestein. The venture planned to export goods after it supplied local Dutch markets.[96] Similarly, in 1949 the company reopened its old relationship with Yokohama Rubber. The Japanese had even set aside the dividends owed Goodrich during the war. With Goodrich using those funds to own a 35 percent share of the new joint venture (up from a prewar share of 9 or 10 percent), the goal was both to supply tires and rubber goods to the Japanese market and to export Goodrich brands to other Asian and South American markets.[97]

Collyer believed that the largest foreign opportunities lay in Latin America, where, he thought, industrialization would occur using motor vehicle, not railroad, transportation. He took a personal interest in multinational expansion in Latin America. Again the expansion occurred through joint ventures: Goodrich continued its alliance in much of the region with the Euzkadi group, a closely knit interest of Basque and Spanish investors. In Cuba and Colombia, Goodrich was the majority stockholder; elsewhere the Euzkadi investments were larger. The policy seemed particularly appropriate in a region where personal relationships were so important in local politics. Thus, the company had expanded into Colombia during the war and looked forward to ventures in Brazil and elsewhere. Board member David Rockefeller, whose interests were primarily in developing international banking opportunities, was sometimes a useful emissary in this regard.[98]

The management of these international activities changed with the reorganization of the company into divisions in 1953. Before the reorganization the company had an International B.F. Goodrich Company, which was reestablished at the conclusion of the war as a division. By 1955 the International B.F. Goodrich Company had affiliates in ten nations, and it was also arranging for tire manufacturing in Peru and the Philippines. The "dollar investment and stock participation" was "relatively nominal," and income came from dividends and technical fees.[99] International B.F. Goodrich was responsible for overseeing the joint ventures (outside of the chemical company) and for sales of products manufactured in the United States for sales abroad.

The multinational activities of B.F. Goodrich proved to be highly competitive and something of a disappointment. American rivals were aggressively investing in foreign ventures. By 1952 Goodyear had tire factories in thirteen nations, Firestone in ten, General in seven, and U.S. Rubber in three; Dunlop was also making tires at ten sites outside Britain. After the Korean War ended in 1953, Goodyear and Firestone continued an aggressive overseas expansion. When Firestone entered the French market in 1959, in competition with Kleber-Colombes, it was that firm's eighteenth tire factory outside the United States.[100] As Goodyear and Firestone were well established abroad with wholly owned subsidiaries, they reaped full overseas profits, and overall Goodrich lost its position as a result. Goodyear and Firestone were better able to weather price competition in the domestic American market than was Goodrich because of their foreign earnings.[101] Although the returns on Goodrich's more limited investments were favorable—better for every division except the chemical company—during Collyer's postwar presidency, they were too small in total to have much impact on the company's consolidated balance sheet.[102]

B.F. GOODRICH CANADA LIMITED

After the war Goodrich continued to play a modest role in the Canadian rubber industry. The goal was to have the Canadian subsidiary operate as a miniature version of the U.S. company, manufacturing tires as well as a wide range of other rubber products. (The Canadian subsidiary did not manufacture products for airplanes, however.) The company's market position in Canada was generally below that in the United States, with the passenger tire market share just under 10 percent in 1954 and 1955. The canvas and rubber footwear market share was well below that in the United States, however, and in 1956 the company decided to end footwear production in Canada. Otherwise, the Canadian company, supplying work to about 1,800 people in 1955, was expanding in comparison to its prewar years. Collyer invested substantial sums in Canada, and sales rose. Profits were commensurate with the returns in other parts of B.F. Goodrich, except for the chemical company.[103]

MANAGEMENT SUCCESSION

As Collyer neared retirement age, the company he had headed for nearly twenty years, and that had once seemed so healthy, was in trouble. Rubber industry profits in general were disappointing, even in the face of mounting sales volumes. The profit-oriented strategy that Collyer had publicized proved to be a failure after 1955 as the company's profits dipped below those of its rivals. Increased competition in the polyvinyl chloride business was responsible for the most significant drop, but the firm was in trouble in other areas as well. Sponge rubber had proven a disappointment as Goodrich had made its investment in that product line at the peak of its market penetration and had paid a heavy price for it. There was no modern tire factory favorably located to sell tires in the original equipment market, and tire sales in the more profitable replacement market were disappointing. Worse yet, Firestone was determined to increase its share of the tire market, and Goodyear was equally determined to maintain its dominant share. Overcapacity in tires had long plagued the tire industry, and in 1959 a price war that Goodrich could ill afford loomed.[104]

Collyer was nearing retirement, and management succession was a serious problem. Collyer had brought William Richardson from the highly successful chemical company to serve as president of B.F. Goodrich in 1954. Arthur Kelly and J. Ward Keener were looked upon as possible successors, but doubts about each executive persisted. Kelly had no marketing experience; Keener, known as a brilliant analyst, had performed several important roles as a senior executive but had no operating experience. Neither man's personality was electrifying, although close associates saw Keener as an affable person, while they saw Kelly as dour.

Collyer privately worried that he had been too demanding as head of the company. When Collyer chose Richardson as president, he did not know that Richardson suffered from high blood pressure. In the summer of 1957 Richardson told Collyer that he had to step down in July or as soon as possible thereafter because, in Collyer's words, "tension associated with his work is bad for his health." In the past, Collyer thought, too many executives had taken early retirement—Jim Tew in the 1930s and, after the war, Tim Graham, George Vaught, and Jim Newman. Arthur Kelly and Jack Hoover, a successful leader in the chemical company, were also considering early retirement.[105]

Richardson's unexpected retirement forced Collyer to select his successor sooner than would otherwise have been the case. He chose J. Ward Keener, who had joined the company to head a business research department and whom Collyer had groomed for leadership. As he prepared to hand over the presidency, Collyer outlined some steps for the company to achieve higher earnings. They included ensuring that selling prices were adequate, improving customer service, bettering manufacturing processes, and developing "more new 'profitable products' and more profit opportunities." Collyer advised that each division undergo a review. In the area of tires in particular, he wanted to know if B.F. Goodrich's actions were contributing to price instability and if the tire division had plans for achieving its goals. Collyer urged the company to assign responsibility for store operation to one executive to help improve replacement tire sales. He recognized that there were serious shortcomings in the tire division, including problems of quality control and of coordinating the work of development engineers with sales and manufacturing. Collyer advised Keener to assume personal responsibility for good relationships with original equipment purchasers by visiting General Motors, Ford, and International Harvester and trying to procure sales at Chrysler, which had heretofore shut out Goodrich.[106]

The chemical company had proven spectacularly successful in the decade after World War II, as measured by return on investment. Now, however, it was in trouble, and Collyer observed that some difficult business decisions had to be made. As the parent company slipped in its traditional rubber markets, chemical company profits became all the more important. Like it or not, Goodrich was becoming more and more a chemical manufacturer, benefiting from the expertise of its scientists as well as from the generally spectacular growth of petrochemicals.

7

Building the Goodrich Chemical
Company, 1945–1971

The chemical company that Goodrich created as a semiautonomous operation was remarkably successful after the war. Three themes stand out in the
history of the B.F. Goodrich chemical company from 1945 to 1972, when it
lost some of its independence from the parent corporation. First, the chemical
company was the most profitable part of Goodrich. Success with polyvinyl
chloride, both in developing products and in perfecting low-cost manufacturing techniques, accounted for the remarkable profits. Second, it enjoyed able
leadership and maintained a high morale among its employees, who believed
that they were successfully participating in a worldwide burst of creativity in
the material sciences, a creativity that followed the success with synthetic rubber during the war. Third, although flourishing in research, production, and
sales of PVC, Goodrich was never able to expand its business into other chemical products in ways that reproduced its favorable results with PVC.

The success of Goodrich Chemical was not uniform, however. As Goodrich's
rubber manufacturing businesses showed signs of faltering after the first bloom
of postwar prosperity faded, troubles besetting the chemical company after
1955 meant that senior management could no longer demonstrate the best financial performance among the large rubber manufacturers. Goodrich's reputation as a blue-chip manufacturing company in the immediate postwar period
was due largely to its success with polyvinyl chloride, the full dimensions of
which were kept a closely guarded secret. As late as 1950 there were five producers of PVC in the United States, a small group of companies in which
Goodrich played a leading role in developing new compounds of the plastic
that enlarged its markets. These few firms maintained an umbrella over PVC
prices, ensuring that they remained at high levels. The result was that, for a
time, Goodrich enjoyed enormous profits in the postwar years. That came to
an end, however, as new competitors entered the PVC field. In 1952 PVC

prices began to weaken, and Goodrich's profits fell accordingly. Sharp declines in vinyl prices during 1955 and 1956 were especially harmful.[1]

The chemical company's operations were an essential part of the strategy of the parent company under John Collyer and David Goodrich. B.F. Goodrich emphasized technological and research leadership to boost earnings without having to make the enormous long-term investments that enlarging market share in tires or industrial products would have required. The chemical company was a central, and successful, feature of this strategy, supported by research efforts both within its own ranks and at the corporate level. In the immediate postwar years Richardson continued to head the chemical company, and Frank Schoenfeld took over corporate research operations when Howard Fritz retired. Both men enthusiastically drove Goodrich to participate in the fruits of new advances in polymer chemistry. Although research, especially in such important products as the tubeless tire, remained central to the rubber company's strategy, it was in the chemical field where research was inextricably linked to the firm's success.

The firm's chemists and chemical engineers were participating in a dramatic development in polymer science—the knowledge of hydrocarbon molecules arranged in long chains—that transformed the world's chemical industry during the middle decades of the twentieth century. The synthetic rubber effort of World War II, and to a lesser extent Goodrich's success with polyvinyl chloride, had demonstrated that the chemical industry could successfully develop new materials and new processes of manufacturing. The result was an explosion of new opportunities in material science as new plastics and rubbers enjoyed new applications and replaced older metallic materials in machinery of all kinds. Goodrich seized opportunities in PVC, grasped for them less successfully in new synthetic rubbers, and explored possibilities in products ranging from artificial leather to pesticides. During this period the chemical company was far more than a PVC company. It sold rubber chemicals, Hycar acrylonitrile synthetic rubbers, and developed new plastics, including Abson, its brand of acrylonitrile-butadiene-styrene engineered plastics, and Estane, a new thermoplastic polyurethane.

The chemical company, like the rest of Goodrich, entered the postwar years as a manufacturing organization devoted to diversity in its product lines. One arm of the company employed engineers who operated synthetic rubber manufacturing plants for the federal government. Another arm continued to make rubber chemicals for its own factories and for sale to other rubber companies. Still another branch was in the nitrile rubber business that Goodrich took over from the wartime venture with Phillips Petroleum, under the brand name Hycar. The most significant part of the company made and sold PVC under the Geon brand name. Both Hycar and Geon had separate sales forces, and as the company developed new product lines, they were placed under their own "general chemicals" organization. A staff organization coordinated operations in functional manufacturing and sales organizations, and ensured collaboration between operating executives and product development researchers.

The chemical company was committed to industrial sales. It flirted with developing products for sale to individual consumers but never fully did so. Goodrich Chemical treated other Goodrich divisions like any other customer, refusing to give them favorable treatment lest external customers become alienated. (This policy produced considerable tension and resentment among industrial products executives.) Salesmen first received training in product development research. After 1960 the company coordinated the work of general chemical, Hycar, and Geon salesmen to meet customers' need for polymer materials, including "polyblends" of PVC and nitrile rubber. Only after 1972, however, were the sales forces of the chemical company fully integrated.[2]

After more than twenty-five years of growth and change, Goodrich Chemical was not fundamentally different from what it had been at the end of World War II. At the end of the war, it had made synthetic rubber at government-owned plants and was a major producer of PVC. A decade later the government was selling its rubber plants to private industry, and Goodrich formed a joint venture with the Gulf Oil Company to purchase and operate a substantial portion of the nation's synthetic rubber capacity. In 1969 the synthetic rubber operation went back to exclusive Goodrich ownership. In the meantime, although new products were developed, PVC was the firm's largest business.

GOODRICH CHEMICAL'S EXECUTIVE LEADERSHIP

For about three decades the chemical company remained semiautonomous, a situation that changed only after O. Pendleton Thomas became the chairman of Goodrich in 1972. The chemical company continued to enjoy a favorable position in the larger structure of Goodrich while Collyer remained in charge. Collyer and William Richardson had a personal and trusting business relationship, and Richardson was able to assemble a talented group of young chemists and chemical engineers around him. In fact, the relative youth of the men in charge of the chemical company attracted some notice. It also gave the members of the company a special esprit de corps, a sense of comradery through building a successful business in a burgeoning industry, that Richardson and his successors deliberately fostered through social activities. Twenty years after the war, the chemical company had a personnel turnover rate one-half the industry average.[3]

Richardson emphasized marketing experience in selecting the leadership of the chemical company, and his successors were able men. When Richardson left for the presidency of B.F. Goodrich in Akron, John Hoover, the vice president for marketing, replaced him as president of the chemical company. Born in 1903, Hoover graduated from Harvard University in 1924 with a degree in chemistry and joined B.F. Goodrich in 1925. After a few years working in the laboratory, Hoover went into chemical sales. Chosen as president of B.F. Goodrich Chemical in 1951, Hoover emphasized the combination of marketing and research as the driving force in the company. The booming growth of

TABLE 7.1
1974 Sales for B.F. Goodrich Chemical Co.
(in millions)

	Pounds	Dollars
Latex and Specialty Chemicals		
Latex	110	40.0
Specialty chemicals	6	10.5
Polymer chemicals	47	32.0
VCM (external sales)	157	14.7
Elastomers		
SBR	376	89.0
CB	167	38.0
SN	92	29.0
Hycar	68	39.0
Epcar	21	5.5
Hydrin	2.3	2.1
Polyvinyl Chloride		
Flexible PVC, wire, & cable	292	80.9
Rigid extrusion (bldg. prod.)	145	47.2
Rigid PVC pipe & fittings	318	68.4
Coating & related resins	145	43.4
Total PVC	900	239.9
CPVC	13.7	8.0
Estane	9.4	11.9
Abson	23.7	10.8

Source: "Plants and Facilities Fact Sheet, 1975," Geon Co. historical files.

the chemical industry in the postwar years excited Hoover, and he wanted Goodrich to be part of that excitement. "The true 'growth' companies," he told a group of Ohio State University students in 1956, "are the ones who have specialized in creative obsolescence." Hoover also emphasized that "the company must be oriented toward marketing." Men who worked with him later recalled Hoover as a warm-hearted, friendly man who knew how to maintain good relationships with customers and, especially, to encourage and reward good performance from those men who reported to him. Along with George Fowles, Hoover also worked outside the company to promote the widespread use of plastics in all kinds of manufactured goods. In 1955 Hoover's peers recognized his exceptional leadership abilities when they elected him chairman of the board of directors of the Manufacturing Chemists' Association, the leading trade group in the industry (in which Goodrich was a relatively small chemical firm). In 1960 Hoover decided to retire early at the age of fifty-seven.[4]

Harry Warner, a brilliant chemical engineer who had taken charge of the first PVC plant in 1940, replaced Hoover in 1960. Warner, who was just forty-three years old, had enjoyed a "somewhat meteoric rise" to the top of the firm, in the estimation of a chemical industry news magazine. After graduating from Ohio State University in 1939 with a degree in chemical engineering, Warner gained wide experience in PVC production, including a tour in England to oversee the construction and operation of a vinyl resin plant. Groomed for a leadership role by Richardson and Hoover, Warner became the chemical company's vice president for development at the age of thirty-seven and, four years later, in 1958, became vice president for marketing. Like Hoover, Warner was an enthusiastic salesman for his business and for the plastic industry. Executives recalled Warner as technically brilliant and entrepreneurial in spirit, an executive who allowed his subordinates to take risks and who supported them in their projects.[5]

Warner's achievements with the chemical company led Keener in 1964, then Goodrich's chief executive officer, to promote him to the corporate office, where he remained until retiring in 1974. In the meantime, the company had been preparing Thomas B. Nantz to succeed Warner. Nantz had joined Goodrich after graduating from the University of Kentucky in industrial chemistry (as chemical engineering was sometimes called) in 1937. After gaining managerial experience at the Lone Star Defense Corporation during the early war years, Nantz rose in the executive ranks through Goodrich's synthetic rubber operations. He served a tour as vice president for manufacturing before being shifted to lead the marketing organization, the post from which Warner and Hoover had ascended to the president's office. Nantz was a down-to-earth executive who, like Warner, understood both the technical aspects of chemical manufacturing and the importance of marketing. Like his predecessors, Nantz was enthusiastic about the prospects of the chemical industry and of his own firm. "The chemical industry is big," Nantz told a publicist in the mid-1960s, "and it's growing faster than the growth rate of the United States. . . . You might even say that large as the chemical industry is today, it's still in its infancy." Nantz also believed that plastics were part of the industry's future growth. "We've just begun to tap the markets for plastics in building products, packaging, leisure and sports products." When the attention of corporate headquarters shifted under Keener's leadership toward resuscitating the tire business, Nantz protected the interests of chemical manufacturing in the allocation of funds for investment.[6]

Each of the executives in charge of Goodrich Chemical faced different business problems as the chemical industry in general, and the PVC industry in particular, expanded and became more competitive during the 1950s and the 1960s. There were several common strategic themes throughout the years of 1945–1971, however. First, the company sought to expand the markets for PVC and to rely on a growing volume of plastic sales to produce profits. Efforts in the 1940s to lower the costs of PVC production intensified as competition increased in the 1950s with the appearance of new firms. Goodrich sought to be the industry's producer with the lowest costs. The competitive setting augmented the desire to increase uses for PVC. Second, each executive valued re-search and cooperated with company scientists in trying to develop new prod-ucts. In this regard Harry Warner was perhaps the most ambitious, or visionary, leader of the chemical company. But his predecessors and successor, too, hoped to use Goodrich's scientific expertise to discover and yield new chemi-cal products that might again produce profits as stunning as PVC's in the 1940s. The business approach of the chemical executives in this sense was consonant with the corporate strategy in rubber.

GOODRICH CHEMICAL'S STRATEGY AND PERFORMANCE

The corporate strategy of growth through research was successful for the chemical company for a decade after the war. Goodrich had emerged from World War II with only one competitor in the PVC field, Union Carbide, and competition was modest at best given the fact that the two firms' PVC prod-ucts tended to go into different markets. Nor did Goodrich chemists and engi-neers become complacent, as new compounds of PVC tumbled forth from the research laboratories and new markets appeared. Within the corporate re-search organization under Schoenfeld, the driving force was developing new ideas and selling them to the operating officers in manufacturing and mer-chandising. Nowhere was there a better reception than in the chemical com-pany, whose top executives included men with backgrounds in sales and who grasped the potential for growth in the chemical industry.

During the decade after the war, Goodrich Chemical fostered improve-ments in PVC compounding to develop new markets for the plastic. When the war ended, Hoover recalled, "we worried about whether we would have enough business to keep the Louisville [PVC] plant in full operation." As late as 1949 Richardson told a reporter that finding outlets for increased produc-tion was "the most pressing problem now facing the industry." In retrospect, the executives need not have worried. In less than a decade, the Louisville fa-cility alone grew from a $1 million investment to $10 million in 1954. Nor was Louisville the only site for PVC manufacturing developed by the firm during the first postwar decade. In 1948 a substantial plant was begun in Avon Lake (a western suburb of Cleveland), and soon plans were under way for a $6 mil-lion facility for manufacturing vinyl chloride monomer (VCM) at Calvert City, Kentucky.[7]

Only in retrospect, however, could the plastics executives realize just how large the postwar demand for their product would become. In fact, for most of the 1950s and 1960s the demand for PVC exceeded even the most optimistic expectations. Using their best foresight in 1945 and 1946, Goodrich Chemi-cal executives believed that it was incumbent upon the firm to enlarge the market for PVC. This foresight led to a strategy of developing new compounds of PVC and then sharing that knowledge with customers in order to widen the usefulness of the plastic and enlarge its market. In effect, the chemical compa-ny sought larger and larger volumes of sales, a strategy that proved successful while demand for PVC grew rapidly. The strategy did not change fundamentally until growth in PVC demand slowed in the 1980s.

The company also tried to maintain the price of PVC while expanding the market. When the number of competitors was small, Goodrich and Union Carbide, as the dominant firms in the field, agreed to compete only on the basis of service, not price. When a few other firms entered the industry, sales executives met informally for breakfast in New York City and reached unspoken agreements to maintain prices. After 1955, when the PVC industry became highly competitive, Goodrich eschewed thoughts of cutting prices in order to win customers. The company cut prices in response to competition, but consistently tried to avoid doing so.[8] Within a decade, Goodrich had pioneered new production techniques that enabled it to be a low-cost producer. The combination of trying to maintain prices while reducing costs proved profitable.

Polyvinyl chloride can be sold either as a basic resin or as a "compound" (a product mixed with various additives that govern both the processing and the final form of the plastic). Resins themselves may have different properties. The particles of resin may be of different size and porosity. Those with a high molecular weight are stronger and more heat-resistant but harder to process. Goodrich scientists worked on three main problems: producing different types of resin, developing new compounds of PVC, and learning and applying lower-cost production techniques. In all three areas Goodrich was an industry leader.[9]

In the first years after the war, the company directed its attention toward developing different resins and compounds, setting research objectives in close association with customers and potential customers. The paste resins first developed on a commercial scale in 1940 were improved. New compounds opened uses for PVC in spread coating, embossing, and molding. Dispersion resins were another significant development. Goodrich scientists learned how to avoid using expensive and dangerous solvents and provide for the dispersion of PVC resin in water, allowing the plastic to be used more readily in coating and, eventually, as sheet vinyl in flooring. Later, in 1951, Goodrich introduced a thermoplastic PVC that was hard and tough. ("Thermoplastic" refers to materials that are flexible, or "plastic," when heated, and that harden when cooled.) Customers could easily process the new thermoplastic PVC compounds in calendering, extruding, and milling machines to make a number of products. These materials were not impact-resistant, however, so Goodrich scientists eventually developed compounds suitable for uses in siding, window frames, gutters, and other building products.[10]

The advances in knowledge about PVC resins and, especially, compounds provoked controversy among Goodrich executives over the firm's basic strategy. The company faced a choice either of retaining its proprietary knowledge and thereby selling a product of high value at a relatively low volume or of sharing its knowledge to expand PVC markets rapidly. This choice divided Goodrich executives over the years and produced arguments, sometimes acri-

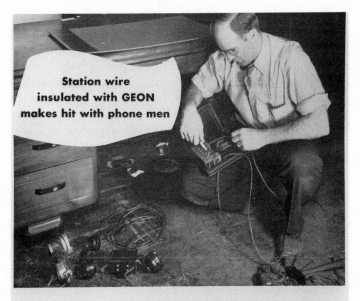

Station wire insulated with GEON makes hit with phone men

Advantages also apply to all types of manufacturing and construction

HERE are some of the things about station wire insulated with GEON that this telephone service man had to say when the picture was taken: it strips faster, cleaner, and easier than any other insulation he's ever seen; it's smooth, not sticky, easy to handle; the colors are clean and bright — easy to spot the wire he's looking for.

He didn't add that the excellent electrical properties of insulation made from GEON permit a thinner coating. That means lighter weight, more conductors per conduit, or

smaller holes to be drilled during construction.

In addition, insulation made from GEON is self-extinguishing — won't support flame. It resists most normally destructive agents such as ozone, oils, acids, air, aging, abrasion, water, and many others.

GEON's applications range from spaghetti for radio hookup wire to heavy insulation for buried service entrance cable. That's why we urge you to specify wire insulated with GEON the next time you order from your supplier. For information about special applications please write Department Y-6, B. F. Goodrich Chemical Company, Rose Building, Cleveland 15, Ohio.

Geon
Polyvinyl Materials

B. F. Goodrich Chemical Company
A DIVISION OF
THE B. F. GOODRICH COMPANY

Wire insulation was an important market for Geon. (BFG Co.)

monious, down to the level of the individual salesman. However controversial the issue might have been within the ranks, senior management generally focused on sales volumes, and during the formative years of the PVC industry the company shared its advances in compounding with customers. In effect, Goodrich gave up its knowledge in order to boost sales volumes, volumes that the company sold at extraordinarily high prices before 1955.

In some respects, the decision to focus on sales volumes instead of compounds of PVC was forced upon the company by the circumstances it faced. Salesmen in the field cooperated closely with product engineers to work on new compounds in order to make PVC fully useful to a wider range of manufacturers. Knowledge of compounds—eventually thousands emerged—disseminated quickly. (Goodrich patent attorneys were not especially aggressive in protecting the knowledge the company's scientists produced.) Nor could the knowledge necessarily be protected by patents. Product engineers left Goodrich for other employment, taking knowledge with them, and they could, with only slight adjustments in formulas, avoid patent violations. Moreover, the largest volume of Goodrich PVC went into wire and cable insulation. Underwriters Laboratories had to approve the insulation, and Goodrich had to reveal the compound formula to obtain the approval. Thus in one important area it was impractical to keep compound formulas as proprietary knowledge.[11]

Nor could Goodrich executives easily change this basic strategy. The growth of competition reinforced the strategy of dispersing knowledge about PVC compounds rapidly, for Goodrich had to share knowledge in order to win customers and retain them in the face of overtures from competitors. As stated in one of the firm's pamphlets, "knowledge or 'know-how' obtained in the laboratory is readily available to consumers."[12] With competition, high prices could no more be maintained on compounds than on the basic resin.

Sales volume grew, and the company soon expanded production facilities in Louisville, Avon Lake, and Calvert City. The expansion began in 1946 when Goodrich bought the government's synthetic rubber plant at Louisville, Kentucky, and began converting it to PVC production. The company continued to expand at Avon Lake, constructing a general chemical plant in 1948 capable of making vinyl plasticizers, a PVC plant in 1950, and its Application Research Laboratory (also called a development center) in 1957. In 1959 Long Beach, California, was added to the list of plant sites, with a PVC facility to service West Coast markets. Expansion continued in the next decade: in 1962 the company began a huge petrochemical complex at Calvert City; in 1964 it began a PVC plant at Henry, Illinois; and in 1967, it decided to build on the East Coast, at Pedricktown, New Jersey, to reach eastern PVC markets.[13]

The result for a decade and more after 1945 was a cascade of profits. And although those profits were hidden in the consolidated reports then issued to stockholders, it did not take observers long to figure out their source. "The only sales field in which Goodrich led its competitors," a feature article in *Fortune* magazine surmised in 1947, "—both absolutely and relatively—was chemicals. And it's well known that profits are currently enormous on the chemical products in which Goodrich specializes." That year, Goodrich executives privately knew, the division had employed $17,851,000 in capital to obtain net sales of $32,090,000. Its operating income of $6,783,000 was 21.1 percent of sales and represented a return of 38 percent on capital. In 1947 the operating income for the entire firm—on sales of $410,180,839—was $48,994,058. For the chemical arm 1947 proved to one of the better years: the peak in terms of income as a percentage of capital employed was 1948 with 40.8 percent, and the nadir for the period 1940–55 was 1953 at 14.8 percent. The demand for PVC was so large that the company allocated the material to its customers. The profits poured in, as the industry maintained its basic PVC price above 35¢ per pound. Even at that price, PVC and other plastics were often competitive with wood, leather, and metals among manufacturers of finished goods. The results affirmed the company's prewar strategy of investing in the chemical field. Moreover, between 1945 and 1972 the chemical company usually led the other manufacturing divisions of B.F. Goodrich in return on investment.[14]

Not surprising, the chemical division was favored within the larger corporate organization. Although its profits were mainly derived from the increasing sales volumes of PVC, specialized rubber chemicals remained a profitable line, as they had been before the war. And Goodrich's nitrile rubbers, branded as Hycar, also dominated their markets. The corporate research organization employed scientists to explore new products that could repeat the commercial success of PVC. Meanwhile, chemical executives were able to obtain the capital they requested from corporate management to build new plants or to expand and improve established factories.

Eventually, however, the price of PVC and the profits it earned began to dwindle owing to competition. As late as 1950 there were just five manufacturers of vinyl resins. As demand and production volumes soared, however, new firms entered the field: by 1959 there were twenty-two "major rivals" making vinyl resins. One result was a continuing round of substantial price decreases for all vinyl manufacturers, including Goodrich. Nor was competition about to ease in the face of a booming plastics market because of new developments in the economics of PVC manufacturing.[15]

THE POSTWAR GROWTH OF THE PLASTICS INDUSTRIES

Goodrich Chemical's successes with polyvinyl chloride were part of a larger pattern of growth in the plastics industry in general in the postwar years. Demand for vinyl and other plastics quite simply boomed beyond even the most optimistic forecasts. However, competition also increased sharply. Companies developed new plastic materials and new synthetic compounds that some classified as "rubber-plastics." As large firms already established in the petroleum and chemical industries rushed to take advantage of increasing demand and plastics production, capacity in some years exceeded demand. Polyvinyl chloride remained the plastic sold most until the end of the 1950s. Even after it lost the lead to polyethylene (PE), demand for PVC grew dramatically in the 1960s and 1970s. However, new entrants like polystyrene, acrylic, polyethylene, and polyesters rapidly penetrated markets. Plastic manufacturers, including Goodrich, could offer end users a variety of materials adapted to specific applications. Plastic materials competed with rubber, ceramic, leather, textiles, and metals; and they also competed with other plastics. The rapid acceptance of styrenes and polyethylene in the market—one even more rapid than that of vinyls—brought Goodrich Chemical a new round of competition for PVC at about the same time that the PVC industry itself was becoming more competitive.

No plastics manufacturer entered all of the new fields, and Goodrich was no exception. Vinyl, which continued to enjoy large and expanding markets, remained its main business as other producers were introducing competing materials. Goodrich had a successful record in developing new PVC compounds to meet its customers' particular needs, and there was no reason to think that the success would somehow evaporate in the future. Nevertheless, the company explored new fields in other plastics, although none ever approached the volumes of Goodrich's PVC. Eventually its polyurethane, branded as "Estane," became an important product. In fact, during the 1940s and 1950s, some executives were critical of Goodrich Chemical's hesitation to invest in competing plastic materials in a timely fashion, allowing Dow and other competitors to expand their penetration of plastics markets.[16]

The Polyvinyl Chloride Industry

After a decade of fantastic profits, the PVC industry underwent fundamental changes. The turning point came in 1955 as a result of a combination of government policy and business strategy by a chemical industry giant, Dow. Dow Chemical was pursuing a strategy of supplying large volumes of industrial chemicals to other firms. During the Korean War (1950–53) the vinyl chloride industry experienced a serious product shortage as it tried to supply both the booming civilian and defense markets. To meet the Korean War emergency, the federal government encouraged companies making raw materials for the plastics industry to enlarge their production capacity by granting so-called "certificates of necessity." These grants allowed Dow Chemical and other suppliers to depreciate their capital expenditures quickly (in effect, the government was underwriting the capital costs for a rapid expansion of the plastics industry). Dow made both chlorine and ethylene and had already made modest investments in vinyl chloride monomer production to provide an outlet for these two raw materials. The government policy allowed Dow to make much more substantial investments, and the firm's executives sought to become a huge supplier of industrial chemicals, including VCM.[17]

Dow's strategy of becoming the dominant producer of VCM irrevocably changed the plastics industry when it began to sell the commodity itself in 1955, creating a new commodity market. (Previously, PVC manufacturers, including Goodrich, had relied on captive supplies of VCM.) Assured of a supply of VCM from the commodity market, other companies began to enter PVC manufacturing, encouraged by the high prices the plastic was commanding. Engineering firms, led by the Scientific Design Company, began to sell PVC manufacturing facilities of a standardized design to companies, including Goodrich customers. Initially, firms buying large quantities of PVC for extrusion and calendering entered the PVC business to integrate backward. They soon learned that small polymer plants were not economical and expanded resin capacity to sell PVC in the open market.[18]

The industry quickly felt the results of Dow's decision. By the end of 1955 there were nine manufacturers of PVC, and industry observers expected two or three more firms to enter the field by 1956; at least four additional firms had announced plans to launch PVC plants, and large European chemical companies were exploring the possibilities of making their own investments. By 1958 there were twenty manufacturers of PVC, and still another was opening a plant in 1959. The industry quickly felt the results, as prices tumbled from 35¢ a pound in 1955 to 18¢ a pound in 1960. "The crying towels were out all over the place," one industry veteran recalled. During those years Goodrich's market share also dropped significantly.[19]

The Impact on Goodrich Chemical

The creation of the commodity VCM market had an extraordinary impact on Goodrich. Immediately, the company had to adapt to the fact that profits in PVC were no longer huge. The industry had become fiercely competitive. In the long term, the company sought to adapt through a combination of new manufacturing processes and marketing strategies that built on successful ventures established before 1955. It also continued to explore new products that might diminish reliance on PVC for profits.

Most significant for the chemical company was the rise of "captive" PVC markets and a resulting loss of market share. Within a few years of the emergence of the commodity VCM market and the availability of "off-the-shelf" polymerization plants from Scientific Design and other firms, executives observed the rise of "captive" markets, wherein the PVC manufacturer and fabricator were linked. Of the twenty-one PVC producers in 1959, ten were making plastic primarily for their own "captive" market, although some firms sold surplus products in the open market. Captive markets comprised a rising share of the nation's total PVC business; by 1964 almost one-fourth of the 1.6 billion pounds of PVC made went into captive consumption. This trend was unfavorable for Goodrich, which did not enjoy especially large sales to the company's industrial products division. Sales of PVC resin to other divisions of Goodrich were a declining share of the chemical company's trade, down to 5 percent in 1964 from 8 percent in 1955. The result was that Goodrich's share of the total PVC market was shrinking, from 30 percent in 1955 to 20 percent in 1964. Within the "free" market, however, the company's share remained at about 30 percent. Executives expected that by 1970 captive consumption nationally would represent 40 to 50 percent of the estimated 2.8 billion pound market.[20] These trends meant that the chemical company would look toward a reconfiguration of its PVC business after 1960.

VENTURES IN THE PETROCHEMICAL INDUSTRY

In the meantime, Goodrich executives sought ways to participate in rapidly expanding fields of petrochemicals that promised a bonanza for American manufacturers. Within PVC, the chemical company sought to exploit its domestic success by establishing ventures in foreign markets. The parent company also hoped to use the skills of the company's researchers to find new chemical fields to enhance profits even further.

Hycar

The company continued to improve and sell the Hycar rubbers, first introduced during the wartime joint venture with Phillips Petroleum. The joint venture ended with the war, a victim of personality clashes between David Goodrich and Frank Phillips. On one occasion, Phillips, a gruff pioneer in Oklahoma oil exploration, was heard referring to the gentlemanly Goodrich as an "old goat," and the two men had almost come to blows. In 1945 the company took all of the physical assets and the Hycar trade name, giving Goodrich Chemical an important line of products.[21]

The new business required the chemical company to modify its structure. All of the Phillips Petroleum personnel assigned to the joint venture returned to their parent company. Because Hycar and Geon went to different markets, the chemical company divided sales responsibilities. It assigned James Richards, who had been managing synthetic rubber production at Borger, Texas, to head the Hycar sales force, while George Fowles remained in charge of PVC sales.[22]

Hycar rubbers never reached the spectacular sales and profits of Geon, but nevertheless were an important product line for the company. The main markets took advantage of the products' oil-resistant properties in gaskets, seals, and hoses. In 1953, after spending five years in research and development, the company announced plans to build a $8.5 million plant in Calvert City to make acrylonitrile, the liquid monomer used to make Hycar and other chemical products. This acrylonitrile plant operated for almost twenty years. The company decided to close it in 1972 because competitors had developed new techniques and facilities and were selling acrylonitrile at prices below Goodrich's cost of production. The company also expanded its Hycar production facilities in Louisville.[23]

International Opportunities

Soon after the chemical company was formed as an independent division under Richardson, it planned to export its knowledge in polyvinyl chloride manufacturing. Opportunities seemed abundant for international sales and manufacturing as the American economy emerged from the war dominant in the world, and most foreign PVC markets were virgin territory. The problem, however, was that the chemical company's resources were too small, and PVC not yet well enough established, for Goodrich to operate independently on a global basis.

Robert Kenney was instrumental in breaking through the impasse between foreign PVC opportunities and Goodrich's limited resources. Before the war was over, Richardson successfully wooed Kenney, a young chemist, to join the firm. Kenney had served the War Production Board allocating PVC to both military contractors and overseas customers. This experience gave Kenney a unique knowledge of the industry, a knowledge that Richardson soon put to use in the international field. Before the war ended he sent Kenney with Frank

Schoenfeld, the director of corporate research, to London on a secret mission to negotiate a joint venture. The team did not know the reason for the secrecy, but suspected it had something to do with avoiding sharing any of the PVC windfall with British Tyre and Rubber. In any event, they negotiated with Distillers Ltd., a large British chemical manufacturer. Having raw materials supplies available and having some limited experience with PVC in its own small pilot plant, Distillers was interested. The result was British Geon, a joint venture—the first of many to come—using expertise from the Goodrich chemical company with a foreign partner to expand the PVC business abroad. The joint venture allowed Goodrich to collaborate with what might have been a powerful competitor, gaining access to markets in Britain and the British Commonwealth without having to make massive investments of its own. In the meantime, the American company profited by collecting royalties on its technology.[24]

This type of expansion evolved over the ensuing years in a global fashion. The next target was the European continent, where Goodrich produced Geon soon after the war, in collaboration with Kleber-Colombes, the Goodrich French tire venture. The most significant venture on the Continent, however, was Ciago, a joint venture between Goodrich and N.V. Chemische Industrie AKU, a Dutch firm. Ciago combined Goodrich products and processes with Dutch manufacturing capabilities. It began producing Hycar rubbers in 1959, and within a decade was making Geon products locally and importing a full line of Goodrich products from the United States. Ciago went on to form alliances with companies in other European countries, giving Goodrich a much needed European distribution system. Problems emerged after 1970 when AKU merged with KZO, a large international chemical company that competed with Goodrich in some product areas, to form AKZO. To avoid the inevitable conflicts of interest, Goodrich purchased Ciago outright in 1973.[25]

The chemical company also extended its reach into Asia. In 1949 James Richards, the vice president in charge of sales for the chemical company, opened negotiations in Japan for what eventually became Japanese Geon, a firm that made both plastics and, eventually, synthetic rubber. The founding of Japanese Geon was related to the Goodrich joint ownership of Yokohama Rubber with the Furukawa group. At the first meeting in Tokyo after the war, Furukawa executives presented their Goodrich counterparts with checks for dividends Yokohama Rubber had earned during the war years. They also expressed interest in PVC, a product they had learned about during the war, for their electrical business. The result was a joint venture, Japanese Geon, which became a significant factor in Asian plastic markets.[26]

These overseas joint ventures allowed Goodrich to reap generous royalties from its technologies. The European and Japanese operations of Goodrich Chemical remained promising for a time, but just as competitors were able to enter the field in the United States, so too were they able to turn PVC into a commodity item worldwide. Eventually, executives were disappointed in their profits in Europe, and Kenney, taking on larger responsibilities for the chemical company's international business, tried after 1958 to shift focus to opportunities in Latin America, Asia, and Australia. Nantz created a separate international department under Kenney in the chemical company to coordinate manufacturing, licensing, and sales. This shift in strategy was difficult to achieve, however. Goodrich was struggling after 1960 (as we will see in chap. 8) to maintain its position as a diversified producer of tires and other rubber products. Keener and his closest advisers approved overseas chemical investments only with great reluctance and after tedious campaigns by executives in the chemical company. Within the chemical company, Nantz helped Kenney secure the necessary approvals from the Akron-based executives. By 1966 the chemical company had joint venture associates in Iran, Australia, New Zealand, Mexico, Brazil, and India.[27]

Not only was it a struggle for the chemical company to gain approval of overseas investments, but B.F. Goodrich actually retreated from two important markets. In 1967 the company decided to sell its 45 percent stake in British Geon to British Petroleum for $7.9 million capital that it needed to shore up lagging rubber fabricating businesses in the United States. The company retreated from Great Britain even though projections of additional capital investments there showed favorable profits. Goodrich now had to compete with a British PVC branded as "Breon." Not long thereafter Goodrich's corporate headquarters raised badly needed capital by selling its interest in Japanese Geon; transactions were completed in 1970. Japanese Geon became Nippon Zeon, a large supplier of synthetic rubbers and plastic materials in its own right.[28]

New Products

Knowledge in polymer chemistry in general during the postwar period was exploding, and Goodrich executives hoped to make breakthroughs in the laboratory and to exploit them in the marketplace, just as they had done earlier with PVC. In 1943 Collyer reassigned Waldo Semon as director of pioneering research to "find new fields for profitable chemical manufacture" so that the company could use its established base of knowledge in rubber and polymer chemistry to expand into other fields. One effort focused upon possible agricultural applications of the sulfur-based rubber chemicals. By 1950 the company planned to introduce "No-Nib'l," a powder to repel rabbits from gardens. Other work was done on an insecticide, and Goodrich entered the fungicide business for a time. In 1956, with organic agricultural chemicals taking over the field, the company decided to abandon its efforts to enter the agricultural chemical business. In the meantime, the company hoped to find new polymers that would allow it to participate more broadly in the rapidly expanding plastics industries.[29]

The chemical company approached the matter of finding and developing new products through two avenues. First, as part of the larger Goodrich corporation, the chemical company maintained close ties to scientists like Semon, who were at the corporate research center in Brecksville at the end of World

War II. Strictly speaking, Goodrich corporate scientists engaged in "basic" research that might lead to new product lines such as agricultural chemicals. At the division level of the chemical company, scientists and engineers engaged in "applied" research. During the construction of the Brecksville research center, the chemical company was launching its own facility at Avon Lake. The idea was to take products developed at Brecksville that showed commercial promise and develop them further at Avon Lake. This plan included working with the important engineering knowledge gained from both small pilot plants and somewhat larger "semiworks" production facilities. Scientists at Avon Lake also worked "to uncover new applications, [to] improve processing techniques, and to furnish customer service" for all of the chemical company's products.[30]

Following DuPont's successful introduction of nylon in 1940, in the postwar period American chemical companies were excited about the possibilities of developing other new artificial fibers. Goodrich was no exception and was eventually almost blinded by a dream of participating in the textile industry. Looking initially for a new tire cord material, for a number of years the company invested substantial sums in work at Brecksville and Avon Lake on a new product eventually called "Darvan." Darvan was a wool-like fiber of vaneldine cyanide that could be woven into garments. By 1950 the company was planning a semiworks plant to make 10,000 pounds per month of the new fiber. Of the senior executives, Harry Warner was especially optimistic about this product. When he rose to the top post of the chemical company, Warner envisioned Darvan establishing Goodrich Chemical as a major supplier for the textile trade. His ambition exceeded reality, however. In 1957 the board of directors took two simultaneous actions, approving $600,000 to study the best applications for the fiber and $10,000,000 to build a plant to manufacture Darvan. However, in 1958, Ward Keener, believing that Goodrich could not compete successfully in the textile market with only one fiber, stopped the venture. Goodrich sold its knowledge about Darvan to the Celanese Corporation in 1960.[31]

A few years later the company also had an unsuccessful experience developing an artificial leather. Goodrich scientists developed a product in the laboratory, called Aztran, that showed promise. Corporate executives in Akron became excited about Aztran, hoping that it would provide Goodrich's industrial products and shoe manufacturing divisions an edge over their competition. But in 1964, before Goodrich could bring its synthetic leather to market, DuPont introduced "Corfam," which actually went into shoes sold to the public. DuPont's product was a failure (it did not stretch and mold to the individual foot), giving artificial leather such a negative reputation that Goodrich had no hope of bringing its product to market. After substantial research and development expenditures, all the company had was a write-off.[32]

Prior to the expensive failure with its artificial leather, Goodrich also suffered a loss from its attempt to enter the automotive finishes business. Apparently instigated by the desire of Collyer and Richardson to broaden the chemical company's business, Goodrich in 1950 spent $3 million for Harmon

Color Works, Inc., a small New Jersey firm that competed with DuPont in supplying paints for the automobile trade. Goodrich hoped to use its knowledge in organic chemicals to expand Harmon's business into supplying pigments for plastics and synthetic fibers as well. The acquisition proved disappointing, however. Goodrich lacked any advantage in polymer science that could give Harmon Color Works an edge over competitors. At first the company had difficulty keeping up with customer demand, but by 1957 the market for the company's finishes had collapsed. Sales forecasts did not justify continued operation of one of the firms's two production plants, but Goodrich was unable to sell its excess capacity. Finally, after a decade of modest investments and unhappy results, Harmon was sold to Allied Chemical.[33]

Although the automotive paint and the artificial fiber and leather businesses ended up as nothing more than expensive failures for the chemical company and its parent corporation, there were successful new products developed in the postwar period. One was Estane, Goodrich's brand name for a thermoplastic polyurethane. The federal government funded research into new elastomers after the war, and there was a great deal of interest in polyurethanes. Eventually, several chemical companies developed different varieties of polyurethane that provided important materials for coatings and wrappings. Goodrich responded to this interest by hiring Charles S. Schollenberger in 1947 to develop a new urethane elastomer. The result was a unique product, a thermoplastic polyurethane. Early in 1952 Schollenberger applied for the first patent. Work on the product proceeded well enough that the company applied for the Estane trademark in 1953. For several years Schollenberger and his colleagues tested various additives and worked on problems of weathering, and Goodrich finally announced Estane in 1958. The only thermoplastic polyurethane on the market, it was capable of being extruded, molded, milled, calendered, and used in standard plastic processing machinery. It enjoyed excellent resistance to abrasion, and was first used in wire and cable jackets. Estane went into adhesives, computer magnetic tape, textile coatings, molded gears, sprockets, and bushings. Although a product of comparatively low production volumes, Estane enjoyed a high value. In 1958 it sold for $1.85 per pound, a price that dropped over the next decade but still remained very profitable. Within a decade Estane was the company's fastest-growing new plastic.[34]

At about the same time, the chemical company had a favorable experience with Abson—its trademark for acrylonitrile butadiene styrene, or ABS—known in the industry as an "engineered plastic." In 1948, Naugatuck Chemical, a subsidiary of U.S. Rubber, brought out ABS commercially. Goodrich's interest in the product stemmed from its work with Hycar nitrile rubbers; ABS resulted from the addition of styrene as a hardening agent. ABS became a rival material to PVC for pipe manufacture, a huge market that Goodrich wanted to exploit. Although PVC pipe had better resistance to abrasion, oxidation, and chemicals than ABS pipe, ABS plastic had real possibilities in molded goods. Goodrich announced its entry into the field in 1960, first making ABS at its Louisville factory.[35]

Four of the fifteen "Goodrich Girls" used in company advertising in the early 1900s are shown here (Sally and Aida to the right, Gwendolen and Marie below). Reproductions of the women graced ads, calendars, handbills, and catalogs.

In the late 1960s and early 1970s Goodrich used Pat Christman, known as "Miss Radial Age," to promote its tires. She appeared in national television and magazine advertisements as part of Goodrich's aggressive advertising campaign.

(Photos courtesy of the BFGoodrich Company)

Presidents and Chairmen
of the
BFGoodrich Company

Benjamin Franklin Goodrich
Founder and President, 1870–88

David M. Goodrich
Chairman, 1927–50

John L. Collyer
President, 1939–54
Chairman, 1950–60

George T. Perkins
President, 1888–1907
Chairman, 1907–10

Bertram G. Work
President, 1907–27
Chairman, 1920–27

J. Ward Keener
President, 1957–67
Chairman, 1967–72

O. Pendleton Thomas
President, 1974–75
Chairman, 1972–79

John D. Ong
President, 1975–84, 1994–95
Chairman, 1979–1997

We Gave Up The Highway For The Runway.

In 1898, we introduced tires for the first commercial automobile sold in America. Ever since, we've been known for high performance.

Of course, our idea of high performance is a lot higher in 1988 than it was in 1898. About 40,000 feet higher.

High performance today means landing a 450-passenger aircraft safely. Time after time. That's why BFGoodrich makes the wheels and new carbon brakes for Boeing 747-400 aircraft.

High performance also means stopping a 100-ton spacecraft smooth as silk. That's why BFGoodrich makes the brakes and wheels for the Space Shuttle.

Today, BFGoodrich is a 2.5-billion-dollar aerospace and chemical company which ranks either first or second in most of its key markets.

We are building higher performance into our balance sheet, t Our debt-to-total-capitalization ratio is now under 30%, dos from 43% just three years ago. Our earnings through Septem were a record — up $74 million over last year.

For more information about the new BFGoodrich, write The BFGoodrich Company, P.O. Box 4658, Akron, Ohio 44.

We gave up the highway. But we're high performance.

BFGoodrich
Chemicals and Aerospace

BFGoodrich left the tire business in the late 1980s. National advertising focused on explaining the company's transformation into a provider of aerospace systems and chemicals.

We Are Out Of Inner Tubes. We Are Into Test Tubes.

Chemical reactions aren't the only ones we know about.

"Huh?"

That's the reaction we get when we tell people that we're out of the tire business and into chemicals.

But the fact is, quality BFGoodrich brand tires are now made by another company, the second largest tire maker in North America, The Uniroyal Goodrich Tire Company.

We're The BFGoodrich Company. Another company entirely. A 2.5-billion-dollar chemical and aerospace producer.

We've been committed to chemical innovation since Charles Goodrich founded the first industrial rubber research laboratory in the United States in 1895.

That's one reason our company is so strong in highly engineered specialty chemicals. Our products add value to our customers' products.

That's also why we are the technology leader in the important vinyl business. And why our Geon brand name is the most respected in the market.

Our earnings through September were a record, up $74 million over last year.

We don't make high-performance tires any longer. But we're high performance.

BFGoodrich
Chemicals and Aerospace

BFGoodrich Aerospace currently operates a global network of service centers that repair and overhaul aircraft and their components. BFG Aerospace is, in the 1990s, the largest independent commercial airframe service provider in North America.

Dr. Poonam Manji, a Goodrich chemist, examines Carbopol EZ-2, an easy-to-mix synthetic thickener manufactured by BFGoodrich.

BFGoodrich inflatable evacuation slides and slide rafts, such as this one installed on a Boeing 747, currently equip many of the world's most widely used commercial and regional business jet aircraft.

All of the personal-care products pictured here contain BFGoodrich Carbopol synthetic thickeners.

Landing gear assembly (including wheels and brakes) manufactured by BFGoodrich is shown here installed on a Boeing 747.

Estane polyurethane thermoplastic materials are used (among many other applications) as binders in the manufacture of magnetic tape for audio and video cassettes and computer disks.

Marketed under the trade name FlowGuard Gold, this pipe manufactured from BFGoodrich high-heat-resistant plastics is replacing copper and other plastic plumbing materials in new home construction and remodeling.

The company was by no means a "first mover" in ABS. In addition to the product from Naugatuck, Marbon Chemical (a division of Borg-Warner) had already entered the field. In fact, Marbon led in developing the use of ABS for molded goods when, earlier in 1960, Remington Rand began using it in portable typewriter housings. Monsanto was also entering the market. Goodrich was a relatively small participant. In the spring of 1961 the company's ABS capacity was 15 million pounds annually, whereas Monsanto had announced a capacity of 40 million pounds, and U.S. Rubber and Marban were established producers each with a 35-million-pound annual capacity, which they were in the process of substantially increasing. While Goodrich advertised three varieties of ABS, Marbon and Naugatuck had fourteen and ten varieties, respectively.[36]

Nevertheless, prospects for ABS production were promising. While the ABS market stood at 45 million pounds in 1960 when Goodrich entered the field, industry observers expected that by the end of the decade it would reach somewhere between 300 and 500 million pounds a year. They expected applications to reach well beyond molded typewriters into the huge automotive industry. Abson compounds were suitable for making refrigerator linings, automotive parts such as dashboards, telephone handsets, and shoe heels, among other goods. Thus, even though Goodrich Chemical was not one of the largest producers of ABS, it proved a profitable product.[37]

Goodrich executives were excited about the possibilities of a new family of hydrophylic polymers (polymers that are soluble in water), two of which the company named "Carbopol" and "Carboset." The company saw a need for products that could serve as thickening agents in a variety of consumer products. While scientists worked on developing a vinyl polymer of extremely high molecular weight, their counterparts in marketing went about the business of testing the applications for the new thickening agent Carbopol. By 1956 the company was reporting "a rapid increase" for Carbopol in the cosmetic, pharmaceutical, and paint industries. Consumer products company Procter & Gamble was an important customer, and Carbopol quickly became a profitable "speciality chemical" product. In 1958 Hoover told the press that Carbopol was "the most versatile agent ever discovered for thickening, suspending, dispersing and emulsifying." In the meantime, Goodrich scientists also perfected Carboset for use in coating the molds in industrial castings. Because it was hydrophylic, Carboset did not require the use of petroleum-based solvents, which created pollution problems. In 1959 Goodrich began manufacturing Carbopol and Carboset at a new $3 million plant in Calvert City, Kentucky, with a capacity of 70,000 pounds per month that could readily be doubled or quadrupled as new markets opened.[38]

The strategy of investing in research and development in hopes of increasing Goodrich's fortunes at the expense of competitors was wide-ranging. The company expended years and millions of dollars trying to develop a new synthetic rubber (EPDM) made from ethylene and propylene, raw materials considerably cheaper than the butadiene and styrene that went into established synthetic rubbers. Harry Warner believed that the new synthetic rubber would

Carbopol, added to a liquid, imparted a suspending property, as seen in this photograph. (BFG Co.)

become the tire rubber of the future, and he and Frank Schoenfeld assigned Edwin Harrington to take charge of the product's research and development at Brecksville and Avon Lake in 1963. The executives, believing that Goodrich basked in superior research capabilities, hoped to capitalize on a scientific breakthrough and gain an advantage over larger competitors.

The project proved a costly disappointment, although the product eventually went into production at a plant in Orange, Texas, in 1971. The new synthetic was not satisfactory for use in tires—it could not be used in treads at all. Harrington and his colleagues did learn, however, that ethylene-propylene rubber had some desirable characteristics, especially in resisting ozone. This rubber eventually went into white sidewalls on tires, and it became an important material for weather stripping. The company unsuccessfully sought to arrange cooperation with DuPont, which had a competing line of weather-resistant rubbers, in developing and marketing the product. Sold as a specialty rubber, the product never met with much enthusiasm from the sales force. Ethylene-propylene rubber remained a failed dream, a successful product that never earned substantial profits.[39]

Strategically, the ventures in new products were a disappointment. The company enjoyed scientific successes and brought important new products to the market, but no new product showed the promise that PVC had once enjoyed. Goodrich earned profits from its research in polymers, but those profits never approached the spectacular figures PVC had earned before 1955. Moreover, this same strategic disappointment proved also to be the case in the synthetic rubbers that Goodrich decided to develop in partnership with Gulf Oil.

GOODRICH-GULF CHEMICALS, INC.

Goodrich Chemical remained largely a PVC company with some additional, more specialized, products. For new enterprises in synthetic rubber, B.F. Goodrich went a different route: a joint venture with the Gulf Oil Company. The two firms had a long-standing relationship. The Pittsburgh-based oil refiner and distributor was an important customer of Goodrich tires, which they sold in Gulf service stations nationwide. In 1952 the two corporate giants, anticipating the eventual disposal of the government-owned industry, entered the synthetic rubber business under a joint venture, Goodrich-Gulf. The match seemed a good one. Gulf had invested relatively less in chemical manufacturing than had other major petroleum refiners, while Goodrich, with less access to capital, had scientific expertise with synthetic rubber. Eventually Goodrich-Gulf sold synthetic rubber under the trade name "Ameripol." Goodrich-Gulf was a privately and jointly held venture between equal partners. Executives of both parent firms controlled the board of directors; operating executives came from both sides of the partnership. William Richardson served as the first president of Goodrich-Gulf, followed by W. I. Burt, the engineer who had been so important in Goodrich's wartime rubber production. In 1958 leadership shifted to Lucien O. Crockett, who had headed Gulf's petrochemical business, followed in 1963 by Z. David Bonner of Gulf.[40] It was within this framework that Goodrich research in synthetic rubber occurred. Scientists at Brecksville conducted the basic research, turning to the Goodrich-Gulf organization for pilot plant and, eventually, production operations.

Synthetic Natural Rubber

The discovery of synthetic natural rubber was a serendipitous moment in the history of science. The wartime synthetic rubber, as we have seen, was splendid for some uses, but for tire sidewalls and some other rubber products, it could not replace the polymer found in nature. There were a number of efforts to synthesize the natural rubber molecule in American laboratories. This effort was a high priority in government research policy because, if successful,

the synthesis would free defense planners from dependence on overseas supplies. In fact, in 1953 Firestone scientists had learned how to make a polyisoprene molecule that was close to the properties of natural rubber, but their
executives had not pursued the finding aggressively.[41]

The world of polymer chemistry in late 1953 was buzzing with news of discoveries by a German chemist named Karl Ziegler. Ziegler was using special
catalysts to make polymers from ethylene, a chemical available in plentiful
quantities from petroleum refineries. Although polyethylene was not a new
plastic, Ziegler's techniques produced a high-quality product at low pressure.
His techniques held the promise of creating a new, inexpensive plastic and
opening a vast commercial opportunity. In 1954 W. I. Burt, then head of chemical engineering at Goodrich, Paul Cornell, a counterpart from Gulf Oil, and
Waldo Semon visited Ziegler's laboratory. Gulf Oil had a working relationship
with Ziegler, and Gulf executives arranged for the use of Ziegler patents in the
United States. They brought back to Akron details of making a polyethylene
that melted only under high temperatures. Goodrich-Gulf executives began
planning to enter the polyethylene business, agreeing to pay Ziegler a
$250,000 license fee for the patent.[42]

The discovery of synthetic natural rubber, or cis 1,4 polyisoprene, came as a
surprise soon thereafter.[43] No one had been able to control the polymerization
of isoprene so as to obtain the cis 1,4 configuration of natural rubber. Research
programs in the field had been abandoned by Goodrich and other firms;
by 1954 there was no active program to synthesize natural rubber.[44] At the
Brecksville research center scientists were working with the Ziegler polyethylene patents for Goodrich-Gulf's entry into the polyethylene business. In early
September the research scientist Samuel Horne conceived of using the Ziegler
catalyst with either butadiene or isoprene. On 30 September Horne began an
experiment using ethylene and isoprene, expecting to find a rigid polyethylene. Horne noted that his result was "different" from normal polyethylene and
sent a sample to the center's analytical department. The analytical chemists,
facing a backlog of work, delayed using their "infrared spectrum" methods on
Horne's product in favor of completing projects analyzing rubber compounds
from competitors' tires. Finally, on 28 October 1954 the analysts observed that
Horne's product contained both ethylene and natural rubber. After learning
that no natural rubber was present, Horne concluded that he had indeed syn-
thesized natural rubber. Upon separating the ethylene, Goodrich scientists
had achieved the manufacture of cis 1,4 polyisoprene in their laboratory.[45]

The announcement on 2 December 1954 of the breakthrough led quickly
to a patent controversy, and Collyer's wartime forebodings about the emergency patent pool began to come true. While some company scientists worked
on research sponsored by the federal government, the firm had always been
careful to keep separate any group working on synthetic natural rubber lest
there be a demand for the pooling of patents resulting from the research. The
caution proved well advised. Within days of the announcement of polyisoprene, Department of Justice attorneys acting on behalf of the government's

Rubber Reserve Corporation, the wartime agency responsible for federal synthetic rubber facilities and research, inquired about the work. They believed that the discovery fell within the patent pool and that Goodrich-Gulf would have to share its knowledge with its competitors.

Goodrich-Gulf disagreed, and a long series of negotiations ensued. The company agreed to make its knowledge available under license while its application for a patent was pending. In the meantime, it constructed a pilot plant at Avon Lake to learn how to manufacture polyisoprene (marketed as Ameripol SN) in commercial quantities, and Goodrich's tire division successfully tested the product. Goodrich-Gulf sold manufacturing licenses for polyisoprene both in the United States and abroad, but it was never able to fully profit from the breakthrough. Because of the cost of isoprene, rubber from efficient plantations competed with the synthetic product. More important to the commercial failure, however, was the fact that soon Goodyear, Firestone, and other competitors learned how to make polyisoprene without the Goodrich license. When the patent was finally secured in 1963, it produced income for the company, but not as anticipated.[46]

The Ziegler catalysts also led to the development of a cis 1,4 polybutadiene rubber that Goodrich-Gulf was able to patent. This rubber had superior abrasion resistance and remained flexible at extremely low temperatures in tire applications. Goodrich-Gulf claimed that this product, sold as Ameripol CB, did not require blending with other rubber, unlike competing polybutadiene rubbers. Although initially the sales volumes were not nearly as large as those for the older butadiene-styrene rubber, the product was a technological success and held great promise for widespread use in tires.[47]

Overall, the scientific breakthroughs in new synthetic rubbers were a business disappointment. Goodrich scientists had enjoyed another "first" with synthetic natural rubber, and their polybutadiene rubber had superior properties; but the company's executives, hampered by the patent dispute over synthetic natural rubber and reluctant to make aggressive investments, were unable to seize those opportunities. This was especially the case with polybutadiene rubber. Goodrich-Gulf converted GR-S facilities at Institute, West Virginia, to cis-polybutadiene rubber but did not keep pace with the growth of the market. When Goodrich-Gulf opened an entirely new plant for Ameripol CB in Orange, Texas, in 1967, the company ranked last among the five producers in the United States. It made 13 percent of the U.S. production, a share sold almost entirely to B.F. Goodrich. Goodrich-Gulf had simply failed to take advantage of an opportunity to be the "first mover" in the field and to establish a position against which competitors had to fight. Instead, Goodrich-Gulf sales personnel had to penetrate markets already visited by adversaries.[48]

High Density Polyethylene

Goodrich-Gulf executives' decision to invest in the manufacture of high density polyethylene (HDPE) produced another frustration. Almost from its

Goodrich-Gulf first manufactured Ameripol CB at this plant in Institute, West Virginia. (BFG Col. UAA)

introduction in 1957, HDPE capacity exceeded demand. The company's access to the Ziegler patents on catalysts proved not to give it an advantage—
one journalist asserted that the company "muffed the opportunity" to reap
"millions in polyethylene"—and soon the HDPE business, as was generally
true of plastics by the end of the 1950s, was beset with overcapacity and depressed prices. Initially, growth of the resin's sales was more dramatic than that
for any other plastic. HDPE leaped from 50 million pounds in 1958—a figure
"inflated because about 15 million pounds went into hula hoops [a popular
toy]"—to 400 million pounds in 1963. Just as hula hoop popularity proved to
be a fad that passed quickly, eager companies, buoyed by optimistic predictions, entered production. In 1960 the base price of HDPE was 35¢ per pound,
but prices soon slipped. In 1962, when Goodrich-Gulf opened a big new plant
in Port Neches, Texas, the polyethylene business was already crowded with fifteen producers and a 2.25 billion pound annual capacity. Part of the problem
was that the material competed with other plastics for such goods as disposable
bottles, and producers therefore could not maintain prices. Overcapacity eventually sunk Goodrich-Gulf's investment in HDPE. In 1965 the industry operated at about 85 percent of capacity at prices that virtually eliminated profits.
In 1967 Goodrich-Gulf announced that it was leaving the HDPE business,
taking a loss of $632,000.[49]

A Synthetic Rubber Manufacturer

Despite the disappointment with the polyethylene business, Goodrich-Gulf entered the synthetic rubber manufacturing business full force. When the federal government finally decided to sell the synthetic rubber plants to private operators in 1954, Goodrich-Gulf became one of the significant firms in the field. In 1955 it bought for $40 million a GR-S plant at Port Neches with a capacity of 90,000 long tons and a half-interest in the adjacent butadiene facility. Later, in 1956, Goodrich-Gulf bought the plant at Institute, West Virginia, with a 122,000-ton annual capacity and modernized it. The strategy was to become a supplier both to Goodrich tire and industrial products factories and to other rubber firms.[50]

Goodrich-Gulf was integrated with its parent firms. In 1966 Gulf provided 38 percent (by value) of the raw materials used, and sales to Goodrich accounted for about 67 percent of the total sales of Goodrich-Gulf products. That year it ranked second in sales among the seventeen producers of butadiene in the United States and third among the thirteen producers of SBR (as styrene-butadiene rubber was then called).

The Goodrich-Gulf joint venture proved to be a short one. In 1969 B.F. Goodrich was the subject of a hostile merger attempt by Northwest Industries (see chap. 8). In order to protect Goodrich's autonomy, Keener arranged for the purchase of Gulf's half-interest in the venture through an exchange of stock. Gulf, now a major stockholder in Goodrich, would not allow the shares to come into the hands of Northwest Industries, and Goodrich-Gulf became Ameripol, Inc., wholly owned by Goodrich. Finally, in 1971 Ameripol became a part of Goodrich Chemical. The synthetic rubber operation that had begun in the crisis of World War II had returned home to B.F. Goodrich.[51]

Although a substantial petrochemical manufacturer, Goodrich-Gulf was not an especially successful business. Once the firm had paid the costs of building its factories, its sales and earnings climbed. The press reported earnings of $6.6 million in 1961 and of $7 million in 1962. The company lost money in 1967 and 1968, however, as plants wore out and as competition kept synthetic rubber prices down. When synthetic rubber manufacturing returned to Goodrich, it was not a line of business poised to help the company's balance sheet.

RESPONDING TO PVC COMPETITION:
MANUFACTURING STRATEGIES

Placing the synthetic rubber and HDPE businesses in the hands of a separate organization freed Goodrich Chemical executives to focus on the firm's established position in the PVC industry. In spite of the buffeting that PVC prices experienced, the outlook for the industry remained favorable. The chemical company executives could look forward to an enlargement of PVC volumes. Given the company's experience with vinyl chloride markets, there seemed enough reason to expand their PVC capacity. In 1958, the most disastrous year ever for PVC prices, industry capacity stood at about 1 billion pounds, while sales barely reached 600 million pounds. However, new markets continued to appear. In 1958, for example, the growth of vinyl flooring markets had offset declines in other markets. Each year industry executives had experienced an upsurge in one or two markets, and they expected sales to reach about 1 billion pounds in 1963 or 1964. Vinyl, in the words of a trade magazine in early 1959, "has by no means reached the age of maturity." The forecast was off the mark: sales of vinyl exceeded 1 billion pounds in 1962. Goodrich had about a 20 percent share of the market.[52]

The answer for Goodrich to the end of the postwar PVC boom was to stay in the industry following a two-pronged strategy that was clearly in place by 1965. First, engineers in the chemical company learned how to manufacture PVC much more cheaply; at about the same time the chemical company worked successfully at backward integration in order to maintain a position as the lowest-cost producer of PVC. Second, the chemical company also cooperated closely with research scientists to develop new products. (The new product ventures enjoyed mixed success, and none proved to have the same dramatic profits that PVC once enjoyed.) Moreover, within the PVC field Goodrich Chemical successfully began producing new compounds that had special applications and that resulted in high profit margins.

Becoming the Lowest-Cost PVC Producer

Establishing Goodrich as the lowest-cost producer of PVC had a number of advantages. Being the lowest-cost producer would discourage competitors from expanding their own manufacturing facilities and discourage new entrants into the industry. This strategy allowed Goodrich, in the cryptic language of the firm's records, "to withstand price pressures and the squeeze on profits from ever-increasing competition."[53]

But the strategy depended on two developments: a new manufacturing technology and backward integration into low-cost raw material sources. The company had developed a significant advance in manufacturing technology in the 1950s when, working with Hoechst, a German chemical firm, Goodrich scientists discovered a commercial method for cracking ethylene dichloride (EDC) to produce vinyl chloride monomer and hydrogen chloride. Although the chemistry was hardly new, the problem was that for each vinyl chloride molecule produced a hydrogen chloride molecule was also produced, a commodity for which there was no special market. The key was a cost-effective process that combined the hydrogen chloride with acetylene to produce more VCM. In 1958 Goodrich began to convert its VCM production facilities to the new process.[54] Acetylene remained a relatively expensive commodity, however, and Goodrich engineers knew that the company would have a jump on the competition if it could use ethylene, a derivative of natural gas. Working with the Badger Company, Goodrich scientists developed the first commercial fluid-bed oxychlorination process, announced in 1964. This breakthrough amounted to a fundamentally new, and lower-cost, technology for manufacturing PVC. The new process pioneered by Goodrich engineers used ethylene. Using a catalyst in a fluid-bed reactor, the hydrogen chloride resulting from the cracking of ethylene dichloride was recycled and combined with ethylene and air to make more EDC.[55]

Goodrich executives hoped the new process would not only give the firm a competitive advantage but would also discourage other companies from expanding into the field and thereby encourage price stability. The chemical company initially invested $23,686,500 in the oxyhydrochlorination of ethylene for manufacturing EDC at Calvert City. Executives believed that because of the overcapacity and depressed profits in the industry, "only those producers who have basic raw material positions are apt to operate profitably in the future, and only those that have large volume sales can really justify integration. With over 20 percent of a billion pound plus per year market, the B.F. Goodrich chemical company is in such a position." To discourage competitors from trying to devise some way around Goodrich patents, the company decided to license its technology.[56]

Their reasoning led executives to integrate the manufacture of chlorine with the manufacture of ethylene dichloride. (Ethylene came from natural gas, and no one considered trying to change Goodrich into a petroleum firm.) The executives decided to spend $15,131,400 for the construction of a chlor-alkali facility at Calvert City capable of making 109,000 tons of chlorine and 122,000 tons of caustic annually. The company expected its chlorine requirements to reach 230,000 tons in 1970. The plant would supply about one-half of that amount at the 1964 market price of $49 per ton, assuring Goodrich of a substantial supply of a raw material for PVC at a price it could largely predict. The problem was disposing of the by-product, caustic soda, and the company postponed making a decision until it had lined up customers for two-thirds of its caustic soda.[57]

After the oxychlorination process was proven a success, the company shifted its strategy slightly. The company expanded its Calvert City VCM capacity in 1969, opening the world's largest facility, capable of producing 1 billion pounds a year. The company's own PVC plants could not use such a large volume of monomer at the time. As Nantz explained, "we've assumed a new role in the vinyl industry, that of being a merchant of vinyl chloride monomer." At a time when PVC production was growing at a rate of 10 percent annually, the strategy projected profits from the large production volume and assured the company of adequate VCM supplies as markets for the plastic expanded.[58]

The bid to become the lowest-cost producer of PVC was a business success. Although vinyl prices continued to soften in the 1960s, from 1961 through 1966 the company's cost of production dropped faster than prices. Chemical sales represented "the most profitable segment of our Company's operations," chairman Ward Keener explained in early 1967. The company, knowing that rivals might be encouraged to develop their own manufacturing innovations, decided to license its new production technology. The licenses yielded profits less sizable than originally envisioned. Nor did the licensing discourage the company's largest competitors from developing new manufacturing processes of their own. By 1969 the company had licensed its oxyhydrochlorination process to three American, four Japanese, and five European companies. Goodrich and Hoechst also licensed their process for cracking EDC. All told, by 1970 40 percent of the world's VCM production occurred with Goodrich licenses.[59]

RESPONDING TO PVC COMPETITION: PRODUCT STRATEGIES

In addition to becoming the lowest-cost producer of PVC, chemical company executives maintained the hope that Goodrich would develop new product lines in PVC and other materials that would again produce dramatic profits. Lawrence Shailer recalled that with Darvan gone, "they were looking for new ways of achieving significant growth." One route was to acquire other chemical companies. Nantz assigned two executives, Shailer and L. F. Reuter, the task of looking for possible mergers. This approach was restricted, however, because corporate executives resisted spending the amounts necessary. The other route was to increase the uses of PVC and its markets. Presumably, if demand for PVC rose, so would its price, especially if demand rose for a Goodrich resin or compound that was superior.[60]

Rigid PVC

The original markets for PVC were in flexible applications, especially wire and cable insulation. Goodrich executives and scientists realized that PVC market opportunities would expand substantially if they could develop compounds that were rigid. Rigid PVC suggested applications in a variety of fields, ideas for which were stimulated in 1945 when Goodrich men traveled to Germany to study the ways the Germans had learned to use PVC as a substitute for materials not available during wartime.

The most startling German wartime PVC application was in pipes. American engineers had not been successful in extruding PVC in a rigid form and believed that the process was simply not viable. Initially, Goodrich engineers paid little heed to the German experience, concentrating instead on improving more established materials for the booming PVC market. However, Clarence Parks, the chief chemist at the Louisville production plant, was personally interested and experimented with extruding rigid PVC. Soon the company moved him to the Avon Lake technical development center to work on a product for the navy, which wanted a lightweight pipe to spray ships with seawater to rinse off radioactive material in the event of a nuclear attack. The navy's successful application of PVC pipes promised to open large civilian markets.[61]

PVC pipe sales were at first a small fraction of what they became after 1960. Announced in 1948, PVC pipes were a proven item by 1953, but only for colder temperatures; in 1955 Goodrich stockholders learned that pipes were an important PVC market. In the civilian sector PVC piping was available for applications such as drainpipes or sewer lines, but its fullest potential awaited a product that could withstand higher temperatures and carry hot water. Not until 1960 did Goodrich have available its "High-Temp Geon," a pioneering chlorinated PVC "so tough that it can be used even in industrial hot-acid piping systems." Harry Warner told the business press that High-Temp Geon, which withstood heat of up to 200°F, "opens the multi-million-dollar plumbing market to the plastics industry for the first time."[62]

The emergence of the plastic pipe industry provided Goodrich with its biggest cause for optimism in the 1960s, but it also provided considerable frustration. Several types of plastics began to be used in pipe manufacturing, including ABS and polyethylene. PVC did not surpass polyethylene in pipe manufacturing until 1965, largely because polyethylene was the most versatile pipe plastic. Before 1960 the difficulty of extruding pipes from PVC resin slowed growth; only thereafter did evolving extrusion techniques allow PVC to enter polyethylene markets and markets of other traditional pipe materials. However, problems with extrusion technology continued to plague Goodrich even after 1960. Strong competition from Monsanto threatened Goodrich's early lead in the plastic pipe market. Goodrich suffered when new extrusion technology appeared that its competitors' resin, but not Hi-Temp Geon, could supply. Hi-Temp Geon proved so difficult to extrude that for a time some industry observers thought of it as a "white elephant."

With the technical problems eventually solved, the company still had to await approval in building codes. That breakthrough occurred in the second half of the decade as the Vietnam War and other factors forced up the demand for copper, traditionally thought of as the most desirable material for residential water pipes. In 1966 the Federal Housing Authority approved plastic pipe for residential uses. At first plumbers' suspicions about plastic pipe relegated its uses to water mains and drainage and vent systems; but soon PVC's price advantages began to overcome their resistance, and a new market for PVC exploded. In 1966, 109 million pounds of PVC went into pipes, surpassing rival plastics in the huge market, and the residential construction market was still to be tapped. Goodrich, as the nation's sole producer of highly chlorinated PVC, was unable to keep up with demand.[63]

Pipes were just one of several possible applications of rigid vinyl. Most promising were other construction applications in siding, doors, and windows. Goodrich, along with Monsanto, led the way in developing vinyl materials for the construction field. By 1962 five firms were producing rigid vinyl. Goodrich chose fabricators of high reputation in developing these new uses for plastic: Andersen for windows and Bird for siding. The Society for Plastics Industries, the trade association, formed a council to establish commercial standards, and in 1963 Goodrich launched a program of awarding a symbol to the siding fabricator who met demanding specifications. Finally, in 1966, Goodrich's long research and development program began to pay off. For the industry as a whole, these markets were still small in 1966, with 13 million pounds of PVC going into windows and 8 million pounds into siding, but prospects for expansion seemed very promising.[64]

FORWARD INTEGRATION

Because of the rising share of captive PVC markets, chemical executives looked for an auspicious venture of forward integration that would be independent of the industrial products division. In 1965 they saw the film and packaging market as highly attractive; they expected it to rise from a level of 55 million pounds of PVC in 1965 to 200–300 million pounds by 1972. They learned that the Thomas J. Little Company had been founded in 1963 in Gloucester, Massachusetts, to develop a new PVC extrusion process for the production of rigid film and sheeting. Little had already developed both a pilot plant for extrusion and a compound superior to anything Goodrich had available. Warner was especially keen on acquiring Little; he thought that the acquisition of Little would allow Goodrich to achieve a significant position in an attractively expanding market and would give the chemical company a larger share of the growing captive PVC market. Goodrich thought that Little's extrusion process might well compete with calendered PVC film with a significantly lower capital investment in plant and machinery. The company also hoped to develop a packaging film from Estane. Thus Goodrich spent $800,000 to acquire Little, and with it the employees whose knowledge held so much commercial promise.[65]

Forward integration never materialized successfully. The acquisition of Little soon ran into trouble, for the vaunted extrusion technology proved not to work. Harry Warner instructed Goodrich engineers to learn as much as they could from Little so that the knowledge might profitably be transferred elsewhere. In the meantime, chemical company executives were thwarted by the corporate treasurer, Fred Moyer, in their attempt to acquire Filmco, a small manufacturer of packaging film, for $14 million. Filmco's owners soon sold their firm to Reynolds for $21 million. The merger allowed Reynolds to become one of the nation's principal suppliers of packaging film.[66]

GOODRICH CHEMICAL AFTER TWENTY-FIVE
YEARS OF GROWTH

The B.F. Goodrich chemical company was, by any measure, a successful business during its period of near autonomy from corporate headquarters in Akron. Goodrich Chemical earned profits every year, and its executives drove it to become larger and larger. By 1970 the chemical division accounted for 33.2 percent of the corporation's total sales, up from 7.4 percent in 1946. During the same period capital invested in Goodrich Chemical rose from $17,851,000 (in 1947), or 8.5 percent of the corporation's capital; the same figures in 1970 were $515,923,000, just over half of the $1,006,313,000 capital-

TABLE 7.2
1971 Results by Division

	Sales	Operating Income	Operating Income as % of Sales
Chemical Company	$346,562	$29,221	8.4
Tire Company	508,774	33,489	6.6
General Products Co.	183,826	131	.1
Footwear Co.	45,500	(3,198)	(7.0)
Aerospace & Defense	52,142	(287)	(.6)
Textile Products	18,730	1,146	6.1
International Co.	126,504	12,777	10.1
BFG Canada	97,010	6,713	6.9
Sponge Products	54,178	1,221	2.2
Total company	1,236,735	94,995	7.7

Source: "Directors Folder," 21 March 1972.

ization of Goodrich. In the twenty-five years after World War II, B.F. Goodrich was reaping the benefits of the diversification into the chemical industry.

Spirits within the executive ranks of the chemical company remained high. Goodrich Chemical employees realized that theirs was the healthiest part of B.F. Goodrich and were proud that their contributions allowed the parent corporation to sustain a public image of a large and successful industrial firm. However, that public image began to wane by the end of the 1960s, and in 1971 the Goodrich board of directors felt forced to recruit an outside leader, O. Pendleton Thomas, to serve as corporate chairman and chief executive officer. Thomas's background included experience in the petrochemical industry. After he took control of Goodrich in 1971, Thomas ended the autonomy of the chemical company and brought its more successful executives into leadership roles at the corporate level.

Although spirits remained high, there were disappointments for the chemical company, mainly due to its response to the changing structure of the polyvinyl chloride industry. Despite the best efforts of the chemical company's executives and scientists, the financial results of becoming the industry's major low-cost PVC producer failed to improve the firm's profits, at least in the short term. The corporation's economists studied product prices by division and found that the chemical company suffered, over its entire product line, a noticeable decline. The decline occurred mostly in PVC. By 1961 (using the average price for 1957–59 as an index of 100), prices had fallen to 86, a 14 percent drop. The downward slide was less precipitous over the next several years but was nevertheless real. By the end of 1967 the index figure was 81.7. Augmenting the price decline was the fact that the other Goodrich divisions fared much better with their prices, and the American economy in general was experiencing inflation, which made the chemical company's price declines all the worse. The operating income return on net capital employed (OIRONCE, a measure of return on investment), for all plastics products (Geon, Abson, and Estane) was below 10 percent in 1966 and slid down below 5 percent in 1970, a far cry from the 41 percent return PVC had enjoyed in 1948.[67]

In 1971, in spite of the price problems with PVC, the chemical company was still B.F. Goodrich's best business. That year—1971 was an especially bad year for the chemical business—the chemical company led the tire and industrial products divisions in operating income as a percentage of sales with an 8.4 percent return. The return for plastic materials (primarily PVC) was 7.4 percent, better than the return for every division except the international division. In 1971 the operating income for plastic materials was $7,426,000, higher than the original equipment tire income of $6,773,000. The strategic decision made in the 1930s to try to turn B.F. Goodrich into something of a petrochemical firm was serving the corporation well in what proved to be troubled times.[68]

By 1969 the events in the plastics industry that had spawned both the booming growth for almost all PVC and other plastics producers and the heightened competition simply did not result in the profits expected by Goodrich executives and by industry observers. The chemical company was in no position to earn the substantial profits that it had enjoyed in the 1940s and 1950s. The decline of its profitability, relative to that of B.F. Goodrich, meant that the parent company was in deep trouble. That trouble, however, was not the responsibility of the chemical company, for the problems lay in Goodrich's traditional policies, which were catching up with senior management and stockholders alike. No longer could the chemical company rescue the parent corporation. After a decade-long struggle to resuscitate the rubber businesses, B.F. Goodrich was in danger for its survival.

8

A Troubled Goodrich: Traditional
Products and Corporate Strategy,
1957–1971

The sins of the past caught up with B.F. Goodrich in the 1960s. The success of Goodrich Chemical was offset by failures in the firm's other businesses. The reliance on research, diversification, and product innovation proved insufficient to overcome the company's failure to invest in the most modern production and distribution facilities outside of chemicals. At the beginning of the decade, Collyer, Keener, and other executives were worried about their firm's profits. At the end of the decade, the company was still struggling to achieve higher profits. In 1971 the board of directors, disappointed by the fortunes of the firm, intervened and removed Ward Keener from his command of the company.

Goodrich's problems were manifold, but nowhere were they worse than in tires. Between 1955 and 1962 the company had seen its earnings decline by 45 percent even as its sales rose by 8 percent. (In contrast, earnings rose 19 percent and 8 percent for Goodyear and Firestone, respectively.) Analysts commonly attributed the trouble to the collapse of vinyl prices. Keener, however, stated clearly that the company's principal problems were in the tire division. Tires represented about half of the company's business, and failures there were difficult to overcome. The profits earned from the chemical business in the 1940s and 1950s proved impressive only in the short run. In the meantime, Goodrich and rival Uniroyal (as U.S. Rubber was renamed) made a "fundamental error" in the eyes of industry observers: "Intoxicated by the glamour of the chemical end of their business, they let their tire plants run down while increasing petrochemical capacity." An anonymous Goodrich executive told a *Forbes* reporter, "If we can straighten out the tire situation, our corporate earnings will really jump."[1] Efforts to catch up in tires consumed much of the attention of top executives. They were unsuccessful. In 1969 Goodrich lagged seriously behind its larger competitors, Goodyear and Firestone, in its profits on sales.[2] Senior executives attempted to rally the company behind programs to improve profits, while offering explanations to directors and investors for the poor showings that pointed to circumstances beyond the firm's control.

LEADERSHIP AND STRATEGY

When Ward Keener was selected to be president, he knew all too well the problems plaguing the company, but he faced them confidently and vigorously. As head of the company, he traveled widely and visited all of the company's manufacturing facilities at home and abroad. Keener was accessible to employees and others; he answered his own telephone.[3] Within a year Keener became chief executive officer and set about reorganizing the corporate headquarters and modifying the company's strategy (Keener was the presiding officer at the meetings of the board of directors and became chairman of the board and chief executive officer in 1967). The changes that Keener inspired occurred, however, with an unspoken assumption: Goodrich as a company was not to depart from its traditions. It would remain a diversified company that made tires and other rubber products. The direction would, however, be somewhat different under Keener, as he brought to bear solutions to problems that arose in Collyer's last years as president.

Keener had plenty of ideas about how to improve Goodrich's prospects in the long term, ideas that emerged from his own background as a staff executive and that reflected the notions circulating among American business executives of Keener's generation. His vision of a newly invigorated Goodrich, expanding in the chemical field and competing more successfully in tires and other rubber products, however, was never fully realized. Keener voiced the right rhetoric about the prospects for improving Goodrich. Unfortunately, Keener proved not to have the managerial presence or the resources needed to make Goodrich into the vigorous, international firm that he envisioned.

The rhetoric that Keener used and the programs that he initiated to revive Goodrich were but one expression of the general confidence felt in American business circles during those years. Goodrich and other American manufacturers had emerged from World War II as dominant in their fields, standing astride domestic and world markets with generally superior technology and relatively ample capital resources. Although recessions had plagued the American economy somewhat after the Korean War ended in 1953, in general the nation was prosperous, with growing material wealth and little questioning about the prospects for the future. There was even greater optimism after the inauguration of John F. Kennedy as president in 1961. Kennedy exuded toughness and confidence and promoted fiscal policies, popular among leaders of large corporations, that promised to dampen the impact of recessions and lead the nation's—and with it the world's—economy to ever higher plateaus of prosperity. Before ills associated with the war in Vietnam surfaced near the end of the decade, Americans in general and business executives in particular enjoyed high levels of confidence in their prosperous future.

Ward Keener and other Goodrich executives were very much a part of this picture. They especially believed that they had the insight necessary to ensure that Goodrich was part of the economic growth. Initially, Keener and Collyer were both confident that their company's net income would improve noticeably between 1960 and 1964. Soon after he became president in 1957, Keener set out a six-point strategy for reinvigorating the company. (1) He wanted to place an even greater emphasis on research and development, but with a different focus: to ensure that efforts were directed toward profitable products. Thus, to the disappointment of chemical company executives, Keener eventually canceled Aztran production. However, he also believed that Goodrich's best prospects for profit were with the chemical company, especially in marketing new adhesives based on the ongoing revolution in polymer science. (2) Keener wanted the company to do more to integrate backward "to achieve lower materials costs for increased profitability." The chemical company's production of VCM was one key example. Forward integration, furthermore, would take advantage of its technical and manufacturing capabilities. (3) Keener set out to invest more vigorously in new plants and equipment, especially for the tire division, the firm's largest single business. He also wanted the company to invest more aggressively in rubber manufacturing abroad than it had traditionally done. (4) He placed greater emphasis on cost analysis and reduction in each of the firm's projects. (5) Keener especially hoped to reorient the company so that its executives adopted what had come to be known as the marketing approach to business. (6) Finally, he sought to refresh management with people hired from outside the company. The "real ambition" of these changes was to achieve the highest profit ratio in the rubber industry "soon" and, eventually, to earn more than Goodrich's larger competitors. Keener and his staff concluded that the combination of ventures should increase net income in the five years 1960–64. Eventually Keener summarized his views in a booklet entitled "Principles and Objectives." Widely distributed among managers, it explained that these principles and objectives transcended the company's operating manuals and were to constitute a common understanding to serve as a basis in reaching decisions.[4]

With his entire business career occupied by staff assignments, Keener not surprisingly considered strengthening corporate staff functions to be an important part of solving Goodrich's problems. Goodrich had never completely decentralized under Collyer; he always retained corporate control over basic divisional decisions. Yet Keener thought that decentralization under Collyer had "gone too far," that the corporate staff must assume even greater authority if the company was to achieve higher profits. The decentralization of 1953 had so fragmented Goodrich that the firm seemed in danger of losing its identity. Advertising themes, for instance, required greater coordination. "Our controls have been about as advanced as any company's," Keener said. The problem was inadequate staff. "You can have all the reports in the world and they are no good unless you are equipped to analyze them properly," he explained.

The result was the creation of a larger, more complex bureaucracy in corporate headquarters. A policy and appropriations council replaced Collyer's operations council. Chaired by Keener, the council was to have a small corps of senior staff executives who attended every meeting. Other executives responsible for operations in tires, chemicals, and other divisions participated in the council meetings when the agenda involved their area. As its title implied, the function of the council was to decide on Goodrich's basic business strategy and to appropriate the capital available for achieving it. Keener required executives seeking approval of capital expenditures to analyze their contribution to the firm's profits. Each proposal had to be accompanied by figures showing the projected impact on sales and profits.

The policy and appropriations council was an umbrella over a series of more focused councils. In 1967, ten years after Keener became president, the company had five other councils. As he explained, the operations review council, which met once a year, involved "all divisional activity." The purchasing council considered rubber and textile materials, while the inventory council was devoted to inventory. "An Employee Relations Council grapples with personnel problems; a Manager's Council is extremely broad, and includes 125–130 people," as Keener summed up the system.

The development and assignment of management personnel necessarily occupied Keener's attention. Soon after he became president, Keener made important personnel changes to strengthen corporate-level control. He appointed W. W. (Bill) Scull as manufacturing vice president. Scull was to ensure that the different manufacturing arms of Goodrich kept their costs low. John N. Hart, a former Ohio State University economics professor, held the new post of controller. His task was to set up controls over the flow of funds to ensure economical operations throughout the company. Frank Schoenfeld, who served as vice president for research starting in 1954, coordinated product development throughout the company. Keener charged Schoenfeld with ensuring that the divisions focused solely on ideas with good prospects for profit. Keener also hired Don C. Miller, an advertising agency executive from Kenyon & Eckhardt in New York, as vice president for marketing, a new corporate function. Meanwhile, Arthur Kelly remained as executive vice president, ensuring that inventories were kept small. As the second in command until his retirement in 1967, however, Kelly's principal role was to serve as Keener's alter ego.

These assignments changed over time. By 1967 Miller, his demeanor too abrasive for Keener's liking, was gone. Manufacturing services, purchasing, and research reported to Arthur Kelly. P. W. Perdriau, who started with the company as a chemist but soon joined management in the rubber products area, became responsible for tires and aeronautics. Harry Warner, who in 1963 had moved from the chemical company, served as a group vice president with industrial products, textiles, footwear, chemicals, and Goodrich Canada reporting to him. When Kelly retired, Warner became president and chief operating officer. Frank Schoenfeld remained in charge of research and development. John Hart served as controller, while Fred Moyer was treasurer. Both Hart and

Moyer reported directly to Keener, who in effect was the company's chief financial officer. Keener also had the international division and the legal department report directly to him.

Recruiting and nurturing managerial talent required Keener's attention. Aware that John Collyer regretted his own inadequacy in grooming managers for leadership positions, Keener very much wanted to rectify the situation. Under Keener's direction, the company began to recruit recent college graduates with liberal arts degrees for junior-level positions in about equal proportion to those it recruited with technical degrees (in 1967, all of the company's top executives except one, J. C. McKinnon of footwear, had earned technical degrees). Keener believed that bright liberal arts graduates enjoyed excellent prospects of developing managerial vision. At a higher level, Keener wanted fresh talent recruited, men who might assume future leadership roles.[5] Although Don Miller did not stay with Goodrich, he left a legacy of several bright, ambitious executives who soon became top managers. Gerard Alexander, an experienced marketing executive from DuPont, took over the international division when William Gullick retired. Patrick C. Ross came from Argus Camera when that company was sold. Ross eventually replaced Alexander as head of the international division, going on to lead the company's tire division.[6] Robert Eisentrout was recruited because of his experience with marketing nationally branded products for Lever Brothers and Procter & Gamble; like Ross, he eventually headed the tire division and also moved to Uniroyal Goodrich (a joint venture created in 1986).

Keener wanted Goodrich executives to assume personal responsibility for important decisions after first carefully reviewing prepared staff reports. Keener appointed the senior executives under a system of "cross-streaming." Executives, in this view, need not have specialized knowledge in the area they were supervising. Broad experience was more desirable. With this in mind, Keener decided to tap the chemical company, which had so successfully nurtured able executives, to help the parent firm. He appointed Harry Warner as group vice president in 1965 and as president of B.F. Goodrich in 1967, a post Warner held until his retirement in 1974. In his organizational and personnel considerations, Keener observed that "decisions never get made by committees." As was the case under Collyer, executives held meetings and discussed ideas and proposals, but the senior executive responsible decided the issue at hand.[7]

KEENER'S INVESTMENT STRATEGY

As the company struggled to deal with its problems, investment strategy necessarily occupied a great deal of attention in the corporate headquarters. The capital requirements for the company were considerable. As we have seen, the chemical company required huge infusions of capital to build the plants required to be the low-cost producer of PVC and to take advantage of profitable opportunities in new products. While the chemical company was making serious demands on Goodrich's capital resources, so too were the more traditional rubber fabricating businesses.

Although there was no basic change in Collyer's financial policies, with Keener's leadership Goodrich proved to be more aggressive in making capital investments. As the economy prospered in the 1960s, all businesses had to plan for growth to take advantage of opportunities. Nowhere was this more true than in rubber manufacturing. In 1965 one business school expert predicted an 82.6 percent increase in tire sales and an increase of 100.3 percent in the demand for other rubber products by 1975 (using 1963 as the base year); the GNP, he thought, would grow by 86.4 percent.[8] Near the end of his tenure, Collyer recognized that his company lagged behind competitors in rubber manufacturing, and in 1956 the company announced a $200 million investment program. But the expenditures in the program fell behind, and Keener vowed to return to the planned schedule. He was concerned that investment expenditures did little more than stay abreast of depreciation: "When you just spend depreciation, you're walking backward." The company also got caught in a tire price war and labor cost increases, conditions that, within a decade of Keener's leadership, required outside financing.[9]

Goodrich invested capital more aggressively under Keener's leadership than under Collyer's presidency, especially in the tire division. That aggressiveness was necessary lest the company slip further behind its larger competitors. Keener had no illusions about gaining ground against Goodyear and Firestone. Investments in modern plants and research would provide the base "for rearranging the profit structure of the four large rubber companies. We do not necessarily want to become the largest rubber and chemical firm in the world, but we are working to make B.F. Goodrich the most profitable."[10] He also wanted to see Goodrich's market share in tires and other products grow. For six of the fourteen years 1958–71, Goodrich investments as a percentage of gross plant were equal to or surpassed those of Firestone and Goodyear. During 1948–57 Goodrich had never led the large rubber manufacturers in that category. From 1956 to 1970 Goodrich always paid dividends as a percentage of earnings that were higher than those of Goodyear, Firestone, and usually also Uniroyal. Keener wanted to maintain a predictable dividend rate, one that would be the same in flush years as in lean years. Unfortunately for him and the firm's stockholders, the lean years proved to be all too common.[11]

Although Keener recognized the need to move aggressively with investments, Goodrich actually lagged further behind its larger competitors during his tenure. His desire to see Goodrich's market share improve, however modestly, was frustrated. Goodyear and Firestone maintained their strong record of capital expenditures, and U.S. Rubber was also undergoing a revitalization program that made it a stronger competitor. In 1967 Keener told company managers that the results of the growth policy were disappointing. The growth of the company's sales was below the growth of the national economy. Keener wanted earnings growth to exceed the growth in sales. The company's earnings were well below the figure needed to generate new capital. After 1967, the situation only worsened.[12] Keener had planned to maintain the company's established practice of investing from retained earnings. Those earnings, however, proved insufficient to meet the investment objectives, and by 1967 the company was resorting to external funding.

One reason was rising interest rates. With the federal government borrowing heavily to finance the Vietnam War and inflation escalating, interest rates rose to a point where long-term financing seemed too costly to Keener. In 1967 he arranged for Goodrich to borrow capital on a short-term basis to allow desired investments in new plant and equipment, anticipating that interest rates would soon become more favorable. When interest rates remained high, the company suffered. Long-term debt payable after one year rose dramatically, from under $50 million in 1958 to $357,290,000 in 1970. Eventually, the company had to borrow money at unfavorable interest rates: $50 million from banks at 9.75 percent interest, and debentures paying 8.25 percent interest.[13]

The high interest charges struck the company just as it was completing its new world headquarters building in 1970. Goodrich executives had long suffered from an inadequate office environment in the old factory buildings on Akron's South Main Street. There they sweltered in Ohio's humid summers and were grimed by carbon black and other effluents from the rubber factory. The new world headquarters building would provide a cleaner, more modern, and air-conditioned environment. Its construction, moreover, was symbolic of Goodrich's commitment to the Akron community, for it was part of a larger project of urban renewal to provide parks and housing along the old Ohio Canal that had originally attracted B.F. Goodrich. The costs, however, were incurred at a time of deepening financial trouble for the company.

RESEARCH AND DEVELOPMENT: THE CONTINUING HOPE OF TECHNICAL INNOVATION

Keener spoke often and with pride of Goodrich's traditional strength in research and development. "B.F. Goodrich holds [the] unquestioned lead in research and development accomplishments among companies with which we compete and has one of the top records in American industry. It is our purpose to maintain and extend this margin of superiority." He and other executives kept hoping for the development of new products that would rival the profits enjoyed by PVC for the ten years following World War II. This wish meant that the corporation's research efforts received higher levels of funding than they had previously. Keener and Frank Schoenfeld, the corporate research director, agreed, however, that some reorganization and reorientation of Goodrich's research efforts were required.[14]

Eventually, Keener spelled out his thoughts about research efforts, reflecting his experience in the field. Keener placed greater emphasis on the commercial opportunities provided by research. The approach was to be "market directed," with research funds spent to protect and improve the company's position in established markets and to achieve "optimum profitable utilization of existing facilities." Research allocations were to go first to the development of products with unsatisfied markets but where Goodrich had established marketing experience. Generally researchers were to extend existing Goodrich businesses rather than invade a field in which the company had no background. Keener was willing to allow the company to go into new fields, but only after a careful analysis of the commercial opportunities and the activities of competitors. In the meantime, research efforts were to go to areas where "the time for successful commercialization is shortest."[15]

With these considerations Schoenfeld and his colleagues observed three problems that especially affected the firm's research efforts. First, although company policy was to have unsurpassed quality standards for its products, there were "several trouble spots in the quality of our goods" that required attention. Second, the scientific complexity of the businesses in which Goodrich engaged was increasing. And third, competitors "had become increasingly competent" in the technical fields in which Goodrich operated. The solution to those problems required reorganization of the research operation. "The facilities of the research laboratory were thrown into the breach to help the operating divisions with their most pressing problems," Schoenfeld told the board of directors. Although the research director did not provide any examples, he concluded that "this has been very successful." The company saved millions of dollars as a result, and the executives responsible for research improved their ability to ensure that technical efforts were more productive. By 1963 Schoenfeld reported that the corporate research staff was able to put more and more energy into developing new products while the operating divisions were working harder "on extensions of existing product lines."[16]

The company's research effort also became more closely tied to government policy, owing to the continuing cold war and armaments race. The 1960s proved to have unprecedented opportunities for government business as President John F. Kennedy increased expenditures for space exploration and announced a program to land an American on the moon by the end of the decade. Goodrich, which had already developed space suits, seized the opportunity to engage in government-funded research and development work. The research projects also led to manufacturing goods such as nose cones, rocket cases, and rocket fuels for the military services and the National Aeronautics and Space Administration. Schoenfeld expected spin-offs from the government work to help the company in civilian markets.[17]

A MARKETING ORIENTATION

Keener attempted to change Goodrich's orientation to what had come to be known as "marketing" in business circles. Marketing, as a concept to apply to business strategy, began in the early twentieth century and blossomed after World War II. The marketing concept involved a number of ideas. Manufacturing executives, like those at Goodrich, were supposed to adopt a marketing orientation toward production—not making goods and offering them for sale but exploring what customers desired and designing and fabricating products accordingly. Under the marketing concept executives throughout the firm were to look at their tasks from the viewpoint of customers, as opposed to looking at the operations of the company from the perspective of technological or organizational problems in manufacturing. Top-level strategists defined goals through market analysis and developed a structure accordingly.

The marketing concept began to flourish in the 1920s. The J. Walter Thompson advertising agency developed a "full service" to its clients, including Goodrich, that included studying the firm's market as well as developing advertisements to reach it. Alfred P. Sloan Jr. of General Motors advanced the marketing concept in the 1920s, defining General Motors's strategy in terms of the automobile market. Breaking the car market into price categories, he organized General Motors divisions accordingly, with each car division assigned a particular market. Under Sloan's tutelage General Motors rose to become the world's largest industrial firm, and when the depression ended, hundreds of other firms tried to emulate Sloan's successes.

The marketing concept was embodied in the American Marketing Association, a professional society of executives and business school professors concerned about the problems of distribution in the American economy and the appropriate orientation of firms. Keener was an active member of the American Marketing Association and announced that the development of a marketing orientation was a priority for his company. As head of Goodrich, Keener stressed what he termed "total marketing"—the idea that "everything starts with the customer." On one occasion he remarked that "marketing is the only reason we are here." Invited to keynote the American Marketing Association's 1959 convention, Keener observed "*everything* business does must be pointed to the Market. It means that every business function must be directed toward and be in tune with the Market." Every department of the firm, from research to personnel, "must, at all times, have their eyes on the Marketing ball." Employees, Keener recognized, had to be educated toward this orientation. At Goodrich the abstraction "The Marketing Concept" became the slogan "Every B.F. Goodrich man must be a 'B.F. Goodrich Customers' man." Keener was convinced that successful companies were market-oriented companies, a status that would only increase as time passed.[18]

As a result of Keener's marketing orientation, Goodrich changed in both its personnel and its structure. Keener quickly reached outside the firm. In 1958 Keener began to devote considerable time to "the strengthening of marketing methods and organizations." He appointed Don C. Miller, the New York advertising executive, to the new post of corporate vice president for marketing. With Miller's assistance Keener began to hire a larger corporate staff to develop market planning, market research, advertising, the commercialization of new products, the design of packages and products, and customer and trade relations. Within three years the divisions were revising their marketing organi-

Under Keener, Goodrich operated Car Care Centers in conjunction with leading department stores, such as this center at John Wanamaker's in Wilmington, Delaware. (BFG Col. UAA)

zations according to what Keener called "the latest good marketing methods." Keener told the stockholders in 1961 that good marketing and efficient production would help overcome the pressures prices were placing on profits.[19]

The new executives were charged especially with the task of attending to distribution problems. Business scholars at the time estimated that 48¢ of every dollar earned in manufactured products went for distribution costs, about 24¢ for physical handling, and about 24¢ for advertising and selling costs. And for tires, Goodrich's biggest source of income, those costs were even higher. Under the new marketing orientation, executives were to serve as a team organized around a product. They were to be supported by increases in advertising expenditures. The 1960 advertising budget was 60 percent higher than the 1959 budget.[20] The tire division in particular was the focus of the new attention being paid to distribution and marketing.

MULTINATIONAL VENTURES

The last major item on Keener's agenda was to strengthen the company in foreign markets. Keener recognized that the risks were greater abroad but that the opportunities for profits were also greater than in the mature American markets. The years after World War II were a time when American companies substantially extended themselves into production and distribution around the globe. The branch factories or affiliated companies of American manufacturers accounted for about one-half of the rubber consumption outside of the United States (except for the Soviet bloc). Goodrich was a latecomer in this postwar multinational expansion, lagging behind Goodyear, Firestone, General, and U.S. Rubber. Collyer had informed the board of directors that one of his company's failings had been the reluctance to expand more aggressively abroad. By the middle of the 1960s, observers thought that Goodyear earned about one-third of its sales, and about 35 to 36 percent of its profit, from foreign operations; Firestone earned about 25 percent of sales, and about 25 to 30 percent of its profit from foreign operations.[21]

Goodrich's leaders recognized that they had to reverse some traditional practices and find resources to invest in tire manufacturing abroad if they were to achieve profits commensurate with those of their larger competitors. Keener revoked Collyer's policy of operating in most foreign markets through a minority interest in subsidiary firms, and began to shift foreign investments out of PVC production in Britain and Japan. Capital from British Geon and Japanese Geon had best be used, he thought, for other projects, including new tire facilities in Europe. When Keener became president, Goodrich manufactured and sold its products abroad through twenty foreign companies, only one of which—B.F. Goodrich Canada—it owned. A decade later Goodrich had thirty-four overseas companies, fourteen of which it controlled. In 1968 international sales accounted for about 18 percent of the firm's consolidated sales. A major thrust of the expansion was in Europe, where postwar prosperity was creating a larger automobile and tire market.[22]

The shift was partly a result of personnel changes in the international division. When William Gullick retired as its president in 1964, some of the company's brightest, most aggressive executives moved to the division's helm. Gerard Alexander brought a keen desire to enlarge international sales. He persuaded Patrick Ross and John Ong, a young attorney with the corporate legal department, to join him in that effort. The largest single effort overseas went into the burgeoning European tire market. In 1965 Goodrich decided to build an $18,330,000 tire factory in Koblenz, Germany, with a daily capacity of 4,000 tires. The factory was to supply the German market primarily, but also serve as a source of products for sale elsewhere in the European Common Market. Company officials were optimistic about the prospects for the Koblenz plant; it would even surpass the capacity of Goodyear's largest foreign tire factory.[23]

Although the Koblenz project was the company's largest overseas investment, there were other important projects as well. Nor were they limited to tires. The international division was responsible for investments in Brazil, Iran, and Australia, and it added to existing ventures in Colombia, Mexico, Peru, Japan, and the Philippines. A special favorite for senior executives was the tire factory built in Iran in cooperation with the Shah. The Iranian venture combined a business opportunity with the nation's strategic objectives in the cold war, while giving executives a chance to travel to a seemingly exotic land.[24]

Overall, however, Goodrich experienced mixed success. Overseas sales as a percentage of total sales reached a high point in 1968, reflecting the relative aggressiveness of the international division with investments. Most important, the international division continued to be profitable relative to other divisions of the company. Nevertheless, the division's profits declined from earlier levels during these years. Operating income for the international division as a percentage of net sales fell during the 1960s, but it stabilized around 11 percent for the years 1967–70. Still, the division was profitable, and the problem of its still fairly small volume of sales paled in comparison with other troubles the company suffered.[25]

The plantation in Liberia, administered separately from the international division, continued to drain resources, yet executives believed they needed to continue their investment there to provide an assured supply of raw material. Goodrich saw profits from natural rubber sustain its competitors during the price war that beset the tire industry after 1958; tree rubber still cost less than synthetic natural rubber. Moreover, as the company began to plan its conversion to radial tires in 1966, engineers discovered that natural rubber was the superior elastomer for parts of the new design. As late as 1970 the production of natural rubber was a promising business. For twelve years natural rubber consumption had grown faster than production. Of the natural rubber imported, American rubber companies used over 40 percent in truck, bus, tractor, and aircraft tires, and almost 30 percent in passenger car tires.[26]

COMPETING IN THE TIRE BUSINESS

Keener's effort to resuscitate the tire business proved an uphill battle, one not won before he left the company. Keener and his counterparts in rival firms remained confident that the tire business was an expanding business, one which American producers would dominate and in which reasonable profits could be expected over the long run. Despite all the problems that beset Goodrich as a large tire producer (albeit one operating by this time in a tier below Firestone and Goodyear) the future still seemed to offer good business prospects. Automobile use was increasing, not declining, and even more so in markets abroad than in the United States. When Keener took the company's reins, tires still seemed like an attractive business. It would befall a younger generation of executives, working in a tire market wherein distribution and manufacturing knew no national boundaries, to think of leaving the tire business as a viable choice for Goodrich.[27]

When Keener became president the tire division was in serious trouble, however. Neglect at the company's tire factories had left them less productive than those of their competitors. Goodrich's market share was well below that of both Goodyear and Firestone, and it suffered especially in the most profitable tire market, replacement passenger tires. Goodrich executives, true to the company's tradition of technological innovation, hoped that the introduction of radial tires, a fundamentally new and improved product, to the American market would provide the company with an edge in the most lucrative premium tire market. However, in the end, the company's hopes for the radial tire sank against the market power of Goodyear.

To make matters worse, just as Goodrich began investing to revive its competitive position in the American tire industry, a price war badgered all of the companies. The price war in tires was mainly the product of overexpansion. Tire manufacturers believed that they would grow as American driving grew. The decision in 1956 to build the interstate highway system was all the more reason to think of the tire business as a growth business. Firestone especially, but other companies also, invested aggressively in tire manufacturing facilities in anticipation of a booming market—and they overinvested, at least for the short term. The growth in manufacturing capacity allowed wholesalers to develop new lines of private label tires and to develop new distribution channels in the discount stores and shopping centers that were rapidly appearing as automobility dispersed the American population into suburbs. In 1955 there were about 50 private label tire brands offered for sale in the United States; by 1965 the number had grown to about 165. By 1965 private label brands enjoyed a 45 percent share of the replacement market.[28]

The price war began in 1959 when Goodyear dropped prices to compete with private label tires. The private label brands offered in discount stores had undercut the tire giant's cheaper lines. The price war eased after 1963, but tire prices remained low. In 1968 prices were on average 95 percent of what they had been in 1957 and 1958, before the price war began. The price war hurt in the original equipment market as well. Automobile manufacturers took advantage of the intense competition in the tire industry to bargain for lower prices, making it difficult for Goodrich to earn much profit in those sales.

The tire companies, including Goodrich, survived the price decline by becoming more efficient. While raw material costs declined about 15 percent, labor costs increased by over one-third between 1957 and 1968. The difference had to be made up through improvements in productivity and reductions in distribution costs. In 1968 Goodrich manufactured 70 percent more tires than it made in 1958 and did so with 80 percent of the number of employees.[29]

In spite of the price war, tire executives remained optimistic about their industry's future. Americans were driving more, and driving heavier cars that wore out tires more quickly. "I can't see anything, barring a major international catastrophe, deterring successful growth of the rubber industry," Earl B. Hathaway, president of Firestone, told a *New York Times* reporter in 1968. Americans, he observed, simply had a love affair with automobiles, "and you can't drive a car without tires." Vic Holt Jr., the president of Goodyear, predicted a 5 to 8 percent growth in tire sales annually for as long "as I can see." Soon, however, Keener had less reason to be optimistic about his company's prospects in the tire industry.[30]

INVESTMENTS FOR THE TIRE DIVISION

Goodrich executives tried to improve their profits in the tire industry by making important investments in both production and distribution. To meet the growing demand, an entirely new tire factory was built near Fort Wayne, Indi-

The Fort Wayne tire factory is shown here in 1962. (BFG Co.)

ana, while established tire factories outside of Akron received new machinery and sometimes additional space. The company also tried to strengthen its distribution by acquiring outlets in new markets. Serious problems with investments in both areas appeared by the end of the 1960s, however.

The construction of the new Fort Wayne tire factory was the most dramatic venture of the tire division. Scull and Kelly began to study possible sites soon after Keener became president. Fort Wayne seemed desirable because of its close proximity to about a quarter of the nation's replacement market and well over half of the automobile factories. The Indiana government promised tax abatements, and its state laws were less sympathetic toward labor unions than those of Ohio. The company announced plans for the new factory in 1960, and production began in 1962. The plant was of the most modern type: single-story, and arranged for an efficient flow of materials and finished products.

Unfortunately, the Fort Wayne plant did not immediately live up to its bright promise. One reason for its location was to win a supply contract with the Chrysler Corporation, a first for Goodrich. The price war raging in 1962, however, meant that Goodrich had to sell tires to Chrysler with little if any profit to gain a portion of that market. The factory simply began making tires at a time when no company was enjoying an especially profitable return on its investment.[31]

Goodrich also tried to improve tire distribution with substantial investments. But the actions, intended to keep abreast of competitors in the replacement market, soon soured as senior executives made poor decisions. The company acquired two firms, the Rayco Manufacturing Company in 1961 and Vanderbilt Tires a year later. Rayco manufactured convertible tops and auto-

Goodrich workers inspect tires at the Fort Wayne factory. (BFG Col. UAA)

mobile accessories, selling them nationally through franchised dealers and six company-owned stores. Vanderbilt had forty-four leased automotive outlets in major department stores and shopping centers. The hope was that the two acquisitions would give the company more profitable outlets for private label tires as well as new facilities for selling premium-priced Goodrich brand tires. Goodrich also opened eight of its new Car Care Centers in connection with leading department stores. Unfortunately, neither venture was very successful. Goodrich left intact the management of Vanderbilt, and its former owner, Harold Leitman, threatened a suit against Goodrich on the grounds that it was selling tires to Sears, Roebuck for lower prices. The company settled the suit in 1965 by agreeing to sell Vanderbilt back to its previous owners, who in turn immediately sold their interests to Goodyear for $10 million. Nor was Rayco a good investment. The company's success had depended in part on shady dealings, which the Federal Trade Commission ordered stopped shortly before Goodrich acquired the firm. Goodrich sold Rayco in 1970 for $7.2 million to Cle-Ware Industries, which was $2.5 million above Rayco's net assets. The deal soured, however, because Goodrich held that profit as a note, and Cle-Ware declared bankruptcy in 1972.[32]

THE DEVELOPMENT OF THE RADIAL TIRE

Having failed to gain an edge over competitors with the development of the tubeless tire, Goodrich hoped that the introduction of the radial tire to the American market would help solve some of the tire division's problems. Michelin, a French firm, had begun radial tire construction in 1948. Goodrich engineers knew about the design and its advantages through their connection with Kleber-Colombes and Vredestein. In fact, the company's European affiliates began to watch Michelin successfully place its radial tires as original equipment with European automobile manufacturers, and they clamored for Goodrich to enter the field. Soon Goodrich realized that the development of radial tires for the American passenger car market offered a great hope for the company. But ultimately these hopes were sadly frustrated, again by the market power of Goodyear.[33]

Radial tires represented a fundamental change in the design and construction of tires. Before radials, tires had belts of fabric underneath the tread that ran diagonally, on a bias, to the direction the tire traveled. In the radial design, the fabric was installed from bead to bead at a ninety-degree angle to the direction the tire traveled. To strengthen the tire and keep it round, designers placed an additional belt underneath the tread that ran in the direction of travel. Initially, the strengthening belts were of fabric; eventually, manufacturers used steel belts.[34]

The radial tire offered advantages and disadvantages to tire manufacturers. The advantages were in better performance. Radial tires provided better control of the vehicle and less rolling resistance; thus, vehicles using radial tires gained improved fuel efficiency. A small disadvantage in performance was a slightly harsher ride at low speeds. A more serious disadvantage to tire manufacturers, however, was that radial tires cost more to build. Existing tire building machinery had to be modified to allow radial construction, and it was most efficient to invest in entirely new tire building machinery. Radial tires also lasted longer, reducing opportunities for replacement tire sales.

Within the ranks of the senior executives, Alexander (who knew what was occurring in the European market, where his international division sold tires) was the special advocate for radial tires. After 1960 foreign automobile manufacturers began to use radial tires as original equipment, and Goodrich's partners developed their own design, the GT100, using rayon belts to avoid Michelin's patents on steel belts. Alexander persuasively argued that radial tires represented clearly superior tire engineering, and being the first to introduce them to the American market would provide the company with an advantage. Best of all, radial tires were premium tires, goods that commanded higher prices and earned higher profits than the private label tires that were a growing share of the nation's replacement tire market and the company's tire business. Company market researchers were learning that the tire market was changing; in purchasing, customers thought less about the tire manufacturer than about the tire's special characteristics and label. It was possible to differentiate the tire market into niches in which Goodrich could reach particular groups of customers and sell them distinctive products.[35]

The company planned to introduce the new product carefully. In the summer of 1965, the policy and appropriations council approved $1,123,000 for a semiworks facility to begin producing radial tires with projected sales of $3.9 million by 1968. The tire division sought first to achieve sales in the replacement market, then to bolster its claims of engineering superiority by convincing original equipment manufacturers to outfit new automobiles with radial tires. Late in 1965 Goodrich first offered radial tires to the market in Dallas. As manufacturing capacity increased, the company over the next year gradually spread distribution into other southern markets. Ford Motor announced that it would supply the radial tire as original equipment on its 1967 Mercury Colony Park station wagons, and it expressed interest in using radial tires on the 1967 Mustang.[36]

There was much reason for optimism about the new product. Dealers reported that there were few problems with radial tires and began offering the premium tires to customers on a satisfaction guaranteed basis. Soon Goodrich dealers were clamoring for greater availability. Finally, in 1968, having gained market experience with the product and having educated its dealers about radial tires' superior features, Goodrich launched its largest ever advertising campaign, "The Radial Age," to reach the general public. Developed by executives from Batten, Barton, Durstine & Osborne, the campaign sought to instill the idea of the radial tire as technologically superior, suitable for customers who wanted the best performance from their car.[37]

Into 1968 company officials remained optimistic about what the new product would mean to their firm's profits. The other large tire manufacturers had rushed to introduce their own radial designs, and there was every sign that customers preferred radial tires once they understood their advantages. Engineers with the automobile manufacturers remained interested. In fact, engineers throughout the tire and automobile industries recognized the radial design as superior in almost all respects. Goodrich was well ahead of its competitors in converting factories to radial tire production. The company seemed poised to take advantage of being the "first mover" in an important new tire technology.

By the summer of 1968, however, their optimism was deflated. Goodyear, reluctant to spend the capital necessary to convert its production lines, and confident of its ability to use its advertising muscle to cloud the reputation of radial tires, refused to follow Goodrich's lead. Goodyear downplayed the advantages of the radial tire, emphasizing that radial tires offered a somewhat less smooth ride at low speeds. Suspension systems needed to be "tuned" to radial tires, Goodyear told replacement tire customers. Apparently not concerned that foreign producers' success with radial tires in the American market would be permanent, Goodyear eschewed converting to the technology. Instead, Goodyear promoted the "bias/belted" tire, using its polyester tire cords instead of nylon or rayon, with a new fiberglass belt under the tread. The resulting product, while technically inferior to radial tires, was superior to conventional bias tires. Best yet, manufacturers could construct bias/belted tires on conventional machinery without making the large investments required to convert to radial tires. Goodrich's hopes that the radial tire would quickly rescue its tire profits finally ended when car manufacturers' purchasing agents refused to buy the radial design, for it was custom that at least two manufacturers supply tires to the assembly lines. Goodrich, as a relatively small supplier, simply had insufficient capacity, and a single supplier provided no insurance against delays in deliveries. The company had to invest over $9 million to convert tire factories to bias/belted production if it expected to maintain its share of the market. Forecasts for 1970 were that conventional tires would have 32 percent of the market and none in original equipment, with bias/belted tires having 57 percent and radial tires just 11 percent.[38]

Sadly, Goodrich managers watched the innovation fail to live up to its full promise. They knew that their company was simply too small, relative to Goodyear, to promote the product on its own. Goodyear's advertising budget was substantially larger, and Goodrich's market share too small to justify larger advertising expenditures. To make matters worse, in 1969 the tire division was caught with an excess inventory of conventional 15-inch tires and insufficient capacity to make the required number of bias/belted tires; executives agreed to make up the shortfall by purchasing 250,000 tires from another manufacturer. They also watched Michelin begin to make inroads in the North American market with its radial tires, as growing numbers of customers learned of their superiority. By 1969 tire imports to the United States were exceeding exports, and radial tires along with the growing popularity of small European cars was the main reason. The radial tire did not become the standard design in the United States until after 1973, when the sudden rise in gasoline costs meant that fuel efficiency became a premier consideration in designing, selling, and driving automobiles. By that time, owing to Goodyear's refusal to invest in the best available tire technology, American tire manufacturers were slipping against foreign competitors, especially Michelin.[39]

A POSSIBLE NEW DIRECTION IN TIRES

By 1969 Ward Keener realized that there was little prospect of Goodrich's following its current course in tires and earning the profits necessary to sustain the company. The radial tire innovation was a technological success but had foundered against the power of Goodyear. The Vanderbilt and Rayco acquisitions had proven unwise investments. Rumors in Akron suggested that the company was in effect abandoning its quest to establish itself over Uniroyal as the third-largest tire supplier and deciding instead to emphasize its other rubber goods. Keener began to search for alternatives. Michelin offered one opportunity. Both companies faced problems that, Keener thought, a partnership might alleviate. The French tire manufacturer wanted to penetrate the American market, then the world's largest, more fully. Michelin announced the construction of a North American tire factory in Nova Scotia capable of producing 12,000 tires a day. Creating a distribution system was the company's largest business problem. Keener thought that perhaps some sort of joint venture with Goodrich, which had original equipment customers and a network of tire stores, was the solution for Michelin. The partnership might provide Goodrich with both capital and greater market power to advertise the superior qualities of radial tires.[40]

Negotiations, for which Goodrich took the initiative, occurred secretly in

Paris between Keener and Michelin officers. Keener, along with a few of Goodrich's top officials—Alexander, Ross, Jeter, and Ong—had reluctantly concluded that Goodrich could no longer follow its traditional pattern in the tire business. Keener was uncertain about just what kind of partnership with Michelin might be desirable, but he wanted to explore some sort of venture in which Goodrich would be the senior partner in the American market. Michelin was interested, but not as a junior partner. When Keener realized that Michelin wanted to control any new joint venture, he broke off the talks and returned to the United States. Fundamental strategic changes would not occur in Goodrich's tire business until John Ong took charge of the company.[41]

Not only was Keener unwilling to consider a relationship with Michelin in which Goodrich was not fully in control, he was also unwilling to concede that his company could no longer hold its own against the much larger Goodyear. Goodyear knew that its knowledge of radial tire technology was inferior to that of its smaller rival, and its chairman, Russell DeYoung, tried to take advantage of Goodrich's relative weakness by, in effect, capturing its tire technology. DeYoung and Keener were friends, having served together in a number of roles in the Akron community and belonging to the same clubs. On a Saturday morning in April 1970, DeYoung called Keener and said, almost in passing, that Goodyear planned to purchase Vredestein in Holland and Reidrubber in New Zealand. Keener was outraged. The deals, if consummated, would give Goodyear his firm's radial tire technology. Quickly he contacted Alexander with instructions for the international division to prevent the sales to Goodyear.[42]

Alexander and his colleagues viewed the Goodyear move as a "double envelopment," a tactic designed to split Goodrich's resources and make it difficult for the smaller rival to fend off the aggressor. Whatever Goodyear's calculations may have been, they failed. Alexander arranged for Donald McClusky, a chemical company executive with international experience in Australia and New Zealand, to work out an arrangement that would prevent Reidrubber from falling into the hands of a competitor. In the meantime, his young lieutenant, John Ong, was already in Europe. Alexander summoned Ong to The Hague to try to prevent Vredestein from being sold to Goodyear.

Ong knew that he was dealing with Dutch executives who were capable of duplicity. The evening before DeYoung's call to Keener, Ong had dined with the Vredestein executives, who were fully cordial and who gave no hint that they were, in effect, working to stab Goodrich in the back. Ong knew a Dutch tax lawyer, who put him in contact with a local investment bank. Together they plotted a defense. Goodrich challenged the purchase of Vredestein in court, arguing that the long-standing technical agreement between Goodrich and Vredestein provided for confidentiality and in effect forbade the sale. Goodrich informed the Dutch court that technology was at risk—technology that, although not necessarily protected by patents, was a valuable asset for which the Goodyear offer was meager compensation.

After weeks of waiting for the ruling, Goodrich won in the Dutch court. An injunction forbade the sale to Goodyear. The battle, however, was not over: it moved to the financial arena of the Amsterdam Bourse. Goodyear offered 380 percent of par value for Vredestein shares. When Goodrich told the Vredestein board of directors that it planned to execute its 1964 agreement allowing it to purchase the shares, the board announced the issuing of 18,300 new shares that it would sell to Goodyear. Again Ong was prepared, and Goodrich ended up owning about 51 percent of Vredestein shares to Goodyear's 49 percent. Goodyear conceded and negotiated the sale of its stake in Vredestein to Goodrich, which became the sole owner of the Dutch company.[43] In the meantime, McClusky had successfully arranged for a new and friendly partner in New Zealand, Feltex New Zealand, to take over Reidrubber, with $755,425 in sorely needed capital to be paid to Goodrich.[44]

All told, the effort to improve the company's profits with the introduction of the radial passenger tire proved a partial success for the company by the end of Keener's leadership. In 1971 executives reported that the tire division was doing well and had enjoyed the second-best operating income in its history. The firm was able to take advantage of economies resulting from earlier capital improvements. The successful introduction of radial tires was serving it well, for Goodrich made more than one-half of the radial tires produced in the United States, albeit for a very small market (radial tires were 2 percent of the original equipment market and 6 percent of the replacement market in 1971). However, the radial passenger tire introduction was a substantial failure in terms of restoring the tire division to long-term profitability. Nor did it help Goodrich regain market share. Goodyear's ability to have the bias/belted tire become the standard tire gave that tire giant a large advantage over all of its competitors, for Goodyear had converted more production faster to bias/belted tires.[45] Even worse for the long term, Goodyear's shortsighted decision to promote bias/belted tires allowed Michelin and other foreign competitors an opportunity to penetrate the American market with superior radial technology. In retrospect, the loss of American firms' dominance of their domestic tire market can be traced to the false promotion of bias/belted tires, something Goodrich was too small and too weak to prevent.

COMPETING IN INDUSTRIAL PRODUCTS

The industrial products division received somewhat less attention from senior management than did the tire division, if for no other reason than its smaller size. The price war that beset the tire division did not extend to other rubber goods, and economic prosperity allowed the company to increase prices for hoses, mechanical goods, and belts in 1965 and 1966. Moreover, price increases for industrial rubber products in general were greater than they were for tires. Markets for hoses and belts, two of the division's mainstays, followed the business cycle, which meant that in the economic boom of the 1960s they prospered.[46]

Keener's effort to stress marketing resulted in a new organization in Goodrich, a consumer products division, which reported to the vice president in charge of industrial products. The firm's consumer products—including Koroseal, foam rubber goods like pillows, and footwear—had little in common with one another. There was simply little common identity and no special esprit de corps in this management area. Keener wanted to change that situation by placing all of the company's goods sold to individual consumers, except tires, under the new consumer products marketing organization. He hoped that the reorganization—with managers employing the most up-to-date market research, advertising, and distribution techniques—would enable Goodrich to emulate successful market-oriented firms like Procter & Gamble. In the meantime, a separate organization would manage sales of products like belts that business customers bought.

The separation stirred controversy among senior executives. Footwear simply refused to participate, and Goodrich's shoe sales remained independent. Unknown to Keener, in complex off-the-record discussions, executives in other areas were offered the opportunity to retain at least part of their traditional marketing organizations. In the end, however, the consumer products division was created in 1961, with offices in New York City.[47]

The principal success for the industrial products division remained in hose, tubing, and flat belts for conveying goods in industrial settings. Those product lines grew across the rubber industry in the 1960s, and forecasters expected the markets to improve even more in the 1970s. Nevertheless, in some areas that the division served, competition was fierce. Foreign manufacturers entered the field earlier than they did in tires and by 1970 were a serious competitive factor.[48]

Keener wanted the industrial products division to solve some serious problems. Part of his desire to have the corporate research staff do more to help solve problems in the divisions stemmed from quality problems in industrial products.[49] In addition, industrial products operations were not well integrated with those of the successful chemical company. Senior executives, watching the chemical company participate in the materials revolution emerging from polymer science, wanted that part of Goodrich's expertise better applied in the industrial products division. They were successful to a considerable extent, as new synthetic rubbers and plastics continued in the 1960s to improve the performance of a wide variety of rubber and mechanical goods.

Although the industrial products division had some success in its traditional product areas, newer ventures into plastics products were, on the whole, disappointing. To try to help, Keener moved James Richards from his post as vice president for sales in the chemical company to head the industrial products division. But Richards soon faced frustrations. For example, the company was struggling in its vinyl floor tile business. Executives thought there would be an advantage to the integration of vinyl production with tile manufacturing, but that proved not to be the case. While Goodrich was struggling, flooring manufacturers were succeeding with vinyl materials. Research scientists tried to help by identifying the technical problems and trying to develop new vinyl compounds. The hope was that the managers newly charged with marketing consumer products would be given a product, integrated with the chemical company, that could garner successful sales volumes.[50] Despite best efforts, Goodrich never became a serious competitor in the vinyl floor tile business. Other plastics areas were more successful, however, as the factory at Marietta operated at capacity. In 1963 the company decided to expand that facility.[51]

One new, if relatively small, area for Goodrich was in supplying flexible vinyl refrigerator gaskets, where long-range forecasts of healthy returns on investment persuaded executives to pursue the field. In 1964, industrial products enjoyed sales of $500,000 to Hotpoint, about half of its gasket business. Then it lost half of its Hotpoint market to a competitor who offered lower prices. The division decided to locate a small plant near the Hotpoint factory, allowing Hotpoint to enjoy reduced shipping, packaging, and inventory costs. When Goodrich built the plant, Hotpoint agreed to buy all of its gaskets from the company. The deal would double Goodrich's sales. Because it saw the refrigerator gasket market as a growing one, the company agreed to make an investment of $174,000, even though the return on that sum it projected as only 6.8 percent in 1965, −4.5 percent in 1966, and 4.9 percent in 1967. The payoff would come in 1967 with a return of 12.7 percent on the $174,000 investment.[52]

Despite such promises, problems continued to plague the division in some very important areas. V-belts were one where Goodrich had fallen by the wayside. The company had left the automotive v-belt market entirely in 1962, and by the end of the decade its market share in v-belts had fallen to about 6 percent. By 1969 v-belts were an unprofitable business for Goodrich; and the losses deepened from $101,000 in 1969 to $409,000 in 1970 and $762,000 in 1971. Tied to the high-cost factory facilities in Akron, Goodrich's productivity in the field had fallen behind that of its competitors. Finally the company tried to rescue its v-belt business by moving production to Elgin, South Carolina, escaping the high labor costs of Akron and allowing the introduction of new manufacturing techniques in a one-story plant. The company justified the expenditure with the achievement of a major marketing goal: a contract with T.B. Woods & Sons, a major pulley manufacturer, to supply belts for five years.[53]

The problems with v-belts were symptomatic of a larger problem. Process technology had fallen behind in a number of important areas. Goodrich simply did not have the modern facilities for making various rubber products efficiently. Often the problems experienced by the industrial products division were like the problems in tire manufacturing. The Akron factory complex was old, poorly designed for the latest machinery, and ill-suited to integrating the movement of goods efficiently. Tires produced higher volumes of revenues than industrial products, and the tire division therefore obtained the lion's share of the new capital spending, especially with the construction of the Fort Wayne plant. Resources were available, however, to deal with some of the worst problems. In 1969 executives decided to spend $2,735,000 to build a plant at Honea Path, South Carolina, to make surgeons' gloves.[54] Nevertheless, the new expenditures could not always solve the division's problems. Sometimes new equipment was installed in the old factory in Akron that engineers could not fully utilize because of awkward requirements in handling the flow of material. Worse, the executives responsible for engineering and production had fallen behind the times. Falsely confident of American technical superiority, they failed to keep abreast of improvements in manufacturing processes developed abroad. When foreign competitors began to penetrate the American market, Goodrich suffered.[55]

Finally, the industrial products division was unmanageable as an entity. James Richards, who headed the division for most of these years, recalled it as the "waste can" of Goodrich. With so many disparate products, and the most promising new areas removed in the aerospace and defense products division, there was little cohesion in production or distribution. Manufacturing processes were often quite different for different products. Worse, there was little commonality in distribution. The marketing reforms envisioned in the creation of the consumer products division failed to realize their full promise. The division was begun in 1961, and sales personnel for consumer products were assigned small territories in which they were supposed to handle all Goodrich products except tires and chemicals. This organization was soon abandoned when executives realized that the range of products was too great for any individual to know in depth. The company went back to assigning a few products to sales personnel and having them work with the manufacturers and distributors who bought carpet cushioning, belts, batteries, and the like from Goodrich. Eventually, Richards concluded that the division should be broken up into more focused parts. When he failed to persuade senior management to make structural changes, Richards chose to retire.[56]

THE MISFORTUNES OF FOOTWEAR

Footwear, another traditional Goodrich business, was an area that looked promising for a time, but that in the long term proved to be disastrous. The market for shoes changed dramatically as the younger American population grew, with the postwar "baby boom," and it looked for a time as if Goodrich would benefit. That it did not, that footwear ended up a serious drain on resources, was as much a product of bad luck and unforeseeable developments as it was of mistaken judgments.

The sales of sneakers—or, more technically, rubber-soled canvas footwear—grew quickly after 1960. Goodrich, with a long history in this area and with a popular line of "P.F. Flyers," expected to succeed in the growing market. The company hoped that with the proper investments in new manufacturing facilities it could make its shoe business a profitable venture that would improve the firm's earnings. However, the United States, generally seeking free trade, lowered tariffs on rubber-soled footwear in 1966. Having failed to anticipate the rapid growth of imported shoes and unable to adapt quickly to changing market conditions, the company ended up losing large sums in footwear.[57]

Sneakers were especially popular among younger Americans, and as the population grew and its average age went down, the market expanded. Executives looking at the situation observed that the sneaker market nearly doubled between 1958 and 1964. With 103 million pairs sold in 1964, they projected continuing expansion to 146.3 million pairs in 1970. To take advantage of this opportunity, Goodrich had introduced new lines of colored canvas shoes. The market share of "Flyers" rose from 15.8 percent in 1958 to 18.7 percent in 1964. Goodrich shoe executives expected the company's market share to grow to 20.5 percent in 1970. They had a solid distribution outlet through an agreement with the J.C. Penney Company, a nationwide merchandiser.[58]

The only problem they anticipated was one of production. In 1962 the company employed a consultant to study shoe manufacturing practices. The firm's factory in Watertown, Massachusetts, acquired through the Hood Rubber merger, was antiquated. Labor costs there were particularly high, and made up about one-half of the cost of manufacturing. The consultant recommended building a new factory, one that allowed for better integration of manufacturing processes and improved product quality control. Acting on this advice, Goodrich decided in 1965 to move its shoe production to new facilities in the South, eventually locating at Lumberton, North Carolina, and Elgin, South Carolina. In Lumberton a well-designed $11,500,000 plant and in Elgin a $1,315,000 plant could turn out shoes with fewer workers and at lower wages than in Massachusetts. The company expected to recover its costs in less than three years. In the meantime, Keener and his colleagues expected to meet foreign competition in part by moving some stitching operations to Puerto Rico, to a subsidiary called Aguadilla Products.[59]

The plans soon went awry. Start-up costs proved to be higher than originally projected, although the company successfully beat back an attempt by the United Rubber Workers to organize the new shoe workers in the Carolinas. Worst, the sneaker market took an unexpected turn. Goodrich had designed its new factory as an up-to-date facility with machinery capable of making long production runs of standardized sneakers inexpensively. The problem, however, was that standardized sneakers faded in the market as customers turned to sneakers of different colors and different designs. Foreign producers, who enjoyed dramatically lower wage costs than any American producer, could quickly change production to meet the changing market; but Goodrich, with its high fixed costs in labor-saving machinery, could not. The results were disastrous. Goodrich lost money in footwear in 1966, and those losses grew deeper every succeeding year. By 1971, when the company completed its move of sneaker manufacturing to the South, the enterprise was hemorrhaging money.[60]

GOODRICH AS AN AEROSPACE COMPANY

Aerospace ventures were a much happier experience for Goodrich, albeit on a smaller scale. In 1961 Goodrich changed the name of the aviation products division to aerospace and defense products. The new division was responsible for

The astronaut John Glenn wore a Goodrich space suit when he orbited the earth. (BFG Co.)

sales to the federal government, which in 1960 constituted 7.3 percent of the company's total sales. The goal was to participate more extensively in supplying products for the military services and the National Aeronautics and Space Administration—which was being developed in the 1960s to place an American on the moon by the end of the decade.[61]

The newly named division enjoyed several successes with new products. It was especially proud of supplying the space suits for the astronauts in Project Mercury, which in 1961 sent John Glenn as the first American to orbit the earth. Goodrich failed to win the contract for the Apollo astronauts who would go to the moon in 1969, but the new division did win important business in other areas.

More substantial for the long-range health of Goodrich was the continuing success of aviation products for civilian as well as military markets. In 1962 the

Goodrich Aerospace tested its evacuation slides for the new Boeing 747 aircraft in 1969. (BFG Co.)

division decided to widen its commercial business and to reduce its dependence on military and space contracts. One result was growth in airplane wheel and brake sales, so much so that by 1965 B.F. Goodrich's aircraft wheel and brake business had grown to the point where the facility at Troy, Ohio, was inadequate. The plant was running overtime, and jobs were being sent to subcontractors over whom Goodrich could not exercise adequate quality control and who took most of the profits. So the company decided to invest an additional $1,560,000 at Troy to take advantage of the expanding business. The planners in the aerospace division expected the sum to produce a return of 13.1 percent in 1966 and 16.9 percent in 1967 and 1968. Even that expenditure proved inadequate for the factory's needs, and in 1967 a building addition and new equipment costing almost $5 million were approved. The company was particularly pleased to be supplying tires and other significant equipment for the Boeing 727 and the Boeing 747 aircrafts. It also supplied wheels, tires, and brakes for the Lockheed L-1011 plane.[62] And the division continued to have a predominant sales position in the general aircraft market. In 1968 sales of general aircraft products were $3,533,000 with an after-tax income of $389,000, a margin of about 11 percent. The company wanted to stay abreast of changing technologies in the field, and it wanted to discourage Goodyear from entering the pneumatic deicer market. Between 1962 and 1972 the division's sales shifted from 25 percent in civilian markets to 58 percent.[63]

LABOR RELATIONS

Goodrich and other rubber companies continued to suffer from poor labor relations during Keener's leadership. Part of the problem was a basic conflict between the desire of rubber workers to improve their standard of living—improvements that they thought should be commensurate with those of workers in the automobile industry, which the rubber companies were supplying—and the intense price competition that forced managers to seek lower production and distribution costs. Part of the problem, for Goodrich at least, was Keener's and other executives' intense dislike of the union movement.

Although in public Keener spoke of his acceptance of collective bargaining, in private he seethed with resentment over having to share power with unions. Keener was unhappy with the course of collective bargaining in the post–World War II period. He believed that the union movement in general, and the United Rubber Workers in particular, had won wage gains at the undue expense of investors, managers, and the men and women who made technological improvements. Typical of manufacturing executives of his generation, Keener voiced the usual rhetoric, accepting the principles of collective bargaining as "a permanent and useful part of American life." But he felt that unions had gone too far. They were too prone to call strikes when the public interest called for harmony, not confrontation. Union leaders expected too large a share of the pie, at the expense of corporations. They were also too quick to accept government help, when labor relations were generally best left to the private sphere. And unions had too many special legal privileges denied companies like Goodrich. His attitudes led Keener to take a greater personal role in major labor disputes than had Collyer.[64]

Not surprising, Goodrich's labor relations were rancorous during the years Keener led Goodrich. Much of the fault, however, lay with the United Rubber Workers. In 1959 the union elected George Burdon president, and negotiations—now on a two-year rather than an annual contract cycle—produced substantial gains in wages and benefits without strikes. That situation changed in 1966 when Peter Bommarito ousted Burdon on a platform that charged Burdon with a failure to act aggressively. Bommarito promised the rubber workers a militant campaign against the rubber companies for higher wages, better security against unemployment, and improved benefits. Given internal union politics, a strike in 1967 was almost inevitable.[65]

The 1967 Strike

With contracts with the four largest rubber companies expiring on 20 April 1967, the United Rubber Workers began negotiations for a new contract in March. The union demanded a substantial wage increase, better benefits and vacation time, and a guarantee that on unemployment the companies would provide 92.5 percent of the worker's wage for a year (called "supplemental unemployment benefit," a contract feature that had spread from the automobile to the rubber industry in 1957). Furthermore, the union demanded that the lower wages of nontire workers be brought up to the level of tire worker wages. The companies' counteroffer was rejected, and the union called a strike against Goodrich, Uniroyal, and Firestone on 20 April. Goodyear remained open until 13 July, its URW members sending benefit funds to the striking union locals.[66]

The strike was long and bitter. It lasted for eighty-six days and disrupted production at nine Goodrich tire and industrial products factories. Knowing that the strike was likely, the tire companies had agreed to help one another withstand it. Goodyear continued to operate, and Goodrich and other manufacturers sent tire molds to its factories, where some tires were made under different labels. Every firm, of course, had built an inventory stockpile. Nevertheless, by the third quarter the strike was hurting Goodrich's revenues and profits. For the workers, strike benefits ran out and, despite help from the United Automobile Workers and other unions, hardships were common.[67]

The most dramatic day of the strike for Goodrich executives was 5 June. Sometimes, during strikes, senior executives stayed overnight in their offices to avoid picket lines; but Ward Keener, not expecting any serious disruption from pickets, had not done so on the evening of 4 June. When he arrived at the factory gate at 7:15 the next morning, Keener found his path blocked by an illegal mass of picketers. Stubbornly, Keener rejected advice from his most experienced labor negotiators to depart, deciding instead to stay in his automobile until company attorneys could obtain an injunction against the picketers. A court issued an injunction ordering the pickets to disperse and allow access into the factory by 10 A.M., but enforcement officers, fearful of provoking violence, refrained from intervening. Keener sat in his car all day, leaving only at 5 P.M. For the head of Goodrich it was a matter of principle—he had the right to go to work. Keener made his point dramatically; he received banner headlines and was much photographed. A writer for *Rubber World* called the episode "a psychological boomerang for the union," but some in the company thought differently: Goodrich was humiliated, their president a flawed leader.[68]

Finally, on 13 July, the URW and General Tire reached an agreement. The new contract in effect set the industry standard, which Goodrich accepted on 15 July. The union did not gain all of the concessions it sought, but it won a substantial victory. Wages were to rise over the three-year life of the contract, vacation and other benefits improved, and the supplemental unemployment benefit was set at 80 percent. Even with these advances, however, the strike was costly to the workers. They had lost wages, and those losses would barely be recovered before the new contract expired in 1970. For Goodrich, already suffering in a competitive industry, the costs of lost revenues and profits were high.[69]

The 1970 Strike

The events of 1967 began what one observer eventually termed "a triennial passion play." Although painful, the 1970 strike was less dramatic for Goodrich. This time the URW focused on Goodyear. Bommarito complained that inflation had wiped out the wage gains of the 1967 union victory and demanded a large increase in wages and improvements in workers' benefits. The Goodyear strike began on 20 April. Goodrich failed to prevent a strike in its plants, however, which the union closed early in May. The company and the union agreed to a contract about a month later, and Goodrich's labor costs rose dramatically as a result.[70]

The company experienced rising labor costs because of the URW victories, and it was unable to offset them with rising prices. Managers believed that the power of the union to compel higher wages and benefits without commensurate increases in productivity cut deeply into Goodrich's profits. Because of the tire price wars and the substantial decline in PVC prices, the company's selling prices overall declined noticeably—from an index of 100 in 1957–59 to 90.6 in 1966. Labor costs per employee during the same period rose by more than one-third. Declines of about 15 percent in raw materials prices helped the company absorb those labor costs. Unable to raise prices for its products, the company tried to compensate with productivity improvements, but those were not infinite. The union victories in 1967 and 1970 were especially painful because Goodrich executives found that further productivity improvements were very difficult to achieve. In 1969 overall productivity in Goodrich's factories actually declined.[71]

THWARTING A MERGER WITH NORTHWEST INDUSTRIES

In 1965–69 American business witnessed a merger movement that mushroomed quickly and died quietly in 1969. Unlike earlier merger movements affecting large firms like Goodrich, this one involved the development of so-called "conglomerate" firms. As the financial markets of the United States had developed, it became possible for a smaller firm to take control of a much larger firm by offering a package of securities whose value was based on the earnings of the larger firm. A belief had arisen among some executives that managerial skills were transferable from one field of activity to another, and that it was possible for a small group of managers in the highest offices in a

company to manage a diversified portfolio of businesses even if those businesses were in very different product or service fields. The conglomerate headquarters staff, in this view, could evaluate performance and manage a diverse
group of businesses through financial controls. This was a finance mentality, as
opposed to the more traditional production or marketing orientations common among manufacturing executives. This relatively new set of beliefs, combined with the desire of some investment houses and banks to earn quick
profits through buying and selling firms, led to companies such as Goodrich
becoming the objects of attempted mergers engineered by entrepreneurs from
very different industries. When it happened to Goodrich, Ward Keener and
his colleagues mounted a defense in what came to be known in business circles
as a classic success.

Late in 1968 and early in 1969, Ward Keener, Ray Jeter, other officers in
Akron, and John Weinberg of Goldman, Sachs (who had taken his father's
seat on the Goodrich board of directors in 1962), ever suspicious that Goodrich
might become a victim of an unwanted merger attempt, learned of unusual
trades of Goodrich stock. They knew that Goodrich was vulnerable because
its relatively poor profits had depressed the price of its stock.[72] Sensing that
they might be a target, Goodrich and Goldman, Sachs executives met to discuss possible defensive strategies.

Keener, Jeter, Weinberg, and the others were right to be suspicious. On 8
January 1969, Lawrence Tisch, the promoter of the Loew's conglomerate,
based on a theater chain, acknowledged that he had purchased a "fair-sized"
portion of Goodrich stock. Keener and his associates planned to discuss how
to respond to Tisch at the 20 January board meeting in New York. While attending the meeting, however, they were surprised. Ben Heineman, a lawyer
turned promoter who had built a conglomerate called Northwest Industries
(whose base firm was the Chicago and Northwestern Railroad, a venerable
company whose tracks ran west from Chicago into rich agricultural districts),
announced an offer worth $1 billion to purchase Goodrich stock, about 30
percent more than the market value of Goodrich's common stock. Tisch, a
member of the Northwest board of directors, had apparently been buying
Goodrich stock as part of the offer. Heineman had recently been hurt in his
attempts to acquire other firms, and Goodrich seemed an attractive target.
He told reporters that Goodrich was undervalued and performing poorly because Keener and the other managers were not aggressive. Heineman invited
Goodrich stockholders to exchange their stock for bonds and shares of stock in
Northwest Industries. Northwest Industries, with 1968 sales of $701 million,
was trying to buy Goodrich, whose sales were just over $1 billion.[73]

Goodrich's defense was swift. Ward Keener was of the old school of executives, intensely suspicious of conglomerate promoters and their motives. He
believed that managers should focus on production processes and markets in
an attempt to improve efficiency and profits. Firms like Goodrich had a responsibility to their customers, their employees, and the communities that
housed them, responsibilities of which conglomerate leaders too easily lost

sight. He wanted no part of a conglomerate constructed with complex financial deals and heavy debt loads, termed by some contemporaries as "Chinese wallpaper." Like Goodrich's executives, members of the board of directors were appalled at the prospect of trading solid assets for what seemed like speculative securities. The offer, in Keener's view, was "a reckless way to combine the businesses of two companies the size of ours and Northwest." Keener warned stockholders that any profits to individuals from the offer were taxable, yet Heineman was not offering any cash that could be used to pay the taxes. Crisis meetings ensued involving all of Goodrich's top executives and their allies in Goldman, Sachs and White & Case, the New York law firm that had served the company for many years. Keener was sure-handed and vigorous in defending Goodrich. Within three days he had met with Heineman and told him that the consummation of the Northwest offer could harm both firms.[74]

The defense moved simultaneously on two basic fronts: political and business. The business front was the least time-consuming. The company planned to stagger the terms of its board members so that even if Heineman were successful he would not control the board of directors for several years. Over the years, originating from business relations, Keener had developed a close personal friendship with executives of Gulf Oil. Calling on that friendship, Keener arranged for the purchase of Gulf Oil's share of Goodrich-Gulf, placing Goodrich stock into the hands of a friendly partner, who now held about 7 percent of the outstanding common stock. (There was a widespread, if unconfirmed, belief among Goodrich managers at the time that if the worst happened, Gulf Oil would take over Goodrich to block Heineman's maneuver.) Soon thereafter, on 5 March, Goodrich purchased Motor Freight, a regional trucking line operating in Indiana and Ohio. Interstate Commerce Commission regulations at the time forbade railroads from owning trucking companies. Two days later Goodrich petitioned the ICC, arguing that Northwest Industries was now obliged to obtain the commission's permission to acquire Goodrich.

The petition to the ICC was just a foretaste of what Heineman would face on the political front. Goodrich officers were well connected politically. More immediately, within days of the offer, Ray Jeter, Goodrich's Arkansas-born corporate counsel, visited his friend Wilbur Mills, the Arkansas Democrat who controlled the powerful Ways and Means Committee of the House of Representatives. Mills agreed to hold hearings on a measure to change the tax laws to discourage conglomerate mergers. Just before the hearings, Jeter introduced Mills to Paul Cabot, a member of the Goodrich board, treasurer of Harvard University, chairman of the State Street Investment Trust, and one of the nation's most respected investment bankers. During the hearings, one observer recalled, "when Cabot testified it was like somebody playing a symphonic concert: Mills was playing the violin and Cabot was playing the viola and they just blended." Mills believed that conglomerate mergers concentrated financial power too highly. Furthermore, Mills cooperated by sending a letter to

Goodrich stockholders—which Keener enclosed with his request for proxies for the annual meeting—supporting the defense and warning that changes in the tax law would soon dampen the financial prospects of conglomerate mergers. No longer would companies issuing bonds in exchange for stock be allowed to deduct the interest expense. Northwest responded by revising its offer to Goodrich stockholders, reducing the number of bonds to be exchanged and adding shares of preferred stock.[75]

On the political front Goodrich defended itself in two other ways. It filed an objection with the Securities and Exchange Commission, pointing out, among other matters, that Northwest did not have a solid financial position with which to back the merger. The bonds it would issue should not be allowed. The company also worked in the judicial arena by suggesting that the merger violated antitrust law. With the help of Akron's congressional representative, William Ayers, and Ohio senator William Saxbe, the company obtained a sympathetic hearing in the antitrust division of the Department of Justice. Late in March government lawyers warned that courts might block the Northwest offer on grounds that it was anticompetitive. It was not an idle threat. In July, when the Justice Department asked for an injunction against the Northwest offer, the presiding judge, while denying the injunction, warned that the case would probably go all the way to the Supreme Court if the merger went through.[76]

Meanwhile, Goodrich managers worked frantically to contact stockholders personally and persuade them that Heineman's offer was a poor one. These combined efforts proved successful. On 11 August, Heineman withdrew his offer and the battle was over. Northwest held just 16 percent of Goodrich's stock; Ben Heineman was the company's largest stockholder. "We are not surprised that Northwest quit," Keener stated. "B.F. Goodrich will remain independent," he continued with pride. "The company has a bright future." It was, company executives and board members alike agreed, Ward Keener's finest hour as a business executive.[77]

THE COMPANY IMPERILED

The successful defense against Heineman was an exhausting affair for senior managers, and for Keener especially. The Goodrich chairman approached the fight vigorously, passionately, and with an astute sense of how to combine his knowledge of financial affairs with skillful manipulation of the legal and political system. He could not bring the same qualities to the long-standing problems of his company, however, and hope to overcome its underlying troubles. The fight with Northwest Industries was a short-lived affair; the fundamental problems of Goodrich were historical and required long-term solutions. The bid by Heineman was provoked in part by the fact that Goodrich was not performing well in the eyes of investors and the stock was not selling at a favorable price. Heineman, or some other corporate raider, could thus package an offer with considerable appeal.

Losing Money

In the mid-1960s, after the tire price war receded, the prosperity of the American economy hid some of Goodrich's underlying weaknesses. The automobile industry boomed; as a result in 1965, tire manufacturers operated at capacity. As Russell DeYoung, the head of Goodyear, explained for his company and the industry in general, sales of tires "were largely limited only by our ability to produce."[78] Nor was the economic boom limited to tires. The high demand for all sorts of rubber products served the industrial products division well. When the boom ebbed, however, all tire companies found it more difficult to earn profits, and Goodrich suffered accordingly. When problems in the footwear and other divisions continued to plague the company, and the profits in plastics, while substantial, were no longer sufficient to cover losses elsewhere fully, management was in trouble. Goodrich did not do well in 1967. Its net sales went down 3 percent from 1966, and its net income fell by 28 percent. Net income would have appeared much worse except for the sale of the firm's equity in British Geon.[79] The sale of assets may have made the balance sheet look better, but it was an ominous sign.

Bad Luck

Some of the ills that befell Goodrich by the end of the 1960s were beyond the company's control. With two of its major products, tires and PVC, it operated in competitive markets wherein administering price increases to compensate for rising production costs was tenuous at best. Nor was it possible for the company to forecast accurately what would happen in two product lines it hoped would earn substantial profits over the next decade: footwear and artificial leather, Aztran. The footwear market shifted, as we have seen, to specialized styles that the company could not supply from its new factory. To compound this unexpected misfortune, Aztran proved a costly failure. Goodrich was spending millions of dollars in its Marietta industrial products plant to manufacture the new poromeric material. It knew that it had to make Aztran available in a wide range of colors and textures for it to succeed in the markets for women's and children's shoes. Goodrich would have to supply a large volume of the material if shoe manufacturers were to accept it over DuPont's artificial leather, Corfam. When Corfam proved a market failure, it gave all artificial leather a terrible reputation, in effect ruining any chance of the Goodrich material being accepted. The company had counted on recovering its substantial investments in Aztran over the long run, a time that never came.[80]

Even worse was the interest rate situation. In 1969 interest charges were fully 43 percent of the company's net income before taxes. This sum was clearly staggering. The debt had to be incurred if the company was going to remain in its traditional tire and rubber fabrication businesses. Not to have invested in the conversion to bias/belted tires would have killed the company's tire business, something Ward Keener was unwilling even to contemplate.[81] The

failure to invest aggressively in a competitive industry—the sins of the past—
simply caught up with B.F. Goodrich. Ward Keener was the individual victim.

The harm that high interest rates did to Goodrich could have been mitigat-
ed somewhat, however. The company and its management were more than
victims of circumstances. They chose to borrow money in order to maintain
dividends. In their judgment, not to maintain the company's dividend in the
face of adversity would have wreaked havoc on equity values and made it difficult for the company to survive. In the near term, however, the decision to
borrow the money was costly indeed.[82]

THE FAILURE OF KEENER'S MANAGEMENT STRUCTURE

A man with great intelligence and a sharp analytical mind, Keener's weakness
as an executive lay in more human qualities. He seemed aloof to less senior executives, a forbidding person lacking in empathy and warmth. A principled
man, dedicated to his company and to his family, he simply lacked any leadership quality that could help him transcend the problem of the moment and
command respect from subordinates. As the company struggled, he and President Warner exhorted managers under them to improve the performance of
their business, but they were themselves unwilling, or unable, to act decisive-
ly in ways that commanded respect.

Keener's requirement that all capital spending proposals be accompanied
by an analysis of their projected impact on the company's sales and profits was
a good idea in theory that did not work out in practice. Savvy executives knew
that projections were essentially hopes and that hopes could be fiction as well
as fact. When someone wanted to have a proposal approved, he simply provided projected sales and profit figures to meet Keener's expectations. The
practical result was terrible business planning and had the net effect of harm-
ing the company.

Nor was the staff work on important acquisitions good enough. Poor judgment in acquiring Rayco in 1961 resulted from inadequate investigation of the
business. In 1960 the Federal Trade Commission had ordered Rayco to stop requiring franchised dealers to buy Rayco products exclusively. When Joseph
Weiss, the head of Rayco, refused to allow Goodrich executives to visit the
dealers prior to sale, they failed to recognize the signs that Rayco was in serious
trouble. The FTC order had in effect ruined Rayco's business, an important
fact that Goodrich executives did not understand. Despite the best efforts of
Akron executives, the company was never able to turn Rayco into a profitable
distributor of Goodrich products. Poor judgment also preceded the acquisition
of Vanderbilt Tire.[83]

The hope of instilling the importance of marketing in Goodrich personnel,
furthermore, was far from fully realized. However much Keener exhorted the
rhetoric of marketing, the company was slow to change. Traditionally the
route to advancement in the executive ranks lay in manufacturing, not marketing. Throughout the firm were managers whose orientation was not fully in

tune with "the marketing concept." The marketing managers Keener brought to the company were at the corporate level, and divisional counterparts often resisted their efforts to change customary ways of doing business. This situation was especially bad in the tire division, where senior executives thwarted efforts to change the image of Goodrich's tire performance and to carve out profitable market niches. Worse, as manufacturing-oriented managers, these men were too often ill informed about process technologies developed elsewhere. While industrial products executives refused to hear the message that better process technologies were in use in Europe, tire managers refused to abandon Goodrich-designed machine tools in favor of better equipment provided by outside suppliers. These older executives became the objects of derision from younger men, themselves ambitious. The company changed toward a marketing orientation, but not completely and not with the speed that Keener desired. Part of the problem was Keener himself, who used marketing rhetoric but who failed to demonstrate that he understood what it meant in practice.[84]

Finally, however much Ward Keener could point with pride to the investments in new plants and equipment made under his leadership, they were almost inevitably inadequate in the rubber manufacturing area. Keener observed that his investments represented record levels for Goodrich. In the meantime, competitors were not standing still. The industry's largest firm, Goodyear, also made record investments. And its investments were adding to an already very large base, whereas Goodrich's investments were not. For instance, as Goodyear expanded overseas, Goodrich was trying simply to gain a base in those markets, especially in Europe.

A Place of Acrimony and Fear

As the company seemed to slip further and further behind its larger competitors, executives knew trouble was brewing. Those who successfully struggled to make profits in their divisions were disheartened to learn that their success was overwhelmed by failure elsewhere. Managers began thinking of protecting themselves. In an age when lifetime loyalty to an employer was highly valued, the most able persons considered leaving for other positions. Some who stayed began to keep secret files about their coworkers, private information they might use to point the finger of blame elsewhere. At the highest levels, Keener and Warner were offering explanations for their firm's problems that sounded more like excuses than plans for meaningful action.

By 1970 Ward Keener recognized that his time for leading Goodrich would soon be over. The question of a successor troubled him. He had inspired Goodrich to employ bright young people to provide a pool of managerial talent, but none were yet experienced or mature enough to assume the full mantle of leadership. He was responsible for bringing Alexander into the company, and Alexander was an able executive. But his dislike of Alexander's aggressive nature and sometimes abrasive personality prevented Keener from anointing him as a successor. Warner was a disappointment. Successful as a leader in the chemical company, where scientific brilliance mattered and where there was a loyal, spirited, and able cadre of supporting staff, Warner had struggled in the corporate office.

Finally, Ward Keener began to discuss with members of the board of directors the need to recruit an executive from outside of Goodrich's ranks to take command. He was surprised, however, by the rapid response and was forced to retire somewhat earlier than he had planned. In September 1971, disgruntled at the continuing problems the firm was experiencing, the board suddenly announced the appointment of O. Pendleton Thomas, an executive from the Atlantic Richfield Petroleum Company, as vice chairman and chief executive officer. Thomas was the heir apparent. Soon a new era of transformation would begin for B.F. Goodrich.

9

New Management, Old Problems,

1972–1979

Orlando Pendleton ("Pen") Thomas, chosen as the new chief executive officer and vice chairman of the board in the fall of 1971 (he became the chairman in 1972), worked with other Goodrich executives to initiate changes
that, over the next two decades, substantially transformed the company. Like
Ward Keener before him, Thomas embraced higher profitability as his fundamental objective. Trained in finance, however, Thomas approached that goal
from a different perspective. He looked on Goodrich as "our business portfolio" and repeatedly called for executives to think about altering the firm's components through acquisitions and divestitures "with an eye to improving our
allocation of capital." "We want to put our money where it will bring the
greatest return," he often explained.[1] Accordingly, under Thomas's leadership
Goodrich placed a growing emphasis on PVC, while downplaying its more traditional tire and industrial products businesses, which appeared less promising. Even so, executives retained a belief that Goodrich should be diversified,
as it had been historically. They viewed tires and industrial products as part of
Goodrich's corporate identity and did not want Goodrich to leave those fields
altogether.

The changes that Thomas brought to Goodrich reflected broader trends of
strategic thinking in American business and the evolving viewpoints of high-
level executives. The modifications involved both strategy and structure, for
the strategic emphasis on financial matters instead of marketing led to structural changes. As Thomas shifted the relative importance of Goodrich's products, he altered the nature of the company's management system. Keener had
stressed centralized management decision making. During Thomas's administration, decentralized decision making began replacing centralized practices, a
movement in the direction back to the management system John Collyer had
favored. This shift aligned Goodrich with other large American manufactur-

ers, most of which by 1970 had at least three divisions turning out products for different markets and had decentralized management structures. Goodrich's direction under Thomas was also in line with the dominant mentality among American business executives at the time. By 1979 a third of the leaders of America's one hundred largest firms had a background in finance, replacing presidents trained in manufacturing and marketing. These finance presidents conceived of their corporations as evolving, flexible collections of businesses.[2]

Growing competition and an increasingly unstable business environment encouraged this development. A severe recession in the early 1970s and a sharp increase in energy prices in 1973 eroded the profits of Goodrich and many other American firms. A second rise in oil prices in 1979 exacerbated an already difficult situation. Goodrich faced increasing competition in tires and PVC in the 1950s and 1960s, and that competition continued in the 1970s. Competition from foreign companies hurt Goodrich, as transportation and communications improvements created a global market. For the most part, foreign competition was a new and unsettling development with which Goodrich and other American executives had not had to deal in the 1950s and the 1960s. Rising competition afflicted much of American industry and influenced managerial decision making. Industrial managers moved their firms into and out of perceived profit opportunities with increasing rapidity.

GOODRICH'S NEW CHIEF EXECUTIVE OFFICER

By the early 1970s Goodrich's directors wanted a new chief executive officer. The fight to avoid an unfriendly takeover by Northwest Industries in 1969 caused them to think anew about Goodrich and led them to wonder if Keener was the proper person to head the firm. There was, remembered one director, "a basic dissatisfaction with the return on investment of the business . . . we knew we were going to have to make some substantial changes." Continuing problems, highlighted by the recession in the early 1970s, led them to question further Keener's ability to rectify the deteriorating situation. In 1970 Goodrich's net sales of $1.1 billion yielded a net income of only $15 million, and in the following year net sales of $1.2 billion resulted in an even smaller net income of $2 million. Goodrich's financial performance lagged far behind that of most other large American industrial companies, and considerably behind that of other rubber manufacturers. Firestone and Goodyear outperformed Goodrich by wide margins. The directors saw Keener as too inflexible in his way of doing business, too remote from others running the company, and too tired to carry Goodrich into the future. Keener had, they thought, "run out of gas."[3]

The Coming of Pen Thomas

The directors looked beyond Goodrich's management ranks for a new chief executive. One of Keener's shortcomings, they belatedly realized, was his failure to groom a successor. One internal prospect was Harry Warner, Goodrich's president, but most directors viewed him as too oriented to the chemical side of the business and not broad-gauged enough.[4] Another internal possibility was Gerry Alexander, who moved from the presidency of the international division to that of the tire division in 1970. But, in the opinion of many, not the least of whom was Keener, Alexander was too brash and abrasive to become the head of Goodrich.[5]

The directors picked Pen Thomas of Atlantic Richfield. Business and personal connections influenced their choice. Gordon Edwards, the Goodrich director who first brought Thomas to the attention of others, knew Thomas as a director of Kraftco, where Edwards was chief executive officer and chairman of the board. John Weinberg and Barry T. Leithead, two other Goodrich directors, were also directors of Kraftco and knew Thomas through that company. Two more Goodrich directors were personally acquainted with Thomas. Herman Nolen had often played golf with him, and Paul Cabot was "a very good friend" of Thomas's.[6] But more than friendships was involved. As the chairman of Atlantic Richfield's executive committee, Thomas was in charge of the company's international and chemical operations and through these responsibilities became involved in petrochemicals.[7] He also oversaw domestic petroleum refining and marketing. Thomas's background in oil and chemicals, products related to Goodrich's, appealed to the directors. Most important in determining their choice were their perceptions of Thomas's character and leadership abilities. They saw Thomas as a strong leader, a real contrast to Keener. As Weinberg later explained, they viewed Thomas as a hard-driving, take-charge executive, and not "a pussycat."[8]

Thomas was available. Born in 1914 in Forney, Texas, near Dallas, he had coached football and taught mathematics at a Dallas high school to pay his way through East Texas State University, from which he graduated in 1935. He received a master of business administration degree from the University of Texas in 1941. Thomas did additional graduate work at the University of Pennsylvania's Wharton School of Finance and at New York University, and he also attended the advanced management program at the Harvard Graduate School of Business Administration. During World War II, Thomas attained the rank of lieutenant in the navy. After the war, he joined the comptroller's department at the Sinclair Corporation, where he quickly moved up the administrative ladder: he became an executive vice president in 1960, was elected president four years later, and became the chief executive officer in 1968. Thomas considered his strength to be "in the general management area," but remarked that he still cultivated "some financial tools." In 1969 Atlantic Richfield purchased Sinclair, and Thomas was disappointed with his position at Atlantic Richfield, where he was third in command. Thomas welcomed the chance to run a major American manufacturing concern again. When he joined Goodrich, Thomas was described as a "tall, lean, silver-haired Texan" who was "elegant, and cultured." He stood six feet, one inch tall and went by the nickname "the Gray Fox," because his hair had turned gray prematurely. Most of his friends simply called him "Pen."[9]

Thomas's Leadership Style

Thomas brought a more forceful leadership than the corporation had experienced for some time. He spent his first few months visiting the company's plants and talking with managers about their operations before making any major changes. He was visible and active, whereas Keener—except for his actions in defending Goodrich against Northwest Industries's takeover attempt—had become passive and almost invisible. Company directors and executives viewed Thomas as an energetic, dominant, and innovative person who got things done.

Beyond agreeing on those qualities, however, Goodrich's directors and executives parted ways. Thomas got along well with the directors, for he viewed them as his peers, his equals. Nolen recalled that Thomas "had a fine personality," which sometimes allowed him to push "through a lot of things with his board" that the directors "weren't necessarily in favor of." David Luke summed up well why the directors favored Thomas: "He was energetic. He was decisive. He was more imaginative by a long shot than Ward Keener, and he seemed ready to solve problems."[10] By contrast, Thomas's relations with executives were sometimes strained. They realized that changes were needed, but many questioned Thomas's approaches. Patrick Ross, who was in charge of the tire division for much of the 1970s, recalled Thomas as a "tough, demanding guy," but admired him for being willing to make decisions rather than engage in "endless debate." Donald McClusky, who headed the chemical division in the late 1970s, agreed that Thomas could be "a very exasperating guy to do business with" but liked "his drive, his focus."[11] The difficulties Thomas had with other executives had important consequences for Goodrich's development. Thomas's strong personality led to clashes with divisional managers. Alexander, who became an executive vice president in charge of one of Goodrich's two groups of operating divisions in 1972, resigned in 1975 partly because of clashes with Thomas. Thomas nearly dismissed Ross, Alexander's successor as head of tires, later in the decade. Thomas was, after all, brought in to make such changes, and his methods could be disruptive.

Renewed Stress on Profitability

When he took the reins at Goodrich, Thomas pushed for a reevaluation of the corporation's businesses. In a series of meetings with top managers in late 1972, Thomas stressed the need to review overall company strategies, including new product development, rather than simply dealing with challenges and opportunities piecemeal. Like Keener, Thomas emphasized that strategy rather than tactics needed to be corporate management's focus. At the root of his thinking, as it had been with Keener, lay a burning desire to boost Goodrich's profitability. In early 1973, Thomas stated that his goal was "to return Goodrich's profit to around 5% of sales," about the same rate of return that Goodyear and Firestone experienced in the late 1960s and early 1970s.[12]

Thomas viewed an increase in earnings as essential if executives were to control their firm's destiny. Only by raising earnings could they secure funds desired to finance new capital-intensive expansion projects.

Contributing to the concern about earnings was a continuing fear in management ranks that Goodrich, whose stock price was generally low, was an attractive takeover target. As late as 1976, Benjamin Heineman of Northwest Industries owned 10 percent of Goodrich's common stock. Meetings with Heineman convinced Thomas that Heineman would sell his holdings, "if we can get the price of our stock back up to a realistic level." The way to do so, Thomas thought, was to "improve our earnings as fast as we can."[13]

Thomas spurred Goodrich executives to raise profits through a program of divestitures and acquisitions, where his background in finance came to the fore. In September 1972 he told executives that they would have to "forgo some expansions and secure the necessary capacity for high-profit items by changing the product mix to eliminate current low-profit items." For the first time in years, Ross recalled, "we came up with financial benchmarks." Those parts of the corporation that failed to measure up would be "pruned and cut back." Thomas wanted to use the returns from the sales of these businesses to diversify into more promising areas, what he called a "redeployment of assets."[14] Officers found themselves selling long-established parts of Goodrich.

The largest divestiture was footwear, but pruning extended well beyond that business. Footwear operations were incurring huge losses by 1971.[15] Growing foreign competition, difficulties in training unskilled workers, and problems in turning out an ever-wider variety of shoes with machinery designed only for long, standardized production runs destroyed any chance of making footwear profitable.[16] As losses mounted, Goodrich sold or leased its footwear facilities to other companies, at a loss of about $16 million.[17] At the same time, Goodrich wrote off investments in a pilot plant in Marietta, Ohio, to make Aztran shoe uppers, taking a loss of $3.2 million.[18] In 1971 Goodrich also discontinued production of golf ball centers, latex catheters and syringes, drug sundries, most molded rubber goods, and reclaimed rubber. Goodrich sold its wholly owned subsidiary, Motor Freight, to the Branch Motor Express Company. These divestitures cost Goodrich about $10 million.[19] Sponge Rubber went in 1974. The development of urethane, which was lighter, cheaper, and could be used as a substitute for sponge rubber, "knocked the dickens out of foam rubber," remembered one Goodrich executive. Dismayed by continuing "unsatisfactory results," Goodrich's directors voted to sell Sponge Rubber in late 1973 and did so the following year.[20]

Diversification through Acquisition

With divestitures well under way, executives turned their attention to acquisitions. Like Collyer and Keener before them, they had no intention of making their company a conglomerate; rather they wanted to build on fields in which they had already become established. The goal of both the divestitures and acquisitions was to focus Goodrich on what it could do best. Diversification within well-established parameters was the watchword. "Don't look for us to engage in what I call 'free-form' diversification," John Ong, Goodrich's president, explained in the fall of 1975; "we will continue to expand and develop on the bases of our strengths, which lie mainly in the marketing and technology in tires, PVC, rubber and special elastomers." In particular, chemicals and some industrial products were targeted for growth, for they would, it was thought, help build a countercyclical balance to the company's automobile industry products.[21]

To develop diversification plans, seventeen top Goodrich executives from around the globe convened at Brecksville in late May 1976. At this and subsequent meetings, they drafted a "Comprehensive Strategic Plan" designed to guide the corporation's growth for the next decade.[22] Placed before Goodrich's stockholders in 1977, the plan intentionally was kept short, only two pages long; for, as Ong remarked, "it sets overall corporate objectives and constraints, as opposed to detailed plans of action." Incorporating Thomas's core ideas, the scheme had two objectives: "The first is that our operating income return on net capital employed shall at least equal the cost of raising capital. The second calls for stated annual earnings growth, which means that we must meet our cost-of-capital objective without shrinking the asset base of the corporation." Higher earnings with continuing growth constituted the heart of the plan. In particular, the plan stressed that returns on new capital investments should at least equal the cost of the capital.[23]

Next came implementation. In 1978 Goodrich hired Booz-Allen & Hamilton, a management consulting firm, to help work out a diversification plan. In early 1979 Booz-Allen, after looking at 3,500 companies in one hundred industries, identified five areas in which Goodrich might profitably make acquisitions: fluid power and control, building products, adhesives and sealants, specialty chemicals, and conveyor systems.[24] Working from Booz-Allen's report, executives drafted a policy statement designed to guide their corporation into the 1980s. Officers announced that they would set aside one-third of all capital investment for acquisitions, because "the Company's present portfolio of businesses has inadequate earnings power, growth potential, and earnings balance." Highest priority, taking about 80 percent of the funding, was to be given to "acquisitions to obtain and help develop and build a major new business base or bases for the Company." Lower priorities were to be given to purchases of companies whose lines were close to what Goodrich already did.[25] Even as Thomas stepped down as Goodrich's chief executive officer in July 1979, the acquisition program began bearing fruit.[26] As we shall see later in this chapter, Goodrich bought a number of firms that proved very important for its future.

DECENTRALIZED MANAGEMENT

Like the chief executives before him, Thomas wrestled with the challenge of devising a corporate structure appropriate for Goodrich's newly defined strategy. Soon after becoming the chief executive officer at Goodrich, Thomas worked with other executives to revamp the firm's management system. They began to replace decentralized with centralized management, delegating more responsibility to divisional management. Thomas believed that Keener's management set-up was too inflexible, that it did not give enough authority over day-to-day decisions to division heads. While Thomas retained control over strategic decision making in the corporate office, he delegated considerable responsibility over operations to divisional managers. Like the executives of many large, complex American corporations in the 1970s, Thomas hoped that by "streamlining the organization and relocating authority and responsibility as far down in the ranks as possible" he could speed up "decision making and response to business opportunities."[27] In the end, however, Thomas failed to institute completely decentralized management. Only in the 1980s and 1990s, under new corporate leadership, was decentralized management fully established.

Steps toward Decentralized Management

Working with the management consulting firm A. T. Kearney, top executives drew up what they called a "restructuring" plan for BFGoodrich.[28] The plan adopted in late 1972 made major changes in Goodrich's management system. As was happening in many other American manufacturing firms, Thomas combined Goodrich's operating divisions in business groups administered by executive vice presidents. Thomas established two major groups. One—a hodgepodge composed of tires, International BFGoodrich, aerospace, Canada, and industrial products—reported to Alexander. The other, made up of chemicals and plastics products, reported to Thomas Nantz.[29]

Those in charge of the divisions in each of these two groups received more authority over operational matters than they had possessed under Keener, and they liked the change. Donald McClusky, who was in charge of chemicals, noted that Thomas "basically pushed out the authority . . . to people who were responsible for the operating divisions." Most fundamental were changes in who controlled the purse strings. "You couldn't even order a wastebasket under the old days of Arthur Kelly and Ward Keener," recalled McClusky. Under Thomas the division chiefs received increased authority over capital expenditures. Thomas raised the limit McClusky could spend without prior corporate approval from $50,000 to $250,000.[30] In 1976 the discretionary spending power of executive vice presidents overseeing the two groups was increased from $250,000 to $500,000.[31]

With the formation of these two groups came the creation of a corporate support group, composed of eight staff divisions: treasury, corporate relations, planning and development, controller, law, systems and computer services, external communications and public affairs, and internal auditing.[32] Staff failures had characterized Keener's administration, and the creation of the corporate support group was a response to those problems. The new staff provided "centralized administrative services" for "the presidents and staffs of the operating divisions."[33] Ong thought that under Keener "the staff organization lacked discipline and lacked quality." Ong became the president of BFGoodrich in 1975, and he fired several of the vice presidents in staff positions and brought in new people "from outside the company who had skills and experience that we just didn't have at Goodrich." Under Ong, staff services took on a new life; at one point 1,100 employees reported to him. Executives with professional training in business management held the new staff positions. In the late 1970s and 1980s, however, Ong reduced the size of this corporate staff by assigning staff officers to the divisions.[34]

Thomas and other executives in the corporate office retained control over strategic decision making through the establishment of a management committee, which functioned like executive committees in most corporations. Initially composed of Thomas and Warner, together with the heads of the two groups of operating divisions, Nantz and Alexander, the management committee made the key decisions for BFGoodrich. (As the head of Goodrich's corporate support group, Ong joined the management committee a few months after its formation.) The management committee reviewed divisional plans, set corporatewide policies, and approved capital appropriations, replacing Keener's many councils. The committee also acted as a sounding board for divisional managers eager to float new ideas. It was, Ong recalled, "a place where division management was encouraged to come forward and talk about specific business opportunities, specific business problems."[35] Most of the management committee meetings, held at least once a month, lasted for a full day. While Thomas was most important at these meetings, he shared responsibility with other officers. A. J. Ashe, who was the secretary for the management committee, recalled that "Pen made the final decision, although I would say that everything was done basically by consensus."[36] Discussion, including occasional debates, was recorded in the minutes of the committee, but not votes.

In the late 1970s Goodrich moved further toward decentralization through the formation of profit centers within several major divisions. A number of industrial firms, especially those in high-tech areas, had taken similar steps in the 1960s. Profit centers were subdivisions usually organized by product line. Profit center managers, like the divisional managers to whom they reported, were given authority over a wide range of issues, from working out the details of how best to run their factories to the hiring of new personnel. The goal, as in the more general movement to decentralized management, was to make companies more responsive to changing business situations. The move to profit centers, it was hoped, would also make their managers more numbers-oriented, more concerned with the financial performance of their business units. In 1978 McClusky established five profit centers within the chemical division: plastics, elastomers, additives and specialty chemicals, latex, and international. This was designed to "enhance ability to react quickly to market conditions." The profit centers were supported by five divisional staff organizations: development, support, employee relations and public affairs, planning and control, and sales.[37] A year later, Larry Pomeroy, who was in charge of the engineered products division, set up four profit centers: industrial products, conveying systems, transportation products, and fabricated products.

While the movement to profit centers gave American companies increased flexibility, their use—if applied incorrectly—could have negative repercussions. Top corporate management sometimes lost touch with what was occurring in the profit centers, especially in firms that had many of them. In their attempts to run highly diverse companies, corporate executives might rely on the rate of return on investment as the sole means by which to judge a profit center's performance. This method could place a premium on short-term results at the expense of long-term investments. Then, too, the adoption of discounted cash flow methodology in capital budgeting, a development that often accompanied the move to profit centers, might contribute to the emphasis on short-term timetables. This system placed a monetary value on time in decisions about capital appropriations, making those projects with short payback periods more likely to be funded than those with long ones. Moreover, some items, which could not be neatly included in any one profit center, but which might be essential for a company's development (such as the training of skilled workers or managers), might not be adequately funded or might be ignored altogether.[38]

For the most part, Goodrich avoided the shortcomings of a management system based on profit centers, incorrectly applied, while benefiting from increased flexibility in its operations. The situation at Goodrich differed from those at corporations with large numbers of profit centers. Top management was able to stay in touch with the needs of the growing, but still relatively small, number of profit centers through the meetings of the management committee. Then, too, the adoption of discounted cash flow accounting in capital budgeting was more a guide than an absolute measure in judging the worthiness of a proposed project.

In 1979 a corporatewide reorganization capped the restructuring move. Working from a plan prepared by Booz-Allen, Goodrich's officers rearranged the operating divisions into three worldwide business groups: chemicals, tires, and engineered products. In the same restructuring, International BFGoodrich was disbanded and its functions absorbed by the three global divisions.[39] Like the establishment of profit centers, the movement to a global structure would, Goodrich officers hoped, stimulate "optimal business growth, entrepreneurial spirit, and development of new managerial talent." The restructuring was undertaken, Ong explained to his company's directors, to complete a "reorganization of management so that it is synchronous with the strategy." That strategy, he reminded the directors, was "to return the Company to the forefront of U.S. corporations in terms of return on the shareholders equity and total assets employed in our businesses."[40]

Tensions between Centralization and Decentralization

Goodrich moved toward decentralized management during Thomas's administration; but, when compared with the more extensive decentralization that would later occur, even the 1978–79 restructuring was, some executives thought, "a false dawn" of decentralization. One officer believed that "operations were truly decentralized in the sense that executives were assigned to run those businesses." However, he also observed that "as time went on, more and more of those executives' time was not spent out in the marketplace trying to develop their businesses, it was spent answering an endless stream of questions and dealing with an endless stream of mandates" from the corporate office.[41] A common complaint of division managers was that, despite the changes instituted in the 1970s, not enough staff support and decision making authority were pushed down to the divisional level.

Nowhere was the tension between centralization and decentralization clearer than in corporate planning. Keener had moved in the direction of companywide planning, but his efforts were inconclusive. "Pen was a devout believer in strategic planning," Ong recalled. Thomas thought that planning should be separate from budgeting. "Budgeting was what accountants did," Ong later explained; "what planning did was to talk about the construction of the portfolio of businesses."[42] In moving toward long-range corporate planning, Thomas aligned Goodrich with changes occurring in other American industrial corporations. The Great Depression of the 1930s and the unsettled times of World War II had encouraged the development of systematic business planning in America, and by the 1960s most large industrial firms had instituted long-range corporate planning.[43]

At Goodrich, every fall the division heads presented to the management committee detailed programs for the upcoming year, along with sketchier outlines for several succeeding years. "You went through Akron [in] October," remembered one division manager, and "presented your program for the following year and what you're going to do with the division . . . for the next five years."[44] The management committee then melded the division plans into a corporate plan. As early as the summer of 1973 the committee considered and approved four-year projections of capital expenditures broken down by division.[45] A staff planning department was established under the economist A. J. Ashe within Ong's corporate support group to assist the management committee.

Problems developed in trying to reconcile the capital requests of the different divisions, for Goodrich was cash- and capital-poor throughout the 1970s, even though Thomas retained a higher percentage of earnings to finance expansion moves than had Keener.[46] In early 1974 Ong noted that "the Operating Divisions' demands for capital funds greatly exceeded the resources of the company." William Wooldredge, who had become Goodrich's treasurer the year before, agreed and recommended a ceiling of $750 million in capital expenditures for 1974–79, a recommendation the management committee accepted. Wooldredge wanted to cap Goodrich's debt ratio at 50 percent. Any further financial leveraging would, he feared, result in a "loss of financial flexibility" and "a greater risk of insolvency" to the corporation.[47]

Capital scarcity and conflict over capital allocations persisted, nonetheless, with division managers repeatedly complaining that Thomas did not consider their desires closely enough. Ashe remembered that Thomas used the corporate plans to try to discipline the divisions. "Thomas just said," Ashe later explained, "that the divisions would make the plans and he would hold them to them."[48] Thomas tightened the screws in the late 1970s by setting up a "Management Information and Control System" to correct any divisional deviations from planned corporate objectives.[49] Many division managers disliked the way Thomas seemed to use the rate of return on investment as a "club" to keep the divisions in line with his desires. Thomas, some believed, was willing to delegate responsibility only so long as the divisions met his earnings goals, which they thought were too high and too short-term. One division manager recalled that to get a capital expenditures project approved, executives first found out Thomas's current expectations on returns, then came up with those returns in their plans, even if they were not real.[50]

Friction between the divisions and the corporate office in the planning process went beyond capital allocation. Planning input from the divisions, while greater than in Keener's days, was insufficient. As Ashe later observed, planning under Thomas was "a tops-down type of planning," with not enough concern for what was actually going on in the divisions. Ong, who oversaw Ashe's work and was deeply involved in the planning process, remembered that planning was too "paper-driven," in which "quantification tended to dominate the projections." The resulting plans were, as a result, "not living documents" and lacked meaning in terms of the day-to-day management of the business.[51] Planning under Thomas failed to foresee major problems and would be addressed anew in the 1980s.

New Management Recruitment and Training Methods

Management recruitment, as well as the corporate structure, changed under Thomas. Like so many alterations made in the 1970s, changes in this realm encouraged an approach to business focused on raising profits quickly. Between 1970 and 1975 some four hundred new college graduates joined Goodrich in engineering, technical, professional, and business administration positions.[52] Recruitment teams of senior managers visited top graduate schools of business administration each year to attract M.B.A. holders to Goodrich, and in the late 1970s about twelve joined the firm's executive ranks each year. Goodrich's treasurer described the advantages he thought they brought to Goodrich: "The company creates a corps of strong, experienced, and high-powered performers who can relate to each other and direct the company toward greater profitability and performance."[53] Not all were as favorably impressed. Some established officers derided the new executives as "financial types" and "bean counters" who often brought conflicting interests in earnings and market share.[54]

Thomas paid less attention to setting up new management training and reward programs within Goodrich. As Thomas admitted in late 1975, career development efforts for managers were only then beginning.[55] Even so, Thomas did more than had Keener. In late 1973, acting on the advice of a management consulting firm, directors tied management compensation more closely to long-run company goals than had been the case before.[56] Additional changes came over the next few years. "By the middle seventies we had implanted management development programs in all of the divisions," Ong observed. "We had planted performance evaluation, tied evaluation to incentive compensation evaluation, [and] formed a training institute." But, as Ong later admitted, "like our approach to planning it was all . . . rather mechanistic paper-ridden kinds of systems." The problem, he thought, was that "we didn't spend enough time winning the hearts and minds of the folks who had to carry this out." The unfortunate result was, Ong concluded, that "we had forms" but not "really good performance reviews [and] people were phoneying them up."[57]

Ethical questions involving management, in fact, occupied a considerable amount of Thomas's time. Thomas inherited a system of illegal political payments. Each year a group of Goodrich officers decided which political candidates the company would support at the local, state, and national levels. To circumvent legal restrictions on corporate political contributions, executives wrote personal checks to the candidates. They were then reimbursed with corporate funds. Such arrangements were common in American business at the time. When Thomas discovered the arrangement, he put a stop to it, and several years later, in 1976, he voluntarily told the Securities and Exchange Commission and the Internal Revenue Service about the payments. At the same time, Thomas revealed that Goodrich had made improper contributions to foreign governments to secure their business. Again, Goodrich was hardly alone. In 1976, for example, Goodyear's officers admitted that they had made improper payments totaling nearly $1 million to foreign governments going back to 1970.[58] To prevent a recurrence of improper domestic and foreign payments by executives, in 1977 Thomas circulated a strong statement on ethical conduct and worked with Goodrich's external auditor, Ernst & Ernst, to enforce it. In addition, the internal auditing division was made directly responsible to the audit committee of the board of directors.[59]

The lack of attention paid to the internal development of managers also led officers to place growing dependence on management consulting firms. A. T. Kearney, McKinsey & Company, and Booz-Allen & Hamilton were tapped to offer advice in various areas of Goodrich's operations—from restructuring the company's management system, to helping plan new growth strategies, to revamping the daily work of some divisions. Goodrich's strategic decisions, such as those involved in setting acquisition paths, if not coming from outside consultants seemed at times to be inordinately influenced by their recommendations. To be sure, many American businesses employed management consultants; but Goodrich went further than most.

Alterations in management practices, including recruitment, were surely needed, given the lethargy into which parts of the organization had fallen in

Keener's later years. A renewed concern for profitability was essential. Nonetheless, the changes caused difficulties. The influx of M.B.A. holders into executive ranks and the reliance on outside management consultants led to friction with established officers, exacerbating an already tense management situation. Genuine cooperation among divisional managers and between them and corporate management became difficult, sometimes making it hard to reach agreements on long-term strategies.

THE CONVERSION TO RADIAL TIRES

Tire developments at BFGoodrich occurred within the larger framework of the corporate hunt for profits. As we have seen, a price war disrupted the American tire industry in 1959, and intense competition marked the 1960s. As this competition continued in the 1970s, executives faced tough decisions. Should Goodrich remain in tires at all? If Goodrich continued to manufacture tires, what types should the firm produce? How should they be marketed and where? Should Goodrich expand or contract overseas tire making? The development of a tire strategy was not easy, for personality conflicts combined with differing viewpoints to make agreement among Goodrich's leaders difficult.

Gerry Alexander—who headed the tire division until 1972, when he became the executive vice president overseeing the group of divisions to which tires belonged—was the strongest champion of tires. Ong recalled that "Gerry just loved the tire business and wanted to see Goodrich grow in it and thought we could be a survivor." Alexander realized, however, that Goodrich faced handicaps in going head-to-head with the industry leaders, Goodyear and Firestone. Goodrich had fallen behind those firms in building modern factories and in expanding marketing networks. Not even the Fort Wayne plant allowed Goodrich to catch up. Like some other executives in the mid- and late 1960s, Alexander consequently pushed high-performance radial tires for the replacement market. Through the niche marketing of specialty tires, Goodrich might, he thought, maintain its place in the American tire industry.[60]

Despite his personal differences with Alexander, Thomas agreed that Goodrich should remain in tire making. Still, Thomas thought that tires should take a back seat to chemicals. Speaking to executives in 1973, Thomas said that he expected continuing profits—and fast ones at that—from chemicals and PVC and, therefore, favored capital investments in those areas. "The market demands for PVC and other chemical products have been strong," he noted, "and the recent expenditures have been providing quick payback and attractive return on the new investment." This emphasis had important ramifications for tires. "It is generally recognized," Thomas told division managers, that "tires will likely grow less rapidly than desired for the corporate total and will likely provide a lower rate of return than is desired."[61] Thomas was willing to invest in tires to try to preserve Goodrich's market share in America's tire sales, but not to expand it. Like Alexander, Thomas came to see the niche marketing of specialty radials as the most fruitful way to keep Goodrich's market share from falling. While favoring chemicals over tires, Thomas could not imagine Goodrich leaving tires altogether.[62]

Other key executives were less enthusiastic. Patrick Ross, who became the president of tires in 1972, was not sanguine about Goodrich's future in tires, especially those for the original equipment market, where he thought profit margins would always be very narrow. By the mid-1970s he was thinking about the possibility of Goodrich leaving tires completely.[63] As John Weinberg, a leading Goodrich director, later recalled, "Pat Ross was a broad-gauged guy; he was running the tire division and still thought, 'What are we going to do, we're going to sell the business.'"[64] As Goodrich's president from 1975, Ong increasingly had to deal with tires, and by the late 1970s—if not earlier—he too wanted to leave tire making, one of his few disagreements with Thomas.[65] Ross and Ong were prepared to support the conversion to radial tires, not as a way of keeping Goodrich in tire making for the long term, but as a way to make tires profitable and thereby attract a buyer for the tire division.

From these various points of view, a reasonably coherent tire strategy emerged, expressed in a plan put forward in 1975, a scheme designed to guide the tire division's activities through 1980. "Growth as an objective would require substantial capital beyond the ability of the present business to generate." Tires would definitely not be an expansion area for Goodrich. Nor was the other extreme, leaving tires altogether, viewed as immediately feasible. "An exit strategy, while conceivably desirable," Goodrich's executives noted, "does not appear possible (although opportunities in this area should be pursued)." Instead, they chose a middle road, hoping to preserve, but not expand, their company's market share in tires. "Hold-reduce-reshape strategy appears to be the most practical broad strategy for the company's domestic tire business to follow."[66]

America's Ailing Tire Industry

The decisions of Goodrich's executives occurred as part of a general restructuring of America's tire industry in the 1970s. The tire industry was hurt by energy crises, especially in 1973, which left people waiting in long lines at gasoline stations and driving less. Recessions bit into new car sales, and thus the sales of original equipment tires. At the same time, the adoption of the long-wearing radial tire decreased replacement tire sales. Major strikes in 1973 and 1976, combined with declining labor productivity in some plants, made a bad situation worse. Underlying many of the difficulties American tire makers faced was the fact that tires had become a global commodity. Foreign competition was a growing problem. By 1978 foreign tires accounted for nearly one-tenth of America's replacement passenger tire sales. Moreover, by 1979 one-quarter of the new cars sold in the United States were foreign and carried foreign tires as original equipment. Unit tire sales made by American companies peaked in 1973 at 202 million tires and then declined at an average annual rate of 4.7 percent to 1980. Not until 1984 would unit tire sales regain their 1973 level.[67]

Tire makers responded by aggressively cutting back unprofitable operations and lowering their labor costs, which were about one-quarter of the total expense of making tires. Between 1969 and 1979, thirteen tire plants were closed, and thousands of workers lost their jobs. Moreover, as tire company executives sought low-cost labor, they continued to move their tire making plants out of the Midwest. Even as plants were shut, mainly in the Midwest, new tire making factories were opened elsewhere, largely in the South. Most of the new plants employed nonunion labor. Of the nine American tire plants built between 1970 and 1986, only one was unionized (by way of comparison, all of the twenty-one such plants put up in the 1960s were). By 1984 nonunion plants accounted for nearly 20 percent of the tires made in the United States, up from just 7 percent in 1967.[68]

The changes hurt Akron, continuing the movement of rubber making out of the city, a trend dating back to the 1930s. In 1957 there were 30,000 rubber workers in Akron, but twenty years later only 12,300 remained. Over 4,000 Akron rubber jobs were lost between 1972 and 1976 alone, and between 1970 and 1975 Akron lost 23,000 residents. By 1977 Goodrich employed only 2,300 hourly workers in Akron, out of a nationwide hourly workforce of 16,000; and Goodyear had only 5,400 hourly workers in the city, of a nationwide total of 34,000. For the first time, Akron was primarily a white-collar and service city. Not only were there fewer people in Akron, wages were also lower: in 1979 manufacturing jobs paid an average of $270 per week, but service jobs only $194.[69]

Switching to Radial Tires

Goodrich's tire strategy for the 1970s was predicated on rapidly converting to the production of radial tires. Prodded by Alexander, Thomas pushed radials. In June 1973 Thomas informed members of the management committee that "every effort must be made to maintain a favorable position in radial tires" and that it was "absolutely necessary that the [tire] division convert to radial tires as rapidly as possible."[70] In radials Goodrich executives thought their company had a rare edge over the other major tire makers, thanks to its early start, giving their company a chance to preserve its market share.[71] In 1972 and 1973 the directors approved the lion's share of the funds available for capital improvements for the tire division, and nearly all of these went into the conversion to radial tire production—$60 million for passenger radials and another $20 million for truck radials.[72] Even tire plants in Akron and Los Angeles, soon to be phased out, received funds to switch to radial production in the early 1970s.[73] This strategy of switching to radial tires was unable to preserve Goodrich's place in the American tire market, but the strategy dominated the thoughts of Goodrich's executives throughout the 1970s.

In 1976 Goodrich announced that the tire plant conversion projects had

A Goodrich worker prepares a radial tire for curing. (BFG Co.)

been "essentially completed." Capital allocations for the tire division were cut back substantially, with more going to the chemical division. Executives in the tire division soon perceived that funds generated by their operations were being used not to benefit tires but to improve other aspects of Goodrich's businesses. Tires were to be less important than in the past in Goodrich's grand strategy. Ray Luebbers took charge of the production side of the tire division in August 1975. Within just a month of taking up this position, Alexander told him that "the plan was to milk tires." A Goodrich director later explained that, in addition to earnings that could be channeled to other parts of Goodrich, tires produced "a lot of depreciation" that could be "charged to earnings" as "a non-cash charge."[74] Only in 1979 did Goodrich's officers again allocate major sums, just over $30 million, to radial tire conversions, mainly to remove bottlenecks in production processes.[75]

Meanwhile, in line with the policy of ending unprofitable operations, Goodrich closed two of its least efficient tire plants. In 1975 it shuttered the Los Angeles factory. Goodyear, Uniroyal, and Firestone had tire plants in Los Angeles, which saturated the West Coast market. In fact, Goodrich's Los Angeles plant often shipped its tires east for sale.[76] Most types of tire manufacturing were also phased out of Akron. The Akron plant remained a hodgepodge of poorly laid out buildings in which tire making was inefficiently intermixed with other forms of rubber manufacturing. Work rules in supplemental labor agreements were more restrictive in Akron than in other Goodrich facilities. Consequently, tire making costs in Akron were about 30 percent higher than in the more modern Fort Wayne and Tuscaloosa plants. Tire making in Akron, except for farm and airplane tires, ended in 1975–76.[77] This marked a major milestone in Goodrich's history, for automobile tires had been made in its Akron facilities since 1896.

Capital spending did not permit the company to catch up with its competitors. Goodrich's capital expenditures on tires, when measured as a proportion of the company's assets devoted to manufacturing tires, were actually a bit higher than those of Goodyear and Firestone in 1975–79: 7.5 percent for Goodrich, compared to 6.8 percent for Goodyear and 6 percent for Firestone. In absolute terms, however, Goodyear and Firestone overwhelmed Goodrich. Between 1973 and 1979 Goodyear spent $1.8 billion on its tire plants, more than six times the $287 million that Goodrich spent. Similarly, Firestone spent $647 million on capital improvements for tires between 1976 and 1979, four times as much as Goodrich's $149 million.[78] Moreover, the lead Goodrich's competitors had amassed from the 1920s on was too large for Goodrich to close during the 1970s, for Goodrich entered the 1970s far behind Goodyear and Firestone in the size and modernity of most of its tire plants.

In addition, difficulties in production, sales, and labor relations made it hard for Goodrich to profit fully from its conversion to radials. Problems in these areas prevented the company from capitalizing on "first-mover" advantages in radial tire making.

Production Problems with Radials

Goodrich's conversion to radials failed to result in completely modern tire plants. Goodrich closed its most antiquated facilities, Akron and Los Angeles, but not even the tens of millions of dollars spent on converting other factories made them as efficient as they might have been. In 1972 Thomas observed that Goodrich was "spending too much effort on product development and not enough on process development." He was correct. Goodrich often used hybrid machinery not well suited to making radials. Funding went "to adapt the existing tire building machines," rather than to install brand-new radial machinery. These conversions left building the tire core a two-step operation—certainly an improvement over the earlier three-step process, but not yet a fully efficient one-step process. In "re-equipping the old bias tire plants," Ong later noted, "a number of compromises were made." Another Goodrich executive remembered the situation even more negatively, concluding that Goodrich was "not willing to be competitive in manufacturing costs" in "tooling up for radial tires."[79] The most brutal assessment came from a Ford engineer, who called Goodrich's machinery "just good for scrap."[80]

In the mid- and late 1970s Goodrich's executives sought, with some success, to improve tire making productivity and quality. Luebbers instituted a "formal improvement program" in 1975 to correct "a trend of declining productivity becoming apparent in our tire plants," and in 1983 he could note with justifiable pride that productivity had increased 30 percent. While Goodrich never faced anything as disastrous as Firestone's fiasco with its radial in the 1970s—tread separation on the "Firestone 500" led to its very costly recall in 1978—lesser quality control problems hindered Goodrich's switch to radials, leading automakers to reject substantial numbers as original equipment. Luebbers and his men improved this situation, just as they had with productivity. By 1977, 83 percent of Goodrich's radials were acceptable as original equipment tires, and 86 percent a year later.[81]

Relations between Labor and Management

Labor problems buffeted production efforts at Goodrich and the other tire makers. Contract renegotiations continued at three-year intervals, often after strikes. As we have seen, major strikes disrupted the tire industry in 1967 and 1970. Another occurred in 1973, and a record-breaking 141-day strike particularly hurt Goodrich in 1976. Only in 1979 were negotiations completed without a strike.

As in the 1960s, there were several reasons for the strikes. Personal ambitions were important. Peter C. Bommarito continued as president of the United Rubber Workers. He was a very outspoken labor leader, and his combative style antagonized tire company executives. Still, probably the most important factor was the jockeying for position between the URW and the tire making companies in a changing economy. The consumer price index soared upward 27 percent between 1973 and 1976, while rubber workers' pay increased by only 17 percent. Fearing continuing inflation and observing greater wage increases won by the United Auto Workers, URW officials demanded major wage hikes. Goodrich executives, joined by other tire makers, resisted, arguing that raises were outpacing productivity gains and thus hurting their company in its growing competition with foreign tire makers.[82]

Tensions ignited in a strike in 1973. In the negotiations that year, Goodyear agreed to a 16 percent wage increase to be spread over three years and improved health and pension benefits.[83] Goodrich offered the same wage increase but lesser health and pension benefits, and was struck. After a twenty-four-day strike, the URW and Goodrich reached an agreement. Wages were to rise as much as those at Goodyear, and in other respects Goodrich went beyond Goodyear. Health and pension improvements were greater. Moreover, responding to cries of Goodrich workers that "we feel more threatened by plant closings than do employees of other rubber companies," the URW received a special job-protection clause. Any Goodrich worker laid off at one plant was to be given hiring preference at other Goodrich facilities and could transfer accumulated benefits to the new job location, something not possible at Goodyear.[84]

In 1974, in the wake of the strike, Ong hired Peter Pestillo of General Electric to head Goodrich's labor relations staff, most of whom Ong thought were incompetent. Over time Pestillo's efforts would greatly improve labor relations at Goodrich, but not right away.[85]

Even greater differences separated labor and management in 1976, and Pestillo could not prevent another strike. The 1976 round of discussions between the URW and the "big four" tire makers focused initially on Firestone, singled out because the firm had been particularly profitable in 1975 and early 1976. Friction soon moved beyond Firestone, however. The 1973 agreement lacked a cost-of-living-adjustment (COLA) clause, for nationwide wage and price controls instituted by President Richard Nixon had prevented the establishment of any COLA. Shortly after the URW reached its 1973 agreement with the tire makers, the restrictions on COLAs were lifted, and the United Auto Workers, whom the URW often emulated, received a contract that included a substantial COLA. In 1976 the URW called for parity with the autoworkers, including an unlimited COLA.

With this demand, the stage was set for a confrontation. On 17 April 1976, the day the 1973 contract expired, URW leaders voted to give Bommarito the power to call a strike (the week before, 95 percent of the rank and file had voted in favor of strike authorization). Working together, the "big four" tire companies offered a $1.05 per hour wage increase over three years and a small COLA. On 18 April federal mediators entered the contract talks between the rubber companies and the URW. Nonetheless, with the union and the companies far apart on wages, benefits, and COLAs, a strike could not be averted. On 20 April seventy thousand rubber workers struck the "big four" rubber companies in a work stoppage involving forty-seven plants and idling two-thirds of the nation's tire making capacity.[86] Negotiations stalled over the next few months. On 5 July Firestone executives offered a $1.30 per hour wage increase over three years, only to have it rejected by the URW one day later. Secretary of Labor William Usery then recessed the talks indefinitely. Industry spokesmen accused Bommarito of torpedoing the talks with his rejection of Firestone's offer, and government officials agreed that Bommarito "seemed unwilling ever to define 'his bottom line.'" Bommarito dismissed this as "company propaganda."[87]

Over time two factors brought the URW back to the bargaining table. First, on the strike's ninetieth day the companies stopped paying for employee hospitalization and health benefits. The workers had to pay the $95 per month on their own, a difficult task since strike benefits ran out after the fifth week. Second, the hope that the automobile companies would have to shut down because of a scarcity of tires was shattered. While car sales were high, the auto makers had large enough inventories to get through their 1976 model year. Usery added to the union's despair by stating that Firestone's last offer was close to the limit the government could endorse as consistent with wage and price stability.[88] In late July talks resumed when Usery invited the representatives of the URW and the companies to Washington, and in early August Firestone's negotiators and union officers reached an agreement. Wages were to rise $1.35 per hour over three years. If the consumer price index went up 6 percent annually, workers would receive an hourly COLA of 75¢ over three years. The URW also won increases in pension and retirement benefits. With only minor differences, the other tire makers, including Goodrich, agreed to this settlement.[89]

The strike hurt Goodrich more than its major competitors, because it affected all of its tire making plants. In 1976 Goodrich's tire sales fell about 12 percent from the previous year. Goodyear and Firestone were less severely hurt. Possessing some nonunion tire plants (and huge tire inventories), both corporations, despite the strike, managed to post record tire sales in 1976.[90]

Faced with the recent history of strikes, the "big four" tire makers and the URW agreed to explore a plan to prevent conflict in the future. Put forward by Usery, the scheme set up a three-person committee to study rubber industry bargaining and report by the end of 1977 on how to avoid protracted conflicts. Goodrich executives undertook their own reassessment of labor relations in the fall of 1976. In late October the directors heard Pestillo make a presentation on the issue. After noting that "at Goodrich it's been worse" than at other tire makers, he outlined a way to avoid "the crisis quality" in labor relations. Pestillo emphasized the need to cooperate more closely with government and labor leaders and the need for Goodrich to assume a leadership role in future negotiations. Over the next two years Pestillo led rubber company officials in working with federal government administrators and labor leaders. In April 1977 he proposed that the companies and the URW adopt a no-strike, binding arbitration agreement, but neither the union nor the other firms were willing to do so. Pestillo renewed his push for binding arbitration in early 1978. Again, the URW rejected his plan, but union officials noted that Pestillo's work was initiating a feeling of goodwill between the company and the union.[91]

Labor negotiations in 1979 went much smoother, especially at Goodrich, than three years before. In 1978 Bommarito was reelected president of the URW, but by 1979 he had lost some of his earlier fire. He may well have realized that an increasing proportion of tires sold in the United States were being made in nonunion plants in America or overseas in non-American firms, a recognition that perhaps made him more amenable to less acrimonious negotiations. Neither union leaders nor company executives wanted a repeat of the 1976 strike. By the late 1970s, John Codrea recalled, "there were level heads that began to see that we must begin to work together." The URW staged a short strike against Uniroyal, but Goodrich and the other "big four" firms concluded negotiations without strikes. The agreement reached between Goodrich and the URW called for a wage increase of $1.14 per hour over three years, a new COLA, and improved pension benefits.[92]

Challenges in Marketing Radials

Goodrich faced challenges in marketing, as well as in making, tires in the 1970s. When Goodrich's competitors, especially Goodyear and Firestone, switched to radials following the energy crisis of 1973, they did so quickly. Their rapid conversion to radials deprived Goodrich of gains from its pioneering technology—at least in the original equipment market which Goodrich left in 1982 (see chap. 10). In the replacement market executives sought to make sales more efficient and profitable. Finding tire prices a mix of inconsistent discounts and rebates, Ross and Robert Eisentrout (who oversaw marketing tires) set just two prices for each replacement tire, one for small and medium-sized dealers and another for dealers ordering more than $75,000 worth of tires annually. At the same time, they streamlined the distribution system by reducing area sales offices from five to four and the number of district sales offices from twenty-five to fifteen.[93] To further rationalize sales they created a central, fully computerized service center in Cincinnati in 1974. Computerization continued for the rest of the decade, culminating in the establishment of a computerized inventory system for all of Goodrich's retail tire centers in 1979.[94]

Even so, efforts to improve retailing proved only partly successful, and Goodrich began selling its retail outlets, a trend that would continue in the 1980s. Many stores were simply too small, selling fewer than 2,000 tires a year, and others were poorly managed. Only about half of Goodrich's 387 stores operated at a profit. Store closures and sales began in 1975, and by the end of 1977, 130 had been sold and another 70 closed in what Goodrich called "Project Independence."[95]

To bolster marketing efforts Goodrich changed its advertising. Worried by consumer surveys that showed a declining recognition of the firm, Goodrich switched advertising agencies. In September 1971 Goodrich moved its advertising from Batten, Barton, Durstine & Osborne to Griswold-Eshleman, which had been handling advertising for the chemical division. A year later Grey Advertising was given responsibility for passenger tires. Grey developed an advertising campaign based on the theme of Goodrich as the "Other Guys," a not-so-veiled reference to Goodyear. The campaign succeeded in winning recognition for Goodrich beyond anyone's wildest dreams. "In all my experience in advertising," recalled Eisentrout, "I never saw a change in the measurements of consumer awareness or change in preference for a brand that occurred with that campaign."[96] The campaign did not, however, increase Goodrich's tire sales as much as had been hoped. "Even though we had a significant increase in awareness and preference for the [Goodrich] brand, it did not bring consumers in to buy the product," remembered Eisentrout.[97] One reason was that, for all of its efforts, Goodrich was outspent by its competitors. Goodyear alone spent four times as much on advertising as Goodrich.[98]

Niche Marketing: The T/A Radial

Finding it increasingly difficult to compete in a broad spectrum of tires, Goodrich emphasized specialty radials for niche markets. In early 1972 Ross called this approach "niche picking," an idea originated in the 1960s. Some success was obtained in farm, truck, and off-the-road tires, but by far the greatest came in making a "T/A" radial for automobiles. Basically a wide version of the Lifesaver radial, the T/A was introduced in January 1971 as a low-profile, wide-tread radial designed for high-powered "muscle" cars. The name was originally meant to stand for TransAm, but it was discovered that a small private-brand tire maker already owned that name, and from that point on "T/A" stood alone as the tire name.[99]

Eisentrout and Ross pushed the T/A's development to create a new identity for Goodrich tires and thereby to increase sales and profits. In Alexander they found a receptive supporter. Alexander's backing, in fact, was an important key to the success of the niche marketing strategy. Eisentrout later recalled that before the advent of the T/A, Goodrich tires had a stodgy image: "people referred to us as Granny Goodrich." Local Corvette clubs, he remembered, "gave as a booby prize . . . a Goodrich racing jacket." Tire division officers spruced up the public image of their tires by campaigning the T/A on a 425-horsepower Pontiac Firebird that they dubbed the "Tirebird." Employed on the Tirebird as a racing tire against cars using tires designed only for racing—the T/A was, of course, intended for passenger car sales—the T/A was successful in races ranging from Sebring to Watkins Glen. In 1971 the T/A was approved by the Sports Car Club of America as the only passenger tire suitable for track use. The T/A, Ross remembered, "gave us some real identity." By 1975 Goodrich was selling 6.5 million T/A radials annually, and these were profitable sales. As Luebbers remembered, "the main T/A lines" were "premium-priced, but still competitive enough to sell at a pretty good volume, and as a result were our profit lines." Eisentrout later recalled that the profit margin on T/A tires was about "two and one-half times" as much "as we were making on anything else."[100]

Foreign Operations in Tires

Facing growing competition in tires at home, Goodrich's executives found little relief abroad. Lacking the resources to compete head-to-head with Goodyear and Firestone overseas—not to mention such foreign giants as Michelin, Dunlop, Bridgestone, and Pirelli—and needing capital to expand nontire operations in the United States, Goodrich reduced its foreign tire making. As one Goodrich executive explained, chemical operations were "just gobbling up lots and lots of capital . . . so those furnaces had to be fed." One source of fuel lay in the sales of overseas tire works.[101] Goodrich's foreign tire operations as a whole were not particularly profitable in the 1970s, so it made sense to divest some of them. As late as 1975 Goodrich's overseas nonchemical manufacturing—mainly tires—accounted for 18 percent of the company's total sales, but just two years later it had fallen to only 12 percent. Those factories that were the least profitable were, in general, the first to go.[102]

In Europe, Goodrich began by selling its operations in Holland. Efforts to improve labor efficiency there failed, as the Dutch unions, backed by their government, refused to consider changes. In the mid-1970s Goodrich wanted to let 762 of Vredestein's 4,700 workers go. The company's plants were never very profitable, and they lost money in 1975.[103] Donald McClusky, who headed BFGoodrich International between 1972 and 1974, later recalled that Vredestein was a "mainstream, bloodletting loser."[104] Unable to shed workers, Goodrich sold Vredestein to the Dutch government and a private foundation in 1976.[105] Goodrich's European operations faced problems beyond the difficulties at Vredestein. Goodrich never had more than 3 percent of the European tire market and lacked the resources to carve out more. "There were so many producers," remembered one executive, "and clearly Goodrich didn't have a market share like the real players such as Michelin or Continental."[106] This realization contributed to the decision to sell Vredestein. Similarly, in 1977 Goodrich closed its German operations at Koblenz. With a capacity of only about 4,000 tires a day, the plant was too small to handle the many tire sizes being demanded by the German market. "We had the wrong-size plant in the wrong place, making basically some of the wrong products," recalled McClusky. He was correct. Koblenz had reported losses or only small profits in the early and mid-1970s.[107]

After selling its unprofitable Australian operation, Goodrich also reduced its presence in Asia.[108] Problems afflicted Goodrich's one-third ownership of Yokohama Rubber in Japan. In 1977 the Dai-Ichi keiretsu, a combine of some thirty Japanese companies of which Yokohama Rubber was now a member, reorganized and expanded. After this move Yokohama Rubber ceased sending reports on its activities to Goodrich. "The Company [Goodrich] no longer saw capital projects proposals and, in spite of significant efforts, has been unsuccessful in even obtaining YRC's management succession plans," management explained to its directors. John Ong later recalled that he received information from Yokohama Rubber only "after the fact and in a fairly summary way." The result, he concluded, was that "we lost confidence over time in the ability of their management." Unable to influence, or even learn about, Yokohama Rubber's plans, executives decided to sell Goodrich's holdings in Yokohama Rubber and by 1981 had disposed of most of them, ending an association that had begun before World War I.[109] By way of contrast, Goodrich's Philippine operations were quite profitable through the 1970s. They attracted $8 million for an expansion of tire making facilities in 1974 and remained an important part of Goodrich's overseas operations as the 1970s came to a close.[110]

The most difficult divestiture was from Iran. Goodrich sold its profitable 68 percent share of BFGoodrich Iran (the Pahlavi Foundation, owned by the shah's family, had most of the rest) under pressure. A nationalistic government, backed by workers, was forcing foreign companies to sell the holdings they possessed in Iranian subsidiaries. Work stoppages, problems in unloading supplies at the docks, and difficulties in arranging necessary financing—problems that Ong believed originated from the Iranian government—hurt Goodrich's tire operations. "It was an absolute pure shakedown," Ong concluded; "we got the message, and our reaction was 'let's get the hell out of here.'" Thomas and McClusky visited Iran in late 1975. "Our conclusion," McClusky later wrote, "was that we should remove ourselves from Iran Tire as soon as we were able." In 1976 a group of public and private interests nominated by the Iranian government, and led by the Pahlavi Foundation, bought Goodrich's share of the tire plant at a reasonable price.[111]

The Western Hemisphere presented a mixed picture. In 1979 Goodrich sold its tire plant in Brazil. With a "limited market share and historically poor returns," the plant seemed a bad investment to officers.[112] Goodrich maintained a profitable investment in Mexico's Compania Hulera Euzkadi, S.A. By expanding its tire making capacity 300 percent in the 1970s, Euzkadi managed to stay abreast of Mexico's booming tire market.[113] Profitable Goodrich operations in Colombia won expansion and modernization funds in 1972 and 1976.[114] So did Goodrich's tire factory in Kitchener, Ontario, which received $9 million to convert to radials in mid-1979.[115]

Divestitures extended to raw materials. In the late 1970s Goodrich decided to sell its rubber plantation in Liberia. Established in 1954, the plantation employed 2,800 wage and 93 salaried employees to produce 19 million pounds of raw rubber in 1976. This operation had become unnecessary to Goodrich, as factory-made rubber prices dropped. In the mid-1970s Goodrich took only about one-fifth of the plantation's output, selling the rest on the open market. Nor was the plantation particularly profitable. Arguing that the "sale of the plantation is consistent with our strategy of redeploying capital from tire-related areas into higher growth/higher return areas," the management committee urged Goodrich's directors to sell the plantation. In May 1976 they agreed to do so, provided that Goodrich obtained at least $15 million for it, and in 1981 they sold the plantation to British interests. At about the same time, Goodrich sold smaller plantation holdings in the Philippines.[116]

Taken as a whole, Goodrich's foreign tire operations were less successful than those of Goodyear and Firestone in the 1970s. Inflation, fluctuating currency exchange rates, energy problems, and recessions hurt the overseas tire making of all American firms, but Goodyear and Firestone were better able to deal with these issues than Goodrich. Rather than cut back their foreign operations, Firestone and Goodyear continued to expand them, though Firestone sold some unprofitable operations in the late 1970s (Firestone also invested in some unprofitable overseas operations). Goodyear, in particular, followed a successful program of what its executives called "geographical diversification." For Goodyear, Latin American markets proved particularly profitable, followed by those of Asia; European markets were more problematic.[117]

BFGoodrich and Its Competitors in Tires

Pioneering in radials did not permit Goodrich to preserve its market share in the American tire industry. The market maintenance strategy put forward in 1975 did not work. The automobile companies moved into radials in the mid-1970s much more quickly than Goodrich had anticipated—prompting its competitors to abandon bias/ply and bias/belted tires and switch to radials speedily. In 1975 radials accounted for 29 percent of the replacement and 65 percent of the original equipment tires sold in the United States; by 1981 the figures were 99 percent and 59 percent, respectively. As the radial revolution was nearly completed, Goodrich saw its share of America's original equipment tire market tumble from 16 percent in 1970 to 10 percent nine years later. Despite the success of the T/A radial, Goodrich had only 5 percent of America's replacement tire market in 1979.[118]

Both Goodyear and Firestone increased their leads in tire sales over Goodrich in the 1970s. In 1973 Goodyear's tire sales came to $3.9 billion, 4.5 times Goodrich's tire sales of $877 million; by 1979 Goodyear's sales had climbed to $6.9 billion, topping Goodrich's sales of $1.3 billion by more than five times. Similarly, Firestone's tire sales of $2 billion were three times greater than Goodrich's sales of $698 million in 1971, but in 1979—despite the recall of the Firestone 500 radial the year before—Firestone's tire sales of $4.1 billion exceeded Goodrich's sales by 3.2 times.[119] In 1979 Goodyear controlled 42 percent of America's original equipment tire market and 14 percent of the nation's replacement market. Firestone sold 23 percent of America's original equipment tires and 11 percent of the replacement tires that year.[120]

Moreover, Goodyear's and Firestone's tire sales were generally more profitable than Goodrich's. Goodyear's *net* income came to an average 8 percent of net sales between 1973 and 1979; in contrast, Goodrich's *operating* income averaged only 4.1 percent of net sales. Even with losses resulting from its problems with radials, Firestone's *net* income came to an average 3.4 percent of net tire sales between 1971 and 1979, nearly as great as Goodrich's *operating* income average.[121] Not surprisingly, Goodyear and Firestone generally performed better financially during most of the 1970s than Goodrich.

CHEMICALS AND PLASTICS: EXPANSION AND INTEGRATION

Chemical products, especially PVC, grew in importance for BFGoodrich in the 1970s. As they began changing the product mix of their company, Goodrich's executives particularly emphasized PVC, until by 1977 PVC sales accounted for 14 percent of all of the company's sales and just under half of the chemical division's sales. The emphasis that Thomas and other executives placed on chemicals was understandable. Chemicals were by far the most profitable of Goodrich's operations and seemed to be the most promising part of its businesses. Moreover, Thomas's background in petrochemicals inclined him to favor chemicals more than had Keener. Ed Osborne, the vice president in charge of marketing chemicals at Goodrich in 1972, recalled that "when Thomas came in it was a real breath of fresh air because he was much more interested in the chemical company than Mr. Keener was, and he was much more knowledgeable about the chemical company and raw material." Begin-

TABLE 9.1
BFGoodrich and Its Competitors in the 1970s

	1968	1969	1970	1971	1972	1973	1974	1975	1976	1977	1978	1979
Net Income as a Percentage of Sales												
All S & P industries	6.10	5.70	5.00	5.00	5.30	6.00	5.30	4.60	5.30	5.00	NA	NA
Tires & rubber	4.90	4.30	3.10	3.90	4.20	3.90	3.10	2.50	1.80	2.60	0.80	1.00
BFG	3.80	3.20	1.00	2.40	3.40	3.40	2.80	1.30	0.80	2.70	2.70	2.80
Firestone	6.00	5.10	4.00	4.60	5.00	5.20	4.20	3.60	2.40	2.50	NM	1.50
Goodyear	5.10	4.90	4.00	4.70	4.70	4.00	3.00	3.00	2.10	3.10	3.00	1.80
Uniroyal	4.00	3.00	1.60	2.60	2.60	2.30	2.10	1.10	0.90	1.40	0.20	NM
Operating Income as a Percentage of Sales												
All S & P industries	15.80	15.30	14.20	14.60	15.10	15.80	15.40	14.40	14.40	14.20	NA	NA
Tires & rubber	13.70	12.80	11.10	12.70	12.60	11.90	10.90	10.00	9.00	10.10	9.30	7.70
BFG	12.00	11.60	11.60	12.40	13.00	12.30	9.80	7.60	8.20	10.00	9.30	8.20
Firestone	15.50	14.20	12.00	13.50	13.90	13.60	12.30	11.60	10.10	10.10	8.70	8.30
Goodyear	14.20	13.90	12.80	14.10	13.60	12.40	11.30	10.70	9.50	11.20	10.90	8.50
Uniroyal	11.50	9.60	7.40	8.70	8.40	7.90	8.70	7.70	6.50	7.00	6.20	3.20
Earnings per Share												
BFG				$0.12	$3.33	$3.76	$3.49	$1.65	$0.95	$3.95	$4.39	$4.89
Firestone				$2.07	$2.36	$2.89	$2.71	$2.36	$1.68	$1.92	($2.58)	$1.96
Goodyear				$2.24	$2.64	$2.42	$2.00	$2.24	$1.67	$2.85	$3.12	$2.02
Uniroyal				$1.42	$1.55	$1.58	$1.65	$0.68	$0.57	$1.13	$0.04	($4.54)

Source: Standard and Poor's Industry Surveys, 1978–80.
Note: S&P = Standard and Poor's; NA = not available; NM = not meaningful.

TABLE 9.2
BFGoodrich Capital Appropriations
(in millions of dollars)

	Tire	Chemical	Other U.S.	Foreign
1973	77.5	28.6	13	27.3
1974	32.5	58.9	33	41.1
1975	28.8	49.4	17	20.3
1976	26.9	57.4	16.5	34.1
1977	25.8	59.6	27	23.2
1978	21.5	84.5	24	13
1979	74	109	64	

Source: "Directors Folders."

ning in 1974, chemicals received the lion's share of capital investments made at Goodrich. Over the next five years, chemicals won twice as much capital as the tire division, and an even greater share than other parts of the company.[122]

As Thomas expanded the production of chemicals, he integrated the chemical division into Goodrich in a way that Collyer and Keener had not. The chemical division had developed from the 1940s almost as a separate company within BFGoodrich. While willing to delegate authority over daily operations down to the divisional level, Thomas ended the chemical division's long-cherished independence. "Keener always had a kind of hands-off position with the chemical business," Ong remembered. Not Thomas. "Now you had a CEO who was very interested in what was going on, who was calling them [chemical division executives] on the phone all the time, visiting the plants," Ong observed. "It was really the end of their autonomy."[123]

Within chemicals Thomas wanted, above all, for Goodrich to remain a low-cost producer of commodity PVC resins and compounds for large markets, much as the company had been in the 1950s and 1960s. Thomas's "real interest," Ong observed, "was exclusively in the PVC business and the general purpose chemical business. The little businesses ... specialty polymers and chemicals, didn't interest him because they lacked size."[124] If the stress on low-cost PVC was the continuation of one decades-old policy at Goodrich, it also represented a muting of a different emerging policy. As competition heated up in PVC markets after 1955, officers sought to diversify chemical production as a way of maintaining profits. With the stress he laid on commodity PVC, Thomas undercut that strategy. While sometimes differing on how best to expand PVC production, executives agreed on the need for that expansion. Only in the very late 1970s did Goodrich begin to return to more diversified chemical production, especially in the realm of specialty chemicals.

By then, however, it had made a basic commitment to the large-scale production of PVC and its feedstocks, a commitment that would wound Goodrich in changed economic conditions during the early 1980s. The emphasis placed on the production of commodity PVC resins and compounds, and the intermediates going into them, required huge capital outlays for new world-scale plants. Those capital needs, requirements much greater than those for the expansion of specialty chemicals, severely strained Goodrich's resources. When a worldwide recession cut the demand for PVC in the early 1980s, Goodrich found itself boxed into a very difficult situation: servicing a large debt incurred in building new facilities with dwindling revenues. That major problems lay ahead for their PVC operations was not recognized by executives in the early 1970s. Far from it; these were expansionary times for the company's PVC work.

The Expansion of PVC Capacity

The early 1970s saw the beginning of a drive to expand PVC production at Goodrich. Optimism abounded. Between 1966 and 1971 the production of PVC in the United States doubled from 1.2 billion pounds to 2.4 billion pounds, and Goodrich's output nearly kept pace, rising from 260 million pounds to 456 million pounds.[125] In 1972 Thomas Nantz, the president of chemicals, observed that the division's "major business is in plastic materials, represented mainly by Geon vinyl plastics," and he identified PVC as having the greatest growth potential in chemicals. PVC accounted for one-third of the chemical division's sales in 1972, and late in that year chemical division executives told the management committee that they expected the demand for PVC in the United States to grow at least 13 percent annually over the next four years.[126]

Such thoughts inspired expansion. In early 1973 Goodrich executives announced the goal of increasing PVC resin production 30 percent by the end of 1974, an essential step if their company were to hold on to its market share. This expansion was almost completed by the end of 1973, as significant expenditures boosted the output of resins at Avon Lake, Long Beach, Pedricktown, Henry, and Louisville. The resins could be used to make both extruded products, such as house siding, garden hose, and pipes, and calendered products, including wall coverings and upholstery materials. Even with the expansion moves, demand for PVC boomed so much that in 1973 Goodrich had to restrict foreign sales to have enough for domestic customers, as had sometimes been the case in earlier years.[127]

Despite a recession that temporarily cut into PVC sales, and despite rising energy and raw materials prices, Goodrich accelerated the expansion of PVC facilities in the mid-1970s. With Goodrich's conversion to radial tires well under way, more funds were available for chemicals. Most of them went into PVC. Especially important, the Louisville plant was modernized and expanded; in 1977 it was making suspension resins at its full capacity of 250 million pounds per year. The Avon Lake plant was also expanded and, with Louisville making suspension resins, was able to switch some of its output to dispersion resins.[128]

PVC products rose in significance for Goodrich during the 1970s. (BFG Col. UAA)

Although its share of America's PVC market fell from 21 percent in 1972 to 18 percent in 1977, Goodrich remained America's largest producer of PVC resins and compounds. In 1977 Goodrich produced 936 million pounds. Trailing Goodrich were Conoco (7.5 percent), Borden (7 percent), Diamond Shamrock (7 percent), and a host of smaller producers. Goodrich was the number one producer of PVC used in vinyl siding (although it was losing market share to newcomers) and the second-largest maker of PVC for pipes, the nation's single largest PVC market.[129] Goodrich's PVC found its way into well over one hundred major types of products in the construction, household consumer, industrial, and transportation markets.[130] Despite growing competition, these were profitable sales. Goodrich's operating income return on net capital employed (OIRONCE) for PVC and plastic products rose from 5 percent in 1970 to 40 percent by 1974, declined to 20 percent in 1975, increased to 22 percent in 1977, and fell to 15 percent in 1978. Even at their lowest,

TABLE 9.3

Performance by Division at BFGoodrich, 1969–1979

	1969	1970	1971	1972	1973	1974	1975	1976	1977	1978*	1979*
	Operating Income as a Percentage of Net Sales										
Tires	5.6	4.4	7.3	8.2	5.4	0.1	3	1.2	8.7	6.8	3.7
Chemical	20	14.3	12.1	14.4	16.6	17	4	6.4	5	6.2	10.4
Industrial products	8.4	6	3.8	2	5	5.5	5.3	8	9.3	6	5.3
	Operating Income as a Percentage of Total Capital Employed at Equity										
Tires	5.9	3.4	8.6	10.7	7.5	5.3	4.9	5.7	18.4	NA	NA
Chemical	17.8	10.1	10.4	15.1	22.7	32	8	13.7	11	NA	NA
General products	5.9	0	1.4	12.75	20.6	23.8	12.2	20.3	15.6	NA	NA
Engineered systems						15.4	19.5	21	26.9	NA	NA
Industrial products				4.8	4.1					NA	NA
International	8.6	8.5	9.9	7.9	9	9.3	8.9	1.6	10.3	NA	NA

Sources: "Directors Folders," 1969–77; "Annual Reports," 1978–79.
*BFGoodrich changed its accounting procedures in 1978.

these returns were higher than what Goodrich was earning in tires or most other products.[131]

Backward Vertical Integration into PVC Feedstocks

The efforts of executives to maintain Goodrich as America's largest low-cost maker of PVC ran headlong into a major problem: a scarcity of raw and intermediate materials at reasonable prices. With other firms also boosting their production of PVC, and with energy prices rapidly rising, the 1970s proved to be a difficult time for PVC production at BFGoodrich. At its core the problem facing executives seemed simple. Goodrich depended heavily on other chemical companies for much of its ethylene dichloride (EDC)—a feedstock used in making vinyl chloride monomers (VCM), which were, in turn, used by Goodrich to make PVC. Worried about rising prices and unavailability of the materials that went into making PVC resins and compounds, Goodrich decided to produce more of those materials itself, a form of backward vertical integration. Goodrich's Calvert City plant had greatly expanded its production of EDC and VCM in the mid- and late 1960s; but not even Calvert City's rising output was enough to meet Goodrich's voracious appetite.

The energy crisis of 1973 heightened concerns. Natural gas prices (propane, which was used in making EDC, was made from natural gas) rose 73 percent between 1973 and 1975, and another 102 percent by 1979, leading to price increases in EDC and VCM. Dow Chemical, Goodrich's main outside supplier of VCM, raised its price from 2.25¢ per pound to 3.25¢ per pound. As one Goodrich executive later remarked, Dow "had us by the short-hair in respect to ethylene dichloride and vinyl chloride manufacturing."[132] Even more distressing was the possibility of not being able to secure enough EDC and VCM during times of peak demand. In February 1973 officers observed with trepidation that "beyond 1975 the Chemical Division has no definite commitment at this time for either a supply of EDC or VCM." Three months later, the management committee learned from executives in the chemical division that, unless steps were quickly taken, Goodrich's "shortfall" of VCM (the amount Goodrich would have to purchase from other chemical companies) would increase from 306 million pounds in 1975 to 1.1 billion pounds by 1980.[133]

Such worries led Thomas to underline "the necessity and urgency of our Company's becoming more basic in the production of raw materials and feedstocks for our Chemical Division's products."[134] All at Goodrich agreed that a solution was desperately needed. Because of his background in petrochemicals—Atlantic Richfield had made large quantities of ethylene—Thomas hoped at first that Goodrich might integrate backward into the making of ethylene as a feedstock for EDC and VCM, perhaps in a joint venture with another company. Executives explored various possibilities along this line, but all proved to be too expensive. Then, too, Goodrich had little use for most of the by-products resulting from the making of ethylene. Consequently,

Goodrich soon decided not to make its own ethylene. At any rate, McClusky later wrote, "we could buy low-cost ethylene by pipeline." "On the rebound," Ong recalled, Goodrich decided to integrate backward into the production of chlor-alkali (chlorine), another feedstock for its EDC and VCM, a somewhat less costly venture than the production of ethylene.[135]

Anton Vittone—who had been the president of the chemical division between 1972 and early 1975, and who had become an executive vice president in 1975—brought the concerns about PVC's raw and intermediate materials to the directors in the fall of 1975. Vittone pointed out that Goodrich had to purchase 540 million pounds of EDC annually, mainly from Dow and Allied. Contracts with these companies, Vittone explained, would expire over the next few years. He feared that Allied would not renew its contract, and that Dow would be able to supply only one-half of Goodrich's outside needs, leaving Goodrich in a "shaky situation." Vittone suggested that Goodrich make its own chlorine (from which EDC could be produced) and EDC. Goodrich would also produce caustic soda as a by-product resulting from the making of chlorine. The caustic soda could be sold on the open market and had the advantage of following a product cycle different from that of PVC. A plant to make chlorine and EDC would, Vittone estimated, cost at least $160 million, more than Goodrich alone could afford. Vittone proposed that Goodrich seek a joint-venture partner to share the huge cost. Because Goodrich and the other company would set up a jointly owned subsidiary to make the chlorine and EDC, the entire venture could be financed "off–balance sheet" without impairing Goodrich's capital base.[136]

In the mid-1970s Goodrich sought a partner for the proposed joint venture. Discussions with many firms fell through.[137] Then in early 1977, Ong later recalled, Steve Bechtel, who headed the global construction firm Bechtel & Company, "understanding that we were having a hard time putting this project together . . . said to me 'well, how would it be if we were to become partners?'"[138] At a series of three meetings in June 1977 members of the management committee discussed in great detail the possibility of working with Bechtel. McClusky, who became the president of the chemical division in 1975, argued persuasively for the joint venture as necessary to "meet most of the Company's needs for chlorine and EDC." More generally, the joint venture would, he thought, lower Goodrich's production costs, allowing the firm to compete better with its "very cost conscious" rivals in making PVC. The "counter-cyclicality" of caustic soda production was also appealing. Altogether, McClusky expected the joint venture to "improve the rate of return on BFG's investments."[139]

While all of the executives agreed that a way had to be found for Goodrich to remain a large, low-cost producer of PVC, some raised questions about the proposed joint venture. Thomas Nantz, who generally favored the project, and Thomas Waltermire, director of corporate finance, pointed out that entering into the joint venture would have a short-term "adverse impact on BFG's net income and cash flow" and that there were also long-term "key vulnerabilities" involved, "such as cost overrun/financing underruns, environmental/political delays." Moreover, they observed that if Goodrich were at some point to buy Bechtel's share of the joint venture, "purchasing the assets of the project could place a severe financial burden on the Company."[140]

The decision to go ahead with the joint venture was, as Ong later recalled, "very controversial." Only after first considering waiting three or four years did executives endorse moving ahead right away. A nonbinding straw vote of those at a management committee meeting of 15 June—a vote of all who would be involved in setting up and running the joint venture, committee members and nonmembers alike—revealed a closely balanced division of opinion. Those at the meeting later recalled that the proposal to enter into the joint venture passed by only one vote, eleven to ten.[141] Four days later the management committee met to decide Goodrich's course of action. "At the end of a very long meeting," remembered Ong, "it was clear that nobody, including Thomas, was 100 percent sure of what we ought to do." By a less than unanimous vote, the committee members decided to go ahead. "It wasn't that the people who voted 'no' didn't understand the strategic value," Ong later observed, "and it wasn't that the people who voted 'yes' didn't understand the financial risk. . . . We all saw both sides of the issue, it just depended a little bit upon who was maybe a little more risk prone . . . or who was a little more cautious."[142] Just one day after this decisive meeting McClusky presented the same arguments he had used in the meetings of the management committee to the board of directors. After what one director recalled as "a fair amount of discussion," the directors voted unanimously in favor of the enterprise.[143]

The Convent Chemical Company

Within a month Goodrich and Bechtel agreed to set up a joint venture to design, construct, and operate a plant to make large amounts of chlorine, caustic soda, and EDC. Bechtel and Goodrich each would put up $8.55 million to finance the venture. The rest, the staggering sum of $250 million, would come from borrowings by the joint venture—not by Goodrich or Bechtel—from banks and insurance companies. Bechtel would construct the new plant. Not interested in long-term investments in the facility, Bechtel agreed to sell its half of the joint venture to Goodrich in 1981.[144] In January 1978 Goodrich and Bechtel incorporated the HCC Chemical Company to make chlorine, caustic soda, and EDC at Bayport, Texas. However, opposition by environmental groups worried about clean air—the projected plant would emit chemical fumes into the atmosphere—killed this venture.[145]

Instead, in September 1978 Goodrich and Bechtel formed the Convent Chemical Company to make the PVC feedstocks in plants at a 675-acre site on the east bank of the Mississippi River at Convent, Louisiana, about twenty miles southeast of Baton Rouge. Convent was an appealing site, easily linked by pipelines to sources of brine and ethylene. Capitalized at $269 million, Convent Chemical received most of its funding from $160 million in loans from insurance companies and $85 million in bank borrowings.[146]

In late 1978 Goodrich announced that Convent Chemical would have two production units: a chlor-alkali plant capable of producing 800 tons of chlorine and 880 tons of caustic soda each day, and a second plant to combine the chlorine with ethylene to make as much as 800 million pounds of EDC annually. Site preparation began in the spring of 1979, and ground was broken for the first building late that summer, with completion scheduled for 1981. Goodrich initially planned for most of Convent Chemical's EDC to be shipped to Calvert City to be made into VCM. In 1979 Goodrich transferred its plant at Calvert City, valued at $68 million, to Convent Chemical. Calvert City's VCM, in turn, would go to five Goodrich plants making PVC resins and compounds across the United States. In 1980 and 1981 Goodrich executives contemplated modifying this scheme. They considered building world-scale VCM and PVC plants to use the EDC right at Convent, only to abandon such plans in the summer of 1981 in the face of a major recession that dried up demand for PVC.[147]

Further Commitment to PVC

The decision to integrate backward into making PVC feedstocks was part of a searching review of Goodrich's PVC strategies. Central to the evolution of those strategies were two reports prepared for Goodrich by McKinsey & Company. A preliminary report presented in late 1978 showed that in the mid-1970s Goodrich's American competitors had expanded faster than Goodrich, often by emphasizing regional or product niche markets. The report revealed further that between 1968 and 1977 Goodrich's PVC mix had shifted toward lower-value-added resins.[148] McKinsey presented a second, more detailed report in early 1979. This report concluded that, while becoming more competitive, the American PVC market "continues to have attractive potential" and estimated that pretax returns on new investments in PVC manufacturing would range from 7 percent for pipe resins to 22 percent for window compounds. Goodrich executives had a choice, the report observed. Goodrich could remain America's number one high-volume producer of PVC resins and compounds. It would take an estimated investment of at least $800 million over ten years for Goodrich to maintain its market position, with much of the money going for "backward integration . . . essential to achieve competitive economics." Or, the report suggested, executives could give up some of their firm's market share, while "increasing [the] importance of high-profit products in the overall mix" and "undertaking selective marketing and manufacturing actions."[149]

Goodrich opted to remain a high-volume PVC producer. In March 1979 Bart A. DiLiddo, the company's general manager of plastics, informed members of the management committee that despite all the expansion moves being

Pipes were a growing market for PVC, as PVC replaced copper. (BFG Co.)

made, he still expected a "substantial capacity gap" to exist in Goodrich's PVC making until 1988.[150] On 31 July 1979 Ong, who had just taken over as Goodrich's chief executive officer, announced that Goodrich was going to expand greatly its production of EDC, VCM, and PVC, along with the raw materials going into them, over the next six years—thus affirming Goodrich's long-standing intent to be America's major low-cost producer of PVC. After noting that he expected American demand for PVC to double in the 1980s, Ong stated, "We are dedicated to maintaining our leadership position in this important industry." PVC earnings would, Ong thought, "be substantial and, therefore, enhance our efforts to raise and stabilize Goodrich profits." By this time, PVC accounted for 20 percent of Goodrich's total sales and 60 percent of its chemical sales.[151]

Executives acted quickly. Even before Ong's announcement, they purchased a PVC plant located in Plaquemine, Louisiana (just a few miles from Convent Chemical), in February 1979. Capable of producing about 165 million pounds of PVC resins annually, the plant was purchased, Thomas observed, as "an expression of Goodrich's confidence in the future of the PVC market."[152] In the fall of 1979 Goodrich officers won approval for a $46-million expansion to double the resin-making capacity of their Pedricktown plant. "While the expansion is attractive financially," Goodrich's executives believed, "strategic considerations are of primary importance, as this project represents the initiation of the new PVC strategy."[153]

The actions of Goodrich executives were understandable, for PVC seemed to have a promising future. The rate of increase in the volume of PVC produced in America slowed in the 1970s from the extraordinary gains made in the two previous decades, but remained high. America's PVC production rose 8.2 percent per year between 1970 and 1974 and 5.4 percent annually over the next four years—very respectable increases, although less than the projections Goodrich's chemical division executives made in 1972. As it had since the mid-1950s, competition was increasing. American companies added to their capacity to produce PVC, bringing 890 million pounds of new production on line between 1972 and 1977.[154] Even so, most experts expected rising demand to keep up with or surpass growing capacity into the 1980s. At the 1979 meeting of the Chemical Marketing Research Association, the head of the plastics division of Conoco Chemicals predicted large gains for PVC as it replaced other plastics in a wide variety of markets.[155] In the fall of 1979 America's leading chemical trade journal observed that "a resurgence in demand during 1980 might even be greater than additions to capacity in 1979, causing producers to press plants as hard as they did earlier this year."[156] Sharing in this optimism, Goodrich executives moved ahead to boost their firm's production of commodity PVC resins and compounds, and the feedstocks that went into them.

Problems with the Environment

Goodrich's expansion of its chemical capabilities, especially PVC, increased the firm's vulnerability to environmental issues, and environmental concerns loomed large across America in the 1970s. Even earlier, Goodrich had responded to state and local environmental laws. Public pressures mounted for stricter regulation of manufacturers whose products harmed the environment. Congress, with President Nixon's reluctant assent, passed legislation creating the Environmental Protection Agency (EPA) in 1970. In the same year Congress passed the Clean Air Act, and two years later it passed the Federal Water Pollution Control Act. To further protect the health and safety of workers, Congress passed legislation establishing the Occupational Safety and Health Administration (OSHA) in 1970. Goodrich executives began to respond to public concerns even before the federal government intervened, and they were proud of their records in living up to the new demands.

No environmental issue involving Goodrich was more in the limelight than a scare about a rare type of cancer of the liver, angiosarcoma, resulting from the exposure of workers to gases released into the air during the conversion of VCM into PVC resins and compounds. The doctor at Goodrich's

Louisville plant—where PVC operations had begun in 1942 and where, therefore, workers had long been exposed to PVC gases—came to suspect a relationship between PVC operations and angiosarcoma in early 1974. The first person in the world's PVC industry to suspect this linkage, he took his suspicions to Dr. Murray N. Johnson in Goodrich's Environmental Health Department in Akron. Johnson and his superior told Ong, then the head of Goodrich's corporate support group; Ong, in turn, informed Thomas.[157]

Thomas immediately called a Sunday afternoon meeting of Goodrich's top executives. The atmosphere of the meeting, recalled Edwin Harrington, who was then in charge of Goodrich's PVC manufacturing, was "absolutely [that of] crisis."[158] Goodrich doctors informed those at the meeting that, although nothing could be absolutely proven, there was most likely a connection between the cancer and the gases. Goodrich's lawyers and outside counsel suggested that, nonetheless, Goodrich's liability might well be limited. Goodrich had been carefully following OSHA standards, set in 1971, limiting gaseous emissions to 500 ppm (parts per million). After "sitting there and listening," Thomas "cut short the presentations," Ong recalled. At around 7:00 P.M. Thomas interrupted to inform everyone that they faced a large potential problem and that the company's employees, other firms making PVC, and the National Institutes of Health had to be informed without delay. "That decision was made early on," recalled Richard Heuerman, Goodrich's top corporate counsel, "to be open and above-board, throw it on the table and get to the bottom of the problem." Harrington recalled the situation similarly. "It was out in the open immediately," he later explained; there was "absolutely no cover-up. Within three days of the time Mr. Thomas knew about it, it became public."[159]

Thomas's decision was not popular with Goodrich's competitors in the PVC industry, for the revelation affected all of them. None had conducted the type of investigations made at Goodrich. "Goodrich was not a hero in the chemical industry for doing that," recalled McClusky; "we were given a fair amount of harassment."[160]

Over the next few months, studies funded by Goodrich and other PVC makers established beyond doubt that too much exposure to PVC gases could cause angiosarcoma. By the end of 1974 researchers had identified thirty-five deaths worldwide from PVC-induced angiosarcoma. Those deaths included five at Goodrich's Louisville facility and eight at a PVC plant in Shawinigan, Quebec, acquired by Goodrich in 1972 (this plant had been making PVC for thirty-three years). In the wake of Goodrich's announcement and the additional tests and investigations, OSHA lowered acceptable exposure levels to PVC gases to 50 ppm in April 1974, and two years later to 1 ppm for an eight-hour exposure. Goodrich and other PVC makers met these requirements by using enclosed production systems, first designed by Goodrich, from which virtually no gas could escape.[161]

Angiosarcoma was only one of many environmental issues Goodrich faced. In 1974 Goodrich completed a $24-million program begun eight years earlier to meet federal and state pollution standards in the company's American operations. In 1975, in the wake of the angiosarcoma scare, Goodrich established a centralized environmental laboratory, began developing environmental profiles of all company operations, and set up an environmental monitoring system to keep abreast of environmental health research. One result was that in 1976 Goodrich ended the production of phenyl betanaphthylamine (PBNA) after research in Europe showed that the human body could metabolize it into a known carcinogen. Goodrich allocated considerable sums to comply with or exceed OSHA and EPA requirements. In 1976–78 alone, it spent $80 million—more than the capital investments for the tire division—with the bulk of the funds going to clean up or safeguard chemical operations.[162]

Specialty Chemicals

While commodity chemicals, especially PVC resins, were the highest priority at Goodrich in the 1970s, Goodrich devoted some resources to the making of specialty chemicals, mainly along lines already laid down. Especially toward the close of the 1970s, the profitability and growing uses of specialty chemicals attracted renewed attention. In 1979 Goodrich went so far as to make an important acquisition in the field.

For years Goodrich had hoped to develop a second polymer beyond PVC into a major commercial success, and in the early 1970s Abson (an acrylonitrile butadiene styrene plastic or ABS) seemed a likely candidate. Abson was used as a rival material for PVC in making pipes and, increasingly, in the production of molded plastic goods. In 1977 Goodrich formed with Cosden Oil a joint-venture company named Abtec to make and market Abson worldwide. New anticipated applications for Abson included telephone, tool, and appliance housings, automobile grills, and industrial safety helmets.[163] Even so, Goodrich did not become the major player in ABS, for Abson had no real technical advantage over rival ABS products, and Goodrich had entered the field later than some of its competitors. In fact, Goodrich's efforts with Abtec never amounted to much. As Ong later recalled, Goodrich's executives looked at Abson "very hard" in the 1970s, but ultimately decided that trying to become a major producer of the plastic would be too expensive. Eventually, they sold their interest in Abtec and left the ABS field.[164]

Estane, a thermoplastic polyurethane developed by Goodrich in the late 1940s and the 1950s, proved much more successful, as it went into a broadening line of products requiring abrasion-resistance and malleability. In the mid-1970s Estane won a new, if initially small, market in molded exterior parts for cars, for it could be used as a substitute for steel among automakers eager to lower the weight of their vehicles. Goodrich's Telcar thermoplastic elastomers also won acceptance in this market. Goodrich substantially increased its sales of thermoplastic polyurethanes to automakers in 1976. Another use also appeared for Estane in the 1970s. In 1974 Nantz reported that the use of Estane as a fabric coating in wearing apparel was rapidly increasing. Estane was used to give the "wet look" to women's clothing, such as raincoats, first in Europe, and a year or two later in the United States.[165]

The hydrophilic polymers Carbopol and Carboset experienced particularly "good sales growth," especially Carbopol, which could be used as a thickening agent in pharmaceuticals, cosmetics, and textile printing inks. By 1974 Carbopol was the largest-volume product of Goodrich's specialty chemical line, and among its most profitable, boasting a 54 percent return on capital. In that year Goodrich initiated a $4.3-million project to increase Carbopol production from 5 million to 8.6 million pounds per year at its Calvert City plant.[166] Carboset resins gained new customers in the mid-1970s, as metal fabricators began shifting from solvent-based to water-based materials for coating metal surfaces, a switch mandated by environmental legislation. This was a use for which Carboset was well suited. With the return on capital devoted to making Carboset resins averaging 42 percent annually, Goodrich executives increased their production at Avon Lake from 3.3 million to 6 million pounds per year in 1976.[167]

Thermoplastic PVC, especially chlorinated PVC (CPVC), which Goodrich trademarked as High-Temp Geon (later called TempRite), won rapid acceptance in pipe making for residential use from the mid-1960s. Worldwide consumption of CPVC soared 22 percent annually in the 1970s, with Goodrich as the only American producer. By 1980 Goodrich had captured 85 percent of the American and 35 percent of the global market for CPVC.[168]

Various other polymer chemicals increased in significance for Goodrich. In early 1972 Nantz labeled polymer chemicals "one of the faster growing segments of the chemical division," and a year later he reported that Goodrich was "strong" in the production of specialty polymers. One was Krylvo, an easily disposable, water-resistant film used in medical and packaging applications. Goodrich's polymer chemicals group set a record for operating income in 1977. Among the polymer chemicals, CureRite, an accelerator made at Goodrich's Henry plant to speed up the curing of rubber compounds, and Hycar reactive liquid polymers (used in making sports balls, electrical encapsulants, structural adhesives, and in applications requiring large molded plastic sheets) performed particularly well, posting a 49 percent gain in sales in 1977.[169]

In the late 1970s Goodrich started to target some specialty chemicals and plastics for additional growth. In 1979 it began a general expansion of the production of additives and specialty polymers. Some $10.5 million were allocated to boost CureRite production. In the same year Goodrich brought its first commercial-size reactive liquid polymer plant on line (liquid polymers were used to enhance the physical properties of plastics such as epoxy and polyester). Noting that general-purpose elastomers had "unacceptable" profit margins, executives observed that they would explore further special-purpose uses for elastomers. They also planned to devote attention to specialty latexes.[170]

The Purchase of Tremco

That Goodrich was taking specialty chemicals seriously became apparent with its purchase of Tremco. A Cleveland-based company, Tremco provided America's industrial and commercial flat-roof markets with coatings and sealants. Tremco also provided maintenance services in these markets. These were expanding and profitable markets, for, as Goodrich's executives observed in late 1978, "energy conscious managers and owners of industrial and commercial buildings have become increasingly sensitive to the need for reliable sealants."[171] Ong was the driving force behind the acquisition. As early as 1977 he had considered the possibility of acquiring specialty chemical businesses for Goodrich. In that year Tremco tried to buy Goodrich's capability in America's reroofing market (a capability based on polymeric membranes made of PVC, which were beginning to displace membranes covered with asphalt). Goodrich executives initially rejected Tremco's approach but later discussed the possibility of a joint venture in this field.[172]

Over time Ong became more and more deeply involved with Tremco. A friend introduced him to Leigh Carter, Tremco's president. Ong asked Carter if Goodrich could buy Tremco, only to be rebuffed, for Carter wanted Tremco to remain independent.[173] Ong and Carter were soon back together. About a month after Ong made his initial offer another firm threatened an unfriendly takeover of Tremco. Alarmed, Carter asked Ong if Goodrich would be willing to buy Tremco in a friendly takeover to allow Tremco to avoid the unwanted, unfriendly takeover attempt. Ong said yes. The immediate danger to Tremco blew over, but thereafter Carter made Ong privy to the details of Tremco's operations and finances, should a quick decision be needed in the future. About every three months the two business leaders met in secret in Cleveland to go over Tremco's affairs (no one else at either Goodrich or Tremco knew of these meetings). In August 1979, while Ong was on vacation with his family at Jackson Hole, Wyoming, another company threatened to acquire Tremco. Interrupted by a message from Carter while out in the hills trailing a moose on horseback, Ong flew back to Ohio and arranged for Goodrich to acquire Tremco.[174]

The purchase of Tremco for about $106 million was in line with recommendations about acquisitions made by Booz-Allen in 1979. Adhesives and sealants had been singled out by the consulting firm as a promising area into which Goodrich might expand. Buying Tremco also fit in well with Ong's plans to boost the production of specialty chemicals at Goodrich. Most important in the long run, the acquisition brought Leigh Carter into the management picture at Goodrich. A Goodrich director later remembered that "we wanted him as much as we wanted the company." Ong agreed. "In my mind," Ong explained, "one of the things we were buying was Carter and his capability." Together, Carter and Ong would lead BFGoodrich through a series of crises in the mid-1980s.[175]

With the internal expansion moves of the late 1970s and with the purchase of Tremco in 1979, Goodrich was moving in the direction of specialty chemicals, which would become very important to the company in the 1980s and 1990s. Most significantly, Goodrich's corporate executives were starting to think in terms of a "specialty chemicals strategy."[176] Even so, specialty chemicals were still in their adolescence at Goodrich. In 1979 specialty chemicals accounted for less than one-fifth of the chemical division's sales.[177]

Synthetic Rubber and Rubber Chemicals

Thomas's interest in pushing commodity chemicals carried over into his treatment of synthetic rubber, for here, too, Thomas generally favored commodity over specialty production. In late 1971 Thomas announced that Goodrich was combining the manufacturing and research facilities of Ameripol with those of the chemical division. Absorbing Ameripol by chemicals (only the brand-name "Ameripol" remained after the merger) would, Thomas hoped, strengthen Goodrich's position in petrochemicals and synthetic rubber at a time when "we are facing the problems of increased competition, an ample supply of rubber, and depressed prices."[178] In the early 1970s Goodrich produced the world's broadest line of synthetic rubbers. The company's plants at Port Neches and Orange, Texas, had the capacity to turn out 650 million pounds of synthetic rubber annually. The synthetic rubber from these plants supplied all of Goodrich's divisions that used rubber and also went to over half of America's rubber fabricating companies. In 1972 synthetic rubber made up a quarter of Goodrich's chemical division's sales.[179]

Goodrich, despite Thomas's reluctance, made some efforts to expand the production of specialty synthetic rubbers. The division's Epcar EPDM rubbers (made at Orange) provided excellent resistance to heat, ozone, and weathering, leading to their growing adoption in automotive applications. Epcar rubbers gained increased acceptance even in the recession of 1975; one new use was as a lubricating oil additive. New nitrile rubbers in the Hycar line found greater automotive and aircraft use, where they were especially prized for applications requiring resistance to oil, solvents, and heat. Hydrin, a very versatile epichlorohydrin rubber, won wide acceptance in automotive and industrial applications. A high grade introduced in 1977 boosted Hydrin's use in making conveyor belts, industrial hose, and sheathings for wires and cables.[180]

Still, most of Goodrich's production of synthetic rubber remained in commodity rubbers, and problems dogged this business throughout the 1970s. There was overexpansion in the production of synthetic rubber worldwide. With about three-quarters of the synthetic rubber going into tires, it "just followed the tire cycle." By the late 1970s some executives wanted to leave synthetic rubber production, a step they would take in the 1980s.[181]

Foreign Operations in Chemicals

Unlike the situation in tires, Goodrich expanded many of its foreign operations in chemicals during the 1970s. The sales of chemicals by its foreign manufacturing subsidiaries nearly doubled from $36 million in 1971 to $70 million in 1977. Even so, the sales of Goodrich's overseas operations failed to keep pace with booming domestic chemical sales: in 1971 they amounted to nearly 13 percent of domestic sales, but by 1977 came to only 9 percent. The profits made by Goodrich's overseas chemical subsidiaries varied considerably. Most reported solid earnings in the early 1970s, but a worldwide recession in the mid-1970s affected them differently.[182] Goodrich responded to opportunities and problems with a selective expansion and contraction program.

Europe seemed least promising, and Goodrich cut back its operations there. As one executive later recalled, chemical division executives "recognized that the European market was going to go down the drain for standard conventional products." Ciago, Goodrich's largest European chemical maker, represented the greatest challenge. Profitable in the early 1970s, Ciago's sales soured in the mid-1970s. The energy crisis of 1973 caused problems. Ciago had entered into long-term contracts to sell its output of nitrile rubber and latex at fixed prices. As Ciago's production costs rose, BFGoodrich forced the subsidiary to break its contracts and raise its prices. This move destroyed sales for many years, for Ciago's customers had "long memories." By the end of the decade Goodrich was thinking of selling Ciago, an action it would take in 1981.[183] Not all European work suffered. In 1977 and 1978 Goodrich established a small cellular vinyl operation in Ireland to provide construction materials, especially synthetic wood trim, for western Europe. Ireland was especially attractive because there was no tax on income from export sales.[184]

Growing problems led Goodrich to shed its chemical operations in Iran. The joint venture in the Abadan Chemical Company—in which Goodrich owned a quarter of the shares, with Iran's National Petrochemical Company owning the rest—became less appealing. In 1973 Goodrich spent $8.6 million to expand the making of VCM, PVC resins, and other products by Abadan, but operations did not prove profitable. When McClusky became the president of the chemical division, he made it a "high priority" to get out of Iran. Officers looked into how best to sell their company's share in the joint venture in 1977 and 1978. Only after very difficult, protracted negotiations following the Iranian revolution in 1979 did they succeed in selling what was left of it— Abadan was bombed at the beginning of the Iran-Iraq War—to the Iranian government in the early 1980s.[185]

Goodrich's officers expanded their Canadian PVC operations much as they did those in the United States. In 1972 they purchased Gulf Oil's PVC plant at Shawinigan, Quebec, about one hundred miles northeast of Montreal, and a year later voted substantial sums for its expansion. Goodrich's production at Shawinigan and at its Niagara Falls, Canada, plant more than doubled in the early 1970s. Expecting continued prosperous growth—in the

1970s, Goodrich earned an average annual return of 20 percent on the capital invested in its Canadian PVC plants—Goodrich launched a $28 million expansion of its PVC operations in Niagara Falls, Canada, in 1976. The expansion doubled the capacity of the plant, so that Goodrich made about half of Canada's PVC resins by the end of 1979. In his speech dedicating the new facilities, Thomas observed that "this dramatic increase will allow us to satisfy the expanding demand for PVC in Canada." Then he and the deputy premier of Ontario cut a festive ribbon, allowing the first truckload of resin to leave the plant.[186]

As new markets for pipes, siding, and other products made from PVC opened in Asia and in Latin and South America, Goodrich increased its presence in those regions. In 1976 and 1977 Goodrich nearly doubled its production of PVC resins in Australia, a market that had been growing an average of 15 percent annually for five years. New Zealand operations, while remaining small, also expanded.[187] In 1978 Goodrich expanded, at a cost of $4 million, a joint venture to manufacture and market pipe and other PVC goods in the Philippines.[188] In 1971 Goodrich entered into a joint venture with Venezuelan interests to make VCM and PVC; Goodrich owned 25 percent of the enterprise, which came on line in 1973. While always small-scale, output tripled over the next four years. Even faster growing, but again small-scale, was the output of a Goodrich plant in Costa Rica, which began making PVC compounds in 1971.[189] Goodrich officers, despite some reluctance owing to fears of creating overcapacity, invested additional sums in a Mexican joint venture in 1978. The result was a new plant at Tampico designed to produce 150 million pounds of PVC annually by 1981; it became Mexico's largest manufacturer of PVC.[190]

Goodrich and Its Competitors in Chemicals

Goodrich's strategies for chemicals contrasted with those of many of its major competitors. While Goodrich emphasized large-scale manufacturing of commodity PVC resins and compounds and vertical integration backward to produce the raw materials and intermediates that went into their production, many of America's largest chemical companies were leaving the production of commodity chemicals, including PVC, for higher-value-added chemicals, specialty chemicals.

As the halcyon days of expansion in petrochemicals in the 1950s gave way to increasing competition, many chemical companies restructured their operations. In 1974 DuPont, already a leader in high-end plastics, set up a corporate planning department to examine the company's business portfolio. While DuPont soon discontinued several mature and less profitable business lines such as cellophane and dyes, specialty polymers and biochemicals won increased support. Dow, which was a major outside supplier of PVC intermediates for Goodrich, remained the nation's leading maker of commodity chemicals throughout the 1970s, with about 85 percent of its business in basic chemicals in the late 1970s. However, in 1978 its executives decided to radically change their company's product line by moving half of their firm's sales and revenues into high-value-added business by 1987. Union Carbide, which made 23 percent of America's PVC in 1959, sold most of its PVC operations to Tenneco in 1977. A large oil-and-gas company by the late 1970s, Tenneco wanted to diversify. Entering PVC seemed a logical step, since through its ownership of oil reserves, Tenneco controlled raw materials used in making PVC (Tenneco would regret the decision to buy the PVC operations and would try, unsuccessfully, to sell them in the early 1980s). Monsanto began moving into high-end polymer products as early as 1949, and from the mid-1960s increasingly emphasized them. Monsanto was America's third-largest producer of PVC in 1959, with 10 percent of the total market share, but it made no PVC by 1977.[191]

This refocusing of operations would accelerate in the 1980s; but already in the 1970s, as one scholar has explained, many chemical companies were "moving into higher value product lines." They "sold off many of their low price, high volume commodity businesses, and their older basic chemicals intermediates."[192] Goodrich did not participate fully in this shift. Instead, along with many oil companies (such as Tenneco), Goodrich expanded its commodity chemical and PVC operations to fill the void left by the exit of the chemical companies.[193] Not until the very late 1970s did Goodrich really begin expanding its output of specialty chemicals.

Goodrich's executives might well have paused to consider more fully the consequences of the growing emphasis they were placing on commodity chemicals. Profits in PVC, while still higher than those earned on most of Goodrich's other products, were falling. Demand for PVC, while still rising, was increasing at a slower rate than in previous years. While most commentators thought PVC still had a promising future in the late 1970s, not all did. As early as 1975 Forbes noted that Goodrich was becoming "inordinately dependent on PVC" and warned that "when a downdraft comes in the PVC market, it can take the whole company down."[194] As events were to show, the commitments made to PVC, especially to the production of feedstocks and intermediates, would hurt Goodrich in the 1980s.

INDUSTRIAL PRODUCTS AND AEROSPACE

Industrial products, which went by several divisional names and which passed through a number of reorganizations in the 1970s, was, for the most part, not a growth area. Larry Pomeroy, who headed industrial products for much of the decade, later observed that it was "a mature business" in which the "main thrust was to improve our production efficiency both in Akron and elsewhere, keep our costs as low as possible, and try to compete in a market that, as we moved towards the mid-1970s and later, became more and more a price market as smaller competitors came in to find niches and as we began to experience some imported competition."[195] Edgar Perry, who was in charge of much of the research and development for industrial products, later pointed out that in the 1970s industrial products "began to lose their 'specialty' status and to revert to commodities, as 'price' replaced 'features and benefits' in the buyer's hierarchy of needs."[196]

Strategies for industrial products developed along several lines. Goodrich divested the most unprofitable product lines: surgical gloves, many latex products, druggists' goods, molded rubber goods, footwear, and sponge rubber. At the same time Goodrich sought to increase the productivity of the Akron plant. When these attempts proved only partly successful, some industrial products were relocated to factories in lower-wage regions. Even as it cut back in some areas of industrial products, Goodrich expanded in more promising ones, most notably in the making of conveyor belts. As the 1970s came to a close, flat belting (that is, conveyor belts and flat transmission belts), industrial hose, v-belts, and sheet rubber and matting were Goodrich's most important industrial products.

Problems with Industrial Products in Akron

Like tire division executives, those in industrial products encountered major problems with Akron operations. The Akron industrial products plant remained, Pomeroy noted, "a tremendous hodge-podge."[197] Its decades-old buildings were poorly designed for modern operations. John Codrea, who was in charge of manufacturing there, considered the factory "forty years behind the times." One example was making braided hose for industrial applications. "They were building hose [by] sending long metal poles through the braiding machines on which the hose was braided, and they didn't have a layout for that," Codrea explained. "So they would pass the hose pole, which was flexible, out of the window and around the corner of the post that held up the roof, and that snake would process through and finally be braided. . . . So here they had a beautiful modern braiding machine, and behind it a supply system that kept it down 50 percent of the time."[198]

Problems in the Akron plant had several sources. Labor difficulties were worrisome. Tied as they were to wages in tire making there, wages in making industrial products were too high, executives thought. Job classifications and work rules were, most Goodrich officers thought, even more harmful, for they made it very difficult to introduce new ways of producing goods. However, more was involved. Perry worked in Goodrich's industrial products plants in Italy and Japan between 1965 and 1970 and returned to the company's domestic operations convinced that they could be improved. Not all shared his outlook. While many executives in industrial products, such as Andy Talalay and Codrea, were willing to try new ideas, including some imported ones, not all executives were.[199]

Those in charge of industrial products addressed the issues hurting their operations sporadically. "We took some of the production departments and began consolidation; some we actually shut down," Pomeroy later explained.[200] Nonetheless, a 1977 study revealed that Akron's manufacturing costs were "too high due to underutilization of facilities, high maintenance cost and inefficient layouts." In the late 1970s corporate management instituted "Project Matrix" to study the operations of industrial products in Akron and make recommendations on how to improve them. The report, completed in early 1979, called for the consolidation of some operations and the movement of others, at a cost of $25 million over four years. Nearly 1 million square feet of space in five older buildings were slated for razing.[201]

In and Out of Akron

In some cases, efforts to improve productivity succeeded, and production remained in Akron. One bright spot in the 1970s was conveyor belts. "Conveyor belting was," Perry observed, "the darling of the industrial division." Conveyor belts, he recalled, "generated the bulk of the profits for the division."[202] Used to carry such products as coal, conveyor belts benefited from the oil shortages of the 1970s. Goodrich's domestic sales of conveyor belts rose an average 17 percent annually between 1972 and 1975, and in 1974 Goodrich spent $6.2 million to raise production capacity from 35 million to 50 million pounds per year (this sum included $1.7 million to install a revolutionary triple-deck curing system for conveyor belts).[203]

One response to the problems in industrial products was to make small acquisitions to round out existing operations that looked most promising.[204] So it was with conveyor belts. Booz-Allen & Hamilton recommended conveyor systems as a possible expansion area in its 1978 and 1979 reports to Goodrich management. Accordingly, Goodrich purchased the Continental Conveyor & Equipment Company for $63 million and moved its operations to Akron in 1978. As Ong recalled, Pomeroy wanted to take a "systems approach" to the making of conveyor installations. In the mid-1970s Goodrich and Continental Conveyor jointly developed a unique intermediate-drive conveyor system. The acquisition of Continental Conveyor allowed Pomeroy to pursue "synergy between the conveyor systems and the belt." As he later explained, "we thought that by being able to offer a complete systems approach, which included both the conveyor belt and the appropriate carrying systems, we could offer a competitive package that others could not."[205]

A second response was to relocate operations to low-wage areas. In 1972 and 1973 Goodrich spent nearly $4 million to move v-belt manufacturing and warehousing from Akron and Columbus, Ohio, to Elgin, South Carolina, where the company had a vacant footwear plant that could be converted to manufacturing.[206] However, Goodrich failed to provide this plant with modern machinery, a factor that would lead to its closing in the 1980s.[207] Similarly, in 1974 Goodrich spent $15 million to move hose and light-belt manufacturing

Goodrich's officers saw a major market in conveyor belts, such as this one, which carried 1,200 tons of coal an hour. (BFG Co.)

from Akron to a plant purchased in Oneida, Tennessee. Goodrich also continued to produce hydraulic control hose at its Marion plant. Since 1967 Akron's hose operations had suffered losses owing to "low productivity, high labor rates, inefficient plant layout, antiquated equipment and technology, and low volume production runs."[208] By this time, Goodrich's industrial hose competitors had either relocated or modernized their plants, and the factory in Oneida would, officers hoped, provide their company with a "new efficient plant layout and equipment, the newest process technology, and labor at a low rate." Labor could be obtained for $3.30 per hour in Oneida, whereas it cost $7.42 per hour in Akron. As the demand for industrial hose boomed owing to the increased use of hydraulic power in machinery, Goodrich spent additional sums to expand production at Oneida and Marion.[209]

Pomeroy summed up well the intent of the relocation moves: "We were gradually moving some of the, I would say, high-labor content products out of Akron to lower-cost and more modern facilities and state-of-the-art equipment."[210] Successful operations in these new plants sometimes led to expansion. In 1979 Goodrich acquired the Carolina Rubber Hose Company, a profitable and growing manufacturer of braided hose, for $12 million. Carolina Rubber Hose operated three nonunion plants: one in North Carolina, another in South Carolina, and a third on the Texas-Mexico border. The purchase fit well the suggestion made by Booz-Allen that Goodrich expand in the hydraulic power field.[211]

Aerospace during the 1970s

Aerospace remained a small part of Goodrich in the 1970s, far from the growth area it would later become. In 1973 the division's sales came to only 4 percent of Goodrich's total sales. Thomas was not particularly interested in aerospace, and aerospace lacked the dynamic divisional leadership needed to win corporate support for expansion, especially in the early 1970s. Under Clint B. McKeown, president of aerospace, it was one of Goodrich's most profitable divisions. Aerospace also continued to win recognition for technical excellence. In 1971, for example, the division secured the contract to supply brakes for the space shuttle. However, McKeown was not aggressive in pushing its expansion and lacked clout with corporate executives, factors contributing to the neglect of the division.[212]

Organizational changes added to aerospace's problems. In 1974 the aerospace and defense products division was combined with the industrial products division to form a new unit called the engineered systems division. This merger hurt aerospace, which had little in common with industrial products. Those who had been running the industrial products division took over most of the leadership positions in engineered systems, including aerospace, but they lacked the expertise to understand the manufacturing and marketing circumstances of aerospace products. These products had different, and often much longer, life cycles than those of industrial products. It was often necessary to invest considerable sums up front in new manufacturing equipment to reap rewards later, especially since many of aerospace's sales were replacement, not original equipment, sales.[213] "It took those of us who were in management at the time a long time to come to understand the aerospace business," recalled Perry. "We were in a period when aerospace was not growing, and we did not understand enough about the long wave cycles of that business to realize that in quieter times you had to reinvest in technology to be prepared for the next major flurry of procurement." Unfortunately, he concluded, "we did not in many instances do a good job of pushing the technology to prepare ourselves for what in the late seventies then became another major buying flurry."[214]

Because they failed fully to comprehend this situation, those running aerospace missed important growth opportunities. Initially, they failed to have Goodrich brakes, wheels, evacuation slides, and other equipment approved for the Boeing 747, the Boeing 767, and the European A-300 Airbus. However, as they became more conversant with its operations, they won more contracts. Boeing soon accepted Goodrich as a supplier of evacuation slides for its 747s. In 1978 Goodrich was selected as an alternative supplier of wheels and brakes for Airbus planes purchased by Eastern Airlines, and in the same year Goodrich became a supplier of wheels and brakes for the Boeing 737 and the

Lockheed L-1011-500. A year later Goodrich received a major contract to provide wheels and brakes for the Boeing 757 and tires for the Boeing 767. Incremental gains occurred in deicing sales, and the manufacturing of deicing systems was shifted from Akron to several plants in West Virginia. As in the move of industrial products out of Akron, the reason was a search for lower wages. Despite some lost chances, then, Goodrich's aerospace division generally performed well. Sales of wheels and brakes nearly doubled between 1973 to 1977, rising to $28 million. These were very profitable sales, boasting an average annual return on capital of 48 percent.[215]

Goodrich's success in airplane wheels and brakes led it into manufacturing disk brakes with antiskid systems for trucks and other vehicles. The U.S. National Highway Transportation Safety Administration mandated the use of such braking systems on heavy-duty, over-the-highway trucks. This was one of the few aerospace areas in which Thomas was interested, and in 1973 Goodrich spent $400,000 to begin making the devices at the aerospace plant in Troy, Ohio. This venture worked out poorly. In October 1978 the Ninth Circuit Court of Appeals declared that trucks did not, after all, have to be equipped with antiskid braking systems, a decision that severely limited the potential market for the brakes. Just two months later, John McKay of aerospace reported to the management committee that many of Goodrich's customers had discontinued use of antiskid brakes, and the committee decided to end most of its production. Goodrich continued to make antiskid brakes for a few specialized uses—for off-the-road earthmoving equipment, for example—well into the 1980s, but the dream of a vast truck market evaporated with the court decision.[216]

The Purchase of Super-Temp

Its experience in brakes led aerospace to make its one major acquisition of the 1970s: that of Super-Temp, a division of Ducommun, a Delaware-incorporated firm. A maker of carbon-carbon composite materials for rocket nozzles and some other uses, Super-Temp operated a single plant in a suburb of Los Angeles. Carbon-carbon could be used in making carbon brakes for airplanes. Carbon brakes offered definite advantages over more-conventional steel brakes: they were much lighter and could withstand more heat. Perry later explained that Goodrich "decided—realistically—that our limited experience with this technology would slow us down if we tried to develop all the expertise in-house." By this time Goodrich's three major competitors—Bendix, Goodyear, and Dunlop—all possessed some carbon-brake capabilities. The purchase of Super-Temp offered Goodrich a way to stay abreast of its competitors in what was seen as the most important technical advance in brake making for the 1980s and beyond. As Ong explained at a meeting of the management committee, "in view of the importance of carbon-brake technology and production capability" Goodrich needed to purchase Super-Temp. Goodrich did, for about $4 million in late 1978.[217]

RESEARCH AT BFGOODRICH

Much changed at BFGoodrich during the 1970s, but the executives remained committed to their firm's tradition of research, as seen in their purchase of Super-Temp. As they had for decades, officers looked to research developments as one way to ensure a profitable future for their company. In the mid- and late 1970s Goodrich spent about the same proportion of its sales on research and development as its competitors in the rubber and chemical industries. Goodrich spent a much higher proportion of its profits on research and development, however.

The thinking of executives on how best to accomplish their research objectives changed from what it had earlier been. Research was among the first areas to be decentralized in the company, as corporate executives sought to link research more closely to divisional needs. Corporate officers also tried to align research activities more closely with emerging areas by allocating a growing share of research dollars to newly developing products, rather than to the refinement of established products.

The Decentralization of Research and Development

In the early and mid-1970s Goodrich decentralized research. A 1972 report by A. T. Kearney concluded that research being done at Goodrich's corporate research facilities at Brecksville was not meeting the needs of the firm's operating divisions and that "divisional control of development activities is essential." Divisional executives agreed. The head of the chemical division, in particular, believed that "Brecksville is doing very little development work for the Chemical Company" and hoped that this situation could be rectified. Over the next two years research activities were reorganized to give "the operating divisions responsibility over their own research and development, including innovation and development of new products and the supply of technical maintenance for existing operations to meet business plans for profit and growth."[218] By late 1975 Thomas could accurately report that "each operating division has its own research and development capabilities," with some research still being done, however, "on a Company-wide level."[219]

Perry, who was charged with reorganizing much of the research, later explained what was involved. "The decision was made to really break up the research organization and divisionalize it and give each of the operating divisions a portion at least of its own research." The research was "still housed at Brecksville, but functionally reporting into [a] division," Perry later observed. "There was a lot of indecision," he recalled, "whether corporate research per se should survive or not, and the decision ultimately favored was to retain a core, a small core, that would really be corporate in nature." The goal in placing the divisions in charge of most of the research was "to bridge what had been a vast chasm between research and development."[220]

TABLE 9.4

Research and Development, 1975–1980

	1975	1976	1977	1978	1979	1980
	R & D Expense as a Percentage of Sales					
Goodrich	2.2	2.1	2	1.5	1.5	1.6
Goodyear	2.2	2	1.8	2	2.1	2.1
Firestone	1.4	1.4	1.4	1.3	1.4	1.7
Uniroyal	2.6	2.5	2.6	1.6	1.6	1.6
DuPont	4.6	4.2	3.9	3.6	3.3	3.5
Dow	3.4	3.3	3.3	3.4	2.9	3
Monsanto	3.2	2.6	2.9	2.9	2.8	3.1
Union Carbide	2.1	2.2	2.2	2	1.8	1.7
Phillips	0.7	0.7	0.8	0.8	0.7	0.6
	R & D Expense as a Percentage of Profit					
Goodrich	163.5	265.2	74.5	57	52.8	80.1
Goodyear	72.8	93.1	59.1	67.1	117.2	84.5
Firestone	38.4	55.7	54.7	−44	97.9	−66.4
Uniroyal	247.4	293.1	189.7	764.9	−34.9	−459.1
DuPont	123.5	76.7	67.3	47.9	44.2	67.6
Dow	27.2	30.6	36.6	40.2	34.3	39
Monsanto	37.8	30.4	48	47.7	52.4	137.4
Union Carbide	31.5	32.3	40.5	39.5	28.9	24.7
Phillips	9.8	9.8	9.4	8.2	7.9	7.9

Sources: Business Week, 28 June 1976, 65–84; 27 June 1977, 62–84; 3 July 1978, 58–69; 2 July 1979, 52–72; 7 July 1980, 47–70; 6 July 1981, 60–75.

The Commercialization of Research

As Perry suggested, the basic objective in giving the divisions more control over research was to boost its commercial applicability. "Research and product development are," Goodrich executives noted in 1973, "key ingredients in the new B.F. Goodrich approach to diversification into profitable new product lines." They stated further that "the objective is to win the race to new markets with unique, premium products offering high growth potential." It was for these reasons, they concluded, that "research and development responsibility was placed directly on individual operating divisions."[221] Throughout the 1970s Goodrich had notable successes in using research to bring products to market. New types of radial tires such as the self-sealing Golden Lifesaver and chemical goods derived from hydrocarbon polymer research (products ranging from vinyl wall coverings to conveyor belts) were among the most important commercial advances. A greater proportion of the research spending went to support developing areas of the company, and by 1979 "approximately two-thirds of planned R&D expenditures" went to "technologies for products in growth businesses," with only one-third allocated to improve products "in mature businesses."[222]

By the late 1970s research had a heightened commercial orientation. In 1979, 77 percent of the $37 million worth of the firm's research was classified as "applied" research, with only 20 percent as "exploratory" or basic research, and with the remaining 3 percent "government-required" research. Most of this research was now "divisional" (although, as Perry said, much of the divisional research was conducted at Brecksville). Of that research classified as "corporate," 55 percent was exploratory and 45 percent applied.[223]

Giving the divisions increased control over much of Goodrich's research may have harmed the company in the long run. With a smaller proportion of research funds going to basic research, Goodrich's historic technological lead over its competitors eroded. Certainly, some advances continued. In 1979 Goodrich allocated $3 million to improve its basic research laboratories for chemicals. These laboratories, executives noted, "have been in constant use for over sixty years with only minor modernization work. For many years laboratories have been well below standard for modern industrial laboratories."[224] Overall, however, Goodrich fell behind some of its competitors in both the rubber and chemical industries in basic research. While Goodrich's competitors spent no higher a percentage of their sales or profits on research than did Goodrich, some companies—such as Goodyear, Firestone, and DuPont—spent much more in absolute terms. And more of their funds often went to basic research. As a result, Goodrich's competitors moved ahead in terms of American patents granted. For 1975 and 1976 combined, Goodrich was granted 173 patents in the United States. The figures for its competitors in the rubber industry were as follows: Goodyear, 288; Uniroyal, 191; Firestone, 118; and General Tire, 83. The figures for its competitors in chemicals and PVC were the following: DuPont, 1,037; Phillips, 609; Dow, 664; Monsanto, 498; Union Carbide, 444; Allied, 309; and Diamond Shamrock, 85. Recognizing this problem, Goodrich instituted an "Inventor Recognition Program" in 1977, and in that year Goodrich's patent applications in the United States rose by a third.[225]

BFGOODRICH AT THE END OF THE 1970S

When Pen Thomas retired at the age of sixty-five and was succeeded by John Ong as BFGoodrich's chief executive officer and chairman in July 1979, the corporation was substantially different from what it had been under Ward Keener's leadership. Problems buffeted all of the divisions in the 1970s, as soaring energy prices, deep recessions, and growing competition at home and abroad bit into profits. Faced with new business realities, Thomas looked at Goodrich with open eyes and worked with other corporate officers to start

TABLE 9.5
BFGoodrich in the 1970s

	Net Income as % of Net Sales	Net Income as % of Assets	Net Income as % of Equity	Profit Margin Ratio: Operating Income as % of Net Sales
1971	0.02	0.01	0.03	7.50
1972	3.30	3.50	7.80	8.20
1973	3.40	3.80	8.50	8.40
1974	2.60	3.20	7.30	6.50
1975	1.30	1.60	3.50	3.70
1976	0.08	0.10	2.20	4.80
1977	2.70	3.50	7.90	7.10
1978	2.70	3.60	8.30	5.70
1979	2.70	3.90	9.10	5.40

Sources: "Annual Reports," 1971–80.

moving Goodrich in new directions. A "willingness to try new things, to accept mistakes, and to push on," Donald McClusky later wrote, characterized Thomas's work.[226] Most noteworthy was the growing importance placed on chemicals, especially PVC, and the declining significance of tires. In 1971 tires accounted for nearly 60 percent of Goodrich's sales, down to only 43 percent by 1979. Conversely, chemicals composed 24 percent of the corporation's sales in 1971, but 35 percent by 1979. In 1971 tires accounted for 55 percent of Goodrich's operating income, but only 25 percent by 1979. Again, it was the rise in importance of chemicals that was responsible for the difference. In 1971 chemicals accounted for 37 percent of Goodrich's operating income, but by 1979 a whopping 58 percent.[227]

Still, executives left unresolved serious problems in their company's operations, some of them inherited from Keener's years. Goodrich was having a difficult time competing in tires, and the future of the tire division had not yet been decided. Radial tires were not going to be the salvation once hoped for. Many of the firm's industrial products operations continued to be carried out in obsolete plants, especially in Akron. More generally, Goodrich seemed to some observers to be a company "adrift" as the 1970s drew to a close. Thomas had lost his early drive, and Ong was just assuming control. "You could say the company lost its way," said one top Goodrich executive about his firm.[228] A business periodical concurred, "Goodrich, for all of Pen Thomas's efforts, reels from crisis to crisis."[229]

Thomas's basic objective of returning Goodrich to stable profitability on par with other American industrial companies remained elusive. In the late 1970s, Goodrich did catch up with Firestone and Goodyear in profitability. Goodrich's return on stockholders' equity rose from an average 4.8 percent during 1971–76, to 7.9 percent in 1977, to 8.3 percent in 1978, and to 9.1 percent in 1979. Even so, Goodrich's returns remained well below the average for American manufacturing companies, which was 12–13 percent in the late 1970s. In late 1978 *Forbes* noted that Thomas had "completely restructured the company and has spent millions of dollars on some of the best outside consultants money can buy." Nonetheless, the journal accurately concluded, Goodrich "was still only marginally profitable."[230] In the years 1971 through 1977 large American manufacturers earned a net income averaging about 5 percent of sales, but the comparable figure for Goodrich was 1.9 percent.[231] Goodrich's quest for profits would continue in the 1980s and 1990s, leading to a fundamental restructuring of the company far beyond what Goodrich executives had imagined in the 1970s.

10

The Restructuring of BFGoodrich, 1980–1988

Dramatic changes occurred in BFGoodrich's product lines during the 1980s, to the extent that the company's officers viewed those alterations as a restructuring of their company. In the early and mid-1980s Goodrich prepared to exit the tire industry, a feat accomplished in 1988. At about the same time Goodrich left the industrial rubber business. Goodrich sold its Louisiana PVC plants in 1985 and, thereafter, tried to concentrate on making specialized PVC resins and compounds. Specialty chemicals and aerospace products developed into leading Goodrich enterprises. Goodrich thereby turned increasingly to specialty goods for niche markets. In this sense BFGoodrich became more like Dr. Benjamin Goodrich's company of the 1870s than it had been for a century, and for much the same reason: facing fierce competition in the commodity rubber product of its day, footwear, Dr. Goodrich's firm had made a wide range of specialty goods. Still, important elements of continuity linked BFGoodrich to its past. The move away from commodity products like tires toward specialty products was foreshadowed by actions taken in the late 1970s and earlier. And company executives continued to decentralize Goodrich's management system, pushing decision making down the line as Thomas had begun to do in the 1970s.

In part the restructuring of the 1980s grew out of changes begun in the previous decade, but the restructuring also developed in response to increased pressures that management faced. The instability of the global economy and increasing foreign competition, both of which had hurt Goodrich and many other American manufacturers during the 1970s, amplified in the 1980s. Even more than before, tires and PVC were commodity products subject to global market forces. Problems in their PVC operations, in particular, left executives scrambling to reposition their company in the world's rapidly changing economy. A deep recession in the early 1980s, the worst economic downturn in fifty years, lent urgency to their efforts. At the same time inflation soared, with interest rates and the cost of living increasing dramatically.[1] Takeover attacks on their firm placed additional pressures on management.

JOHN ONG AND THE MANAGEMENT OF BFGOODRICH

John Ong became Goodrich's chairman of the board and chief executive officer when Pen Thomas retired at the age of sixty-five in July 1979. Thomas had groomed Ong for leadership. As Ong later recalled, Thomas first indicated that he was eventually to head Goodrich as early as 1973 and 1974, when he backed Ong's election as the vice chairman of the firm.[2] As one director remembered, Ong was "the heir apparent."[3] Ong's selection was, according to many within Goodrich, almost a foregone conclusion.[4]

A Business Leader

Born in 1933 in Uhrichsville, a small Ohio town, Ong came from a family of farmers and professionals, mainly doctors and lawyers. After graduating from local schools, he went on to Ohio State University, the third generation in his family to attend that institution. There he majored in history, participating in an arts graduate program that emphasized individual study. Ong later recalled that the program stressed "the interdisciplinary approach and the seamlessness of knowledge." He graduated with a B.A. and an M.A. in history in 1954. "From an early age it was assumed by everyone, myself included, that I would become a lawyer," Ong later explained; and in July 1957 he received his law degree from Harvard. That same month he married Mary Lee Schupp. Faced with the draft, he entered the army, in which he became a special agent in the counterintelligence corps. In his spare time Ong continued to study law, and on a three-day leave passed the Ohio bar examination in early 1958. Ong became a first lieutenant in the judge advocate general's office in the regular army (he had been in the reserves).[5]

After leaving the army in 1961, Ong considered several careers, ranging from politics to practicing law in an Ohio county seat; but he put those aside after reading an advertisement for a legal counsel for the international operations of a large Ohio manufacturer. That company was BFGoodrich. Interviewed by Ray Jeter, then the head of the legal department, Ong was impressed by the friendliness of those he met and by the generous starting salary he was offered, $7,500 annually. In March 1961 he joined Goodrich as assistant counsel. "I was a sort of dog's body who picked up the leads and ran errands," Ong remembered. The position was instrumental in Ong's advancement, for it brought him into contact with top management, including John Collyer and Ward Keener. Most of Ong's work had to do with international issues, especially financial matters related to the establishment of overseas subsidiaries.

Ong rose quickly through managerial ranks. His legal work attracted the attention of Gerry Alexander, the president of the international division. Asked by Alexander to join him in the international division and wooed by Fred

Moyer to work with him in the corporation's treasury office, Ong chose the former. "I thought," he later explained, that "if you are going to be a business-man and you are going to work for a corporation, maybe you should, just by God, be one and not play around at being a lawyer." Ong was Alexander's ad-ministrative assistant, performing a wide variety of tasks, and under his guid-ance Ong thought he was "learning how to manage an organization."[6]

Further education in corporate governance soon followed. Ong was select-ed by Keener to participate in Goodrich's 1969 defense against the hostile takeover bid made by Northwest Industries. For five months, Ong later re-called, "I was a junior patrol leader on the team, but I . . . was in on everything." After fending off Northwest Industries, Keener made Ross the president of the international division in 1969, and Ong became the vice president in charge of that division's manufacturing facilities. When Ross joined the tire division in June 1970, Ong became the president of the international division. Ong continued his rapid advancement as Thomas's protégé in the 1970s: group vice president, 1972–73; executive vice president, 1973–74; vice chairman, 1974–75; president and director, 1975–77; and president, chief operating offi-cer, and director, 1978–79.

Ong thrived in unsettled situations, which he saw as fascinating challenges. Thinking back to his work in the international division under Alexander, Ong recalled that "it was like the Arts Graduate Program, two sort of formless things . . . amorphous things without much precedent." His studies at Ohio State and his work in the international division, Ong concluded, "were prob-ably the two things that shaped the course of my career more than anything else in my life." His experiences during the rapidly changing business condi-tions of the 1960s and 1970s helped prepare him for the still more uncertain times of the 1980s and 1990s.

Ong's leadership style differed dramatically from Thomas's. Whereas Thomas had been domineering, Ong led more by persuasion. As Robert Eisen-trout, who headed Goodrich's tire operations for part of the 1980s, put it, "I saw a different management style totally. John Ong was a communicator, an understanding kind of guy, bright guy. Pen Thomas . . . expected everything his way, just had no patience with people."[7] Larry Pomeroy, who was in charge of Goodrich's engineered products division in the early 1980s, remembered Ong as having a "collegial style" in running Goodrich. "His style," observed Pomeroy, "was that we work together very much as a management team."[8] Ong's persuasive talents were crucial in the mid-1980s, when he led the re-structuring of BFGoodrich. By working closely with diverse constituencies—other executives in top management, the many divisional and subdivisional managers, the directors of the company, labor organizations, and stockhold-ers—Ong was able to lead Goodrich rapidly in new directions.

EXPECTATIONS FOR THE 1980S

As Ong and other Goodrich executives initially viewed matters, their firm's strategy for the 1980s would evolve from changes begun in the 1970s. "Today's blueprint for profitable growth," Ong observed in the winter of 1982, "stems from efforts initiated in the early 1970s to revitalize a financially troubled company."[9] Ong viewed Goodrich's renewal as having passed through two stages by the early 1980s. In the first phase Thomas had pruned unprofitable operations and focused the firm on core businesses. Then "a second phase of BFG's transformation began in 1979, when the Company announced plans to double production of PVC by the mid-1980s." Thus, "the stage was set," Ong believed, "for the final and most difficult stage of the transformation—the implementation of a coordinated business plan."[10] Through planning Ong hoped to guide Goodrich to greater sales and consistently higher earnings.

Growth Plans for the Early 1980s

Like Thomas, Ong looked at Goodrich's businesses mainly from a financial point of view. In the fall of 1979, Ong and other executives worked with Braxton Associates, a Boston management consulting firm, to prepare growth plans for Goodrich. Braxton's report, finished in December 1979, called on Goodrich officers to "map out broad alternatives for existing businesses" and to "identify target industries, companies" for acquisition. Goodrich, the Braxton report stressed, remained an "evolving portfolio" of businesses.[11] Exactly which businesses composed that portfolio, officers agreed, should depend on how profitable they were. The hunt for profits that had dominated Ward Keener's and Pen Thomas's years also permeated Ong's administration. In what would become a refrain echoing through the 1980s, officers announced in 1981 that "the Company's strategic plans are based on the goal of reaching a return on equity by 1985 that matches the five-year average of similar industrial corporations. Currently, this industrial average is about 13 percent." By "similar" they meant the five hundred largest industrial firms in the United States. As they achieved greater profitability, executives also expected to build a larger company. "By 1985," they observed, "BFGoodrich plans to achieve sales of approximately $5.5 billion, nearly double 1980 sales."[12]

Goodrich executives began their quest for increased profitability with an approach similar to that of the 1970s. Mature businesses would be used as sources of earnings or "cash cows" to support more promising parts of Goodrich. Mature businesses that failed to earn adequate profits would be sold. The proceeds from the divestitures, expected to total about $150 million in the early 1980s, would be used to "expand high-growth, high-return businesses." Executives targeted five areas for growth: PVC resins and compounds, specialty polymers, specialty chemicals, materials-conveying systems, and waterproofing products for buildings. To nurture these areas, Goodrich announced a massive five-year capital spending program of $1.5 billion. In 1980 the five business areas accounted for one-third of Goodrich's sales; by 1985 they would, executives hoped, account for two-thirds.[13]

While Goodrich's executives thus planned to alter radically their company's product mix, their goal in doing so was a traditional one. For decades officers had sought to build a company whose products operated on different business cycles, thereby providing a basis for stable growth and profits. Expansion in the five areas designated in 1980 and 1981 shared that objective, for executives believed that "the businesses taken together provide opportunities for major participation in markets whose demand cycles do not move in concert."[14]

Observers of America's business scene, while pointing out that there were risks involved in Goodrich's plans, generally applauded them. "The biggest potential problem may be the stability of PVC prices," reporters for *Business Week* cautioned in 1981. Then, too, industry observers noted that Goodrich's debt was increasing. William Wooldredge, Goodrich's executive vice president in charge of finance, announced in 1981 that his company was willing to see its debt ratio rise from its current 40 percent to as high as 48 percent to help pay for the planned capital improvements. "If the debt is going to go that high," the vice president of Standard & Poor's commented, "then improved profitability better not be far behind." Nonetheless, most analysts viewed the plans favorably. The same reporters who recognized the dangers inherent in PVC conceded that Goodrich was on the right track in moving away from tires and into PVC and chemicals. "While there are problems with both tires and PVC," they noted, the firm was wise in "picking the industry in which it is a leader instead of an also-ran." Writers for *Forbes* were even more optimistic. "By 1985," they noted in late 1980, "Goodrich will be much larger, with different sources of earning power."[15]

PRELUDES TO RESTRUCTURING

Such optimism was understandable, but misplaced. America's economy grew dramatically in the late 1970s, and few expected a major downturn in the 1980s. However, the recession of the early 1980s combined with high interest rates to devastate the economies of the United States and much of the industrialized world, unraveling many of Goodrich's plans. No area of Goodrich's operations was hurt more than its PVC business.

Problems in America's PVC Industry

That major difficulties in PVC would affect Goodrich was not at first apparent. Executives remained committed to the PVC expansion announced in 1979 and acted on the assumption, predicted in the 1978 and 1979 McKinsey & Company reports, that markets would grow. Ong later stressed that "we all made the decision to go forward" with the development of new PVC facilities "in the context of those reports."[16] Goodrich's officers expected America's home construction and automobile industries, major consumers of PVC, to continue growing at least as rapidly as they had in the 1970s. Moreover, because of its "relatively low energy content," PVC would, they anticipated, continue to replace aluminum and other materials in many uses. Consequently, PVC sales would expand, they expected, about 6.7 percent annually during the 1980s.[17]

The recession of the early 1980s brought to a head problems that had been developing in America's PVC industry for decades, and those problems destroyed Goodrich's plans for PVC. By the late 1950s, and certainly by the 1960s, most PVC had become a commodity product whose production processes were well understood. Plants to make PVC and its feedstocks, while expensive, were no longer technologically difficult to put into operation. Consequently, competition increased in the 1960s and 1970s, and in the early 1980s it rose still more. In what one of America's leading chemical trade journals called "a stunning reversal" of fortunes, America's PVC market collapsed in 1980.[18] Housing construction, hurt by both the economic downturn and rising interest rates, dropped 27 percent between 1980 and 1982 and did not regain 1979 levels until 1985. (Housing construction took about 75 percent of the output of America's PVC.)

Consequently, PVC sales and prices crumbled. Sales of PVC dropped 18 percent in the United States in 1980, and the list price of PVC resin fell from 35¢ to 31¢ per pound (the actual market price was even lower, owing to extensive discounting below list). The nadir was reached in mid-1982. America's foremost chemical trade journal observed in the fall of 1982 that "one need hardly be told that the polyvinyl chloride market is in a shambles" and concluded that "PVC is a crippled product with nothing but rough sailing ahead."[19] By the spring of 1983 some "signs of recovery" were appearing.[20] By mid-1984, with demand continuing to rise, many PVC makers were, according to one trade journal, "smiling again."[21] Even so, overproduction continued. America's PVC making capacity rose faster than demand, as new plants launched in the halcyon days of the 1970s came into full production. Even as demand for PVC rose by 700 million pounds in 1983, 1.1 billion pounds of new capacity came on line in the United States.[22]

Not surprisingly, the early 1980s witnessed a major restructuring of America's PVC industry, as a number of producers left the business. Firestone, Imperial Chemical Industries (a British firm), Diamond Shamrock, Ethyl, and Stauffer Chemical abandoned making PVC in the United States. Still other companies—such as Air Products & Chemicals, Tenneco, and Pantasote—tried to sell their PVC operations, but could not find buyers.[23] While many companies cut back their PVC operations, a few expanded them. Only companies willing and able to invest large sums of capital in new, modern facilities did well. Low-cost, efficient production was the key to whatever success could be found in the depressed PVC market.

In this context, the growth of two foreign producers in the United States was particularly noteworthy. Shintech, a subsidiary of Shin-Etsu Chemical of Japan, had emerged as a global competitor in the 1970s. In 1980 and 1981 Shintech doubled the capacity at its Houston PVC facility to 660 million pounds per year. In 1984 Shintech announced a further capacity increase of 330 million pounds per year. Shintech's plant featured very large reactors in which to make the PVC, computer controls to enhance efficiency, and new procedures designed to prevent scale build-up on the reactor walls.[24] Formosa

Plastics was part of Yung Ching Wang's Formosa Plastics Group, Taiwan's largest conglomerate. Formosa Plastics began manufacturing in America through the purchase of thirteen PVC plants, including those of Imperial Chemical Industries and Stauffer Chemicals, in the late 1970s and early 1980s. Able to buy the plants cheaply during the recession, Wang sunk $200 million into their modernization. Moving into the construction of its own facilities, Formosa Plastics opened a massive plant at Point Comfort, Texas, in 1983. Like Shintech, Formosa Plastics built a state-of-the-art plant specifically designed to capture commodity business. Using equipment imported from Taiwan, the Point Comfort facility, according to Wang, made PVC for one-third less than the cost of making it at his Taiwan plants. In fact, all of Formosa Plastics's operations were low-cost producers. In case after case, Wang increased the productivity of the American plants he acquired. For instance, by moving new equipment from Taiwan into the plant he purchased from Stauffer Chemicals, Wang was able to reduce the payroll from 380 to 200 people, while boosting output by one-third.[25]

Some American producers, operating from the same premises as Goodrich, also expanded their output of PVC. Borden spent $105 million to expand the capacity of its PVC operations in Louisiana by 300 million pounds per year. The timing was poor: Borden's chemical division's sales fell 12 percent in 1981, and its operating earnings dropped 29 percent.[26] Occidental Petroleum, soon to become Goodrich's leading competitor, expanded its presence in America's PVC industry. In 1979 Occidental operated a single small PVC plant in Burlington, New Jersey. In the following year Occidental bought Firestone's 700 million pounds of annual PVC manufacturing capacity. Even so, Occidental Petroleum's main interest in the early 1980s remained in oil and gas. In late 1982 the firm spent $4 billion to acquire Cities Services, whose vast reserves of domestic oil helped Occidental offset its declining reserves. To pay off its huge $8.8 billion debt, in 1983 Occidental considered selling many of its chemical operations, on which it lost $3 million that year.[27]

The Downturn in PVC Demand

Goodrich executives remained optimistic about PVC in the face of falling sales and prices, for they viewed the slumps as only temporary. The strategic plan adopted in late 1980 by Goodrich called on the chemical division to "remain the lowest cost PVC producer" and "to strengthen its feedstock position." The chemical division was to try to boost its share of America's plastics market (especially PVC) to 27 percent by 1988, up from 20 percent in 1980.[28]

Goodrich continued construction of the Convent, Louisiana, complex. Goodrich plans assumed that "energy and feedstock-related matters will not improve" over the next five years. Oil and gas prices were expected to rise about 20 percent annually.[29] In 1980 and 1981 Goodrich broadened its original plans for Convent to include building world-scale plants to make VCM and PVC (the plants at Convent had initially been intended only to produce feedstocks for VCM and PVC). Engineering work was completed for facilities capable of turning out 1.6 billion pounds of VCM and 1.1 billion pounds of PVC resins annually, a capacity 20 percent greater than that of its largest American competitor.[30] In 1981 Goodrich acquired Bechtel's half share of the Convent Chemical Corporation, which thereupon became a wholly owned Goodrich subsidiary. By this time the first phase of the Convent project had been completed on time and under budget, with $259 million spent on capital improvements for PVC facilities in 1981 alone. In May 1981 the Convent facilities began making chlorine and ethylene dichloride (EDC), both of which were prime feedstocks for PVC, and caustic soda, a by-product sold on the open market.[31]

Goodrich expanded its PVC capacity in other ways. Modernization of EDC and VCM plants at Calvert City increased operating efficiencies. Then, too, Goodrich added 150 million pounds to the annual suspension-resin capacity of its Pedricktown plant, along with a 50 percent increase in the facility's dispersion-resin capacity. The company also started expanding resin production at its Avon Lake plant. The conversion and modernization programs boosted the productivity of the PVC facilities. Even so, it is unlikely that their operating efficiencies reached those of newer plants constructed from the ground up by Shintech and Formosa Plastics. At many of Goodrich's plants, PVC operations intermingled inefficiently with other chemical operations, a situation difficult to correct without wholesale changes costing more than what Goodrich, with large sums committed to Convent Chemical, could spend.[32] Acquisitions also played a part in the expansion of PVC capacity. In late 1981 Goodrich paid $125 million to purchase two Texas plants from the Diamond Shamrock Company, one capable of making 1 billion pounds of VCM a year, the other able to produce 260 million pounds of PVC annually. The purchase of the VCM plant doubled Goodrich's VCM capacity and aimed at making the company "self-sufficient in this crucial feedstock for the next several years."[33]

Even the enthusiasm of Goodrich executives, who were more optimistic than many of their counterparts in the industry about the future of PVC, faltered as the PVC market worsened in 1981 and 1982. In September 1981 they halted further work on the Convent complex, canceling building the VCM and PVC plants. The announced suspension was to last just six months. Bart DiLiddo, president of the chemical division, insisted that his company's assessment of the long-term prospects for PVC remained favorable. "Ours is a very sound strategy," he said, "and what we'll do is just keep those projects in a hold position."[34] In fact, Convent Chemical faced very serious problems by this time, and Goodrich would never build its VCM and PVC plants.

Bad luck in timing its vertical integration backward into PVC feedstocks at Convent was a major part of Goodrich's difficulty. As Ong later noted, "the problem was that we started it up right at the beginning of the worst recession since the 1930s. There was an enormous amount of vinyl chloride monomer and particularly PVC resin capacity under construction as we went into that recession. . . . So not only did demand go down, but with each passing year more and more capacity came on-stream. [As a result,] margins shrank and shrank and finally disappeared."[35] As other companies brought not only PVC facilities into production but also plants making VCM (and sometimes EDC and chlorine), their actions threw into question the rationale for Convent Chemical. Backward vertical integration seemed less attractive with PVC intermediates and feedstocks on the market in copious supplies at reasonable prices. Looking back at Goodrich's heavy investment at Convent, Ong noted in 1985 that "we were dead wrong" on the assumptions made about feedstock prices and PVC demand.[36]

Two additional problems hurt Goodrich's PVC operations. Energy prices and the prices of raw materials failed to rise as much as expected.[37] Ironically, this slowdown in price increases hurt Goodrich. The company's officers, expecting continuing rapid price rises, had entered into long-term contracts with outside suppliers at prices that turned out to be well above market rates. As Goodrich's treasurer later explained, "the [Convent] plant came on stream with raw materials contracts that turned out to be too expensive."[38] Then, too, the market for caustic soda failed to develop as expected. Goodrich's executives had anticipated that sales of caustic soda would balance any temporary fall in PVC sales. This did not occur. One Goodrich officer later called the caustic soda problem "the biggest fiasco" Goodrich had at the Convent plant.[39]

In late 1984 Goodrich remained America's leading producer of PVC, with 18 percent of the nation's total capacity, the same as its share in 1977. Goodrich also had 39 percent of the United States' VCM manufacturing capacity. But competitors were following much more closely than before, as a number of American firms challenged Goodrich. Tenneco had 11 percent of the nation's PVC capacity; Georgia Gulf, 10 percent; Borden, 10 percent; Vista Chemical (just spun off from Conoco), 8 percent; Occidental Chemical (a subsidiary of Occidental Petroleum), 6 percent; and Air Products & Chemicals, 6 percent. Some of these same companies competed with Goodrich in making VCM. Georgia Gulf controlled 20 percent of America's VCM capacity; Vista Chemical, 14 percent; and Borden, 12 percent. Foreign firms had been insignificant as PVC makers in the United States in the 1970s, but Shintech had 12 percent of America's PVC capacity in 1984, with Formosa Plastics controlling another 10 percent. Formosa Plastics had, in addition, 16 percent of America's VCM capacity.[40] Consequently, Goodrich officers found little cause for optimism about their company's basic PVC operations. These were, Ong thought in 1985, devastated by "overcapacity, intense competition, and operating losses."[41]

Faced with growing competition, Goodrich executives began changing their PVC strategy. In 1984 they announced a two-pronged approach. First, they still wanted Goodrich to remain "competitive in the high-volume, general-purpose PVC resin markets." But they realized that more was needed to insure profitability. Thus, second, they proclaimed that Goodrich would place a growing emphasis on "higher-margin, special-purpose resins and compounds."[42] This second prong represented a shift from the emphasis Goodrich had placed on commodity PVC in the 1970s. A growing emphasis on specialty PVC (or, as many at Goodrich called it, "specialized" PVC) would guide Goodrich's strategy into the 1990s. By producing a growing share of specialty PVC, officers hoped to blunt some of the competition and cyclicality in America's PVC market.[43]

Several types of specialty PVC were enticing. Goodrich was aggressive in developing a family of "super-clean" PVC resins that could be used for medical and food-packaging applications. In 1982 the company won a major contract to sell PVC resins to the health care giant Baxter Travenol. After winning this account, Goodrich went on to develop super-clean resins for food packaging.[44] Chlorinated PVC (CPVC), which Goodrich trademarked as Temprite, was also appealing.[45] In 1980 Goodrich—which remained, as it had been throughout the 1970s, the sole American maker of CPVC—controlled 85 percent of the United States market and 35 percent of the world market. Nippon Carbide was Goodrich's main competitor. Expecting consumption of CPVC to soar 40 percent annually in the 1980s, Goodrich hoped to increase its production to 100 million pounds per year by 1985. In 1980 it spent $30 million to expand the CPVC capacity at the Louisville plant by 50 percent.[46] Demand for CPVC "increased substantially" in 1981, and further advances occurred in 1982. By 1983 and 1984 CPVC was being used in a broadening range of applications, such as pipes, fire-sprinkler systems, appliances, business machines, and handrails for hospitals.

Goodrich converted some of its general-purpose PVC facilities to special-purpose ones. Between 1983 and 1985 work at the Avon Lake and Shawinigan plants raised Goodrich's compounding capacity by 70 million pounds annually. As DiLiddo noted, "special-purpose resins and compounds provide greater margins and a steadier source of earnings than general-purpose resins." In 1984 DiLiddo announced the development of "Super Cubes," a new family of special-purpose PVC compounds for rigid applications, and in the same year Goodrich purchased a modern compounding plant in Terre Haute, Indiana.[47]

Even so, movement into specialty PVC resins and compounds was only beginning. Special-purpose resins composed just 15 percent of Goodrich's PVC sales in 1984, with compounds making up another 19 percent. CPVC sales came to only $26 million. A more fully developed specialty PVC strategy awaited corporate restructuring in 1985 and 1986.[48]

Growing Emphasis on Specialty Chemicals

Specialty chemicals offered opportunities even more promising than those in specialized PVC. Like PVC, chemicals in general had become a mature industry by the 1970s and 1980s. As one scholar explained, "in the 1970s and 1980s the chemical industry hunkered down and tried to survive environmental regulation, oil shocks, and recessions." The industry was characterized by "slowing growth, lower profit margins, and falling product prices."[49] As Ong saw it, cycles in America's general chemical industry had come to "follow the pace of the general economy." Moreover, he thought that cycles of boom and bust in demand would be "a constantly accelerating trend." Specialty chemicals promised a way to avoid this cycle. A specialty chemical, as Ong explained, was "sold primarily on the basis of what it does for the customer's product as opposed to how much it costs per pound [and was] tailored to a customer's particular use." It was sold with "a lot of aftermarket technical service" and tended "to be a small part of the cost of goods sold by the customer." All of these characteristics, Ong thought, would make sales of specialty chemicals "much less price-sensitive" than sales of general chemicals.[50]

In fact, specialty chemicals experienced renewed emphasis at Goodrich in the late 1970s. As we have seen, executives began thinking in terms of a specialty chemicals strategy—the purchase of Tremco was one result of that thinking. In 1980 and 1981 Goodrich announced that it hoped to capitalize on the firm's expertise as "one of the leading polymer chemical producers of the world" by expanding operations in markets that "are growing at rates averaging 10–15 percent a year."[51]

Several specialty chemicals won increased attention. Demand for Estane continued to grow for use as cable jackets, molded wheels, specialty films and sheets, and exterior automobile parts. Estane's sales of $68 million composed about one-third of Goodrich's sales of specialty chemicals in 1984. Specialty hydrophilics also increased in importance. Particularly significant were the company's well-established Carbopol polymers, Carboset resins, and Goodrite K-700 polymers (used for water treatment and detergents). Sales of Goodrich's hydrophilic resins rose about 30 percent in 1981 and 1982. Goodrich doubled its production of Carbopol at its Calvert City plant and tripled its output of Carboset and Goodrite at Avon Lake over several years beginning in 1980. In 1984 Goodrich sold $38 million worth of hydrophilics, one-fifth of the sales derived from specialty chemicals.[52]

Tremco, which Goodrich had purchased as part of its emerging effort in specialty chemicals, performed well. Within Goodrich's organizational scheme, Tremco was located in the engineered products division, not the chemical division. This step was taken at the insistence of Tremco's president, Leigh Carter, who feared that Tremco would be out of place in Goodrich's chemical division, amid its commodity operations. Moreover, Carter asked that he be left alone by corporate management to continue Tremco's development. Ong agreed. Carter's entrepreneurial spirit served Tremco well. Tremco's highly motivated sales force of three hundred pushed new products into new markets throughout the early 1980s. Despite the recession that savaged the housing market, Tremco prospered through the sales of specialty products. In 1980 Tremco began selling a single-ply roofing membrane trademarked as Tremply. Three years later, Tremco introduced Therm 100, a multi-ply roofing system that used a proprietary hot-applied rubberized adhesive, a roofing system that would become popular in the mid- and late 1980s. By 1984 Tremco had enjoyed nine years of steadily rising sales and, except for a brief dip in 1982, soaring profits as well.[53]

Problems in Chemicals

Despite developments in specialty chemicals and specialized PVC, the chemical division was not a moneymaker for Goodrich in the early 1980s. Starting as it did from a small base, specialty chemicals could not offset the problems Goodrich encountered in making and selling PVC. Specialty chemicals boasted a very respectable return on investment, but even in 1984 sales of specialty chemicals amounted to only one-fifth of the sales of PVC resins and compounds. Nor was the fundamental change occurring in Goodrich's PVC product mix—the shift from commodity to special-purpose resins and compounds—far enough advanced to make overall PVC sales profitable. Distress in commodity PVC operations pulled chemicals down. Despite receiving the bulk of capital expenditures between 1979 and 1983, the chemical division's share of Goodrich's operating income fell from 57 percent to only 36 percent of the total. The chemical division's profit picture was dismal. As a proportion of its assets, chemical's operating income fell from 18 percent in 1979 to just 3 percent four years later.[54]

Profits in Tires

Tires kept Goodrich afloat during the early 1980s. Far from becoming less important, as had been predicted in strategic plans put forward in 1980 and 1981, tires temporarily increased in significance. Between 1979 and 1983 the tire division's share of Goodrich's operating income soared from 25 percent to 65 percent. Of the three major divisions—chemicals, tires, and engineered products—only the tire division approached the profit goals laid out in the early 1980s.[55] Nonetheless, the ultimate objective was to leave the tire industry. Executives were pleased with the success of tires but generally viewed the future of the tire industry, and their place in that industry, unfavorably. "The combination of downsized domestic vehicle production, more extensive use of longer wearing fuel efficient radial tires and cost-induced driving curtailment," Patrick Ross, the president of tires, observed in 1980, "results in a flat outlook for domestic small tire demand." "Downward pressure on prices and margins" could, he thought, be expected.[56] Ong explained more bluntly, "this wasn't a business we were going to be a survivor in." In fact, in the early 1980s Ong and Ross "padded around the world" looking for a buyer of Goodrich's tire operations or, failing that, another company with which Goodrich might enter into a joint venture in the tire industry. Yokohama Rubber, Bridgestone, Michelin, Pirelli, Continental, and Dunlop were approached, but negotiations "never really got very far," Ong recalled. Antitrust considerations precluded Goodrich from approaching Goodyear or Firestone, but Ong did briefly talk with Joseph Flannery, the chief executive officer and chairman of Uniroyal.[57]

Unable to attract a buyer or joint-venture partner, Goodrich took steps to leave some fields of tire making and to become more profitable in those realms in which it remained. Goodrich announced in 1981 that it would not make original equipment passenger car tires in 1982. This action, Ong recalled, was considered "revolutionary."[58] After all, Goodrich had been making original equipment tires since 1896. But the original equipment market had been competitive for decades, and Goodrich's presence in it had been shrinking. By 1980 Goodrich commanded only 10 percent of America's original equipment tire market—compared to 28 percent for Goodyear, 22 percent for Firestone, and 20 percent for Uniroyal.[59] By this time Goodrich's original equipment sales accounted for less than 10 percent of its tire sales.

Executives said they would "redeploy" their firm's assets into "the higher-return replacement tire business," with "the goal of becoming the leading North American marketer of premium replacement tires."[60] In 1982 Eisentrout pointed out that "focused marketing—or niche picking" had been "our approach to tires since the early seventies, when we introduced the first of our line of T/A tires."[61] (In fact, as we have seen, it started even earlier, in the 1960s.) This strategy resembled the growing emphasis being placed on specialty chemicals by the chemical division. In both tires and chemicals Goodrich was moving away from commodity products. The strategy worked, at least temporarily. Despite a deepening of the recession, in 1982 Goodrich increased its replacement tire shipments 13 percent over those of the previous year. Recovery from the recession brought an additional 11 percent upswing in Goodrich's replacement tire shipments in 1983, considerably better than the 7 percent industrywide increase.[62]

Goodrich continued to develop its high-performance T/A tires for the replacement market. In 1980 the company introduced T/A tires for luxury cars, sports cars, and off-the-road vehicles, such as dune buggies. A year later, Goodrich launched a major marketing campaign for its full line of T/A tires and brought out the "Comp T/A," an "ultra-high-performance tire." Still more types of T/A tires followed, including one designed for speeds of up to 130 miles per hour. Nonetheless, the future for even Goodrich's specialty tires dimmed. "Many of our competitors," Ong told his company's executives in 1985, "have made great strides in recent years in lowering their costs and, coupled with foreign competition, this has put continual pressure on margins." Even the T/A line was being affected. "Our strongest business, 'performance tires,' is currently under fierce attack and price competition for these products is becoming the norm."[63]

While no longer making original equipment tires for passenger cars, Goodrich continued to produce them for trucks, farm equipment, and off-the-road vehicles. Here Goodrich experienced mixed fortunes. Sales of all three types of nonautomobile tires proved disappointing in 1980. Sales of truck tires recovered a bit in 1981, and in that year Goodrich introduced a radial light-truck tire designed as original equipment for General Motors trucks around the world. Additional new radials for trucks appeared in 1982, and truck tire sales continued to recover in 1983 and 1984. The sales of original equipment farm and off-the-road tires failed to rebound from drops incurred in the recession and remained mired in the doldrums in 1983 and 1984.[64]

To support its remaining production of tires, Goodrich transferred its general-purpose styrene-butadiene synthetic rubber (SBR) plant in Port Neches, Texas, from the chemical division to the tire division in 1983 in a move expected to "lead to better integration of raw-materials needs with manufacturing scheduling." Initially, Goodrich had considered selling all of its SBR operations to another company (for a while Uniroyal seemed interested in buying them), for there was an excess of SBR on the market and it no longer seemed essential to maintain a captive supply. In 1981 Goodrich sold its synthetic rubber complex at Orange, Texas. Only the intercession of Ross, who believed that it was necessary to preserve some in-house supply, along with a failure to find a buyer for the other SBR plants, kept some SBR facilities within the Goodrich fold.[65]

Problems in Engineered Products and Aerospace

Engineered products fared poorly in the early 1980s, as the division's operating income fell during the recession years. Engineered products accounted for slightly more than one-fifth of Goodrich's sales between 1979 and 1983. These were not profitable sales. Engineered products incurred losses in 1982 and 1983. When not suffering from losses, engineered products earned only about 5 percent on its capital.[66]

Industrial products, the largest business unit in engineered products, had the most difficulties. As we have seen, Goodrich took tentative steps in the late 1970s to make some of industrial products' operations more efficient, but to little avail.[67] Following the completion of a study by McKinsey & Company, industrial products was restructured in 1982 and 1983. This included consolidating the production of hoses in two plants in Oneida, Tennessee, and Salisbury, North Carolina. Plants in Marion, Ohio, and Kitchener, Ontario, were sold.[68] Other changes included the "physical and organizational restructuring" of operations in Akron, but these steps failed to solve the problems of continuing "high costs and operating losses." The Akron facilities remained a hodgepodge of buildings and operations that defied rationalization, as they had for decades. Between 1980 and 1984 industrial products lost a staggering $84 million on its Akron operations.[69]

Even more disappointing was the performance of the Continental Conveyor & Equipment Company, for Goodrich had high hopes for this business. Continental Conveyor saw its major market, conveyor systems to move coal, slump in the early 1980s. As Larry Pomeroy, who headed engineered products into 1982, recalled, "we were convinced that domestic energy sourcing would push the country toward greater coal utilization and we would be in an excellent position to capitalize on that." Unfortunately, he observed, "it did not happen." In 1981 the officers running Continental Conveyor began to develop new markets in above-ground (rather than underground) conveyor belt systems. Continental Conveyor boasted record sales in 1982, but this success did not last. As the coal mining industry continued to languish, purchases of underground conveyor systems plummeted, pulling Continental Conveyor's sales down. Not even the introduction in 1983 of a revolutionary high-angle conveyor system designed to replace trucks in removing ore from steep-sided open-pit mines could offset the decline in the sales of below-ground systems, for technical snags arose in the development and deployment of this system. Continental Conveyor reported losses in 1983 and 1984.[70]

Aerospace's potential was not fulfilled in the early 1980s. Its fortunes faltered in 1980 and 1981, as the recession hurt airline companies, with some recovery occurring in 1982 and 1983. In 1982 aerospace earned $5.7 million on sales of $175 million, and a year later it reported earnings of $5 million on sales of $174 million.[71] Aerospace was composed of seven business units by 1984, but three of them accounted for the bulk of the division's sales: wheels and brakes, with 44 percent of the total; tires, with 20 percent; and deicing systems, with 11 percent. Brakes for off-highway construction vehicles, a section closely associated with aerospace, performed poorly. In 1980 the recession had not yet hit this unit's sales, and Goodrich committed $17 million to acquire and renovate a plant in Bloomington, Indiana.[72] This timing proved to be unfortunate, for the plant became fully operational in 1982, just as "poor market conditions" led to "disappointing sales."[73]

A Company in Trouble

By 1983 and 1984 BFGoodrich was a company in trouble. Because of the problems with PVC and engineered products, Goodrich did not begin to approach its target of a 13 percent return on equity. The firm's annual return on equity averaged only 4.5 percent between 1979 and 1983. Returns for 1982 and 1983 were particularly depressing: −3.3 percent and 1.6 percent, respectively. By comparison, the Fortune 500 industrial companies, which Goodrich strove to emulate, averaged returns of 14 percent in 1980 and 1981 and around 12 percent in 1982 and 1983.[74] Nor did Goodrich grow in size the way company executives had hoped. Far from showing the increases needed to double by 1985, sales rose only slightly: from $2.98 billion in 1979 to $3.2 billion six years later.

THE BEGINNING OF RESTRUCTURING, 1984–1985

In the mid-1980s Ong and others in top management responded to the intensifying problems by undertaking a full-fledged review of the firm's activities and prospects. That review resulted in restructuring. The basic goal, expressed in a "Corporate Investment Strategy" formulated by Ong in late 1984, was to improve Goodrich's profits, which had been "unsatisfactorily low for many

years." The stated objective was to reach the 13 percent return on equity averaged by the Standard & Poor's 500 companies. After installing a new management team, Ong further decentralized Goodrich. More was involved than a
reorganization of management, however. Central to the restructuring were basic changes in Goodrich's product lines, particularly a growing focus on specialty products.[75]

Internal Pressures for Change

Internal pressures led to the restructuring at Goodrich. Stockholders and
directors, worried about Goodrich's worsening problems, brought pressure on
management to solve them. As early as 1982 at least one outside director informally raised questions about Goodrich's commitment to Convent Chemical. After a board meeting held during a visit to Tremco's Canadian plant, the
director, Ong later explained, "took me on about the PVC business," asking
"were we realistically going to be able to dig ourselves out of this hole?" By late
1983 the board was discussing PVC developments on a regular basis, and, Ong
felt, had "put more pressure on me." "I was feeling pressure," he later stated,
"from within myself, and from our management, and from our board of directors."[76]

Much of the impetus for change originated from top management. Corporate executives held a retreat each year at the Rolling Rock Club in Ligonier,
Pennsylvania, to review corporate strategy. It was in part at these meetings in
1983 and 1984 that the decision to restructure Goodrich came. There was a
growing recognition of the seriousness of the problems Goodrich faced and a
realization that only drastic changes could rectify them.[77]

That problems beyond the ordinary faced them became apparent to officers
at the Rolling Rock meeting in 1983. There they decided that Goodrich was
not likely "to earn a high enough return in the tire business to merit reinvestment," and they also expressed concern about the problems in engineered
products. However, they spent much of the time talking about the deteriorating situation in PVC, especially "regarding ways of reducing loss at Convent."
Executives discussed "the PVC specialty strategy" and "concluded that we
need to do capital expenditures for specialties." Specialty chemicals, particularly Tremco, also deserved increased funding, they decided. Still, executives
remained fairly confident about the future. They concluded that they could
spend about $330 million annually to "fund businesses we want to grow" and
expected sales to double to $6.3 billion by 1987.[78]

By the time of the meeting in 1984, the atmosphere was gloomier. Executives expressed "a sense of urgency" about "the need to reach our financial objectives." Discussion of engineered products focused on the manufacturing
facilities for industrial products at Akron. "In order for Akron to have any
chance for survival," officers agreed that "a totally new labor contract, management change, and further consolidation of facilities" were necessary. Tires
also attracted attention. Worried about the "productivity improvements and

other cost reductions of our competitors," as well as "import competition," executives realized that they were "at a strategic crossroads—growth or structural change." As in 1983, however, Goodrich's PVC operations occupied most of their energy. After recognizing that the business "environment has changed dramatically since we built the plant," they discussed options for "divestment or reducing operating costs" at Convent Chemical. Ong, McClusky, and DiLiddo were delegated "to sell or swap" the plant—and had already been contacted by another firm interested in acquiring the Convent facilities. Officers noted, too, that they needed "to find a way to add value to PVC, including examining forward integration."[79]

Takeover Attempts: External Pressures on Goodrich

External pressures added to the internal pressures for change. The early and mid-1980s were years of increased merger activity in the United States, with hostile takeovers much in the nation's business news. With its stock price low, Goodrich was a tempting target for individuals or other companies on the prowl; and that vulnerability was on the minds of officers, just as it had been during the late 1960s. Ong had participated in Goodrich's defense against the takeover attempt by Northwest Industries in 1969 and later recalled that "my antennae vibrated" at any threat of a takeover. "Right from the beginning" of the 1980s, he observed, Goodrich "faced a series of outside pressures or threats."[80]

In late 1980 Charles Bluhdorn, the head of Gulf & Western Industries, began buying Goodrich's common stock, until by April 1981 he owned just under 10 percent. Alerted to these purchases, Ong, joined by John Weinberg, who, in addition to being a Goodrich director, was a general partner of Goldman, Sachs—he later became the senior chairman of the investment firm—visited Bluhdorn in his New York City office. It was "a bizarre episode," Ong recalled. Bluhdorn's desk was elevated on a dais so that he looked down on his visitors. Behind his desk a large American flag was fastened to the wall. Weinberg later remembered that he and Ong explained to Bluhdorn, "Charlie, here's an American company . . . we are not in favor of losing control, we think we've got a program, we've got plans for the future." Bluhdorn, he remembered, replied, "I am for the American way," and assured Weinberg and Ong that "I don't do unfriendly tenders." For whatever reason, Bluhdorn bought no more Goodrich common stock and sold much of what he had purchased over the next year, until he owned just 6.5 percent in late 1982.[81]

A raid by Carl Icahn several years later was viewed by Goodrich executives as a serious threat. In early 1984 Icahn bought just under 5 percent of Goodrich's shares. It is unlikely that Icahn intended to take over Goodrich, for he was stretched thin by other projects at the time. He was probably holding the company up for "greenmail," a common practice for corporate raiders in the 1980s. By purchasing Goodrich's stock, Icahn sought to make it look as if he was mounting a takeover bid—thus convincing officers to buy back his stock at a premium price. Icahn's actions worried Goodrich's outside directors, several of whom had just experienced attacks on their companies, as well as the firm's management. Once again Weinberg joined Ong in defusing the threat. Together they met with Icahn. Weinberg came away from the meeting, he later recalled, convinced that Icahn simply "wanted money." He received it. Believing that Icahn's attack was, in the words of Goodrich director David Luke, "a potentially destabilizing thing," Goodrich's directors authorized Ong to buy Icahn's stock at 25 percent above the market price, which he did in the fall of 1984.[82]

Restructuring: The Old and the New

There were several pressures on management to restructure their company. Difficulties in Goodrich's PVC operations—especially the attempt to control feedstocks and intermediates—were simply a trigger, if an extremely important one, to restructuring that probably would have taken place in any event. That restructuring combined the old with the new. "What happened around 1985," Ong thought, was "a further development of strategies in place." The basic goal of improving profits had motivated management since Collyer's last years as head of the firm. A move toward decentralized management had been started by Thomas in the 1970s and was pushed further by Ong in the early 1980s. Similarly, some of the changes in Goodrich's product lines, especially the shift toward specialty products, had been foreshadowed by actions in the late 1970s and the early 1980s, especially the growing emphasis on specialty chemicals. The move out of tires and engineered products also had begun earlier. Yet there was much that was new in the restructuring of the mid-1980s. The selling of Convent Chemical heralded a very different future for Goodrich's PVC operations than what had been envisioned just a few years before. Aerospace, still largely ignored by most executives in the early 1980s, emerged for the first time as a key Goodrich business.[83]

New Executives and a New Management Structure

Restructuring began with top-level managerial changes. Larry Pomeroy (who headed engineered products), Donald McClusky (the vice chairman of the board), William Wooldredge (treasurer), and Richard Heuerman (chief legal counsel) all left BFGoodrich between 1982 and 1985. In 1984 Ong created a corporate executive office consisting of himself as the chairman and chief executive officer, Leigh Carter as vice chairman, and Patrick Ross as president (both Carter and Ross also served as operating officers). There was some functional division of authority within the corporate executive office. While Ong supervised the development of Goodrich as a whole, Ross took charge of the "capital-intensive and commodity-oriented" tire and PVC businesses. Carter focused on "the smaller high-growth specialty units." Ong completed building what he later called "a really strong" management team with the hiring of Jon Heider as general counsel in 1984 and D. Lee Tobler as chief financial officer in January 1985. Thinking that it had become too unwieldy, Ong abolished the management committee. In its place Ong established an eleven-person operations board. Not a decision making body—for strategic decisions were made by the corporate executive office—the board "functioned more like a think-tank than a ruling hierarchy," a place where ideas could be floated and discussed.[84]

Of special importance for Goodrich's restructuring was Leigh Carter. After graduating from a preparatory school in 1943, Carter served in the army air force as a fighter pilot for two years. Following World War II, he attended Washington and Lee College, graduating with a degree in commerce in 1949. Carter then joined Tremco, moving up through marketing and management positions to become the firm's president and chief executive officer in 1972. Carter joined Goodrich as the president of Tremco in 1979, and in 1982 he became the executive vice president heading engineered products. In 1984 Carter was elected Goodrich's vice chairman and operating officer, as well as a director. Two years later he became the corporation's president and chief operating officer, positions he would hold until he retired in 1990.[85]

Carter and Ong complemented each other and worked smoothly as a team. "Leigh and I were able to get along very well," Ong later recalled. "We were very different people [with] different styles, different backgrounds, but we shared [the same] values."[86] Carter was particularly important for the emphasis on specialty products and entrepreneurship that he brought to Goodrich. "Leigh brought to the Company a very strong background, knowledge, and temperament for running specialty businesses, with an equally strong feeling for profit center management," Ong stated in mid-1990. "He probably realized sooner than anyone else the potential that was in our aerospace businesses."[87]

Structural alterations and changes in managerial style accompanied the personnel changes. Specialty chemicals and aerospace became divisions on par with PVC, industrial products, and tires. Divisional presidents were allowed greater scope than before, as Ong, Ross, and Carter sought to further decentralize decision making. Within the divisions additional profit centers were created; and their managers were, like the divisional presidents above them, given more autonomy. Profit centers had existed at Goodrich since 1978, but now they became *the* way by which Goodrich was run. The creation of the new divisions and profit centers was intended, Ong said, to encourage "quicker response to market conditions and increased innovation by our business management teams." Looking back on these changes, Ong later recalled that "we needed a different management structure, and that's what caused me to reorganize the company in the summer of 1984."[88]

The move to profit centers was an organizational change that both acknowledged and furthered a basic modification in Goodrich's corporate culture: that the firm was trying to be more entrepreneurial. Weinberg remembered the shift "down to smaller units . . . money units, profit centers" as the most important change that occurred in Goodrich's corporate culture during his thirty years as a director. Profit centers reinvigorated Goodrich, Weinberg thought. "These guys [those running the profit centers] are proud," Weinberg explained. "You see these guys standing up there proudly and saying 'hey, look, we just did this . . . we're on our way.' "[89] Another director recalled that he supported the formation of profit centers as a way of "emphasizing more smaller businesses and businesses that were more responsive and more imaginative."[90] Goodrich had forty-two profit centers by 1988.

Corporate Investment Strategy, 1984–85

Even as Ong was establishing a new management team and organization, he and other executives turned their attention to altering Goodrich's product lines. Discussions on how to increase profits continued after the management meeting at Rolling Rock in early 1984. By this time, "management was engaged in a kind of thought process looking at options," Ong later recalled. "We were feeling very vulnerable."[91] At a series of meetings in the summer and fall of 1984, Ong repeatedly raised the issue, Eisentrout recalled, of "ways to improve our return on capital."[92] From these meetings, Ong went on to prepare a new planning document. In contrast to Thomas's extensive use of management consultants, Ong and those laboring with him did the work themselves. "I came out of all that experience in the seventies thinking management consultants are bullshit," Ong later recalled. Ong continued to use management consultants, but only sparingly and only for precise purposes, mainly at the operating, not the strategic, level.[93]

Drafted in November 1984, Ong's "Corporate Investment Strategy" began by setting forth general objectives. Ong stressed, as had Goodrich executives for decades, that "our principal objective is to provide a financial return to our stockholders." Ong emphasized that Goodrich must achieve a 13 percent return on its equity to be competitive with Standard & Poor's 500 companies. Obtaining this goal would, Ong admitted, be difficult. After noting that Goodrich's "competitive strengths include our heritage, name, and quality image," he observed that the firm faced daunting problems. Too much of Goodrich's capital and sales were, he thought, "concentrated in mature, capital-intensive businesses" and not enough in "our successful specialty businesses." This mix needed to be changed. Sounding much like Thomas a decade earlier, he stated that businesses "with losses or returns below the levels indicated" should be quickly improved or divested. Businesses "with high capital intensity . . . or low capital turnover" should be viewed as "less attractive than those with the opposite characteristics." Conversely, businesses with "low capital intensity and high asset turnover" should be "expanded vigorously," and Ong stressed that "we need an active program to conceive and incubate businesses of this variety."[94]

Working toward these objectives would, Ong thought, have varied consequences for Goodrich's divisions. He wanted to "push the growth and product line expansion" of specialty chemicals by "product development and by acquisition," making this division "the single largest component of Company earnings within five years." Tremco, now transferred to specialty chemicals, should be expanded "to provide renewed growth opportunities." Similarly, Ong believed that Goodrich should "reinvest and expand vigorously" most aspects of its aerospace businesses by "logical product development work or by acquisition." Off-highway brakes were, however, a good candidate for divestiture. Within PVC, Ong believed that future investments should go only to "business units where value-added opportunity exists." He hoped tires would "produce cash beyond reinvestment requirements" each year, thus generating funds that could be used elsewhere in Goodrich. Much of industrial products needed, Ong thought, to be divested, including all of the operations remaining in Akron. Continental Conveyor, unless able to succeed quickly with its high-angle system, was also a logical candidate for divestiture.[95]

Winning Support for the Plan

Ong moved quickly to win acceptance for his plan. He circulated it to Carter and Ross on 26 November 1984, and within four days received replies. The "challenge," Ong emphasized, "lies in the execution of strategy calling for the expansion of our successful specialty businesses," an assessment with which Carter agreed "whole-heartedly." Carter made the most suggestions for changes in Ong's plans, but generally found Ong's ideas to be "simple [and] honest." He found special praise for those sections calling for the nurturing of specialty businesses.[96] After revising the scheme, Ong, Ross, and Carter presented it to a general meeting of managers in early December. Ong explained the philosophy and goals of the investment strategy, Carter discussed the future of specialty businesses, and Ross talked about tires and PVC. Carter then led "intensive discussions" with the profit center managers. Throughout the remaining presentations that day, the three stressed the need for the continued "decentralization of operations" through the formation of "autonomous units." They pointed out that the corporate office would shrink to no more than 250 people and that the head office would "spin off" many "shared service" departments, such as accounting and legal services, to the profit centers.[97]

During the month following the December meeting, the division heads were individually called on to draw up plans, and in early 1985 their ideas were combined with those emanating from the corporate executive office to form the "1985 BFGoodrich Corporate Investment Strategy and Strategic Plans." This document would guide Goodrich's restructuring. Its main points were the same as those put forward by Ong, but now more details appeared. "Backward integration (particularly at Convent)" into the making of PVC feedstocks was formally recognized as "a liability." Similarly, the goal of "sell[ing] all small tire capacity at acceptable margins" was specifically endorsed. It was decided to try to increase aerospace's sales by 15–20 percent annually, with half of the growth coming from acquired companies. Specialty chemicals would, executives hoped, experience sales increases of 8–12 percent per year.[98]

With managers committed to the plan, Ong, Carter, and Ross presented it to the board of directors at a series of meetings in New York City between December 1984 and June 1985. They informed the directors that tires were "still Okay, but a concern long-term," and that PVC "fails to meet the earnings potential test." More promising were specialty chemicals, which were "doing nicely," and aerospace, which had "emerged as a growth opportunity." Underlying their presentations was the realization that Goodrich was not performing well: the firm was not achieving the desired return on equity, it was not paying adequate dividends, and its debt was too high. The solution to these problems, executives repeatedly asserted, could not come simply from increasing sales and earnings. In addition, it would be necessary to "liquidate [the] least productive assets." Several scenarios were presented, but the Convent PVC operations, Continental Conveyor, some tire plants, off-highway braking facilities, and Akron's industrial products operations were consistently singled out for divestiture.[99]

It was hoped that Goodrich would emerge as a smaller, but much more profitable, corporation. For the first time, executives seriously considered the notion of running a smaller company. Throughout the 1970s, Thomas had emphasized growth and increased market share—as well as profitability—as key company objectives. As late as 1983 Ong and others in top management postulated a doubling of their company's sales over five years. Now, Ong and other executives recognized that such goals would at least temporarily have to take a backseat to the overriding necessity of boosting their firm's profits.

The directors' meetings involved considerable discussion. "We'd bring things up, then they'd bring up that thing," Weinberg recalled; "we used plenty of dialogue at these meetings."[100] Ultimately, it was decided to address Goodrich's most pressing problems at one time. As Ong remembered, "We figured it was better to try to solve, if not all, a good many of our problems in one fell swoop." The stock market would, Goodrich's directors and executives hoped, respond better to one quick, if painful, charge against earnings than to a long, drawn-out series of write-offs. The decision that Goodrich would be restructured—though not all of the details of that restructuring—was announced publicly after a final board meeting in June. Ultimately, officers took a one-time charge against earnings of $365 million in 1985, in recognition of divestitures and write-offs completed that year.

The Initial Impact of Restructuring

Goodrich's PVC operations experienced the greatest immediate changes. In the fall of 1985 Goodrich sold its complex at Convent, Louisiana, to the Diamond Shamrock Chemicals Company—the same firm from which Goodrich had purchased VCM and PVC plants in 1981—at a loss of about $177 million. While legally two separate transactions, Goodrich, in effect, swapped its Convent facilities for PVC facilities Diamond Shamrock possessed in Fort Saskatchewan, Alberta. With the sale of their Convent facilities, executives acknowledged "our mistaken assumptions in making backward integration investments during 1979–81." Goodrich increasingly emphasized the making of specialized PVC resins and compounds, a strategy Ong later called a "reversal of the policy of the sixties and seventies." In addition, to resolve a long-standing problem, Goodrich set aside $30 million to clean up pollution at PVC facilities, especially at Calvert City.[101]

Executives wanted to leave tire making altogether but, lacking a buyer for its plants, Goodrich remained in the business. While staying in tire making, Goodrich cut back its operations. It left the markets for farm, off-the-road, and heavy-duty truck tires, "where margins are lowest." As a result, the Miami, Oklahoma, plant where these tires were made was closed. Moreover, Goodrich shut down its smallest and least efficient passenger car tire plant in Oaks, Pennsylvania. Tire sales and production were affected as Goodrich sold or shuttered nearly all of its remaining retail tire stores.[102]

Restructuring affected still other segments of Goodrich's businesses. Officers planned to sell Continental Conveyor, gave thoughts to divesting the off-highway braking operations, and decided to close all industrial products facilities still left in Akron. More positively, they predicted that over the next few years growth areas would be developed in aerospace and specialty chemicals.[103] They hoped that by the end of 1987 those two businesses would account for over one-third of Goodrich's sales and one-half of its income.

BFGoodrich and the Restructuring of American Business

Many large American manufacturers underwent restructuring during the 1980s. The unstable global economy, combined with a revival of merger activity, often based on hostile takeovers, placed pressures on chief executive officers. As one financial journal noted in early 1987, "spinoffs, mergers and acquisitions have become the norm for the way American business operates." Some 143 of the largest 500 industrial firms in the United States were acquired by other companies in the 1980s, and the total value of business assets changing hands in America during the decade came to $1.3 trillion. Restructuring was often triggered by specific events similar to Goodrich's PVC problems and involved a search for profits, which, in turn, led to an increased focus on what business executives considered the core activities of their corporations. About 60 percent of the unrelated acquisitions made by American manufacturing companies during the 1970s had been divested by 1989.[104]

Restructuring was particularly pronounced among chemical companies. "Numerous mergers, asset sales and swaps, and demerging," one scholar has noted, reshaped the American and world chemical industry in the 1970s and 1980s.[105] The energy crisis and recession of the early 1980s, combined with heightened foreign competition, led many American chemical companies to focus their attention on specialty, as opposed to commodity, chemicals and to divest unprofitable business units—much as Goodrich was doing. This trend began in the 1970s, but accelerated in the 1980s. In 1984, for example,

DuPont began moving out of its polymer lines into higher-margin products, among other steps selling its 50 percent share in a commodity polymer joint venture with Mitsubishi Chemicals. Dow restructured its operations so that by 1988 over one-half of its revenues came from higher-value-added products. Similarly, beginning in 1984 Monsanto reshaped its product mix through a growing emphasis on biotechnology and other high-margin products.[106]

In many respects, then, the restructuring that took place at Goodrich resembled that of other American manufacturing enterprises, but Goodrich's restructuring differed from most in two ways. First, Goodrich's reshaping of product lines went further than that at most companies. In leaving tires and industrial rubber products completely—both accomplished by 1988—executives made especially bold moves. Second, Goodrich differed in who led the changes. In most companies, a complete turnover in management was a necessary precursor to restructuring, often through the forced resignation of top executives. And, indeed, management changes occurred at Goodrich. Nonetheless, it was John Ong, Goodrich's president since 1975 and chief executive officer since 1979, who led Goodrich in its restructuring during the 1980s and who would continue to lead additional alterations in the 1990s. Flexible enough to change without giving up his core values, Ong remained the driving force behind Goodrich's evolution for two decades.

A Continuing Research Tradition

Well aware of their company's strong research tradition, officers sought to invigorate research and development efforts in the early 1980s. They boosted spending on research and development from $37 million in 1978 to $49 million in 1980 and to $63 million in 1982. In 1983 they formed a science and technology board "to help ensure superior technical capability within the Company." In 1983 the president of Bell Telephone Laboratories was elected a Goodrich director in a move hoped to "provide still further guidance for our business and technology decisions."[107] Research and development expenditures dropped in the mid-1980s, but came to about $56 million in 1988.

Throughout the 1980s Goodrich devoted funds equal to about 2 percent of its sales to research and development—roughly the same proportion as Goodyear, Firestone, and Uniroyal, but only about one-half the percentage spent by America's leading chemical companies. Goodrich compared better to its rivals in terms of the proportion of its profits spent on research and development. In many years Goodrich spent about the same or a higher proportion of its profits on research and development than did its competitors in the rubber and chemical industries, although between 1987 and 1989 Goodrich lagged behind most of them.

As part of the restructuring in the mid-1980s, Goodrich executives continued to link research closely to the commercial needs of the operating divisions. "Technology," Ong emphasized in late 1984, "is one of the keys to our busi-

TABLE 10.1

Research and Development, 1980–1989

	1980	1981	1982	1983	1984	1985	1986	1987	1988	1989
	R & D Expense as a Percentage of Sales									
Goodrich*	1.6	1.7	2	2	1.7	2	2.2	2.4	2.4	2.7
Goodyear	2.1	2.3	2.7	2.6	2.7	3.1	3.2	2.7	2.8	2.8
Firestone	1.7	1.8	2.1	1.8	2.1	2.1	2.5	2.2	—	—
Uniroyal	1.6	1.6	2	1.9	2	—	—	—	—	—
DuPont	3.5	2.8	2.6	2.7	3.1	3.9	4.3	4	4	4
Dow	3	3.4	4.3	4.5	4.4	4.7	5.4	5	4.6	5
Monsanto	3.1	3.2	4	4.6	5.5	7	7.6	7.3	6.9	6.9
Union Carbide	1.7	2	2.6	2.7	2.8	3.1	2.3	2.3	1.9	2.1
Phillips	0.6	0.7	0.9	0.8	0.8	0.7	0.9	0.9	0.9	1.1
Uniroyal-Goodrich									0.8	0.8
	R & D Expense as a Percentage of Profit**									
Goodrich	80.1	59.9	−178.7	254.4	71.7	—	89.2	34.1	22.5	26.3
Goodyear	84.5	86.1	94.4	46.9	40.7	64.5	117.1	30	54.8	62
Firestone	−66.4	98.7	4000	40.7	80.8	—	237.8	41.4	—	—
Uniroyal	−459.1	81.7	152.4	48.8	28.8	—	—	—	—	—
DuPont	67.6	58.4	98.3	28.3	27.8	35.8	38.7	33.4	34.5	32.1
Dow	39	71.6	134.5	110.3	75.1	1823.3	48.9	31.4	20	22.2
Monsanto	137.4	49.6	77.8	50.9	52.3	—	82.2	82.8	64.4	58.9
Union Carbide	24.7	31.9	77.4	242.6	43.7	—	65.5	39.3	13.6	19.8
Phillips	7.9	13.4	21.4	5.1	6.1	5.5	12.9	35.3	9.1	24.8
Uniroyal-Goodrich									87.7	295.2

Sources: Business Week, 6 July 1981, 60–75; 5 July 1982, 54–74; 20 June 1983, 122–45; 9 July 1984, 64–77; 8 July 1985, 86–104; 23 June 1986, 134–54; 22 June 1987, 139–58; 20 June 1988, 139–49; special issue, "Innovation," 1989, 1977–96; special issue, "Innovation," 1990, 194–207.
*Goodrich is categorized as a tire and rubber company until 1986, after which it is categorized as a chemical company.
**In the sources, the years 1980–82 and 1988–89 are labeled "% of profits." The years 1983–87 are labeled "% of pretax profits."

nesses." Goodrich was, just as he had stressed a decade earlier, "a diversified industrial company, not a conglomerate." As such, it needed, Ong thought, to have its market prospects and technologic capabilities closely connected.[108] One of the "common threads" uniting Goodrich divisions was that "all our core businesses depend upon and are developing advanced technology to grow successfully." It was "vital [that] BFG continue to establish product differentiation through technological advantage."[109]

While some research remained corporate research conducted at Brecksville, most research and development—including, as in the previous decade, much of that done at Brecksville—was controlled by the divisions.[110] For instance, the executives in the PVC division formed an advanced polymers and technology business unit in 1986 to help their division switch to higher-value-added products. The goal was to "create an entrepreneurial business development team skilled in research and development and market research." Specifically, members of the unit were to look into the development of "proprietary process and technology focused sharply on well-analyzed market needs." In doing so, the "target application" was for "plastics with inherently higher cost characteristics."[111]

Between 1986 and 1988 the annual growth in research and development investments at Goodrich averaged 35 percent for aerospace, 19 percent for PVC, and 14 percent for specialty chemicals. The corresponding figure for corporate research was 9 percent. Divisional research aimed at the "adaptation of existing technology to new applications." Corporate research "emphasize[d] projects that involve[d] longer-range, more fundamental research."[112] Goodrich's research effort brought important improvements to existing products but, as in the 1970s, resulted in few breakthroughs. No discoveries comparable to the 1926 discovery of how to plasticize PVC or the 1947 discovery of how to construct tubeless tires were made.

GROWTH AREAS, 1985–1988

Even as they scrambled to restructure their company, Goodrich executives tried to look to the future strategically. From their discussions came three-year strategic plans, beginning with "Strategic Objectives and Key Events, 1985–87."[113] In this plan three areas emerged as growth segments for Goodrich. Aerospace and specialty chemicals were singled out for expansion. Officers also hoped that PVC, now freed of the drag imposed by the former Convent operations, would perform well. These three fields composed what Ong called in 1987 Goodrich's "core" businesses. The officers looked for growth in the future. Their flirtation with running a smaller company, it turned out, was only temporary. They predicted that by 1995, the 125th anniversary of their firm, BFGoodrich would have sales of $5 billion, twice the $2.4 billion in sales made in 1988.[114] Executives wanted their company to improve its stature in the national and international business arenas.

Expansion in Aerospace

Aerospace became one of Goodrich's leading divisions after 1985. Robert C. Langford, a British businessman trained in aeronautical engineering, was brought in as president of the division in 1983 and was responsible for much of the growth. Langford emphasized the importance of profit centers and raised the prices of aerospace products, thereby increasing profits. When he retired in 1987, Langford was succeeded by David Burner, who remained president of the division into the mid-1990s. Burner had joined Goodrich in 1983 as the financial vice president of engineered products and had become the executive vice president of aerospace in 1985.[115] Aerospace's share of Goodrich's sales tripled from 5 percent in 1983 to 16 percent four years later, and during these years returns on investment averaged nearly 14 percent annually.[116] By 1987 aerospace was composed of fourteen profit centers.

Some of aerospace's growth was generated internally. Wheels and brakes grew in this manner, accounting for 40 percent of aerospace's revenues by 1988. Carbon brakes were of increasing significance, as the purchase of Super-Temp in 1978 paid off in the 1980s. Goodrich became a major supplier for Boeing planes and the European Airbus.[117] Even Goodrich's off-highway braking unit enjoyed success, and executives decided temporarily to retain it as part of the aerospace division.

Acquisitions were very important for aerospace. Most of the markets for Goodrich's aerospace products were narrow, making growth difficult except through acquisitions, a situation that was in contrast with specialty chemicals.[118] In 1985 Goodrich bought a large facility in Norwood, North Carolina, to make aircraft tires, and within two years most such production had been moved there. Larger acquisitions followed in 1986: Castleberry Instruments & Avionics, which overhauled aircraft flight control systems, and Jet Electronics & Technology, which manufactured and serviced instruments controlling the flight surfaces of aircraft.[119] These purchases led Goodrich into the servicing of aircraft, which officers viewed as a field with lucrative prospects. As deregulation reshaped America's airline industry, many small airlines challenged the nation's well-established carriers. Few of these small airlines could afford their own service facilities, and even many larger carriers sought to cut expenses by turning to firms like Goodrich for some of their servicing needs. Goodrich began setting up the service businesses as profit centers separate from manufacturing in the late 1980s, and they soon became "fantastic little businesses."[120]

The Purchase of Tramco

The growing emphasis on services led Goodrich into a major acquisition, that of Tramco. Based in Everett, Washington, Tramco provided maintenance, repair, and overhaul (MRO) services for commercial aircraft. Owned by the two entrepreneurs who had founded it, Tramco had sales of about $50

Tramco offered maintenance, repair, and overhaul services to America's airlines. (BFG Co.)

million in 1988, the year Goodrich purchased the company for $78 million. Goodrich agreed to expand Tramco greatly, while retaining the former owners as its top executives. Those at Goodrich viewed Tramco as capable of becoming a company with annual sales of $250 million within just five years, something Tramco's former owners realized they could not achieve on their own without heavy borrowing.[121] Goodrich executives observed that the acquisition would immediately make their company "a major competitor in the large and growing aircraft MRO market" and began an expansion of Tramco's facilities.[122]

Divestitures of less profitable operations accompanied acquisitions. In 1988 Goodrich sold its engineered rubber products business, which had made life rafts, inflatable tanks, and other products for aircraft. Even some recent acquisitions were jettisoned, for not all worked out as well as had been hoped. In the fall of 1988 Goodrich announced that it was selling the aircraft tire operations at Norwood to Michelin, and in early 1989 the transaction was completed.[123]

The Growing Importance of Specialty Chemicals

As expected, specialty chemicals also played a growing role in Goodrich's development. Specialty chemicals' share of Goodrich's sales doubled from 16 percent to 32 percent between 1985 and 1987, and its return on assets averaged about the same as in aerospace, 13 percent annually.[124] Three major businesses composed specialty chemicals: specialty polymers and chemicals,

Tremco, and elastomers and latex. For the most part, improvements to existing products, not breakthroughs into new areas, occurred.

Specialty polymers and chemicals saw an expansion of product lines already under development. The corporate plan for 1987–89 called on the business unit to "exploit new opportunities for Estane and Hydrophilics based on recent technical progress."[125] Several new types of hydrophilics (Quick Break, a Carbopol used in creams and lotions) and polyurethanes (Estaloc, a fiber-reinforced polyurethane that could be employed in exterior components for cars) were introduced in 1987. While most new products in the late 1980s were elaborations of earlier developments, two original advances took place. One was the development in 1988 of a new technology that would become important in the plastics fabrication market, Telene dicyclopentadiene reaction injection-molding resin. This technology would soon be used in automobile, marine, farm equipment, and recreational vehicle applications. In a move that would later become important, Goodrich scientists also began experimenting with reverse-osmosis water treatment technologies at their Louisville plant in the same year.[126]

To handle the growing demand for these products, Goodrich expanded production facilities. In 1986 it completed additions to plants at Avon Lake and Calvert City and purchased three small specialty chemical operations for $8 million. Most sales continued to be made within the United States, but foreign markets became increasingly important. About 11 percent of sales were made abroad in 1984, and 25 percent in 1985. Over the next few years, specialty polymers and chemicals "substantially" increased the number of its sales and service representatives abroad, especially in Europe and Asia, until by 1988, 40 percent of its sales came from outside of North America.[127]

Tremco, which continued to develop autonomously, consisted of two major subdivisions. Its Incon unit made sealants and glazing products for industrial and commercial construction and polymeric goods used in insulating glass assemblies, automobiles, trucks, and manufactured housing. Tremco's roofing unit was a supplier of commercial roofing maintenance and replacement systems. Most of the new products introduced between 1985 and 1988 were offshoots of older ones. Spectem, a silicone construction sealant introduced in 1985, was designed to "augment Tremco's broad line of construction sealants." Similarly, Swiggle Strip tape—a combined sealant, spacer, and desiccant developed in the early 1980s—was improved through many refinements. Goodrich also decided to "build new businesses through complementary acquisitions."[128] In 1986 Tremco bought Concrete Products, a California company, Kamia-Chemical GmbH, a West German maker of sealants for insulating glass, and the Tretol Group, a London-based manufacturer of protective coatings, adhesives, and specialty paints. Overseas markets increased in importance, just as they had for specialty polymers and chemicals. By 1987 international sales, including those made in Canada, came to nearly half of Tremco's total sales.[129]

Elastomers and latex had acrylic products as its major line of goods. Good-rich emphasized high-value-added specialty products—again, increasingly for foreign markets. In 1985 it introduced a new line of Hycar nitrile elastomers, and a year later it expanded an agreement to make and sell some types with a Taiwanese affiliate. As in the case of Tremco, purchases of "additional comple-mentary" businesses were part of Goodrich's plans for elastomers and latex.[130] In 1987 it bought an epichlorohydrin plant in Mississippi from Hercules Inc., making Goodrich the world's largest producer of this specialty elastomer. In that year Goodrich also introduced Elastoplast, another specialty elastomer combining the best properties of elastomeric and acrylic latexes. By 1988 em-phasis was being placed on the development of new products for plastics mod-ification, which was viewed as having a growing global market.[131]

PVC: A Return to Profitability

PVC resins and compounds produced by the newly named Geon Vinyl division composed the third growing component of Goodrich's operations. Between 1985 and 1987, PVC sales climbed from 27 percent of Goodrich's to-tal sales to 49 percent. As a proportion of assets, Geon Vinyl's operating in-come came to 20 percent in 1987, placing PVC ahead of even specialty chemicals and aerospace in profitability—a major change from just a few years before. "We were making all of the money in the world," Ong later re-marked.[132]

Goodrich's PVC operations prospered, as demand recovered from the deep slump of the early 1980s. American consumption of PVC rose 6.4 percent in 1986, another 7.3 percent in 1987, and a further 1 percent in 1988, as the American economy, and with it housing sales, perked up. By 1987 American PVC plants were operating at 95 percent of capacity, up from 83 percent two years before. An industry trade journal rejoiced that "The concerns of U.S. polyvinyl chloride (PVC) producers have been transformed radically. . . . Gone are complaints about capacity surpluses, underutilized production facilities, and bulging producer inventories." The journal concluded that "in their place are worries about churning out enough resin to supply domestic as well as over-seas customers."[133]

PVC attracted renewed support from Goodrich's executives. In 1985 they wrote off $235 million in PVC assets, mainly in Convent Chemical, but after that poured funds into PVC operations. In 1986 and 1987, PVC facilities at-tracted $70 million in new capital, about one-third of Goodrich's total capital expenditures. Goodrich finished modernization projects designed to "contin-ue efforts to shift pounds sold to the highest possible mix of value added resins and compounds."[134] One result was the introduction in 1987 of a new type of CPVC called Flowguard for use in making water pipes. Some other com-panies adopted a similar strategy. By late 1988 Georgia Gulf claimed that three-quarters of its line of three hundred PVC products were in higher-margin goods ranging from cosmetics packages to blow-molded bottles.[135]

Nonetheless, even with the recovery in PVC sales and profits, executives harbored doubts about the future of PVC operations and started to "explore approaches for liquidating part of the manufacturing capacity of the Geon Vinyl Division." For decades officers had looked to PVC sales and profits to offset declines in sales and profits in other products, especially tires. By the late 1980s they were abandoning such hopes, recognizing that PVC sales and profits would themselves always be very cyclical. The profits PVC experienced in 1986 through 1988 were, they feared, only temporary. As Ong explained, "We knew this was just the latest and, as it happened, the greatest peak in the cycle."[136]

Executives also realized that competitors, especially Occidental Petroleum, were catching up with their company in productive capacity. Improvements in Occidental's PVC fortunes began when Ray R. Irani became the chairman and chief executive officer of Occidental Chemical in 1983. Irani brought in a new management team to revive Occidental's faltering PVC operations. Occidental poured hundreds of millions of dollars into expanding and upgrading its production facilities, slashing costs, and boosting output. Like Goodrich, Occidental sought to make specialty PVC goods; but, like their counterparts in Shintech and Formosa Plastics, Occidental's executives also thought that their company could earn substantial profits by producing commodity resins in ultramodern, efficient plants. In PVC and chemicals Occidental sought buffers to downturns in other businesses, especially petroleum. Occidental's expansion in PVC was part of a broader shift the company was making into chemicals, and by 1988 Occidental had become America's sixth-largest producer of chemicals.[137]

Expansion by Occidental continued to reshape America's PVC industry. In 1986 Occidental purchased Tenneco's PVC business and bought the chlor-alkali facilities that Diamond Shamrock had purchased from Goodrich.[138] In late 1987 Goodrich had 19 percent of America's PVC capacity, and Occidental had 18 percent. They were trailed by Formosa Plastics with 13 percent, Shintech with 11 percent, Georgia Pacific with 10 percent, Vista Chemical with 8 percent, Borden with 7 percent, Air Products & Chemicals with 6 percent, and a number of smaller firms.[139] By this time Occidental claimed to be the nation's largest producer of PVC resins.

Occidental's expansion alarmed Goodrich executives. They recognized that the moves made by Occidental's executives were "creat[ing] a strong, vertically integrated competitor with a clear mission to become the lowest cost PVC producer" and lamented that "clearly the Oxy acquisitions weaken our competitive position." In 1987 Occidental secured captive supplies of VCM by purchasing Shell Oil's operations in Deer Park, Texas. Occidental also bought a large chlor-alkali plant from DuPont.[140] Goodrich's executives recognized that their company was no longer "the low cost producer [of PVC] and can not be in the foreseeable future." Possessing large, new, efficient PVC facilities, Occidental, Shintech, and Formosa Plastics had lower-cost PVC operations than many of Goodrich's plants. Looking ahead, Ong, Carter, and

Tobler "began to ask a lot of questions about PVC"—a line of thought that would lead Goodrich to divest most of its PVC operations in 1993.[141]

DIVESTITURES: INDUSTRIAL PRODUCTS AND TIRES

Even as Goodrich executives expanded their company's specialty chemicals, aerospace, and, to some extent, PVC operations, they divested two other areas that had been central to the firm's history: industrial products and tires. Industrial products had long faced growing difficulties. When not even Carter could solve those problems as the head of engineered products between 1982 and 1984, Goodrich left the field in the mid- and late 1980s. Tires had also presented problems for decades. Goodrich stopped making original equipment tires in 1982, and Ong's restructuring plans of 1984–85 called for the company to leave all tire making when favorable circumstances to do so arose. That opportunity came in the late 1980s.

Leaving Industrial Products

Industrial products played a shrinking role in Goodrich's mix of businesses. The basic problem continued to be low profitability, just as it had been for decades. Industrial products piled up operating losses in 1985, 1986, and 1987. Not surprisingly, Goodrich sold off parts of industrial products. It disposed of Continental Conveyor in 1986 for $11 million, and in the same year sold the industrial hose and belt businesses for $38 million. As a result, by 1987 Goodrich's work in industrial products consisted of little more than the fabrication of polymers for wall coverings, and industrial products' sales amounted to only 4 percent of Goodrich's total sales, half of what it had been just three years before. Executives sought to move the fabrication of polymers into new areas of specialty products, as they put it, "out of mature, commodity businesses and into higher-technology, specialty products." When this effort did not succeed, Goodrich sold nearly all of what was left of its industrial products businesses in 1988.[142]

With these moves, little remained of Goodrich's century-long presence near downtown Akron. Plans were prepared in 1987 to raze all vacant manufacturing buildings by the end of 1989.[143] Goodrich called the shuttering of most of its manufacturing in Akron "Operation Greengrass." As Dennis Oleksuk, who was in charge of Goodrich's physical facilities in Akron, observed, "We were preparing the complex for demolition—ultimately for green grass."[144] A survey of Goodrich's forty-five Akron buildings, completed in 1986, resulted in recommendations to end most operations there.[145] In 1987 Goodrich moved its headquarters to a new building constructed on the outskirts of Akron, about fifteen miles west of downtown. By the end of 1986, Goodrich had only 1,421 workers left in Akron factories, with plans to let 921 of them go over the next few years.

As events transpired, many of Goodrich's Akron buildings found new uses. In mid-1988 Goodrich reached an agreement with the Covington Capital Company—a New York real estate development firm specializing in redeveloping old buildings—through which Covington became the owner of twenty-seven Goodrich buildings just south of Akron's downtown. Called "Canal Place" after the nearby remnants of the Ohio Canal, whose presence had helped attract Benjamin Goodrich to Akron in 1870, this complex became the home for small manufacturing and service businesses.[146] Comprising a mammoth 3.5 million square feet of floor space, the buildings housed 113 businesses employing 2,700 people by 1993. While the new firms were welcome, the number of jobs they offered were a far cry from the tens of thousands Goodrich had once had.[147]

The Formation of Uniroyal Goodrich

For years many of Goodrich's executives had wanted to leave tire making, and in the late 1980s they achieved that goal on favorable terms. Goodrich's exit from tires occurred in two stages. In 1986 Goodrich entered a joint venture with Uniroyal to manufacture and sell automobile and truck tires through the formation of the Uniroyal Goodrich Tire Company (UGTC). Then in 1988 Goodrich sold its share in UGTC, leaving tire making altogether.[148]

It was Goodrich that approached Uniroyal to propose the joint venture. In the summer of 1985 Ong initiated a series of meetings with Joseph Flannery, Uniroyal's chief executive officer.[149] Uniroyal executives were open to suggestions from their counterparts at Goodrich. To avoid an unfriendly takeover by Carl Icahn, the same corporate raider who had attacked Goodrich the previous year, Uniroyal—aided by the investment banking firm of Clayton & Dubilier—had borrowed large sums to purchase the company's stock and take it off the market. The resulting interest payments, along with underfunded pension liabilities, led executives to look favorably on the proposal from Goodrich.[150]

Spinning off their tire divisions into a joint venture offered immediate advantages to Uniroyal and Goodrich. Both companies would receive hefty infusions of cash for the tire plants going into the joint venture. Like Uniroyal, Goodrich needed capital. The firm was going through its costly restructuring, which included reporting a large loss in 1985. Then, too, both firms would benefit from continuing income should the joint venture prove successful. But from the beginning Goodrich officers looked beyond these advantages to what they saw as their ultimate goal, leaving tire making completely. They hoped that UGTC would prove attractive to a buyer, more attractive than Goodrich's plants were. Protracted negotiations between Ong and Flannery resulted in Uniroyal and Goodrich setting up UGTC as a joint venture in August 1986. The formation of UGTC brought $251 million in sorely needed cash into Goodrich's coffers. Established as a partnership, UGTC paid that sum to Goodrich, and a lesser $225 million to Uniroyal, each in return for their tire plants (in Goodrich's case the Tuscaloosa, Fort Wayne, and Kitchener facilities). The joint venture financed these payouts with loans from CitiBank and other financial institutions.[151]

Uniroyal and Goodrich each owned one-half of UGTC through subsidiaries and expected to earn income each year through that ownership. Profits were important not just for what they could do for immediate cash flow; Goodrich's executives intended to use the joint venture as a vehicle by which to leave tire making. They wanted, their corporate strategic plan for 1987–89 stated, to "manage our Uniroyal Goodrich Tire Company investment so as to provide the optimum opportunity for its liquidation on attractive terms." More specifically, they hoped to "encourage Uniroyal Goodrich Tire Company management to manage earnings levels and cash flow so as to accommodate an initial public offering at the earliest possible date."[152] Ong, especially, desired the joint venture to "generate an interesting earning track" that would allow UGTC "to be taken public ... the sooner the better."[153] That is, Goodrich executives hoped to make the UGTC profitable to attract buyers for their share of it.

The contributions of Goodrich and Uniroyal to UGTC complemented each other, which seemed to bode well for the success of the joint venture. While Uniroyal was strong in the original equipment tire business, especially as a supplier for General Motors, Goodrich's strength lay in the replacement tire business. The "result," thought Goodrich executives, was "a well-balanced company both in terms of markets and in its ability to cope with the cyclical nature of the tire business."[154]

Problems with Uniroyal Goodrich

However, the predicted benefits proved elusive. Eisentrout, who handled the details of the merger negotiations for Goodrich, had from the first thought that expectations, especially on the part of Uniroyal, were too high. He later recalled that "in a number of these [negotiating] meetings they would start talking about what the savings would be, like if we say we'll put these two plants together in Canada the synergies there will save us $10 million; and I'd be saying, 'wait a second, I don't think there'll be $10 million.' ... All of a sudden they had projections of ... huge, huge earnings."[155] David Devendorf, Goodrich's treasurer and later the treasurer of UGTC, also recalled that savings expectations were unrealistic: "$80 million of synergy arising out of the amalgamation."[156]

Manufacturing and marketing problems afflicted UGTC. Many of the UGTC plants proved to be less efficient than those of their competitors. Synergistic savings failed to materialize. On the contrary, factory costs increased as a result of start-up expenses because of the diverse technologies employed. For instance, the tire molds used by the two companies had different venting systems, making it difficult to move molds from one factory to another. Nor were problems limited to the factory floor. Goodrich and Uniroyal found it hard to harmonize their different cost accounting systems.[157] Marketing problems arose. When General Motors's market share for new automobiles sold in the United States dropped from 42 percent in 1985 to just 35 percent two years later, UGTC's original equipment tire sales suffered, for Uniroyal had been a major General Motors supplier. Even so, in 1987 UGTC was the third-largest manufacturer of automobile tires in the United States, after Goodyear and Firestone.[158] The result was that UGTC was a big, but unprofitable, company. In 1987 earnings came to $11 million on sales of $2 billion.[159]

Underlying the poor performance of UGTC was an inability of the Goodrich and Uniroyal executives to work together. Ong noted that "we just couldn't agree on how to run it."[160] Patrick Ross became chairman and CEO of UGTC, with Sheldon Salzman of Uniroyal as his vice chairman and chief operating officer. The two found it hard to cooperate. As Eisentrout, who was in charge of marketing for UGTC, later explained, "they got along very badly." This lack of cooperation extended throughout the organization. "At meetings there was never much overt hostility or any that I remember, but behind the scenes they fought about everything," Eisentrout observed. One example of the lack of cooperation lay in marketing. "Shel did not turn the marketing organization over to me," remembered Eisentrout; "he kept Uniroyal people still running sales, if you can imagine, private brand sales, bidding against us."[161] Such sentiments were shared by those from Uniroyal. As one Uniroyal executive put it, "The joint-venture became a 'we-they' situation, and the interplays interfered with the process and the progress." All too often, as a consequence, "decisions just didn't get made."[162]

The End of Goodrich as a Tire Manufacturer

Faced with paltry profits from its share of UGTC, Goodrich left the joint venture to abandon tire making altogether. In June 1988 Goodrich sold its half-interest in the partnership to the UGTC Holding Corporation, which was owned by a group of investors organized by Clayton & Dubilier. In return, Goodrich received $225 million in cash. Altogether, then, Goodrich received $476 million from its involvement in the joint venture—considerably more, most Goodrich executives thought, than could have been obtained from the sale of Goodrich's tire plants on the open market. At one point in the mid-1980s, Eisentrout recalled, Continental Tire (of Germany) offered Goodrich only $250 million for all of its tire making facilities.[163] "We were happy as clams" with this profitable exit from tire making, remembered Ong.[164]

Goodrich was wise to leave the joint venture when it did. Leonard Bogner of Prudential Bache spoke for many investment analysts when he called Goodrich's move "a very clever and positive development." Harry Millis of McDonald Securities thought that the sale would give Goodrich "a good cash position and strong balance sheet upon which to grow chemicals."[165] The UGTC never performed well as an American company and was acquired by Michelin in 1990. This purchase by Michelin was part of a more general trend.

Continental Tire bought General Tire from the GenCorp in 1987. In 1988 Bridgestone (of Japan) purchased Firestone, and Pirelli (of Italy) bought Armstrong Tire. Only Goodyear remained independent among the United States' major tire makers by the mid-1990s.

A REVITALIZED COMPANY: BFGOODRICH IN 1988

Talking to a reporter from the *New York Times* in early 1989, John Ong described the changes that had occurred at BFGoodrich over the previous four years. "You know how they say that in every fat man, there's a thin man dying to get out?" he asked rhetorically. "Well, I always knew," Ong explained, "that inside this bad, fat company was a great, thin company dying to get out."[166] Goodrich was a smaller, but much more profitable, firm in 1988 than it had been just three years earlier. Goodrich's sales had dropped from $3.2 billion to $2.4 billion, but its net income had risen from the break-even point to nearly $200 million. Corporate debt had been reduced from $812 million to $351 million. In 1988 Goodrich's return on equity stood at 19 percent, well above the 13 percent sought by the firm's executives and higher than the 17 percent averaged by its competitors.[167] Indeed, much had changed at Goodrich with the emphasis on specialty products and the exit from tires and industrial products. As Carter observed, Goodrich had long had some specialty products, but for decades "if one poked up its head to ask for capital, its head would get bitten off." Now specialty businesses came into their own, to be further developed in the 1990s.

Even so, restructuring was incomplete. Far from all of Goodrich's sales came from specialty businesses. PVC accounted for slightly more than one-half of the firm's sales in 1988; and, despite the efforts of Goodrich's executives to move into specialized PVC, most of Goodrich's PVC sales remained in commodity products. As a result, profits were insecure, as would be revealed by a recession in the early 1990s. The search for consistent profits on par with other American industrial companies would continue. More generally, it was unclear in the late 1980s exactly where restructuring was leading Goodrich, and especially how the firm might best be presented to the public. In 1988 Goodrich executives felt compelled to sponsor a new advertising campaign. To differentiate Goodrich from Goodyear, a long-standing problem, and to begin placing a new corporate image emphasizing their company's exit from tires before the American public, Goodrich ran a series of advertisements on the theme of "Just Read Our Lips: No Blimps, No Tires."[168] The company was truly transformed, and its leaders now faced the future with the desire that BFGoodrich be a technological leader in its manufacturing fields while maintaining the best of its traditions.

11

Tradition and Transformation: BFGoodrich in the 1990s

The dramatic changes that BFGoodrich underwent in the 1980s as it left its traditional rubber manufacturing businesses were not the end of the story. The 1990s were years of further dramatic transformation as John Ong sought to preserve those parts of Goodrich's tradition he thought valuable. The company sold its polyvinyl chloride business, announcing the decision in 1993. The result was a diversified BFGoodrich focused on two main lines of business, specialty chemicals and aerospace. The capital available from the sale of the PVC business went into corporate acquisitions designed to strengthen what were now Goodrich's core activities. Since the formation of Uniroyal Goodrich less than a decade earlier, Goodrich had been changed more substantially than at any time in its history. The rebuilding of BFGoodrich required a balance between the expectations of investors for high and regularly reported profits and the requirement that Goodrich, to be a successful manufacturing firm, remain true to its traditions by investing for the future.

Goodrich remained, of course, a unique institution, a product of its own history. Nevertheless, as the company rebuilt in the 1990s, its strategy reflected the fashion of the time, when many large companies "restructured" and rearranged their businesses to lower production and distribution costs, enhance profits, and boost returns on investment. Goodrich fit this pattern, while also maintaining some of the company's traditional values. A common theme in strategy discussions was achieving a "fit" among diverse parts of the company. For Goodrich, "fit" meant that advantages would flow from a common organization, from sharing resources of knowledge, technology, and capital. This concern for integration hearkened back to an earlier perspective held in the company—and in American manufacturing more generally—of valuing the integration of materials, production, technology, and knowledgeable people so that the sum was greater than the total of the parts. Concern for integration pervaded strategic thinking at Goodrich, as executives sought to strengthen their chemical manufacturing and aerospace businesses. Ideas about integration also led to transformations as Ong and his colleagues shifted capital to acquire other firms and fold them into BFGoodrich operations.

Although relying on certain traditions, the company's executives also followed new trends in strategic thinking in the American business community. Most important, perhaps, were ideas about structure. As we have seen, the notion of creating semiautonomous divisions within large manufacturing firms had grown slowly at first from its origins in DuPont and General Motors in the 1920s. At Goodrich, too, these ideas were slow to permeate the practices of the company. By the middle of the 1980s, however, Goodrich had become a highly decentralized business firm. As Goodrich rebuilt itself after the sale of its rubber and polyvinyl chloride businesses, it remained highly decentralized, with two segments, BFGoodrich Aerospace and BFGoodrich Specialty Chemicals. At the base of each segment stood divisions, small units sometimes referred to as "profit centers." The divisions formed into groups of related activities, and each group reported to the headquarters of either aerospace or specialty chemicals. At the lowest level of organization, executives had considerable autonomy to understand the business in which they competed, with responsibility for earning profits in it. By 1994 divisions with related activities formed intermediate groups of business units, each group with a middle manager who ensured that the operating arms shared knowledge about markets and technologies. At each level executives presented plans to their superiors, and still other executives in the small corporate headquarters reviewed their goals and measured their performance.

In 1995, when the company celebrated its 125th anniversary, it was on a strategic course that was articulated in early 1991. It was also, inevitably, shaped by economic forces beyond its control. In 1991 John Ong outlined a growth strategy for the coming decade stressing the development of specialty products for niche markets and entrepreneurship in management, sustaining policies laid out in the mid-1980s. Insofar as it was possible, Goodrich was not to be a company making generic goods for commodity markets. The goal was to earn an average 15 percent return on stockholder equity. The company did not achieve its goal, at least in the short term, in part because of adverse trends in both American and foreign economies. A worldwide recession began in 1990, as industrial economies everywhere struggled to adjust to the end of the cold war. Military spending dropped with the disappearance of the Soviet Union, and at the same time the airline industry was delaying the purchase of large numbers of new aircraft, slowing sales growth for BFGoodrich Aerospace. Specialty chemicals markets also suffered from slowed economic activity. But recovery, well under way in the United States by the end of 1993, offered hope for renewed profits to Goodrich and other manufacturing firms.[1]

Goodrich management was briefly joined by John N. Lauer. Lauer came from Hoechst Celanese to assume duties as executive vice president, and the company planned to have him serve as president upon Leigh Carter's retirement. Lauer's first assignment was as head of Goodrich's Geon Vinyl division in early 1989. A chemical engineering graduate from the University of Maryland, Lauer had been in charge of Hoechst's engineering plastics group. In September 1990, when Leigh Carter retired, Lauer was elected as Goodrich's president and chief operating officer, positions he held until he resigned in the summer of 1994 to pursue other personal and business interests.

CORPORATE STRATEGY AND PLANNING

In developing the strategy for the new BFGoodrich, John Ong and other corporate executives sought to clarify a vision of a company deeply rooted in its heritage. The quantitative aspect of the strategy was clear: above-average returns on investment for manufacturing firms. Ong, however, viewed defining the broader vision of the company's strategy as supremely important. When he reviewed older documents about Goodrich's investment strategy, going back to 1984, and as he reflected on decisions going back to the middle of the 1970s, Ong was intrigued that those statements had provided "an accurate outline . . . of the strategies which we have pursued over the intervening years." Because the company had changed so much over such a short period of time, he decided that a statement about values and vision could provide a similar function: to serve as an overarching strategy for the future, a stable platform for strategic planning in the coming years. Such a document would explain the company's mission to its employees and guide them in their business decisions.

Although most of the senior executives, and all of the other officers at the corporate level, had begun their careers with other firms, Ong's long experience with Goodrich and his training in history at Ohio State lent a focus to this effort. He had begun with the firm when it was a very different organization operating in rubber markets, and Ong had led the company through the most dramatic transformations of its history—the divestment of the rubber (and, soon, the polyvinyl chloride) businesses. Nevertheless, Ong believed that Goodrich had preserved a particular orientation toward business, a concern for values that could provide guidance for the future. That orientation, he believed, included promoting technological advances, establishing and maintaining a caring and supportive work environment for employees, promoting social responsibility in areas of vital interest (especially in environmental concerns), and insisting on prudent financial management.

Ong—believing that it was important to express the company's strategic vision—began working in 1991 with Lauer, Tobler, and Jon V. Heider (the senior vice president and general counsel, who had joined the company in 1984) to write a new statement outlining the rebuilding of the company. This document, Ong thought, would clarify the company's mission to its employees, owners, and to investors. Especially for managers, Ong expected the document to define the scope of their work and their performance targets. Indeed, the strategic vision was to become part of the planning process. Managers—responsible for operating the various parts of Goodrich's portfolio of business-es—were to present senior corporate executives with clearly stated annual plans for their approval, these plans also looking two or more years into the future.[2]

When Ong reflected on Goodrich's history, he observed that the firm had consistently maintained two important continuities in its long history. The founder, Benjamin F. Goodrich, had instructed his colleagues to focus on high-quality service, which the modern-day Goodrich, although much transformed, maintained through its marketing orientation, working to satisfy customers' needs. Also, Goodrich had always been a diversified manufacturer, at first sup-plying several different rubber products and, eventually, operating in several industries. The modern-day Goodrich, with its core businesses in only aero-space and specialty chemicals, was less diverse than the company had once been, but it nevertheless maintained that link with its past. In addition, Ong's three decades of experience with the company instructed him that Goodrich, as an organization, had developed and perpetuated a set of unspoken assump-tions conveyed by one generation of executives to another about decency, character, community, and social responsibility. His idea was to articulate those continuities, and especially the values Goodrich fostered and practiced. In fact, Ong called his draft statement a "vision and values" document.[3]

Recognizing that scientific research had in the past given the company im-portant commercial openings, Ong was particularly interested in taking advan-tage of the opportunities afforded by new technology. Operating executives were responsible for maintaining "substantial technical competence" in both "product and process" technology. Ong expected managers to stay abreast of their special areas, to stay focused on customers' needs while seeking to replace sales revenues from old products with revenues from new products. The corpo-rate research and development organization was to aid the managers in achiev-ing their "market-defined technical goals." "Our aim," Ong summarized, "will be to achieve constant process and product improvement in every business so as continually to increase the performance of our products, reduce our cost of manufacturing and thus stay ahead of our competition."[4]

To accomplish that objective, corporate management was to focus on strategic planning, while decentralized business units were to operate Good-rich's manufacturing and service functions. In Ong's scheme, he and other se-nior corporate officers would set forth the specific long-term goals for each division. As the operating units developed their strategic plans, the senior management would review them; plans were to be "debated on qualitative grounds with divisional management before being agreed upon." Once the corporate office accepted the strategic plan of an operating unit, that plan then provided the performance standard against which senior executives judged the operating officers. Meanwhile, Goodrich would remain decentral-ized, in small business units grouped together into divisions "based on common technology employed, common markets served or common approaches for taking products to market." As a "basic principle," each general manager enjoyed "full responsibility for the results of that business and substantial authority to manage the assets employed in it."[5]

In setting forth Goodrich's vision and values, and in designing the firm's structure, Ong was conscious of the company's need, insofar as was possible, to remain loyal to its employees. By 1991 Goodrich was operating in a general social environment in which many Americans had lost a sense of security in their employment. Ong wanted Goodrich employees to feel secure in their jobs as long as they performed their tasks well. Moreover, Goodrich would provide educational opportunities and training programs to allow its employees to stay abreast of dynamic technologies and business conditions. The company was to judge the performance of all employees on merit. Goodrich was to "provide equal opportunities for employment and advancement to all." "Decency and fairness" were "widely perceived" as "Goodrich values," and Ong and the other senior executives wanted to ensure that these values continued to guide everyone in the company.[6]

Finally, Goodrich was to follow a socially responsible course. This responsibility, in Ong's view, should include "a vigorous advocacy for public policy issues at every level of government" insofar as public policy touched the company's business either directly or indirectly. Public policy, he recognized, influenced "the fundamental forces underlying our continued competitiveness." Goodrich was affected by government policies on education, health care, savings and investment, the promotion of new knowledge, and, especially, environmental concerns. Goodrich had spent huge sums over the years to meet and exceed environmental standards.[7] "We are committed," the 1992 annual report observed, "to achieving the highest possible standard of excellence in every aspect of our business relating to the environment, health and safety."[8]

LEAVING THE PVC BUSINESS

Goodrich's departure from the polyvinyl chloride manufacturing industry was the single most important change in the early 1990s. PVC manufacturing was a business that acutely reflected the nation's business cycle, with sales and income dropping as other manufacturing industries (especially building construction) slowed. Aware of this fact, Goodrich officers had explained that the economic cycle for PVC manufacturing was different from that of its other businesses, especially aerospace. Fortunately, plastics and aerospace worked countercyclically, offsetting one another to some extent. Even so, Ong and the other officers harbored doubts about the long-term prospect of PVC manufacturing for Goodrich. Virtually all large chemical manufacturers questioned staying in the business of making bulk chemicals that sold in commodity markets.[9]

The recession of the early 1990s brought such doubts to a head. As housing construction slumped, American consumption of PVC dropped 7 percent to 8.5 billion pounds in 1991. Commodity PVC prices and margins fell dramatically; and, despite continuing efforts to leave the manufacturing of commodity PVC, in 1990 "higher performance vinyl resins and compounds" still represented only about "25 percent of Geon's sales volume."[10] The Geon Vinyl division suffered operating losses in 1991 and 1992. Goodrich executives concluded that their PVC operations would always be, as Ong explained, "a very, very cyclical business." PVC would never, they thought, become consistently profitable. "We just felt we needed to get out of the business," Ong later recalled.[11] Thus, in 1993, Goodrich sold most of its PVC operations.

PVC Operations in the Early 1990s

William F. Patient was the executive directly responsible for PVC manufacturing when Goodrich decided to leave the industry. Patient had been recruited to become the new president of Geon Vinyl, joining Goodrich after a twenty-six-year career with Borg-Warner. Patient had overseen Borg-Warner's chemical operations in Europe and, just before joining Goodrich, served as the vice president of Borg-Warner's chemical marketing. Borg-Warner sold its plastics unit to General Electric for $2.3 billion in mid-1988, and, unhappy with his new position at General Electric, Patient had left the firm. He was eager to move to Goodrich. Patient first tried to redirect the division toward producing and selling specialized PVC. When that effort proved only partly successful, he helped Goodrich sell most of its PVC operations to a new firm, Geon, which he would head.[12]

The aim of developing specialized compounds of PVC was to reduce the impact of the general business cycle on the company. For several years Goodrich PVC executives had sought to turn their division in this specialized product and niche market direction, and Patient brought a renewed sense of purpose to those desires. Patient and other Geon executives "pledged to reforge polyvinyl chloride (PVC) into a true engineering material" for use in a wide variety of specialty injection-molding applications.[13] This proved a difficult goal to achieve, however. Goodrich's sales of custom-injected molding compounds rose 9 percent even in depressed 1991, but the majority of Goodrich's output of PVC resins and compounds remained commodity products. Moreover, markets for even specialty PVC became more competitive. Patient recognized the difficulty: "The segments are still there and still growing, but it's tougher to make money in them." A new problem, he noted, was that "several large customers [had begun] mixing their own compounds."[14]

With the commodity segment of its PVC business still dominant in the Geon division's profile, Goodrich was at a competitive disadvantage. Too many of the company's plants were inferior to the modern, efficient facilities operated by Occidental, Shintech, and Formosa Plastics. After considering many different possibilities in the summer of 1991, Goodrich announced in December that it would phase out resin manufacturing at the firm's Avon Lake, Henry, and Plaquemine plants over two years. With an annual capacity of 530 million pounds, the plants represented about one-quarter of Goodrich's North American resin manufacturing capacity. The facilities had per-pound production costs 40 percent higher, on average, than Goodrich's other PVC resin operations. Geon Vinyl's 1991 loss included a pretax charge of $117 million incurred in closing unprofitable plants. Some 225 workers lost their jobs.[15]

Those decisions improved the performance of the Geon division in 1992 and 1993. In addition to closing inefficient plants, Geon Vinyl executives raised the productivity in their remaining resin manufacturing facilities 7 percent in 1992. They continued trying to shift their division's product mix to higher-margin items. Geon Vinyl's 1992 strategic plan called upon the division to "shift to value-added products [to] achieve consistent financial performance"; in that year Goodrich's sales of custom-injected molding compounds rose 12 percent, and of extrusion compounds, 19 percent.[16]

The Formation of the Geon Company

Over time, the improvements made in PVC operations aimed less at keeping Geon Vinyl a part of Goodrich than at boosting its profits to make it an attractive candidate for divestiture. By late 1991, executives had decided to sell Geon Vinyl because the cyclical nature of its business did not permit the division to enjoy the steady growth in earnings desired for BFGoodrich. In December of that year, Ong and Tobler went to New York City to discuss that step with executives at Goldman, Sachs. Goodrich executives wanted to turn the Geon Vinyl division into a new freestanding company to be named the Geon Company. Goodrich would contribute most of its PVC plants to the new concern in return for common stock in the enterprise. Goodrich would then sell that stock to the public. Goldman, Sachs executives were "intrigued" by the idea. After considerable staff work, Goodrich's board of directors approved the divestiture in April 1992. Just then, however, the stock market soured, and the plans were delayed.[17]

A revival of the stock market in late 1992 and early 1993 allowed Goodrich to establish the Geon Company. In February 1993 it was created as an independent enterprise with Patient as Geon's chairman and chief executive officer. The Geon Company took over all of Goodrich's PVC facilities except operations at Calvert City. The new firm had the capacity to make about 1.75 billion pounds of PVC per year. Goodrich retained half of the common stock in Geon, selling the other half to the general public for about $223 million. Goodrich also received $160 million in a special tax-free distribution from the Geon Company.[18]

Nonetheless, it soon became apparent that officers had not done enough to prepare their company's stockholders for the divestiture. As Ong later observed, "We underestimated the shock that would occur." A Goodrich scientist had first plasticized PVC in 1926, and Goodrich had pioneered in demonstrating the commercial value of PVC. The divestiture caught unaware many people long associated with Goodrich. David Luke, who had retired as a Goodrich director in 1992, recalled that the step "came as a great surprise to me."[19] By 1993, about 70 percent of Goodrich's common stock was owned by institutional investors, as was typical of publicly held American companies. Their initial response to the divestiture was largely negative. About 70 percent of Goodrich's common stock changed hands that year as fund managers, who had bought Goodrich stock in anticipation of rising PVC sales, sold their shares. Those investment analysts were simply unwilling to wait for the fulfillment of the promise of better returns that the operating executives in the manufacturing firm envisioned.[20]

Goodrich, following the conventions of the market and its agreement with the underwriters, sold no more of its holdings in Geon until late November 1993. This policy served to stabilize the market for Goodrich stock. In a second public offering Goodrich disposed of the remaining half of its Geon stock. From then on, Goodrich had no ownership role in the Geon Company, and by the spring of 1994 Ong was the only Goodrich officer on Geon's board of directors. Altogether, Goodrich obtained about $630 million from the divestiture of its PVC operations, funds sorely needed if it was to expand the company's aerospace and specialty chemical businesses.[21]

The sale of Geon represented a dramatic change in the nature of BFGoodrich and reflected senior executives' desires to transform their firm into one that emphasized the commercialization of advanced technologies rather than the sale of products undifferentiated from those of competitors. The new Geon Company was a significant firm in the PVC industry, which itself was changing. Geon was one of fourteen PVC resin producers in North America, and, along with Occidental Petroleum, Shintech, and Formosa Plastics, was in the top tier of producers. Occidental Petroleum and Shintech focused on producing and selling resins for commodity markets, especially pipes, while Formosa Plastics was the most fully integrated competitor, owning feedstocks and converting about half of its resin production into either pipe or film. Geon, like the Goodrich division that preceded it, tried to sell its resins as compounds suitable for special applications.

Geon faced a difficult future, but one in which it was possible to make substantial profits. Its competitors had invested aggressively in huge, state-of-the-art resin factories in Texas and Louisiana. As the economy began to recover from recession in 1992, they expanded even further.[22] Nevertheless, Geon remained a large producer able to take advantage of expanding markets in the prospering economy. Geon's chairman, William Patient, modified strategy and sought to become a low-cost producer of commodity PVC. Patient had begun cost-reduction efforts when he took charge of the Geon division of Goodrich, and he continued those efforts as head of the new Geon Company. Geon, implementing a decision reached when it was still part of Goodrich, shut three factories, cutting capacity by one-fourth, and laid off more than one-third of its workforce. The company also simplified its product offerings, deemphasizing specialty compounds that were not earning desired profits—

which gave customers fewer choices, but seemed necessary if Geon were to earn profits. When the economy recovered in 1993 and 1994, the company was profitable. Geon executives planned to lower costs to the point where the company would continue to earn profits during inevitable downturns in the business cycle.[23]

GOODRICH AND THE SPECIALTY CHEMICALS BUSINESSES

For most of the twentieth century, Goodrich had been a company manufacturing and selling specialty chemical products to other manufacturers. The strategic decisions of the 1990s placed a renewed emphasis on this tradition and sought to take advantage of the company's research heritage in the field. With the sale of the Geon Vinyl division, specialty chemicals now comprised about half of Goodrich. Ong and the other officers had long admired the way some Goodrich chemical products led in or captured particular niche markets and earned handsome returns as a result. Their vision for a rebuilt Goodrich thus included specialty chemicals as an area of entrepreneurial opportunity that would enlarge upon Goodrich's established strengths in polymer chemistry, explore new related materials and technologies, and thereby improve the company's balance sheet. Best of all, they expected specialty chemicals to enlarge their sales through internally generated growth rather than through the acquisition of other firms. The purchase of other specialty chemical manufacturers that complemented Goodrich's strengths was not, they learned in 1988, easily accomplished, for larger firms carried high price tags. Acquisition strategy in this part of the company focused on small firms whose technical and distribution resources held promise for rounding out and enlarging Goodrich's established businesses in the field.[24]

This strategy conformed to the long-term requirements of Goodrich as a manufacturer of specialty chemicals, but it did not immediately help the company earn above-average profits. Aiming to develop long-term advantages with products and service was a response to the general conditions that pervaded the specialty chemicals field in the larger economy. The common pattern in the chemical industry over the preceding twenty years, as we have seen, was for the largest chemical manufacturers to shift investments away from products that were "commodities" and thus price-sensitive to the business cycle, toward products that were "specialized" and price-insensitive. Goodrich was part of this shift—all the more so upon the creation of the Geon Company—but at the same time Goodrich was a relatively small firm in the specialty field. Worse, specialty chemicals in general, and some of Goodrich's products in particular, were becoming less "specialized" (in the traditional distinctive sense) and so more subject to competition and less profitable. Scientific breakthroughs were harder to achieve, moreover, and the entire specialty chemical industry, while remaining profitable, was losing some of the financial glamour that had once seemed so attractive. After rising from $40 billion in 1985 to $56 billion in 1990, sales of specialty chemicals in America increased more slowly, to just over $60 billion in 1992. A leading chemical industry journal reported in the summer of 1993 that "specialty chemical companies continue to wrestle with pinched markets, increasing cost pressures, and tougher global competition."[25]

Thus the specialty chemicals arm of Goodrich was, more than ever, feeling the economic influence of the 1990s. Helped by a buoyant American and world economy, in 1989 and 1990 Goodrich witnessed profits in specialty chemicals of over 13 percent of assets, not far from the targeted 15 percent return on equity for the entire company. When the economy fell into recession, however, returns tumbled to about 6 percent of assets, well below the desired goal. Clearly, specialty chemicals no longer were as price-insensitive as before. To make matters worse, several new products were introduced during these years; they all held much promise for future profits, but their introductory costs also depressed profits in the short run. When economic recovery took place, the fortunes of specialty chemicals improved a bit, but even in 1993 the performance of specialty chemicals was well below what executives desired. These results led to intensive questioning and, in 1993 and 1994, to a restructuring of specialty chemicals operations.[26]

The Specialty Polymers and Chemicals Division

At the beginning of the 1990s, most of Goodrich's specialty chemicals business was in its own specialty polymers and chemicals division, where Kent H. Lee Jr. served as division president. (The division was made up of four parts: specialty plastics, polymer chemicals, hydrophilics and latex, and water management.) Lee had joined Goodrich-Gulf as a sales associate in 1968. He held several international marketing positions in Goodrich's chemical group and served as general manager of the international division before moving into specialty polymers and chemicals, becoming its president in 1985.[27] Lee announced general development principles in early 1991, just as the recession was biting into profits. Specialty polymers and chemicals would, Lee asserted, continue to develop "unique, protectable technology or service capability" and would emphasize "selling an integrated 'package' of technical expertise, product, and service." The division would focus on "narrow market niches," in which it could control at least one-fifth of the market. Continuing work begun earlier, Lee stressed the need for "empowering managers in each profit center to take responsibility for every facet of operations."[28]

Despite the recession, Lee adhered to those principles. Well-established products remained the backbone of specialty polymers and chemicals. The returns on Estane, TempRite, hydrophilics, and latexes, which together accounted for about 70 percent of the division's business in 1991, continued at desired healthy levels. There were few competing firms or products, and in some product lines Goodrich had no competitors. Naturally, Lee and the other executives sought to expand sales and product lines in those areas.[29]

Lee and his division planned for that expansion through a combination of investments in established and new products. Telene, a new thermoset dicyclopentadiene resin—on which the company had done research for about twenty years—seemed especially promising. The product had excellent prospects as a plastic used by injection molders who sought impact resistance, flexibility, and heat deflection. During 1993 the number of molders making parts from Telene increased by half. Advances also took place in Estaloc, a fiber-reinforced type of Estane especially desirable for molded items like gears and pulleys, in machine housings, and in the development of new generations of Carbopol and Carboset. In 1993, Goodrich introduced Carbopol ETD (easy to disperse) polymers, a new generation of synthetic thickeners. While promising to pay dividends in the future, all of these projects required funding at a time when Goodrich, owing to the recession, new accounting requirements, and growing health care costs for current and retired employees, was not reporting desirable profits. All the new products came on line at about the same time, and, although there was reason to be optimistic about their future, some initially lost money.[30]

Although officers had good reason to be optimistic about improving older products and offering new ones, there was cause for concern in some areas of the division. Since the first part of the century, Goodrich had made chemicals for rubber manufacturing (initially, of course, developed to improve its own rubber products) that it continued to sell. Goodyear and Michelin were both important customers with which Goodrich dealt directly, and Goodrich sold to a wide range of smaller rubber manufacturers through its long-standing distribution arrangement with RTVanderbilt. The problem, from Goodrich's perspective, was that, although its specialty rubber chemicals enjoyed advantageous positions in the market, rubber manufacturing was a cyclical industry. When the industry's purchases shrank, Goodrich profits suffered, and the specialty polymers and chemicals division was unable to report the returns on investment that met corporate goals.

Water management chemicals and systems was a newer, and auspicious, area. In response to the chemical company's need to control its own effluent water, Goodrich had become a premier supplier of intermediate water treatment chemicals to other firms by the end of the 1980s. The Nalco Chemical Company was its most important customer, providing about 60 percent of Goodrich's business in the field. "Our relationship with Nalco is excellent," Lee told corporate headquarters in 1989, "and they look upon BFG as their technical partner and primary supplier." Moreover, after acquiring Chemical Sciences, Inc., in 1983, Goodrich had developed a full line of chemicals for reverse osmosis treatment facilities. By 1989, as fresh water supplies dwindled and environmental regulations grew more stringent, Lee and other chemical executives believed that reverse osmosis water treatment technology was a promising, growing field. They realized that reverse osmosis water treatment firms had not become especially large and that the business was geographically scattered. Capital requirements, moreover, would be substantial. Nevertheless, Goodrich executives and scientists were confident that they could improve the operation of reverse osmosis plants.

As a result, Goodrich forward integrated in 1989 with the purchase of Arrowhead Industrial Water, a company with about $40 million in annual sales that provided both emergency supplies of pure water and pure water service contracts. The prospects of acquiring a business not dependent on the business cycle (water required purification no matter what the level of economic activity), and a business that Goodrich's technical expertise could improve, seemed promising for a time. Nevertheless, in 1995 Goodrich sold Arrowhead. Aware that the capital costs of water treatment plants were high, the company decided that it could best use its resources in other businesses.[31]

Growing Difficulties at Tremco

The specialty polymers and chemicals division was, like the rest of its industry, readjusting to new scientific and business conditions, and there seemed every prospect that new products would soon produce the sought-after profits. Tremco presented a very different set of problems of its own. When Goodrich purchased Tremco, it solidified its position as a provider of specialty chemicals. Because Tremco was such a successful firm, and fearing that a close integration with other parts of Goodrich chemicals might disturb a healthy venture, Goodrich allowed it considerable autonomy. H. David Warren became the president of Tremco in 1988, just seven years after joining Tremco Canada as its executive vice president.[32] Under his leadership, Tremco performed better than the specialty polymers and chemicals division in the early 1990s; but even Tremco's returns began to slip.[33] The changing business circumstances that Tremco faced caused Goodrich to reverse the policy of autonomy that had served it so well for over a decade.

Tremco had prospered as a service-oriented company whose sales personnel kept in close contact with customers. Tremco provided excellent products, but sales and service were its hallmarks. By 1988, however, Tremco's products began to face stiff competition from other materials and firms, and there were no significant proprietary materials in the pipeline. Although profits for Tremco continued to be handsome, executives were concerned about the future. "We have not been able to create sufficient unique value adding products in our core markets to keep us ahead of encroaching competition," Tremco reported to corporate headquarters near the end of 1988. The whole experience was "humbling," and managers sought to improve their own leadership qualities, trim costs, and improve products, while staying focused on markets that promised profitable performance.[34]

In addition, international events especially affected Tremco's profits. In 1990 a recession in Canada, where Tremco did over half its business, reduced sales dramatically, and Canadian sales went to just 35 percent of Tremco's total sales that year. Worse, the North American Free Trade Agreement, which the United States and Canada signed in 1992, brought about increased competition. In Canada Tremco had a consumer products division that held a dominant share (55 to 60 percent) of that nation's rust paint market, and about one-third of the Canadian consumer sealant market. The treaty allowed American firms—especially Dow Corning, which had a successful line of silicone products, along with private label product manufacturers—to penetrate those important Canadian markets.[35]

A Reorganized and Refocused Business

There was reason to remain optimistic about the future prospects of Goodrich in the specialty chemical field, in spite of the problems encountered with the recession of the early 1990s and the trend of the entire industry toward products that sold as commodities rather than as specialties. In the face of this industrywide transformation, Goodrich officers remained true to their manufacturing tradition of maintaining a strong scientific and technological base. They believed that reorganizing and refocusing Goodrich efforts in specialty chemicals would, within a few years, rebuild on that tradition to produce the desired profits.

Attention in the early 1990s especially focused on Tremco. Goodrich executives realized that they had not been doing enough to commercialize product and process innovations to enable Tremco to stay ahead of competitors.[36] As Ong later explained, Tremco suffered from "tired technology" in its product lines. Moreover, because of Tremco's organizational separation from specialty polymers and chemicals, its executives found it difficult to use technologies developed there or, for that matter, in other parts of Goodrich. Tremco, as we have seen, had been left on its own by corporate management in the 1980s. By the 1990s Ong thought that this situation was no longer tenable. "We really got to the point," he recalled, "where our organizational structure was working against us."[37]

Early in 1993 Ong delegated to Lauer the task of examining specialty chemicals; and in January of that year, Lauer laid down characteristics he thought specialty polymers and chemicals and Tremco should have. "We are looking," Lauer said, "for a mix of revenues which are predominantly systems based, i.e., not products in the classical sense, but integrated systems of several chemicals/polymers providing uniqueness for the ultimate consumer." Producing individual products was not enough. Specialty chemicals—like aerospace and a growing number of other American chemical producers—should, Lauer believed, produce fully developed components designed for the needs of specific customers. In addition, the businesses should "be *global*" and should operate only in markets in which they could be the number one or two producers. In such markets they should be able to make annual sales of at least $100 million, or have the clear potential of reaching that level, by 1998.[38] Discussions based on Lauer's ideas resulted in the drafting of a growth plan by Lee in February 1993. Lee reemphasized that specialty chemicals should be "an international manufacturer and marketer of high performance chemical products, services, and systems." He hoped to more than double the sales of specialty polymers and chemicals by 1995.[39]

However sensible this approach seemed from the manufacturing perspective, Ong was concerned that it was insufficient. In 1993 he and Lauer employed Peter Spitz, an Austrian-born chemical engineer and historian of the petrochemical industry, to conduct an analysis of the specialty chemical industry. The objective was to provide realistic goals for Goodrich operations in the industry and benchmarks against which to measure Goodrich managers' performance. One result would be a clearer understanding of investor expectations. What Spitz learned was not comforting: investment analysts viewed specialty chemical manufacturers strictly from the viewpoint of their returns on investment, and that viewpoint was not a long-term one. In other words, Goodrich was likely to encounter impatient Wall Street analysts who cared little and knew less about the importance of scientific, product, manufacturing, and distribution integration to long-term success. As Ong recalled, Spitz discovered that "it isn't so much what you do as how you do it" that mattered.[40]

This realization bolstered Ong's inclination to reorganize the specialty chemicals and polymers division and integrate its operations with those of Tremco. To help in that regard, as Spitz was preparing his report, Ong and Lauer hired the Delta Consulting Group, New York City–based experts on management organization, to prepare recommendations that later helped the senior executives move forward with reorganization. The Delta consultants confidentially interviewed sixteen Goodrich executives in Tremco, specialty polymers and chemicals, and the corporate office about their understanding of the company and its prospects.

The consultants' analysis revealed that Goodrich faced a difficult rebuilding process. Like Spitz, the Goodrich executives and the Delta consultants were concerned that the short-term profit expectations of investment analysts would interfere with the long-term needs of a manufacturer always needing to renew its product lines. In order to meet those short-term expectations, the consultants observed that Goodrich needed more integration of production, research, and sales between Tremco and the other business units in specialty chemicals and polymers. "Tremco and SP&C are not distant relatives," said one executive; "they are unrelated strangers." An officer in specialty polymers and chemicals noted, "We don't know much about Tremco." "They have put up boundaries," he continued, "that prevent us from understanding their business." He was echoed by a counterpart at Tremco: "I know very little about SP&C. Therefore, I have difficulty answering your questions about potential synergies." The report also revealed that the vision and values expressed by the corporate office had not yet fully permeated the company in its day-to-day operations.[41]

The solution lay in a reorganization during the second half of 1993, through which Tremco ceased to operate as an independent unit. Goodrich formed a new specialty chemicals segment with four business groups: specialty plastics, including Estane, Telene, and TempRite; specialty additives, including Carbopol; specialty sealants, coatings, and adhesives, including the products so successfully sold by Tremco in the 1980s; and water systems and services. The Delta consultants forecasted that such a reorganization would bring benefits. Tremco brought a "client and market focus," a strong sales orientation, and international experience and facilities. Specialty chemicals and polymers brought a historic research and development capability, a "strong market share position in key areas," and some products, like Carbopol, that enjoyed high returns and others that showed high growth potential.[42]

The purpose of the reorganization was to improve the perception (and actual abilities) of Goodrich as a specialty chemical provider. Two important developments soon followed. Lee retired as head of the specialty polymers and chemicals division late in 1993; and in April 1994 Wayne O. Smith assumed a new position as president of the specialty chemicals segment. Recruited by Goodrich at the age of fifty, Smith had worked for Air Products and Chemicals between 1974 and 1990, becoming the general manager of that firm's specialty chemicals operations in 1988. From 1990 to 1993, he was the chief executive of the industrial gases business of the BOC Group, Ltd., in North and Latin America. In 1993, Smith served as a consultant to a venture capital firm seeking to acquire a specialty chemicals or industrial gases business.[43] Meanwhile, Goodrich continued with its specialty chemicals acquisitions. In late 1993 Goodrich purchased Sanncor Industries, a privately held maker of waterborne urethane polymer resins for printing inks, coatings, adhesives, and fabrics. The acquisition complemented Goodrich's acrylic emulsions business. Located in Leominster, Massachusetts, the firm had $14 million in sales and employed fifty-two people in 1993.[44] Internally generated growth would, the purchase suggested, be augmented by small acquisitions in the future.

CONTINUING GROWTH IN AEROSPACE

Goodrich was more successful, in the short run at least, in the aerospace business than in the specialty chemical businesses that remained after the divestiture of Geon. In both integration and decentralization the aerospace division expressed a clear vision, and practiced it. The company had flirted with the small American aircraft industry before 1939 but had hesitated to focus resources on aerospace ventures even when that industry grew to substantial size. With the redirection of the 1980s and 1990s, it became a significant factor in aerospace. BFGoodrich Aerospace was not an aircraft manufacturer, but it was an important supplier of aircraft components, both mechanical and electronic, and of aircraft maintenance services.

Unlike specialty chemicals, where products in niche markets might have only a remote relationship to one another, the aerospace division competed by supplying entire aircraft systems and after-sale service. The division's president, David Burner, believed that it was important to expand in both manufacturing and service for at least two reasons. First, such expansion could fit the larger corporate goal of achieving stable profits at the targeted level. The company had learned from its aircraft tire and brake businesses that production and service operated on different business cycles. Second, in addition to the fact that aircraft services were themselves a profitable business, Goodrich's expanding ability to service airplanes facilitated its ability to sell the aircraft systems that it manufactured. Burner and others in the division believed that the future lay in a company's ability to supply entire systems—such as landing gear together with the wheels, brakes, and antiskid components, constituting the entire undercarriage subassembly of an aircraft. As Burner observed, "we want to be an integrated systems provider."[45]

Burner convinced Ong and other corporate executives, and Ong authorized expenditures for major acquisitions. Aerospace, Ong and Burner realized, held very large market shares, but in limited markets. If the company was to grow as an aerospace venture, it could not rely on internal growth alone; new businesses were necessary. The acquisitions that resulted allowed Goodrich to integrate its wheels and brakes into landing gear systems, continue with deicers, venture into avionics (the application of advanced computing and electronic technologies to aircraft navigation and control), and expand in servicing aircraft.[46] Investments in both acquisitions and research and development allowed BFGoodrich Aerospace to become a technological leader in wheels and brakes, composite materials, deicing and evacuation systems, and avionics.

Aerospace Acquisitions

The growth of BFGoodrich Aerospace through acquisitions was substantial. In 1990 Goodrich purchased Simmonds Precision Products from Hercules for $162 million. A maker of fuel-measurement and fuel-management systems, speed- and torque-sensing devices, ignition systems, and electromechanical actuators, Simmonds had annual sales of about $200 million and was, Burner thought, "a good fit with our existing businesses." In particular, Burner predicted that the acquisition would give his division "a strong market position in engine systems and components."[47] Simmonds was also known to be working on combining many of the smaller control systems for airplanes into a centrally controlled integrated utility system, basically combining all systems except those for guidance and propulsion. Goodrich was involved with Simmonds on part of this work in a joint venture; and, as Ong later observed, "we wanted into that."[48] The company also began to expand into avionics, in what soon became a business unit, BFGoodrich FlightSystems, formed after the purchase of Foster Airdata. FlightSystems, which produced the Stormscope line of thunderstorm-detection devices, built a new facility in Columbus, Ohio, to expand production.[49]

Goodrich followed up the additions made in 1990 and 1991 with two large purchases in 1993. In June, Goodrich bought the Cleveland Pneumatic Company for $193 million. Goodrich had been interested in Cleveland Pneumatic as early as 1988, but the asking price had been too high. A leader in the manufacture and overhaul of aircraft landing gear (including some for the Boeing 747 and 767), the firm had sales of $272 million in 1992. "The acquisition," Ong announced, "is an important step in our strategy to enlarge our earnings from our aerospace businesses. . . . [The purchase] continues the transformation of BFGoodrich into an aerospace and specialty chemicals company."[50]

Even as they were buying Cleveland Pneumatic, executives were negotiating for the purchase of an even larger company, Rosemount Aerospace in Burnsville, Minnesota, a subsidiary of Emerson Electric. It was their desire to produce complete airplane systems that led them to make this purchase. Employing twelve hundred workers, Rosemount Aerospace was America's foremost firm in the making of electronic sensors for airplane components, sensors Goodrich was already using in manufacturing deicers and some other products. "Acquisition of Rosemount's sensor technology and software capabilities would," Goodrich executives believed, "provide BFGoodrich Aerospace with the ability to move toward sensor and component integration." The purchase would also complement their earlier acquisition of Simmonds Precision Products. Officers considered Rosemount Aerospace an "exceedingly well-run" company, estimating that in 1992 its sales of $150–55 million generated an operating income of $29–30 million.[51]

Negotiations to purchase Rosemount Aerospace lasted through much of 1993. They began when Ong called the head of Emerson Electric, with whom he was personally acquainted, to inquire about the possibility of buying Rosemount Aerospace. Ong pointed out that Rosemount Aerospace did not fit in with Emerson's product mix. Emerson Electric's head agreed, but was quick to point out that Rosemount Aerospace was very profitable. Additional phone calls and visits between Goodrich and Emerson Electric officials ensued. In April 1993 Burner met with Emerson Electric's vice president of strategic planning in St. Louis, only to learn that Rosemount Aerospace was "not for sale." Nonetheless, Burner was encouraged, because he was also told that Rosemount Aerospace was "not considered a strategic fit" by Emerson. A follow-up telephone call between Ong and the chairman of Emerson led to the purchase of Rosemount Aerospace for about $300 million in December 1993. Ong thought that Goodrich "paid a high price for Rosemount" but believed that the technologies Rosemount Aerospace brought to Goodrich amply justified the acquisition.[52] More specifically, Goodrich officers thought that "the acquisition of Cleveland Pneumatic and Rosemount Aerospace strengthens our ability to develop and supply integrated systems and subsystems."[53]

Internal Developments in Aerospace

Internal developments, especially in the servicing of airplanes, which Goodrich had begun developing in the 1980s, also fueled aerospace's growth. In 1989, Tramco doubled its capacity by opening a new hanger. In the following year, aerospace expanded its maintenance services by nearly a third with the establishment of new wheel and brake service centers in Louisville and London. In 1990, too, Goodrich set up a British subsidiary to handle the maintenance of aircraft landing gear systems. Tramco boosted its sales 28 percent in 1992 and began constructing a huge $81-million hangar that would permit the overhaul of four wide-body planes at one time. By late 1993, Tramco operated three large hangars with 1 million square feet of space. Employing two thousand workers in 1994, up from six hundred just six years before, Tramco had sales of about $200 million. By 1994, Goodrich operated eleven repair and overhaul stations around the world from London to Singapore, and its main competitor, Bendix, had copied Tramco's strategy.[54]

While servicing aircraft became more and more important for Goodrich, manufacturing also remained significant. In 1991, Goodrich won acceptance as a leading provider of wheels and carbon brakes for Boeing's proposed 777 aircraft. By early 1994, Goodrich, as one of two suppliers of wheels and brakes for that airplane, had won 72 percent of the airline orders. With the first delivery of the 777 scheduled for 1995, this contract was expected to generate $3 billion for Goodrich over the following forty years. In 1991, Goodrich also became the sole supplier of wheels and brakes for Cessna's Citation business aircraft and began deliveries of carbon brakes for F-16 fighters. Production of Goodrich's carbon brakes reached a new all-time high in 1992. In 1993 Goodrich won a position as a supplier of wheels and brakes for Airbus A-321 aircraft.[55]

CORPORATE POLICIES FOR A REBUILT COMPANY

In 1994, with a promising future for the aerospace business and optimism about growing sales in specialty chemicals, the corporate office faced challenges affecting the entire company. Not the least were the hardships caused by the deep recession of 1990–93. In addition, corporate executives had to solve the problem of how to cover health care insurance costs for employees and retirees adequately. True to its promise of social responsibility, Goodrich also followed recommendations of the Chemical Manufacturers' Association for occupational health and environmental responsibility. And, perhaps most important for the future of Goodrich, the company had to ensure that its expenditures for research and development were both substantial and designed to foster commercially viable technologies for the future. Those challenges, moreover, were interrelated.

Research and Development

Goodrich had long valued research and development, and expenditures for research, at least since the days of John Collyer, had been an integral part of the company's business strategy. Goodrich sold manufactured products in competitive global markets in which rival firms were constantly seeking to improve their own proprietary knowledge about material science, electronics, and aeronautics, among other fields. Ong and his colleagues knew that to survive in the long term, Goodrich had to maintain and even enlarge its investments in research and development. Despite the recession, Goodrich increased its spending on research and development from just under $60 million in 1989 to nearly $80 million in 1992. Still, they realized, those expenditures alone would not ensure that Goodrich remain competitive in the aerospace and specialty chemicals markets in which it participated.[56]

The problem was simple: Goodrich competed with considerably larger chemical manufacturers that could afford to spend more for research. Moreover, Goodrich's research expenditures went partly to developing new aerospace technologies. Aware of this situation and knowing that Goodrich had to compete in research in order to survive, the senior executives decided to rethink their research and development strategy in 1994. The company's "core competency," executives decided, lay in "materials and systems and their integration." Victoria Haynes, who had joined Goodrich in 1992 as vice president for research and development, led the effort. She and other corporate executives agreed to redirect corporate-sponsored research and development efforts toward strategically aligned longer-range research for the company, as well as to leverage technology across the company. Haynes concluded that "technology belongs to the corporation" and that technological advances made in one area might well benefit Goodrich in another.[57]

To help guide the company Haynes classified three types of research and development: that which improved the company's "base technology," designed to "maintain current business"; that which developed "key technology" to protect Goodrich's competitive position and provide a foundation for future growth; and that which provided "pacing technology" capable of transforming Goodrich's products and markets. Goodrich's executives decided to "concentrate primarily on pacing technology," which "has leverage across *all* BFG businesses." They hoped that by the beginning of the twenty-first century, the creation of pacing technologies would compose three-quarters of their firm's corporate (separate from divisional) research efforts, up from just one-half in 1994. Specifically, they planned to "realign research . . . around Pacing Technologies directed toward a few specific advanced materials and systems projects." As they did so, they would be careful to "champion and promote the synergies which exist across BFG." Meanwhile, business units in both aerospace and specialty chemicals would sponsor research on "base" and "key" technologies.[58]

In order to increase Goodrich's investment in pacing technologies, the company created a pacing research fund at the corporate level, available to anyone in the company. Under this scheme, project teams, supported by a business unit, requested funding for a research program in pacing technology. The company evaluated proposals, using referees from both within and outside Goodrich, according to their strategic importance for the business, their likely return on investment, their technical quality, and their fit with competencies important to Goodrich. In 1995 Goodrich funded eleven pacing technology projects under this system.

This organization of corporate research, designed to ensure focus on pacing technologies vital for the long-term well-being of Goodrich, attracted considerable attention from executives of other companies interested in promoting "discontinuous innovation" (breakthrough ideas and technologies) and transferring pacing technologies to practical—and profitable—products and services. The program that Haynes began in 1995 assured the transfer of technology from the corporate level to the operating units of the company by having those units help fund each approved project. Each project received promise of funding for three years (with a possibility of renewal), with the business units' contributions increasing proportionately each year.

Goodrich executives were pleased with the process, which assured that all corporate-level research efforts went to pacing technologies that clearly fit the firm's business strategy. Executives at the highest level saw the process as assuring that research efforts were strategically focused and accountable for their projected return on investment. Haynes, moreover, observed the program enhancing and facilitating innovation, soliciting and supporting ideas that may have been in the organization for years but never had the opportunity to surface and receive funding. "We have allowed the organization to express innovation," Haynes remarked. She was confident that the company had developed a way of administering research that facilitated and supported discontinuous innovation and the transfer of technology to the company's operating units, vital for Goodrich's long-term growth.[59]

Social Responsibility

Before corporate executives decided to renew their research expenditures, they had to face issues in employee and retiree health insurance costs, and in meeting public and governmental demands for environmental responsibility. The problem of health care costs originated in a long-standing national policy that almost all health insurance provided to Americans would come from employers. This system served most Americans well for a time, but beginning in the early 1970s the costs of providing health care began to escalate dramatically, putting pressure on Goodrich and other employers. The problem worsened as markets in which American manufacturers competed became global; foreign firms operating outside the United States did not usually face the same health insurance costs because their employees had access to publicly funded insurance programs.[60] When health care costs continued to rise much faster than the general rate of inflation in the 1980s, Goodrich faced a real dilemma in trying to remain true to its tradition of caring about the welfare of its employees.

The matter came to a partial resolution in 1992, but it was a resolution that affected the balance sheet. The matter occupied considerable attention from senior Goodrich executives. In 1989 Goodrich, like most American employers, had begun to shift more of the costs of health insurance to its employees. The changes in benefits programs would help "mitigate the effect of these expenses on current earnings and will slow future cost increases," the company told its stockholders in its 1992 annual report. That year Goodrich used a new accounting standard required by the government to estimate and charge current earnings for the future health and life insurance costs for retirees. The result was a one-time charge of $286.5 million in 1992. This extraordinary charge, along with the continuing economic recession and other adjustments designed to reduce future costs, meant that Goodrich's balance sheet suffered dearly.

The story was happier in the area of environmental matters. Since about 1970 the company, like all manufacturers, had been subject to environmental and safety regulations from federal and state governments. Chemical manufacturers were especially susceptible to public suspicions about corporate spoilage of the natural environment and about production processes that harmed workers. Although Goodrich had already spent substantial sums on environmental controls and had taken the lead in protecting the safety of workers in the vinyl industry, the company went even further in the 1990s. Goodrich employed a vice president for the environment, health, and safety management systems, appointing Carl A. Mattia to the post in 1990. Each operating unit had executives responsible for health and environmental issues, and corporate headquarters demanded that each unit conform to a high standard.

The standards Goodrich used came from the "Responsible Care" program of the Chemical Manufacturers' Association. Adopted in 1988 by the association, which adopted a model developed in Canada, the program was designed to improve the public reputation of the American chemical industry by improving its performance in environmental and safety matters. The association required member firms to adopt the standard as a condition of membership. In 1990 the Goodrich board of directors formed an oversight committee for environment, health, and safety, ensuring attention to those matters at the highest level. Goodrich conducted biennial audits of its performance in both specialty chemicals and aerospace (and, before 1993, in Geon Vinyl) using both its own staff and outside consultants. Executives believed that, despite the heavy expenditures, the program was necessary for the company's very survival.[61]

TRADITION AND TRANSFORMATION:
BFGOODRICH IN PROCESS

As the company celebrated its 125th anniversary, Ong and his colleagues took great pride in the financial success of their efforts to rebuild Goodrich. The firm's earnings had improved dramatically, growing from 28¢ per share in 1993 to $2.24 per share in 1994. The board of directors had approved an aggressive three-year business plan for 1995–97, and even before the close of the plan's first year the company was exceeding its own optimistic forecasts. In 1995 investors recognized the improvements, and Goodrich's share price advanced faster than the generally booming stock market. Ong observed that "the 'new company' we envisioned is now in place," and the investors' recognition of Goodrich's performance very much pleased the chairman. "Many challenges lie ahead," Ong noted, "but we have well-articulated plans and a proven management team. We look forward with confidence to the next 125 years."[62]

Ong's pride reflected the fact that the rebuilt company was very much a product of its own history. Both core areas, specialty chemicals and aerospace, were rooted inescapably in that past. Both had grown out of rubber manufacturing, and both were a product of the company's participation in the mobilization for World War II. Specialty chemicals originated from the need to improve the characteristics of manufactured items made from natural rubber and had grown and changed as a result of the revolution in polymer chemistry fostered by the war mobilization efforts. Similarly, aerospace had begun from the initially small opportunities to provide rubber products to aircraft manufacturers, and it had grown in importance when the military services had to create the modern American aircraft industry during the 1940s.

The historical roots of the company also extended deeper than its product lines of the 1990s might suggest. The roots extended all the way back to Dr. Benjamin Franklin Goodrich and his commitment to providing different products to different markets, and to focusing on constantly ensuring that those products were of the highest possible quality. The roots extended outward to encompass a set of values, enunciated again in the 1990s, about the company's commitment to its employees, its customers, and to social responsibility. Perhaps most important, as the company changed, became smaller, and then began to grow again, its executives realized that at Goodrich's core was an ability to synthesize materials and technical knowledge into systems and products that met customers' needs.[63]

The company in process was traditional; it was also a dynamic, changing institution responding to business opportunities. Its two principal lines of business were different, united by history but by little else—or so it may have seemed on the surface. Underneath that surface, there was an underlying business unity. Both BFGoodrich Aerospace and BFGoodrich Specialty Chemicals enjoyed a valuable reputation in their respective fields, a commonality extending much deeper than the Goodrich name. BFGoodrich was not merely a holding company, a small central office that held the assets of subsidiaries. As the company grew and expanded its sales, its integration allowed the corporate office to provide important financial services, moving funds from one part of the company to another as various business units encountered different cyclical business opportunities and faced research and development needs for new products. In addition, executives with managerial talent moved from one part of the company to another, bringing fresh perspectives and renewed energy to new assignments. Finally, the company was one in which executives, scientists, and engineers sought new technologies in which expertise from specialty chemicals helped aerospace, and vice versa. Both aerospace and specialty chemicals involved material science, and in fact the two segments were joined in common research teams. As BFGoodrich grew, expanded its sales, and looked toward its future, its executives remained focused on the demands of investors. The men and women of BFGoodrich understood that they were part of a common manufacturing enterprise renewing its technologies, products, and services with a view toward providing value, not just for the present, but for future generations as well.

APPENDIX A

Financial Data, 1881–1994

Date	Total Assets	Sales	Net Income
1881	$233,000	$319,000	$69,000
1882	292,000	443,000	77,000
1883	418,000	490,000	74,000
1884	366,000	451,000	86,000
1885	404,000	377,000	77,000
1886	396,000	456,000	67,000
1887	548,000	585,000	47,000
1888	548,000	696,000	106,000
1889	714,000	722,000	182,000
1890	1,034,000	954,000	173,000
1891	1,106,000	1,145,000	205,000
1892	1,286,000	1,413,000	257,000
1893	1,226,000	1,838,000	304,000
1894	1,217,000	1,790,000	299,000
1895	2,039,000	2,292,000	469,000
1896	2,368,000	2,379,000	397,000
1897	2,811,000	2,781,000	366,000
1898	3,250,000	3,563,000	634,000
1899	4,726,000	4,568,000	782,000
1900	4,380,000	4,941,000	718,000
1901	3,869,000	4,816,000	796,000
1902	4,107,000	5,888,000	1,094,000
1903	6,345,000	6,480,000	729,000

(*continued*)

Financial Data   (Continued)

Date	Total Assets	Sales	Net Income
1904	6,807,000	7,555,000	1,495,000
1905	7,733,000	8,820,000	1,910,000
1906	12,503,000	10,474,000	2,073,000
1907	12,473,000	12,930,000	2,324,000
1908	12,700,000	12,611,000	2,757,000
1909	13,329,000	17,166,000	3,350,000
1910	21,807,000	23,807,000	1,605,000
1911	18,800,000	27,407,000	3,393,000
1912	98,786,000	45,304,000	4,391,000
1913	94,512,000	39,509,000	2,600,000
1914	94,937,000	41,764,000	5,440,000
1915	107,086,000	55,417,000	12,266,000
1916	115,637,000	70,991,000	9,569,000
1917	146,127,000	87,155,000	10,545,000
1918	141,238,000	123,470,000	15,637,000
1919	175,716,000	141,343,000	17,305,000
1920	139,910,000	150,007,000	2,711,000
1921	89,031,000	86,687,000	(8,893,000)
1922	92,311,000	93,650,000	3,048,000
1923	88,274,000	107,093,000	3,025,000
1924	84,886,000	109,818,000	8,823,000
1925	108,992,000	136,250,000	12,744,000
1926	107,296,000	148,391,000	5,065,000
1927	115,261,000	151,685,000	11,780,000
1928	117,071,000	148,805,000	3,513,000
1929	163,696,000	164,495,000	7,446,000
1930	159,022,000	155,256,000	(8,374,000)
1931	139,111,000	115,156,000	(8,807,000)
1932	113,603,000	74,502,000	(6,930,000)
1933	114,390,000	79,294,000	2,273,000
1934	117,600,000	103,872,000	2,535,000
1935	124,021,000	118,669,000	3,430,000
1936	140,750,000	141,097,000	7,320,000
1937	135,436,000	149,972,000	(879,000)
1938	132,009,000	115,038,000	2,240,000
1939	129,828,000	135,736,000	6,629,000
1940	140,000,000	145,000,000	6,000,000
1941	157,000,000*	211,000,790	9,000,000
1942	184,000,000*	239,000,000	10,000,000
1943	229,000,000*	374,000,000	12,000,000
1944	244,000,000*	419,000,000	12,000,000
1945	222,000,000*	372,000,000	12,000,000
1946	239,000,000*	361,000,000	25,000,000

Financial Data   (*Continued*)

Date	Total Assets	Sales	Net Income
1947	265,000,000*	410,000,000	23,000,000
1948	288,000,000*	420,000,000	24,000,000
1949	291,000,000*	388,000,000	21,000,000
1950	354,000,000*	543,000,000	35,000,000
1951	416,000,000*	638,000,000	35,000,000
1952	421,000,000	624,000,000	32,000,000
1953	437,000,000	675,000,000	32,000,000
1954	464,000,000	631,000,000	39,000,000
1955	508,000,000	755,017,000	47,000,000
1956	519,000,000	724,000,000	44,000,000
1957	528,000,000	735,000,000	39,000,000
1958	547,000,000	697,000,000	35,000,000
1959	559,000,000	772,000,000	38,000,000
1960	613,000,000	765,000,000	30,000,000
1961	646,000,000	758,000,000	31,000,000
1962	648,000,000	812,000,000	26,000,000
1963	658,000,000	828,000,000	27,000,000
1964	679,000,000	872,000,000	34,000,000
1965	746,000,000	980,000,000	41,000,000
1966	850,000,000	1,006,000,000	49,000,000
1967	918,000,000	1,039,000,000	35,000,000
1968	1,035,000,000	1,140,000,000	45,000,000
1969	1,256,000,000	1,229,000,000	39,000,000
1970	1,304,000,000	1,205,000,000	16,000,000
1971	1,342,000,000	1,237,000,000	2,000,000
1972	1,400,000,000	1,507,000,000	49,000,000
1973	1,475,000,000	1,661,000,000	56,000,000
1974	1,646,000,000	1,966,000,000	52,000,000
1975	1,596,000,000	1,901,000,000	25,000,000
1976	1,568,000,000	1,996,000,000	16,000,000
1977	1,699,000,000	2,222,000,000	60,000,000
1978	1,931,000,000	2,594,000,000	70,000,000
1979	2,082,000,000	2,988,000,000	82,000,000
1980	2,224,000,000	3,080,000,000	62,000,000
1981	2,727,000,000	3,185,000,000	109,000,000
1982	2,425,000,000	3,005,000,000	(32,000,000)
1983	2,578,000,000	3,192,000,000	18,000,000
1984	2,625,000,000	3,438,000,000	61,000,000
1985	2,263,000,000	3,200,000,000	(317,000,000)
1986	1,821,000,000	2,553,000,000	13,000,000
1987	1,940,000,000	2,168,000,000	105,000,000
1988	2,073,000,000	2,417,000,000	196,000,000

(*continued*)

Financial Data   (*Continued*)

Date	Total Assets	Sales	Net Income
1989	2,277,000,000	2,420,000,000	172,000,000
1990	2,416,000,000	2,433,000,000	136,000,000
1991	2,273,000,000	2,472,000,000	(81,000,000)
1992	2,454,000,000	2,525,000,000	(296,000,000)
1993	2,360,000,000	1,818,000,000	128,000,000
1994	2,469,000,000	2,199,000,000	76,000,000
1995	2,490,000,000	2,409,000,000	118,000,000

Sources: "Directors Meetings," 1881–1920; Leavitt, "History of and Statistics Appertaining to the B.F. Goodrich Co."; "Annual Reports," 1919–95.
*Adjusted per 1951 "Annual Report" to include all marketable securities in current assets (1941–51).

APPENDIX B

Chairmen of the Board

1907–10	G. T. Perkins
1912–17	F. A. Hardy
1920–27	B. G. Work
1927–50	D. M. Goodrich
1950–60	J. L. Collyer
1967–72	J. W. Keener
1972–79	O. P. Thomas
1979–	J. D. Ong

When no chairman was named, the president presided over meetings of the board of directors.

APPENDIX C

Presidents

1870–88	B. F. Goodrich
1888–1907	G. T. Perkins
1907–27	B. G. Work
1927–28	H. Hough
1928–37	J. D. Tew
1937–39	S. B. Robertson
1939–54	J. L. Collyer
1954–57	W. S. Richardson
1957–67	J. W. Keener
1967–74	H. B. Warner
1974–75	O. P. Thomas
1975–84	J. D. Ong
1984–86	P. C. Ross
1986–90	L. Carter
1990–94	J. N. Lauer
1994–95	J. D. Ong
1995–	D. L. Burner

APPENDIX D

Board of Directors, Listed Chronologically by Date of Retirement, from 1912

Director	Dates Served
Albert T. Pelz	5/2/12–5/8/12
W. K. Means	5/2/12–6/12/12 6/27/12–7/24/12
Howard H. Bryant	5/2/12–9/12/12
W. A. Fuller	5/2/12–9/12/12
O. C. Barber	6/12/12–3/10/15
Philip Lehman	6/27/12–3/10/15
A. H. Wiggin	5/8/12–3/8/16
Harold E. Joy	5/2/12–6/12/12 3/8/16–1/30/18
Henry Goldman	6/12/12–3/13/18
F. A. Hardy	6/12/12–3/13/18
Guy E. Norwood	6/27/12–3/13/18
E. C. Shaw	5/2/12–4/21/26
H. K. Raymond	3/8/16–4/20/27
Bertram G. Work	5/2/12–8/30/27 (d. 1927)

(continued)

Board of Directors   (Continued)

Director	Dates Served
Lorenzo D. Brown	3/12/19–9/?/27 (d. 1927)
F. C. Van Cleef	3/13/18–11/1/27
W. O. Rutherford	3/18/16–1/4/28
Harold Stanley	4/20/21–1/4/28
W. C. Geer	3/8/16–1/25/28
Harry Hough	1/30/18–7/25/28 (d. 1947)
H. E. Raymond	5/2/12–6/12/12
	7/24/12–10/24/28 (d. 1928)
W. A. Means	5/2/12–4/22/30
Joseph R. Swan	1/25/28–4/22/30
A. A. Tilney	4/20/21–4/22/30 (d. 1937)
A. H. Noah	6/12/12–6/10/30
Frank H. Mason	5/2/12–7/10/31 (d. 1931)
T. G. Graham	1/4/28–9/8/31
Frank H. Hobson	4/22/30–1/12/32
C. M. Keys	4/17/29–2/9/32
Charles C. Goodrich	6/27/12–8/9/32 (d. 1932)
Waddill Catchings	3/13/18–5/3/33
George M. Moffett	1/4/28–2/19/37
C. B. Raymond	5/2/12–12/21/37
W. D. Ticknor	4/12/32–3/24/38 (d. 1938)
J. D. Tew	4/20/27–4/19/38
C. E. Sullivan	1/12/32–2/14/39 (d. 1939)
A. H. Marks	6/12/12–4/20/21
	4/22/30–5/9/39 (d. 1939)
S. B. Robertson	2/16/37–9/12/39
William A. Evans	5/6/36–10/25/39 (d. 1939)
T. B. Tomkinson	3/23/28–11/19/40
A. B. Newhall	8/16/38–4/1/42

Board of Directors   (*Continued*)

Director	Dates Served
V. I. Montenyohl	3/23/28–6/16/42
A. A. Sprague	4/22/30–8/16/38 12/17/40–4/6/46 (d. 1946)
David M. Goodrich	5/2/12–6/12/12 3/13/13–5/17/50 (d. 1950)
George K. Funston	6/18/46–9/7/51
Sir Walrond Sinclair	5/2/34–4/15/52
T. H. McInnerney	5/2/34–10/21/52 (d. 1952)
Wesson Seyburn	6/10/30–7/30/55
Charles S. McCain	4/22/30–9/18/56
A. B. Jones	3/8/16–4/20/21 12/21/37–11/30/57
Cleveland E. Dodge	5/21/42–4/15/58
G. W. Vaught	12/16/41–12/26/41 1/16/51–4/21/59
Reuben B. Robertson Jr.	12/15/53–7/22/55 9/2/57–3/13/60 (d. 1960)
Langbourne M. Williams Jr.	8/16/38–10/18/60
W. S. Richardson	11/18/52–12/19/61
R. S. Rauch	1/12/32–4/17/62
Sidney J. Weinberg	6/10/30–4/17/62
John L. Collyer	9/12/39–4/21/64 (d. 1981)
David Rockefeller	6/19/56–4/21/64
Amory Houghton Jr.	1/20/59–3/21/67
Deane W. Malott	6/19/51–3/25/69
Paul C. Cabot	6/20/50–4/22/70
Elmer L. Lindseth	6/21/55–4/18/72
Arthur Kelly	1/17/61–4/17/73 (d. 1990)
Herman C. Nolen	5/31/60–4/17/73 (d. 1992)
J. W. Keener	8/1/57–1/1/74 (d. 1981)

(*continued*)

Board of Directors *(Continued)*

Director	Dates Served
Harry B. Warner	7/19/66–4/15/74 (d. 1991)
Barry T. Leithead	2/19/52–7/15/74 (d. 1974)
Boone Gross	2/20/62–4/21/75 (d. 1979)
Gerard Alexander	6/20/72–9/16/75 (d. 1983)
Anton Vittone	9/15/75–7/6/77 (d. 1977)
Thomas B. Nantz	6/20/72–2/1/78 (d. 1979)
Fred G. Fusee	4/17/73–2/21/78 (d. 1978)
Gordon Edwards	12/19/67–4/17/78 (d. 1988)
James N. Purse II	1/20/75–6/3/82 (d. 1982)
R. Stanley Laing	3/25/69–4/16/84
William F. Laporte	4/17/78–4/16/84
M. Donald McClusky	9/15/80–11/19/84
O. Pendleton Thomas	9/8/71–2/8/85 (d. 1985)
William P. Stiritz	5/16/83–4/15/85
C. E. Meyer Jr.	4/15/85–4/18/88
David V. Ragone	6/21/82–4/18/88
Patrick C. Ross	7/3/84–4/18/88
Thomas C. Simons	5/17/82–8/17/88 (d. 1988)
G. Jack Tankersley	6/16/75–4/16/90 (d. 1995)
Leigh Carter	7/3/84–4/15/91
John C. Duncan	2/22/78–4/15/91
David L. Luke III	1/16/62–4/15/91
Jeanette Grasselli Brown	4/15/91–
George A. Davidson Jr.	4/15/91–
James J. Glasser	4/15/85–
Thomas H. O'Leary	4/18/88–
John D. Ong	6/18/73–
Joseph A. Pichler	9/1/88–
Alfred M. Rankin Jr.	4/18/88–
Ian M. Ross	3/1/83–

Board of Directors (Continued)

Director	Dates Served
D. Lee Tobler	4/18/88–
William L. Wallace	4/16/90–
John L. Weinberg	5/15/62–
A. Thomas Young	4/17/95–

NOTE ON SOURCES

We were privileged to have access to an array of sources for this study. Although BFGoodrich historically, as a matter of policy, does not retain the correspondence of its executives, we were able to piece together our story from a variety of sources, as we have indicated in the notes for each chapter. These sources include published materials as well as manuscripts housed at the National Archives, Cornell University, and the Ohio Historical Society. The company's own records, however, provided the bulk of our information.

We enjoyed the full cooperation of the company in pursuing any sources we believed were important for this history. John Ong even provided several cartons of documents from his office, including reports from consultants and records of meetings among high-level executives during his tenure with Goodrich. The legal department made available its record books, consisting mainly of minutes from meetings of the board of directors and other executive bodies. For much of the firm's history, the minute books provided very little information, but during James Tew's time of leadership the records included some appendices that gave important insight into the company's problems and its strategic decisions. Similarly, when Pendleton Thomas led the company, there were minutes of meetings that told us far more than the bare record of what was decided. We also had access to the so-called "board books," the material provided to individual members of the board of directors for each meeting, for almost the last three decades of the company's history.

During the 1960s Goodrich began a company archive and employed a professional archivist to administer its records. Soon, however, the firm abandoned the project and turned over the archives to the American History Research Center in the University of Akron library (we have used the abbreviation *BFG Col.* to designate these records). During the course of our project we collected some additional materials, most notably the papers of Waldo Semon and George Fowles, and deposited them in the University of Akron Archives' Goodrich collection. In addition, interviews with a number of current and former Goodrich associates were extremely important sources of information and insight. In all but a very few cases, the recordings and transcriptions of those interviews are also on deposit with the Goodrich materials housed in the University of Akron library. The persons who granted us interviews included the following: A.J. Ashe, Felix Bellini, Thomas Blazey, Z. David Bonner, Walter Brodine, John Codrea, David Devendorf, Robert Eisentrout, George Fowles, Leonard Freeman, Keith Funston, Charles Goff, Earl Gunn, Edward Harrington, Victoria Haynes, Richard Heuerman, Archie Japs, Ray Jeter, Benjamin Jones, Jefferson Keener, Robert Keener, Robert Kenney, Stanley Laing, Raymond Luebbers, David Luke, Deane Malott, Jean Malone, Donald McClusky, John McCool, John Nelson, Herman Nolen, Thomas Norman, John Ong, Edward Osborne, Marvin Patterson, William Perdriau, Edgar Perry, Lawrence Pomeroy, James Richards, David Rockefeller, Patrick Ross, William Scull, Waldo Semon, Glen Sengpiel, Lawrence Shailer, Richard Silver, Elmer Stevens, Charles Stockman, Anselm Talalay, E. F. Tomlinson, Alvin Ulle, Thomas Waltermire, and John Weinberg.

Finally, we used a few materials housed in the records center of the Geon Company; we have noted these materials as Geon Company historical files. Records cited without a location are retained in Goodrich's files.

NOTES

CHAPTER I

1. Benjamin Franklin Goodrich, "List of the Articles Used in Manufacturing Heavy Rubber Goods with the Prices of the Same in This City, October 5, 1870," no folder, box M-1, BFG Col.
2. "Directors Meeting," 8 January 1907, reprints semiannual balance sheet; and P. W. Leavitt, "History and Statistics Appertaining to the B.F. Goodrich Co. for Forty Years from 1870 to 1910," typescript, 54, 59, folder 14, box NA-1, BFG Col. (Leavitt joined Goodrich as its bookkeeper in 1881 and became its chief accountant in 1889.)
3. Many of the histories of Akron and Summit County contain biographical data about Benjamin Goodrich. See *A Centennial History of Akron, 1825–1925* (Akron: Summit County Historical Society, 1925); Karl H. Grismer, *Akron and Summit County* (Akron: Summit County Historical Society, 1952); S. D. Kenfield, *Akron and Summit County, Ohio, 1825–1928: Historical and Biographical* (Chicago: S. J. Clark Publishing, 1928); George Knepper, *Akron: City at the Summit* (Tulsa: Continental Heritage Press, 1981); Samuel Lane, *Fifty Years and Over of Akron and Summit County* (Akron: Beacon Job Department, 1887); Oscar Eugene Olin, *Akron and Environs: Historical, Biographical* (Chicago: The Lewis Publishing Company, 1917); William Henry Perrin, *History of Summit County with an Outline Sketch of Ohio* (Chicago: Baskin & Battey, 1881).
4. "Original Manuscript of Elbert Hubbard," typescript, 14–17, folder 23, box NA-1, BFG Col.
5. Benjamin Goodrich to Julia Dinsmore, 10 April 1869, MS-1016, box 10, file 501, Dinsmore family papers, Arizona Historical Society Archives, Tucson, Arizona.
6. *Akron Beacon Journal*, 4 August 1888 (the newspaper that became the *Akron Beacon Journal* was published under several titles in the late nineteenth century; for the sake of clarity it will be referred to as the *Akron Beacon Journal* throughout

this history); "Biography of Benjamin Franklin Goodrich," typescript, p. 1, no folder, box NA-1, BFG Col.; Lane, *Fifty Years*, 469; P. W. Leavitt, "History and Statistics"; and Perrin, *History*, 708.

7. "Biography," 1.
8. *Akron Beacon Journal*, 4 August 1888; "Biography," 2; and "Original Manuscript of Elbert Hubbard," 18–19.
9. David Goodrich, "Reminiscences," folder 48, box NA-1, BFG Col.
10. Ibid., 4.
11. Frances W. Gregory, "The American Industrial Elite in the 1870s: Their Social Origins," and William Miller, "The Business Elite in Business Bureaucracies: Careers of Top Executives in the Early Twentieth Century," in William Miller, ed., *Men in Business: Essays on the Historical Role of the Entrepreneur* (Cambridge: Harvard University Press, 1952).
12. Benjamin Franklin Goodrich to [name unclear], 6 September 1865, letter in the private possession of Mrs. Jefferson Patterson, Washington, D.C.
13. "Biography," 2.
14. David Goodrich once recalled that his mother told him that his father had at one time held nearly $500,000 in New York real estate. If so, Goodrich had lost most of it by the late 1860s, for he entered the rubber industry short of capital. See David Goodrich, "Reminiscences," 2. Some accounts suggest that Goodrich may have first met Morris in Jamestown; see Howard and Ralph Wolf, *Rubber: A Story of Glory and Greed* (New York: Covici Friede Publishers, 1936), 403.
15. "Price List of the Hudson River Rubber Company, April, 1869," and "Statement of Hudson River Rubber Company, June 8, 1869."
16. John P. Morris, "Statement, June 17, 1896."
17. Ibid. Goodrich's son David later recalled matters in a similar vein: "Father seems to have had one major failing in a business way. He was too much inclined to loan money to a great many people who didn't seem to have too much collateral. I think probably that is the real reason he got into the rubber business. He loaned a lot of money to a little rubber company at Hastings-on-Hudson, and I think eventually he found that his only chance to save face and get out was to take over the company." See Goodrich, "Reminiscences," 3.
18. On the development of the early rubber industry see Andrea C. Dragon, "Wild Men: The First Twenty-five Years of the American Rubber Industry," *Essays in Economic and Business History* 13 (1995): 217–30.
19. *A Compendium of the Ninth Census (July 1, 1870)*, (Washington, D.C.: Government Printing Office, 1872), 804, 902–3.
20. Morris, "Statement," 3.
21. Ibid., "Biography," and Leavitt, "History and Statistics," n.p. Morris never regained any of the money he had invested in Goodrich's rubber ventures in Hastings or Melrose. Nor was he a partner in Goodrich's later enterprise in Akron.
22. "Third Annual Report of the Akron Board of Trade, April, 1870," one-page flyer, folder 42, box NA-1, BFG Col.
23. See especially *A Centennial History of Akron*, chap. 20; Knepper, *City at the Summit*, chap. 3; and William D. Overman, "The Rubber Industry in Ohio," *Ohio Historical Quarterly* 66 (1957): 278–89.
24. Hugh Allen, *Rubber's Home Town: The Real-Life Story of Akron* (New York: Stratford House, 1949), chap. 10.
25. *Akron Beacon Journal*, 6 January 1912; Doyle, *Centennial History of Summit County*,

353–54; Kenfield, *Akron and Summit County*, 631–34; Lane, *Fifty Years*, 152; and Perrin, *History of Summit County*, 694–95.

26. James S. and Margot Y. Jackson, *At Home on the Hill: The Perkins Family of Akron* (Akron: Summit County Historical Society, 1983).

27. Ibid., chap. 5; *Akron Beacon Journal*, 8 September 1910; Lane, *Fifty Years*, 157; and Perrin, *History*, 754.

28. Grismer, *Akron and Summit County*, 211–12; and untitled typescript, folder 24, box NA-1, BFG Col. Four pledged $1,000 apiece, one $600, and the rest $500 each.

29. Carl Abbott, *Boosters and Businessmen: Popular Economic Thought and Urban Growth in the Antebellum Middle West* (Westport, Conn.: Greenwood Press, 1981).

30. "Articles of Co-Partnership, December 31, 1870." See also "Limited or Special Partnership Certificate, December 31, 1870."

31. *Akron Daily Beacon*, 17 March 1871.

32. *Akron City Times*, 3 May 1871.

33. *Akron Beacon Journal*, 25 November 1872; and B.F. Goodrich Company, "Rubber in Industry: A Story of the Development, Manufacture, and Uses of Rubber Belting, Hose, Molded Goods, Packings, Floor Coverings, Miscellaneous Rubber Articles, and Rubber Insulated Wire," pamphlet, 1918, 44.

34. *Akron City Times*, 3 May 1871.

35. Ibid.

36. R.G. Dun, Ohio vol. 180, p. 394, R.G. Dun & Co. Collection, Baker Library, Harvard University.

37. GNP per capita was $223 in 1869–73, $254 in 1872–76, and $327 in 1877–81. These figures are in 1929 prices.

38. *A Compendium of the Tenth Census (June 1, 1880)* (Washington, D.C.: Government Printing Office, 1888), part 2, 940–41.

39. R.G. Dun, Ohio vol. 180, p. 457, R.G. Dun & Co. Collection.

40. "Agreement, September, 1874," no folder, box M-1, BFG Col.

41. R.G. Dun, Ohio vol. 180, p. 457, R.G. Dun & Co. Collection.

42. *A Centennial History*, 95.

43. "Agreement Made This First Day of April 1875 by and between the Firm of B.F. Goodrich & Co. of Akron, Ohio and Geo. T. Perkins of Akron, Ohio." In return, Perkins received an annual salary of $2,000 and a large say in the management of the firm.

44. R.G. Dun, Ohio vol. 180, p. 457, R.G. Dun & Co. Collection.

45. R.G. Dun, Ohio vol. 180, p. 520, R.G. Dun & Co. Collection.

46. B.F. Goodrich, "Ledger D," oversize ledger book, BFG Col.

47. Ibid.; "Sales Data, 1875–1880"; and R.G. Dun, Ohio vol. 180, p. 520, R.G. Dun & Co. Collection.

48. R.G. Dun, Ohio vol. 180, p. 520, R.G. Dun & Co. Collection.

49. Ibid., 613.

50. "Agreement between George Crouse and B.F. Goodrich & Co., September 4, 1878."

51. "Articles of Incorporation of the B.F. Goodrich Company, May 10, 1880." The percentage of shares held by the various stockholders thus differed some from what was specified in the 1878 agreement, with Crouse and Perkins combined owning 48 percent and Goodrich 40 percent of the shares.

52. "Directors Meeting," 23 February 1882.

53. R.G. Dun, Ohio vol. 180, p. 682, R.G. Dun & Co. Collection.
54. "Directors Meeting," 1 January 1881; and "Settlement of Differences between B.F. Goodrich, A. Work, G. W. Crouse and G. T. Perkins with B. T. Morgan and H. F. Wheeler, December 31, 1880."
55. "By-Laws of the B.F. Goodrich Company, May 12, 1880."
56. "Directors Meetings," 19 January 1881, 19 January 1882, 17 January 1883, 16 January 1884, 21 January 1885, 13 January 1886, 12 June 1886, 13 October 1886, 12 January 1887, 9 November 1887, and 14 January 1888.
57. Akron Beacon Journal, 31 October 1881; Doyle, Centennial History of Summit County, 419; Grismer, Akron and Summit County, 715–16; and Perrin, History of Summit County, 801.
58. Goodrich, "Reminiscences," 2.
59. Leavitt, "History and Statistics," 9.
60. "Directors Meetings," 13 April and 12 October 1881; Akron Beacon Journal, 5 March 1881.
61. "Directors Meetings," 9 July 1884 and 8 July 1885.
62. Doyle, Centennial History, 815–16; Goodrich, "Reminiscences," 8; and Grismer, Akron and Summit County, 715.
63. "Directors Meetings," 1 January 1882 and 11 July 1888; Leavitt, "History and Statistics," 54.
64. "Directors Meetings," 11 January 1882 and 9 January 1884.
65. R.G. Dun, Ohio vol. 180, p. 682, R.G. Dun & Co. Collection.
66. Centennial History of Akron, chap. 22; and Lane, Fifty Years, 532.
67. Leading Manufacturers and Merchants of the City of Cleveland and Environs (New York: International Publishing Company, 1886), 208.
68. Benjamin F. Goodrich, "Specification Forming Part of Letters Patent No. 270,303 dated January 9, 1883," folder 19, box F-1, BFG Col.
69. "Directors Meetings," 11 January 1882, 21 January and 8 July 1885, 12 January 1887, and 2 April 1888.
70. Goodrich, "Reminiscences," 2; and Leavitt, "History and Statistics," 47.
71. "Goodrich Epistles, 1885–88," no folder, box BE-1, BFG Col.
72. R.G. Dun, Ohio vol. 180, p. 793, R.G. Dun & Co. Collection.
73. Compendium of the Eleventh Census: 1890 (Washington, D.C.: Government Printing Office, 1897), vol. 3, 682.
74. B.F. Goodrich Company, "Raw Rubber Invoice Ledger, 1877–1898," oversize volume, BFG Col. The prices are for the Para fine grade.
75. As quoted in Glenn D. Babcock, History of the United States Rubber Company, Indiana Business Report Number 39 (Bloomington: Indiana University, 1966), 24. It is unclear precisely what Goodrich may have had in mind. Perhaps he saw the combination as a way of cashing out of the enterprise he had worked so hard to build. By this time his health was beginning to fail.
76. "Directors Meeting," 10 January 1883.
77. Ibid., 11 April 1883.
78. India Rubber World 3 (15 February 1891): 134; 4 (15 May 1891): n.p.; 6 (15 May 1892): 244; and unsigned letter to Dr. Benjamin Goodrich, n.d. (probably 1886), folder 35, box F-1, BFG Col.
79. Kittieger, "Reminiscences," 4.
80. Goodrich, "Reminiscences," 14–15.
81. "Directors Meetings," 11 January, 11 July, and 13 August 1888.

82. *Akron Beacon Journal*, 11 August 1888.
83. "Last Conference between Dr. B. F. Goodrich, Mr. Corson, Mr. Mason and Mr. Perkins, July 11, 1888," folder 28, box NA-1, BFG Col. See also *Akron Beacon Journal*, 11 August 1888; "Certificate of Death, Benjamin F. Goodrich," folder 28, box NA-1, BFG Col.; and "Directors Meeting," 11 July 1888.
84. *Akron Beacon Journal*, 31 August 1927; Doyle, *History of Summit County*, 818; Goodrich, "Reminiscences," 6–7; Grismer, *Akron and Summit County*, 716; and *New York Times*, 31 August 1927.
85. Leavitt, "History and Statistics," 40. As early as 1900, the editor of the *India Rubber World* was calling Goodrich's laboratory "the finest laboratory now underway or completed" by any rubber company. See *India Rubber World* 22 (1 April 1900): 198.
86. Leonard Reich, *The Making of American Industrial Research: Science and Business at GE and Bell, 1876–1926* (Cambridge: Cambridge University Press, 1985).
87. H. W. Maxon, "Research and Rubber," typescript manuscript, chap. 6, n.d., BFG Col.
88. "Board of Control Minutes," 21 April 1902. One was hired in 1902 at an annual salary of $2,500.
89. "B.F. Goodrich Chemical Company History," typescript, n.p.
90. Goodrich, "Reminiscences," 11. Benjamin Goodrich's notebooks containing the compounding formulas in code are in the vault at Goodrich's research facility in Brecksville, Ohio.
91. Chester F. Conner, "Remarks on Retirement," August 1950, box C-2, BFG Col.
92. "Directors Meeting," 12 January 1898; "Rubber in Industry," 97.
93. *India Rubber World* 18 (August 1, 1898): 306; on the development of the golf ball, see Goodrich, "Reminiscences," 13–14.
94. B.F. Goodrich, "For Earth, Sea, and Sky: A Story of the Development, Manufacture, and Uses, of Rubber Footwear and Rubberized Fabrics," pamphlet, 1920, 11.
95. "Directors Meetings," 11 January 1905 and 1 January 1907; and "Rubber Footwear," 12.
96. Charles Hoffman, "The Depression of the Nineties," *Journal of Economic History* 16 (June 1956): 137–64.
97. *India Rubber World* 15 (January 10, 1897): n.p.
98. Eric Thompson, *The History of the Pneumatic Tyre* (Lavenham, England: Eastland Press, 1981).
99. *Akron Beacon Journal*, 30 December 1893.
100. Ibid.; *India Rubber World* 14 (10 April 1896): 209; 14 (10 May 1896): 249; 14 (10 August 1896): 353; and 15 (February 1897): 130.
101. *India Rubber World* 18 (10 February 1898): 141.
102. "Directors Meetings," 14 July 1897 and 26 September 1898; and *India Rubber World* 18 (November 1898): 52.
103. *India Rubber World* 15 (10 October 1896): 18; 16 (10 April 1897): 174; 17 (10 October 1897): 2, 19; and 17 (10 December 1897), 63–64.
104. "Directors Meetings," 10 October 1888, 10 April, 10 July, and 9 October 1889.
105. *Akron Beacon Journal*, 11 May 1895; "Directors Meetings," 11 January, 29 March, and 12 July 1893, 1 January and 10 July 1895; and *India Rubber World* 11 (10 April 1895): 7.
106. "Directors Meeting," 1 May 1899.
107. *India Rubber World* 18 (1 September 1898), 347.

108. French, *U.S. Tire Industry*, 10–14.
109. "The B.F. Goodrich Company Chronological Highlights," typescript, p. 2, folder 1, box NA-1, BFG Col.; Richard Wager, *Golden Wheels* (Cleveland: John T. Zubal, Inc., in cooperation with the Western Reserve Historical Society, 1986), 5; and Alexander Winton, "Get a Horse," *Saturday Evening Post*, 8 February 1930, 39.
110. French, *U.S. Tire Industry*, 15–16.
111. Leavitt, "History and Statistics," 37.
112. *India Rubber World* 19 (1 January 1899), 89.
113. Babcock, *United States Rubber*, chaps. 2–4.
114. Maurice O'Reilly, *The Goodyear Story* (Kent, Ohio: Kent State University Press, 1984), 13, 14, 21; and French, *U.S. Tire Industry*, 10, 16. See also Hugh Allen, *The House of Goodyear* (Cleveland: Corday & Gross, 1949), book 1.
115. Alfred Lief, *The Firestone Story* (New York: McGraw-Hill, 1951), chaps. 1–3; and French, *U.S. Tire Industry*, chap. 2.
116. Babcock, *United States Rubber*, 117; and French, *U.S. Tire Industry*, 17.
117. *India Rubber World* 21 (1 December 1899): xxv, 65; 21 (1 January 1900): 105; 21 (1 February 1900): xxv, 137; 21 (1 March 1900): xxv, 166; 22 (1 April 1900): xxxi, 188; 23 (1 October 1900): 4; 23 (1 December 1900): 94; 23 (1 March 1901): 189; 24 (1 April 1901): 207; and 25 (1 January 1902): 109.
118. French, *U.S. Tire Industry*, 19; Lief, *Firestone Story*, 25–26.
119. Leavitt, "History and Statistics," 47–48.
120. *India Rubber World* 14 (10 September 1896): 379; 15 (February 1897): 13.
121. W. W. Leigh, "The Wholesaling of Automobile Tires," *Journal of Marketing* (October 1936): 91.
122. "Directors Meetings," 10 June 1893, 13 January 1897, 12 January and 29 June 1898.
123. Leavitt, "History and Statistics," 48–49.
124. "Directors Meeting," 5 February 1900.
125. *India Rubber World* 24 (1 July 1901): 308.
126. Ibid., 17 (10 December 1897): 87; 18 (1 April 1898): 206; 20 (1 July 1899): 283; 21 (1 February 1900): 125; and 24 (1 June 1901): 277.
127. Ibid., 6 (15 November 1892), 59.
128. Ibid., 14 (10 May 1896): 250; 14 (10 June 1896): n.p.; and "Directors Meeting," 12 January 1898.
129. B. G. Work, "Report on European Trip, 1899," folder 41, box F-1, BFG Col. The company did expand its overseas marketing some in the early 1900s. In the summer of 1901, for example, B.F. Goodrich was the only rubber manufacturer to display its goods at the Chemist's Exhibition held in London's Covent Garden. See *India Rubber World* 25 (1 October 1901): 16.
130. Derived from Leavitt, "History and Statistics."
131. Grismer, *Akron and Summit County*, 216; see also *Akron Beacon Journal*, industrial supplement, 3 December 1892.
132. Knepper, *City at the Summit*, chap. 3.
133. Bureau of the Census, *Bulletin 58: Census of Manufactures, 1905, Ohio* (Washington, D.C.: Government Printing Office, 1906), 6–7, 42–44.
134. B.F. Goodrich's capitalization was as follows: $100,000 in 1881, $200,000 in 1882, $500,000 in 1889, $750,000 in 1890, $1 million in early 1895, $1.5 million in late 1895, $2 million in 1896, $3 million in 1899, $5 million in 1903, and $10 million in 1906.

135. "Directors Meeting," 19 June 1899.
136. Ibid., 10 January 1907.
137. F. W. Taussig and W. S. Barker, "American Corporations and Their Executives: A Statistical Inquiry," *Quarterly Journal of Economics* 40 (November 1925): 19.
138. "Directors Meeting," 12 October 1881.
139. Kittieger, "Reminiscences," 1–2.
140. Goodrich, "Reminiscences," 10.
141. *Akron Beacon Journal*, 2 January 1878.
142. Kittieger, "Reminiscences," 2.
143. *India Rubber World* 19 (1 February 1899), 133.
144. *Akron Beacon Journal*, 5 November 1896; and *Akron News*, undated newspaper clipping in the possession of Patterson.
145. *Akron Beacon Journal*, 16 June 1891, 20 April 1892, and 23 July 1895.
146. "Directors Meeting," 29 March 1894; and "Stockholders Meetings," 9 January 1895, and 9 January 1901.
147. Charles Traxler, "Reminiscences and Map of B.F. Goodrich, 1882," no folder, box F-1, BFG Col.
148. Leavitt, "History and Statistics," 21.
149. Ibid.
150. *India Rubber World* 26 (1 September 1902): 402.
151. Harold S. Roberts, *The Rubber Workers: Labor Organization and Collective Bargaining in the Rubber Industry* (New York: Harper and Brothers, 1944), 26–28.
152. Bureau of the Census, *Census of Manufactures, 1914* (Washington, D.C.: Government Printing Office, 1919), vol. 2, 793.
153. *Akron Beacon Journal*, 14 August 1888, and 18 January 1896.

CHAPTER 2

1. John B. Rae, *The American Automobile Industry* (Boston: Twayne Publishers, 1984), 180.
2. Tires and tubes composed 48 percent; boots and shoes, 17 percent; hose, 6 percent; belting, 3 percent; druggists' goods, 3 percent; and all other rubber products, 13 percent. Derived from U.S. Bureau of the Census, "Abstract of the Census of Manufactures, 1914," Table 168 (Washington, D.C.: Government Printing Office, 1917), 257; and U.S. Bureau of the Census, *Historical Statistics of the United States, Colonial Times to 1957* (Washington D.C.: Government Printing Office, 1960), series P, 250–306.
3. B. G. Work to executive committee members, 18 March 1915, in "Executive Committee Meeting," 18 March 1915.
4. "Directors Meeting," 13 January 1904, reprints the letter.
5. "Directors Meeting," 15 July 1908.
6. Ibid., 21 October 1908, 20 January 1909; *India Rubber Review* 9 (15 March 1909): 102; and 9 (15 November 1909): 487–88.
7. *Akron Beacon Journal*, 20 July, 24 August, 26 October, and 15 December 1910; B.F. Goodrich Company, "Proceedings for the Increase of the Capital Stock, the Creation of Preferred Stock, and the Disposition Thereof," no folder, box M-1, BFG Col.; "Directors Meeting," 19 October 1910.
8. Howard and Ralph Wolf, *Rubber: A Story of Glory and Greed* (New York: Covici, Friede Publishers, 1936), 427–28. The Wolfs covered the rubber industry as writers for the *Akron Beacon Journal*.

9. *Akron Beacon Journal*, 19 August and 27 August 1914, 31 August 1927; *India Rubber World* 51 (1 October 1914): 26; and 53 (1 December 1915): 142; *New York Times*, 31 August 1927.
10. "Executive Committee Meeting," 3 March 1919.
11. "Directors Meeting," 23 April 1913.
12. "Executive Committee Meeting," 11 December 1920.
13. "Directors Meeting," 27 March 1912; and "Agreement between the B.F. Goodrich Company and Bertram G. Work, Frank H. Mason, Charles B. Raymond, and Goldman, Sachs & Co., Lehman Brothers, and Kleinwort Sons & Co."
14. *Akron Beacon Journal*, 6 May 1912.
15. *India Rubber Review* 8 (15 November 1908): 507.
16. *Akron Beacon Journal*, 10 June and 3 August 1910; and "Directors Meeting," 21 July and 21 October 1910, and 20 July 1911.
17. B.F. Goodrich to Messrs. Goldman, Sachs & Co.; Messrs. Lehman Brothers; and Messrs. Kleinwort Sons & Co., 11 May 1912.
18. *Akron Beacon Journal*, 5 December 1910; and *India Rubber Review* 11 (15 December 1911): 653.
19. Bertram Work to Stockholders of B.F. Goodrich, 1908, in "Directors Meeting," 1908 record book.
20. *Akron Beacon Journal*, 12 October and 26 October 1895; and *India Rubber World* 8 (15 September 1893): 380. Initially called Sherbondy Rubber, the new company was called Diamond Rubber from the spring of 1894.
21. William Franklin Fleming, *America's Match King: Ohio Columbus Barber, 1841–1920* (Barberton, Ohio: Barberton Historical Society, 1981), 223.
22. *Akron Beacon Journal*, 3 May 1939; and A. B. Jones, "A Saga of Interesting Years in the Rubber Industry, 1908–1918," typescript manuscript, 1–3, folder 5, box NA-1, BFG Col.
23. William C. Geer, *The Reign Of Rubber* (New York: The Century Company, 1922), 88–97. See also Wolf & Wolf, *Rubber*, 336 (the source of the quotation).
24. "A Chemical History of the B.F. Goodrich Company," typescript manuscript, 4–7. See also Geer, "Twenty-five Years of Rubber Chemistry," *Industrial and Engineering Chemistry* 17 (October 1925): 4–5; James Cooper Lawrence, *The World Struggle with Rubber, 1905–1931* (New York: Harper & Row, 1931), 8–11; and Wolf & Wolf, *Rubber*, 345–56.
25. David Goodrich, "Reminiscences," folder 48, box NA-1, BFG Col.
26. "Directors Meeting," 13 July 1904.
27. *India Rubber News* 25 (1 December 1901): 85; and 25 (1 January 1901): 124.
28. "Agreement between the Diamond Rubber Company and the B.F. Goodrich Company, May 8, 1912," in B.F. Goodrich Record Book 1.
29. Goodrich, "Reminiscences," 9.
30. "Directors Meeting," 24 February 1910.
31. Ibid., 8 May 1912.
32. "Agreement between the Diamond Rubber Company and Goldman, Sachs & Co.; Lehman Bros.; Kleinwort Sons & Co.; and F. A. Hardy on May 8, 1912," in B.F. Goodrich Record Book 7.
33. *India Rubber World* 51 (1 March 1915), 339.
34. B. G. Work to Goldman, Sachs & Co., Lehman Bros., and Kleinwort Sons & Co., 10 June 1912, in B.F. Goodrich Record Book 7.

35. "Agreement . . . May 8, 1912."
36. Ibid.
37. Chester F. Conner, "Remarks on Retirement," August 1950, box C-2, BFG Col.
38. Frank Seiberling to J. C. McFadyean, 19 March 1912, in Goodrich folder, box 8, Frank Seiberling Collection, Ohio Historical Society.
39. *Akron Beacon Journal*, 10 February 1913; and *New York Times*, 15 February 1914.
40. "Executive Committee Meeting," 16 September 1912; *India Rubber World* 47 (1 January 1913): 200.
41. "Annual Reports," 1913 and 1914.
42. "Executive Committee Meeting," 13 March 1913.
43. "Annual Report," 1917; and "Executive Committee Meeting," 14 March 1917.
44. *India Rubber World* 52 (1 May 1915): 459; and 52 (1 July 1915): 551.
45. *Akron Beacon Journal*, 2 August 1919; *India Rubber Review* 21 (15 May 1921): 414; and *India Rubber World* 52 (1 June 1915): 505; 52 (1 September 1915): 669; and 53 (1 October 1915): 27.
46. *Akron Beacon Journal*, 13 February and 19 February 1915; and "Annual Reports," 1914 and 1915. Goodrich became the single largest taxpayer in Ohio in 1915.
47. *Akron Beacon Journal*, 23 June and 30 October 1915; and *India Rubber World* 52 (1 July 1915): 562–63.
48. *Akron Beacon Journal*, 28 April 1916.
49. "Annual Report," 1916.
50. *India Rubber World* 50 (1 July 1914): 555; 51 (1 January 1915): 215, 217; 52 (1 April 1915): 383; 53 (1 October 1915): 15–16; and 53 (1 March 1916): 287–88.
51. Ibid., 47 (1 October 1920): 60; 60 (1 August 1919): 637; "Lumina Aeroplane Cloth," pamphlet in box BC-6, BFG Col.; and "Operating Committee Meeting," 5 March 1917.
52. "Report and Accounts of the B.F. Goodrich Company for the Nine Months Ending December 31, 1912," folder 1, box A-1, BFG Col. See also *India Rubber Review* 12 (15 November 1912): 626–27; and *India Rubber World* 47 (1 November 1912): 103.
53. "Executive Committee Meeting," 10 July 1913; and *India Rubber Review* 13 (15 April 1913): 189.
54. *Akron Beacon Journal*, 15 April, 4 May, 16 July, and 14 October 1915; "Executive Committee Meetings," 24 March and 8 September 1915; and *India Rubber World* 52 (1 August 1915): 618–19.
55. For an overview see Daniel Nelson, "Mass Production in the U.S. Tire Industry," *Journal of Economic History* 47 (June 1987): 329–39.
56. "Executive Committee Meeting," 23 October 1913.
57. P. W. Barker, "Rubber Statistics, 1900–1937," U.S. Department of Commerce, Bureau of Foreign and Domestic Commerce, "Trade Promotion Series—No. 181" (Washington, D.C.: Government Printing Office, 1938), iv, 5. See also Lawrence, *World's Struggle with Rubber*, 14, 67; and Charles R. Whittlesley, *Governmental Control of Crude Rubber: The Stevenson Plan* (Princeton: Princeton University Press, 1931), 12.
58. Glenn D. Babcock, *History of United States Rubber* (Bloomington: Indiana University, Bureau of Business Research, 1966), 83–88; Alfred Lief, *The Firestone Story* (New York: McGraw-Hill, 1951), 90–91; and Maurice O'Reilly, *Goodyear Story* (Elmsford, New York: Benjamin Company, 1983), 25.
59. *Akron Beacon Journal*, 20 July 1910.

60. W. T. Easly, "Plantation Rubber in the East," typescript report, 36–37, folder 31, box F-1, BFG Col.
61. *Akron Beacon Journal*, 18 November, 19 November, and 23 November 1914; *India Rubber World* 51 (1 December 1914): 147; and 51 (1 January 1915): 181.
62. "Directors Meetings," 12 and 27 January 1915; "Executive Committee Meeting," 9 January 1915; and *India Rubber World* 51 (1 February 1915): 241, 248, 285.
63. *India Rubber World* 51 (1 March 1915): 338.
64. "Executive Committee Meetings," 27 February 1918 and 12 February 1919.
65. H. L. Trumbull, "Goodrich Plantations," two-page memo, box A-3, BFG Col.
66. For accounts of the strike see Daniel Nelson, *American Rubber Workers and Organized Labor, 1900–1941* (Princeton: Princeton University Press, 1988), chap. 2; and Kevin Michael Rosswurm, "A Strike in the Rubber City: Rubber Workers, Akron, and the IWW, 1913," masters thesis, Kent State University, 1975. For contemporary testimony, including the testimony of Goodrich workers, see "Majority and Minority Reports of the Senate Select Committee Appointed to Investigate Causes and Circumstances of the Strike of Employees of the Akron Rubber Industries," in *Ohio Senate Journal*, 1913.
67. Rosswurm, "A Strike," 72.
68. W. W. Leigh, "The Wholesaling of Automobile Tires," *Journal of Marketing* (October 1936): 91.
69. "Annual Reports," 1913–16.
70. Leigh, "Wholesaling," 92.
71. Ibid., 1912.
72. *India Rubber World* 50 (1 June 1914): 488.
73. *Akron Beacon Journal*, 2 March 1916.
74. "Executive Committee Meeting," 24 October 1916.
75. W. W. Leigh, "Some Marketing Problems of the Tire Industry," Ph.D. diss., Northwestern University, 1936, 38.
76. *India Rubber Review* 13 (15 August 1913): 457; *India Rubber World* 50 (1 August 1914): 602; and 51 (1 October 1914): 25.
77. B.F. Goodrich advertisements, 1909, in advertising file, box BA-2, BFG Col.
78. Michael French, *The U.S. Tire Industry* (Boston: Twayne Publishers, 1991), chap. 3; Lief, *Firestone Story*, 28–29; and O'Reilly, *Goodyear Story*, 23, 44.
79. The standard accounts of the expansion of American multinationals are Mira Wilkins, *The Emergence of Multinational Enterprise: American Business Abroad from the Colonial Era to 1914* (Cambridge: Harvard University Press, 1970); and Wilkins, *The Maturing of Multinational Enterprise: American Business Abroad from 1914 to 1970* (Cambridge: Harvard University Press, 1974).
80. Babcock, *United States Rubber*, 91–93; O'Reilly, *Goodyear Story*, 25, 27; and Wilkins, *Maturing*, 75.
81. "Annual Reports," 1913, 1918, and 1927.
82. *India Rubber World* 60 (1 May 1919): 445.
83. Leigh, "Some Marketing Problems," iii.
84. With a less well developed foreign sales network than Goodrich possessed, U.S. Rubber made 7 percent of its sales abroad in 1917. See Babcock, *United States Rubber*, 91.
85. *India Rubber Review* 8 (15 February 1908): 82.
86. *Akron Beacon Journal*, 26 December 1910; "Directors Meetings," 20 July 1910 and 17 January 1912; *India Rubber Review* 11 (15 January 1911): 17; and 11 (15 April 1911): 194.

87. "Annual Report," 1912; "Directors Meetings," 12 March and 27 May 1913; "Executive Committee Meeting," 21 February 1913; *India Rubber World* 47 (1 October 1912): 39–40; and 48 (1 June 1913): 480.
88. "Directors Meeting," 28 July 1914.
89. *India Rubber World* 47 (1 October 1912): 39; 48 (1 October 1913): 16; and "Operating Committee Meeting," 19 February 1917.
90. "Annual Report," 1915.
91. "Operating Committee Meeting," 19 March 1917.
92. "Contract between the B.F. Goodrich Company and the Bogatyr Company, March 8, 1917," in the private possession of Anselm Talalay; and interview by the authors with Anselm Talalay, 15 January 1993.
93. On Goodyear-Goodrich relations see the Goodrich file, box 8, Frank Seiberling Collection, Ohio Historical Society.
94. *India Rubber World* 51 (1 December 1914): 173; 51 (1 January 1915): 203; 51 (1 March 1915): 318; 52 (1 April 1915): 396; 52 (1 May 1915): 455; 52 (1 August 1915): 611; 53 (1 October 1915): 29; 53 (1 November 1915): 77, 53 (1 December 1915): 137; and 53 (1 February 1916): 252.
95. Ibid., 52 (1 April 1915): 393.
96. While Goodrich increased its total assets 18 percent between 1913 and 1916, Goodyear boosted its assets 158 percent and U.S. Rubber raised its assets 20 percent (comparable figures are not available for Firestone). During the same years, Goodrich's sales rose 43 percent, but those of Goodyear increased 93 percent, and those of Firestone soared 175 percent. U.S. Rubber's sales rose 38 percent. Goodrich fared better in raising its profits, in large part because the company began from a low base. In the three years following 1913, Goodrich's net profits increased 269 percent, Goodyear's rose 250 percent, Firestone's went up 212 percent, and U.S. Rubber's increased 39 percent. Derived from the annual reports of the companies.
97. French, *U.S. Tire Industry*, 38; Lief, *Firestone Story*, 53; Nelson, *American Rubber Workers*, 47; and O'Reilly, *Goodyear Story*, chaps. 3 and 4.
98. "Operating Committee Meeting," 6 November 1916.
99. "Annual Reports," 1914–16.
100. Goodyear, "Annual Reports," 1914–16; and Lief, *Firestone Story*, 416. Comparable dividend figures for Goodyear are not available.
101. French, *U.S. Tire Industry*, 25–27; and Wolf and Wolf, *Rubber*, 430–31.
102. Babcock, *United States Rubber*, 134–35; Lief, *Firestone Story*, 48–49, 113; and O'Reilly, *Goodyear Story*, 26.
103. *India Rubber Review* 22 (October 1922): 27–29, 58; 24 (October 1924): 116; and *India Rubber World* 58 (April 1918): 425.
104. "B.F. Goodrich Chemical Company History," typescript, chap. 1; *India Rubber Review* 11 (15 July 1911): 365; and H. W. Maxon, "Research and Rubber," typescript manuscript, 27, BFG Col.
105. "Chemical History," chap. 1; "Executive Committee Meeting," 12 January 1914; and Arthur Marks, "Laboratories," typescript, box H-4, BFG Col.
106. "Laboratory Notebooks of F. H. Martin, 1915;" folders 2–10, box H-2, BFG Col.; and "Laboratory Notebooks of J. Young, 1912–15," folder 9, box H-2, BFG Col.
107. R. Y. Lochhead, "BFGoodrich, Then and Now," typescript; "The B.F. Goodrich Company Chronological Highlights," typescript; and Geer, *Reign of Rubber*, 46, 59–61.
108. "Annual Report of the Work Carried on in the Research Laboratories of the B.F.

Goodrich Company during the Year 1918," folder 1, box H-8, BFG Col.; "Chemical History," chap. 1; and "Plant 3," typescript.

109. "Executive Committee Meetings," 2 April, 17 April, and 8 July 1918; and "Operating Committee Meetings," 8 February and 12 March 1917.

110. *Akron Beacon Journal*, 6 March and 12 March 1917.

111. *Akron Beacon Journal*, 6 March 1917; and "Industry File," box 22, Federal Writers Pro-ject, Works Project Administration (WPA) Collection, Ohio Historical Society.

112. "Executive Committee Meeting," 25 September 1918; and "Industry File."

113. "Executive Committee Meeting," 3 December 1918.

114. French, *U.S. Tire Industry*, 37; and O'Reilly, *Goodyear Story*, 43.

115. Geer, *Reign of Rubber*, chap. 19.

116. "Executive Committee Meetings," 13 March and 25 September 1918; and *India Rubber World* 57 (1 December 1917): 161; 57 (1 February 1918): 296–97; 57 (1 March 1918): 360; 58 (1 May 1918): 478; 58 (1 June 1918): 546; 58 (1 July 1918): 609; 58 (1 September 1918): 730; and 59 (1 November 1918): 67, 102.

117. Rae, *American Automobile Industry*, 180. See also *India Rubber World* 57 (1 December 1917): 134; and 58 (1 June 1918): 516.

118. French, *U.S. Tire Industry*, 37.

119. *India Rubber Review* 17 (15 September 1917): 498; *India Rubber World* 57 (1 October 1917): 43; 57 (1 March 1918): 343; and "Operating Committee Meetings," 19 February and 28 February 1917.

120. Leigh, "Wholesaling," 92.

121. "Annual Reports," 1916 and 1918.

122. "Executive Committee Meeting," 2 October 1918; and "Operating Committee Meeting," 1 January 1917.

123. *Akron Beacon Journal*, 17 January and 18 October 1917; and "Operating Committee Meeting," 12 March 1917.

124. "Executive Committee Meeting," 3 April 1918.

125. Ibid., 24 January and 17 August 1917, and 10 April 1918; "Operating Committee Meeting," 24 January 1917.

126. "Executive Committee Meeting," 24 January 1917.

127. Babcock, *United States Rubber*, 90; and O'Reilly, *Goodyear Story*, 21.

128. "Operating Committee Meeting," 29 November 1916.

129. Ibid.

130. Ibid., 21 November 1916.

131. Ibid.

132. Ibid., 29 November 1916.

133. On the development of welfare capitalism in America, see Stuart D. Brandes, *American Welfare Capitalism, 1880–1940* (Chicago: University of Chicago Press, 1970). Lizabeth Cohen, *Making a New Deal: Industrial Workers in Chicago, 1919–1939* (Cambridge: Cambridge University Press, 1990), chap. 4, offers a provocative interpretation of what welfare capitalism meant to workers.

134. *Goodrich Circle*, June 1916; and "Operating Committee Meetings," 26 February and 19 March 1917.

135. "Executive Committee Meetings," 9 September and 3 October 1918.

136. Ibid., 26 February 1917.

137. *Akron Beacon Journal*, 18 October 1918.

138. "Executive Committee Meeting," 7 May 1918.

139. Ibid., 2 October 1918; and *India Rubber World* 57 (1 December 1917): 141.

140. *India Rubber Review* 25 (January 1925): 5–6.
141. Ibid., 17 (15 September 1917): 494; 17 (15 October 1917): 560; and 17 (15 December 1917): 674; and *India Rubber World* 55 (1 February 1917): 256; 57 (1 October 1917): 32; 57 (1 November 1917): 73; 57 (1 January 1918): 224; 57 (1 February 1918): 271, 278–79; and 57 (1 March 1918): 355.
142. Goodrich charged a 10 percent profit on all goods carrying a full overhead (such as taxes and selling expenses). For products from which the overhead had been eliminated Goodrich charged a 12½ percent profit. See "Executive Committee Meetings," 26 February, 28 May, and 25 September 1918.
143. Box H-2, BFG Col., contains a large, detailed map of Goodrich's production complex.
144. Between 1916 and 1919 Goodyear's assets soared 144 percent, and Firestone's rose 109 percent. Goodrich's assets increased only 51 percent, while U.S. Rubber's rose 44 percent. During the same years, Goodyear increased its sales 164 percent, and Firestone raised its sales 107 percent. Goodrich boosted its sales a lesser 99 percent, while U.S. Rubber increased its sales 78 percent. Similarly, while Goodyear's net earnings jumped 233 percent, Goodrich's increased 80 percent. U.S. Rubber's increased 70 percent, and Firestone's rose 55 percent. Derived from the annual reports of the companies.
145. *Akron Beacon Journal*, 27 October 1916; "Directors Meeting," 25 October 1916; "Executive Committee Meeting," 25 October 1916; and "Operating Committee Meeting," 20 November 1916. The operating committee was disbanded in the early 1920s.
146. "Directors Meetings," 1 January and 25 October 1916; and "Executive Committee Meetings," 25 October 1916, and 18 February and 2 April 1918.
147. Fred Barton, "His Figures Made Goodrich Hum," *Forbes*, 15 January 1928, 12.
148. William B. Doyle, ed., *Centennial History of Summit County, Ohio, and Representative Citizens* (Chicago: Biographical Publishing Company, 1908), 754.
149. Ibid., 904–5; and Karl Grismer, *Akron and Summit County* (Akron: Summit County Historical Society, 1952), 738–39.
150. *India Rubber World* 64 (1 April 1921): 520.
151. *India Rubber Review* 25 (January 1925): 100.
152. *India Rubber World* 58 (1 September 1918): 736; and 63 (1 February 1921): 352.
153. Derived from Goodrich's annual reports.
154. Derived from stockholder lists of 1907, 1916, and 1920.
155. *Akron Beacon News*, 17 May 1928; *India Rubber Review* 24 (February 1924): 110; *India Rubber and Tire Review* 25 (September 1925): 114; *India Rubber World* 51 (1 March 1915): 342; and *New York Times*, 9 October 1928.
156. *Akron Beacon Journal*, 7 February 1917.

CHAPTER 3

1. Between 1921 and 1927 the number of rubber manufacturers in the United States rose from 477 to 516, the number of workers employed in the industry increased from 103,000 to 142,000, and the value of the rubber goods they produced climbed from $705 million to $1.26 billion. See U.S. Department of Commerce, *Biennial Census of Manufacturers 1927* (Washington, D.C.: Government Printing Office, 1930), 780.
2. In 1921, 178 companies employing 56,000 workers turned out 31 million tires.

By 1927 the number of companies had dropped to 109. This smaller number of firms employed 78,000 workers to make 62 million tires.

3. The average return on capital in making rubber products between 1924 and 1930 came to only 2.3 percent, well below the 9.2 percent average return for all of American industry. United States National Recovery Administration, Division of Economic Research and Planning, "Material Bearing on the Rubber Tire Industry," 5–8, in Record Group 9, National Archives.

4. Michael French, *The U.S. Tire Industry* (Boston: Twayne Publishers, 1991), 37–39. For a contemporary assessment of the problems, see *India Rubber Review* 22 (January 1922): 35.

5. Alfred Lief, *The Firestone Story* (New York: McGraw-Hill, 1951), chap. 7; and Maurice O'Reilly, *The Goodyear Story* (Elmsford, New York: Benjamin Company), chap. 4.

6. "Executive Committee Meetings," 6 June, 13 July, 9 August, 14 September, 3 November, 15 November, and 30 December 1920, and 5 January, 25 January, 6 April, 29 April, 24 May, and 21 December 1921. B.F. Goodrich led the industry in cutting tire prices; see *India Rubber Review* 21 (June 1921), 515–17.

7. "Executive Committee Meetings," 6 August 1919 and 26 August 1920.

8. Ibid., 3 November and 6 November 1921, and 4 January 1922.

9. *Akron Beacon Journal*, 8 January, 19 April, and 24 June 1920; *India Rubber World* 60 (1 September 1919): 715; and 61 (1 February 1920): 314.

10. "Directors Meeting," 19 January 1921; and "Executive Committee Meeting," 23 May 1921.

11. "Executive Committee Meetings," 30 June 1920 and 17 September 1921.

12. *Akron Beacon Journal*, 16 April 1919.

13. "Executive Committee Meetings," 20 May and 7 August 1919; *India Rubber World* 61 (1 November 1919): 108.

14. *J. Walter Thompson News*, 14 May 1921, in J. Walter Thompson Col., box 1, folder 9, Duke University.

15. "Executive Committee Meeting," 25 January 1921.

16. *Akron Beacon Journal*, 18 February 1922; *India Rubber Review* 22 (February 1922): 58; and 22 (March 1922): 50.

17. Between 1919 and 1922 Goodrich's assets dropped by 47 percent, while Firestone's fell 16 percent, U.S. Rubber's decreased 1 percent, and Goodyear's rose 41 percent. Goodrich's sales dropped 33 percent, U.S. Rubber's declined by 25 percent, Goodyear's decreased 27 percent, and Firestone's fell 29 percent. Part of the drop in Goodrich's assets can be accounted for by the company's decision in 1920 to stop carrying $58 million of goodwill on its books as assets. Derived from the annual reports of the companies.

18. *Akron Beacon Journal*, 7 February and 16 March 1920; "Directors Meeting," 7 February 1920; and Howard and Ralph Wolf, *Rubber: A Story of Glory and Greed* (New York: Covici, Friede Publishers, 1936), 446.

19. French, *U.S. Tire Industry*, 38–39.

20. Leigh, "Some Marketing Problems," 17.

21. *India Rubber World* 64 (1 June 1921): 683.

22. *India Rubber Review* 23 (September 1923): 1105.

23. "Annual Report," 1922.

24. *India Rubber Review* 24 (February 1924): 108.

25. *Akron Beacon Journal*, 5 July 1922; "Annual Report," 1924; "Directors Meeting,"

3 July 1922; and "Executive Committee Meeting," 10 July 1923; *India Rubber Review* 25 (March 1925): 86.

26. *India Rubber Review* 25 (February 1925): 86. For another favorable assessment of Goodrich's improvements, see *Financial World* 54 (30 August 1924): 269.

27. Moody's Investors Service, *Moody's Investment Letter*, 20 May 1926, 164.

28. Harris, Winthrop & Co., "A Study of the B.F. Goodrich Company, 1928," pamphlet, 13–14, box M-1, BFG Col.

29. "Annual Report," 1927.

30. "Executive Committee Meeting," 8 October 1923.

31. Ibid., 27 August 1924.

32. *India Rubber Review* 24 (June 1924): 17, 120.

33. "Executive Committee Meetings," 20 June 1922, 17 July 1923, and 12 April and 10 June 1924.

34. "The Brunswick Tire Corporation," a one-paragraph historical sketch in file 25, box F-1, BFG Col.; and *India Rubber Review* 23 (December 1923): 1514.

35. "Executive Committee Meeting," 31 October 1922.

36. Leigh, "Some Marketing Problems," 255–57.

37. *Akron Beacon Journal*, 5 November 1925; "Executive Committee Meetings," 17 January and 31 October 1922, 5 January, 3 April, and 19 November 1923, 30 September 1924, and 23 October 1925; and *India Rubber Review* 23 (January 1923): 995; 25 (January 1925): 58; and 25 (February 1925): 37.

38. Frank Robert Chalk, "The United States and the International Struggle for Rubber, 1914–1941," Ph.D. diss., University of Wisconsin, 1970, chap. 3.

39. Hugh Allen, *The House of Goodyear* (Cleveland: Corday & Gross Company, 1949), 124–25.

40. Chalk, "Struggle for Rubber," chaps. 5 and 6.

41. Ibid., 61.

42. *India Rubber Review* 23 (April 1923): 487.

43. Harris, Winthrop & Company, "A Study of the B.F. Goodrich Company, June 30, 1928," 6.

44. Randolph Resor, "Rubber in Brazil: Dominance and Collapse, 1876–1945," *Business History Review* 51 (Autumn 1977): 341–66.

45. "Executive Committee Meetings," 12 October and 16 December 1920, and 17 July 1923.

46. Ibid., 23 October 1916.

47. Ibid., 8 April, 17 May, 6 June, and 13 July 1920, and 15 May 1923.

48. Ibid., 23 February 1926; and "Directors Meeting," 27 January 1926.

49. Chalk, "Struggle for Rubber," chap. 11.

50. "Executive Committee Meetings," 2 January and 10 June 1919, and 26 February 1925; and "Operating Committee Meeting," 5 March 1917.

51. "Executive Committee Meeting," 2 January 1920.

52. Glenn D. Babcock, *History of the United States Rubber Company*, Bloomington: Indiana University Press, 1966), 89.

53. Lief, *Firestone Story*, 155.

54. O'Reilly, *Goodyear Story*, 37, 41, and 76.

55. "Annual Report," 1929.

56. "Executive Committee Meetings," 17 February and 30 July 1923; Daniel Nelson, *American Rubber Workers and Organized Labor, 1900–1941* (Princeton: Princeton University Press, 1988), 96–98.

57. *Goodrich Circle*, 6 March 1920.
58. Ibid., 3 April 1920; and "Executive Committee Meeting," 20 April 1920.
59. Cyrus F. Raymond to E. C. Shaw, 12 December 1916, box F-1, BFG Col.; and "Operating Committee Meetings," 11 December 1916 and 19 March 1917.
60. "Executive Committee Meeting," 26 May 1926; and Sengpiel interview. On Bedaux see Daniel Nelson, ed., *A Mental Revolution: Scientific Management since Taylor* (Columbus: Ohio State University Press, 1992), 156–74.
61. The Bedaux system is described in detail in "About Goodrich," an employee handbook published by the company in 1936. See also Sengpiel interview.
62. While Goodrich's assets increased 25 percent between 1925 and 1927, Goodyear's rose 26 percent and Firestone's soared 64 percent. U.S. Rubber's assets climbed 8 percent. Sales presented a similar picture. Goodrich's sales rose 62 percent and U.S. Rubber's increased 14 percent, but Goodyear's climbed 81 percent and Firestone's advanced an even greater 97 percent. In terms of profits, Goodrich fared better, mainly because it started from a lower point than its competitors. Goodrich's profits climbed 293 percent, Goodyear's rose 198 percent, and Firestone's increased 89 percent. The profits of U.S. Rubber fell 10 percent. Derived from the annual reports of the companies.
63. French, *U.S. Tire Industry*, 47.
64. *India Rubber Review* 24 (February 1924): 8.
65. Lief, *Firestone Story*, 139, 142.
66. "Executive Committee Meetings," 25 February and 16 October 1925; and *India Rubber Review* 23 (July 1923): 928.
67. French, *U.S. Tire Industry*, 50.
68. Fred B. Barton, "His Figures Made Goodrich Hum," *Forbes*, 15 January 1928, 12.
69. Philip J. Kelly, *The Making of a Salesman* (New York: Abelard-Schuman, 1965), 91.
70. Wolf and Wolf, *Rubber*, 461.
71. *Akron Beacon Journal*, 6 January, 24 March, and 21 September 1928; *India Rubber and Tire Review* 27 (May 1927): 60; 27 (October 1927): 18; 28 (April 1928): 56; *Silvertown Cavalier* 8 (4 May 1937): 1–4.
72. Harry Hough to David Goodrich, 21 March 1928, in B.F. Goodrich Supplemental Record Book 5H.
73. *Akron Beacon Journal*, 27 September 1927; and *New York Times*, 18 May 1950.
74. Wolf and Wolf, *Greed*, 462.
75. *Akron Beacon Journal*, 21 September 1927.
76. Moody's, *Investment Newsletter*, 20 December 1928, 511.
77. Clarence R. Jung Jr., "Business Expectations and Plant Expansion with Special Reference to the Rubber Industry," Ph.D. diss., The Ohio State University, 1953, 134.
78. Lief, *Firestone Story*, 171–73.
79. Moody's, *Investment Newsletter*, 20 December 1928, 514.
80. "President's Reports," 23 January, 7 August, and 6 November 1929. See also Goodrich's file of the shoe advertisements.
81. French, *U.S. Tire Industry*, 54–55; and Leigh, "Some Marketing Problems," chap. 4. Sears sold automobile tires as early as 1910 but did not become a major retailer of them until the mid-1920s.
82. Roland Marchand, "Creating the Corporate Soul," an unpublished manuscript, chap. 10. The quotations are from p. 19. For contemporary accounts see *India*

Rubber and Tire Review 29 (March 1929): 46; 29 (November 1929): 144; and 29 (December 1929): 119. For biographical information on Kelly see *India Rubber and Tire Review* 28 (September 1928): 52.

83. "Minutes of J. Walter Thompson Representatives Meeting," 8 October 1929, folder 2, box 2, J. Walter Thompson Col., Duke University.

84. W. W. Leigh, "The Wholesaling of Automobile Tires," *Journal of Marketing* (October 1936): 93.

85. *India Rubber and Tire Review* 29 (December 1929): 62–63, 98, 144; "President's Report," 6 November 1929.

86. Goodyear accounted for 13 percent of the replacement tires sold in 1926, but three years later its share had risen to 18 percent. Firestone's share of the replacement market stood at 12 percent in 1926, and at 13 percent in 1929. U.S. Rubber saw its share drop from 7 percent to just 6 percent. See United States, Federal Trade Commission, Docket 2116, Exhibit 22090, Record Group 122, National Archives, Washington, D.C.; and French, *U.S. Tire Industry*, 47.

87. "Organization Declaration of the Rubber Institute, Inc.," in folder 3, box 1, series 1, J. Penfield Seiberling Collection, Ohio Historical Society.

88. L. C. Andrews to F. A. Seiberling, 13 June and 28 August 1928, folder 3, box 1, series 1, J. Penfield Seiberling Collection.

89. *India Tire and Rubber Review* 28 (May 1928): 22.

90. L. C. Andrews to the Attorney General of the United States, and L. C. Andrews to J. D. Tew, both letters dated 12 November 1928, folder 3, box 1, series 1, J. Penfield Seiberling Collection.

91. L. C. Andrews to F. A, Seiberling, 25 April 1929, in folder 3, box 1, series 1, J. Penfield Seiberling Collection.

92. James McLain, "The Theory of the Firm and Competition in the American Rubber Industry," Ph.D. diss., The Ohio State University, 1959, 192.

93. *Los Angeles Herald*, 2 May 1928. The downtown Los Angeles public library has an extensive newspaper clipping file dealing with Goodrich's Los Angeles plant. We want to thank Jane Nowak and Betty Ellison of the library for helping us locate and use that file.

94. "Annual Reports," 1928 and 1929.

95. Stephen Erie, "How the Urban West Was Won," unpublished paper presented at the annual meeting of the Organization of American Historians, April 1991, in Louisville, Kentucky.

96. Babcock, *U.S. Rubber*, 313–14; Lief, *Firestone Story*, 412; and O'Reilly, *Goodyear Story*, 45.

97. *Akron Beacon Journal*, 3 May 1928; and *Los Angeles Times*, 4 May 1928.

98. *Petroleum World* 13 (April 1928): 30.

99. *Los Angeles Times*, 4 May 1928.

100. *Akron Beacon Journal*, 13 March 1929; and "Executive Committee Meetings," 12 March and 4 October 1929.

101. Babcock, *United States Rubber*, 39; and "Hood Rubber," one-page typescript history, folder 25, box F-1, BFG Col.

102. Maxon, "Research and Rubber," 63–65.

103. *India Rubber World* 21 (November 1899): 54.

104. Hood Rubber, "Annual Report," 1918; and *India Rubber World* 64 (1 April 1921): 513. Scattered copies of Hood Rubber's annual reports are available at the Baker Library at Harvard University in Cambridge, Massachusetts.

105. *India Rubber World* 56 (1 May 1917): 470; and 61 (1 January 1920), 238.
106. Hood Rubber, "Annual Report," 1928.
107. "Agreement between Hood Rubber Company and the B.F. Goodrich Company, August 19, 1929"; *Akron Beacon Journal*, 19 August and 30 August 1929; and "Directors Meeting," 19 August 1929.
108. "Annual Report," 1929.
109. "Preliminary Report on Goodrich Heavy Footwear, June 25, 1928," microfilm reel 196, J. Walter Thompson Col., Duke University.
110. *India Rubber and Tire Review* 19 (November 1929): 138.
111. "Minutes of Discussion of B.F. Goodrich Directors," n.d.
112. *India Rubber World* 58 (1 June 1918): 261.
113. "Comparative Income Account, Miller Rubber, December 31, 1917," in the Baker Library; *India Rubber Review* 22 (March 1922): 52.
114. *India Rubber Review* 24 (June 1924): 101; and 24 (July 1924): 58.
115. Miller Rubber, "Annual Reports," 1920, 1925, and 1928, in the Baker Library.
116. "Agreement Between the B.F. Goodrich Company and the Miller Rubber Company, January 15, 1930"; *Akron Beacon Journal*, 21 January and 23 January 1930.
117. "Annual Report," 1929.
118. Ibid., 1927.
119. Babcock, *United States Rubber*, 91–93; O'Reilly, *Goodyear Story*, 25, 27.
120. "Executive Committee Meeting," 5 January 1922.
121. "Directors Meeting," 19 January 1921; and "Executive Committee Meetings," 6 February, 11 February, and 7 July 1919, 10 August 1920, 10 November 1921, 5 January 1922, 15 January, 4 April, 17 July, and 9 October 1923, and 28 October 1924.
122. W. C. Arthur, vice president, the International B.F. Goodrich Corporation, "Memo," 13 April 1923, bound volume, BFG Col.
123. "Executive Committee Meeting," 11 August 1923.
124. "Executive Committee Meeting," 16 January 1915; and *India Rubber World* 50 (1 April 1914): 384.
125. "Directors Meetings," 25 June, 25 July, and 6 November 1917; "Executive Committee Meeting," 24 July 1917; and *India Rubber World* 57 (1 November 1917): 114.
126. Yokohama Rubber Editorial Committee, *Forty Years of Yokohama Rubber* (Tokyo: Yokohama Rubber Company, 1959), chap. 1. We are indebted to Kimio Tsuji for a translation of this volume.
127. Thomas McCormick, *China Market: America's Quest for Informal Empire, 1893–1901* (Chicago: Quadrangle Books, 1967).
128. Mark Mason, *American Multinationals and Japan* (Cambridge: Harvard University Press, 1992), chap. 1.
129. "Company Contract of Yokohama Gomu Seizo Kabushiki-Kaisha."
130. "Minutes of the First General Meeting of Promoters of the Yokohama Gomu Seizo Kabushiki Kaisha," 13 October 1917, bound volume, box A-3, BFG Col.; *Forty Years*, chap. 1.
131. A. B. Jones, "Memo on Plant Administration, December 11, 1917," in bound volume, box A-3, BFG Col.
132. "General Features of the Company's Workings"; *Forty Years*, chap. 1.
133. H. E. Raymond to W. C. Geer, 19 November 1917, in bound volume, box A-3, BFG Col.

134. Raymond to Taiji Komura, 19 November 1917, in bound volume, box A-3, BFG Col.
135. *Forty Years*, chap. 2.
136. "Executive Committee Meeting," 11 July 1923; *Forty Years*, chap. 1.
137. "Executive Committee Meeting," 11 August and 2 October 1922.
138. Ibid., 21 January 1924.
139. "Executive Committee Meetings," 23 May and 12 July 1923.
140. Ibid., 11 July 1923.
141. Ibid., 4 December 1922; *Akron Beacon Journal*, 23 August 1924; "Directors Meetings," 21 April and 28 July 1920; *India Rubber Review* 21 (15 April 1921): 319; and *India Rubber World* 64 (1 May 1921): 598.
142. *India Rubber Review* 9 (15 March 1909): 105; and *India Rubber World* 52 (1 June 1915): 514.
143. "Operating Committee Meeting," 19 February 1917.
144. Ibid., 19 February 1917.
145. "Executive Committee Meeting," 11 February 1919.
146. *Akron Beacon Journal*, 2 May 1924; and "History of BTR Industries Limited," chap. 1, typescript obtained from BTR Industries in Great Britain.
147. "History of BTR Industries," 9–11.
148. "Executive Committee Meeting," 18 June 1913. See also ibid., 21 June 1912; and *India Rubber Review* 13 (15 February 1913): 72; and 13 (15 April 1913): 178–79.
149. "Directors Meeting," 30 January 1918; "Executive Committee Meeting," 28 March 1919; and "Operating Committee Meeting," 26 February 1917.
150. Maxon, "Research and Rubber," 56–58, looks at the history of Ames Holden before its relationship with Goodrich.
151. "Executive Committee Meetings," 25 May 1921, 10 October, 23 November, and 4 December 1922, and 15 January and 12 April 1923.
152. "Annual Report," 1928; "Executive Committee Meetings," 18 July and 3 December 1923, and 9 November 1925.
153. "Directors Meeting," 27 July 1921; *India Rubber Review* 21 (15 July 1921): 635; and *India Rubber World* 64 (1 July 1921): 752. The details of the work of International B.F. Goodrich may be followed in the "Minutes of the Meetings of the Executive Committee of International B.F. Goodrich," 1921–24.
154. "Annual Report," 1929; and "President's Report," 7 August 1929.
155. "President's Reports," 7 August and 6 November 1929.
156. *India Rubber and Tire Review* 29 (January 1929): 44.
157. *Akron Beacon Journal*, 2 February 1929 (*Akron Beacon Journal* clipping file at the newspaper); "Directors Meeting," 25 July 1928; and *India Rubber and Tire Review* 28 (April 1928): 64.
158. "Annual Report," 1928; "President's Reports," 23 January and 7 August 1929.
159. "President's Reports," 23 January and 7 August 1929.
160. John Crawford, "Memorandum on the visit of Messrs Caywood and Aspell of the BFGoodrich Rubber Co to Mr. Ford's office," 15 October 1936, box 85, asc. 390, Ford Motor Company Archives. Provided by Professor Mira Wilkins of the Florida International University.
161. *Akron Beacon Journal*, 15 September and 2 November 1929, in newspaper clipping file.
162. Geer, *Reign of Rubber* (New York: Century Company, 1922), 118.

163. "Executive Committee Meetings," 18 October 1919, 5 January 1922, and 3 May 1923; and *India Rubber Review* 22 (March 1922): 5; and 22 (April 1922): 50.

164. B.F. Goodrich, "Chemical Research Laboratories Report, 1927," box H-8, BFG Col.; and Waldo Semon, "Stories about Mill 3," typescript, April 1978.

165. *Akron Beacon Journal*, 9 December 1926; "American Anode," typescript, folder 25, box F-1, BFG Col.; "Anode Process," typescript, box GA-3, BFG Col.; "Directors Meetings," 27 October 1926 and 22 April 1938; and "Executive Committee Meetings," 21 March and 31 October 1938.

166. "Stories about Mill 3."

167. Silver interview.

168. "Chemical Research Laboratories Report, 1927."

169. H. E. Fritz and J. R. Hoover, "The Chemical Resistance of Rubber as an Engineering Material," *Symposium on Rubber*, American Society for Testing Materials, Philadelphia, 1932.

170. "A Man of Ideas: The Biography of Dr. Waldo Semon, Inventor of Plasticized Polyvinyl Chloride," typescript, 1991.

171. "Chemical Laboratories Report," 1927; and "Executive Committee Meeting," 28 October 1924.

172. Waldo Semon and G. Allan Stahl, "The History of Vinyl Chloride Polymers," paper presented at the annual meeting of the American Chemical Society, 26 March 1980.

173. Semon interview, 30 July 1990.

174. Ibid.

175. Goodrich, "Reminiscences," 5.

176. Between 1926 and 1930 Goodrich's margin of operating profit (the percentage of profit remaining from sales after deducting costs of expenses and depreciation) averaged 2.9 percent per year, while Goodyear's was 7.7 percent and Firestone's was 7.7 percent. U.S. Rubber's was 2.4 percent. Derived from Moody's, *Newsletter*, 6 July 1931, W-333.

CHAPTER 4

1. "History of the Code of Fair Competition for the Rubber Manufacturing Industry," 11–12, box 7598, NRA Col., Record Group 9, National Archives, Washington, D.C.; and John B. Rae, *The American Automobile Industry* (Boston: Twayne Publishers, 1984), 180.

2. "History of the Code of Fair Competition for the Rubber Manufacturing Industry," 12; and "History of the Code of Fair Competition for the Rubber Tire Manufacturing Industry," 6—both in NRA Col. Record Group 9, the National Archives.

3. Howard Wolf and Ralph Wolf, *Rubber: A Story of Glory and Greed* (New York: Covici, Friede Publishers, 1936), 460. Concentration remained the norm, as the market share of the "big four" rubber manufacturers—Goodyear, Firestone, Goodrich, and U.S. Rubber—in tire sales remained about what it had been in the late 1920s, around 70–75 percent of the nation's total. See "Sales and Financial Data," folder 53, box 8, J. Penfield Seiberling Collection, Ohio Historical Society.

4. "President's Report to Directors," 5 February 1930.

5. *India Rubber and Tire Review* 30 (May 1930): 28; 30 (June 1930): 32; and 30 (September 1930): 93.
6. "Annual Report," 1930; and "Consolidated Sales and Earnings Statement, 1929–1930."
7. "Annual Report," 1931; and "President's Report," 9 February 1932.
8. "President's Report," 12 January 1932.
9. "Consolidated Balance Sheet, 1932–33"; and "President's Reports," 12 April, 9 August, and 13 December 1932.
10. "President's Report," 6 November 1929.
11. "President's Reports," 4 February, 10 March, 10 November, and 8 December 1931.
12. Ibid., 8 March 1932.
13. "Annual Report," 1932; "Directors Meeting," 21 December 1937; and "President's Report," 13 September 1932.
14. *Akron Beacon Journal*, 12 November 1930 (in newspaper clipping file), 15 January 1931; *India Rubber and Tire Review* 31 (January 1931): 24; and "President's Reports," 9 September 1930, 13 January 1931.
15. "President's Report," 9 June 1931.
16. *Akron Beacon Journal*, 10 June and 27 June 1931; and *India Tire and Rubber Review* 31 (August 1931): 17.
17. "President's Report," 8 December 1931.
18. Ibid., 8 March, 4 May, 14 June, and 9 November 1932.
19. W. W. Leigh, "Wholesaling of Automobile Tires," *Journal of Marketing*, October 1936.
20. "President's Report," 5 February 1930.
21. Moody's Investors Service, *Newsletter*, 13 February 1930, I-63.
22. "Annual Report," 1931; and "President's Reports," 13 September 1932, 10 January and 14 February 1933.
23. Moody's, *Newsletter*, 19 January 1931, W-485. In 1919 car owners bought an average of five replacement tires per car, by 1930 only 1.65.
24. Standard & Poor's, "Investment Survey, The Rubber Industry, September 8, 1939," 1, in the J. Penfield Seiberling Collection.
25. Philip J. Kelly, *The Making of a Salesman* (New York: Abelard-Schumm, 1965), 103.
26. *Akron Beacon Journal*, 23 April and 24 April 1931; and "Minutes of the Meetings of the Rubber Manufacturers Association," 6 April and 15 September 1932, in folder 38, box 1, series 1, J. Penfield Seiberling Collection.
27. "President's Report," 14 February 1933.
28. "Dealer Investigation for B.F. Goodrich Company, June, 1930," in J. Walter Thompson Col., Duke University.
29. "Consumer Report, Goodrich Tire Investigation," in J. Walter Thompson Col., Duke University.
30. *Super-Service Tire Review* 31 (December 1931): 28–29.
31. "President's Report," 8 March 1932.
32. "B.F. Goodrich Company, Analysis of Advertising Expenditures, September, 1932," microfilm reel 45, J. Walter Thompson Col., Duke University.
33. "President's Report," 13 January 1931.
34. "President's Reports," 6 May 1931 and 9 August 1932.
35. Ibid., 11 April 1933.

36. "Directors Meeting," 8 July 1930.
37. "Sales and Financial Data."
38. Kelly, *Making of a Salesman*, 91.
39. Between 1929 and 1933 the firms reduced the number of branch houses from 418 to 340. By 1934 Firestone operated 322 wholly owned retail tire outlets and another 101 partially owned tire stores. Goodyear possessed 262 retail outlets for tires and continued to sell through Sears. U.S. Rubber owned 19 tire stores and sold as well through independent dealers, mail-order houses, and gas stations. The proportion of replacement tires sold through independent dealers continued to shrink. By 1933 dealers accounted for only 66 percent of the sales, down from 76 percent four years before. The proportion moving through mail-order houses had risen to 15 percent and the share sold through tire-company stores had increased to 11 percent. Outlets controlled by oil companies accounted for an additional 8 percent. Altogether the number of independent tire dealers halved from about 120,000 in 1927 to just 60,000 by the mid-1930s.
40. *Akron Beacon Journal*, 11 September 1930; and "President's Report," 9 September 1930.
41. "President's Reports," 13 January and 4 February 1931.
42. Ibid., 4 February and 10 March 1931; *Akron Beacon Journal*, 28 February and 4 April 1931; and "Executive Committee Meeting," 29 December 1932.
43. Babcock, *United States Rubber*, 275–78, 292–99; and Alfred Lief, *The Firestone Story* (New York: McGraw-Hill, 1951), 191, 222.
44. "President's Report," 4 May 1932.
45. Moody's, *Newsletter*, 6 July 1931, W-333.
46. Michael French, *The U.S. Tire Industry* (Boston: Twayne Publishers, 1991), 46; Lloyd G. Reynolds, "Competition in the Rubber-Tire Industry," *American Economic Review* 28 (September 1938): 460; and U.S. Bureau of the Census, *Historical Statistics of the United States, Colonial Times to 1957* (Washington, D.C.: Government Printing Office, 1960), 75, 412.
47. *Akron Beacon Journal*, 19 June and 21 June 1937.
48. B.F. Goodrich, "Statement to the Army Price Adjustment Board, Ordnance Division, 1942," in box M-1, BFG Col.
49. "Executive Committee Meeting," 17 February 1933.
50. Ibid., 20 March 1934.
51. "Press Release to the *Wall Street Journal*, February 5, 1934, in 'Consolidated Approved Code Industry File,' Retail Rubber Tire Code, Code 410," folder 2, box 4761, NRA Col., Record Group 9, National Archives.
52. "Annual Report," 1938; "Directors Meeting," 30 November 1936; "Executive Committee Meeting," 9 April 1934; and "Statement to Army Price Adjustment Board." For the mid-1930s the inventory turnover rate in company-owned stores was as follows: 2.9 times for Goodyear, 3.3 times for Firestone, 3.6 times for Goodrich, and 3.7 times for U.S. Rubber. See "Executive Committee Meeting," 11 August 1938.
53. Ellis W. Hawley, *The New Deal and the Problem of Monopoly* (Princeton: Princeton University Press, 1966).
54. "President's Report," 9 August 1932.
55. "Report to the Rubber Manufacturers Association of America in Respect to the National Industrial Recovery Act, June 23, 1933," pamphlet in box SA-1, BFG Col.

56. In additional to codes for the tire industry, the NRA also prepared codes for other aspects of rubber manufacturing. See "History of Fair Competition for the Rubber Manufacturing Industry."

57. Moody's, *Newsletter*, 21 August 1933, 531.

58. *Akron Beacon Journal*, 6 September and 20 December 1933; "Executive Committee Meetings," 2 October and 20 December 1933; and "History of the Code of Fair Competition for the Rubber Tire Manufacturing Industry." See also French, *U.S. Tire Industry*, 66–69; and Lief, *Firestone*, 198–202.

59. "History of Fair Competition for the Retail Rubber Tire and Battery Trade," box 7632, NRA Col., Record Group 9, National Archives; see also French, *U.S. Tire Industry*, 67–68.

60. B.F. Goodrich to NRA, 24 January 1934, in folder 2, box 4761, "Consolidated Approved Code Industry File," NRA Col., Record Group 9, National Archives.

61. J. Penfield Seiberling to J. A. Walsh (president of Armstrong Rubber), 19 March 1934, folder 14, box 5, series 1, J. Penfield Seiberling Collection.

62. "Petition to NRA Administration," folder 21, box 4775, "Consolidated Approved Code Industry File, Rubber Tire Code 410," NRA Col., Record Group 9, National Archives.

63. R. E. Wood to Hugh S. Johnson, 19 March 1934, file 21, box 4775, "Consolidated Approved Code, Industry File, Rubber Tire Code 410," NRA Col., Record Group 9, National Archives.

64. "Executive Committee Meeting," 25 May 1934; French, *U.S. Tire Industry*, 68–69.

65. Moody's, *Newsletter*, 25 January 1934, 951.

66. Ibid., 30 July 1934, 566.

67. Ibid., 20 June 1935, 654.

68. "United States of America before the Federal Trade Commission, in the Matter of Goodyear Tire & Rubber Company, 2 January 1936," box 2116, Docketed Case Files, 1915–43, Records of the Federal Trade Commission, Record Group 122, National Archives. See also French, *U.S. Tire Industry*, 70.

69. "Directors Meeting," 11 August 1936; "Memoranda, 1939," Legal Document Files, 1914–73, U.S. Rubber, Federal Trade Commission Records, Record Group 122, National Archives.

70. Daniel Nelson, *American Rubber Workers and Organized Labor, 1900–1941* (Princeton: Princeton University Press, 1988), especially chaps. 6–8.

71. For a look at Akron during the early years of the depression see Mary-Ann Blasio, "Akron and the Great Depression, 1929–1933," master's thesis, University of Akron, 1987.

72. *Goodrich Circle*, 13 February 1933, 2.

73. Sengpiel interview.

74. "Operating Committee Meetings," 31 August 1934 and 14 August 1936.

75. *Circle*, 13 February 1933, 2, and 1 March, 1–3.

76. Nelson, *American Rubber Workers*, 117–24.

77. Sengpiel interview.

78. Ibid.

79. *Circle*, 20 December 1933, 2; 28 February 1934, 1; and 18 September 1934, 2.

80. Ibid., 15 March 1935.

81. Irvin Sobel, "The Economic Impact of Collective Bargaining upon the Rubber Industry," Ph.D. diss., University of Chicago, 1952, 14–15.

82. Nelson, *American Rubber Workers*, 130.
83. "Operating Committee Meeting," 25 January 1935.
84. Nelson, *American Rubber Workers*, 144–48.
85. Ibid., 154–55; and "Operating Committee Meeting," 12 May 1934.
86. Nelson, *American Rubber Workers*, 156–59.
87. Ibid., 159–62.
88. "Executive Committee Meeting," 16 April 1934.
89. Nelson, *American Rubber Workers*, 183.
90. Nelson, *American Rubber Workers*, 205–6.
91. Nelson, *American Rubber Workers*, 219–20.
92. Charles A. Jeszak, "Plant Dispersion and Collective Bargaining in the Rubber Industry," Ph.D. diss., University of California, Berkeley, 1982, 47.
93. Sobel, "The Economic Impact of Collective Bargaining," 10.
94. Ibid., 14–18.
95. Sengpiel interview.
96. *Akron Beacon Journal*, 9 September 1936; "Directors Meeting," 9 June 1936; "Executive Committee Meeting," 8 June 1936; and "Operating Committee Meeting," 5 June 1936.
97. *Akron Beacon Journal*, 9 February and 9 June 1937; "Directors Meeting," 21 December 1937; and "Executive Committee Meetings," 18 December 1936, and 26 September 1938.
98. "Annual Report," 1939; *Business Week*, 6 May 1939, 17; "Executive Committee Meetings," 23 January and 14 February 1939; and "Directors Meeting," 14 February 1939.
99. Sengpiel interview.
100. *Newsweek*, 4 April 1938, 35; and "Statement to Army Price Board."
101. T. G. Graham, "Must Goodrich Move Out of Akron?" address dated 16 February 1938, box E-8, United Rubber Workers Local 5 Collection, University of Akron Archives.
102. Ibid.
103. Nelson, *American Rubber Workers*, 272–78.
104. *Akron Beacon Journal*, 27 February 1939.
105. "Directors Meeting," 14 March 1939; and "Executive Committee Meeting," 21 March 1939.
106. Stevens interview.
107. Babcock, *United States Rubber*, 352–59; and Lief, *Firestone Story*, 207–8.
108. Stevens interview.
109. *Akron Beacon Journal*, 14 March 1934; and "Directors Meeting," 5 November 1930.
110. "Executive Committee Meeting," 20 August 1936.
111. Ibid., 18 January 1937. The Philadelphia Rubber Works Company lay totally idle between 1932 and 1937. See H. W. Maxon, "Research and Rubber," typescript manuscript, BFG Col.
112. Ibid., 21 December 1934.
113. "Directors Meetings," 14 November and 12 December 1933; and "Executive Committee Meetings," 28 August 1933 and 22 August 1934.
114. "Executive Committee Meetings," 11 August, 13 November, and 30 December 1936.
115. Babcock, *United States Rubber*, 347–50; French, *U.S. Tire Industry*, 123–24; Lief,

Firestone Story, 173–75, 205–8; and Maurice O'Reilly, *The Goodyear Story* (Elmsford, New York: Benjamin Company, 1983), 78.

116. "Directors Meeting," 8 December 1936.

117. "Executive Committee Meetings," 3 January and 23 February 1934, 25 October 1935, and 11 July 1938.

118. *Akron Beacon Journal*, 24 December, 25 December, 27 December, and 28 December 1937, and 8 January 1938, all in the newspaper's clipping file.

119. *Akron Beacon Journal*, 27 May 1932; "Executive Committee Meeting," 23 February 1934; and *New York Times*, 6 July 1939.

120. "Executive Committee Meeting," February 1934.

121. Ibid., 25 May, 19 September, and 2 October 1934, 13 May and 25 November 1935, 7 May 1936, and 15 December 1939; and "Directors Meetings," 10 April, 2 May, 12 June 1934, 8 January, 10 October 1935, 13 October 1936, 28 February 1938, and 13 June 1939.

122. "Directors Meetings," 11 December 1934 and 15 November 1938.

123. Ong interview, 5 August 1992.

124. *Akron Beacon Journal*, 24 January 1936; "Directors Meeting," 8 August 1939.

125. "Directors Meeting," 16 November 1937; and "Executive Committee Meetings," 15 May and 25 May 1934.

126. "Directors Meetings," 16 August and 13 December 1938; and "Executive Committee Meetings," 16 August, 15 September, and 10 October 1938, and 9 January and 21 March 1939.

127. Kimio Tsuji to Mansel Blackford, 4 May 1992. Some of the sales of shares may have been voluntary. A Ford Motor executive reported in 1936 that Goodrich executives sold the majority of their shares because they were alarmed about the situation in Asia and did not want to have their money tied up there. See John Crawford, "Memorandum on the visit of Messrs Caywood and Aspell of the BF Goodrich Rubber Co to Mr. Ford's office," 15 October 1936, Ford Motor Archives. Provided by Professor Mira Wilkins of the Florida International University.

128. K. B. Davis, "B.F. Goodrich History," typescript, 18 August 1954, 7.

129. Lief, *Firestone Story*, 174, 197, 209, 246.

130. Michael J. French, "The Emergence of a US Multinational Enterprise: the Goodyear Tire and Rubber Company, 1910–1939," *Economic History Review* 40 (1987): 64–79; and O'Reilly, *Goodyear Story*, 77–79.

131. Jacob Vander Meulen, *The Politics of Aircraft: Building an American Military Industry* (Lawrence: University Press of Kansas, 1991), 65, 92, 99.

132. Moody's, *Newsletter*, 17 July 1929, 1.

133. Richard K. Smith, "The International Airliner and the Essence of Airplane Performance, 1929–1939," *Technology and Culture* 24 (Fall 1983): 428–49.

134. Moody's, *Newsletter*, 5 July 1937.

135. *Akron Beacon Journal*, 15 May 1937; and R. Y. Lochhead, "BFGoodrich, Then and Now," typescript; "Report on Airplane Tires by the J. Walter Thompson Advertising Agency, November, 1929," in the J. Walter Thompson Col., Duke University.

136. Miscellaneous press releases and advertisements on airplane brakes, 1937–39, BFG Col.

137. On Hayes Industries see "Annual Reports" and supporting data available in the Baker Library, Harvard University.

138. B.F. Goodrich, Machine Development Department, "Problem #4825," 22 December 1930, BFG Col.
139. J. Earl Gulick, "Pneumatic Deicers," typescript manuscript, BFG Col.
140. William Geer, "Comments on the Deicer Story," 27 March 1940, BFG Col.
141. Ibid.
142. Akron Beacon Journal, 16 October and 17 October 1930; and Super-Service Tire Review 31 (March 1931): 82.
143. Miscellaneous advertisements, 1938–39, boxes BA-4 and BA-6, BFG Col.
144. Akron Beacon Journal, 28 November 1935; and "Products-Airplanes," 1935 and 1938," pamphlets, BFG Col.
145. Akron Beacon Journal, 16 July, 17 July, and 19 July 1928.
146. India Rubber Tire Review 29 (May 1929): 109; and 29 (August 1929): 36; and Super-Service Tire Review 29 (October 1929): 161; 30 (August 1930): 106; and 30 (October 1930): 82.
147. Benjamin Jones, "History of BFGoodrich's Aerospace Division," handwritten sketch prepared for the authors, 15 May 1992.
148. "Report on Airplane Tires."
149. Ibid.
150. "President's Report," 6 November 1929.
151. "Annual Reports," 1930–38; and Alfred D. Chandler Jr., Strategy and Structure (New York: Doubleday, 1966), 435.
152. "Operating Committee Meeting," 20 April 1934; "President's Report," 9 December 1930; and Wolf and Wolf, Rubber, 339.
153. "Adjourned Special Meeting of Stockholders, July 16, 1935"; "Directors Meeting," 5 June 1935; and "Executive Committee Meeting," 28 May 1935.
154. Akron Beacon Journal, 6 June, 29 June, 11 July, 12 July, 15 July, 16 July, 19 July, and 27 July 1935; "Annual Report," 1935; Time, 29 July 1935; and Wall Street Journal, 24 July 1935.
155. Akron Beacon Journal, 29 July 1935.
156. Ibid., 11 October 1935.
157. Ibid., 24 January and 26 August 1936; "Annual Report," 1936.
158. "Annual Report," 1936; "Directors Meetings," 10 March and 21 July 1936; and Time, 21 September 1936, 70.
159. Akron Beacon Journal, 5 May 1937.
160. This report is in B.F. Goodrich, Supplemental Book 13, n.p.
161. "Executive Committee Meetings," 9 April 1934, 3 October 1935; David Goodrich to R. S. Rauch, 4 June 1936; and R. S. Rauch to David Goodrich. The letters are in B.F. Goodrich Supplemental Book 12, 58–59.
162. "Executive Committee Meeting," 20 August 1936.
163. Ibid., 27 May and 14 June 1937.
164. Silvertown Cavalier, 4 May 1937, 1, 4, in box C-3, BFG Col.
165. James Tew to Shelby Jett, 30 April 1937.
166. "Directors Meeting," 16 February 1937.
167. Akron Beacon Journal, 6 May 1937; Super-Service Tire Review 31 (September 1931): 72.
168. Press release, 25 April 1939, folder p 1.20, box 124, the 1939 New York World's Fair Collection, New York Public Library.
169. Ibid.; and Rubber Age 44 (December 1938): 165.
170. Press release.

171. Ibid.
172. "B.F. Goodrich Bulletin," folder p 1.20, box 124, World's Fair Collection; and Vincent Coletti to B.F. Goodrich, 1 March 1939, folder p 1.20, box 124, World's Fair Collection.
173. Moody's, *Newsletter,* 23 November 1936, bond survey, 134–35.

CHAPTER 5

1. Stevens interview; Kenneth Attiwill, *Fortress: The Story of the Siege and Fall of Singapore* (Garden City, N.Y.: Doubleday, 1960), 24–29; John George Smyth, *Percival and the Tragedy of Singapore* (London: McDonald & Co., 1971), 120–21.
2. "Executive Committee Meeting," vol. 10, 82; Beasley, *History,* 178–81; Walrond Sinclair to Goodrich, 19 December 1938, Collyer papers, Cornell University Archives.
3. Goodrich to Sinclair, 12 May 1939; Collyer Oral History Memoir, Collyer papers, 12–13.
4. Collyer wanted to work under a contract, but dropped the matter when he learned that contracts with executives were not a customary policy. Goodrich agreed to a year's salary as severance pay in case Collyer's employment was terminated. He would receive initially a salary of $85,000, with a profit sharing plan to bring his income to about $150,000 per year; if the board did not approve the bonus, Goodrich agreed to increase Collyer's salary. "Discussion Held Tuesday July 11th 1939," Collyer papers.
5. Goodrich to Sir Walrond Sinclair, 18 September 1939; 2 October 1939; Goodrich to Collyer, 18 September 1939, Collyer papers.
6. Scull and Jones interviews; Jeter interview, 10 July 1990.
7. John L. Collyer Oral History, Collyer papers, 114–15.
8. Ibid., 121. Soon after Collyer became president of B.F. Goodrich, the board of directors approved a new plan for rewarding salaried employees with bonuses. Persons receiving less than $4,000 annually in salary received a 3 percent bonus each year during the war. Salaried employees earning between $4,000 and $10,000 per year received merit bonuses. In 1941 the board of directors also approved incentive compensation for top executives. In 1942 the officers of the company were given thus $140,000; in 1943, $177,000; and in 1944, $178,000. Goldman, Sachs & Co. Prospectus, 1 May 1945, Competitors folder, 1945, J. Penfield Seiberling Collection, Ohio Historical Society; Tomlinson interview.
9. Goodrich to Collyer, 18 August 1939; John L. Collyer Oral History, Collyer papers, 108–9, 115–16. Collyer wanted only outside directors at first, but later added executives to the board. He was aware that his policy was different from that of other major industrial firms at the time, which typically had boards almost exclusively composed of inside directors. See also Jeter interview, 10 July 1990. Jeter recalled that when he joined the firm in 1948 Collyer did not allow his executives to sit on other firms' boards of directors.
10. John L. Collyer Oral History, Collyer papers, 109–10; Goldman, Sachs & Co. Prospectus, 1 May 1945, Competitors folder, 1945, J. Penfield Seiberling Collection; Jeter interview, 10 July 1990; "Operations Council Minutes," 12 June 1942. L. L. Smith replaced Vaught as treasurer after six months. *New York Times,* 19 December 1940. No evidence survives that Vaught significantly changed the orientation of Goodrich toward marketing.

11. "A Statement to the Army Price Adjustment Board Ordnance Division," 27 November 1942, file M-1, BFG Col.
12. "A Statement to the Army Price Adjustment Board Ordnance Division."
13. Japs interview.
14. Ong interview, 9 August 1990; John L. Collyer Oral History, Collyer papers, 139.
15. Collyer to Wayne C. Taylor, 6 May 1942, General Records of the Department of Commerce, file 82218/14, RG 40.
16. Goodrich, "Annual Report," 1940, 3; John L. Collyer Oral History, Collyer papers, 32. When he arrived in the United States to take charge of B.F. Goodrich, however, Collyer was unwilling to make alarming forecasts. He assured reporters that supplies of natural rubber were adequate for the immediate needs of the war, and shipping lanes would remain open. New York Times, 3 November 1939.
17. "Synthetic Rubber," 31 December 1931; "Mr. Paull" to Collyer, 16 January 1936, Personal & Dunlop file, Collyer papers.
18. Interview of Waldo Semon by Herbert A. Andres, 19 January 1966, BFG Col.; Avery, "Milestones in the Progress of the Rubber Industry," 80.
19. Interview of Waldo Semon by Andres.
20. Standard Oil of New Jersey and Farben had formed an American subsidiary, JASCO, to control patents in the United States. They had approached Goodrich in 1932 for joint projects to overcome problems of using synthetic rubbers in manufactured goods. Frank A. Howard, Buna Rubber: The Birth of an Industry (New York: D. Van Nostrand Company, 1947), 38; Interview of Waldo Semon by Andres; "A Man of Ideas: The Biography of Dr. Waldo L. Semon, Inventor of Plasticized Polyvinyl Chloride," typescript, 1991, 75–77.
21. Semon, "Achievements of the Chemical Engineer in the Synthetic Rubber Industry," Speech, National Industrial Chemical Conference, Chicago Coliseum, 16 November 1944, Historical File, Charles Cross Goodrich Library; Beasley, "History of Goodrich," 191; "The Government's Rubber Projects," II, 357; Japs interview. In their war planning, the military services were interested in synthetic rubber, and explored the prospects with Goodrich in the summer of 1939. George W. Auxier, Rubber Policies of the National Defense Advisory Commission and the Office of Production Management (Washington, D.C.: War Production Board, Historical Reports on War Administration, Special Study No. 28, 1947), 93.
22. Avery, "Milestones in the Progress of the Rubber Industry," 82; Waldo Semon, "Achievements of the Chemical Engineer in the Synthetic Rubber Industry," National Industrial Chemical Conference, 16 November 1944.
23. Semon and Schade to T. G. Graham, 26 January 1940, file 3–1, Semon papers.
24. Waldo Semon, "Achievements of the Chemical Engineer in the Synthetic Rubber Industry," National Industrial Chemical Conference, 16 November 1944; Avery, "Milestones in the Progress of the Rubber Industry," 83; interview of Waldo Semon by Andres; New York Times, 3 January 1939; Harrington interview. Goodrich was not the only company working on these problems. DuPont had already developed neoprene, useful in some industrial and footwear applications, and Goodyear had its own research program under way, but apparently its scientists were not as far along as Semon's group. Peter J. T. Morris, The American Synthetic Rubber Research Program (Philadelphia: University of Pennsylvania Press), 7–9.
25. "Executive Committee Meeting," 29 January 1940; "The Government's Rubber Projects," 2: 411.

26. The company kept secret the chemical combined with butadiene. "Ameripol," undated, Select Document File "Rubber," Records of the War Production Board, RG 179. The company coordinated the announcement with a presentation by A. L. Viles of the Rubber Manufacturers' Association to E. R. Stettinius Jr. of the government's National Council of Defense.

27. "Liberty Rubber Made with Ameripol," booklet in Goodrich legal department files; "The B. F. Goodrich Company Chronological Highlights," typescript.

28. Interview of Waldo Semon by Andres; "Meeting—July 1, 1940," Policy Documentation File 571.2, RG 179; "Executive Committee Meeting," 12 June 1940. By August 1940, B.F. Goodrich expected the daily production of Ameripol tires to reach 150 tires. "Operating Committee Meeting," 9 August 1940.

29. John Collyer, "A Report on Rubber to Americans Alert to the Meaning of Independence and Preparedness," easel talk, 5 July 1940; Collyer to A. L. Viles, 5 June 1940, Select Document File "Rubber," RG 179.

30. Gerald T. White, *Billions for Defense: Government Financing by the Defense Plant Corporation during World War II* (Tuscaloosa: University of Alabama Press, 1980), 38–41; "Meeting—July 1, 1940," Policy Documentation File 571.2, RG 179; Collyer, "A Report on Rubber to Americans Alert to the Meaning of Independence and Preparedness"; *New York Times*, 9 October 1940; May 1, 1941, "A Confidential Summary of the Rubber Position in the United States." Collyer sought a $10 million government investment in a 36,000-ton plant to come to full production in eighteen months.

31. Synthetic Rubber Conference, 7 August 1940, Policy Documentation File 574.1; A. L. Viles to rubber manufacturers, 4 September 1940, Policy Documentation File 571.2; E. R. Stettinius Jr. to Roosevelt, 13 September 1940, Policy Documentation File 574.1, RG 179. The rubber manufacturers were asked but not required to buy stock in the government's Rubber Reserve Corporation. They insisted on limiting their collective liability to $1,000,000. Notes on the meeting of the board of directors of the Rubber Manufacturers' Association, 14 June 1940, Select Document File "Rubber," RG 179.

32. Robert E. Wilson memo, 15 July 1940, Policy Documentation File 574.8, RG 179; Williams Haynes, *American Chemical Industry*, vol. 5, *Decade of New Products* (New York: D. Van Nostrand Company, 1954), 211; Goodrich, "Annual Report," 1940, 3; Harrington interview. The initial plant was capable of making six tons of rubber a day. In the spring of 1941, an explosion at DuPont's neoprene plant enlarged the venture's market, because its rubber was directly competitive. Memo of a telephone conversation, 7 March 1941, Brandt to Major Early of Wright Field, Select Document File, RG 179, box 698. At the start of the war, there was a surplus of oil-resistant rubbers on the market. F. H. Carman, Chief, Synthetic Rubber Section, to A. I. Henderson, Deputy Director, 18 December 1941, File 574, Policy Documentation File, War Production Board, RG 179.

33. "Executive Committee Meeting," 24 June 1941; "Annual Report," 1942; Docket 111–13769-D, Records of the National War Labor Board, RG 202, National Archives. The government also contracted for 10,000-ton plants with Goodyear, Firestone, and U.S. Rubber. Michael J. French, *The U.S. Tire Industry: A History* (Boston: Twayne Publishers, 1990), 9.

34. Howard, *Buna Rubber*, 172, 175, 291; B.F. Goodrich Company, "Annual Report," 1942, 4. In 1942, thanks to its early lead, Goodrich produced more synthetic rubber than any other firm.

35. Avery, "Milestones in the Progress of the Rubber Industry," 90, 95; Scull inter-

view, 10 September 1990; Peter J. T. Morris, *The American Synthetic Rubber Research Program*, 33–35. When copolymerization occurred at low temperatures, the resulting rubber was superior. Goodrich held nine patents on cold rubber, but shortages in refrigeration equipment seemed to dictate against the process in the emergency. Robert Solo, *Synthetic Rubber: A Case Study in Technological Development under Government Direction*, reprinted as *Across the High Technology Threshold: The Case of Synthetic Rubber* (Norwood, Pa.: Norwood Editions, 1980), 100. After the war, the government adopted the cold rubber process in the plants it owned. Goodrich always used the process in its privately financed plant in Louisville.

36. French, *U.S. Tire Industry*, 81. The cheaper butadiene from petroleum provided better long-term commercial prospects, and it took much political pressure from farm interests to promote the emergency use of alcohol as a raw material even though it was a proven technology. In 1942 the government responded by ordering whisky distillers to convert to producing industrial alcohol. The operation at Borger, Texas, was threatened for a time by an acute housing shortage. T. G. Graham to W. M. Jeffers, 30 November 1942, Policy Documentation File 574.4, RG 179.

37. "A Statement to the Army Price Adjustment Board Ordnance Division."

38. "List of 252 Corporations," War Production Board File, 1943, J. Penfield Seiberling Collection.

39. "A Statement to the Army Price Adjustment Board Ordnance Division." In general, American manufacturers did not invest in war plants whose postwar uses were not readily apparent. Substantial government investments helped spur the economic mobilization.

40. "A Statement to the Army Price Adjustment Board Ordnance Division."

41. *War Production News*, 7 August 1942.

42. Edward W. Hassell, "Report on the Rubber Industry," Policy Documentation File 570.1, RG 179.

43. "A Statement to the Army Price Adjustment Board Ordnance Division."

44. "A Statement to the Army Price Adjustment Board Ordnance Division."

45. James J. Newman to A. L. Viles, 6 October 1942, RMA folder, 1942, J. Penfield Seiberling Collection.

46. *Akron Beacon Journal*, 2 April 1942.

47. R. Y. Lochhead, "BFGoodrich, Then and Now," typescript. The sharing of synthetic rubber patents began a week after the attack on Pearl Harbor. Eventually the companies agreed to have an independent scientist, Dr. E. R. Weidlein of the Mellon Institute, take charge of the patent sharing. Agreements had to be reached on the production of butadiene, styrene, and the compounding and processing of the new synthetic rubber. The companies left open the issues of royalty payments for the use of other firms' patents, only in 1943 accepting a plan of Collyer and Frank Howard of Standard Oil to submit disputes to arbitration. Howard, *Buna Rubber*, 173–75, 179, 231–32; Robert Solo, *Synthetic Rubber*, 40.

48. *Akron Beacon Journal*, 1 April 1945.

49. Senate Small Business press release, 31 May 1942, Burger file, 1942, J. Penfield Seiberling Collection.

50. Burger to Seiberling, 30 June 1942; Small Business Committee press release, 11 September 1942, Burger file, 1942; H. D. Dawson to William M. Jeffers, 21 October 1942; L. D. Tompkins to W. M. Jeffers, 19 October 1942, War Production

Board Folder, 1942; Seiberling to Newman, 24 March 1943, Competitors file, 1943, J. Penfield Seiberling Collection; "Operations Council Minutes," 7 December 1942.

51. Figures compiled by Seiberling, Competitors folder, 1944; Goldman, Sachs & Co. Prospectus, 1 May 1945, Competitors folder, 1945, J. Penfield Seiberling Collection. Seiberling's figures showed Collyer's 1944 earnings of $145,000 substantially higher than his counterparts' at Firestone ($93,750) and Goodyear ($91,097). Docket 111–3441-D, RG 202. The United Rubber Workers had won a 6 percent pay increase in the 1941 contract after difficult negotiations. *Akron Beacon Journal*, 19 May 1941.

52. Hillman telegram, 11 December 1941; Sidney C. Suffrin to Thomas Burns, 13 December 1941, File 574.4, Policy Documentation File, War Production Board, RG 179; Karl H. Grismer, *Akron and Summit County* (Akron: Summit County Historical Society, n.d.), 507; Goldman, Sachs & Co. Prospectus, 1 May 1945, Competitors folder, 1945, J. Penfield Seiberling Collection. T. G. Graham reported that Goodyear Aircraft alone was employing about 31,000 persons. "Operations Council Minutes," 29 January 1943. In the summer of 1941 federal officials placed restrictions on the use of rubber in civilian goods, including automobiles, and Goodrich, which had lagged behind rival firms in contracting for defense work, faced the prospect of laying off large numbers of employees. A juggling of vacation schedules avoided the problem, and workers left voluntarily for jobs in nearby defense plants, especially Goodyear Aircraft. At the end of the year, federal officials stepped in to assure dislocated rubber workers of seniority rights protection in case they shifted to a defense industry. *Goodrich Circle*, September 1941, 2; Sidney C. Suffrin to Thomas Burns, 13 December 1941, File 574.4, Policy Documentation File, War Production Board, RG 179.

53. *War Production News*, 23 October 1942.

54. *Circle*, August 1943, 5; Grismer, *Akron and Summit County*, 507; T. G. Graham to William M. Jeffers, 1 July 1943, Policy Documentation File 574, RG 179. In 1944 Collyer and Graham reported that the URW had resisted allowing women to take on jobs traditionally reserved for men. "Meeting with Officials of Six Major Tire Companies in the Akron Area," 6 July 1944, Select Document File "Rubber," RG 179.

55. "Operations Council Minutes," 15 May 1942; 29 January 1943; Report of the Activities of the Office of Labor Production, WPB, in Increasing the Production of Heavy Duty Truck Tires, 1 December 1944, Policy Documentation File 579.44, RG 179. At the National Association for the Advancement of Colored People's request, in 1942 Goodrich named L. L. Smith, the firm's new treasurer, to the board of the civil rights organization. The goal was to strengthen efforts to achieve racial justice and harmony in Akron.

56. Seiberling to H. H. Stafford, 3 May 1944, Conference Board folder, 1944, J. Penfield Seiberling Collection.

57. *Akron Beacon Journal*, 7 October 1941.

58. *Akron Beacon Journal*, 29 March 1942. Copies of *War Production News* are in file K-4, folder 21, BFG Col. The CIO took Goodrich's labor management committee to other rubber companies.

59. *War Production News*, 29 April and 6 May 1942.

60. *Akron Beacon Journal*, 11 June 1942; *War Production News*, 18 June 1942; Seiberling to C. Tyler Wood Jr., 15 June 1942, War Production Board folder, 1942,

J. Penfield Seiberling Collection. State draft board officials and the War Production Board supported the company's position.

61. Rubber czar William Jeffers brought pressure to bear for cooperation. One of his first public actions in 1942 was meeting in Akron with labor representatives, where he observed that "proper cooperation on the part of management, as well as on the part of the workers, will avoid a calamity in this country." Jeffers to Seiberling; to Robert L. Cruden, 4 September 1943, War Production Board file, 1943, Rubber Manufacturers' Association folder, 1943, J. Penfield Seiberling Collection.

62. *War Production News*, 18 June 1942; 6 November 1942.

63. Dockets 111-13769-D, 111-1896-D, 111-10013-D, 111-2719-D, RG 202; *Akron Beacon Journal*, 29 September 1942; Nelson Lichtenstein, *Labor's War at Home: The CIO in World War II* (New York: Cambridge University Press, 1982), 197.

64. Lichtenstein, *Labor's War at Home*, 52, 97–98, 197.

65. *Circle*, January 1941, 2; *Akron Beacon Journal*, 20 May, 21 May, 22 May, and 3 June 1942; Docket 111-3441-D, RG 202. At the end of 1942 Goodrich, following President Roosevelt's directive, moved to give every worker one day off per week. *War Production News*, 25 December 1942.

66. The Akron locals were thereafter united in their hatred of Dalrymple. They supported Bass for the United Rubber Workers presidency in 1944, but could not outvote the war-born locals that remained loyal to Dalrymple. Wayne Morse of the National War Labor Board drafted an executive order seizing the Goodrich factories. Lichtenstein, *Labor's War at Home*, 163–65; *Akron Beacon Journal*, 3 April, 11 May, 12 May, 13 May, 15 May, 18 May, 22 May, 23 May, 24 May, 26 May, and 27 May 1943.

67. *Akron Beacon Journal*, 15 June 1944; Docket 111-3441-D, RG 202.

68. Fred W. Climer to A. L. Viles, 22 February 1944; minutes of meeting, 22 March 1944, Rubber Manufacturers Association folder, 1944, J. Penfield Seiberling Collection.

69. *Akron Beacon Journal*, 20 July 1944.

70. *Akron Beacon Journal*, 23 April 1945.

71. John L. Collyer Oral History, Collyer papers, 123; "Operating Committee Meeting," 9 July 1941; "Executive Committee Meeting," 14 July 1941. The other large rubber companies also operated ordnance factories.

72. Goodrich earned $420,554 in 1942 from the Lone Star operation. "A Statement to the Army Price Adjustment Board Ordnance Division"; Goff and Freeman interviews; "Annual Report," 1945, 4.

73. Tomlinson interview.

74. Ibid.; "A Statement to the Army Price Adjustment Board Ordnance Division"; *Akron Beacon Journal*, 10 December 1940, 22 July 1941.

75. "A Statement to the Army Price Adjustment Board Ordnance Division"; *Rubber Age* 51 (August 1942): 421; and 51 (September 1942): 513.

76. Tomlinson interview, 3 January 1991; French, *U.S. Tire Industry*, 83. General Tire purchased a missile manufacturer, Aerojet.

77. Collyer to William S. Knudsen, 27 November 1941, file 317.0422, Policy Documentation File, War Production Board, RG 179, National Archives; "Operating Committee Meeting," 26 December 1941. Not all went smoothly, in part because of the haste with which aircraft designs went into production. During 1941, as the aircraft industry was expanding to meet defense needs, Goodrich

sold $2,800,000 worth of the devices and suffered a loss of $1,219,000 on the business. It lost on the B-25 alone because of changes in the plane's specifications. By 1942, management had aligned costs and prices for fuel cells.

78. *Life*, 24 July 1943, 3.
79. Collyer to William M. Jeffers, 30 June 1943; T. G. Graham to Jeffers, 1 July 1943, Policy Documentation File 574, RG 179. Truck tires combining natural and synthetic rubber took 15 to 30 percent more time to build than prewar types. "Report on Crude and Synthetic Rubber Position," Rubber Manufacturers' Association folder, J. Penfield Seiberling Collection.
80. "Operations Council Minutes," 8 July 1944; 15 December 1944; "Meeting with Officials of Six Major Tire Companies in the Akron Area," 6 July 1944; "Report on Tire and Tube Industry Conference," 22 November 1944; Select Document File "Rubber"; Report of the Activities of the Office of Labor Production, WPB, in Increasing the Production of Heavy Duty Truck Tires, 1 December 1944, Policy Documentation File 579.44; Collyer to J. A. Krug, 25 June 1945, Policy Documentation File 570.1, RG 179. The government was investing large sums in equipment to improve truck tire production, but Goodrich did not receive an allocation because its factories were already at capacity. Its executives thought the government should build entirely new plants, which could be dismantled at the end of the war if the industry then had an overcapacity.
81. Executive committee of the Rubber Footwear Manufacturing Industry to Rubber Bureau, War Production Board, 15 February 1945; to George K. Hamill, 22 March 1945, Select Document File "Rubber," RG 179.
82. "Operations Council Minutes," 1 July 1944, 20 July 1945; Goldman, Sachs & Co. Prospectus, 1 May 1945, Competitors folder, 1945, J. Penfield Seiberling Collection.
83. "Operations Council Minutes," 15 December 1944, 20 July 1945.
84. John L. Collyer Oral History, Collyer papers, 48, 129.
85. *New York Times*, 27 February 1940; *Akron Beacon Journal*, 19 March 1943; "Annual Report," 1944, 4, 1945, 4; Ong interview, 9 August 1990. Government funding of plant expansion extended to American owned plants in Canada. "Operations Council Minutes," 23 December 1944.
86. "Operations Council Minutes," 4 September 1944, 17 August 1945; "Executive Committee Meeting," 3 January and 4 January 1945.
87. Don Whitehead, *The Dow Story: The History of the Dow Chemical Company* (New York: McGraw-Hill, 1968), 188; "Annual Report," 1945, 4.
88. "A Man of Ideas," 67.
89. Williams Haynes, *American Chemical Industry*, vol. 5, *Decade of New Products* (New York: D. Van Nostrand Company, 1954), 338; Peter H. Spitz, *Petrochemicals: The Rise of an Industry* (New York: John Wiley, 1988), 250–53.
90. "A Chemical History of the B.F. Goodrich Company," anonymous typescript, n.d.
91. *Circle*, January 1942, 12.
92. Semon to J. D. Tew, 3 November 1937, file 3–1, Semon papers.
93. Semon, "The Present Koroseal Situation," 3 November 1937, Semon papers.
94. Semon to J. D. Tew, 3 November 1937; "Application of Research Products to Factory Production," 4 February 1938, file 3–1, Semon papers.
95. Japs interview.
96. "Operating Committee Meeting," 16 May 1940.

97. "Executive Committee Meeting," 30 September 1940; press release, 25 March 1941, file JF 1–2, BFG Col.
98. "Operating Committee Meeting," 17 May 1939.
99. Goodrich Products 1939; "Annual Report," 1939, 3; Circle, April 1941, 10–12.
100. N. S. Prime, "Memorandum to Be Presented to Chemical Advisory Committee on Priorities," Policy Documentation File 539.6132; "Meeting—July 1, 1940," Policy Documentation File 571.2, RG 179. By 1938 the Bureau of Engineering in the Navy Department was exploring the availability of plastics that it could use in ship construction. The bureau, for instance, wrote to the Dow Chemical Company and the Hercules Powder Company in 1938 requesting information about plastics available from those manufacturers. D. Williams to Bureau of Engineering, 28 December 1938, and J. H. Steel to Bureau of Engineering, 29 December 1938, Bureau of Engineering General Correspondence, Records of the Bureau of Ships, RG 19, National Archives.
101. John L. Collyer Oral History, Collyer papers, 11–12; undated (1941) press release, file JF 1–1, BFG Col. The company decided to suspend attempts to expand civilian sales. "Operating Committee Meeting," 11 April, 2 May, and 9 May 1941.
102. Collyer to C. A. Jones, Bureau of Ships, 5 September 1941; H. B. Stevens to Admiral Ben Moreell, 20 April 1945; Route Slip, 23 April 1945, B.F. Goodrich file, General Correspondence, 1940–1945, Bureau of Ships, RG 19, National Archives.
103. "Operations Council Minutes," 10 April 1942; John L. Collyer Oral History, Collyer papers, 11–12; Collyer, "Raw Material Outlook in the Rubber Industry," India Rubber World 111 (February 1945): 559–60. As we have seen, Goodrich had briefly flirted with a multidivisional structure a few years earlier.
104. Harlan Trumbull, "A Chemical History of the B.F. Goodrich Company," has a two-page appendix on Richardson. Tomlinson and Kenney interviews.
105. Rubber Age 52 (December 1942): 256; "Operations Council Minutes," 12 February 1943; Fowles interview, 4 January 1991.
106. Fowles interviews.
107. Fowles interviews.
108. Kenney interview; "Operations Council Minutes," 11 February 1944; "Executive Committee Meeting," 20 March 1944. Before the expansion, Goodrich was capable of making 2 million pounds of PVC per month, and Union Carbide 3.25 million pounds.
109. "Distribution of Polyvinyl Chlorides in October, 1942," File 537.5513, Policy Documentation File, War Production Board, RG 179, National Archives.
110. Fowles interview, 4 January, 1991. In 1944 the government urged a further expansion of PVC capacity. "Operations Council Minutes," 11 February 1944; "Annual Report," 1943, 4.
111. "Annual Report," 1945, 3; Fowles interviews; Joseph Del Gatton, "BFG Chemical: Technological Dominance," reprinted from Rubber World 152 (September 1965).
112. "Post-War Planning for Koroseal," 26 June 1943, file JF1–15, BFG Col.
113. "Executive Committee Meetings," 3 January, 4 January, 16 July, and 20 August 1945.
114. Kenney interview; "Operations Council Minutes," 29 December 1944. In 1944 Distillers and Goodrich had agreed on a distribution arrangement.

115. Unsigned "Memorandum to Editor," *Wall Street Journal*, 24 September 1943, folder 15, J. Penfield Seiberling Collection.
116. James J. Newman, "The Place and Problems of the Sales Manager in the Postwar Period," 20 October 1944, file C-3, BFG Col.; Goldman, Sachs & Co. Prospectus, 1 May 1945, Competitors folder, 1945, J. Penfield Seiberling Collection.
117. Goldman, Sachs & Co. Prospectus, 1 May 1945, Competitors folder, 1945, J. Penfield Seiberling Collection.
118. "B.F. Goodrich—The Pathfinder," 5, reprinted from *Rubber World* 156 (July 1967). Keener quickly rose in the company, becoming Collyer's assistant in 1944.
119. *Akron Beacon Journal*, 28 July 1945.
120. Telephone conversation on 20 April 1945; E. L. Cochrane, Vice Admiral, to the Rubber Bureau, 30 April 1945; memo, B.F. Goodrich file, n.d., General Correspondence, 1940–1945, Bureau of Ships, RG 19, National Archives; "Annual Report," 1946, 2–3.
121. John L. Collyer Oral History, Collyer papers, 125; "A Statement to the Army Price Adjustment Board Ordnance Division." The company also developed a pressure sealing zipper during the war. *Rubber Age* 56 (November 1944): 195.
122. Goldman, Sachs & Co. Prospectus, 1 May 1945, Competitors folder, 1945, J. Penfield Seiberling Collection.
123. The figures are from Neiman, "A Study of Rubber Industry Profits."

CHAPTER 6

1. Collyer to Industrial Group, New York Society of Security Analysts, 18 October 1943, Collyer papers.
2. Remarks of George Vaught to Security Analysts of Boston, 26 January 1948, box C-4, BFG Col.
3. Research-minded executives were willing to explore the application of new technologies to manufacturing. For example, in 1953 they assigned Goodrich scientists to learn atomic energy. Stockman interview.
4. Remarks of George Vaught to Security Analysts of Boston, 26 January 1948, box C-4, BFG Col.
5. "Directors Meeting," 17 January 1950.
6. Rockefeller interview.
7. Mallott interview.
8. "Trouble in Synthetic Rubber," *Fortune* 35 (June 1947): 114–19; "Gentleman of Akron," *Forbes*, 15 January 1954, 14; "Comparison of Net Income 1949–1956 as Estimated from Published Tax Amounts," Collyer papers.
9. *Akron Beacon Journal*, 16 July 1952; Mahmoud Sadik Said Bazaraa, "An Analysis of the Financial Expansion of Business Corporations Engaged in the Manufacture of Rubber Tires and Tubes, 1946–1960," Ph.D. diss., University of Illinois, 1965, 68.
10. *Akron Beacon Journal*, 3 January 1951.
11. Interview with John Ong, 9 August 1990. The comparative data are in "Rubber Fabricating," *Standard & Poor's Industry Surveys*, 23 March 1961, R134-R139, and 16 April 1970, R196-R201.
12. "Richardson of B.F. Goodrich, *Fortune* reprint, July 1954, BFG Col.; "Steering toward Profitability," *Business Week*, 7 November 1959, 170.

13. Remarks of John L. Collyer, Interdivisional Meetings, 22 November 1952, Keener papers, held by family.
14. W. S. Richardson before Boston Analysts' Society, 21 March 1955, box C-3, BFG Col.
15. L. N. Freeman, "Method for Application of Statistical Quality Control in the Manufacture of Rubber Products," *Rubber World* 138 (April 1958): 107–9; Freeman interview.
16. *Rubber Age* 73 (July 1953): 518–19; Tomlinson interview; Blazey interviews; Keener interview.
17. "Executive Committee Meeting," 26 October 1942; Jones interview.
18. Telephone conversation on 20 April 1945, E. L. Cochrane, Vice Admiral, to the Rubber Bureau, 30 April 1945; memo, B.F. Goodrich file, n.d., General Correspondence, 1940–1945, Bureau of Ships, RG 19, National Archives; "Annual Report," 1946, 2–3. The original cost projections were optimistic in the face of postwar inflation, and the company had to allocate additional capital to finish the facility. "Directors Meeting," 19 March 1946.
19. Collyer to New York Society of Security Analysts, 20 January 1948, box C-1, BFG Col.
20. H. L. Trumbull, "B.F. Goodrich Research Center," 6 February 1948, typescript; *Inaugural Meeting, B.F. Goodrich Research Center,* 15 June 1948; Sharon L. Butcher, "Historically Speaking," *R&D Spectrum: BFGoodrich Research Newsletter* 4 (Summer 1990): 1–7; Japs interview.
21. Perdriau interview. John Ong recalled that when he was assigned responsibility for labor relations shortly after Ward Keener's retirement in 1972 he observed the attitude of distinguishing union members from employees. Ong interview, 10 May 1993.
22. Blazey interviews, 17 July and 10 September 1991.
23. *Akron Beacon Journal,* 11 January 1946; *New York Times,* 6 February 1946.
24. *Akron Beacon Journal,* 30 March 1952.
25. *Akron Beacon Journal,* 29 March 1952; *India Rubber World* 126 (June 1952): 392–93; Jeter interviews, 9 July and 10 July 1991.
26. *Akron Beacon Journal,* 16 July and 17 July 1956; *Rubber World* 134 (August 1956): 740.
27. *New York Times,* 28 August 1949; *Akron Beacon Journal,* 16 September 1949.
28. *Rubber World* 140 (May 1959): 283; and 140 (June 1959): 461–62.
29. "Trouble in Synthetic Rubber," *Fortune* 35 (June 1947): 114–19.
30. "Annual Report," 1945, 5; 1947, 5; *Rubber Age* 63 (July 1948): 469; H. B. McCoy to Henry A. Wallace, 12 November 1946, file 82218/14, Records of the Department of Commerce, RG 40, National Archives; "Trouble in Synthetic Rubber," *Fortune* 35 (June 1947): 114–19.
31. Harley Hise to John R. Steelman, 27 June 1950, Rubber Development Corporation, Miscellaneous Committees, Records of the Reconstruction Finance Corporation, RG 234.
32. Charles F. Phillips Jr., *Competition in the Synthetic Rubber Industry* (Chapel Hill: University of North Carolina Press, 1963), 45–59.
33. Collyer to William L. Batt, 11 July 1946, Batt Committee File, Rubber Development Corporation, Records of the Reconstruction Finance Corporation, RG 234; Anti Trust Division, U.S. Department of Justice, "Synthetic Rubber Patents and the Influence on Post War Competition," 14 February 1946, in Records of

the Secretary of Commerce, RG 40; R. Y. Lochhead, "BFGoodrich, Then and Now," typescript; Robert Solo, *Synthetic Rubber: A Case Study in Technological Development under Government Direction*, reprinted as *Across the High Technology Threshold: The Case of Synthetic Rubber* (Norwood, Pa.: Norwood Editions, 1980): 94.

34. Remarks of George Vaught to Security Analysts of Boston, 26 January 1948, box C-4, BFG Col.; Collyer prepared remarks, October 1950; "Annual Report," 1953: 7–8; John L. Collyer Oral History Memoir, Collyer papers.

35. The Liberian investment soon encountered cost over-runs. In 1957 the company discovered it needed a total of $5,570,000 through 1958, to include the planting of a total of 13,500 acres. The saving grace was the expectation of higher yields than originally planned and therefore of higher profits. In practice, the company actually cleared and planted 6,400 acres through 1958. "Executive Committee Meeting," 19 November 1957; National Production Authority, U.S. Department of Commerce, *Materials Survey: Rubber* (Washington, D.C.: Government Printing Office, 1952): xii–4.

36. W. S. Richardson speech to Boston Analysts' Society, Mar. 21, 1955, Box C-3, BFG Col.; *Circle-News*, 15 April 1955; *B.F. Goodrich Citizen*, 1 April 1963.

37. "Directors Meeting," 15 July 1952; Jeter interview, 9 August 1990.

38. "National Defense Bulletin #253," 28 December 1954, Rubber Manufacturers' Association, J. Penfield Seiberling Collection, Ohio Historical Society.

39. "1958/59 Review and Preview of the Rubber Industry," *Rubber Age* 84 (January 1959): 601–6.

40. Minutes of meeting, 9 July and 10 July 1945, Rubber Manufacturers' Association folder, 1945, J. Penfield Seiberling Collection; Bazaraa, "An Analysis of the Financial Expansion of the Business Corporations Engaged in the Manufacture of Rubber Tires and Tubes, 1946–1960," 53.

41. For the years 1951–60 the company predicted an annual average production of passenger cars of 5,070,000 and of trucks and buses 1,290,000. The actual outcomes were 5,770,770 and 1,156,270, respectively. "Trends and Prospects in the Automotive, Rubber and Allied Industries, 1950–1960," B.F. Goodrich pamphlet, February 1952, Labor-Management Documentation Center, Cornell University.

42. Winfield Travis Hutton, "Price Formulation and Price Behavior in Three Heavy Manufacturing Industries," Ph.D. diss., The Ohio State University, 1959, 239; "Directors Meeting," 19 June 1951.

43. "Executive Committee Meeting," 21 October 1952.

44. "The B.F. Goodrich Company, Report on Operations for the Year 1955," Collyer papers.

45. M. G. Huntington, "Your 1955 Merchandising Challenge, The Tubeless Tire," speech before the Western Division of the Oil Industry T.B.A. Group, 21 February 1955, BFG Col.

46. "Proposed Time-Table for General Motors Meeting," Collyer 1948 speech file, BFG Col.; "Goodrich Makes Up Its Mind," *Business Week*, 16 May 1953, 140–46; Perdriau interview.

47. H. B. Sanders to R. C. Riggs, 22 March 1949, P.R. series, BFG Col.

48. Goodyear, "Supervisional Newsletter," 24 April 1950, BFG Col.

49. *Wall Street Journal*, 13 July 1954.

50. "B.F. Goodrich Co. v. United States Rubber Co.," 147 *F. Supp.*, 40.

51. Hutton, "Price Formulation," 199. In 1957 Goodrich decided not to begin manufacturing nylon on its own. "Executive Committee Meeting," 5 June 1957.

52. The figures are from "The B.F. Goodrich Company, Report on Operations for the Year 1955," Collyer papers. Exact market share data among firms were kept secret. Advertising vendors did studies of market share, however, that showed Goodrich in, at best, a stable position in passenger car tires.

53. Blazey interview, 10 September 1991; Perdriau interview.

54. Perdriau interview.

55. "Calender Train Boosts Tire Production by 20% for Goodrich," *Rubber Age* 77 (July 1955): 549–50; Freeman, "Method for Application of Statistical Quality Control," *Rubber World* 138 (April 1958): 107–9; Freeman interview; Paul R. Cone et al., *Executive Decision Making through Simulation*, 2d ed. (Columbus: Charles E. Merrill Publishing Co., 1971), 154–55. See also "Automation in Rubber Manufacturing: Report of a Symposium Sponsored by the Akron Rubber Group," *Rubber Age* 78 (December 1955): 393–403. Although there were presentations by Firestone and Goodyear employees, there were none by Goodrich men.

56. Tomlinson interview.

57. Fremont A. Shull Jr., "The Advertising Appropriation in the Rubber Tire Industry: A Study in Decision-Making," Ph.D. diss., Michigan State University, 1958, 167.

58. *New York Times*, 19 August 1947.

59. "The B.F. Goodrich Company Discusses Anti-Trust Allegations," 22 August 1947, Labor-Management Documentation Center, Cornell University.

60. *New York Times*, 22 October 1948.

61. Ploesser to Garland S. Ferguson, Chairman, Federal Trade Commission, July 3, 1947, File 203-1-3-2-1, Records of the Federal Trade Commission, RG 122, National Archives.

62. Everette McIntyre to the Federal Trade Commission, 26 August 1949, file 203-1-6-1, Records of the Federal Trade Commission, RG 122, National Archives; *New York Times*, 4 January 1952.

63. *The B.F. Goodrich Company v. Federal Trade Commission et al.*, in Hariette H. Esch, comp., *Statutes and Court Decisions Pertaining to the Federal Trade Commission, 1949–1957*, vol. 5 (Washington, D.C.: Government Printing Office, 1957).

64. Warren W. Leigh, *Rubber Industry, with Particular Reference to the Tri-County Region of Ohio* (Akron: Tri-County Regional Planning Commission, 1965), 40.

65. The terms "flat" and "conveyor" belts were largely synonymous.

66. *Rubber World* 141 (December 1959): 403.

67. Tomlinson interview.

68. Arnold Zack papers, Labor-Management Documentation Center, Cornell University.

69. Recollections of Edgar Perry, 3 August 1992, typescript; Perry interview; Alfred Lief, *The Firestone Story: A History of the Firestone Tire and Rubber Company* (New York: McGraw Hill, 1951), 340.

70. *New York Times*, 6 March 1953; W. S. Richardson speech to Boston Analysts' Society, 21 March 1955, box C-3, BFGoodrich Archives; recollections of Edgar Perry, 3 August 1992, typescript; Perry interview.

71. "Annual Report," 1954, 7.

72. William L. Smith, "The New Belting Plant of The B.F. Goodrich Co. at Akron, O.," *India Rubber World* 126 (August 1952): 641–44.

73. Tomlinson interview; Perry interview.

74. W. J. Sears, "Growth Trends in the Rubber Industry," *Rubber World* 135 (January 1957): 553–58.

75. "Directors Meeting," 20 July 1948.

76. *News about BFG Industrial Products* 1 (31 July 1944): 3; *Rubber Age* 60 (October 1946): 86.

77. "Operations Council Minutes," 14 July 1945. The initial cost of the Marietta factory was $3,767,086. "Directors Meeting," 20 November 1945; Graham remarks of 21 February 1947, Graham speech file; Collyer to New York Society of Security Analysts, 20 January 1948, box C-1, BFG Col.; "A Man of Ideas: The Biography of Dr. Waldo L. Semon, Inventor of Plasticized Polyvinyl Chloride," typescript, 1991, 90–91.

78. "Annual Report," 1954, 7.

79. "Report on Operations for the Year 1955," Collyer papers; Lief, *The Firestone Story*, 365; minutes of the authorizations council, 13 August 1954; *Akron Beacon Journal*, 19 February 1957. Industrial products executives quietly accused chemical company executives of undermining their plastics operations, although no evidence survives that such was the case.

80. Docket 6043, Records of the Federal Trade Commission, RG 122, National Archives; "Report on Operations for the Year 1955," Collyer papers.

81. In 1954 the aeronautical division had 1,645 employees, down to 1,092 in 1955. "Report on Operations for the Year 1955," Collyer papers. William Perdriau, appointed in 1956 to head aerospace when it became a new division, recalled that it was earning profits in the range of 25 to 35 percent. Perdriau interview.

82. "Operations Council Minutes," 20 December 1945, and 31 January and 15 August 1946; "Executive Committee Meeting," 6 February 1946. The total cost of the purchase and relocation was $551,825.

83. *American Aviation*, 25 August 1958, 18; Jones interview.

84. Perdriau interview.

85. *American Aviation*, 15 July 1947; Jones interview.

86. Jones interview.

87. The maximum possible investment for a two-year program was $1,346,414, and the minimum requirement $586,414. "Executive Committee Meeting," 18 June 1957; 18 February 1958; Stockman interview; Japs interview.

88. W. E. Glancy, "The Manufacture of Rubber Footwear," *India Rubber World* 122 (August 1950): 529–33.

89. "Executive Committee Meeting," 4 February 1953; "Report on Operations for the Year 1955," Collyer papers; W. S. Richardson speech to Boston Analysts' Society, 21 March 1955, box C-3, BFG Col.

90. *News about BFG Industrial Products* 3 (21 June 1946): 2; "Annual Report," 1953, 5–7; "Executive Committee Meeting," 20 April 1954; "Report on Operations for the Year 1955," Collyer papers; W. S. Richardson speech to Boston Analysts' Society, 21 March 1955, box C-3, BFG Col.

91. Talalay interview; W. J. Sears, "Growth Trends in the Rubber Industry," *Rubber World* 135 (January 1957): 556.

92. "Report on Operations for the Year 1955," Collyer papers.

93. "Report on Operations for the Year 1955," Collyer papers; Jeter interviews, 9 July and 10 July 1991; "Annual Report," 1954, 1955.

94. Although the general policy in this period was for executives not to serve on the boards of other firms, an exception was Collyer's service on the board of J.P. Morgan Co., which provided valuable international contacts. John L. Collyer Oral History Memoir, Collyer papers, 48, 129.

95. "A Statement of the Position of the B.F. Goodrich Company Regarding Colombes-Goodrich," Supplemental Record Book, vol. 19, 35; "Directors Meeting," 16 April 1946; 16 July 1946.

96. New York Times, 30 October 1947; Rubber Age 62 (November 1947): 205; J. W. Keener remarks, Ciago opening, 24 September 1959, BFG Col.

97. "Operations Council Minutes," 8 February 1949; "Directors Meeting," 21 June 1949.

98. B.F. Goodrich News, 29 October 1945, 2; "The World Outlook in Rubber, An Interview with John L. Collyer," U.S. News and World Report, 6 January 1950; Rockefeller to Collyer, 25 February 1958, David Rockefeller papers, Chase Manhattan Bank Archives.

99. W. S. Richardson speech to Boston Analysts' Society, 21 March 1955, box C-3, BFG Col.

100. National Production Authority, U.S. Department of Commerce, Materials Survey: Rubber (Washington, D.C.: Government Printing Office, 1952): xi–2, 3; Akron Beacon Journal, 8 October 1959.

101. Collyer's typewritten notes, 19 May 1958, Collyer papers.

102. "Report on Operations for the Year 1955," Collyer papers.

103. Collyer to New York Society of Security Analysts, 20 January 1948, box C-1, BFG Col.; "Annual Report," 1953, 5–6; "Report on Operations for the Year 1955," Collyer papers.

104. "Remarks of Collyer to the Rubber Manufacturers' Association," 21 November 1957, box C-2, BFG Col.; Jeter interview, 9 August 1990.

105. Collyer's handwritten notes, 1 May 1957, Collyer papers.

106. Collyer's handwritten notes, 1 August 1957, Collyer papers.

CHAPTER 7

1. Moody's Stock Survey, 26 March 1958, 385; Collyer's typewritten notes, 19 May 1958, Collyer papers. In 1950 Goodrich and Union Carbide each had a 41 percent share of the PVC market, with Uniroyal, Goodyear, and Monsanto far behind with shares of 6 percent, 6 percent, and 4 percent, respectively. "Polyvinyl Chloride and BFGoodrich's Role in the Industry," typescript, n.d. (1980s), Geon Co. historical files. An important sketch of the history of the chemical industry in the twentieth century is John Kenly Smith, "The Evolution of the Chemical Industry: A Technological Perspective," in Chemical Sciences in the Modern World, Seymour H. Mauskopf, ed. (Philadelphia: University of Pennsylvania Press, 1993), 137–57.

2. Joseph Del Gatto, "BFG Chemical: Technological Dominance," Rubber World 152 (September 1965): 82; Fowles interviews, 4 January 1991, 28 August 1991; Malone interview. Rubber chemicals continued to be sold through an independent distributor.

3. Richards interview; Del Gatto, "BFG Chemical," 83.

4. "Goodrich Gets a Young, New Top Team," *Chemical and Engineering News*, 2 May 1960, 22–24; McClusky interview, 18 July 1991; Osborne interview.

5. Stevens interview; Fowles interview, 28 August 1991; Jones interview; Codrea interview; "Goodrich Gets a Young, New Top Team," 22–24.

6. Typescript about Nantz, Geon Co. historical files, n.d.; Fowles interviews, 4 January 1991, 28 August 1991; McClusky interview, 18 July 1991; Harrington interview. In general, chemical executives recalled being able to obtain needed capital from both Collyer and Keener.

7. "Topper," *Forbes*, 1 July 1949, 18; *Moody's Stock Survey*, 26 March 1958, 385. The Calvert City monomer plant opened in 1953 using hydrogen chloride and acetylene supplied by Pennsalt and Air Reduction, respectively, as well as inexpensive electricity supplied by the government-owned Tennessee Valley Authority.

8. Fowles interview, 4 January 1991; Osborne interview.

9. "Polyvinyl Chloride and BFGoodrich's Role in the Industry," typescript, n.d. (1980s), Geon Co. historical files.

10. Waldo L. Semon and G. Allan Stahl, "The History of Vinyl Chloride Polymers," reprint from the *Journal of Macromolecular Science*, part A, Chemistry, vol. 15, Geon Co. historical files. In the early postwar years Goodrich advertising attempted to teach potential customers about the wide possibilities of applying PVC. See, for example, *Modern Plastics Encyclopedia*, vol. 1 (1947), 257–72.

11. On the other hand, when Goodrich developed compounds of rigid PVC, it succeeded in keeping knowledge proprietary. Malone interview.

12. "Customer Service Provided by B.F. Goodrich Chemical Co.," pamphlet, 1955, Geon Co. historical files; Kenney interview; McClusky interview, 18 July 1991; Fowles interview, 28 August 1991; Malone interview.

13. "Policy and Appropriations Council Minutes," 13 November 1967.

14. "Trouble in Synthetic Rubber," *Fortune* 35 (June 1947): 158–62; "What Your Dollar Buys in Molded Plastics," *Modern Plastics* 27 (September 1949): 75–78; "Vinyl Chloride," *Modern Plastics* 33 (January 1956): 92–95; Osborne interview; "Report on Operations for the Year 1955," Collyer papers. Had the Goodrich figures been made public, they would have stunned the financial community. When officers of the Hercules Powder Company, a medium-sized American chemical firm during this period, studied their industry, they learned that Dow Chemical led the field in growth. Using the period 1935–39 as a base, Dow's sales in 1954 had increased 1,682 percent. Hercules' increase was 407 percent. Between 1940 and 1954, Goodrich Chemical's sales rose 5,543 percent, although from a much, much smaller base. Davis Dyer and David Sicilia, *Labors of a Modern Hercules* (Boston: Harvard Business School Press, 1990): 289.

15. "Deflated Akron?" *Barron's*, 11 July 1960, 15, 19.

16. George R. Vila, "A New Era in Synthetics to Match Plastics?" *Rubber World* 133 (January 1956): 519–22; Kenney interview.

17. *India Rubber World* 124 (June 1951): 345; R. L. Van Boskirk, "The Plastiscope," *Modern Plastics* 206–10.

18. Peter H. Spitz, *Petrochemicals: The Rise of an Industry* (New York: John Wiley, 1988), 397–99; *Modern Plastics* 39 (July 1962): 197.

19. *Modern Plastics* 33 (January 1956): 92–95; 38 (January 1961): 91–95; Shailer interview. Exact market share figures are not available.

20. "Policy and Appropriations Council Minutes," 10 September 1965.

21. R. Y. Lochhead, "BFGoodrich, Then and Now," typescript; Semon interviews, 30 July and 31 July 1990; Kenney interview.
22. Richards interview.
23. Press release, 19 May 1953; "Notes for off-the-record comments by O.P. Thomas at Paducah Luncheon," 24 February 1972, Geon Co. historical files.
24. Kenney interview. Kenney recalled that he and Schoenfeld procured a supply of the new wartime wonder drug developed in Britain, penicillin.
25. By 1972 Ciago sold $26,043,000 of goods with a net income of $1,503,000. "Directors Folder," 18 June 1973.
26. Fowles interview, 4 January 1991; Kenney interview; Richards interview.
27. When Kenney observed that Keener had decided to build a tire plant in Australia, he was able to persuade the company to construct a PVC plant also. Kenney interview. The chemical company did not produce PVC in Canada, but left that task to B.F. Goodrich Canada. Its Canadian market share was 25 percent in 1965 and 27 percent in 1971. "Policy and Appropriations Council Minutes," 8 March 1972.
28. "Policy and Appropriations Council Minutes," 12 June 1967; Kenney interview; Richards interview. No records about profits and losses in international chemical survive; executives interviewed recalled the disappointment, however.
29. "Operations Council Minutes," 6 November 1947; interview of Waldo Semon by Herbert A. Andres, 19 January 1966, BFG Col.; McCool interview. The agricultural chemicals were part of the firm's "Good-rite" line.
30. B. M. G. Zwicker, "Industrial Research and Development Techniques, "Rubber World 132 (September 1955): 745–57; Del Gatto, "BFG Chemical," 81–85.
31. Initially, the fiber was called Zetek. "Operations Council Minutes," 17 June 1949, 1 July 1949, 9 June 1950; Shailer interview; Stockman interview; Business Week, 22 October 1955, 92; New York Times, 22 June 1958. L. F. Reuter was the sales development manager for Darvan. Celanese already had a line of artificial fibers.
32. Ashe interview; Fowles interview, 28 August 1991; Pomeroy interview; New York Times, 16 February 1967.
33. "Executive Committee Meeting," 15 August 1950, 18 September 1950, 16 April 1957; "Directors Meeting," 18 May 1954; "Annual Report," 1960, 4; Richards interview.
34. C. S. Schollenberger, H. Scott, and G. R. Moore, "Polyurethane VC, a Virtually Cross-Linked Elastomer," Rubber World 137 (January 1958): 549–55; "The Urethanes Grow Up," Modern Plastics 36 (June 1959): 101–202; Frank Schoenfeld's remarks to stockholders, 20 April 1960; press release, 28 May 1969, Geon Co. historical files; Fowles interview, 28 August 1991.
35. Fowles interview, 28 August 1991.
36. Modern Plastics 37 (May 1960): 92; 38 (April 1961): 82–86, 156–59.
37. Modern Plastics 38 (September 1960): 47.
38. Press release, 14 December 1956, Geon Co. historical files; "Carbopol . . . Goodrich's Versatile New Polymer," Plastics Industry 17 (January 1959): 36–37.
39. Harrington interview; Brodine interview. The EP plant was operated by Goodrich-Gulf.
40. The relationship within the venture always remained friendly. Bonner interview.
41. Peter J. T. Morris, The American Synthetic Rubber Research Program (Philadelphia: University of Pennsylvania Press, 1989), 43–47.
42. "Chronological History of Synthetic Rubber Research," Legal Working Paper,

box H-5, BFG Col.; "Personal Experience of Waldo Semon," typescript. Goodrich and Gulf each invested equal amounts in the firm. Semon's recollection of his own close personal involvement with the discovery of polyisoprene is not sustained by the written records.

43. As Paul Cornell explained, *cis* is a Latin word meaning "on the same side" or "on this side." "In a cis molecule, therefore, certain important atoms are all on the same side." Natural rubber was a cis molecule. *Stereo-regular* was another term applied to this rubber. "Stereo-regular describes a series of atoms in a chain which are all arranged in a uniform way in space." "The Rubber of the Future," *Orange Disc* (January/February 1963): 18.

44. "Chronological History of Synthetic Rubber Research," Legal Working Paper, box H-5, BFG Col; W. L. Semon and M. A. Reinhart, "The Use of Ameripol SN in Tires," typescript, Geon Co. historical files.

45. "Chronological History of Synthetic Rubber Research," Legal Working Paper, box H-5, BFG Col.

46. Robert Solo, *Synthetic Rubber: A Case Study in Technological Development under Government Direction*, reprinted as *Across the High Technology Threshold: The Case of Synthetic Rubber* (Norwood, Pa.: Norwood Editions, 1980): 106–7; Morris, *The American Synthetic Rubber Research Program*, 43–47; "Annual Report," 1963, 19.

47. "Personal Experience of Waldo Semon," typescript; "A More Rubbery Rubber," *Business Week*, 22 December 1962, 76–77; "An Anniversary for Goodrich-Gulf," *Orange Disc* 18 (November/December 1967): 25–27.

48. "Description of Business of Goodrich-Gulf Chemicals, Inc.," n.d., Geon Co. historical files.

49. *Modern Plastics* 41 (January 1964): 89; 43 (May 1966): 135; "Directors Folder," 20 February 1968, 35; Anthony J. Piombino, "Goodrich-Gulf," *Chemical Week*, 14 April 1962, 50.

50. "President's Report to the Stockholders," 11 April 1956, Geon Co. historical files; "National Defense Bulletin #253," 28 December 1954, Rubber Manufacturers Association, J. Penfield Seiberling Collection. The Goodrich-Gulf investments were disproportionate to Goodrich's share of the rubber market. In 1955 Goodyear purchased plants with 114,800 tons; Firestone, with 129,600; and U.S. Rubber, just 22,200 tons.

51. "Ameripol, BFG Now Combined," press release, 30 December 1971, Geon Co. historical files. Bonner recalled that Gulf had no interest in being a synthetic rubber producer alone. Bonner interview.

52. *Modern Plastics* 36 (January 1959): 79–81; 39 (July 1962): 197.

53. "Policy and Appropriations Council Minutes," 30 April 1965.

54. "Executive Committee Meeting," 19 August 1958. Goodrich had sent Robert Kenney to Europe for two years as an "industrial spy" to learn about new processes. Kenney learned about the German developments in making VCM from EDC.

55. Spitz, *Petrochemicals*, 403–5; Del Gatto, "BFG Chemical."

56. "Policy and Appropriations Council Minutes," 11 July 1962, 14 July 1964.

57. "Policy and Appropriations Council Minutes," April 30, 1965.

58. Press releases, 23 February 1967 and 16 August 1968, Geon Co. historical files.

59. Ward Keener, "B.F. Goodrich—Managing for the Future," remarks to the New York Society of Security Analysts, 28 February 1967; "BFG Chemical Technology Sets Pace for 'Free World's' Vinyl Output," press release, 15 May 1969, Geon Co. historical files.

60. Shailer interview.
61. Ibid. Goodrich also learned that it was possible to ship VCM, freeing executives in deciding where to locate new plants.
62. "Annual Report," 1955, 5; "Shaping the Future," *Barron's*, 6 July 1960, 19; "A Study of Vinyl Chloride," mimeographed, 1953, Jean Malone private papers.
63. "Plastics Sales Reach New High as Market Penetration Deepens," *Modern Plastics* 44 (January 1967): 94–95; "The Plastics Pipe Industry," *Modern Plastics* 45 (October 1967): 100–105, 204; Fowles interview, 4 January 1991; Policy and Appropriations Council Minutes, 28 June 1963.
64. Gordon M. Kline, "The Year 1962 in Review," *Modern Plastics* 40 (February 1963): 140; "Plastics Sales Reach New High," 94–95, 119. The use of PVC in blow-molded applications also offered some promise; by 1965 Goodrich was selling 7 million pounds annually in the market, with forecasts indicating an increase to 66 million pounds by 1970. "Policy and Appropriations Council Minutes," 26 November 1965.
65. "Policy and Appropriations Council Minutes," 10 September 1965; Shailer interview.
66. Shailer interview.
67. "B.F. Goodrich Corporate Indexes, Selling Prices and Purchased Raw Materials Prices," 10 January 1968; "Directors Folder," 16 January 1968; McKinsey & Co., "Developing a North American PVC Strategy," presentation, 30 January 1979.
68. "Directors Folder," 21 March 1972.

CHAPTER 8

1. *Forbes*, 1 June 1963, 26.
2. *Business Week*, 14 March 1970, 142. In 1969 Goodyear and Firestone enjoyed a return on sales about average for all manufacturing, while Goodrich's (and Uniroyal's) return was considerably below average.
3. Keener interview.
4. "B.F.G.—1960–1964," Collyer papers; Keener, "B.F. Goodrich Today and Tomorrow," 7 March 1960; "B.F. Goodrich—Managing for the Future," 28 February 1967, New York Society of Securities Analysts; "Principles and Objectives, The B.F. Goodrich Company," n.d. (copy loaned to the authors by J. W. Keener Jr.).
5. Otto Scott, "B.F. Goodrich—The Pathfinder," *Rubber World* 156 (July 1967): 6.
6. When Goodrich left the tire business in 1986 through the establishment of a joint venture, Uniroyal-Goodrich, Ross left to serve as one of its top two officers.
7. "Steering toward Profitability," *Business Week*, 7 November 1959: 169–76. Keener did not succumb to the ideology of his time that executive skills were transferable from one business to another. This view had led to a so-called "conglomerate" merger wave during the 1960s in which companies bought firms in widely disparate fields with the view that management skills and financial controls transcended specialized knowledge.
8. Warren W. Leigh, *Rubber Industry, with Particular Reference to the Tri-County Region of Ohio* (Akron: Tri-County Regional Planning Commission, 1965), 221.
9. "The Diverse Treads of B.F. Goodrich," *Investor's Reader*, 18 March 1959, 20–24.
10. "The B.F. Goodrich Company," reprinted from the *Christian Science Monitor*, 1959.
11. Keener, "Principles and Objectives." In contrast to Goodrich's planned invest-

ments of $200,000,000 over five years announced in 1956, Goodyear had capital expenditures of over a half billion dollars for the period 1955–61. *Akron Beacon Journal*, 1 February 1961.

12. George Fowles's private papers, unfiled handwritten notes.
13. *Akron Beacon Journal*, 4 October 1967; "Annual Report," 1971, 28.
14. Keener, "Principles and Objectives," 6; Schoenfeld remarks to board of directors, 15 January 1963, box C-3, BFG Col.
15. Keener, "Principles and Objectives," 6–8.
16. Schoenfeld remarks to board of directors, 15 January 1963, box C-3, BFG Col.
17. Ibid.
18. Keener, keynote address, 17 June 1959, box C-3, BFG Col.; Keener, "Marketing's Job for the Future," *Journal of Marketing*, January 1960 reprint, box C-3, BFG Col.; "Steering toward Profitability," *Business Week*, 7 November 1959, 169–76; "Goodrich Is Racing on Radial Tires," *Business Week*, 17 August 1968, 48–53.
19. Keener, "B.F. Goodrich Today and Tomorrow," 7 March 1960, New York Society of Securities Analysts, box C-3, BFG Col.; Keener's remarks to the annual meeting of stockholders, 18 April 1961, box C-3, BFG Col.
20. Leigh, *Rubber Industry*, 81. There was dispute within the company, however, over who spent the advertising funds: the corporate advertising campaign or the divisions. Keener brought Lawrence Shailer to corporate headquarters to take charge of advertising at the corporate level, but Shailer was unable to persuade Keener to making a full commitment toward projecting a coordinated image of Goodrich. This situation pleased the division level executives, who thereby had more funds to spend on their particular campaigns. Shailer interview.
21. Collyer typewritten notes, 19 May 1958, Collyer papers; Leigh, *Rubber Industry*, 153; National Production Authority, U.S. Department of Commerce, *Materials Survey: Rubber* (Washington: Government Printing Office, 1952): xi–2, 3.
22. John N. Hart, remarks before Boston Security Analysts Society, 19 September 1968, box C-2, BFG Col.
23. "Policy and Appropriations Council Minutes," 13 October 1965. The company would provide $8,000,000 of the Koblenz investment and borrow the balance.
24. Codrea interview.
25. Ong interviews, 5 and 6 August 1992.
26. *Rubber World* 150 (April 1964): 3; 162 (January 1970): 65; *Chemical Week*, 3 September 1966, 23.
27. Ong interview, 9 August 1990; Blazey interview, 17 July 1991.
28. *Moody's Stock Survey*, 23 August 1965, 498.
29. John N. Hart, remarks for Financial Analysts of Philadelphia, 27 April 1967, box C-2, BFG Col.; *New York Times*, 22 November 1968.
30. *New York Times*, 11 August 1968.
31. "Annual Report," 1960: 3; Blazey interview, 10 September 1991.
32. "Annual Report," 1961: 8; remarks of Harry Warner to stockholders, 22 April 1970, box C-4, BFG Col.; "Directors Folder," 18 November 1969, 34; "Directors Folder," 16 March 1971, 7; Blazey interview, 19 July 1991.
33. Ross interview.
34. Goodrich's first passenger radial tires used rayon belts. By 1963, however, the company was experimenting with steel belts in truck tires. "Policy and Appropriations Council Minutes," 27 September 1963.
35. Ross interview; Charles F. Huber, "The Tire Companies: Can They Shake Detroit

and Make More Money?" *Rubber World* 157 (December 1967): 53. The use of rayon in the GT100 also avoided the problems associated with developing the machine tools necessary for steel belt manufacture.

36. "Policy and Appropriations Council Minutes," 14 July 1965. Goodrich explained to Ford that radial tire prices would be higher than prices for conventional tires, 28 January 1966; *New York Times*, 19 August 1966.

37. Bill Whitney, "The Radial Age; Is It, Really?" *Tire Review*, February 1968.

38. "Policy and Appropriations Council Minutes," 30 August 1968.

39. "Policy and Appropriations Council Minutes," 12 May 1969; "Year End Report: Rubber in 1968—A Complete Recovery," *Rubber World* 157 (January 1969): 33.

40. Art Zimmerman, "The New, Smart Ways of Tire Companies," *The Exchange*, January 1969, "Tire Industry and Trade" clipping file, Akron Public Library; *Rubber World* 162 (January 1970): 57.

41. Ong interview, 9 July 1990; Jeter interviews, 9 July and 10 July 1991; Ross interview.

42. Although Keener was outraged with the duplicity of his erstwhile friend, when DeYoung later asked Keener to sponsor him for membership in the yacht club of Naples, Florida, Keener, always dignified, did so. Keener interview.

43. "Directors Folder," 19 May 1970, 24; Ong interviews, 5 and 6 August 1992. Ong speculated that the Dutch tire executives were predisposed to sell to Goodyear because they disliked working with Alexander, and decided to consummate a deal with Goodyear when Goodrich was battling a merger with Northwest Industries.

44. "Directors Folder," 16 February 1971, 46.

45. *Rubber World* 162 (January 1970): 50–51; "Annual Report," 1971, 3.

46. *Rubber World* 154 (September 1966): 102.

47. Talalay interview.

48. "Rubber Fabricating," *Standard & Poor's Industry Surveys*, vol. 139, 12 August 1971, R 194.

49. Frank Schoenfeld to board of directors, 15 January 1963, box C-3, BFG Col.

50. Keener, "B.F. Goodrich Today and Tomorrow," 7 March 1960, New York Society of Securities Analysts; Frank Schoenfeld to board of directors, 15 January 1963, box C-3, BFG Col.

51. "Policy and Appropriations Council Minutes," 29 March 1963.

52. Ibid., 13 April 1965.

53. Records of the Policy and Appropriations Council, 8 March 1972.

54. Ibid., 8 September 1969.

55. Perry interview.

56. Richards interview; William Daley to authors, 1 August 1994.

57. *Rubber World* 155 (January 1967): 10.

58. Records of the Policy and Appropriations Council, 9 June 1965. With different categories of reporting, government statistics for sneakers differed from those used by Goodrich, but the trends were the same. See "Rubber Footwear Production," *Congressional Record*, 20 November 1969, 35277–78.

59. Records of the Policy and Appropriations Council, 12 September 1967.

60. Gunn interview. In 1969 Warner admitted to the directors that there were problems with the footwear division, but was optimistic that the new, efficient plant would soon allow the company to profit in shoes. "Directors Folder," 20 January 1970, 28. Other than the Puerto Rican operation, Goodrich did not consider

moving its own footwear production to overseas areas with low labor costs. In making their investments executives believed that improved technology could offset the relatively higher labor costs in the United States.

61. *New York Times,* 9 July 1961.
62. "Policy and Appropriations Council Minutes," 30 April 1965, 14 March 1967; "Annual Report," 1969, 3, 6.
63. Policy and Appropriations Council Records, 22 April 1969; "Annual Report," 1972.
64. Keener, "Free and Responsible Collective Bargaining and Industrial Peace," White House Conference on National Economic Issues, 21 May 1962, box C-3, BFG Col.; Sengpiel interview.
65. "A Push for Blue-Collar Salaries," *Business Week,* 25 February 1967, 150–52.
66. *New York Times,* 21 April 1967. Allowing one company to operate also reduced chances of the federal government ordering a "cooling-off" period under the terms of the Taft-Hartley Act of 1947.
67. *Akron Beacon Journal,* 2 July 1967.
68. Otto Scott, "B.F. Goodrich: The Pathfinder," *Rubber World* 156 (July 1967): 60; Sengpiel interview; Ong interviews, 5 August and 6 August 1992.
69. *Akron Beacon Journal,* 16 July 1967. The chemical company also suffered the longest strike in its history in 1967 when the Association of Machinists walked off the job at the Calvert City plant for six months. Supervisory personnel struggled to keep the plant operating. *New York Times,* 13 October 1967.
70. *Akron Beacon Journal,* 13 June and 14 June 1970, 25 February 1979.
71. John N. Hart, remarks for Financial Analysts of Philadelphia, 27 April 1967, box C-2, BFG Col.; *Rubber World* 162 (September 1970): 30.
72. "Up Again?" *Forbes,* 15 October 1968, 42.
73. *New York Times,* 21 January 1969; Jeter interview, 10 July 1990. Heineman's statements in retrospect reveal ignorance of the reality of Goodrich at the time. He declined a request for an interview for this history. Both he and Tisch denied any collusion.
74. "Managers' Notice," 20 January and 23 January 1969, box E-2, BFG Col.
75. Ong interview, 5 August and 6 August 1992; Mills's press release, 10 February 1969; Keener to stockholders, 21 February 1969, box E-2, BFG Col.; *New York Times,* 6 March 1969. Lawyers working for Goodrich, Goldman, Sachs, and White & Case drafted an amendment to the Internal Revenue code that was an important factor in stopping the wave of conglomerate mergers.
76. "Northwest Industries, Inc., Second Registration Statement," typescript analysis in John Weinberg files, Goldman, Sachs; "Managers' Notice," 11 July 1969, box E-2, BFG Col.
77. "Managers' Notice," 12 August 1969, box E-2, BFG Col.
78. *Rubber World* 153 (January 1966): 67.
79. John N. Hart, remarks before the Boston Security Analysts Society, 19 September 1968, box C-2, BFG Col.
80. John M. Hart, remarks before the Boston Security Analysts Society, 15 September 1968, box C-2, BFG Col.
81. "Rebound for Goodrich?" *Financial World,* 7 October 1970, 7.
82. Blazey interview, 10 September 1991.
83. Blazey interview, 19 July 1991; *Federal Trade Commission Decisions,* vol. 57 (Washington, D.C.: Government Printing Office, 1962): 96–107.
84. Eisentrout and Perry interviews.

CHAPTER 9

1. "Transcript of an interview with Pen Thomas," 4 November 1975, n.p.
2. Neil Fligstein, "The Intraorganizational Power Struggle: The Rise of Finance Personnel to Top Leadership in Large Corporations, 1919–1979," *American Sociological Review* 52 (February 1987): 55. On the transformation in management and management thinking, see Alfred D. Chandler Jr., "The Competitive Performance of U.S. Industrial Enterprises since the Second World War," *Business History Review* 68 (Spring 1994): 1–72; Chandler, *Scale and Scope: The Dynamics of Industrial Capitalism* (Cambridge: The Belknap Press of the Harvard University Press, 1990), 605–31; Jon Didrichsen, "The Development of Diversified and Conglomerate Firms in the United States, 1920–1970," *Business History Review* 46 (Summer 1972): 202–19; and Robert Locke, *Management and Higher Education since 1940* (Cambridge: Cambridge University Press, 1989), especially chap. 5.
3. Laing, Luke, Nolen, and Weinberg interviews. See also *Wall Street Journal*, 13 September 1971.
4. *Chemical Week*, 22 September 1971, 23.
5. Ong later recalled that Keener simply could not get along with Alexander and did not want him to become Goodrich's chief executive officer: "Deep down he didn't like Alexander. Alexander was just too abrasive and aggressive, too fast for him, too talkative." See Ong interview, 9 August 1990.
6. Laing, Nolen, and Weinberg interviews; and Kraftco, "Annual Reports," 1970 and 1971.
7. Ong interview, 10 May 1993.
8. Weinberg interview. While stepping down as Goodrich's chief executive officer, Keener remained a Goodrich director until January 1974. He died in early 1980.
9. *Forbes*, 27 November 1978, 73.
10. Luke, Nolen, and Weinberg interviews.
11. Gunn, Luebbers, McClusky (18 July 1991), Osborne, Pomeroy, and Ross interviews.
12. "Management Committee Meetings," 15 November, 4 December, and 15 December 1972; Ross interview; and "Transcript of Press Conference with Ralph Winter of the *Wall Street Journal*, March 13, 1973." By a 5 percent profit, Thomas meant net income divided by net sales: in 1971, this was a miserable 0.02 percent.
13. Ibid.
14. Blazey, Laing, Luke, Ong (10 May 1993), and Ross interviews; and "Management Committee Meetings," 12 September 1972 and 20 April 1973.
15. In 1971, footwear reported an operating loss of $2.8 million on net sales of $46 million. See "Directors Folders," 21 March and 24 March 1972.
16. "Annual Reports," 1970 and 1971; and Ashe, Blazey (10 September 1991), Gunn, Luke, and Perdriau interviews.
17. Converse leased and ultimately bought the Lumberton facility, and the Waserman Development Company purchased the Watertown property. Goodrich turned the Elgin plant to other uses and liquidated the Clarkesville plant. See "Directors Folders," 21 March, 20 June, and 21 November 1972.
18. This synthetic leather, which Goodrich had hoped might become a competitor for DuPont's Corfam in the 1960s, did not develop the expected demand and, like Corfam, proved to be a market failure. See "Directors Folder," 21 March

1972. After investing an estimated $100 million in Corfam's development, DuPont announced that it would stop making the synthetic leather in March 1971. See *New York Times*, 17 March, 11 April, and 20 October 1971.

19. "Annual Report," 1972; "Directors Folders," 21 March and 19 December 1972; and "Directors Meeting," 18 April 1972.

20. Goodrich sold its sponge rubber operations to Ohio Decorative Products. Goodrich's sponge (foam) rubber sales of $61 million in 1973 had resulted in an after-tax loss of $49,000. See "Directors Folder," 15 February 1972; "Directors Meetings," 17 December 1973 and 20 February 1974; Gunn interview; "Management Committee Meeting," 8 March 1974; Talalay interview; and *Wall Street Journal*, 15 March 1974.

21. *Chemical Week*, 3 September 1975, 42.

22. "Corporate Investment Strategy Defines BFG's Future."

23. John D. Ong, "Remarks to Shareholders," BFGoodrich Annual Stockholder's Meeting, 18 April 1977.

24. Ibid., 2 February 1979; Booz-Allen & Hamilton, "Discussion Outline, Corporate Diversification/Acquisition Strategy, BFGoodrich Company," 20 December 1978.

25. "BFGoodrich Policy Statement: Corporate Diversification and Acquisition Strategy, April 24, 1979." See also "Management Committee Meeting," 7 June 1979.

26. Goodrich's 1979 capital appropriation budget of $343 million, the largest annual budget of the decade, set aside $75 million for new ventures. See "Directors Folder," 15 October 1979.

27. "Annual Report," 1972; and *Financial World*, 24 November 1971, 5, 27.

28. "Management Committee Meeting," 14 July 1972.

29. On this administrative trend and problems it often caused, see Chandler, *Scale and Scope*, 623–24. Too often the vice presidents in charge of the divisions in American companies lost contact with what was going on in the divisions.

30. Ashe, Gunn, McClusky (18 July 1991), and Pomeroy interviews. Ong also remembered that when he was the president of BFGoodrich International in 1970–71 he had to ask the corporate office for any expenditure exceeding $25,000. See Ong interviews, 5 August and 6 August 1992.

31. "Directors Folder," 18 February 1976.

32. "Management Committee Meeting," 6 July 1972.

33. "Annual Reports," 1972 and 1973.

34. Ong interview, 10 May 1993. See also "Directors Meeting," 19 December 1977.

35. Ong interview, 10 May 1993.

36. Ashe, Ong (10 May 1993), and Ross interviews.

37. "Annual Report," 1978. See also "Directors Folders," 16 October 1978 and 21 May 1979; "Managers' Notice, No. 53, August 1, 1978"; and Harrington and Malone interviews.

38. Chandler, "Competitive Performance," 18–20; and Carliss Y. Baldwin and Kim B. Clark, "Capital-Budgeting Systems and Capabilities Investments in U.S. Companies after the Second World War," *Business History Review* 68 (Fall 1994): 73–109, especially 82–83.

39. "Annual Report," 1979; and "Directors Folder," 21 May 1979.

40. "Directors Folder," 21 May 1979.

41. Perry interview.

42. Ong interview, 10 May 1993.
43. David Cleland, *The Origin and Development of a Philosophy of Long-Range Planning in American Business* (New York: Arno Press, 1976).
44. "Directors Meetings," 18 June 1973 and 21 January 1974; and Ashe, Gunn, Malone, McClusky (19 July 1991), and Ong (10 May 1993) interviews.
45. "Management Committee Meeting," 20 August 1973.
46. Between 1956 and 1971, Goodrich paid out an average 59 percent of its earnings as dividends each year. Beginning in 1974, the company adopted the policy of paying out only about 30 percent. This policy was adopted "to signal investors that our target for future corporate growth is much higher than actual growth achieved between 1956 and 1971." See "Dividend Policy," in BFGoodrich, "Directors Folder," 19 November 1973.
47. "Management Committee Meetings," 30 July 1973, 6 August and 19 August 1974, and 12 May 1977.
48. "Annual Reports," 1977 and 1978; and Ashe, Gunn, and McClusky (18 July 1991) interviews.
49. "Annual Report," 1978; and "Directors Folders," 18 April 1977 and 15 January 1979.
50. Codrea, Luebbers, McClusky (19 July 1991), Norman, Perdriau, Ong (10 May 1993), and Pomeroy interviews.
51. Ash and Ong (10 May 1993) interviews.
52. "Annual Report," 1975.
53. William Wooldredge, "Do They Really Work?" *Management Review* (April 1979): 12.
54. Harrington, Heuerman, Norman, Ong (10 May 1993), and Ulle interviews. Thomas was far from alone in his use of holders of M.B.A.s. Between 1954 and 1964, the number of M.B.A.s awarded by American universities doubled to 6,375, and over the next four years it tripled to 19,335, with a growing proportion specializing in finance. Thomas's goal in hiring consultants was, he said, twofold: "first, to get the objectivity that an outsider can provide; and, second, to acquire for a short period of time a great number of highly trained and experienced analytical people." See "Transcript of Interview," 4 November 1975.
55. "Transcript," 4 November 1975, n.p.
56. "Directors Folder," 19 November 1973.
57. Ong interview, 10 May 1993.
58. Blazey (17 July 1991), Laing, Luke, and Ong (10 May 1993) interviews; and O. Pendleton Thomas, "Remarks at BFGoodrich's Annual Meeting, April 18, 1977." On Goodyear, see *New York Times*, 4 March 1976.
59. Thomas, "Remarks . . . 1977." See also "Management Committee Meeting," 7 September 1978.
60. Ong interviews, 10 May 1993 and 2 May 1994. On Alexander's commitment to tires, see also Ross interview.
61. "Management Committee Meetings," 20 April and 14 May 1973.
62. Codrea, Laing, Luebbers, Ong (10 May 1993), and Weinberg interviews.
63. Ross interview. See also Ong interview, 10 May 1993.
64. Weinberg interview.
65. Ong interview, 10 May 1993.
66. BFGoodrich, "Tire Division Long-Term Strategic Plan, 1976–1980," n.p., from Benjamin Jones.

67. Michael French, *U.S. Tire Industry* (Boston: Twayne Publishers, 1991), chap. 9, surveys changes in the tire industry during the 1970s. See also Charles Jeszeck, "Structural Change in CB: The U.S. Tire Industry," *Industrial Relations* 25 (Fall 1986): 229–48.
68. Jeszeck, "Structural Change," 234–35.
69. *New York Times,* 20 April 1977 and 15 April 1979.
70. "Management Committee Meeting," 25 June 1973.
71. "Directors Folders," 20 June 1972 and 20 March 1973.
72. Ross, "Remarks . . . May 20, 1974."
73. "Annual Reports," 1971–73; "Directors Folders," 17 September 1973 and 15 June 1974; "Directors Meeting," 10 February 1973; and "Management Committee Meetings," 22 December 1972 and 10 September 1973.
74. Laing, Luebbers, and Ulle interviews.
75. "Directors Folder," 16 July 1979.
76. "Annual Report," 1975; and Blazey, Codrea, and Luebbers interviews. Goodrich completed the sale of the Los Angeles plant to Don Kroll in 1977 for just under $5 million. See "Directors Folder," 19 September 1977.
77. Luebbers, Ong (10 May 1993), and Ross interviews; and "Management Committee Meetings," 10 October 1972 and 23 July 1974.
78. Derived from the annual reports of the companies, and from Goodrich's "Directors Folders."
79. Ong (10 May 1993), Ross, and Perdriau interviews; and "Management Committee Meetings," 5 June 1972 and 16 July 1973.
80. Daniel-Guy Denoual, "The Diffusion of Innovation: An Institutional Approach," Ph.D. diss., Harvard University Graduate School of Business Administration, 1980, 329.
81. "Annual Report," 1972; "Directors Folders," 19 September 1977, 22 February 1978, and 16 July 1979; and Harrington interview.
82. For an overview of the changing nature of collective bargaining in the tire industry in the 1970s, see Jeszeck, "Structural Change."
83. *New York Times,* 26 April 1973.
84. Ibid., 8 May, 10 May, 11 May, 14 May, 15 May, and 1 June 1973; *Rubber Age* (January 1974): 41–42. See also Ong interview, 10 May 1993.
85. Blazey, Devendorf, Ross, and Ong (10 May 1993) interviews.
86. *New York Times,* 18 April, 19 April, 20 April, 21 April, and 23 April 1976. Goodrich executives estimated that the economic package offered by Firestone would cost their company $2.26 per hour over the life of a three-year contract, if the URW accepted it. See BFGoodrich, "Operations Report," June 1976.
87. *New York Times,* 7 July 1976. See also "Directors Meeting," 19 July 1976.
88. *New York Times,* 16 July and 24 July 1976.
89. *Akron Beacon Journal,* 6 September and 12 September 1976.
90. Firestone, "Annual Reports," 1975–76; and Goodyear, "Annual Reports," 1975–76.
91. *Akron Beacon Journal,* 21 April 1977; "BFGoodrich Board Presentation, October 20, 1976"; and handwritten notes misfiled in "Directors Folder," 20 October 1975.
92. *Akron Beacon Journal,* 14 June and 16 June 1979; and Codrea interview. See also Devendorf, Luebbers, Ross, and Ong (10 May 1993) interviews.
93. "Directors Folder," 15 July 1974.

94. "Annual Reports," 1976 and 1979; Eisentrout and Ross interviews; and *Rubber World* 170 (August 1974): 13.
95. *Business Week*, 14 November 1977, 83; "Directors Meeting," 19 January 1976; and Eisentrout and Ross interviews.
96. Eisentrout interview. See also "Directors Meetings," 18 January 1972, and 20 February and 17 December 1973; and Ross interview.
97. Eisentrout interview. In the late 1970s, Goodrich switched its ads to emphasize the reliability of its radials. The ads pictured Goodrich as "the company you can trust." See "Directors Folder," 17 January 1977.
98. Denoual, "Diffusion of Technology," 327.
99. Eisentrout and Ross interviews. On the introduction of the T/A see *Akron Beacon Journal*, 6 January 1971.
100. "Annual Reports," 1975–79; and Eisentrout, Luebbers, and Ross interviews.
101. Heuerman interview. See also Devendorf and Ross interviews.
102. These figures are for the sales of International BFGoodrich. International BFGoodrich made all of Goodrich's nonchemical foreign sales (except those made in Canada) until 1979. These sales were generally more profitable than domestic tire sales, but less profitable than other nontire Goodrich sales in the United States. BFGoodrich International's operating income averaged 6.9 percent of net sales between 1972 and 1977 (the last year for which figures are available). This statistic is derived from figures in the "Directors Folders."
103. "Directors Folders," 18 July 1972, 12 February and 16 December 1974, 17 November 1975, and 18 February and 19 April 1976. On the problems with labor and the Dutch government, see also McClusky (18 July 1991) and Ong (10 May 1993) interviews.
104. McClusky (18 July 1991) interview.
105. "Annual Report," 1976.
106. Devendorf interview. On Goodrich's market share see *Business Week*, 26 July 1976, 50–51.
107. "Directors Folder," 18 January 1972, 20 February 1974, and 18 February 1976; and McClusky (18 July 1991) interview.
108. "Directors Meeting," 19 February 1975.
109. "Annual Report," 1981; "Directors Folders," 19 September 1972 and 21 November 1977; and Ong interview, 2 May 1994.
110. "Management Committee Meeting," 21 June 1974.
111. McClusky to the authors, 17 February 1995; and Norman and Ong (2 May 1994) interviews.
112. "Annual Report," 1979. See also "Directors Folder," 18 June 1979.
113. "Annual Report," 1980.
114. "Directors Folders," 19 September 1972 and 20 August 1976.
115. "Directors Folder," 16 July 1979.
116. "Annual Report," 1981; "Directors Folder," 17 May 1976; "Management Committee Meeting," 6 May 1977; and Ong interview, 9 August 1992.
117. Derived from the annual reports of Goodyear and Firestone for the 1970s.
118. French, *U.S. Tire Industry*, chap. 9.
119. These figures are derived from Goodyear's and Firestone's annual reports.
120. *Modern Tire Dealer*, 28 January 1980.
121. The figures for Goodyear and Firestone are derived from their annual reports.

122. Osborne and Shailer interviews. Between 1974 and 1979, chemicals received appropriations of $417 million, while tires got only $211 million.

123. Ong interview, 10 May 1993. In 1971, the chemical division moved its headquarters to a new office building in Independence, Ohio, ten miles south of Cleveland. Worried that this location might continue to give the division too much freedom from corporate headquarters, Thomas threatened to move chemical's headquarters to Akron, unless its executives cooperated fully with corporate plans. See Ashe interview.

124. Ong interview, 5 May 1993. On Thomas's abiding interest in commodity chemicals and PVC see also Harrington, Luebbers, Perdriau, and Ross interviews.

125. "Directors Folder," 21 March 1972.

126. "Annual Reports," 1971–73; "Directors Meeting," 16 January 1973; and "Management Committee Meeting," 12 November 1972.

127. "Annual Report," 1973; "Directors Folders," 8 March 1972 and 15 July 1974; "Management Committee Meetings," 14 November, 12 December, and 22 December 1972, 10 September 1973, and 9 July 1974; and Shailer interview. Not all plants were expanded. In 1971, Goodrich's original—but now small and inefficient—PVC installation at Niagara Falls, New York, was closed.

128. "Annual Reports," 1975–77; "Directors Folder," 19 April 1976; "Management Committee Meeting," 15 November 1977; and Malone interview.

129. McKinsey & Co., "Developing a North American PVC Strategy," presentation, 30 January 1979, 41–45.

130. "Annual Report," 1977, contains a special report on how Goodrich's PVC was used.

131. McKinsey & Co., "Developing a North American PVC Strategy," 14, 28. The figures include Estane and Abson with PVC, but PVC composed the great bulk of the output of these three products.

132. Norman interview. See also Heuerman and Ong (2 May 1994) interviews. Ong later recalled that the overriding concern of Goodrich executives was that they had "to get more leverage on costs."

133. "Management Committee Meetings," 16 February and 11 May 1973.

134. Ibid., 24 April 1974.

135. McClusky to the authors, 17 February 1995; and Ong interview, 2 May 1994.

136. "Directors Folder," 20 October 1975, contains Vittone's presentation to the board. On Vittone as a manager, see Malone interview.

137. Ibid.; "Management Committee Meeting," 15 March 1976; and Ong interview, 10 May 1993. In early 1976 Goodrich entered into a $100 million contract with Dow, in which the chemical company agreed to supply Goodrich with 550 million pounds of VCM over five years beginning in 1978. Goodrich executives thought that, at best, this contract would provide their company with half of the VCM it needed to acquire from external sources. The need for greater supplies of VCM remained. In 1978 Goodrich entered into a contract with Shell Chemical, by which Shell would supply Goodrich with up to $77 million worth of VCM over the next five years. However, this contract could be canceled at the end of 1982, should Goodrich build its own VCM plant.

138. Ong interview, 10 May 1993.

139. "Management Committee Meetings," 13 June, 15 June, and 19 June 1977; and Ong interview, 10 May 1993.

140. Ibid.; and Harrington interview.
141. Ong interview, 2 May 1994, Ulle interview, and telephone interview with Thomas Waltermire, 28 March 1994.
142. "Management Committee Meetings," 15 June and 19 June 1977; and Ong (10 May 1993) and Ulle interviews. Ong recalls the vote of the management committee to go ahead as three-to-two; McClusky remembers it as four-to-one.
143. "Directors Meeting," 20 June 1977; and Luke and Weinberg interviews.
144. Ibid; see also *Wall Street Journal*, 21 July 1977. Goodrich could not borrow additional large sums itself without violating already existing debt covenants. See Devendorf and Ulle interviews.
145. "Management Committee Meeting," 27 July 1978; and "Operations Council Meeting," 13 June 1978.
146. "Directors Folders," 18 September 1978 and 16 October 1979; and Malone interview.
147. "Management Meeting," 23 October 1979.
148. McKinsey & Co., "North American PVC Strategy Project, Plastics Profit Center, November 7, 1978."
149. McKinsey & Co., "Developing a North American PVC Strategy," 30 January 1979, especially pages 85 and 87.
150. "Management Committee Meeting," 10 March 1979.
151. Press release, 31 July 1979; and *Wall Street Journal*, 1 August 1979.
152. "Directors Folder," 15 January 1979; "Management Committee Meeting," 8 January 1979; and press release, 1 February 1979.
153. "Directors Folder," 17 September 1979.
154. Malone interview; Shailer interview; and McKinsey & Co., "Developing a North American PVC Strategy," 20, 34, 47. America's output of PVC rose 15.5 percent annually in 1960–65, and 10.1 percent annually over the next five years. About 6 billion pounds of PVC were made in the United States in 1979.
155. *Chemical Week*, 23 May 1979, 44–45.
156. *Chemical and Engineering News*, 3 September 1979, 13.
157. "Annual Report," 1974; and "Directors Folder," 17 June 1974 (this includes a report by Johnson); and Ong interview, 10 May 1993.
158. Harrington interview.
159. Harrington, Heuerman, Malone, McClusky (18 July 1991), and Ong (10 May 1993) interviews.
160. McClusky interview, 18 July 1991.
161. "Annual Report," 1974; "Directors Meeting," 20 February 1974; "Management Committee Meetings," 12 February, 5 March, and 24 June 1974; and Malone interview.
162. "Annual Reports," 1971 and 1976; "Directors Folder," 19 June 1978; and "Directors Meeting," 19 February 1975.
163. "Annual Report," 1976; and "Directors Folder," 23 February 1977.
164. "Directors Folder," 23 February 1977; and Ong interview, 2 May 1994.
165. "Annual Reports," 1971–74; and Ong interview, 2 May 1994.
166. "Directors Folder," 18 November 1974; "Management Committee Meetings," 29 May and 17 June 1974; and Shailer interview.
167. "Directors Folder," 18 October 1976.
168. BFGoodrich, "1980 Chemical Strategy Plan," 15–17.
169. "Annual Reports," 1975–77.

170. "Annual Report," 1979.

171. "Directors Folder," 20 November 1978.

172. Ibid.; "Management Committee Meeting," 30 April 1979; and Blazey and Gunn interviews.

173. Ong interview, 26 March 1994.

174. Ibid.

175. Luke, McClusky (18 July 1991), Ong (10 May 1993), Pomeroy, Ross, and Ulle interviews; and Wall Street Journal, 16 January 1980.

176. Ong interview, 2 May 1994.

177. "Annual Report," 1979; "Directors Folder," 16 July 1979; and Business Week, 14 November 1977, 78.

178. Press release, 3 December 1971.

179. Ibid.; and "Annual Report," 1972.

180. "Annual Reports," 1970–80.

181. "Annual Report," 1975; and Ong interview, 10 May 1993.

182. In 1971 Goodrich's overseas chemical manufacturing subsidiaries in Australia, Holland, New Zealand, Venezuela, and Costa Rica reported earnings averaging 7.7 percent (operating income as a percentage of net sales), and in 1972 earnings averaged 8.1 percent. By 1976 earnings had fallen to 4.4 percent and a year later to only 3.4 percent. Goodrich's chemical operations in Canada continued to be handled by BFG Canada and are not included in these figures. See "Directors Folders," 20 February 1973 and 22 February 1978.

183. Press release, 2 July 1981; "Directors Folder," 18 June 1973; and Norman and Shailer interviews. Ciago's sales came to about $60 million in 1980.

184. "Annual Reports," 1977–78; press release, 9 August 1994; and Shailer interview.

185. Press release, 8 September 1971; "Directors Folder," 19 June 1978; "Management Committee Meeting," 9 April 1973; McClusky to the authors, 17 February 1995; and Ong (2 May 1994) and Shailer interviews.

186. Press releases, 16 May 1972 and 8 June 1979; "Directors Folder," 20 March 1978; "Management Committee Meetings," 13 February 1973 and 11 May 1976; and O. P. Thomas, "Niagara Opening," 8 June 1979.

187. BFGoodrich, "Ventures in Vinyl: BFGoodrich in Australia, 1961–1991"; press release, 6 July 1976; and "Management Committee Meetings," 21 November 1972, 19 April 1976, and 19 December 1977.

188. "Management Committee Meetings," 5 October and 8 December 1978.

189. "Annual Report," 1971; press release, 16 August 1971; and Shailer interview.

190. Press release, 18 July 1971; "Directors Folder," 22 February 1978; and "Management Committee Meetings," 10 November 1977, and 23 January and 8 February 1978.

191. Chandler, "Chemicals and Electronics: Winning and Losing in Post-War American Industry," 16 November 1993, especially pp. 3, 13–14, 22, 27, 31–32. We are indebted to Chandler for allowing us access to this unpublished manuscript. McKinsey & Co., "Developing a North American PVC Strategy," 62, examines Goodrich. On Tenneco see Barron's, 17 May 1980, 42–43; Business Week, 23 November 1981, 80–91; Chemical Week, 17 December 1980, 17; Financial World, 1 May 1980, 44–45; and Fortune, 12 January 1981, 48–49.

192. Chandler, "Chemicals and Electronics," 61.

193. As Chandler has observed, "oil and other companies whose capabilities rested on the exploitation of economies of scale inherent in continuous-process produc-

tion expanded their output of commodity chemicals." See Chandler, "Competitive Performance," 34.

194. *Forbes*, 1 December 1975, 68.
195. Pomeroy interview.
196. Perry interview.
197. Pomeroy interview.
198. Codrea interview. On the failure to modernize, see also Ong interview, 9 August 1990.
199. Codrea, Ong (10 May 1993), and Perry interviews.
200. Pomeroy interview.
201. "Directors Folder," 15 January 1979; "Management Committee Meeting," 15 November 1978; and *Wall Street Journal*, 5 January 1979.
202. Perry interview. See also Codrea and Pomeroy interviews.
203. "Annual Reports," 1970–75; and "Management Committee Meetings," 24 April, 13 May, and 9 July 1974.
204. Ulle interview.
205. "Annual Reports," 1976 and 1980; "Management Committee Meeting," 30 March 1978; and Devendorf, Heuerman, Ong (10 May 1993), Perry, and Pomeroy interviews.
206. "Directors Folder," 19 December 1972.
207. Codrea, Perry, and Pomeroy interviews.
208. "Directors Folder," 20 February 1974.
209. Ibid., 20 February and 15 July 1974, 19 July 1976, and 7 June 1979.
210. Pomeroy interview.
211. "Directors Folder," 19 March 1979.
212. On sales of $58 million in 1972 and $71 million a year later, aerospace earned an average 14 percent on its capital. Commercial sales were 25 percent of the division's total in 1962, but 58 percent a decade later. See "Annual Report," 1972; "Directors Folders," 20 March 1973 and 18 March 1974; and Ashe, Codrea, Ong (5 August and 6 August 1992, and 10 May 1993), Perry, and Pomeroy interviews. Ong later explained, "we [corporate management] viewed them [aerospace's management] as being very unaggressive." See Ong interviews, 5 August and 6 August 1992.
213. McClusky (18 July 1991), Perry, and Pomeroy interviews.
214. Perry interview.
215. "Annual Reports," 1977–79; "Directors Folders," 17 April and 7 September 1978; Perry and Pomeroy interviews; and "Management Committee Meetings," 22 August 1978 and 25 September 1980.
216. Ong (10 May 1993), Perry, and Pomeroy interviews; and "Management Committee Meetings," 27 March 1973, 9 April 1974, and 15 December 1978.
217. "Annual Report," 1983; "Directors Folder," 7 September 1978; and Heuerman and Ong (10 May 1993) interviews.
218. "Directors Meeting," 18 March 1974.
219. "Management Committee Meeting," 14 July 1972; and "Transcript of interview," 4 November 1975, n.p.
220. Perry interview.
221. "Annual Report," 1973.
222. For reports on Goodrich's research see "Annual Reports," 1973, 1976, and 1977.
223. "Management Committee Meeting," 10 December 1979.

224. "Directors Folder," 21 May 1979.
225. These figures are derived from "Directors Folders," 21 July 1975, 19 January 1976, 17 January 1977, and 16 January 1978.
226. McClusky to authors, 17 February 1995.
227. Industrial products remained steady at 17–22 percent of sales in the 1970s. Industrial products' share of the company's operating income fluctuated during the 1970s, coming to about 18 percent in 1979.
228. Norman interview.
229. *Forbes*, 1 December 1975, 68.
230. *Forbes*, 27 November 1978, 73. See also *Business Week*, 14 November 1977, 78.
231. Derived from *Standard & Poor's Industry Surveys*, 1978–80.

CHAPTER 10

1. America's gross national product (GNP) climbed from $1.7 trillion in 1976 to $2.7 trillion in 1980. Then economic growth slowed to a trickle. America's GNP rose to $3.1 trillion in 1982 and to $3.3 trillion in 1983. America's consumer price index moved upward 13 percent in 1979, another 13 percent in 1980, and 9 percent in 1981. Only in 1982 did the rate of increase fall to 4 percent, the level at which it stayed through 1985. See U.S. Department of Commerce, "Business Statistics, 1963–91" (Washington, D.C.: Government Printing Office, 1992), appendix II, A-96, A-98. The GNP figures are in constant dollars.
2. Ong interview, 5 May 1993.
3. Laing interview.
4. Ashe interview. America's business press also viewed Ong's election as CEO as a natural progression. See *Wall Street Journal*, 19 June 1979.
5. Most of the following biographic sketch is drawn from our interviews with Ong, 5 August and 6 August 1992.
6. John Ong to Marc de Logeres, 22 September 1983.
7. Eisentrout interview.
8. Pomeroy interview.
9. Ong interview, 2 May 1994.
10. "Annual Report," 1981. See also *Wall Street Journal*, 17 January 1980.
11. Braxton Associates, "Strategic Priorities for the Eighties," 20 December 1979.
12. "Annual Report," 1981.
13. Ibid., 1980–81.
14. Ibid., 1980.
15. *Business Week*, 9 March 1981, 49–50; *Forbes*, 15 September 1980; and *Wall Street Journal*, 17 January 1980. In 1981, however, Moody's lowered Goodrich's senior debt rating from A to Baa.
16. Ong interview, 26 March 1994.
17. BFGoodrich, "1980 Chemical Strategic Plan," 6–8.
18. *Chemical and Engineering News*, 6 October 1980, 13.
19. Ibid., 6 September 1982, 12–13.
20. Ibid., 18 June 1984, 27, shows graphs of PVC consumption in America for 1979–84.
21. *Chemical Week*, 4 April 1984, 24–25.
22. "Annual Reports," 1983 and 1984.
23. *Business Week*, 6 August 1979, 90, 92; 29 September 1980, 41–42; 8 December

1980, 73; 26 July 1982, 74–75; *Chemical and Engineering News*, 6 October 1980, 16; 5 April 1982, 20; 12 July 1982, 7; 14 February 1983, 8; and *Chemical Week*, 24 September 1980, 14; 17 December 1980, 16; 13 January 1982, 12; 23 February 1983, 11–12; 30 November 1983, 20.

24. *Business Week*, 29 September 1980, 41–42; *Chemical and Engineering News*, 31 August 1981, 16; *Chemical Week*, 4 May 1983, 27; 4 April 1984, 25; McClusky interview, 3 August 1994; Ong interview, 26 March 1994.

25. *Business Week*, 1 August 1983, 37; and *Forbes*, 15 July 1985, 88–93.

26. *Chemical and Engineering News*, 21 July 1980, 17; *Chemical Week*, 16 July 1980, 19; 10 February 1982, 56–57.

27. *Business Week*, 22 October 1979, 178–80; 21 September 1981, 32; 30 August 1982, 22–23; 11 July 1983, 78–79; *Chemical Week*, 30 May 1979, 18; 24 November 1982, 13–14; and *Fortune*, 21 March 1983, 95–96.

28. "1980 Chemical Strategic Plan," 11, 14.

29. Ibid., 1, 11.

30. "Annual Report," 1980.

31. "Annual Reports," 1980–82.

32. Ibid., and McClusky interview, 3 August 1994.

33. "Annual Reports," 1980–83.

34. *Chemical Week*, 30 September 1981.

35. Ong interview, 10 May 1993.

36. *Business Week*, 1 July 1985, 27.

37. For the decline in prices of chlorine and ethylene, see *Chemical and Engineering News*, 5 April 1982, 20.

38. Devendorf interview.

39. Ross interview.

40. Derived from figures in *Chemical Week*, 24 October 1984, 10.

41. "1985 Corporate Investment Strategy."

42. "Annual Report," 1984.

43. Ong interview, 26 March 1994. Not all shared high hopes for specialty PVC. As he later recalled the situation, McClusky believed that Goodrich's output of commodity PVC was simply too great to convert to specialty PVC—that the market for specialty PVC was simply much smaller than the market for commodity PVC. See McClusky interview, 3 August 1994.

44. "Annual Reports," 1981–83.

45. Ong interview, 26 March 1994. Goodrich made CPVC by increasing commodity PVC's chlorine content by about 10 percent. This step made it more resistant to heat and impacts. See *Chemical Week*, 20 October 1982, 40.

46. "1980 Chemical Strategic Plan," 15–17.

47. "Annual Reports," 1982–84.

48. Ibid.; and "1985 Corporate Investment Strategy."

49. John Kenly Smith Jr., "The End of the Chemical Industry? Organizational Capabilities and Industry Expansion," unpublished paper presented at the Business History Conference, Williamsburg, Virginia, March 1994. Cited and quoted with the permission of the author.

50. Ong interview, 26 March 1994.

51. "Annual Reports," 1980 and 1981.

52. "Annual Reports," 1980–84; and "1985 Corporate Investment Strategy."

53. Ibid.; and Ong interview, 26 March 1994. With an average annual OIRONCE of

nearly 14 percent for the years 1981 through 1984, Tremco was a star performer. See also "Tremco Notebook and Strategy Plan, 1980."

54. Ibid. The average annual OIRONCE for specialty chemicals was 13.5 percent between 1981 and 1984. Between 1981 and 1984, PVC operations had the miserable average annual OIRONCE of 0.6 percent. These figures do not include those for Tremco.

55. Ibid. The tire division's profits (as measured by OIRONCE) averaged 12 percent between 1981 and 1984. To use a slightly different measure, the division's operating income as a proportion of its assets came to 6 percent in 1979, 9 percent in 1980, and 12 percent annually from 1981 through 1983.

56. BFGoodrich, "1980 Tires Strategic Plan," n.p.

57. Ong interview, 26 March 1994. See also correspondence between Goodrich's officers and executives at Dunlop and Michelin, 1981–83.

58. Ong interview, 26 March 1994. On this decision, see also Eisentrout, Luebbers, and Ross interviews.

59. Michael J. French, The U.S. Tire Industry: A History (Boston: Twayne, 1991), 111.

60. "Annual Report," 1980.

61. Ibid., 1982.

62. Ibid., 1982 and 1983.

63. "1985 Corporate Investment Strategy."

64. "Annual Reports," 1980–84.

65. Ibid., 1981–84; and "Management Committee Meeting," 6 February 1981. By 1984 Goodrich was consuming only about half of the synthetic rubber made in its plants, selling the rest on the open market.

66. "Annual Report," 1982. The figures include those for Tremco.

67. Industrial products suffered severe losses in 1982. Of the $40 million lost by engineered products that year, $35 million resulted from a charge against industrial products.

68. "Annual Reports," 1983 and 1984.

69. Ibid. Nor did the fabricated polymers division, which manufactured pond liners, wall coverings, and industrial plastics, do well. Loosely associated with the industrial products division, fabricated polymers was also hurt by the recession. Its officers sold their Los Angeles plant and began upgrading their Marietta, Ohio, plant in 1980.

70. "Annual Reports," 1980–84. Product liability suits also hurt Continental Conveyor, for some of its early above-ground systems performed poorly. See Ong (26 March 1994) and Pomeroy interviews.

71. "Annual Reports," 1980–81.

72. Wall Street Journal, 6 May 1980.

73. "Annual Report," 1982.

74. Ibid., 1979–84. Another measure of profitability, Goodrich's operating income expressed as a percentage of its assets, was equally dismal: a paltry annual average of 5.6 percent from 1979 through 1983.

75. John Ong, "Corporate Investment Strategy, November 26, 1984," 2.

76. Ong interview, 26 March 1994.

77. There was a lot of the discussion at the 1982 conference about PVC. The drop in market demand led Goodrich officers to "recognize the new realities in raw materials markets through adjustment in purchasing and manufacturing plans."

There was, as yet, no real sense of urgency, however. See "Rolling Rock Conference Summary of Discussion," 1982.

78. Ibid., 1983. They also expected net income to increase sevenfold by 1987, rising to $412 million.
79. Ibid., 1984.
80. Ibid.
81. Ong (26 March 1994) and Weinberg interviews; and *Wall Street Journal*, 11 March, 17 March, 15 April, 12 August, and 2 September 1981, and 13 August and 2 September 1982. Precisely what occurred at Bluhdorn's office is unclear. Ong does not recall Weinberg's presence.
82. "Annual Report," 1985; Luke, Ong (26 March 1994), and Weinberg interviews.
83. Ong interview, 26 March 1994.
84. Ibid.
85. "BFG Today," June/July 1990, 1; BFGoodrich, "Biographical Sketch of Leigh Carter."
86. Ong interview, 26 March 1994.
87. "BFG Today," June/July 1990, 1.
88. Ong interview, 10 May 1993.
89. Weinberg interview.
90. Luke interview.
91. Ong interview, 26 March 1994.
92. Eisentrout interview. See also Ong interview, 10 May 1993.
93. Ong interview, 26 March 1994.
94. Ong, "Corporate Investment Strategy, November 26, 1984," 1–3.
95. Ibid., 5–8.
96. "Corporate Investment Strategy, November 26, 1984"; and Carter to Ong, 30 November 1984.
97. "Managers Meeting," 3 December 1984.
98. "1985 Corporate Investment Strategy."
99. "Presentations Given to Board of Directors, December 17, 1984, and February 20, 1985."
100. Weinberg interview.
101. "Annual Reports," 1985 and 1986; Ong interview, 26 March 1994; and "Presentation to BFG Board of Directors Meeting, May 20, 1985."
102. Blazey (17 July 1991), Codrea, Eisentrout, and Ross interviews.
103. However, a $25 million charge resulted from writing off obsolete chemical equipment in plants at Calvert City and Avon Lake and from closing the Long Beach plant completely. See "Presentation, May 20, 1985."
104. *Industry News*, January 1987, 12.
105. Smith, "The End of the Chemical Century?" 2. For a listing of chemical company mergers in the 1980s, see *Chemical Week*, 2 August 1989, 102–10.
106. Chandler, "Chemicals and Electronics: Winning and Losing in Post-War American Industry," unpublished paper, 4, 15–16, 24, and 34.
107. "Annual Report," 1983.
108. Ong, "Corporate Investment Strategy, November 26, 1984."
109. "Annual Report," 1986.
110. "Managers Meeting," 3 December 1984.
111. "Strategic Objectives 1987–89."
112. "Annual Reports," 1983 and 1991; and "BFGoodrich, 1984–88."

113. "Strategic Objectives and Key Events, 1985–87," and "Strategic Objectives and Key Events, 1987–89." For the background thoughts leading to these plans, see "Minutes of Rolling Rock Meetings, 1985–88."

114. "Annual Reports," 1988 and 1993.

115. BFGoodrich, "Biography of David L. Burner"; and Ong interview, 26 March 1994.

116. As measured by operating income divided by capital investment.

117. "Annual Reports," 1985–88.

118. "Annual Report," 1988; and Ong interview, 26 March 1994.

119. "Annual Reports," 1986–88; and "Strategic Objectives 1987–89."

120. Ong interview, 26 March 1994.

121. Ibid.

122. "Annual Report," 1988.

123. Ibid.

124. "Strategic Objectives 1987–89."

125. Ibid.

126. "Annual Reports," 1985–88.

127. Ibid.

128. "Strategic Objectives 1987–89."

129. "Annual Reports," 1986–88.

130. "Strategic Objectives 1987–89."

131. "Annual Reports," 1985–89.

132. Ong interview, 26 March 1994.

133. *Chemical Week*, 18 March 1987, 70. On the recovery in PVC demand, see also *Chemical and Engineering News*, 3 June 1985, 36; 7 July 1986, 14; 24 August 1984, 47; 14 December 1987, 9; and *Chemical Week*, 23 November 1988, 6. Nearly all of the PVC consumed in America was made in America. Of the 8.5 billion pounds consumed in the United States in 1988, only 140 million pounds were imports. See *Chemical Week*, 24 May 1989, 16.

134. "Annual Reports," 1986–88; and "Strategic Objectives 1987–89."

135. *Chemical Week*, 12 October 1988, 12.

136. Ong interview, 26 March 1994.

137. On Occidental's PVC strategy, see *Chemical Week*, 1–8 January 1986, 12–14; 2 September 1987, 30–33; *Chemical and Engineering News*, 2 May 1988, 19–22; and Occidental Petroleum, "Annual Report," 1987. In 1988 Occidental spent $1.25 billion to buy Cain Chemical, a Houston-based maker of high-density polyethylene and ethylene glycol. See *Chemical Week*, 27 April 1988, 9–13. Looking back at the 1980s in early 1990, Armand Hammer, the chairman and chief executive officer of Occidental Petroleum, observed that during the decade his company had consciously "expanded our chemical business from a minor player in commodity chemicals to a highly integrated and highly profitable market leader."

138. Occidental Petroleum, "Annual Report," 1989.

139. Derived from figures in *Chemical Week*, 4 November 1987, 57. For figures on company capacity, see also *Chemical Week*, 1–8 January 1986, 14.

140. See the Occidental Petroleum File, 1986. See also *Chemical and Engineering News*, 26 May 1986, 6; 2 May 1988, 19–22; *Chemical Week*, 25 January 1984, 12; 16 January 1985, 11; 4 March 1987, 11–12; and Occidental Petroleum, "Annual Report," 1987.

141. Ong interview, 26 March 1994.

142. "Annual Reports," 1986–89.
143. "Strategic Objectives 1987–89."
144. John Case, *From the Ground Up: The Resurgence of American Entrepreneurship* (New York: Simon & Schuster, 1992), 166.
145. BFGoodrich, "Akron Complex Building Survey, May 27, 1986."
146. Case, *From the Ground Up*, 162–83.
147. *Akron Beacon Journal*, 10 April 1994, has a feature story on Canal Place. Goodrich's employment nationwide, as well as in Akron, fell with the restructuring of the 1980s. In 1985 Goodrich had 26,000 employees, and by the end of 1988 only 12,000. Some of these workers, of course, found jobs with firms buying businesses divested by Goodrich.
148. "Uniroyal-Goodrich Tire Company," Case Study 9–390–005, prepared by the Harvard Business School, 29 October 1991, offers insights into the joint venture—especially its later stages.
149. Ong interview, 26 March 1994.
150. Devendorf interview.
151. "Annual Reports," 1986 and 1987; and Devendorf and Ong interviews. The $225 million listed in the Harvard case study is incorrect.
152. "Strategic Objectives 1987–89."
153. Ong interview, 26 March 1994. Eisentrout also recalled that "John Ong thought, 'here's real capital coming in [that] I can take and put into businesses where I think they belong—the long-range tire business is a dog business.'" See Eisentrout interview.
154. "Annual Report," 1985.
155. Eisentrout interview.
156. Devendorf interview.
157. *Business Week*, 30 November 1987, 35.
158. In 1987, UGTC had 19 percent of the original equipment tire market and 7 percent of the replacement tire market. Goodyear made 33 percent and Firestone 22 percent of America's original equipment tires. Goodyear also manufactured 16 percent and Firestone 9 percent of the replacement tires. See "Uniroyal-Goodrich Tire Company," 12, 20, and 21.
159. "Annual Report," 1988.
160. Ong interview, 26 March 1994.
161. Eisentrout interview.
162. Richard Tedlow, "Hitting the Skids: Tires and Time Horizons," paper presented at the Harvard Business School, 9 August 1991, 74. Quoted with permission.
163. Eisentrout interview.
164. Ong interview, 26 March 1994. See also Devendorf interview.
165. *Chemical Week*, 6 January 1988, 13–14.
166. *New York Times*, 12 March 1989.
167. "BFGoodrich Presentation." The profit figures are net income return on equity. Goodrich's successes attracted the interest of the British corporate raider Sir James Goldsmith. In 1988 Goldsmith, who mounted a major attack on Goodyear, bought some of Goodrich's common stock. Whether he sought control of Goodrich or was simply investing in the firm is unclear. See Sir James Goldsmith File.
168. *Wall Street Journal*, 30 September 1988.

CHAPTER 11

1. "Annual Reports," 1990–93. Helped by a buoyant American and world economy, Goodrich had come close to reaching its profit goal in 1989 and 1990.
2. Ong to Lauer and Tobler, 29 May 1991; Ong interview, 26 March 1994.
3. Ong to Lauer and Tobler, 29 May 1991; Ong interview, 26 March 1994.
4. Ong to Lauer and Tobler, 29 May 1991.
5. Ibid.
6. Ibid.; and Ong to Lauer and Tobler, 28 March 1991.
7. Ong to Lauer and Tobler, 29 May 1991.
8. When Ong and his colleagues completed their statement about mission and values, the company summarized it as a mission statement for public consumption. The 1992 annual report began, for the first time, with the BFGoodrich "Mission": "The basic purpose of the BFGoodrich Company is to provide customers with quality products, systems and services that represent the best use of our technological, financial and human resources. We achieve leadership positions in specialty markets by helping our customers improve the performance of their products and reducing their costs. By creating economic advantages for our customers, we generate wealth for our shareholders, provide rewarding careers for our employees and build our worldwide business in a profitable and responsible manner." In 1995 Goodrich revised the wording slightly.
9. Karen Heller, "Repeating History—with Hindsight," Chemical Week, 29 May–5 June 1991, 28. The likelihood of Goodrich selling its Geon Vinyl division was the subject of speculation among industry observers.
10. "Annual Reports," 1990 and 1991; the quotation is from the 1990 report.
11. Ong interview, 26 March 1994.
12. Chemical and Engineering News, 6 April 1987, 5; 20 April 1987, 4; Chemical Week, 6 May 1987, 21; 22 June 1988, 12–13; Financial World, 10 March 1987, 6; Institutional Investor, January 1988, 109–10; and Ong interview, 26 March 1994. For more detail on Patient's career, see BFGoodrich, "William F. Patient, Biography."
13. Modern Plastics 67 (February 1990): 9–10; and "1991–1995 Division Business Plans."
14. "Annual Report," 1990.
15. BFGoodrich, "1990–1992 Division Business Plans," and "1991–1995 Division Business Plans"; "Geon Vinyl Division, Restructuring Opportunities, July 31, 1991"; "Annual Report," 1991. See also Chemical Week, 25 March 1992, 9.
16. "Annual Report," 1992; and BFGoodrich, "Geon Vinyl Division—Strategic Plan, 1992."
17. BFGoodrich, "Report to Stockholders, First Quarter, 1993"; "UPI News," 18 February and 15 April 1993; and Ong (26 March 1994) and Waltermire interviews. For details on America's initial public offering market in the early 1990s, see Economist, 8 October 1994, 88. Initial public offerings are the sales of stock in new companies to the public.
18. Ibid.; "Annual Report," 1993; and Chemical and Engineering News, 22 February 1993, 6.
19. Luke interview.
20. Ong interview, 26 March 1994. The price of a share of BFGoodrich's common stock fell from about $54 on 12 February 1993 to $42 on 26 February 1993 (just a

few days before the Geon Company was set up), and recovered only to $46 on 30 April 1993.

21. "Annual Report," 1993; Ong and Waltermire interviews; "UPI News," 29 September 1993. There was still a remnant of the PVC business in Goodrich. Even with the establishment of the Geon Company, Goodrich retained ownership and operation of its chlor-alkali and ethylene facilities at Calvert City. For legal reasons, these could not be included in the divestiture. In 1993, the Calvert City plants made PVC intermediates for the Geon Company and the Westlake Monomers Corporation, under contracts due to expire in 1996. Byproducts, such as caustic soda, went to merchant chemical markets. In 1993, sales came to $133 million, and operating income was $4 million. "Annual Report," 1993.

22. Occidental Petroleum, "Annual Reports," 1989–93; *Chemical Week*, 20 September 1989, 13; 8 May 1991, 12; Gale Research, "Polyvinyl Chloride, Share of Capacity, 1990," Market Share Reporter; and Donald P. Knechtges, "The Outlook for PVC."

23. Dyan Machan, "Starting Over," *Forbes*, 4 July 1994, 53–56.

24. In 1988 an acquisitions task force, aided by the consultants McKinsey & Co., Goldman, Sachs, Shearson Lehman, and Salomon Brothers on Wall Street, explored the possibility of buying another large specialty chemical business. Goodrich sought a friendly merger with a firm whose integration with Goodrich would expand product and market opportunities for both. The task force soon learned the possible mergers posed undesirable difficulties, and chose to focus instead on friendly mergers with "two or more specialty chemical companies linked to BFG technology and/or businesses." Gordon D. Harnett to Leigh Carter, 31 January 1989.

25. "Specialty Chemicals," *Chemical Week*, 11 August 1993, 25; BFGoodrich, "Specialty Chemicals & Polymers—Strategic Plan, 1991."

26. Ibid., 1989–93; and "UPI News," 14 April 1994.

27. BFGoodrich, "Biography of Kent Lee."

28. "Annual Report," 1990.

29. Specialty Chemicals and Polymers Division strategic plan, 1992.

30. Specialty Chemicals and Polymers Division strategic plan, 1989; "Annual Reports," 1989–93; Ong interview, 2 May 1994.

31. Specialty Chemicals and Polymers Division strategic plan, 1989; Ong interview, 1 December 1995.

32. BFGoodrich, "Biography of H. David Warren." Tremco did about half of its business in Canada.

33. Tremco's average annual OIRONCE for 1990–91 was 17.7 percent, which compared favorably to the 9.6 percent for specialty polymers and chemicals, and which was only slightly less than it had been in the late 1980s.

34. Warren, "Strategic Overview," 22 November 1988.

35. Tremco Strategic Plan, 1991.

36. BFGoodrich, "Tremco, Business Plan, January 3, 1992."

37. Ong interview, 2 May 1994.

38. John Lauer to K. H. Lee and H. D. Warren, 15 January 1993.

39. Kent Lee, "SP&C Working Document, February 23, 1993."

40. Ong interview, 2 May 1994, and correspondence between Spitz, Ong, and Lauer, June 1993. Spitz had begun his career with Scientific Design, the company whose

innovations in PVC manufacturing had ended the very handsome profits earned in that business during the Collyer years.

41. Delta Consulting Group, "BFGoodrich Specialty Chemicals: Organizational Challenges and Opportunities, July, 1993."
42. Delta Consulting Group, "BFGoodrich Specialty Chemicals: Organizational Challenges and Opportunities, July, 1993"; and "Annual Report," 1993.
43. BFGoodrich "Biography of Wayne O. Smith"; and "UPI News," 5 April 1994.
44. *Akron Beacon Journal*, 16 December 1993; "Annual Report," 1993; *Chemical Week*, 22/29 December 1993, 5; and *New York Times*, 16 December 1993.
45. Ong interview, 26 March 1994. On the movement into making entire components, see also "Annual Report," 1993; and *Aviation Week and Space Review*, 15 March 1993, 32.
46. Ong interview, 2 May 1994.
47. "1991–1995 Division Business Plans."
48. Ong interview, 26 March 1994.
49. "Annual Reports," 1989–92. Some divestitures accompanied acquisitions, as Goodrich sought to develop a coherent and profitable aerospace product line. In 1990, Goodrich sold its off-highway braking unit, because "it lacked strategic fit with other BFGoodrich Aerospace units."
50. "UPI News," 17 May 1993; on the early negotiations see "Rolling Rock Meeting Materials, 1992."
51. Ong interview, 26 March 1994; and "Rolling Rock Meeting Notes," 1993.
52. Ibid.; and *Wall Street Journal*, 11 November 1993.
53. "Annual Report," 1993.
54. Ibid., 1989–93; and Ong interview, 26 March 1994.
55. "Annual Reports," 1990–93.
56. When Goodrich sold its Geon Vinyl division, it kept the corporate research facility in Brecksville.
57. BFGoodrich, "Executive Office Discussions, May 2, 1994."
58. Ibid.
59. Haynes interview.
60. Mitigating this situation somewhat was the fact that foreign companies generally paid higher taxes than did American firms. The problem was that the health care costs of American employers were rising rapidly.
61. "Annual Report," 1991; Andrew Wood, "Responsible Care: BFGoodrich," *Chemical Week*, 17 June 1992, 118–20; Karen Heller, "Responsible Care," *Chemical Week*, 6 July 1994, 31; Marc S. Reisch, "Chemical Industry Tries to Improve Its Community Relations," *Chemical and Engineering News*, 28 February 1994, 8, 21. Among his other duties, Ong held leadership posts in the Chemical Manufacturers' Association.
62. Ong to the authors, 27 November 1995.
63. Ong interview, 2 May 1994. One undesirable aspect of the company's tradition, the bitterness and rancor that had so often pervaded labor relations, had largely disappeared. In particular, the tire industry had long had a record of acrimonious labor relations, and Goodrich had left that business. In general, a new climate of cooperation also developed in labor relations that was not limited to Goodrich.

INDEX

Abadan Chemical Company (Iran), 338
ABS (acrylonitrile butadiene styrene),
246–47, 334
Abtec, 334
accelerators, organic, 66, 106
acid process, 50. *See also* reclaimed rubber
acrylonitrile, 154, 159, 242
acrylonitrile butadiene styrene (ABS),
246–47, 334
advertising: of airplane products, 136–38;
of consumer goods, 58–59; marketing orientation, 270; post–World
War I, 79; of radial tires, 317; by radio, 84; of tubeless tires, 212, 215;
during World War II, 151, 157,
176–77
Aeronautical Chamber of Commerce,
133
aerospace: in 1945–59, 221–23; in
1957–71, 284–87; in the 1970s,
344–45; in the 1980s, 365, 377–78;
in the 1990s, 401–4
Agerite resin, 106
agricultural chemicals, 244
Airbus, 344, 377
aircraft industry: instrumentation, 377;
integrated systems, 402, 403; leadership in the 1930s, 132–38; as new
area, 54; servicing aircraft, 377–78,
403–4; tires, 83, 133–34, 286–87,
377, 378; World War II, 174–75. *See*

also Boeing planes; brakes: aircraft;
wheels, aircraft
airships, 67
Ajax Rubber Company (Leyland, England), 103–4
Akron: business climate in the 1880s,
14–15; housing shortage, 70; industrial products, 340–44; manufacturing operations, 53–55; move to,
13–17; new factory buildings, 48;
"Operation Greengrass," 382; outdated facilities, 282, 283, 340–41,
364; relocation from, 127–29, 195,
311–13, 342–43; as rubber center,
36–39; stadium construction, 129;
world headquarters building, 267
Akron Board of Trade, 9, 14, 15
Akron Employer's Association, 42
Akron Rubber Shoe Company, 30, 35
AKU (N. V. Chemische Industrie AKU),
243
Alexander, Gerard: and decentralization,
303; as head of international division, 271; as head of tire division,
309; as potential CEO, 295, 299;
and radial tires, 276; and Reidrubber, 279; resignation of, 300
alkali process, 49, 50, 86. *See also* reclaimed rubber
Alkali Rubber Company, 50, 85
Allen, William T., 16

Historical Perspectives on Business Enterprise Series

MANSEL G. BLACKFORD AND K. AUSTIN KERR, EDITORS

The scope of the series includes scholarly interest in the history of the firm, the history of government-business relations, and the relationships between business and culture, both in the United States and abroad, as well as in comparative perspective.